C000050181

1 MONTH OF
FREE
READING

at

www.ForgottenBooks.com

By purchasing this book you are eligible for one month membership to ForgottenBooks.com, giving you unlimited access to our entire collection of over 1,000,000 titles via our web site and mobile apps.

To claim your free month visit:

www.forgottenbooks.com/free960390

* Offer is valid for 45 days from date of purchase. Terms and conditions apply.

ISBN 978-0-260-62548-9
PIBN 10960390

This book is a reproduction of an important historical work. Forgotten Books uses
state-of-the-art technology to digitally reconstruct the work, preserving the original format
whilst repairing imperfections present in the aged copy. In rare cases, an imperfection in
the original, such as a blemish or missing page, may be replicated in our edition. We do,
however, repair the vast majority of imperfections successfully; any imperfections that
remain are intentionally left to preserve the state of such historical works.

Forgotten Books is a registered trademark of FB &c Ltd.
Copyright © 2018 FB &c Ltd.
FB &c Ltd, Dalton House, 60 Windsor Avenue, London, SW19 2RR.
Company number 08720141. Registered in England and Wales.

For support please visit www.forgottenbooks.com

UNITED STATES CIRCUIT COURT OF APPEALS
FOR THE NINTH CIRCUIT

STATE OF OREGON, acting by and through its
State Forester, and KLAMATH FOREST PRO-
TECTIVE ASSOCIATION, an Oregon nonprofit
corporation,

Appellants.

vs.

UNITED STATES OF AMERICA,

Appellee.

E

Appeal From the United States District Court
for the District of Oregon

APPELLANTS' BRIEF

ROBERT Y. THORNTON
Attorney General of the
State of Oregon

THOMAS C. STACER
Assistant Attorney General

CLARENCE R. KRUGER
Assistant Attorney General
2600 State Street
Salem, Oregon
Attorneys for Appellants

ene

ne_

st_

FILED

APR 20 1962

FRANK H. SCHMID, CLERK

TOPICAL INDEX

TABLE OF AUTHORITIES CITED

CASES AND AUTHORITIES

TABLE OF AUTHORITIES CITED—Continued

STATUTES

No. 17574

IN THE

UNITED STATES CIRCUIT COURT OF APPEALS

FOR THE NINTH CIRCUIT

STATE OF OREGON, acting by and through its
State Forester, and KLAMATH FOREST PRO-
TECTIVE ASSOCIATION, an Oregon nonprofit
corporation,

Appellants.

vs.

UNITED STATES OF AMERICA,

Appellee.

Appeal From the United States District Court
for the District of Oregon

APPELLANTS' BRIEF

STATEMENT OF JURISDICTION OF UNITED STATES DISTRICT COURT

This is an appeal by the State of Oregon and Klamath
Forest Protective Association, an Oregon nonprofit corporation, from that order of the United States District
Court for the District of Oregon which dismissed the
second amended complaint of plaintiffs, and the action
stated therein, due to lack of jurisdiction of the court
(**R**. 53-54).

The order for dismissal was entered by the District
Court on its own accord after the court had considered

and denied a motion for summary Judgment filed by the defendant (**R**. 53-54).

By the second amended complaint (R. 13-15), brought under the Federal Tort Claims Act, 28 U.S.C.A. Sec. 1346(b), 2671 to 2680, the plaintiffs sought to recover the expenses incurred in fighting, controlling and extinguishing an uncontrolled fire on forest lands in the State of Oregon.

In paragraph II of the second amended complaint (R 13) plaintiffs allege that:

> "Plaintiff State of Oregon is acting by and through the duly appointed and authorized State Forester of Oregon."

In paragraph III of the second amended complaint (R 13) plaintiffs allege that:

> "Plaintiff Klamath Forest Protective Association is an Oregon nonprofit corporation duly registered and authorized to do business in the State of Oregon."

In paragraph IV of the second amended complaint (R. 13-14) plaintiffs allege that:

> ". . . servants, agents and employees of the Forest Service Department of Agriculture, United States of America, while acting within the course and scope of their employment, negligently and carelessly set a forest fire, which forest fire they then negligently and carelessly permitted to escape and burn into the State and District of Oregon as hereinafter stated."

In paragraph VI of the second amended complaint (R. 14) plaintiffs allege:

> "That defendant failed, neglected and refused to

control and extinguish said fire in the State and District of Oregon."

In paragraph VII of the second amended complaint (R. 14) plaintiffs allege that:

"As approximate result of said negligence and carelessness the plaintiffs were required to . . . and did so fight, control and extinguish said fire . . ."

And it is further alleged in paragraph VIII of the second amended complaint that·

". . . plaintiffs suffered damage in the sum of $26,999.41, being moneys expended by plaintiffs to fight, control and extinguish said fire on forest lands in the State of Oregon."

On defendant's motion for summary Judgment, the court denied the motion of defendant, but ordered a dismissal of the complaint and action as aforementioned (R. 53-54). The reasons for dismissal were detailed in the opinion of the court (R. 49-52)

Jurisdiction to hear and determine such cause of action is conferred on the United States District Court under the provisions of 28 U.S.C.A. Sec. 1346(b) which reads as follows:

"(b) Subject to the provisions of chapter 171 of this title, the district courts, together with the United States District Court for the District of the Canal Zone and the District Court of the Virgin Islands, shall have exclusive Jurisdiction of civil actions on claims against the United States, for money damages, accruing on and after January 1, 1945, for injury or loss of property, or personal injury or death caused by the negligent or wrongful act or omission of any employee of the Government while acting within the scope of his office or employment, under circumstances where the United States, if a private person, would be liable to the claimant in accordance with the law of the place where the act or omission occurred."

JURISDICTION OF COURT OF APPEALS FOR NINTH CIRCUIT TO HEAR THE APPEAL

On June 26, 1961, the district court entered its order of dismissal on the ground of lack of jurisdiction over the subject matter (R. 53-54). August 25, 1961, plaintiffs filed their notice of appeal (R. 55) from the order of dismissal entered by the United States District Court for the District of Oregon.

Jurisdiction is conferred on this court to review said order of dismissal under the provisions of 28 U.S.C.A., Sections 1291 and 1294(1).

STATEMENT OF CASE

The United States Forest Service, an agency of the defendant United States of America, set fire to lands located in the vicinity of Bogus Creek area in the County of Siskiyou, State and Northern District of California (R. 13) The fire was set by the servants, agents and employees of the United States, while acting within the course and scope of their employment (R. 13). The fire escaped and burned over an area of Northern California, and into forest lands in the State and District of Oregon.

The fire burned uncontrolled into the State of Oregon (R. 14); the United States failed to take action to prevent the spread of the fire (R. 14) in Oregon

Klamath Forest Protective Association and the State of Oregon, the latter by and through its State Forester, incurred expenses in the sum of $26,999.41 in controlling and extinguishing that part of the fire which had burned uncontrolled into the State of Oregon (R. 12, 14).

The United States failed to exert an effort to suppress and extinguish the fire which burned on the lands in the State of Oregon. The fire burned over both private and federal lands in the State of Oregon. The federal lands were under the jurisdiction of the Department of the Interior of the United States, and are commonly referred to as "O. & C." lands or Bureau of Land Management lands; the private lands, in part, were owned by members of plaintiff Klamath Forest Protective Association (R. 3-12).

On June 23, 1959, the original complaint was filed against the United States of America alleging negligence of defendant in the setting and control of Bogus Mountain Fire. By the complaint, under the aforementioned Federal Tort Claims Act, plaintiffs sought to recover the expenses incurred by them in fighting, controlling and extinguishing the fire on forest lands in the State of Oregon.

On November 29, 1960, the second amended complaint was filed (R. 15). The action was based upon Oregon law, with particular reference to ORS chapter 477, and 477.064 to 477.071.

The defendant filed a motion for summary judgment

(R 15, 16); thereafter, on June 26, 1961, the district court denied the motion, but on its own initiative determined the court lacked Jurisdiction and entered its order of dismissal of the second amended complaint (R 53-54). The court had prefaced its order by an opinion issued June 22, 1961 (R 49-52). By its opinion the district court made reference to and in effect adopted the ruling of Judge Louis E. Goodman, United States District Court for the Northern District of California (Southern Division), entered on June 1, 1961, in the case entitled "People of the State of California, Plaintiff, vs. United States of America and First Doe to Twentieth Doe, both inclusive, Defendants" (R. 52), which case is also on appeal in this court by the State of California (CCA, No. 17534).

The question on appeal is whether the Federal Tort Claims Act subjects the United States to liability for the fire-fighting expenses incurred by plaintiffs in suppressing and extinguishing a forest fire negligently set by the United States on Federal lands in the State of California and allowing the fire to escape and burn to and upon forest lands in the State of Oregon The plaintiffs hereinbefore mentioned are now appellants.

SPECIFICATION OF ERROR

1. The district court erroneously held that the Federal Tort Claims Act does not confer Jurisdiction upon it to adjudicate the claim of plaintiffs for fire suppression costs against the defendant United States, and in so doing, erred in dismissing the second amended complaint and cause of action of plaintiffs.

SUMMARY OF ARGUMENT

The cause of action stated by the State of Oregon and Klamath Forest Protective Association, and the claim of $26,999.41 asserted therein against the United States of America, are within the purview of the Federal Tort Claims Act. The following is a summary of argument:

1. The uncontested facts of the second amended complaint and the answers to the written interrogatories reveal negligence in the origin, escape and control of Bogus Mountain Fire.

2. The admitted negligence of the United States is within the scope and provisions of the Federal Tort Claims Act.

3. The rule of *lex loci delicti* is applicable to the facts of the case, thereby a tort was committed within the District and State of Oregon.

4. The Oregon laws authorize collection of the fire suppression costs against a person who wilfully or negligently originated a fire or permitted a fire to burn uncontrolled on forest land in Oregon.

5. The fire suppression efforts of the State of Oregon and Klamath Forest Protective Association were done in order to protect, and to prevent continued damage to, property and natural resources in Oregon.

ARGUMENT

This appeal brings an important issue to the appellate court, namely, whether or not an action may be brought against the United States under the Federal Tort Claims Act for the recovery of fire suppression costs incurred by the appellants due to a fire burning uncontrolled on forest land in Oregon, which fire was negligently set and allowed to escape by the officials and employees of the United States.

1. **The uncontested facts of the second amended complaint and the answers to the written interrogatories reveal negligence in the origin, escape and control of Bogus Mountain Fire.**

In its decision, the lower court ignored the facts set forth in the complaint and answers to the written interrogatories. The facts, for purposes of the question before the lower court, were uncontested.

The second amended complaint clearly states that the United States negligently and carelessly set a fire which was allowed to escape and burn onto forest lands in the State and District of Oregon (R. 13-14). Further, the complaint sets forth the uncontested allegations that the United States failed and neglected to control and extinguish that part of Bogus Mountain Fire which burned into Oregon (R. 14).

The motion for summary judgment required an admission of the alleged facts by the United States. Similarly, the lower court by its own notice and decision was required to review the alleged facts as admitted.

For all purposes of this appeal, the tort of the United States is revealed. Appellants assert their claim for $26,999.41 against the United States, based upon the admitted allegations of tort liability. The State of Oregon and Klamath Forest Protective Association were required by Oregon Revised Statutes, chapter 477, hereafter fully cited by pertinent provisions, to fight, control and extinguish that part of Bogus Mountain Fire which burned into Oregon; the requirement was based upon the failure and neglect of the United States to do any effort on the fire. Therefore, this action was brought by appellants against the United States under the provisions of the Federal Tort Claims Act· 28 U S.C.A., Sec 1346(b), 2671 to 2680 (R. 13).

The allegations of the second amended complaint assert that the ". . . plaintiffs suffered damage in the sum of $26,999.41, being moneys expended by plaintiffs to fight, control and extinguish said fire on forest lands in the State of Oregon." (R. 14) By its opinion the lower court was fearful that it lacked jurisdiction because the allegations of the complaint and answers to the interrogatories did not reveal that the appellants sustained damage to property. As will be later shown, appellants incurred the fire suppression costs in order to protect property and natural resource values. The latter was not considered by the lower court and it erred in failing to do so

2. **The admitted negligence of the United States is within the scope and provisions of the Federal Tort Claims Act.**

By the Federal Tort Claims Act, Congress has changed the concept of sovereign immunity in so far as the United States is concerned. In essence, the enactment provides for civil actions against the United States for injury or loss of property, or because of personal injury or death due to negligence or wrongful act or omission of any employee of the Federal Government while acting within the scope of the office or work—provided such was under circumstances where the United States, if as a private person, would be liable in accordance with the law of the place where the act or omission occurred: *Wiltse v. United States,* 74 F. Supp. 786; *Lavitt v. United States,* 177 Fed. 2d 627. In *Jones v. United States,* 126 F. Supp. 10, 228 Fed. 2d 52, 97 U. S. App. D. C. 81, the court asserted that the federal statute was remedial in nature and was intended to waive the sovereign immunity in the field of tort; the statute did not create a new cause of action but merely under stated circumstances made the United States liable in the same way and extent as a private individual· 1 ALR 2d 224, citing *Jones v. United States,* supra.

Although courts have given the Federal Tort Claims Act a literal and narrow construction, yet there have been an equal number of courts that have avowed that the Act should receive a liberal construction because of its benevolent purposes: *Bates v. United States,* 76 F. Supp. 57; *Panella v United States,* 216 Fed. 2d 622.

As revealed above, there are exceptions to actions which may be brought against the United States: 28 U.S.C.A. Sec 2680. However, the present action is within the scope of the Federal Tort Claims Act, as the negligence and carelessness of the officials and employees of the United States was the proximate cause of the damages sustained by the appellants, namely, $26,999.41 expended by the appellants in fighting, controlling and extinguishing Bogus Mountain Fire on forest lands in Oregon.

The state law governs when the cause of action comes into existence: *Bizer v. United States*, 124 F. Supp. 949. The substantive law of the place where the tort occurred is to be applied: *Hess v. United States*, 259 F. 2d 285, 358 US 923, 79 S. Ct. 604, 3 L. Ed. 2d 627. Under the allegations set forth in the second amended complaint of appellants, Oregon law is applicable to the acts and omissions of the United States in originating Bogus Mountain Fire and in the failure and neglect of the United States to fight, control and extinguish the fire on forest lands in Oregon.

3. **The rule of lex loci delicti is applicable to the facts of the case, thereby a tort was committed within the District and State of Oregon.**

The rule under the Federal Tort Claims Act compelled Congress under practical procedures to adopt the principles of local law to define tort liability; therefore the rule of *lex loci delicti* should be reviewed. Both in Oregon and in other jurisdictions the rule is as set forth in Restatement of Conflict of Laws, Sec. 377·

"The place of the wrong is in the state where the last event necessary to make an actor liable for an alleged tort takes place."

The above rule was stated in *Jordan v. State Marine Corporation of Delaware, et al*, 257 Fed 2d 232, wherein it was held that the place of wrong is the state in which the *last event* is necessary to make the actor liable for the alleged tort; also, *Otey v. Midland Valley R. Co.*, 108 Kan. 755, 197 P 203. In the latter case the barn of the plaintiff in Oklahoma caught fire allegedly from sparks of defendant's engine; the defendant claimed that if the fire was set by a spark which escaped from the engine in Kansas, there would be no recovery; the court stated:

> "Such is not the law. . . . a recovery was proper whether the engine was in Kansas, or on the state line, or in Oklahoma. The damage occurred in Oklahoma. If it was caused by defendant's engine, that was all that was necessary . . ."

A similar situation as in the Otey case arose in *Connecticut Valley Lumber Co v. Maine Central Railroad*, 78 NH 553, 103 A 263, wherein the court stated:

> "While the defendant's negligent acts occurred in Canada, the resulting injury to the plaintiff's property occurred in this state. If one, while in one jurisdiction, performs a negligent act which is the proximate cause of damage to property in another Jurisdiction, the locality of the act is deemed at common law to be the same as that of the damage."

Also in *Dallas v. Whitney*, 118 W. Va. 106, 188 SE 766, the court confronted with the *lex loci delicti* problem concluded:

> "The rule seems to be that where a cause is put in motion in one jurisdiction that results in injury in another, the law of the latter jurisdiction is the law by which the substantive rights of the parties are to be determined."

The second amended complaint alleges that Bogus Mountain Fire originated through the negligence and carelessness of the United States. Under the above cited cases and rule, the event which caused the liability of the United States to the appellants occurred when and after the fire burned into Oregon. In so far as the claim of appellants set forth in the second amended complaint, Oregon law governs the rights and liabilities of the parties to this action. See *Jordan v. State Marine Corporation of Delaware*, 257 Fed. 2d 232, supra; also, *Nadeau v. Power Plant Engineering Co.*, 216 Or 12, 17, 337 P2d 313. See 133 ALR 260 wherein it is stated that the law of the situs of the tort governs the liability therefor, and on page 266 of said annotation is cited *Connecticut Valley Lumber Co. v. Maine Central Railroad*, supra. Further, see *United States v. Marshall*, C.A. Idaho (1956) 230 F. 2d 183.

In the present action the alleged negligence in the origin of Bogus Mountain Fire, as aforementioned, was a continuing act of negligence causing injury and damage to appellants in Oregon.

4. The Oregon laws authorize collection of the fire suppression costs against a person who wilfully or negligently originated a fire or permitted a fire to burn uncontrolled on forest land in Oregon.

The action brought by the State of Oregon and Klamath Forest Protective Association is based upon the provisions of ORS chapter 477, particularly ORS 477.002 and ORS 477.064 to 477.071. The statutes define forest lands and require the owner to fight and extinguish fires occurring thereon: ORS 477.066. A fire burning uncontrolled on forest lands without proper action being taken to prevent its spread is a public nuisance: ORS 477.064. When the public nuisance exists, the State of Oregon is required to fight, control and extinguish the fire ORS 477.066. If the fire originated through negligence of an owner, *or* if the owner fails, refuses or neglects to make a reasonable effort to control and extinguish such fire, the costs of the state may be collected by an action at law from the owner: ORS 477.068. See *State v. Gourley Bros. et al,* 209 Or 363, 305 P2d 396, 306 P2d 1117; *State v. City of Marshfield,* 122 Or 323, 259 P 201. Also, see *State v. The California-Oregon Power Co.,* 225 Or 604, 358 P2d 524.

For the convenience of the court, the Oregon statutes are hereinafter set forth:

ORS 477.002 (1) (d) "Forest land" includes any forest, woodland, brushland, cutover land, slashing, chopping or clearing containing any inflammable forest debris.

ORS 477.064 Any fire on any forest land in Oregon burning uncontrolled or without proper action being taken to prevent its spread, notwithstanding its origin, is declared a public nuisance by reason of its menace to life and property. The spread of fire in forest land across an ownership boundary is prima facie evidence of fire burning uncontrolled.

ORS 477.066 The owner, operator and person in possession of land on which a fire exists, or from which it may have spread, or any of them, notwithstanding the origin or subsequent spread thereof on his own or other land, shall make every reasonable effort to control and extinguish such fire immediately when its existence comes to his knowledge, without awaiting instructions from the forester, warden or ranger and shall continue until the fire is extinguished If the owner or operator or person in possession fails so to do, or if the fire is burning uncontrolled, the forester, or any forest protective agency under contract with the State Board of Forestry for the protection of forest land against fire, and within whose protection area the fire exists, shall summarily abate the nuisance thus constituted by controlling and extinguishing the fire

ORS 477.068 (1) In case such owner, operator and person in possession, or any of them, shall fail to make the effort required by ORS 477.066, or where such owner, operator or person in possession is wilful, malicious or negligent in the origin of the fire, the actual cost of controlling or extinguishing the fire shall be recovered from such owner, operator or person in possession when necessary by action for debt prosecuted in the name of the State of Oregon or such forest protective agency or both

(2) The cost in cases covered by ORS 477 066 shall constitute a general lien upon the real and personal property of such owner, operator or person in possession, but the lien shall be limited to the real and personal property situated within the external boundaries of the area over which the fire has burned A written statement and notice of the lien, containing a description of the property and a statement of the cost, shall be certified under oath by the forester or any warden and filed in the office of the county clerk of the county in which the lands and personal property are situated within six months after extinguishment of the fire, and may be foreclosed by suit in the manner provided by law for foreclosure of liens, for labor and material. The lien provided for in this section shall be inferior to any existing lien.

(3) Upon request of the forester, the district attorney for the district in which the lands and personal property are situated shall prosecute such action for debt or foreclose the lien in the name of the State of Oregon or such forest protective agency or both. Liens provided for in this section shall cease to exist unless suit for foreclosure is instituted within six months from the date of filing the same.

ORS 477.069 Notwithstanding ORS 16.220 and 16.230, or any other law, in the instance of a fire occurring as described in ORS 477.064, or any other fire or spot fire therefrom, wherein the owner, operator or person in possession, or any of them, has been wilful, malicious or negligent in the origin of the fire and also has failed to make the effort required by ORS 477.066, the plaintiff, in bringing the action authorized by ORS 477.068, may unite in the same complaint such causes permitting collection of the cost incurred by the plaintiff under ORS 477.066 The provisions of this section shall not apply to any acts, omissions, actions, suits or proceedings occurring or commenced prior to April 19, 1957.

ORS 477 070 If the owner regularly pays a fire patrol assessment on the lands described under ORS 477.068 or is a member in good standing of an organization approved by and under contract with the board, which organization has undertaken the control and suppression of fires on such land and which is actually engaged in the control and suppression of fire entering upon or burning on such land, the owner, operator or person in possession shall not be subject to the penalties prescribed by ORS 164.070, or be held as maintaining a nuisance as defined in ORS 477 064, unless he or his agent is wilful, malicious or negligent in the origin of the fire. But payment of fire patrol assessments or membership in an organization under contract with the board shall not relieve any owner, operator or person in possession of land from the obligation imposed by ORS 477.066 and 477.068 to control and prevent the spread of fires if that land has theretofore become an operation area and if, as a result thereof, an additional fire hazard has been created and exists thereon and has not been released by the forester.

ORS 477.071 For the purpose of ORS 477.066, notification to the owner, operator and person in possession of the land, or any of them, shall be considered good and sufficient notice to the owner of the existence of a fire.

The above statutes sound in tort. Such has been the long interpretation of the Oregon Supreme Court: *State v. City of Marshfield,* 122 Or 323, 259 P 201, 259 P 203: *State v. Gourley Bros. et al,* 209 Or 363, 305 P2d 396, 306 P2d 1117. See also, *State v. The California-Oregon Power Co.,* 225 Or 604, 358 P2d 524.

Liability under the cited Oregon statutes is a tort liability, even though the statutes refer to an action of debt. The last cited cases substantiate this argument. By its omissions and acts, the United States becomes responsible to the State of Oregon, and its contracting fire protective agency, for the costs incurred by the state and agency in fighting and extinguishing Bogus Mountain Fire. A private person would be liable in similar circumstances, and as a consequence of the Federal Tort Claims Act, the appellee United States is rendered responsible.

The lower court erred in ignoring the decisions of the Oregon Supreme Court cited above, and in failing to consider the tort liability of the United States under the above Oregon laws

5. The fire suppression efforts of the State of Oregon and Klamath Forest Protective Association were done in order to protect, and to prevent continued damage to, property and natural resources in Oregon.

Although the action and claim of the appellants is for fire suppression costs, none the less, each appellant has an interest in the forest lands and natural resources which were burned or threatened by Bogus Mountain Fire. The lower court erred in overlooking such property interests.

(a) Forest land interests of the appellants:

Referring to Oregon Revised Statutes, chapter 477, particularly ORS 477.033, the state and association are entitled to budgeted costs for providing protection of forest lands from fire. The court may take notice that ORS 477 033 authorizes the costs of such protection to become a lien upon the forest lands involved. The lands are those for which the owner has neglected and failed to provide proper protection against fire: ORS 477.022 to 477.055. In effect, the statutes of the State of Oregon give a lien interest in forest lands of a fire protection district The lien interest may be foreclosed "like taxes": ORS 477.033.

The lien interest is derived as follows.

Under the provisions of ORS 477.022, as such existed

at the date of Bogus Mountain Fire, unprotected forest
land is not authorized; the statute states in full:

> "The preservation of the forests and the conserva-
> tion of the forest resources through the prevention
> and suppression of forest fires hereby are declared to
> be the public policy of the State of Oregon. To
> achieve this end the need for a complete and coordi-
> nated fire protection system is acknowledged."

Also, under the provisions of ORS 477.024, every
owner of forest land " . . shall provide adequate
protection against the starting or spread of fire thereon
or therefrom which protection shall meet with the approval of the board." The unquoted parts of ORS 477.024
require the State Forester of Oregon to provide fire
protection for those lands neglected by the owner. Under
ORS 477.026, the State Forester establishes fire protection districts in order to set up the protection required
of him by ORS 477.024. Each year the State Forester
and Oregon State Board of Forestry estimate the cost of
such protection and cause the cost to be levied and
assessed, "like taxes", against the forest lands involved:
ORS 477.030 to 477.035. Such cost so levied are a lien
upon the privately owned property: ORS 477.033. Thus,
at the time Bogus Mountain Fire raged uncontrolled onto
forest lands in Oregon, by statute the State of Oregon
had an interest in the forest lands. In those instances
where assessments were not levied, then Klamath Forest
Protective Association was involved with land interest,
namely, association members owned forest lands burned
or threatened. References to statutes and land ownership are a part of this court record (R. 3-12, 51). The

uncontrolled nature of Bogus Mountain Fire in Oregon
and the failure of the United States through its servants,
agents and employees of the Forest Service, Department
of Agriculture, (R. 13) to exert any effort to fight and
control the fire in Oregon (R. 14), was the direct reason
and proximate cause for appellants incurring $26,999.41
fire suppression costs. The costs were incurred for the
protection of the forest lands and interests therein of
appellants.

The Oregon Supreme Court made an analysis of the
predecessor statute to ORS 477.022 to 477.055. In *First
State Bank v. Kendall,* 107 Or 1, 213 P 142, the court
stated on page 9:

"The general object and purpose of this act was
to prevent the destruction by fire of the forest lands
within the state. *To accomplish this purpose all private owners of forest lands are required by this act
to maintain a fire patrol over their lands during the
dry season of each year.* Recognizing that some timber land owners might not comply with the law, the
legislature properly included in the act a provision
whereby, *through the state forester, a system of
patrolling such private lands could be maintained at
the expense of the delinquent land owner, and provided a method whereby this expense could be collected from such owner.* As the means thus adopted
tended to prevent the destruction of forests by fire,
and was essential to the accomplishment of the purpose of the act, it was proper to include this provision
in the act. Without some such provision, obedience
to the law could not be enforced." (Emphasis supplied)

The Oregon court further stated in the Kendall case on page 12:

"Under this statute every owner of timber lands within the state is commanded to patrol them during the dry season of the year, when fires are liable to occur. If any owner fails to patrol his own lands, it is made the duty of the state forester to furnish a fire patrol therefor. The law provides that the amount of the expense of the state forester in patrolling privately owned lands, which the owner has failed or neglected to patrol, shall be reported by the state forester to the appropriate County Court, and that this amount shall be extended on the assessment-roll of the county and shall become a lien upon the lands so patrolled, and that this amount shall be collected in the same manner and at the same time that taxes are collected, and when collected, shall be repaid to the state forester, and makes the procedure applicable to the collection of taxes and delinquent taxes applicable to the collection thereof"

Because of the nature of the statute, it has been referred to as the Compulsory Forest Patrol Act of Oregon The court in the Kendall case further stated on page 13·

" . . This statute was not designed for the purpose of raising revenue, and its enactment was not an exercise of the taxing power of the state The act is a reasonable and proper police regulation designed to protect the forests of the state from destruction by fire. The method adopted by the legislature to compel the delinquent owner to reimburse the state for the moneys so expended provides merely for the collection of an indebtedness imposed under

the police power of the state, and not the collection
of a tax."

From the above citations and quotations it is obvious
that the State of Oregon has an interest in forest lands
in order to regain its costs of protection. It was such an
interest in property that the Bogus Mountain Fire damaged and threatened to burn. Contrary to the lower
court opinion (R. 49), the appellants did have property
interests which were damaged and threatened by the
fire negligently started and permitted to escape by
appellee. The lower court failed to consider the nature
and scope of the pertinent Oregon statutes.

(b) Natural resources were damaged and threatened

The court may take notice that the State of Oregon
has a property interest in its natural resources. Trees,
forests, watershed areas, fish and wildlife are threatened
by a fire in forest lands burning uncontrolled. Both
appellants were committed to the protection of such
resources The fire suppression costs incurred by appellants in fighting Bogus Mountain Fire were expended
to prevent further damage to such resources. This
factor the lower court fully ignored. The lower court
declared an absence of property damage (R. 51). It was
in error.

Oregon has affirmed its right in water and watershed
resources: ORS, chapters 536 and 537. Also, Oregon has
exerted its rights over fish and wildfowl and wild animals: ORS, chapters 496 to 505 The Oregon court has
acclaimed such rights in several decisions, particularly

in *State v. Blanchard,* 96 Or 79, 189 P 421, where on page 87 the right was affirmed:

> "The argument also ignores the repeated decisions of our own and other courts, that nobody has an absolute right to fish in the waters of this state; that the property in fish, abounding in the waters of this state, so far as they can be said to be property, is in the state in trust for the people, and, so long as it does not discriminate between citizens, the legislature may prescribe the time in which and the method by which the fish may be taken, and the waters from which they may be taken."

The Oregon court reaffirmed the right of the state in *Anthony et al. v. Veatch et al.,* 189 Or 462, 486, 220 P2d 493, 221 P2d 575, 71 S.Ct. 499, 340 U.S. 923, 95 L.Ed. 667. Other Oregon decisions relating to wild game· *Thompson v. Dana,* 52 F.2d 759, 285 U.S. 529, 76 L.Ed. 925; *Fields v. Wilson,* 186 Or 491, 207 P2d 153.

It is here asserted that the action taken by appellants in fighting, controlling and suppressing that part of Bogus Mountain Fire in Oregon was for the preservation and protection of natural resources in Oregon. The sum of $26,999.41 was so incurred. It is a proper amount to assert against the United States under the previously cited provisions of the Federal Tort Claims Act.

CONCLUSION

In view of the above-cited arguments and authorities, appellants urge the order of the lower court be overruled and reversed on this appeal; and further, that said cause of action and claim of plaintiffs be deemed within the purview of the Federal Tort Claims Act.

Dated· Salem, Oregon
March 28, 1962

Respectfully submitted,

ROBERT Y. THORNTON
Attorney General of the
State of Oregon

THOMAS C. STACER
Assistant Attorney General

CLARENCE R. KRUGER
Assistant Attorney General

2600 State Street
Salem, Oregon
Attorneys for Appellants

...be deemed within the
...ms Act.

...omitted,

...ER. Y THORNTON
...orney General of the
...ate of Oregon

...MAS C STACER
...stant Attorney General

...RENCE R. KRUGER
...istant Attorney General

...0 State Street
...em Oregon
    Attorneys for Appellants

INDEX

CITATIONS

Cases:

In the United States Court of Appeals for the Ninth Circuit

No. 17574

STATE OF OREGON, ET AL., APPELLANTS

v.

UNITED STATES OF AMERICA, APPELLEE

Appeal from the United States District Court
for the District of Oregon

BRIEF FOR APPELLEE

JURISDICTIONAL STATEMENT

This is an appeal from an order entered by the District Court for the District of Oregon on June 26, 1961, dismissing appellants' action for lack of jurisdiction over the subject matter (R. 53-54). Appellants sought recovery under the Federal Tort Claims Act of fire suppression costs incurred in suppressing a fire allegedly negligently started by employees of the United States. This appeal was noted on August 25, 1961 (R. 55). The jurisdiction of this Court is invoked under 28 U.S.C. 1291 and 1294 (1).

(1)

STATEMENT OF THE CASE

In September, 1957, in pursuance of a project of reforestation of its lands in the State of California, the United States Forest Service (Department of Agriculture) set a fire on those California lands (R. 13). This fire went out of control, crossed into Oregon, and burned lands in Oregon owned by the United States and other private landowners. Alleging negligence on the part of the Forest Service in setting the fire in California (R. 13), appellants brought this action under the Tort Claims Act to recover their costs incurred in suppressing the fire in Oregon (R. 14), premising their rights on Chapter 477 of the Oregon Revised Statutes which provide for recovery of such costs.

The United States moved for summary judgment, contending (1) that the complaint did not state a claim upon which relief could be granted, and (2) that the district court lacked jurisdiction over the subject matter (R. 16).

The district court dismissed the action for lack of jurisdiction over the subject matter, on the ground that the asserted claim was not for any damage to property (R. 49-52). It is from that dismissal that appellants prosecute this appeal.[1]

---

[1] Also on appeal to this Court is the identical ruling of the District Court for the Northern District of California in a Tort Claims Act suit brought by the State of California to recover expenses incurred by it in fighting the same fire. Like this case, the California suit is based on a fire suppression cost statute (California Health and Safety Code, Section 13009). *People of the State of California* v. *United States* (No. 17,534).

STATUTES INVOLVED

1. 28 U.S.C. 1346(b) provides as follows:

Subject to the provisions of chapter 171 of this title, the district courts, together with the United States District Court for the District of the Canal Zone and the District Court of the Virgin Islands, shall have exclusive jurisdiction of civil actions on claims against the United States, for money damages, accruing on and after January 1, 1945, for injury or loss of property, or personal injury or death caused by the negligent or wrongful act or omission of any employee of the Government while acting within the scope of his office or employment, under circumstances where the United States, if a private person, would be liable to the claimant in accordance with the law of the place where the act or omission occurred.

2. The relevant provisions of the Oregon Revised Statutes are as follows:

477.064. *Uncontrolled fire declared nuisance.* Any fire on any forest land in Oregon burning uncontrolled or without proper action being taken to prevent its spread, notwithstanding its origin, is declared a public nuisance by reason of its menace to life and property. The spread of fire in forest land across an ownership boundary is prima facie evidence of fire burning uncontrolled.

477.066. *Duty of owner or possessor of land to abate fire; abatement by authorities.* The owner, operator and person in possession of land on which a fire exists, or from which it may have spread, or any of them, notwithstanding the origin or subsequent spread thereof on his own or other land, shall make every reasonable effort to control and extinguish such fire immediately when its existence comes to his knowledge, without awaiting instructions from the forester, warden or ranger and shall continue until the fire is extinguished. If the owner or operator or person in possession fails so to do, or if the fire is burning uncontrolled, the forester, or any forest protective agency under contract with the State Board of Forestry for the protection of forest land against fire, and within whose protection area the fire exists, shall summarily abate the nuisance thus constituted by controlling and extinguishing the fire.

477.068. *Liability of owner or possessor for cost of abatement; lien; foreclosure.* (1) In case such owner, operator and person in possession, or any of them, shall fail to make the effort required by ORS 477.066, or where such owner, operator or person in possession is wilful, malicious or negligent in the origin of the fire, the actual cost of controlling or extinguishing the fire shall be recovered from such owner, operator or person in possession when necessary by action for debt prosecuted in the name of the State of Oregon or such forest protective agency or both.

(2) The cost in cases covered by ORS 477.066 shall constitute a general lien upon the real and personal property of such owner, operator or person in possession, but the lien shall be limited to the real and personal property situated within the external boundaries of the area over which the fire has burned. A written statement and notice of the lien, containing a description of the property and a statement of the cost, shall be certified under oath by the forester or any

warden and filed in the office of the county clerk of the county in which the lands and personal property are situated within six months after extinguishment of the fire, and may be foreclosed by suit in the manner provided by law for foreclosure of liens, for labor and material. The lien provided for in this section shall be inferior to any existing lien.

(3) Upon request of the forester, the district attorney for the district in which the lands and personal property are situated shall prosecute such action for debt or foreclose the lien in the name of the State of Oregon or such forest protective agency or both. Liens provided for in this section shall cease to exist unless suit for foreclosure is instituted within six months from the date of filing the same.

477.070. *Effect of payment of fire patrol assessment or membership in control organization.* If the owner regularly pays a fire patrol assessment on the lands described under ORS 477.068 or is a member in good standing of an organization approved by and under contract with the board, which organization has undertaken the control and suppression of fires on such land and which is actually engaged in the control and suppression of fire entering upon or burning on such land, the owner, operator or person in possession shall not be subject to the penalties prescribed by ORS 164.070, or be held as maintaining a nuisance as defined in ORS 477.064, unless he or his agent is wilful, malicious or negligent in the origin of the fire. But payment of fire patrol assessments or membership in an organization under contract with the board shall not relieve any owner, operator or person in pos-

session of land from the obligation imposed by
ORS 477.066 and 477.068 to control and prevent
the spread of fires if that land has theretofore
become an operation area and if, as a result
thereof, an additional fire hazard has been created and exists thereon and has not been released
by the forester.

SUMMARY OF ARGUMENT

1. As the district court correctly held, appellants'
claim does not come within the scope of the Federal
Tort Claims Act because the complaint failed to allege
an injury or loss of property, let alone sought recovery for such an injury or loss. By reason of 28
U.S.C. 1346(b), the jurisdiction of the district court
is limited to claims "for injury or loss of property,
or personal injury or death." This limitation applies
whether or not state law would impose liability in
the circumstances of the case, and plainly bars this
action.

2. Appellants' assertion—advanced for the first
time in this Court—that the fire which it suppressed
damaged or endangered property subject to a state
lien interest, as well as fish and game, watersheds
and like public resources, should not be considered.
Since the complaint contained no such allegation, and
it was not pressed upon the district court, it is not
before this Court. Further, appellants' position would
not be improved if they were allowed, in effect, to
amend their complaint at this juncture. For one
thing, the claim would still not be "for loss or injury

of property" but for fire suppression costs. For another, appellants could not cast themselves in the role of a landowner having been required to incur expense in the protection of their own property from the consequences of another's negligence. The state's lien interest in forest lands creates no right of action in it for harm to those lands resulting from negligence, or any other similar property interest. And the natural resources which appellants now insist were endangered are not the property of appellants— or, indeed, of anyone else. Those resources are common to all, and the state has simply the power to control their use. In protecting them against fire, appellants do no more than carry out their function of providing for the general welfare. And while Congress could have provided that the Tort Claims Act remedy should embrace expenses incurred in the performance of this function, in its wisdom it chose not to do so.

II

The Tort Claims Act also does not embrace actions which are not grounded in tort. For this additional reason, the complaint was appropriately dismissed. Statutory provisions such as those of the Oregon Revised Statutes here involved do not confer rights in tort but, rather, rights having a quasi-contractual footing. For the purpose of Tort Claims Act jurisdiction, it is the nature of the right and not the label placed on it by a particular state which controls. Thus it is irrelevant here how the Oregon courts would characterize the liability of a landowner for

the cost of the assumption by the state or a quasi-public agency—to protect the general welfare—of obligations belonging to the landowner.

ARGUMENT

I

Appellants' Claim Is Not Based Upon "Injury or Loss of Property" and Therefore Is Not Within the Scope of the Tort Claims Act

By this action, appellants seek a recovery under the Federal Tort Claims Act, which, insofar as we are aware, is without precedent. Appellants here seek the recovery of expenses they incurred as public firemen, wholly unrelated to any damage to their property. We submit that the district court correctly held that appellants' claim was not within the Act.

1. The waiver of immunity from suit in tort contained in the Tort Claims Act is, of course, not unlimited. One indication of this fact is that, in 28 U.S.C. 2680, Congress expressly excluded from the ambit of the waiver many types of torts which would be actionable were a private defendant involved; *e.g.*, (in subsection (h)) assaults, batteries, misrepresentations. Within the past year, the Supreme Court invoked the misrepresentation exclusion in holding that damage resulting from a negligent FHA appraisal was not recoverable under the Act. *United States* v. *Neustadt*, 366 U.S. 696. In the course of its opinion, the Court noted that whether under state law the claim would be regarded as based upon a mispresentation "does not meet the question of whether this

claim is outside the intended scope of the Federal Tort Claims Act, which depends solely upon what Congress meant by the language it used in § 2680 (h)". 366 U.S. at 705-706. In other words, state law does not shape the boundaries of the waiver of immunity.

To be sure, none of the Section 2680 exceptions have been brought into play here. But what is involved is an even more fundamental jurisdictional provision—28 U.S.C. 1346(b), *supra*, p. 3. This is the keystone of the entire Act and unless the claim can be brought within the scope of the limited jurisdiction conferred upon the district courts by the terms of that Section, there is no occasion to consider whether it falls within any of the other exclusionary provisions of Section 1346(b).

The conditions precedent to jurisdiction contained in Section 1346(b) are several: (a) the suit must be "for money damages"; (b) the claim must have accrued after January 1, 1945; (c) the sought recovery must be "for injury or loss of property, or personal injury or death"; (d) that injury, loss or death must have been "caused by the negligent or wrongful act or omission" of a Government employee "while acting in the scope of his employment"; and (e) state law must impose liability on a private person in like circumstances.

All of these conditions must be met and, thus, the absence of but one is necessarily fatal to the claim. For example, in *United States* v. *Ure*, 225 F. 2d 709, this Court reversed judgments under the Act based upon damage sustained by the plaintiffs when a break

in a government-operated irrigation supply canal
caused the flooding of their lands in Oregon. The
district court recovery had been founded primarily
upon the principle of absolute liability enunciated in
Rylands v. *Fletcher*, 225 F. 2d. at 711. But, as this
Court pointed out, the *Rylands* doctrine, although
accepted by the Oregon courts, could not support a
claim under the Tort Claims Act. This was because
of the jurisdictional requirement that the claim be
founded on a negligent or wrongful act or omission—
a requirement that precludes the entertaining of any
claim based upon absolute liability. See also *People
of the State of California* v. *United States*, 146 F.
Supp. 341 (S.D. Cal.).[2]

In this case, negligence on the part of Government
employees is alleged. The second amended complaint,
however, does not assert that, as a result of the pur-

---

[2] In that case, the State of California sought recovery
under the Tort Claims Act for damage resulting from the
flooding of one of its highways. The district court, per
Judge Jertberg dismissed the action, relying in large measure upon this Court's decision in *Ure*. As the Court's opinion
pointed out (146 F. Supp. at 344):

> The plaintiff contends that the settled law of Cali-
> fornia holds actionable a diversion and concentration
> of waters onto lower properties never before subjected
> to these waters. I do not question that under the laws
> of the State of California, under appropriate allegations
> and proof, upper land owners may become liable to a
> lower land owner, where the upper land owner by
> artificial means causes surface waters, as distinguished
> from flood waters, to change their natural flow and
> thereby cause damage to the lower land owner. How-
> ever, jurisdiction of this Court must be founded upon
> Federal statutes and not upon State law.

ported negligence, there was "injury or loss of property". Indeed, even a cursory examination of that complaint reflects that no damage to any property of the appellants is claimed.

Instead, the gravamen of the complaint is that, as a result of the charged negligence, public firemen in the employ of appellants were called upon to extinguish a fire. And, what is sought to be recovered is simply the expenses which appellants purportedly incurred by reason of the activities of its public firemen. For a basis of entitlement to such recovery, the complaint points to Chapter 477 of the Oregon Revised Statutes (R. 49).[3] This chapter imposes

---

[3] The act of negligence upon which appellants' action rests occurred in California (R. 13-14), *i.e.*, appellants allege negligence on the part of agents or employees of the Forest Service (United States Department of Agriculture) in setting and controlling the Bogus Mountain fire. Section 1346(b) of the Tort Claims Act provides that "the law of the place where the act or omission occurred" controls. The Supreme Court had occasion to construe this provision in *Richards* v. *United States*, 369 U.S. 1. The Court held (1) that the courts must look, under Section 1346(b), to the law of the state in which the negligent act or omission occurred and (2) in looking to that law, the courts must look to the whole law, *i.e.*, the substantive as well as the conflicts of law rules of such state.

Thus, since appellants here allege an act of negligence in California, the law of California must be first applied in order to determine which law controls this case for Tort Claims Act purposes. California, following what is the majority rule, looks to the law of the place of the wrong. See 11 Cal. Juris. 2d § 79. That place would, in this case, be Oregon (*Ibid.*).

It should be noted, however, that the application of Oregon law might be giving an unintended extraterritorial effect to the Oregon statutes upon which appellants here rely. Gen-

liability for fire suppression costs upon the owner, operator or person in possession of land on which there is a forest fire, where such person is negligent in the origin of the fire or fails to make an effort to suppress the fire. ORS 477.068, *supra*, pp. 4-5. The cost of suppressing the fire may be recovered, pursuant to these provisions, by the State or the forest protective agency which fought the fire (*Ibid.*). This reimbursement is not dependent to any extent upon the fire endangering, let alone damaging, property owned by the State or the agency. Negligence, or inaction on the landowner's part, is enough.

It is readily seen upon analysis that statutes of this type confer rights of a quasi-contractual nature and that recovery under them is in no real sense recovery in tort. See pp. 17-21, *infra*. But even if a particular state were, for one reason or another, to characterize the remedy as one in tort (as Oregon is claimed to have done), and that characterization

---

erally, Oregon statutes are not intended to have such an effect. *Union Pac. R. Co.* v. *Anderson*, 167 Ore. 687, 120 P. 2d 578. And here, although the United States is a landowner in the State of Oregon, in order to reach the act of negligence alleged the Oregon statutes would have to be construed to impose their duties on the activities of the United States as the owner of land in California. It would nevertheless appear permissible for Oregon law to be applied. Cf. *Young* v. *Masci*, 289 U.S. 253, Cavers, *The Two Local Law Theories*, 63 Harv. L. Rev. 822 (1950), casenote, 71 Harv. L. Rev. 1351 (1957-58). See also *Sayles* v. *Peters*, 11 C.A. 2d 401, 54 P. 2d 94. Should, however, this Court find as a matter of construction that Oregon law does not apply, and that California law controls this case, we incorporate by reference, and make a part hereof, our brief in *People of the State of California* v. *United States* (No. 17,534).

were to be accepted,[4] it still could not provide the
basis for an action under the Tort Claims Act.

In the context of the *Ure* and *Neustadt* cases, Congress could have subjected the United States to absolute liability and liability for misrepresentation where state law imposed such liability upon a private person. In its wisdom, it chose not to do so and its judgment in this regard has been given effect—as it must—irrespective of considerations of state tort law. So too, Congress could have provided that the United States should be responsible for any expenses incurred by reason of negligence of Government employees—but did not. The plain mandate of Section 1346(b) is that it is only where the governmental negligence occasions injury to person or property that the Act may be looked to as a means of redress. Stated

---

[4] That the label that the state might attach to a particular form of action is totally irrelevant was recognized by the Fourth Circuit in *Stepp* v. *United States,* 207 F. 2d 909, certiorari denied, 347 U.S. 933. In that case, the plaintiff endeavored to argue that the claim was not barred by the "assault and battery" exception in Section 2680(h) because the conduct of the Government employee did not constitute an "assault and battery" under Alaska law. Rejecting this contention, the court stated (207 F. 2d at 911):

> * * * We think, however, that where the United States excepts itself from certain liabilities, as in Section 2680 of the Federal Tort Claims Act, such exceptions must be interpreted under the general law rather than under some peculiar interpretation of a State or Territory. Stated differently, we do not think that a State may circumvent this intended exception to Government liability by merely abolishing the crime commonly known as an assault and battery and entitling such acts, instead, as a "hurting." * * *

otherwise, it was only *that* type of loss or expense
that Congress felt should be recoverable judicially
from the United States.

It is these considerations, we think, that explain
the inability of appellants to point to a single instance
in the 16 year history of the Tort Claims Act where
recovery was permitted in the absence of injury to
person or property. What appellants ask of this
Court is a rewriting of the terms of Section 1346(b)
to enable them to pursue a remedy which has been
generally understood to be unavailable under the Section
as enacted.

2. For the first time in the entire litigation, appellants
assert in their brief in this Court (pp. 18-
23) that public property was damaged and threatened
by the fire. The short answer to this assertion is
that it should not be considered by the Court. As
above noted, appellants' complaint (R. 13-15) sought
recovery solely on the basis of Oregon statutes relating
to the reimbursement of expenses incurred by
public firemen—and contained no allegations respecting
any fire fighting activities in the capacity of landowner protecting his own property from possible
damage. Likewise, the complaint did not assert damage to state property and did not ask for recovery
of any such damage. What is before this Court is
the question of the correctness of the dismissal of
that complaint; not whether some other complaint,
setting forth different allegations of fact and grounded upon some different theory of liability, might have
stated a cause of action within the ambit of the Tort
Claims Act.

Moreover, even with their new factual representations, appellants do not claim an entitlement to a recovery for any loss of their property. Instead, their present insistence is—as it was in the court below—that they should be given judgment simply for the expenses which were incurred in fighting the fire. Thus, whether or not their property was threatened or damaged, the claim is not for "injury or loss of property" within the meaning of 28 U.S.C. 1346(b).

While this Court need not reach the point, we think it perfectly obvious why appellants did not bring suit under the Tort Claims Act to recover for property loss. The reason is that neither appellant has a sufficient property interest in any of the resources referred to in their brief to maintain such a suit.

For example, while appellants claim (Br., p. 19) that individual *members* of the appellant Klamath Forest Protective Association owned forest lands which were burned or threatened, there is no assertion that the Association itself was the owner of such property. Any damage sustained by an Association member would, of course, have to be recovered in a suit brought by that member.

The appellant State of Oregon's claim (Br., pp. 19-22) of a lien interest in Oregon forest land stands on no better footing. The lien is created by virtue of an allocation of budgeted costs for fire protection, which costs are then assessed against forest land. These assessed costs are, by statute, a lien against the forest land (see App. Br., pp. 18-19). Such a lien creates no interest in the land to which it attaches. Cf., *Schleff* v. *Purdy, et al.*, 107 Ore. 71, 214

P. 137. Rather, it merely secures an indebtedness (*Ibid.*). The holder of such an interest, moreover, has no right to sue for the negligent damage of the property to which his lien is attached. Cf., 2 Jones on Mortgages § 859 at 178 (Eighth Ed. 1928), Anno: Remedy of Mortgagee or other holder of lien on real property against third person for damage to or trespass on property. 37 ALR 1120. Compare *Northern Pac. R.* v. *Lewis*, 162 U.S. 366.

Insofar as the now asserted threat or damage to natural resources is concerned, fish and game, watershed areas and the like are not generally regarded as property which is owned by the State. As to them, the State merely exercises "its undoubted authority to control the taking and use of that which belong(s) to no one in particular, but [is] common to all." *Geer* v. *Connecticut*, 161 U.S. 519, 529. See also *State* v. *Blanchard*, 96 Ore. 79, 189 Pac. 421, quoted at page 23 of appellants' brief.

In the final analysis, then, appellants' new theory based upon damage or threat to natural resources does not alter the situation to any extent. With or without regard to their present claim as to the significance of their fire fighting activities, the undeniable fact is that those activities were undertaken as part of the burden of the sovereign to provide for the general welfare of its citizenry. In Oregon, the burden of affording protection against fire is reflected by Chapter 477 of the Oregon Revised Statutes, which establishes a comprehensive fire control program. Participating in this program, for the benefit of the citizenry at large, is not only the appellant State, and associations like the other appellant here, but the Federal Government itself (R. 20-48).

As previously noted, there is nothing which would have precluded Congress from permitting states, in given circumstances, to transfer the obligation for expenses incurred in the exercise of its police powers to the United States through the vehicle of the Tort Claims Act. We have seen, however, that Congress decided not to make costs involved in providing for the general welfare recoverable under the Act. The express terms of Section 1346(b) must be given their plain meaning, under which appellants can make claim only for damage to or loss of their property. Such damage is nonexistent here (or at least is not sought to be recovered) and, for this reason, the district court properly dismissed the action for lack of jurisdiction.

II

ORS 477.068 Creates a Right in Contract, Which Is Not Within the Tort Claims Act.

There is still another, independent although related, reason why this suit must fail. As its very title reflects, the Tort Claims Act was designed (with certain clearly defined exceptions) to "remove the sovereign immunity of the United States from suits in tort." See *Richards* v. *United States*, 369 U.S. 1, 6. Thus a right created by state law, in order to be within the class of rights with respect to which the Congress waived sovereign immunity, must be a right in tort. We submit that whatever right appellants have under Oregon law is a right in contract, and thus not cognizable under the Tort Claims Act. Cf.,

Drake v. *Treadwell Construction Co., et al.*, 299 F. 2d 789 (C.A. 3) ; *Jones* v. *United States*, 89 F. Supp. 980 (D. Iowa).

The starting point is, necessarily, that the label that a state places on a particular type of action is not determinative for Tort Claims Act purposes. See *e.g., Stepp* v. *United States*, discussed n. 4, *supra*, p. 13. Thus, for example, if a state were to purport to confer a right "in tort" for a breach of contract which was negligent rather than intentional, it would scarcely follow that a Tort Claims Act suit could be maintained on such a breach of a Government contract. For it could not be said that Congress thought of that type of conduct as tortious, and thus subject to an action under the Tort Claims Act instead of the Tucker Act.

We have already suggested that, whatever the label which Oregon might have chosen to place on the right which is conferred by ORS 477.068, that right cannot be regarded as being, in any real sense, in tort. For the right comes into existence under the statute wholly independently of whether the conduct complained of gave rise to any risk at all to property of the appellants. So long as the appellants undertake to fight a forest fire which is deemed a public nuisance, they have a statutory entitlement to reimbursement of their expenses no matter how distant may be their own property (and thus remote the risk).

Where recovery is allowed of expenses involved in the performance of a general public duty owing the citizenry at large, it must be on a quasi-contractual

basis—unless a penalty rationale is involved. When
public firemen attack a fire which has been negligently set, or permitted to spread, by a landowner,
they are assuming an obligation which rests principally upon the landowner. Cf., ORS 477.066.
Having thus bestowed a benefit upon the wrongdoer,
they are entitled to obtain reimbursement under the
quasi-contracts doctrine that no one shall be allowed
to enrich himself unjustly at the expense of another.
Keener on Quasi-Contracts, p. 16 (1893).

As we have developed in our brief in *People of the
State of California* v. *United States* (No. 17,534),
(see n. 3, *supra*, p. 11), the California fire suppression cost statute (California Health and Safety
Code § 13009) is recognized by the California courts
as creating rights of a quasi-contractual character.
Of course, California's characterization of the nature
of the right conferred by this kind of statute is no
more controlling for Tort Claims Act jurisdiction
purposes than is the Oregon characterization. But
we submit, the view of the California courts represents the application of long-standing and well understood concepts underlying the dichotomy between
actions in tort and actions having a quasi-contractual
basis. See *People* v. *Zegras*, 165 P. 2d 541 (C.A.
Cal.), affirmed on other grounds, 29 C. 2d 67,
172 P.2d 883; *Ventura County* v. *So. Calif. Edison
Co.*, 85 C.A. 2d 529, 193 P. 2d 512.

ORS 477.068 is concededly not identical to its California counterpart. While the California statute is
only operative if the fire had spread beyond the negligent landowners' property, Oregon requires simply

that the fire be "burning uncontrolled or without proper action being taken to prevent its spread." ORS 477.064. Nonetheless, the two statutes do not differ in any respect which is material here.

On the contrary, just as the California statute refers to a "charge" against the negligent landowner which "shall constitute a debt," ORS 477.068 refers to the recovery of 'fire suppression costs "by action for debt" and creates a lien to cover the debt. Of greater significance, under the Oregon statute as under the California statute, the negligent conduct need give rise to no risk to property of the plaintiffs. The *sine qua non* of liability under both statutes is a failure on the part of the landowner properly to assume his statutory obligations to prevent the spread of fire, with the result that a public fire fighting agency is required to assume it for him. And the measure of that liability is the expense to the fire-fighter of assuming the obligation.

For these reasons, we submit that this Court need not consider whether, as appellants insist (Br., p. 17), the Supreme Court of Oregon has affixed a label of "tort" to actions to recover fire suppression costs. Once again, what is involved here is an issue of jurisdiction under a federal statute—and its resolution is wholly dependent upon whether Congress regarded the term "tort" to apply to actions brought by public or quasi-public agencies to recover costs incurred in performing a service for the general welfare which allegedly should have been performed by the defendant. Since there is no evidence in the Act or its legislative history that Congress intended to depart so radically from conventional notions of what constitutes a tort liability as opposed to a contractual or quasi-contractual obligation, the answer to that inquiry must be in the negative. In sum, the result here must be the same as in the *California* case, where even under state law there is no room for doubt as to the contractual nature of the right to recover 'fire suppression costs from the negligent landowner.

CONCLUSION

For the reasons stated, it is respectfully submitted that the judgment of the district court should be affirmed.

WILLIAM H. ORRICK, JR.,
Assistant Attorney General.

SIDNEY I. LEZAK,
Acting United States Attorney.

ALAN S. ROSENTHAL,
STANLEY M. KOLBER,
Attorneys,
Department of Justice,
Washington 25, D. C.

MAY 1962.

No. 17585

In the

United States Court of Appeals
For the Ninth Circuit

RAY B. WOODBURY,
Appellant,
v.
UNITED STATES OF AMERICA,
Appellee.

APPELLANT'S BRIEF

Appeal from the Judgment of Dismissal of the
United States District Court for
the District of Oregon

THE HONORABLE JOHN F. KILKENNY, *Judge*

KING, MILLER, ANDERSON, NASH & YERKE,
NORMAN J. WIENER,
JEAN P. LOWMAN,
 1200 American Bank Building,
 Portland 5, Oregon,
  Attorneys for Appellant.

SIDNEY I. LEZAK,
 Acting United States Attorney,
 District of Oregon,
ROGER G. ROSE,
 Assistant United States Attorney,
 District of Oregon,
 P. O. Box 71,
 Portland, Oregon
MORTON HOLLANDER,
 Chief, Appellate Section, Civil Division,
 Department of Justice,
 Washington 25, D. C.,
  Attorneys for Appellee.

INDEX

INDEX—(Continued)

TABLE OF CASES AND AUTHORITIES

Cases

TABLE OF CASES AND AUTHORITIES—(Continued)

Statutes

Other Authorities

No. 17585

In the
United States Court of Appeals
For the Ninth Circuit

RAY B. WOODBURY,
Appellant,

v.

UNITED STATES OF AMERICA,
Appellee.

APPELLANT'S BRIEF

Appeal from the Judgment of Dismissal of the
United States District Court for
the District of Oregon

THE HONORABLE JOHN F. KILKENNY, *Judge*

STATEMENT OF JURISDICTION

This action was filed on September 30, 1957 (R. 17), in the United States District Court for the District of Oregon (R. 3). The original jurisdiction of the District Court was invoked under the provisions of the Federal Tort Claims Act, 28 USCA Section 1346 (b) and 28 USCA Sections 2671-2680 (R. 4). The question of whether the District Court had jurisdiction of the cause is before this court on this appeal.

On February 14, 1958, appellee filed its motion to dismiss and in the alternative for summary judgment (R. 17-19). By stipulation of the parties contained in the pre-trial order (R. 45), the issues raised by the motion to dismiss were segregated for hearing in advance of other issues in the case (R. 116). The segregated issues came on for trial before the court without a jury on December 12, 1960 (R. 122-123). February 8, 1961, the court entered its opinion in favor of appellee (R. 79-117). February 24, 1961, the court entered its judgment of dismissal, dismissing appellant's complaint and the causes of action therein contained (R. 117-118).

Appellant filed his notice of appeal on April 11, 1961 (R. 118), within the time allowed by Rule 73 (a), Federal Rules of Civil Procedure. April 21, 1961, the court entered its certificate and order nunc pro tunc to appear of record as of February 24, 1961, that in entering its judgment of dismissal it intended to make the same final pursuant to the requirements of Rule 54 (b), Federal Rules of Civil Procedure. It found that there was no just reason for delay in the entry of final judgment on appellant's complaint and directed that final judgment be entered on such complaint (R. 121-122).

Consequently, this court has jurisdiction to review the judgment of dismissal of the District Court under 28 USCA Section 1291 and Rule 54 (b), Federal Rules of Civil Procedure.

⸗llee filed its motion to
⸪ ∴ summary judgment
· ue parties contained in
∴ ∵ues raised by the
∴ ∴ for hearing in ad-
∴ 116). The segre-
∴ the court without
∴ 122-123). February 8,
∴ in favor of appellee
∴ court entered its
∴ ant's complaint
∴ R 117-118).
∴ April 11, 1961
∴ Rule 73 (a), Fed-
∴ 1961. the court
∴ tunc to appear
∴ in entering its
∴ make the same
∴ Rule 54 (b), Fed-
∴ there was no
∴ judgment on
∴ final judgment
∴).
∴ tion to review
∴ Court under 28
∴ eral Rules of

STATEMENT OF THE CASE

A. Preliminary Statement.

This case relates to the purview of the Federal Tort Claims Act and, as such, it has a significance which extends far beyond its impact upon appellant. The legal principles involved in this case and the question before this court are basic to the application of the Act, and it is, therefore, inevitable that the outcome will have considerable nation-wide importance.

There is no question as to the facts in this case. The issues before this court are of law. Appellant agrees with and accepts the District Court's findings (infra, page 22). He challenges only the court's conclusion, that is, that it does not have jurisdiction of this cause under the provisions of the Federal Tort Claims Act.

B. Nature of the Action.

Appellant's claims arose out of the construction of the Aleutian Homes housing project in Kodiak, Alaska, which was intended to provide housing for naval personnel stationed at Kodiak Naval Base and for civilians employed on the Base.

The basis of appellant's claims may be summarized as follows: By entering into a completion agreement under which construction of the project was to be concluded, Housing and Home Finance Agency (an agency of the federal government hereinafter referred to as "HHFA") and the Housing and Home Finance Agency Administrator (hereinafter referred to as "the Administrator") entered into a fiduciary relationship with appellant, the project creditors and other interested parties. HHFA, its agents and employees breached this fiduciary relationship (1) by failing to obtain or provide permanent long-term financing of the project and (2) by satisfying its own interests as a creditor from the project assets to the exclusion of other interested parties, and specifically appellant (R. 69, 102).

Appellant seeks to recover the damages resulting from appellee's breach of its fiduciary duty (R. 70) under the provisions of the Federal Tort Claims Act. His damages include:

1. Certain payments made by him for which he would have been reimbursed if appellee had not breached its fiduciary duty, that is, (a) $75,000 paid to the project manager appointed under the completion agreement for overhead in the completion of the construction, (b) $164,594.80 paid to the Bank of California, N. A. pursuant to the provisions of the completion agreement, and (c) $35,955.02 paid to General Casualty Company of America in satisfaction of a judgment obtained by the latter for the unpaid premium on a bond executed in connection with the Aleutian Homes project (R. 1-13, 70).

2. The sum of $150,000, which appellant had advanced from his personal funds to pay expenses incurred during preparation for the project. (Shares of preferred stock of Aleutian Homes, Inc., amounting to $150,000 issued to appellant would have been redeemed if appellee had not breached its fiduciary duty (R. 13-14, 70).)

3. The sum of $428,127, as the damage to and destruction of the equity of Aleutian Homes, Inc. in the Aleutian Homes project (R. 15-16, 70).

C. Summary of Facts.

The facts which gave rise to this action are complicated, and consequently it is necessary to outline the same in more than the usual detail. Because of the large number of private and public agencies and organizations involved (see Ex 1177), the attention of the reader is directed to the opinion of the District Court (R. 79-89) in which a full statement of the same is set forth, as well as a summary of the relevant federal statutes.

The relevant federal agencies and personnel thereof will be referred to herein as follows:

1. Housing and Home Finance Agency, "HHFA."

2. The Housing and Home Finance Agency Administrator, "the Administrator" (also referred to by the District Court as "the Lender").

3. Federal Housing Administration, "FHA."

4. Federal National Mortgage Association, "FNMA."

5. Community Facilities Administration, "CFA" (formerly Community Facilities and Special Operations Branch, "CF&SO").

6. Reconstruction Finance Corporation, "RFC."

Background of Aleutian Homes Project. In 1949, discussions commenced among officials of the Navy, the Alaska Housing Authority, the City of Kodiak and the FHA relative to obtaining additional housing for naval and civilian personnel stationed and employed at Kodiak Naval Base. These officials considered the possibility of obtaining such housing under the provisions of the Wherry Act (National Housing Act, Title VIII, as amended), but discarded the same. They then caused studies to be made as to the prospects of constructing an off-base project, consisting of 350 to 400 houses, with conventional FHA assistance under the National Housing Act, Title II, Section 203, as amended (R. 53, 89).

In 1950 and 1951, arrangements were made to secure a site for the project, consisting of lands owned by the Federal Government and under the control of the Bureau of Land Management of the Department of the Interior. The property was to be conveyed to the Alaska Housing Authority, which would reconvey the same to the City of Kodiak. The city was to use this property for construction of a housing project by a sponsor of its selection. Thereafter, the Alaska Housing Authority conveyed the land directly to the approved sponsor (R. 53, 89).

Streets for the project were to be provided by the city, water and sewer facilities and schools by the city and the Department of Interior through Alaska Public Works, and power by the local REA (R. 53-54, 89-90). In 1951, the city received a commitment from the Alaska Public Works program for funds to construct the water and sewer facilities (R. 54, 90).

In 1950 and 1951, the project site was surveyed and engineering was performed for the city and for a proposed sponsor, Raymond Lewis of Los Angeles. However, at the conclusion of the year 1951, Lewis was no longer interested (R. 54, 90).

Background of Appellant's Interest in Aleutian Homes Project. In 1951, appellant, a businessman in Portland, Oregon, financed a trip to Alaska by three associates, S. C. Horsley, R. A. Blanchard and G. K. Gosling, in order that they might ascertain whether a house panel invented by Horsley could be sold in the territory. Gosling on this trip contacted Lee C. Bettinger, Mayor of Kodiak, who thereupon met appellant and

8

interested him in becoming the sponsor of the proposed housing project (R. 54, 90).

In February, 1952, appellant caused Aleutian Homes, Inc. to be incorporated under the law of the State of Oregon. In February or March, 1952, the City of Kodiak approved the new corporation as sponsor of the project. The property chosen as the project site was thereafter conveyed to Aleutian Homes, Inc. by the Alaska Housing Authority (R. 54, 90).

Financing of Project. The proposed financing of the Aleutian Homes project had two phases: the long-term financing, and the short-term interim financing for construction purposes. These phases will be discussed in that order.

1. Long-Term Financing. The proposed long-term financing was to consist of funds advanced by a private lending agency, Brice Mortgage Co., to be secured by individual mortgages on each of the houses in the project. These funds in turn were to be based upon a firm commitment of FHA to insure such private mortgages and upon a further firm commitment of FNMA to purchase the mortgages so insured.

It was originally intended that the project be financed under the provisions of the National Housing Act, Title II, Section 203, as amended, which contemplated that a private mortgage agency would take out individual long-term mortgages on each house. Brice Mortgage Co. was selected as permanent mortgagee, but before it could sell any mortgages on the houses to FNMA, it of course first had to obtain an FHA commitment to insure such mortgages (R. 55, 91; and see Ex. 289/A2).

In accordance with FHA requirements, the Secretary of the Navy twice certified to FHA (in 1951, with respect to Raymond Lewis, and in 1952, with respect to Aleutian Homes, Inc.):

a. The Navy's critical need for 385 family dwellings to be used by military and civilian personnel at the Kodiak Naval Base;

b. The permanency of the Kodiak Naval Base; and

c. The ability of such personnel to pay rentals in the amounts of $100, $130 and $150 for two- and three-bedroom units (R. 55-56, 91; and see Ex. 115/48).

In 1952, FHA appraised the value of a completed 344-unit project at $5,904,250. In April of that year it issued a firm commitment to Brice Mortgage Co. to insure long-range individual mortgages on each home in a total amount of $4,706,400. This figure was based upon 80 per cent of the FHA appraised value (R. 55-56, 91-92).

In the same year, FNMA also issued a firm commitment to Brice Mortgage Co. to purchase the individual long-range mortgages at par after they were insured by FHA (R. 56, 92).

Aleutian Homes, Inc. was to use the amount received from the long-term financing for the following purposes:

a. Repayment of the $4,230,900 short-term interim construction loan from HHFA;

b. Payment of the costs of taking out permanent individual mortgages (estimated to be several hundred thousand dollars); and

c. Any balance remaining as capital (R. 56, 92).

2. Short-Term Interim Construction Loan. In 1952, Aleutian Homes, Inc. and Brice Mortgage Co., because of the difficulty of attracting risk capital to Alaska, were unable to obtain from private sources the funds required for construction of the project before long-term financing should be realized. As a result, they sought assistance from HHFA. Negotiations then ensued between Brice Mortgage Co., on behalf of Aleutian Homes, Inc., and CF&SO with respect to an interim loan for construction purposes (R. 56-57, 92).

In the latter part of 1952, Aleutian Homes, Inc. made its final application for an interim loan, and the same was approved in January, 1953. This loan was in the sum of $4,230,900, constituting 90 per cent of the FHA and FNMA commitments for long-term financing. According to the application, the difference between the projected costs and the loan was to be supplied by Aleutian Homes, Inc. (R. 57, 92-93).

The loan authorization was signed by the Administrator and effectuated by documents required under a building loan agreement. These documents included appellant's guaranty of the loan agreement and the construction contract and a promissory note and deed of trust. A loan and disbursement agreement, executed on April 27, 1953, by appellant as president of Aleutian Homes, Inc., described the procedure for disbursements. The construction contracts and appellant's capital stock in Aleutian Homes, Inc. were assigned to the Administrator, as security. Appellant executed a standby agreement, individually and as president of Aleutian Homes, Inc. Performance bonds were executed in favor of Aleutian Homes, Inc. and the Administrator (R. 57-58, 93).

Upon the completion of the foregoing, firm arrangements finally had been made to provide the financing for this large housing project.

Contractual Arrangements for Construction. The contracts relating to construction of the Aleutian Homes

12

project under the HHFA interim loan were signed on April 27, 1953 (R. 58, 93).

Simultaneously, and in accordance with its understanding with HHFA, Aleutian Homes, Inc. entered into a general contract with Kodiak Construction Co. whereby the latter agreed to construct the project for $4,230,-900, the total maximum amount of the HHFA loan. Kodiak Construction Co. at the same time entered into the following subcontracts:

1. A "supply contract" with Alex B. Carlton, doing business as Carlton Lumber Company, for the purchase of prefabricated house packages;

2. A "site construction contract" with Pacific Alaska Contractors, Inc., for preparation of the site; and

3. A "construction contract" with Leo S. Wynans, Inc., for erection of the prefabricated houses on the prepared sites.

In addition, Kodiak Construction Co. entered into a contract with Coastwise Steamship Lines for transportation of prefabricated house packages and other materials from Portland, Oregon, to Kodiak. The total payment under these four contracts equaled $4,230,900 (R. 58-59, 93-94), the exact amount of the HHFA construction loan. At this stage all details appeared to have been ironed out successfully.

Cessation of Construction. In the summer of 1953, serious problems developed with respect to site preparation. As a result, a dispute arose between Kodiak Construction Co., acting through Leo S. Wynans, its agent, and Pacific Alaska Contractors, Inc., and the latter discontinued such work. Thereafter, Kodiak Construction Co., under Wynans' direction, furnished the labor and materials required under the site construction contract (R. 59, 94).

Financial problems arose in October and November, 1953, primarily due to lack of operating capital. November 6, 1953, when the project was approximately 75 per cent completed, Pacific Alaska Contractors, Inc. filed a lien claim against it for $150,504.43. Construction then ceased (R. 59, 94-95).

Completion Agreement. When construction was halted, various plans were considered by HHFA to remedy the situation. These included foreclosure, completion of the project by the sureties, demand upon appellant for performance, and introduction of additional money, either in conjunction with or in substitution for the Aleutian Homes, Inc. sponsorship. In addition, it was suggested that the project might be completed under a completion agreement (R. 59-60, 95).

14

Demand was made on appellant under his guaranty in November, 1953, but he did not comply (R. 60, 95).

Representatives of HHFA and Aleutian Homes, Inc. formulated a 'completion agreement" in January, 1954, and it became effective in substantially the same form on April 23, 1954. During the intervening period, the consent necessary to effectuate the agreement was obtained (R. 60, 95).

The completion agreement (Ex. 583/1-140, 512/4) provided for completion of construction. It provided that appellant was not to have any further control or direction over the project until the then scheduled long-range financing came into effect, and further, that appellant was to advance substantial funds for the overhead of the project during the completion of construction. It also provided for payment of claimants, creditors and completion costs, to be made in four stages. In order to effectuate this agreement, Aleutian Homes, Inc., Kodiak Construction Co. and Leo S. Wynans Co., Inc. agreed that a project manager would be vested with exclusive authority to take any and all action in connection with the project that they would have been authorized to take. By the agreement, HHFA was vested with overall supervision and control of the project, including the receipt and disbursement of all funds of the project during the completion period and until the long-range financing by the constituent agencies of HHFA had been effected (Exs. 583/1-140, 562/A-4, 891/A-21, 1021/A-22, R. 60, 95-96).

In the words of the District Court:

> "It is clear from all pertinent parts and provisions of the completion agreement, taken together and considered in light of the facts and circumstances surrounding the transaction at the time of execution, and the actions of the parties subsequent thereto, that the obligation of the Lender to furnish long-term financing was within the contemplation of the parties and was necessary to carry their intentions into effect." (R. 110)

> "Already I have mentioned that the only source of long-term financing in the area was through the federal loan agencies. In my opinion an agreement to provide such long-term financing was as much a part of the completion agreement as if it had been specifically mentioned. The providing of such financing was one of the duties of the Lender when it moved in and took complete control of the project." (R. 111)

Completion of Project. Harry M. Langton was appointed project manager under the completion agreement. He had prescribed duties, responsibilities and authority with respect to completion of construction and payment of claims (R. 60-61, 96), subject however, to the overall direction and control of HHFA.

Scott J. Cross was appointed construction superintendent (also by HHFA) to oversee the physical completion of the project (R. 61, 96).

By October 26, 1954, construction of 343 houses had been completed. The remaining house was never constructed for the reason that the lot upon which it was to be located was not suitable for building purposes. By April 12, 1955, 341 houses had passed final inspection by FHA. The two remaining houses were not acceptable for reasons which pertained to their foundations. At that time all claims in stages 1 and 2 were paid, as were a portion of the claims in stages 3 and 4 (R. 61, 96).

Long-Term Financing Commitments Permitted to Expire. Despite the fact that by April, 1955, FHA had approved virtually all the houses in the project, no permanent individual mortgages ever were taken out on any of these houses. In June, 1955, ostensibly in order to avoid payment of further commitment fees to FHA and FNMA, HHFA permitted the FHA commitments (to insure the mortgages) and the FNMA commitments (to purchase the same at par) to expire (R. 61, 96; Exs. 832/A-1-207, 849/49-4, 850/20, 851/A-20, 859/20). As late as November, 1955, HHFA still planned to obtain long-term financing so the short-term HHFA loan could be paid off and the project placed on a sound long-term financial basis (Exs. 974/21, 976/21, 983/21; and see Ex. 1019/22).

Occupancy of Project. During the period from July, 1954, to August, 1959, the project was from 60 per cent to 95 per cent occupied, by personnel connected with the naval base at Kodiak (R. 62-63).

In the summer of 1957, the Navy indicated that it would reduce its service personnel by 10 per cent and its civilian personnel by approximately 33⅓ per cent (R. 63, 97).

Payments relating to Project Made and Received by Government Agencies. The advances made by HHFA to or for the benefit of Aleutian Homes, Inc. for project construction amounted to $4,192,717.10, from a total authorized loan of $4,230,900. The difference resulted from nonconstruction of one house (supra, page 16) and the failure of two others to pass FHA inspection (supra, page 16). From June 25, 1953, until November 24, 1953, that is, prior to the completion agreement, HHFA advanced $3,330,062.68. After the completion agreement became effective, it advanced an additional $862,654.42 on the project manager's requisition (R. 64, 98).

In March, 1955, HHFA authorized advances in addition to the original loan in an amount not to exceed

$160,000. These advances were to be utilized by the project manager for the care and preservation of the project. March 15, 1955, HHFA advanced $56,239.19 to the project manager. This sum was repaid on May 5, 1956, with 7 per cent interest (R. 64, 97-98).

HHFA received payments totalling $909,675.58 for or on behalf of Aleutian Homes, Inc. Individually, these payments were: (1) $35,134.14 from June 25, 1953, to October 31, 1953, prior to the completion agreement; (2) $402,241.44 from the project manager after he assumed his duties under the completion agreement; (3) $122,300 withdrawn by HHFA from the project manager's bank account immediately prior to foreclosure; and (4) $350,000 from the court-appointed receiver (R. 65, 98).

FHA received fees of $22,360 for its commitments to insure and extension of the same, and FNMA received fees of $106,422.77 for its commitments to purchase and extension (R. 65, 98).

Rentals Received by Project Manager. During the period from July 1, 1954, to June 14, 1957, the project manager received $1,114,800.20 in rentals (R. 65-66, 98-99).

Payments Relating to Project Made by Appellant Subsequent to Completion Agreement. After the completion agreement was formulated, appellant made the following payments relating to the Aleutian Homes project:

1. During 1954, 1955 and 1956, appellant made payments totaling $164,594.80 to The Bank of California, N. A., in payment of the latter's claim against the project, as set forth in the completion agreement. Certain of these payments were credited to principal and others to interest (R. 66, 99).

2. In 1954, appellant paid Brice Mortgage Company $35,000 in settlement of all claims of the latter and of Brice Realty Company against the project for alleged work done and services performed prior to execution of the completion agreement (R. 66-67, 99).

3. In 1954, appellant paid the Administrator $75,-000 in accordance with provisions of the overhead agreement and the completion agreement requiring him to pay certain overhead expenses relating to the completion of the project (R. 67, 100).

4. September 18, 1956, appellant paid General Casualty Company $33,542.09 in satisfaction of a judgment obtained by the latter on July 24, 1956, for the unpaid premium on a bond issued on behalf of Kodiak Construction Co. and expenses. In defending this action, appellant incurred legal fees and other expenses in the sum of $2,412.93 (R. 67, 100).

Seizure of Funds and Foreclosure Suit. It should be noted that from approximately February, 1954, through May, 1957, HHFA through the project manager had absolute control and direction of this project. It made all the decisions, received and disbursed all funds. During this period it completed the project and thereafter rented the houses. It made the decision to permit the existing commitments for long-range financing to expire. By the terms of the completion agreement, appellant had absolutely no control or direction of the project during this period. In the words of the trial court:

> "* * * evidence is overwhelming that the Lender (HHFA) in truth and in fact took over absolute control of and proceeded with the completion of the project." (R. 106)

Furthermore, as the trial court indicated in its opinion, there was no available source of long-range financing for this project, except the United States itself or one of its agencies, a fact of which HHFA was well aware. (R. 103, 111).

Despite all this, and despite the fact that private capital was not available, HHFA on May 21, 1957 (Exs. 1142/A-22; 1144/23; 1150/A-32; and see Ex. 1025/A-32), without advance warning seized for its own account $122,300 out of the bank account of the project. Immediately thereafter it instituted suit to foreclose its interim short-term loan mortgage in the United States District Court for the District of Alaska. This suit was brought in the name of the United States of America against Aleutian Homes, Inc., Pacific Alaska Contractors, Inc., Alex B. Carlton, doing business as Carlton Lumber Company, the city of Kodiak, certain individuals as trustees, and "Also all other persons or parties unknown claiming any right, title, estate, lien or interest in the real estate described in the complaint herein" (R. 67-68, 100-101). June 14, 1957, M. G. Gebhart was appointed receiver of the property on the plaintiff's motion. June 20, 1958, the court authorized the receiver to pay HHFA $200,000 from the proceeds of operating the project, and this was thereafter done. On or about September 12, 1958, the plaintiff amended its complaint, adding the Territory of Alaska, Kodiak Construction Co., Leo S. Wynans Co., Inc., and United States of America as defendants. On or about April 10, 1959, the court authorized the receiver upon the latter's request to pay HHFA $150,000 from the proceeds of operating the project, and he subsequently did so (R. 68, 101).

From the foregoing it is evident that by May, 1957, appellee had made its decision to foreclose appellant's investment in the project and ultimately to obtain title to the entire project through foreclosure proceedings. By so doing, it effectively renounced its previously stated position that long-range financing would be provided for the project so that the short-term interim construction loan of HHFA could be repaid.

D. Findings and Conclusion of District Court.

The findings of the District Court, which are undisputed, are in part as follows:

1. Appellee could and did occupy the status of a fiduciary.

> "I am of the opinion that the Lender could legally occupy the legal status of a fiduciary in connection with the completion of the housing project in question. Furthermore, I find and hold that the Lender took over full and complete control of such project and, in so doing, was acting in a fiduciary capacity with the plaintiff" (R. 108-109).

2. Appellee breached its fiduciary duty to appellant.

> "I have already concluded that defendant could act as a fiduciary and was acting in a fiduciary or confidential capacity in assuming control over the completion of the project and the long-term financing. Assuming, arguendo, and I would so hold if I felt I had jurisdiction, that defendant in truth and in fact breached its duty in failing to provide, without justification, said long-term financing, is said breach of duty 'negligent or wrongful act or omission' within the meaning of the phrase as used in the Federal Tort Claims Act?" (R. 112)

However, the court concluded that breach of fiduciary duty does not constitute tortious conduct within the meaning of the Federal Tort Claims Act (R. 113-114), and that it therefore does not have jurisdiction of appellant's claims (R. 116, 117).

E. Question Presented.

In the foregoing state of facts, the following question is presented for decision on this appeal:

Under the provisions of the Federal Tort Claims Act, does the District Court have jurisdiction of appellant's claims for damages arising from appellee's breach of fiduciary duty?

SPECIFICATION OF ERROR

The District Court committed error when it concluded as a matter of law that it did not have jurisdiction of appellant's claims under the Federal Tort Claims Act and thereupon dismissed appellant's complaint and the causes of action set forth in said complaint.

SUMMARY OF ARGUMENT

I. The District Court committed an error of law when it held that it does not have jurisdiction of appellant's claims under the provisions of the Federal Tort Claims Act and thereupon dismissed appellant's complaint and the causes of action therein set forth.

A. Breach of fiduciary duty constitutes tortious conduct for which appellant would be liable, if a private person, under the applicable law.

B. Apart from the provisions of the Federal Tort Claims Act, appellee is amenable to suit for breach of fiduciary duty.

C. Governmental immunity from liability for breach of fiduciary duty has been waived under the provisions of the Federal Tort Claims Act.

1. Breach of fiduciary duty is within the scope of the clear and unequivocal provisions of the Federal Tort Claims Act, which constitutes a waiver of governmental immunity from liability as to all torts which would give rise to individual liability except those expressly removed from the operation of such waiver.

2. The Congressional intent was not such as to exclude breach of fiduciary duty from the scope of the Federal Tort Claims Act.

3. The provisions of the Federal Tort Claims Act must be given a liberal construction.

4. The cases relating to the Federal Tort Claims Act show that the Act constitutes a waiver of governmental immunity from liability for breach of fiduciary duty.

II. In the event that this court affirms the conclusion of the District Court that breach of fiduciary duty is not within the purview of the Federal Tort Claims Act, it should require the District Court to transfer this case to the Court of Claims.

ARGUMENT

Point I

The District Court committed an error of law when it held that it does not have jurisdiction of appellant's claims under the provisions of the Federal Tort Claims Act and thereupon dismissed appellant's complaint and the causes of action therein set forth.

After finding that appellee was in a fiduciary relationship with appellant, and that it had breached its fiduciary duty to him (supra, page 22), the District Court stated the issue thus: "* * * is such breach of duty a 'negligent or wrongful act or omission' within the meaning of the phrase as used in the Federal Tort Claims Act?" (R. 112). The court answered "No," and dismissed appellant's complaint. Appellant respectfully urges that the answer should have been "Yes," and that judgment should have been entered in his favor.

Under the provisions of the Federal Tort Claims Act 28 USCA Section 1346 (b)

the District Courts have exclusive jurisdiction of

"* * * civil actions on claims against the United States, for money damages, accruing on and after January 1, 1945, for injury or loss of property, or personal injury or death caused by the negligent or wrongful act or omission of any employee of the Government while acting within the scope of his office or employment, under circumstances where the United States, if a private person, would be liable to the claimant in accordance with the law of the place where the act or omission occurred."

In concluding that breach of fiduciary duty is not within the scope of these provisions, the court reasoned as follows:

1. Immunity from liability as to all torts was not waived under the Act;

2. Immunity was waived only as to the "ordinary common-law type of tort," i.e., negligence; and

3. If violation of fiduciary duty constitutes tortious conduct, it is not within the provisions of the Act, as so limited (R. 112-116).

However, the conclusion must fail, for the reasoning is not correct. Breach of fiduciary duty is a tort under Oregon law, and it is conduct for which governmental immunity from liability was waived under the Federal Tort Claims Act.

A. Breach of fiduciary duty constitutes tortious conduct for which appellee would be liable, if a private person, under the applicable law.

Before c
Claims Act
whether the
appellee's e
would be lia
of the State
resolved. Br
under Orego
a private ins
pellant.

Breach o
tortious cons

Restatemen

"A pe
another
from a b

"Com

"b. A
duty as a
the perso

This rule
Harper v. In
P2d 757

This wa-
leged that t

loss of property,
by the negligen
of any employee of th
the scope of his
circumstances when
private person, would b
cordance with the law
omission occurred."

of fiduciary duty is not
the court reasoned

all torts was not

as to the "ordinary
negligence: and

constitutes tortious
sions of the Act, as

for the reasoning
duty is a tort under
which governmental
under the Federal

constitutes tortious conduct
liable, if a private person,

Before considering the scope of the Federal Tort Claims Act specifically, it is necessary to determine whether the breach of fiduciary duty committed by appellee's employee constitutes conduct for which it would be liable, if a private individual, under the law of the State of Oregon. This problem is, however, easily resolved. Breach of fiduciary duty is an actionable tort under Oregon law, and, consequently, if appellee were a private individual, it would be liable therefor to appellant.

Breach of fiduciary duty is generally regarded as tortious conduct.

4 Restatement of Torts, Section 874

"A person standing in a fiduciary relation with another is liable to the other for harm resulting from a breach of duty imposed by such relation.

"Comment: * * *

"b. A fiduciary who commits a breach of his duty as a fiduciary is guilty of tortious conduct to the person for whom he should act."

This rule obtains in the state of Oregon.
Harper v. Interstate Brewery Co. (1942) 168 Or 26, 120 P2d 757

This was a tort action in which the plaintiffs alleged that the defendants had breached their fiduciary duty to the plaintiffs. This fiduciary duty related to certain property conveyed by the plaintiffs to the defendants in reliance upon certain representations made by the latter. In affirming a judgment for the plaintiffs, the court stated (168 Or 42, 120 P2d 764):

> "The contract between plaintiffs and the defendant brewery expressly required the defendant to 'use its best efforts to obtain as much as it reasonably can for said property', but that is not all. Pursuant to the contract the defendant company received deeds as security with a purported power of sale. It thereby assumed a relationship to the plaintiffs upon which the law imposed a duty to act in good faith, using reasonable efforts to make the sale beneficial to the mortgagor by obtaining the best price reasonably obtainable. This was a duty 'independent of contract' imposed by law and irrespective of similar contractual provisions. *A breach of that duty was an actionable tort* under the authorities cited." (emphasis added)

And see

> *Fergison v. Belmont Conv. Hospital*
> (1959) 217 Or 453, 464-466,
> 343 P2d 243, 247-248

There is, therefore, no doubt that if appellee were a private individual, its conduct would have given rise to tort liability under Oregon law.

B. Apart from the provisions of the Federal Tort Claims Act, appellee is amenable to suit for breach of fiduciary duty.

As the facts of this case bring it within the scope of the Federal Tort Claims Act, our principal concern is with that statute. However, it must be noted that even apart from the provisions of the Federal Tort Claims Act, appellee would be amenable to suit by appellant for its breach of fiduciary duty.

The statutory powers of the Administrator (R. 82-84) show that he is clothed with all the attributes of a private enterprise "launched * * * into the commercial world," and that as such he is given the power to "sue and be sued." Patently, in vesting him with such rights and powers, Congress removed his governmental immunity from liability for conduct which would give rise to liability on the part of a private enterprise.

> *Federal Housing Administration v. Burr*
> (1939) 309 US 242, 245, 84 Led 724,
> 728-729

And see

> *Reconstruction F. Corp. v. J. G.*
> *Menihan Corp.*
> (1940) 312 US 81, 85 Led 595
>
> *Keifer & Keifer v. Reconstruction*
> *Finance Corp.*
> (1938) 306 US 381, 83 Led 784

Acting in his capacity as a private entrepreneur, the Administrator committed a breach of his fiduciary duty to appellant. A private enterprise would be liable for such conduct, and, in the absence of the Federal Tort Claims Act, appellee would be similarly liable. However, as breach of fiduciary duty is within the scope of the Act, appellant's remedy must perforce be under that statute.

28 USCA Section 2679(a)

> "The authority of any federal agency to sue and be sued in its own name shall not be construed to authorize suits against such federal agency on claims which are cognizable under section 1346(b) of this title, and the remedies provided by this title in such cases shall be exclusive."

C. Governmental immunity from liability for breach of fiduciary duty has been waived under the provisions of the Federal Tort Claims Act.

The tort committed by appellee, i. e., breach of fiduciary duty, is clearly within the scope of the Federal Tort Claims Act, and, as a result, governmental immunity from liability for such conduct has been waived. To limit the scope of the Act so as to exclude this tort from its provisions would be contrary to the unequivocal language of the Act and to judicial decision relative to the same.

1. Breach of fiduciary duty is within the scope of the clear and unequivocal provisions of the Federal Tort Claims Act, which constitutes a waiver of governmental immunity from liability as to all torts which would give rise to individual liability except those expressly removed from the operation of such waiver.

In order to determine whether breach of fiduciary duty is within the scope of the Federal Tort Claims Act, the first step is to examine the language of the Act. This reveals a clear, unambiguous statute waiving governmental immunity from liability as to all torts which would give rise to individual liability other than those expressly excepted from such waiver.

The Federal Tort Claims Act is part of a statute vesting the District Courts with jurisdiction over certain actions to which the United States is a defendant. 28 USCA Section 1346

"(a) The district courts shall have original jurisdiction, concurrent with the Court of Claims, of:

"(1) Any civil action against the United States for the recovery of any internal-revenue tax alleged to have been erroneously or illegally assessed or collected, or any penalty claimed to have been collected without authority or any sum alleged to have been excessive or in any manner wrongfully collected under the internal-revenue laws;

"(2) Any other civil action or claim against the United States, not exceeding $10,000 in amount, founded either upon the Constitution, or any Act of

Congress, or any regulation of an executive department, or upon any express or implied contract with the United States, or for liquidated or unliquidated damages in cases not sounding in tort.

"(b) Subject to the provisions of chapter 171 of this title, the district courts, together with the United States District Court for the District of the Canal Zone and the District Court of the Virgin Islands, shall have exclusive jurisdiction of civil actions on claims against the United States, for money damages, accruing on and after January 1, 1945, for injury or loss of property, or personal injury or death caused by the negligent or wrongful act or omission of any employee of the Government while acting within the scope of his office or employment, under circumstances where the United States, if a private person, would be liable to the claimant in accordance with the law of the place where the act or omission occurred."

And see

28 USCA Section 2674

"The United States shall be liable, respecting the provisions of this title relating to tort claims, in the same manner and to the same extent as a private individual under like circumstances, * * *"

When the provisions of the Federal Tort Claims Act,

28 USCA Section 1346 (b)

are examined alone, it appears that the language thereof is sufficiently broad to include any civil wrong including actions *ex contractu* and those *ex delicto*. However, when the statute is considered as a whole, it is apparent that such is not the case, and it is a simple matter to delineate the wrongs actually covered by the Act.

A perusal of the preceding subdivision of the chapter,

28 USCA Section 1346 (a) (2)

reveals that actions on contract not exceeding $10,000 in amount are covered by that subdivision, and are within the concurrent jurisdiction of the District Courts and the Court of Claims. Additionally, under the provisions of

28 USCA Section 1491

the Court of Claims has jurisdiction "to render judgment upon any claim against the United States founded * * * upon any express or implied contract with the United States." As contract actions are fully treated by these provisions, it is manifest that an action *ex contractu* is not included in the "negligent or wrongful act or omission" of subdivision (b).

With actions *ex contractu* eliminated from consideration, the Act can only apply to actions sounding in tort, that is, actions *ex delicto*. Thus, "tort" has been defined as follows:

Black's Law Dictionary (4th Ed, 1951) page 1660

> "A private or civil wrong or injury. A wrong independent of contract."

Prosser on Torts (2d Ed, 1955) Section 1, page 2

> "* * * a civil wrong, other than breach of contract, for which the court will provide a remedy in the form of an action for damages."

Furthermore, the provisions of the Act, which embrace the "negligent or wrongful act or omission" of government employees, patently extend to *all tortious conduct* which would give rise to liability if the United States were a private individual. The language employed admits of no exceptions. This conclusion is confirmed when it is observed that Congress expressly excluded certain types of tortious conduct from the operation of the statute. Thus, see

28 USCA Section 2680

> "The provisions of this chapter and section 1346 (b) of this title shall not apply to—
>
> "(a) Any claim based upon an act or omission of an employee of the Government, exercising due care, in the execution of a statute or regulation, whether or not such statute or regulation be valid, or based upon the exercise or performance or the failure to exercise or perform a discretionary function or duty on the part of a federal agency or an

employee of the Government, whether or not the discretion involved be abused.

"(b) Any claim arising out of the loss, miscarriage or negligent transmission of letters or postal matter.

"(c) Any claim arising in respect of the assessment or collection of any tax or customs duty, or the detention of any goods or merchandise by any officer of customs or excise or any other law-enforcement officer.

"(d) Any claim for which a remedy is provided by sections 741-752, 781-790 of Title 46, relating to claims or suits in admiralty against the United States.

"(e) Any claim arising out of an act or omission of any employee of the Government in administering the provisions of sections 1-31 of title 50, Appendix.

"(f) Any claim for damages caused by the imposition or establishment of a quarantine by the United States.

"(g) Any claim arising from injury to vessels, or to the cargo, crew, or passengers of vessels, while passing through the locks of the Panama Canal or while in Canal Zone waters.

"(h) Any claim arising out of assault, battery, false imprisonment, false arrest, malicious prosecution, abuse of process, libel, slander, misrepresentation, deceit, or interference with contract rights.

"(i) Any claim for damages caused by the fiscal operations of the Treasury or by the regulation of the monetary system.

"(j) Any claim arising out of the combatant activities of the military or naval forces, or the Coast Guard, during time of war.

"(k) Any claim arising in a foreign country.

"(l) Any claim arising from the activities of the Tennessee Valley Authority.

"(m) Any claim arising from the activities of the Panama Railroad Company."

Subdivision (g) was repealed in 1950, and at the same time subdivision (m) was amended and a new subdivision (n) added, as follows:

"* * * (m) Any claim arising from the activities of the Panama Canal Company.

"(n) Any claim arising from the activities of a Federal land bank, a Federal intermediate credit bank, or a bank for cooperatives."

This specific enumeration of classes of tortious conduct removed from the operation of the Act definitely belies any suggestion that other classes of torts are excepted from its provisions. See, in this connection, *Employers' Fire Ins. Co. v. United States* (9 Cir., 1948) 167 F2d 655

This case involved the negligence aspect of the Federal Tort Claims Act, and specifically the question of whether a subrogated claim is within the scope of the Act. This court stated at page 656:

"In the Federal Tort Claims Act, Congress,

though granting jurisdiction generally to the Federal Courts to render judgment on 'any claim', designated twelve categories of claims of which the Federal Tort Claims Act was not meant to apply. Claims of subrogees were not included therein. *Had Congress intended to exclude subrogated claims, it would have undoubtedly designated them as one of the categories which the Act was not meant to cover.*" (emphasis added)

The same question was before the court in

Wojciuk v. United States (ED Wis, 1947) 74 F Supp 914, 916

"Congress exercised great care in designating twelve different categories of claims which the Federal Torts Claims Act was not intended to cover. The claims here in question were not included in any such classification. The familiar maxim of interpretation, expressio unius est exclusio alterius, may be invoked. It is my opinion that plaintiff Casualty Company, as a subrogee of Wojciuk, is a proper claimant under the act."

And see

Richards v. United States (1962) 369 US 1, 7 Led2d 492

This case involved a question as to the applicable law in an action brought under the Federal Tort Claims Act which was based upon an act of negligence occurring in one state and resulting in death and injury in another. The court stated (369 US 6-7, 7 Led2d 496-497):

> "The Tort Claims Act was designed primarily to remove the sovereign immunity of the United States from suits in tort and, with certain specific exceptions, to render the Government liable in tort as a private individual would be under like circumstances. It is evident that the Act was not patterned to operate with complete independence from the principles of law developed in the common law and refined by statute and judicial decision in the various States. Rather, it was designed to build upon the legal relationships formulated and characterized by the States, and, to that extent, the statutory scheme is exemplary of the generally interstitial character of federal law. If Congress had meant to alter or supplant the legal relationships developed by the States, it could specifically have done so to further the limited objectives of the Tort Claims Act. That is, notwithstanding the generally interstitial character of the law, Congress, in waiving the immunity of the Government for tortious conduct of its employees, could have imposed restrictions and conditions on the extent and substance of its liability." (emphasis added)

Consequently, the courts should not read additional exceptions into the Act.

Rayonier Inc. v. United States (1957) 352 US 315, 320, 1 Led2d 354, 358-359

"There is no justification for this Court to read exemptions into the Act beyond those provided by Congress. If the Act is to be altered that is a function for the same body that adopted it."

Analysis of the plain provisions of the Federal Tort Claims Act thus leads inevitably to the following conclusion: Because breach of fiduciary duty is a tort for which the United States would be liable if it were a private individual (supra, pages 26-28), it is within the scope of the Act. It was not included in the list of torts excepted from the application of the Act, and it is therefore within the waiver of governmental immunity from liability effectuated by the Act.

2. The Congressional intent was not such as to exclude breach of fiduciary duty from the scope of the Federal Tort Claims Act.

In concluding that the Federal Tort Claims Act encompasses only negligent conduct, the District Court relied upon alleged legislative intent to limit the waiver of governmental immunity from liability for torts grounded on negligence. This reliance is misplaced. As appellant has demonstrated (supra, pages 31-39), the provisions of the Act are clear and unequivocal, embracing other wrongful acts or omissions, such as breach of fiduciary duty, as well as negligent acts or omissions. Consequently, reference to the legislative intent is not necessary. In any event, however, the intent of Congress was not to confine the act in the manner suggested by the District Court, but was rather in complete accordance with the clear language of the Act.

The Federal Tort Claims Act was enacted in order to relieve Congress from the necessity of determining the merits of myriad private bills presented for the redress of individual tort claims, a process both inequitable and burdensome. Of course, a large percentage of the claims presented in this way arose out of the negligent conduct of government employees, and there is no doubt that the Act does cover such claims, a fact which Congress discussed in some detail. This does not, however, militate against the fact that the Act also covers tort claims arising from other wrongful conduct of government employees, such as breach of fiduciary duty.

In discussing legislative intent, the District Court quotes (R. 113) from

Dalehite v. United States (1952) 346 US 15, 97 Led 1427

a case which has been abandoned or overruled by the Supreme Court. See

> *Indian Towing Co. v. United States* (1955)
> 350 US 61, 100 Led 48

> *Rayonier Inc. v. United States* (1957)
> 352 US 315, 1 Led2d 354

In the *Dale...*
97 Led 1436-...

"The
Congress...
ity from...
occasione...
ing withi...
templated
to liabilit...
ture or fu...
tion. Up...
were the
example...
peated p...
to tort li...
vehicles.'

At most, this
common-law
thinking, ar...
ticles receiv...
coverage of t...
constitutes a
whether the
many comm
which was n
and breach o
such a tort.
most" in Con
cate that ot...
its thinking.

In the *Dalehite* case, the court states (346 US 27-28, 97 Led 1436-1437):

> "The legislative history indicates that while Congress desired to waive the Government's immunity from actions for injuries to person and property occasioned by the tortious conduct of its agents acting within their scope of business, it was not contemplated that the Government should be subject to liability arising from acts of a governmental nature or function. Section 2680 (a) draws this distinction. Uppermost in the collective mind of Congress were the ordinary common-law torts. Of these, the example which is reiterated in the course of the repeated proposals for submitting the United States to tort liability is 'negligence in the operation of vehicles.' "

At most, this statement would indicate that "ordinary common-law torts" were uppermost in Congressional thinking, and that negligence in the operation of vehicles received frequent mention as an example of the coverage of the Act. However, it is not clear as to what constitutes an "ordinary common-law tort," or even whether the example fits into this category. Certainly, many common-law torts arose out of wrongful conduct which was not negligent in character, such as trespass, and breach of fiduciary duty may be regarded as being such a tort. Furthermore, if negligence were "uppermost" in Congress' collective mind, this would not indicate that other wrongful conduct was not also within its thinking.

In addition, the District Court quotes (R. 112-114) a statement made to a Congressional committee by Francis M. Shea, Assistant Attorney General, again referring to the "ordinary common-law type of torts" and citing negligence in vehicular operation as an example of the same. This does not necessarily enlighten us as to the Congressional intent, and, at any rate, the same criticisms are applicable.

The legislative history of the Federal Tort Claims Act is extensive, going back for a number of years prior to its enactment in 1946. Consequently, an examination of some of the remarks made by various members of the Congress during the course of this history are helpful. Thus, see

69 Congressional Record (70th Congress, First Session, 1928)

On this occasion, the House of Representatives had resolved itself into a Committee of the Whole House to consider H. R. 9285, to provide for settlement of claims against the United States on account of property damage, personal injury or death. The following statements were made:

> "Mr. RAMSEYER. The committee reporting out this bill goes beyond negligence and includes, and the gentleman will see on page 1, line 8, and page 2, line 2, not only negligence but wrongful acts or omissions.

"Mr. BULWINKLE. Yes.

"Mr. RAMSEYER. Now wrongful does not necessarily involve negligence, neither does omission.

"Mr. BULWINKLE. That is true.

"Mr. RAMSEYER. Under the act where you make the Government liable for injury to private property not in excess of $1,000, you specifically state, 'Caused by negligence of an officer or employee.'

"Mr. BULWINKLE. Yes.

"Mr. RAMSEYER. You expand in this bill beyond what you went under this limited liability of $1,000 to private property.

"Mr. BULWINKLE. We do.

"Mr. RAMSEYER. Now, what is your reason for it?

"Mr. BULWINKLE. The reason for it is in order that these meritorious cases, whether they arise from negligence, wrongful acts, or wrongful omissions of any of the agents of the Government shall be settled or shall be adjudicated by some one instead of waiting from year to year on Congress." (page 2191)

"Mr. RAMSEYER. * * *

"We first attempted to relieve the Committee on Claims in 1922 when we conferred jurisdiction upon the heads of the departments to adjudicate claims up to a thousand dollars for injury to private property on account of the negligence of Government employees. I ask members to note this language in that statute:

'caused by the negligence of any officer or employee.'

"In this bill we go further. We confer jurisdiction for damages or loss to private property—

'caused by the negligence or wrongful act or omission of any officer or employee of the Government.'

"There can be no question that we are widening the scope of the statute that we passed in 1922." (page 2203)

86 Congressional Record (76th Congress, Third Session, 1940)

Here, the House of Representatives had resolved itself into a Committee of the Whole House to consider H. R. 7236. The following was a discussion with Mr. Celler, Chairman of the Committee on the Judiciary:

"Mr. O'CONNOR. I believe the bill is a good one. However, I should like to get the gentleman's interpretation of just what limitation is to be placed in the bill in the nature of the actions that may be determined. For instance, I call the attention of the gentleman to line 4 on page 2, beginning with the words—

'Caused by the negligent or wrongful act or omission of any officer or employee of the United States, including any member of the military and naval forces, while acting within the scope of his office or employment.'

"What I am trying to get at is, does this bill limit the nature of the claims to the acts specified in that clause?

"Mr. CELLER. No. In the first place, this section, section 1, involves the settlement of claims, not actions brought.

"Mr. O'CONNOR. In other words, is there any limitation in this bill as to the nature of the claims that may be passed upon by the department heads as outlined in the bill?

"Mr. CELLER. Yes; if the gentleman will look at section 303, on page 6, and the pages following, he will find this language:

'The provisions of this act shall not apply to'

"And then we enumerate the types of claims that cannot be brought or settled under this bill?

"Mr. O'CONNOR. Other than that, the bars are down?

"Mr. CELLER. Absolutely." (page 12019)

In the course of this same discussion, it became apparent that Congress considered that assault and battery would have been covered by the Act in the absence of the express exception now contained in

28 USCA Section 2680(h)

"Mr. O'CONNOR. Paragraph 9, on page 7, it seems to me ought to be stricken out. Suppose an officer goes into one of the parks or goes on an Indian reservation and gets into trouble there with an Indian or somebody else and beats him up and assaults him, why should not an action of that kind be determined by a court or be determined in the manner provided rather than requiring a special act here in Congress?

"Mr. CELLER. We considered those possibilities that the gentleman has mentioned, and we were afraid that there would be terrifically exaggerated claims brought if we took away those exemptions, and that is why we included the phrase as you have it there." (page 12020)

Certainly, this is not a tort grounded in negligence.

A recent comment made by the Supreme Court will serve to summarize the legislative intent.

Richards v. United States (1962) 369 US 1, 8, 7 Led2d 492, 497-498

> "* * * The concern of Congress, as illustrated by the legislative history, was the problem of a person injured by an employee operating a government vehicle *or otherwise acting within the scope of his employment,* * * *" (emphasis added)

Clearly, the intent of Congress was not such as to exclude wrongful conduct other than negligence from the operation of the Federal Tort Claims Act. Breach of fiduciary duty is therefore within the scope of the conduct encompassed by the Act.

3. The provisions of the Federal Tort Claims Act must be given a liberal construction.

Statutory consent to sue the sovereign is to be construed liberally. In the oft-quoted words of Judge Cardozo:

Anderson v. John L. Hayes Const. Co. (1926) 243 NY 140, 153 NE 28, 29-30

> "The exemption of the sovereign from suit involves hardship enough, where consent has been withheld.

- unded in negligence.

...e Supreme Court will

...intent.

- 359 US 1, 8, 7 L ed 2d

...ws, as illustrated by
...problem of a person
'perating a government
...in the scope of his
...added)

- ...was not such as to

- than negligence from

...ims Act. Breach of

...the scope of the con-

d ral Tort Claims Act

...tion is to be con-

...ds of Judge Car-

...(1926) 243 NY

.rn from suit involves
...been withheld.

We are not to add to its rigor by refinement of construction, where consent has been announced."

And see

United States v. Shaw (1939) 309 US 495, 501, 84 L ed 888, 892

"A sense of justice has brought a progressive relaxation by legislative enactments of the rigor of the immunity rule. As representative governments attempt to ameliorate inequalities as necessities will permit, prerogatives of the government yield to the needs of the citizen. * * * When authority is given, it is liberally construed."

These statements are particularly apposite to a consideration of the Federal Tort Claims Act, and they have often been quoted or cited by the courts in discussing the provisions of the Act.

> *United States v. Yellow Cab Co.* (1950)
> 340 US 543, 554-555, 95 L ed 523, 532
>
> *United States v. Aetna Cas. & S. Co.* (1949)
> 338 US 366, 383, 94 L ed 171, 186
>
> *American Exch. Bank of Madison, Wis.*
> *v. United States* (7 Cir., 1958) 257 F2d
> 938, 941
>
> *Somerset Seafood Co. v. United States*
> (4 Cir., 1951) 193 F2d 631, 634
>
> *Rushford v. United States* (ND NY,
> 1950) 92 F Supp 874, 875

48

Consequently, the Act must not be whittled away by stringent construction, but, rather, it must be liberally construed to afford full efficacy to its provisions. When this guiding principle is applied to the clear provisions of the Act, the conclusion is unavoidable. Breach of fiduciary duty is one of the torts for which governmental immunity from liability has been waived.

4. The cases relating to the Federal Tort Claims Act show that the Act constitutes a waiver of governmental immunity from liability for breach of fiduciary duty.

In construing the provisions of the Federal Tort Claims Act, the District Court limited the words "negligent or wrongful act or omission" to negligent conduct (R. 115), and thus concluded that the Act does not encompass breach of fiduciary duty. Appellant has shown (supra, pages 31-39) that this construction is contrary to the clear provisions of the Act. It is equally certain that the court's holding is contrary to the relevant body of judicial decision.

It is true that most litigation under the Act arises in the field of negligence, and this fact must be considered when examining the cases construing the Act. However, it is by no means true that the operation of the Act is limited to cases of negligent conduct, and the falsity of this suggestion is made apparent by a consideration of the relevant authorities. The Act does extend to more than negligent conduct, and it does encompass breach of fiduciary duty.

Before examining the cases, it is well to note with some precision the meaning of the words "negligent" and "wrongful." Thus, "negligent" has been defined as follows:

Webster's New International Dictionary (2d ed, 1950)

"Guilty of, or given to, neglect or disregard; neglectful; characterized by negligence; heedless; culpably careless; as in *negligent* order; *negligent* of traffic rules."

Webster's Third New International Dictionary (1961)

"1. That is marked by or given to neglect: that is neglectful esp. habitually or culpably * * *; *specif:* not exercising the care usu. exercised by a prudent person * * *."

"Wrongful" is defined:

Webster's New International Dictionary (2d ed, 1950)

"1. Full of wrong; injurious; unjust; unfair; as *wrongful* acts or dealings.

"2. Not rightful, esp. in law; unlawful, illegitimate; without legal sanction * * *."

Webster's Third New International Dictionary (1961)

"1: full of wrong: INJURIOUS, UNJUST, UN-
FAIR * * *

"2: not rightful esp. in law: having no legal
sanction: UNLAWFUL, ILLEGITIMATE * * *."

It is clear, then, that, although a negligent act may
be wrongful, all wrongful conduct is not negligent. The
words "wrongful act or omission" are broader in scope
than the words "negligent act or omission." See
Clark's Adm'x v. Louisville & N. R. Co. (1897) 101 Ky
34, 39 SW 840

In discussing the words "wrongful act" as they appeared in the phrase "negligent or wrongful act" of the
wrongful death act, the court stated at page 841:

"* * * It is a more comprehensive term than
the word 'negligence.' Necessarily, in every case of
negligence there must be a 'wrongful act,' either
of omission or of commission. There may be an actionable 'wrongful act' which is not the result of
negligence; neither is there an element of negligence in it. It may be willfully or unintentionally
done. The words 'wrongful act' denote or embrace
all acts other than those constituting mere negligence which are wrong, * * *."

Consequently, when the District Court equated a
"negligent" act or omission with a "wrongful" act or

omission, it rendered the latter language meaningless. Such construction is patently erroneous.

Parcell v. United States (SD W. Va., 1951) 104 F Supp 110, 116

> "* * * Under Sec. 1346(b) of the Act the United States is made liable for '* * * loss of property, or personal injury or death caused by the negligent *or wrongful* act or omission of any employee of the Government * * *.' (emphasis added.) The words, 'wrongful act,' in that portion of the statute set out above must be given some meaning. To say that 'wrongful act' is a tautological phrase meaning negligence is inconsistent with the general rule of statutory interpretation, namely, that no portion of a statute susceptible of meaning is to be treated as superfluous."

Thus, in commenting upon the meaning of the word "wrongful" as used in the Act, the courts have uniformly indicated that it encompasses more than negligent conduct.

Hatahley v. United States (1955) 351 US 173, 181, 100 Led 1065, 1074

> "We note also that § 1346(b) provides for liability for 'wrongful' as well as 'negligent' acts. In an earlier case the Court has pointed out that the addition of this word was intended to include situations like this involving ' "trespasses" which might not be considered strictly negligent.' "

52

Aleutco Corporation v. United States (3 Cir., 1957) 244 F2d 674, 678

> "The act was primarily directed towards eliminating the congressional preoccupation with the enactment of private bills compensating individuals for losses sustained as a result of the negligent torts of government employees. S.Rep. No. 1400, 79th Cong. 2d Sess. (1946). However, the act was written broadly to include losses 'caused by the *negligent or wrongful* act or omission of any employee of the government.' (Emphasis supplied.) See *Hatahley v. United States*, 1956, 351 U.S. 173, 181, 76 S.Ct. 745, 100 L.Ed. 1065."

The District Court suggests (R. 115) that the word "wrongful" has been deprived of its full meaning through inferential application of the rule of ejusdem generis. However, by definition that rule is not relevant to a consideration of the provisions of the Federal Tort Claims Act.

Black's Law Dictionary (4th ed, 1951) page 608

"EJUSDEM GENERIS. * * *

"In the construction of laws, wills, and other instruments, the 'ejusdem generis rule' is, that where general words follow an enumeration of persons or things, by words of a particular and specific meaning such general words are not to be construed in their widest extent, but are to be held as applying only to persons or things of the same general kind or class as those specifically mentioned. * * * The rule, however, does not necessarily require that the general provision be limited in its scope to the identical things specifically named. Nor does it apply when the context manifests a contrary intention."

Furthermore, the District Court does not cite any cases in which this rule has been applied to the provisions of the Act. It is clear that this case must be determined upon some basis other than the use of ejusdem generis.

The pertinent inquiry is, therefore, as to whether the courts permit recovery under the Federal Tort Claims Act for damages resulting from wrongful conduct other than negligence. The answer is clearly "Yes."

Hatahley v. United States (1955) 351 US 173, 100 Led 1065

This was an action brought by eight families of Navaho Indians under the Federal Tort Claims Act to recover damages for destruction of their horses by agents of the federal government. The Supreme Court reversed the judgment of the Court of Appeals for the Tenth Circuit, which had in turn reversed the judgment of the District Court allowing recovery.

After the enactment of the Taylor Grazing Act, permits were issued to white livestock operators, permitting

54

them to graze their animals on lands used by the Indians. Disputes thereafter arose between the two, resulting in suits by the government and by the stockmen to remove the Indians from such lands. In addition, however, government agents carried on an active campaign to round up and destroy the Indians' horses. In so doing, they purportedly acted under the provisions of the Utah Abandoned Horse Statute, but the record showed that the statute was applied in a discriminatory manner against the Indians.

The Supreme Court held that the Utah Abandoned Horse Statute was not properly invoked, and, further, that there was liability under the provisions of the Federal Tort Claims Act. In so holding, it noted that the word "wrongful" as used in the Act includes conduct which is not negligent in character (see supra, page 51).

The District Court dismissed the *Hatahley* case as one which is "closely related to negligence" (R. 115). However, as this case involves a trespassory invasion which is not akin to negligence, it cannot be disposed of in this summary fashion.

Aleutco Corporation v. United States (3 Cir., 1957) 244 F2d 674

55

This was an action brought under the Federal Tort Claims Act to recover damages for conversion of war surplus property which the plaintiff had purchased from the government. Judgment for the plaintiff was affirmed.

In May, 1948, the plaintiff purchased from the government miscellaneous surplus property located in the Aleutian Islands and in the custody of the Navy. The property was to be removed by November 30, 1948, but the removal date was later extended to October 30, 1949, and the plaintiff did thereafter take portions of the property. March 22, 1951, the plaintiff received permission from the Navy to remove additional property, but when the plaintiff's representatives went to the site to arrange for such removal, they were refused permission by a civilian employee of the Navy. The matter of ownership was referred to the Navy Department, and the plaintiff thereafter wrote the General Services Administration that (1) the War Assets Administration had advised it that there was no urgency for removal of the property and (2) the commander of the naval base at Adak, Alaska, had given it specific written permission for an indefinite extension of time for such removal. Various correspondence and conferences ensued, following which the plaintiff was notified that it had forfeited any rights to the property, and the same was sold to another firm. This action resulted.

After noting the use of the word "wrongful" as well as of "negligent" in the Federal Tort Claims Act (see supra, page 52), the court stated at pages 678-679:

> "Aleutco's complaint is a sufficient statement of a cause in tort for conversion, and it would seem that Aleutco could have equally well made out a complaint for breach of contract. See 3 Williston on Sales § 595 (Rev. Ed. 1948). Aleutco has chosen to prosecute its action on the basis of tort in the District Court. That it failed to avail itself of an action in the Court of Claims is not a valid jurisdictional objection. So long as immunity of the United States to suit depended upon the distinction between tort and contract, the Supreme Court was careful to preserve the distinction. Thus prior to the Tort Claims Act, rather than extend the liability of the United States under the Tucker Act, the common law privilege of waiving the tort and suing on the contract implied by law was denied. * * * However, requiring strict enforcement of the distinction in the situation presented in the instant case would be contrary to the purpose for which the Tort Claims Act was enacted. The waiver of the immunity of the United States to suit was the primary purpose of the various enactments conferring jurisdiction on the federal courts to hear such suits. There is little doubt as to Aleutco's ability under the statutes to bring this suit. While only cases 'not sounding in tort' are cognizable in the Court of Claims, the jurisdiction of that court has been sustained where elements of both contract and tort were involved in the claim. * * * Likewise, as a result of the Tort Claims Act, there is no policy in the law which requires that the forum of the district court be denied a plaintiff who pleads and proves a classic case in tort. To do so would neither further nor accomplish Congress' purpose in waiving the immunity of the United States to suit."

Again, the District Court in the case at bar attempted to bring the *Aleutco* case within the purview of its holding by stating that the latter case is "closely related to negligence" (R. 115). Appellant respectfully disagrees with this analysis. The conduct complained of in the *Aleutco* case was, as the court therein indicated, "wrongful," but not negligent.

United States v. Praylou (4 Cir., 1953) 208 F2d 291

This was an action brought under the provisions of the Federal Tort Claims Act to recover damages resulting when an airplane operated by government employees on government business fell from the sky. Judgments for the plaintiffs were affirmed.

Liability was under the provisions of the Uniform Aeronautics Act, which provided for absolute liability regardless of negligence where injuries were caused by the descent of an airplane. The court noted that the effect of this statute was to make the infliction of injury or damage by the operation of an airplane of itself a wrongful act giving rise to liability. It held that cases involving liability of this sort are clearly within the purview of the Federal Tort Claims Act.

The *Praylou* case was followed in

Hahn v. U.S. Airlines (ED NY, 1954) 127 F Supp 950

which also involved damages resulting from the crash

58

of a government airplane. The court therein stated at pages 951-952:

> "It is hard to see in logic why liability should not follow such an invasion of plaintiffs' premises. Restatement of the Law, Section 165, subdivision (c), recognizes the liability for such intrusion, and illustration 8 is of particular interest.
>
> 'A is skillfully navigating an airplane far above the surface of B's premises. Stress of weather renders the plane unmanageable, and it comes to land in B's field, damaging his crops. A is liable to B.'
>
> Judge Parker, in *United States v. Praylow* [sic], 4 Cir., 208 F.2d 291, 292, at page 294, wrote:
>
> 'In other words, the flight of an airplane at a proper altitude is recognized as lawful but the person operating it is charged with the responsibility of preventing injury to persons and property beneath. Not to prevent such injury, whether negligent or not, renders the person operating the plane liable at law on the theory that it was his duty under the law to prevent it if he undertook to operate the plane. As said by Judge Moore in *Parcell v. United States*, D.C., 104 F. Supp. 110, 116, "To say that a tort giving rise to absolute liability is not a 'wrongful act' would be a technical refinement of language incompatible with that liberal interpretation of the sovereign's waiver of immunity which the highest court in the land has admonished us to employ. See *United States v. Aetna Casualty & Surety Co.*, 1949, 338 U.S. 366, 70 S.Ct. 207, 94 L.Ed. 171; *United States v. Yellow Cab Co.*, 1950, 340 U.S. 543, 71 S.Ct. 399, 95 L.Ed. 523." ' "

The discu
Hahn case is
District Court
of fiduciary c
in a volume se
same is true o

Parcell v. Uni
110

This was a
Claims Act a
Force planes
ment for the

The court
was applicab
ility is a "v
Federal Tort

In additic
numerous cas
arise from a
cept of such
See, for exam

Rayonier Inc
L.ed2d 354

These we

The discussion of the Restatement of Torts in the *Hahn* case is also interesting. In the case at bar, the District Court placed reliance upon the fact that breach of fiduciary duty is classified as tortious by that work in a volume separate from that treating negligence. The same is true of the section relied upon in the *Hahn* case.

Parcell v. United States (SD W. Va., 1951) 104 F Supp 110

This was an action brought under the Federal Tort Claims Act and resulting from the crash of two Air Force planes on the plaintiff's land. There was judgment for the plaintiff.

The court held that the principle of absolute liability was applicable and that a tort giving rise to such liability is a "wrongful act" within the meaning of the Federal Tort Claims Act.

In addition to the foregoing authorities, there are numerous cases which, although relating to negligence, arise from a duty divorced from the common-law concept of such conduct envisaged by the District Court. See, for example, the following:

Rayonier Inc. v. United States (1957) 352 US 315, 1 Led2d 354

These were actions brought under the Federal Tort

Claims Act to recover damages resulting from the negligence of Forest Service employees in allowing a forest fire to start on government land, and in failing to use due care to extinguish such fire. Judgments of dismissal were reversed.

The court stated (352 US 319-320, 1 Led 2d 358-359):

> "It may be that it is 'novel and unprecedented' to hold the United States accountable for the negligence of its firefighters, but the very purpose of the Tort Claims Act was to waive the Government's traditional all-encompassing immunity from tort actions and to establish novel and unprecedented governmental liability. The Government warns that if it is held responsible for the negligence of Forest Service firemen a heavy burden may be imposed on the public treasury. It points out the possibility that a fire may destroy hundreds of square miles of forests and even burn entire communities. But after long consideration, Congress, believing it to be in the best interest of the nation, saw fit to impose such liability on the United States in the Tort Claims Act. Congress was aware that when losses caused by such negligence are charged against the public treasury they are in effect spread among all those who contribute financially to the support of the Government and the resulting burden on each taxpayer is relatively slight. But when the entire burden falls on the injured party it may leave him destitute or grievously harmed. Congress could, and apparently did, decide that this would be unfair when the public as a whole benefits from the services performed by Government employees. And for obvious reasons the United States cannot be equated with a municipality, which conceivably might be rendered bank-

rupt if it were subject to liability for the negligence of its firemen. There is no justification for this Court to read exemptions into the Act beyond those provided by Congress. If the Act is to be altered that is a function for the same body that adopted it."

Indian Towing Co. v. United States (1955) 350 US 61, 100 Led 48

This was an action brought under the Federal Tort Claims Act to recover damages allegedly resulting from the negligence of the Coast Guard in (1) permitting the light in a lighthouse maintained by it to become extinguished, and (2) failing to repair such light or to give notice that it was not functioning. Judgment of dismissal was reversed.

The court stated (350 US 69, 100 Led 56):

"The Coast Guard need not undertake the lighthouse service. But once it exercised its discretion to operate a light on Chandeleur Island and engendered reliance on the guidance afforded by the light, it was obligated to use due care to make certain that the light was kept in good working order; and, if the light did become extinguished, then the Coast Guard was further obligated to use due care to discover this fact and to repair the light or give warning that it was not functioning. If the Coast Guard failed in its duty and damage was thereby caused to petitioners, the United States is liable under the Tort Claims Act."

American Exch. Bank of Madison, Wis. v. United States
(7 Cir., 1958) 257 F2d 938

This was an action brought under the Federal Tort Claims Act to recover for personal injuries sustained by the plaintiff's decedent when she fell on steps leading to an entrance of a federal post office building. Judgment for the defendant was reversed, and the cause was remanded for further proceedings.

The District Court held that neither the Wisconsin Safe Place Statute nor the rules and orders of the Wisconsin Industrial Commission were applicable to the post office building, and that the United States could not be found negligent for its failure to comply with the same. The Court of Appeals held that the same were applicable, and that violation of an order relating to handrails should have been considered in determining the government's liability for negligence in violating such order.

United States v. Lawter (5 Cir., 1955) 219 F2d 559

This was an action brought under the Public Vessels Act and the Federal Tort Claims Act to recover damages for the death of the plaintiff's wife, allegedly caused by the negligence of the Coast Guard in conducting an air-sea rescue. Judgment for the plaintiff was affirmed. The court stated at page 562:

" * * * the uncontradicted evidence shows that the Coast Guard, pursuant to long established policy, affirmatively took over the rescue mission, excluding others therefrom, and thus not only placed the deceased in a worse position than when it took charge, but negligently brought about her death, and it is hornbook law that under such circumstances the law imposes an obligation upon everyone who attempts to do anything even gratuitously, for another not to injure him by the negligent performance of that which he has undertaken. 38 Am.Jur., 'Negligence', Sec. 17, p 659."

Somerset Seafood Co. v. United States (4 Cir., 1951) 193 F2d 631

This was an action brought under the Federal Tort Claims Act to recover damages for the sinking of the plaintiff's ship as a result of the government's negligent marking of a wrecked vessel. Under the Wreck Acts, 33 USCA Sections 409, 736, 14 USCA Section 86, the government had a mandatory duty to remove or mark such wreck. Judgment dismissing the complaint was reversed and the cause remanded for further proceedings.

Otness v. United States (D Alaska, 1959) 178 F Supp 647

This was an action brought under the Federal Tort Claims Act to recover damages allegedly caused by a collision between the plaintiff's vessel and a maritime aid known as Channel Light No. 54. It was found that the damages were caused by the defendant's negligence, and there was judgment for the plaintiff.

The court held that the defendant breached its duty to exercise due care in its efforts to locate the aforementioned maritime aid after it was discovered that the same was missing. The basis of the duty was stated at page 650:

> " * * * One who voluntarily creates or maintains a condition for the use of others is in the absence of some privilege, charged with the duty to exercise care to prevent that condition from becoming a source of danger to those who use it. * * * The Coast Guard maintains the maritime aids to navigation in Wrangell Narrows and had done so for a number of years. Evidence was introduced showing that these aids assisted the mariners in negotiating the dangerous passage of Wrangell Narrows and mariners relied upon these aids in traversing the passage. Based on the rules above, the voluntary assumption of caring for these aids to navigation placed a duty upon the defendant to exercise due care in maintaining the aids."

Claypool v. United States (SD Cal , 1951) 98 F Supp 702

This was an action brought under the Federal Tort Claims Act to recover damages sustained when the plaintiff was injured by a bear while camping in Yellowstone National Park. There was judgment for the plaintiff.

When the plaintiff asked a ranger whether it was safe to sleep in the park, he was advised that it was, although the ranger had knowledge that a bear had recently attacked several campers.

The court stated at page 706:

> "We do not believe it is necessary, for the purposes of this opinion, to make any fine distinction as to the exact status occupied by plaintiff when he entered the Park; nor do we deem it necessary to formulate a broad and inclusive definition of the quantum of care owed by defendant to plaintiff. It is enough to say that regardless of whether plaintiff was expressly or impliedly invited into the Park, regardless of whether he had the right to expect protection from injury, he was in the Park by permission of the defendant, and his activities there in no way transgressed the permission given. A danger to plaintiff known by the employees of the Park existed. Under similar conditions, the minimum duty which a private individual would owe a person coming upon premises maintained by such individual would be 'an honest disclosure of the danger known' to provide 'an opportunity for an intelligent choice' as to whether he wished to incur the risk incident to coming upon the land."

In reasoning that the Federal Tort Claims Act does not encompass breach of fiduciary duty, the District Court stated that immunity was not waived as to all torts. In this connection, it pointed to certain types of conduct allegedly outside the scope of the Act (R. 114-115), which will now be considered seriatim.

First, the court stated that immunity was not waived for conduct amounting to a nuisance, citing

Dalehite v. United States (1952) 346 US 15, 97 L ed 1427

This was an action brought under the provisions of the Federal Tort Claims Act to recover damages resulting from the explosion of ammonium nitrate fertilizer, manufactured for the government and under its direction, while it was being loaded for export. The District Court entered judgment for the plaintiffs, but was reversed by the Court of Appeals, and the Supreme Court affirmed the judgment of the Court of Appeals.

It is interesting first to note that the principal holding of the Dalehite case, that liability is not imposed upon the government for acts performed in a "uniquely governmental" capacity, has been abandoned or overruled by the Supreme Court.

> *Indian Towing Co. v. United States*
> (1955) 350 US 61, 100 L ed 48
>
> *Rayonier Inc. v. United States*
> (1957) 352 US 315, 1 Led2d 354

At any rate, in mentioning nuisance (346 US 44-45, 97 L ed 1445), The Supreme Court noted by way of dictum that a residue of a theory of absolute liability without fault was reflected in the District Court's finding that the fertilizer constituted a nuisance and in one of the plaintiff's contentions. Consequently, the discussion of this case will be combined with a consideration of the next points raised by the District Court, that is, that the Act does not impose liability for the ownership and operation of a dangerous instrumentality or liability without fault.

Once again, reference must be made to the language of the Act, which relates to the "*negligent or wrongful act or omission*" of government employees. However, conduct for which absolute liability is imposed may be neither negligent nor wrongful. Thus, the court in the *Dalehite* case stated that the Act is to be invoked (346 US 44-45, 97 L ed 1445):

> " * * * only on a 'negligent or wrongful act or omission' of an employee. Absolute liability, of course, arises irrespective of how the tortfeasor conducts himself; it is imposed automatically when any damages are sustained as a result of the decision to engage in the dangerous activity. The degree of care used in performing the activity is irrelevant to the application of that doctrine. But the statute requires a negligent act. So it is our judgment that liability does not arise by virtue either of United States ownership of an 'inherently dangerous commodity' or property, or of engaging in an 'extrahazardous' activity."

(It must be remembered that the *Dalehite* case dealt with the negligence aspect of the Act.)

The other cases cited by the District Court on the

subject of absolute liability or liability without fault merely follow the dictum of the *Dalehite* decision and do not require further discussion.

Therefore, under the foregoing authorities, the government would not be subject to liability where its employees have not been guilty of a "negligent or wrongful act or omission," but this does not negate the principle that the government is liable when its employees do commit a negligent or wrongful act or omission. In the case at bar, a government employee did commit a wrongful act, i. e., breach of fiduciary duty. The authorities cited by the court do not detract from the conclusion that the same is within the purview of the Federal Tort Claims Act.

The District Court also points out that "although fraud and deceit may constitute tortious conduct, such conduct does not fall within the provisions of the Act" (R. 115), relying upon

> *United States v. Gill* (WD Pa, 1957)
> 156 F Supp 955

It is true that governmental immunity from liability has not been waived as to such conduct, but this is by express statutory exception.

> 28 USCA Section 2680(h)

69

The statutory exception was the basis of the decision in the *Gill* case, wherein the court stated at page 958:

> "Although the defendant cites 28 U.S.C.A. § 1346 (b) as the requisite statutory authority for his counterclaim, section 2680(h) of that title specifically excludes from the scope of section 1346(b) any claim based on, inter alia, deceit or misrepresentation."

Consequently, this principle is not relevant to a consideration of whether governmental immunity from liability has been waived as to breach of fiduciary duty, for Congress did not remove that tort from the operation of the Act.

Thus, the authorities demonstrate fully that the waiver of immunity from liability embodied in the Federal Tort Claims Act extends to the wrongful acts or omissions committed by government employees. Breach of fiduciary duty is a wrongful act, and as such, it is unquestionably within the purview of the Act.

Point II

In the event that this court affirms the conclusion of the District Court that breach of fiduciary duty is not within the purview of the Federal Tort Claims Act, it should require the District Court to transfer this case to the Court of Claims.

Appellant believes he has shown conclusively that the District Court committed reversible error when it concluded that appellee's breach of fiduciary duty is not within the purview of the Federal Tort Claims Act and consequently dismissed appellant's complaint. However, in the event that this court should affirm the District Court's conclusion, appellant respectfully urges that the latter should be required to transfer this case to the Court of Claims.

If it is in the interest of justice, the District Courts are required to transfer cases within the jurisdiction of the Court of Claims to the latter court.

28 USCA Section 1406(c)

> "If a case within the exclusive jurisdiction of the Court of Claims is filed in a district court, the district court shall, if it be in the interest of justice, transfer such case to the Court of Claims, where the case shall proceed as if it had been filed in the Court of Claims on the date it was filed in the district court."

In the case at bar, the District Court found that appellee was in a fiduciary relationship with appellant and that it breached the fiduciary duty which it owed to him. This breach of fiduciary duty resulted in a very substantial injury to appellant. If the District Court does not have jurisdiction to grant relief to appellant, it is clearly in the interest of justice that this case be transferred to a court which does have such jurisdiction.

CONCLUSION

The uncontroverted facts in this case clearly disclose that the government in early 1954 determined to proceed with the completion and management of a private housing project at Kodiak, Alaska, which it deemed vital to national defense. This decision was effectuated pursuant to the terms of a so-called "completion agreement," through the medium of a project manager, who was subject to appointment, control, direction and removal by the government. The completion agreement and the acts thereunder created duties and obligations, as well as rights, on the part of both appellant and the government.

By exercising its rights under the completion agreement, the government occupied a fiduciary relationship to appellant, who in reliance upon this fiduciary capacity advanced further personal funds to the project after the completion agreement was executed.

By reason of this fiduciary relationship, the government was under a legal duty through HHFA to conform to a standard of conduct commensurate with such relationship.

HHFA by its seizure of funds in May, 1957, and its filing of a foreclosure suit in June, 1957, failed to conform to the standards required by it by said fiduciary relationship and committed a wrongful act.

Such wrongful act resulted in damages to appellant which he seeks to recover in this action.

The test of whether this action is cognizable under the Federal Tort Claims Act is this: Would a private person be liable to appellant under the uncontroverted facts of this case?

This action is unique in the jurisprudence relating to the Federal Tort Claims Act and the question presented by this appeal, that is, whether breach of a fiduciary duty is within the purview of the Act, is one of first impression.

We respectfully urge that the question posed by this appeal is easily answered in the affirmative under the clear and unequivocal provisions of the Act and the applicable judicial decisions.

Thus, the Act waives governmental immunity from liability as to the tortious conduct of government employees acting within the scope of their employment, where such conduct would render the United States liable if it were a private person. Breach of fiduciary duty is such conduct. Consequently, it is within the purview of the Act, and the District Courts are vested with jurisdiction of claims arising from such breach.

In the case at bar, appellee was in a fiduciary relationship with appellant and breached its fiduciary duty to him. As a result, the District Court had jurisdiction of his complaint under the Federal Tort Claims Act. In entering judgment dismissing such complaint, the District Court committed manifest error.

Appellant respectfully urges that the judgment of dismissal of the District Court be reversed and judgment entered in his favor.

Respectfully submitted,

KING, MILLER, ANDERSON,
NASH & YERKE,

NORMAN J. WIENER,

JEAN P. LOWMAN,

1200 American Bank Building
Portland 5, Oregon

Attorneys for Appellant.

APPENDIX

Exhibit No.	Identified	Offered	Received
115/48	R. 129-130	R. 129-130	R. 130
289/A2	R. 130-131	R. 130	R. 131
512/4	R. 132-133	R. 132	R. 133
562/A-4	R. 133-134	R. 133	R. 134
583/1-140	R. 135-146	R. 135	R. 146
802/65	R. 146-148	R. 146	R. 148
832/A-1-207	R. 148-151	R. 148	R. 151
849/49-4	R. 151-152	R. 151-152	R. 152-153
850/20	R. 153	R. 153	R. 153
851/A-20	R. 153-154	R. 153	R. 154
859/20	R. 154-156	R. 154	R. 157
891/A-21	R. 157	R. 157	R. 158
983/21	R. 158-159	R. 158	R. 159
997/A-22	R. 159-160	R. 159	R. 160
1019/22	R. 160	R. 160	R. 160
1021/A-22	R. 160-163	R. 160	R. 163
1025/A-32	R. 163-166	R. 163	R. 167
1091/22	R. 167	R. 167	R. 167
1144/23	R. 167-168	R. 167-168	R. 168
1150/A-32	R. 168-170	R. 168	R. 170
1177	R. 128	R. 128	R. 128-129

ON APPEAL

No. 17,585 ✓

IN THE UNITED STATES COURT OF APPEALS
FOR THE NINTH CIRCUIT

RAY B. WOODBURY, Appellant

v.

UNITED STATES OF AMERICA, Appellee

✓ APPEAL FROM THE UNITED STATES DISTRICT COURT FOR THE
DISTRICT OF OREGON

BRIEF FOR THE UNITED STATES

JOSEPH D. GUILFOYLE,
Acting Assistant Attorney General,

SIDNEY I. LEZAK,
Acting United States Attorney,

ALAN S. ROSENTHAL,
JOHN W. BOULT,
Attorneys, Department of Justice,
Washington 25, D.C.

CITATIONS

Cases:

(1)

Statutes:

Miscellaneous:

No. 17, 585

RAY B. WOODBURY, Appellant

v.

UNITED STATES OF AMERICA, Appellee

ON APPEAL FROM THE UNITED STATES DISTRICT COURT FOR THE
DISTRICT OF OREGON

BRIEF FOR THE UNITED STATES

JURISDICTIONAL STATEMENT

This suit was filed on September 30, 1957, in the United
tes District Court for the District of Oregon against the
ted States under the Federal Tort Claims Act, 28 U.S.C.
6(b), 2671, *et seq*. On February 14, 1958, the Government
ed a motion to dismiss the complaint and in the alternative
summary judgment, alleging, *inter alia*, that the suit was
within the purview for the Federal Tort Claims Act and
refore the court was without jurisdiction(R. 17-19). On
ruary 24, 1961, the district court dismissed the complaint
the ground that it had no jurisdiction of the claim under
Tort Claims Act (R. 117-118). Notice of appeal was filed
April 11, 1961. The jurisdiction of this Court is invoked
er 28 U.S.C. 1291.

I. Summary

In general, the present suit arises out of a borrower-lender
relationship between appellant and the Housing and Home Finance
Agency (referred to hereinafter as HHFA), an agency of the Unite
States Government. This relationship was created in January 195
when appellant, who had become interested in sponsoring a housin
project near a military installation in the vicinity of Kodiak,
Alaska, applied for, and was granted, a construction loan by HHF
in the sum of $4,230,900. In order to describe with clarity the
precise nature of appellant's various claims urged against the
Government in the court below, there is set forth below a detail
discussion of (1) the negotiation with preceded the basic loan
agreement and supplementary agreements, (2) the nature of the
loan agreement and its pertinent conditions, (3) the difficultie
which arose in completing the housing project and repaying the
loan, and (4) the subsequent negotiations, conducted in an effor
to rescue the housing project from these difficulties, which
culminated in the so-called 'completion agreement" between
appellant, his corporation, subcontractors, and creditors of the
project. None of the recited facts are in dispute; indeed most
appear in the Agreed Statement of Fact which was incorporated in
the pretrial order (R. 46-68).

I. The Alaskan Project

   A. Preliminary Negotiations

   In 1949 discussions took place between officials of the Navy,
he Alaska Housing Authority, and the City of Kodiak, Alaska, cor
erning the possibility of securing additional off-base housing
or naval personnel connected with the Naval Base in Kodiak.
uring 1950 and 1951, arrangements were made to transfer to the
ity of Kodiak certain Government land, as a site for this housir
roject to be built by a sponsor selected by the City of Kodiak.
uring this same period the site was surveyed and some engineer-
ng performed on behalf of one Raymond Lewis of Los Angeles,
alifornia, a proposed sponsor of the project. However, in
ate 1951, Mr. Lewis abandoned interest in the project. (R. 53-
4)

   Also during 1951, appellant became interested in the promotic
f a prefabricated house panelling of recent invention. Conse-
ently, in late 1951 he financed a trip by the inventor, and
hers, to Alaska to investigate the possibility of selling the
anelling there. In the course of this promotion, appellant's
ssociate approached the Mayor of Kodiak, and as a result appel-
nt became interested in becoming the sponsor of the off-base
using project near Kodiak. (R. 54)

   Accordingly, in February 1952, Aleutian Homes, Inc., was
corporated under the laws of the State of Oregon for the pur-
se of sponsoring the project. Appellant became the president

f Aleutian Homes, Inc., and the owner of virtually all

utstanding shares of stock issued by the corporation.

ebruary or March 1952, the City of Kodiak approved Aleu

omes, Inc., as the sponsor of the housing project, and

ite land was subsequently conveyed to the corporation.

B. Financing of the Project

The financing of the project became divided into two

hich may be termed long-term financing, and short-term

he long-term financing was to be accomplished under the

f Section 203 of Title II of the National Housing Act,

ursuant thereto the Brice Mortgage Company was selected

s the permanent mortgagee by receiving long-term mortga

ach house included in the project. In order to assure

uture marketability of these mortgages, Brice Mortgage

pplied to the Federal Housing Administration (referred

nafter as FHA) for a commitment to insure the mortgages

arly 1952, FHA appraised the value of the project at $5

nd, in April 1952, issued its conditional commitment, to

pril 24, 1953, to insure the mortgages in the amount of

r 80% of the appraised value. Also in 1952, the Federa

ortgage Association (referred to hereinafter as FNMA) i

onditional commitment, to expire May 15, 1953, to purch

ar the individual long-term mortgages as they were obta

rice Mortgage Company and insured by FHA. The funds re

Aleutian Homes, Inc., through this long-term financing were to b(
ed in large part to repay an interim short-term construction loan
   55-56)

The second phase of the financing of the project was necessitated
 the need for immediate funds required for the construction of th(
oject prior to obtaining the long-term financing. Being unable t(
tain from private sources the financing required for the construc·
on of the project, Brice Mortgage Co., and Aleutian Homes, Inc.,
gan negotiations with the Community Facilities and Special Projec'
anch of the HHFA. Aleutian Homes, Inc., filed a formal loan appl.
tion in late 1952. The application was approved through a Loan
thorization signed by the Administrator of HHFA in January 19£3.
. 57). This document authorized a loan in the total amount of
,230,900, or 90% of the FHA and FNMA commitments, to be used sole'
 finance the housing project. The loan authorization, by its ter
ntemplated the negotiation and execution of a number of supportin(
cuments prior to the disbursement of any portion of the loan. (R.
Thereafter, on April 27, 1953, the basic loan documents were exec\
ese included (1) the Building and Loan Agreement, (2) the Loan an(
sbursement Agreement, (3) Borrower's Promissory Note in the amoun·
,230,90Q signed by Aleutian Homes, Inc., R. B. Woodbury, Presiden1

(4) Guaranty by R.B. Woodbury covering performance of t

tion contract by Kodiak Construction Company,[1]/ the ger

tor for the housing project, which contract was contemp

assigned by Aleutian Homes to HHFA, (5) Guaranty by R.I

covering performance of the Loan Agreement, (6) Standby

executed by R.B. Woodbury, (7) general contract betweer

Homes, Inc., and Kodiak Construction Company, (8) Suppl

between A.B. Carlton, d/b/a/ Carlton Lumber Company and

Construction Company for the prefabricated houses at a

price per house, (9) Erection Contract between Kodiak (

Company and Pacific Alaska Contractors, Inc., to prepar

and lay house foundations. (R. 57-59) As a condition r

to the disbursement of any part of the loan, each of tr

listed construction contracts was assigned to the Admir

of the HHFA together with the stock of Aleutian Homes,

Also, as a condition to the granting of the loan, Aleut

agreed to advance all sums necessary for the completior

project in excess of the amount of the loan, and at the

of HHFA were subject to deposit with HHFA sums to insur

resources adequate for that purpose. (R. 57)

---

[1]/ This corporation was formed under the laws of the $
Oregon to act as general contractor in the construction
project. Appellant was the president of this corporati
the owner of a substantial amount of its outstanding st

paration of the site. In August 1953 the site constructio
contract between Kodiak Construction Company and Pacific
Contractors, Inc., which contract had been assigned to HH
April 27, 1953, was terminated. (R. 59) In September 195;
site preparation operation was taken over by Kodiak Const:
Company. (R. 59-94)

On November 6, 1953, Pacific Alaska Contractors, Inc.
a lien against the project for more than $150,000 (R. 95)
upon, construction came to a standstill with the project
mately 75 per cent completed.

Repayment of the HHFA loan became in default and HHFA
appellee of his obligation under his personal guarantee t
additional funds to complete the project free of all lien:
lee informed HHFA that he was unable to meet this obligat
60)

D. The Completion Agreement.

In November 1953, with loan payments in default, the
could have declared expended loan funds, and interest, du
payable. However, the Government had no disposition to e:
its right of foreclosure if there was any reasonable mean:
overcoming the difficulties upon which the project had fo
The project sponsor (Aleutian Homes) its president (appel
general contractor, subcontractors, and other project cre

-7-

ere equally interested in keeping the project, and its .

live, if at all possible. To this end negotiations were

etween the sponsor and the project creditors, which resu

plan prepared by Aleutian Homes' attorney which was pre

) creditors for acceptance and to HHFA to serve as a ba:

irther disbursement of undisbursed loan funds.2/ Meetin;

inducted concerning this plan during which it became mai

iat (1) Aleutian Homes owed creditors large amounts of i

id (2) owed HHFA principal and interest on the loan, and

:oject could not be completed within the contract time.

:sult of the negotiations was the execution of a comple<

;reement (Exhibit 583/1-140) by appellant, Aleutian Home

idiak Construction Company, the Subcontractors, corpora<

iarantors, stockholders, permanent mortgagee, and princ:

'editors and claimants against the project.3/

In the completion agreement itself it was stated tha<

imstance which prompted the agreement was the unwilling:

FA to make further loan disbursements in view of unpai<

' At the time default occurred, construction ceased, and
' funds terminated, approximately $3,330,062 had been d:
FA to Aleutian Homes under the Building and Loan Agreer

' Neither HHFA nor any other Government agency was lis<
ipletion agreement as a party thereto, nor was the doci
any Government official.

ursements.

In order to accomplish this the parties to the agreer
ed therein to a schedule of the amounts of their then
claims against the project, agreed to a schedule for
the costs of completing the project including repayment
interim loan, and agreed to refrain from legal procee
enforce claims while the agreement was in effect. (Ex)
1-140).

The efficacy of these agreements was conditioned upo
lingness to modify appropriately the loan disbursement
and the maturity date of the loan, and defer collectio
rest until completion of the project. Further, also
; of the completion agreement, appellant, individually
provide necessary overhead expenses to complete the pr
to preserve the FHA and FNMA mortgage commitments, in
oximate amount of $15,000 per month.

Finally, the parties agreed to the appointment of a
ger and a Construction Superintendant acceptable to tl
would be "vested with full and exclusive authority" t
and all actions in connection with the project. The
ger was to be subject to removal and replacement by H
time. His compensation was to be considered an overh
ise payable out of the funds to be supplied by Woodbu
ntee.

-9-

The agreement also contained the following provision:

> The obligations of any party signatory hereto shall
> not be released, discharge, or in an way affected, nor
> shall claimants or any other parties signatory have any
> rights or recourse against lender (HHFA) by reason of
> any action lender may take or omit to take under the
> foregoing powers; nor by reason of any action taken by
> lender which in its opinion may be necessary to keep
> the project free from liens.

E. Operations Under the Modified Loan Agreement

On the basis of the foregoing arrangements, construction was
resumed and loan disbursements continued. Under the amended
disbursement procedures, project funds were to be expended solely
y the Project Manager in paying the cost of completion and in
atifying the claims scheduled for payment in the completion
greement. (R. 60-61)

However other expenditures were made by appellant, without
nowledge of the Government, beginning on June 2, 1954 (R. 66).
hese were payments made to the Bank of California on a claim
hich was part of the completion agreement. The payments con-
inued through July 6, 1956 and through a period when the pro-
ect was in financial difficulties. Although obligated under
is overhead agreement to pay $15,000 per month for adminis-
rative expenses, and to maintain FHA and FNMA commitments,
ppellant ceased to make such payments (R. 67) although he con-
inued to make payments to the Bank of California in disregard
f other claimants. Thus, with the mortgage commitments to
xpire in June 1955, appellant, on May 18, 1955, paid the Bank
f California $59,731.43 (R. 66). Again, on June 13, 1955, the

.rtual eve of commitment expiration, he paid the Bank of
.lifornia $2,352.75 (R. 66).

Thus, permanent individual mortgages were not taken out
ι any of the houses and the FHA commitment to insure the FNMA
ιmmitment to purchase such mortgages expired and were not
:newed by the payment of appropriate fees.

On or about June 11, 1957 foreclosure proceedings were
ιstituted by the United States in the United States District
ιurt for the District of Alaska pursuant to the deeds of trust
·curing the indebtedness of Aleutian Homes under the Building
ιd Loan Agreement and promissory note.

:I. Nature of Appellant's Claims

The complaint filed by appellant in the district court under
ιe Tort Claims Act sets forth six "Causes of Action" against
ιe United States, each alleging damages in a specified amount.
.ese claims may be summarized as follows:

> 1. HHFA breached a fiduciary duty owed to appellant in
> failing to secure long-range financing of the housing
> project by reason of which appellant suffered damage in
> the amount of $75,000, this sum representing the funds
> advanced by appellant under his overhead agreement.
>
> 2. HHFA failed to pay the claims of the Bank of Calif-
> ornia by reason of which appellant, under his liability
> as an accommodation endorser, suffered damages in the
> amount of $164,594.80.
>
> 3. HHFA failed to pay a claim of the General Casualty
> Company of America, as a result of which appellant by
> reason of his personal guaranty of this claim, suffered
> damages in the amount of $35,955.02.

4. HHFA failed to secure long-term financing for the
project by reason of which appellant suffered damages
in the amount of $150,000, this sum representing fund
advanced by appellant between 1951 and 1953 in prepar
tion for the project.

5. HHFA failed to secure long-term financing for the
project by reason of which appellant suffered damages
in the amount of $9,297.04, this sum representing cla
satisfied by appellant subsequent to the completion
agreement.

6. HHFA failed to secure long-term financing for the
project, and wrongfully seized appellant's bank accou
and foreclosed on appellant's equity in the project,
reason of which appellant suffered damages in the amo
of $428,127, this sum representing the alleged value
appellant's equity in the project.

V. Proceedings in the District Court

The Government responded to the complaint by filing a

o Dismiss and in the Alternative for Summary Judgment (R.

9). In support of this motion, appellee urged that the s

f limitations had run on appellant's claims, and that the

ere not within the perview of the Federal Tort Claims Act

On April 28, 1958, after the Government's alternative

ad been withdrawn, the district court denied the motion t

ith leave to renew the motion at the time of the pretrial

On June 2, 1958, the Government filed its answer (R. 2

a which it denied each of appellant's substantive allega

d renewed its contentions that the complaint was not ccg

der the Federal Tort Claims Act and that the complaint w

rred by the statute of limitations.

On July 15, 1960, the district court entered a pretria

roceed to try the segregated issue of whether HHFA became appel-
ant's fiduciary (R. 77).

On November 4, 1960, the court ordered that decision on the
otion to dismiss be reserved, and that trial be held on the
ontroverted issue of an alleged fiduciary status (R. 78-79).

On February 8, 1961, after hearing, the court held that it
ad no jurisdiction over the complaint under the Federal Tort
laims Act (R. 116). This appeal followed.

STATUTE INVOLVED

The Federal Tort Claims Act, Act of June 25, 1948, 62 Stat.
33, 982, 28 U.S.C. 1346(b), 2671, *et seq.*, as amended, provides
c pertinent part as follows:

> 1346(b) Subject to the provisions of chapter 171 of
> this title, the district courts, together with the United
> States District Court for the District of the Canal Zone
> and the District Court of the Virgin Islands, shall have
> exclusive jurisdiction of civil actions or claims against
> the United States, for money damages, accruing on and
> after January 1, 1945, for injury or loss of property, or
> personal injury or death caused by the negligent or wrong-
> ful act or omission of any employee of the Government
> while acting within the scope of his office or employment,
> under circumstances where the United States, if a private
> person, would be liable to the claimant in accordance with
> the law of the place where the act or omission occurred.

> 2679. Exclusiveness of remedy

> (a) The authority of any federal agency to sue and
> be sued in its own name shall not be construed to authorize
> suits against such federal agency on claims which are cog-
> nizable under section 1346(b) of this title, and the remedies
> provided by this title in such cases shall be exclusive.

2680. Exceptions

The provisions of this chapter and Section 1346(b) of
:le shall not apply to:

(a) Any claim based upon an act or omission of a
employee of the Government, exercising due care, in th
execution of a statute or regulation, whether or not
such statute or regulation be valid, or based upon the
exercise or performance or the failure to exercise or
perform a discretionary function or duty on the part
of a federal agency or an employee of the Government,
whether or not the discretion involved be abused.
*   *   *   *   *

(h) Any claim arising out of assault, battery fa
imprisonment, false arrest, malicious prosecution, abu
of process, libel, slander, misrepresentation, deceit
interference with contract rights.

waiver of sovereign immumity contained in the Tort Claims
es not extend to claims based on the allegedly wrongful
e of employees of the Government to fulfill obligations
ɔ arise by reason of a contractual relationship between
vernment and the plaintiff. On the contrary, the Tucker
ɔvides the sole basis for suit on such claims and, where
ɔovery sought exceeds $10,000, the Court of Claims is the
ɔrum. Since it is clear in this case that appellant's
ɔf action is bottomed entirely on a breach of duties which
ant claims arose from the completion agreement, the district
lacted jurisdiction to entertain it under the Tort Claims

II

ɔ if the contractual footing of appellant's claim were
ɔ, Tort Claims Act jurisdiction would still be lacking.
e claim comes within two of the exceptions contained in
.C. 2680.

Section 2680(a) bars, inter alia, claims based upon the
ɔe of a discretionary function. An examination of the
ɔry provisions underlying HHFA's lending activities reveals
ɔngress conferred broad discretion upon the agency in the
t of those activities. All of the actions complained of

by appellant were performed in the exercise of that discretio
and involved policy judgments as to the most appropriate mann
in which to carry out the Agency's statutory functions.

B. The claim is also barred by the Section 2680(h) exclus
of claims arising out of interference with contract rights.
exclusion has been judicially interpreted to apply not only t
interference with existing contractual rights, but also to in
ference with prospective or potential economic advantage. An
the gravamen of appellant's complaint is that the alleged wro
ful acts of HHFA deprived him of the benefits of long-term fi
cing arrangements.

Moreover, the abuse of process and malicious prosecution e
tions in the same subsection apply, respectively, to the alle
tion that the Aleutian Homes' bank account was wrongfully sei
and the complaint of an improper commencement of foreclosure
ceedings against the project.

I

APPELLANT'S CLAIM ARISES FROM CONTRACT AND
IS THEREFORE OUTSIDE THE SCOPE OF THE FEDERAL
TORT CLAIMS ACT.

1. As its very title reflects, the Tort Claims Act was
designed, with certain exceptions, to "remove the sovereign
immunity of the United States from suits in tort* * *." See,
Richards v. United States, 369 U.S. 1,6. That claims based
upon breach of contract are wholly alien to the Tort Claims
Act is beyond question. As early as 1887, Congress surrender
the Government's sovereign immunity cn claims based upon contracts which are express or implied in fact by enacting the
Tucker Act.4/ Today the Tucker Act constitutes the sole basi
for a suit against the United States sounding in contract and
the district court's jurisdiction under that Act is very limi
As recently stated in Drake v. Treadwell Construction Company
299 F. 2d 789,791 (C.A. 3):

> The generalized consent of the United States to be
> sued in contract appears in the Tucker Act, 28 U.S.C.
> §1491. But the Tucker Act divides jurisdiction over
> claims against the United States, whether founded in
> express or implied contract, between the court of
> claims and the district courts. Only claims for less
> that $10,000 are cognizable in the district courts.
> 28 U.S.C. §1346(a)(2).

4/ Act of May 3, 1887, 24 Stat. 505, 28 U. S. C. 491, as
amended.

Thus, by the enactment of independent, mutually exclusive, consenting statutes, the Congress has drawn a clear and signifi-cant line of distinction between governmental liability in tort on the one hand, and contract on the other. It follows that, when the Tort Claims Act refers in 28 U.S.C. 1346(b) to a "negligent or wrongful" act or omission of a Government employee it contemplates negligent or wrongful conduct in the tort sense and not such conduct which amounts to nothing more a breach of obligations which arise, if at all, solely by reason of a con-tractual relationship between the United States and the plain-tiff. For any other reading of the jurisdictional keystone to the Act would essentially obliterate that line of distinction.

2. Whether a particular claim sought to be asserted under the Tort Claims Act is based upon a right in tort, rather than one created by contract, must be determined on the basis of the nature of that claim. Stated otherwise, the particular label that the claimant may choose to place upon the claim -- or the words that are used in the complaint in describing it-- are not decisive. As has been generally recognized by the courts, Congress did not intend that the bounds of the waiver of immunity in the Tort Claims Act be conditioned by linguistic considerations. Rather, as the Tenth Circuit has pointed out in a case under that Act, the obligation of the court is to 'look beyond the literal meaning of the language (used in the pleadings) to ascertain the real cause of complaint". Hall v.

United States, 274 F. 2d 69, 71. See also Klein v. United
States, 268 F. 2d 63, 64 (C.A. 2); Miller Harness Co. v.
United States, 241 F. 2d 781, 783 (C.A. 2); Stepp v. Unite
States, 207 F. 2d 909 (C.A. 4); Broadway Open Air Theatres
Inc. v. United States, 208 F. 2d 257 (C.A. 4).

We submit that scrutiny of the present allegations will
reveal that appellant's claim is founded solely on a breac
f asserted contractual obligations. Indeed, the fundamen
ontractual character of the claim is clearly betrayed by
asic allegations (R. 7-9): (1) that HHFA "entered into
ompletion argeement" with appellant "in which HHFA undert
o pay all creditors" and to "complete construction of the
roject", (2) that "Pursuant to said completion agreement"
ssumed control over the project, (3) that "in carrying ou
aid completion agreement" HHFA selected a project manager
nd directed disbursement and receipt of all project funds
4) that "in the carrying out of said completion agreement
HFA permitted the commitments of FHA and FNMA, with resp
o long-term financing, to terminate, and (5) that appella
n reliance upon the "completion agrsement" advanced certa
unds to the project manager which were to be repaid out o
NMA funds.   The damage complained of is asserted to have
esulted from the manner in which HHFA performed its purpo
bligations under the completion agreement.

In short, it is abundantly clear that HHFA's duties

appellant begin and end with the completion agreement-

tract. Indeed, as appellant himself concedes in the c

of his brief, (p. 71) the entire basis for the present

is that: "The completion agreement and the acts there

created duties and obligations, as well as rights, on

of both appellant and the government." Thus, the righ

appellant asserted in this action arise solely from cc

and being in excess of $10,000 in amount, can be asser

in a Tucker Act suit in the Court of Claims.

THE CLAIM IS BARRED BY 28 U.S.C. 2680(a) & (h).

In Point I, we have shown that, since appellant's compl
is, in essence, that the United States failed to fulfill c
tractual obligations running to appellant, Tort Claims Act
jurisdiction is absent. We now will demonstrate that, eve
if the contractual footing to the claim were disregarded,
appellant's position would not be improved. For the Tort
Act does not represent a total waiver of the Government's
from suit in tort. On the contrary, Congress expressly se
in 28 U.S.C. 2680 several specific types of claims in tort
which the waiver would not apply.

If appellant's claim is deemed to be in tort, it is pre
by subsections (a) and (h) of that Section. They provide,
material part, that the Act does not extend to:

> (a) Any claim based upon * * * the exercise or per-
> formance or the failure to exercise or perform a
> discretionary function or duty on the part of a
> federal agency or employee of the Government, whether
> or not the discretion involved be abused.

> (h) Any claim arising out of * * * malicious prose-
> cution, abuse of process * * * misrepresentation, dec
> or interference with contract rights.

A. The Present Claim is Based Upon the Exercise of a
   Discretionary Function Within the Meaning of 28
   U.S.C. 2680(a)

1. The HHFA was created by the Reorganization Plan No.
947, 61 Stat. 954, 5 U.S.C. 133y-16. Under this plan the
is functions and programs of the Government related to ho

were consolidated within the HHFA. Among the functions alloted
to HHFA was that of assuring that the nation's industrial capacity for the production of prefabricated housing to be available for national defense, by making loans to business concerns
involved in the production and distribution of such housing.
See, 12 U.S.C. 1701g-1. In connection with this loan program,
12 U.S.C. 1701g-2(2) empowers the HHFA Administrator to:

> * * *take any and all actions determined by him
> to be necessary or desirable in making, servicing,
> compromising, modifying, liquidating, or other-
> wise dealing with or realizing on loans* * * .

Further, by 12 U.S.C. 1749a(c)(4), (8) and (9), the Administrator is empowered to:

> (4) foreclose on any property or commence any
> action to protect or enforce any right conferred
> upon him by any law, contract, or other agree-
> ment* * *.

> (8) * * * Consent to the modification, with res-
> pect to rate of interest, time of payment of any
> installment of principal or interest, security,
> or any other terms of any contract or agreement
> to which he is a party or which has been trans-
> ferred to him* * *.

> (9) * * * include in any contract or instrument
> made pursuant to this subchapter such other con-
> venants, conditions, or provisions as he may deem
> necessary to assure that the purposes of this sub-
> chapter will be achieved.

These provisions constitute the statutory basis for the partici-
ation of the HHFA in the initial loan negotiations, the basic
uilding and loan agreement, and the subsequent modification of
he loan documents, including the so-called completion agreement
rom which appellant contends the Government's liability arises.

ese statutory provisions grant the Administrator broad

etion in fulfilling his statutory duties. They carve

oad areas within which the Administrator is authorized

e his judgment in determining the best course to follo

2. There can be no question that the acts of which a

mplains were all based upon the Administrator's exerci

e discretion given him by statute. For example, the c

leges (R. 7) that HHFA entered into a completion with

which it took complete control over the project and u

pay all creditors then existing, and to complete cons

the project. This, of course, took place at a time w

using project was in jeopardy and when appellant was i

the basic loan. (R. 59-61) In an effort to salvage

ct, and in connection with the completion agreement, H

extend the maturity date of the loan and to defer the

on of interest until the project was completed. The c

reement, then, represented, in the fullest sense, a mo

the existing loan conditions. Surely, therefore, the

rticipation in the completion agreement procedures was

ercise of the Administrator's power to "take any and a

;ermined by him to be necessary or desirable in making

;, compromising, modifying, or otherwise dealing with

loans", (12 U.S.C. 1701g-2(2), supra, p. 22.) and h

"consent to the modification" of the "terms of any co

eement to which he is a party". (12 U.S.C. 1749a(c)(

The insistence, if any, by HHFA upon control over th
truction of project as condition to the further advanc
f loan funds and its subsequent actions taken in the e
f that control was surely an exercise of the Administr
ower to "include in any contract or instrument" such "
ions" as he determines to be necessary to accomplish t
urposes of the loan program. 12 U.S.C. 1749a(c)(9), su
. 22 . The allegation (R. 9) that the Government wron
eized the Aleutian Homes bank account, and wrongfully
ited foreclosure proceedings is clearly based upon an
ormed under the Administrator's power to "foreclose on
roperty or commence any action" to enforce the rights
pon the Administrator by contract or otherwise. 12 U.
749a(c)(4), supra, p. 22.

It is, of course, eminently reasonable and necessary
1e head of a Government lending agency be given broad
lon in carrying out a loan program. Such activity in
equires the daily exercise of judgment and policy deci
·der to cope with the many unpredictable difficulties
ivaribly arise and to protect the federal funds which
iployed. Indeed, such programs require, and this case
·ecisely the kind of discretion described by the Supre
ι Dalehite v. United States, 346 U.S. 15, 34, as being o
ie scope of the Tort Claims Act:

> the "discretion" protected by the section * *
> is the discretion of the executive or adminis

to act according to one's judgment of the best-
course, a concept of substantial historical an-
cestry in American law.

Later, in the same context, the Court said:

Where there is room for policy judgment and
decision there is discretion. 346 U.S. at 36. 5/

In addition to the landmark Dalehite decision, there are
any other cases in which Section 2680(a) was held to bar claim
ased, as the one here involved, upon the allegedly improper
xecution of activities involving policy determinations or the
xercise of broad judgment. 6/ Of course, these cases involved

---

/ There is no merit to appellant's suggestion (Br. p. 40) tha
hat portion of Dalehite relating to Section 2680(a) was overru
n Indian Towing Co. v. United States, 350 U.S. 61, and Rayonie
nc. v. United States. 352 U.S. 315. Neither of those cases
nvolved the applicability of the "discretionary function"
xception. Rather, in both, the only part of the Dalehite hold
nder consideration was that the dealing with the liability of
nited States for uniquely governmental activities such as fire
ighting. See, 346 U.S. at 43-44. As recently at June 27, 1962
ne Third Circuit passed on this very point. In holding that
ction 2680(a) barred a claim based upon the Federal Governmer
articipation in the design of a highway built with federal fir
ial assistance, the court quoted from that part of Dalehite wh
ncerned Section 2680(a) and pointed out in a footnote that:
lthough there are portions of the Dalehite opinion which are
nger authoritative, we do not read Rayonier, Inc. v. United
tates, 352 U.S. 315 (1957) or Indian Towing Co. v. United Stat
50 U.S. 61 (1955), as having retracted the language quoted."
hler v. United States, (C.A. 3, No. 13726), slip opinion, p.
1 13.

/ See, e.g., Goddard v. District of Columbia Redevelopment La
ency, 287 F. 2d 343 (C.A.D.C.); Chournos v. United States, 19
2d 321 (C.A. 10), certiorari denied, 343 U.S. 977; Schmidt v
ited States, 198 F. 2d 32 (C.A. 7), certiorari denied, 344 U.
6; Weinstein v. United States, 244 F. 2d 68 (C.A. 3), certior
nied, 355 U.S. 868; Coates v. United States, 181 F. 2d 816 (C

lvers factual situations, some more closely akin to the p

ase than others. However, the common thread which unites

f them is found in the fundamental proposition articulate

he court in Coates v. United States, 181 F. 2d 816, 818 (

s follows:

> The Congress had a sound basis for use of the
> words (discretionary function or duty) in the
> Exceptions of the Act and used them in recognition of
> the separation of powers among the three branches of
> the Government and the considerations of public polic
> which have moved the courts to refuse to interfere
> with the actions of officials at all levels of the
> executive branch who, acting within the scope of thei
> authority, were required to exercise discretion or
> judgment.

It is submitted that a proper application of the fore

inciple compels the conclusion that the claims in the pr

se were barred by the discretionary function exception o

ction 2680(a).

Appellant cannot escape the fact that, as we have see

tion of the complexity of the federal housing program, a

e compelling need for immediate day-to-day and case-to-c

cision and action, the HHFA Administrator was endowed by

th broad authority to exercise his own best judgment and

on in "making, servicing, compromising, modifying, liqui

otherwise dealing with or realizing on loans." Once ag

pellant's complaint is wholly addressed in the manner in

e administrator and his subordinates exercised that disc

As heretofore noted, 28 U.S.C. 2680(h) excluded claims
ter alia, upon interference with contract rights. As h
cognized by the Third Circuit, this exclusion embraces
aims founded upon interference with existing contractua
t also wrongful acts which are alleged to have interfer
ospective or potential advantage from business relation
ird persons. Dupree v. United States, 264 F 2d 140 (C.A
us, in Dupree, the court held that Section 2680(h) barr
tion brought by a licensed shipmaster based upon the al
gligent withholding of a security clearance by the Coas
e gravamen of the complaint had been that, as a result
tholding, the shipmaster was unable to obtain employmen
The Dupree holding is plainly applicable here. The gr
appellant's complaint is that, as a result of the alle
ongful acts on the part of HHFA employees, appellant wa
obtain the benefits of the long-term financing for the
which he had obtained conditional commitments from FH
IA. In other words, the claim is that HHFA's conduct o
interference with an economic advantage which appellan
ed would be the end product of its activities in conne
Kodiak project. And see also, Fletcher v. Veterans A
n, 103 F. Supp. 654 (E.D. Mich.); Builders Corporation
rica v. United States, 148 F. Supp. 482 (N.D. Cal), re

-27-

n other grounds, 259 F. 2d 766 (C.A. 9); Roxfort Holding Co. v
Inited States 176 F. Supp. 587 (D.N.J). As the court pointed out
n Builders (148 F. Supp. at 484):

> The alleged wrongful act of the Base Commander
> for which plaintiffs seek a recovery * * *
> appears to be the tort of "interference with
> prospective advantage" (Prosser on Torts, p. 745
> [2d Ed. 1955]), sometimes labeled "interference
> with prospective contracts or business relations"
> * * * Since Congress has decided not to surrender
> the immunity of the United States from tort actions
> based on interference with contract relations, 28
> U.S.C. §2680(h), the essential issue which this
> Court must decide, then, is whether the tort of
> interference with prospective advantage or pro-
> spective contracts is properly includable within
> the aforementioned exception to the Tort Claims
> Act. It would seem to be quite illogical to
> conclude that Congress intended to exclude one
> tort from the operation of the Act, and, at the
> same time, waive the Government's immunity from
> actions sounding in a substantially identical
> tort; the distinction between the two being
> one of degree, only, in the elements necessary
> to establish liability."

Moreover, to the extent that the complaint is based upon
he allegation that (R. 9-10):

> [T]he HHFA, its agents and employees * * * in breach
> of said fiduciary duties and obligations * * * did
> seize the bank account of Aleutian Homes, Inc * * *
> and * * * Commenced foreclosure proceedings * * *
> against Aleutian Homes, Inc * * * to collect the
> balance of moneys due on the interim loan.* * *

t is barred by other exclusionary provisions in 28 U.S.C.
680(h). The alleged seizure of the corporation bank account,
f wrongful, amounted to an abuse of process. Prosser on Torts
2d Ed., 1955) pp. 667-669. And, since the majority rule in the
nited States is that the tort of malicious prosecution embraces

titution of civil as well as criminal proceedings,(Ibi

allegedly wrongful commencement of foreclosure procee

es within the exclusion of such claims.

It is also worthy of note that, while Section 2680(h)

ited in scope to deliberate torts (United States v. Ne

U.S. 696), the legislative purpose was to exclude all

ts from suit under the Act. 7/ In this case, the comp

not based upon proportedly negligent or inadvertent co

her, the allegedly wrongful acts upon the part of HHFA

ended to accomplish the ends which were achieved. For

foreclosure proceedings were deliberately instituted

orce the Government's rights under the deed of trust s

interim loan and appellant's promissory note. The ba

ount of Aleutian Homes was seized for the purpose of a

funds to the amount due the United States from appell

ther, the payment, during the completion period, of so

ims by the project manager and the non-payment of othe

sciously done in a deliberate attempt to achieve the p

the agreement, and to complete construction of the pro

3ee H. Rept. 2246, 77th Cong. 2d Sess.; Hearings befor
:ommittee of the Senate Committee on the Judiciary on
), 76th Cong., 3rd Sess., p. 39; Hearings before the H
iittee on the Judiciary of H.R. 5373 and H.R. 6463, 77
;., 2d Sess., pp. 33-34.

For the foregoing reasons we respectfully submit that

:trict court was clearly correct in its conclusion tha

:ked jurisdiction over appellant's claim. To avoid an

:understanding, we feel compelled to add -- even thoug

.ieve the court need not reach the point -- that appel

error in its statement (Br. p. 22) that it is undispu

?A breached a fiduciary duty arising by reason of its

.ationship with appellant. On the contrary, we streno

: existence of any such duty and, if one did exist, it

It is true that we have not developed the point in th

an alternative basis for affirmance of the judgment in

it's favor. We do not think, however, that there was

do so. The district court's expression of opinion on

: purely gratuitious in view of its disposition of the

:, accordingly, the court stated (R. 109) that it did

'necessary or desirable" to make detailed findings in

: conclusion. It seems likely that this court in no e

.ld wish to consider the question without such finding

: documentary evidence bearing on the issue is volumin

onstration of the insubstantiality of appellant's cla

its thus would have required the undue burdening of t

ore this court on an appeal from a judgment of dismis

k of jurisdiction.

Brief note must also be made of appellant's suggestio

this court agrees with us that the district court lac

f Claims. Appellant has given no reason why this Court

invoke 28 U.S.C. 1406(c) (Supp II) to order such a trans-

we know of none.

CONCLUSION

the light of the foregoing, it is respectfully submitted

e dismissal order of the District Court should be affirmed.8/

JOSEPH D. GUILFOYLE,
Acting Assistant Attorney General.

SIDNEY I. LEZAK,
Acting United States Attorney.

ALAN S. ROSENTHAL,
JOHN W. BOULT,
Attorneys, Department of Justice,
Washington 25, D.C.

---

course, appellant's contention (Appellant's brief, pp 29-30)
e present suit should lie apart from the provisions of the
aims Act, since the HHFA Administrator is entitled by
 to ".sue or be sued" (R. 82) constitutes no valid reason
ver for overturning the district court's order. In the
lace, 28 U.S.C. 2679(a) provides that the Tort Claims Act
onstitute the exclusive remedy against the Government for
n tort, regardless of the "sue and be sued" attributes of
eral government agencies. In the second place, the present
s a suit against the United States only, and the HHFA Admin-
r was never made a party to it. Under such circumstances,
e and be sued" characteristics of an alleged offending
cannot be used to sustain a suit against the United States,
States v. Waylyn Corp., 130 F. Supp. 783, aff'd 231 F. 2d
A. 1), cert. den. 352 U.S. 827.

RAY B. WOODBURY,

        Appellant,

   v.

UNITED STATES OF AMERICA,

        Appellee.

APPELLANT'S REPLY BRIEF

Appeal from the Judgment of Dismissal of the
United States District Court for
the District of Oregon

THE HONORABLE JOHN F. KILKENNY, Judge

KING, MILLER, ANDERSON, NASH & YERKE,
NORMAN J. WIENER,
JEAN P. LOWMAN,
   1200 American Bank Building,
   Portland 5, Oregon,

     Attorneys for Appellant.

JOSEPH D. GUILFOYLE,
   Acting Assistant Attorney General,
SIDNEY I. LEZAK,
   Acting United States Attorney,
ALAN S. ROSENTHAL,
JOHN W. BOULT,

     Attorneys, Department of Justice,
     Washington 25, D. C.,

     Attorneys for Appellee.

TABLE OF CASES AND AUTHORITIES

Cases

Statute

Appellant,

v.

UNITED STATES OF AMERICA,

Appellee.

_____

APPELLANT'S REPLY BRIEF

_____

Appeal from the Judgment of Dismissal of the
United States District Court for
the District of Oregon

THE HONORABLE JOHN F. KILKENNY, Judge

_____

PRELIMINARY STATEMENT

It is apparent from a perusal of appellee's brief
that the issue before this court, i. e., whether breach of
fiduciary duty is cognizable under the Federal Tort Claims
Act, is unpalatable to appellee. Indeed, as a result of
appellee's unwillingness and/or inability to meet this issue,
it is often difficult to recognize that appellee's brief is
purportedly addressed to the same case as that decided by the
trial court and discussed by appellant in his opening brief.

- 1 -

1. Many of the "facts" recited therein are inaccurat
and unsupported by the record.

2. The alleged arguments urged therein are based upo
a misapprehension as to the posture of the case, and, as
such, are directed to matters not in issue.

3. There is no discussion or even mention of the
issue which is before this court for determination.
These defects will be discussed in order.

ARGUMENT

I

Appellee's brief is factually inaccurate.

In the portion of its brief entitled "Statement of
the Case," appellee purports to set forth the facts giving rise
to this action. However, its statement is so slanted as at
times to be inaccurate, and at other times to be patently incorrect. This is demonstrated by the following examples:[1]

Page 2. At page 2 of its brief, appellee states that
"* * * appellant, who had become interested in sponsoring a
housing project near a military installation in the vicinity of
Kodiak, Alaska, applied for, and was granted a construction loa
by HHFA * * *." This is the first of many attempts by appellee
to equate appellant with Aleutian Homes, Inc., an Oregon corporation. The latter was incorporated under the laws of the stat

---

[1] Page references are to appellee's brief

- 2 -

of Oregon for the purpose of becoming sponsor of the Aleutian
Homes housing project (R. 54, 90). It applied for and obtained
the construction loan from HHFA (R. 57, 92-93). Aleutian
Homes, Inc., is not a party to this action, and it is not the
appellant on this appeal. Appellant is an individual, Ray B.
Woodbury, who seeks to recover funds he personally expended
after the execution of the completion agreement and for his
interest as a shareholder in Aleutian Homes, Inc.

Page 7. In discussing the background of the completion agreement, appellee states "the Government had no
disposition to exercise its right of foreclosure if there was
any reasonable means of overcoming the difficulties upon which
the project had foundered." It is not surprising that appellee
does not support this statement with a citation to the record,
for the same is anything but factual. It is rather a mere
conclusion of the writer, and as such is not properly found in
a supposedly objective recital of facts relative to this case.

Pages 7-8. Appellee's discussion of the circumstances leading to the formation of the completion agreement
is typical of its one-sided presentation. Thus, in this portion
of its brief it suggests that the purpose behind the completion
agreement was a desire on the part of appellant to secure money.
This is simply not correct. The completion agreement was entered
into in order to obtain further funds, but such funds were to
be used to complete the project, to obtain the long-term financ-

sented to creditors for acceptance and to HHFA to serve as
basis for further disbursement of undisbursed loan funds."
course, the completion agreement was finally formulated in
Washington, D. C., in conferences between appellant, his
attorney, and HHFA representatives. Many portions of the
agreement were presented by and insisted upon by HHFA. The
after, the plan was submitted to the project creditors for
their approval. In this connection, the District Court sta
(R. 104):

> "The evidence is undisputed that HHFA played
> a major part in all of the negotiations leading up
> to the signing of the completion agreement on
> April 23, 1954."

It ill befits appellee now to suggest that the agreement wa
appellant's product.

Page 8, Footnote 3. In this footnote, appellee s
that neither HHFA nor any other government agency was liste
the completion agreement as a party. In fact, HHFA is refe
to throughout the completion agreement as "the Lender." Fu
more, there is no significance to the fact that HHFA did no
the agreement. Thus, the District Court stated (R. 105-106

> "It is true that neither HHFA nor the Administrator
> signed the completion agreement. However, it is
> crystal clear that all parties to the agreement an-
> ticipated that HHFA would formally accept such
> obligations as it had under the terms of this agreemen

disburse further proceeds of the loan. The parties agreed to sign all documents required by the Lender. All income from the project and other proceeds were to be assigned to the Lender. Plaintiff agreed to provide certain overhead expenses required by the Lender estimated at $16,000 per month. The Project Manager had to be acceptable to the Lender and was vested with full and exclusive authority to take all action necessary in connection with the project, subject to the general direction of the Lender. Any and all subcontractors had to be approved by the Lender. The Project Manager was subject to removal on the request of the Lender. In truth and in fact, the Lender had an absolute right to designate the Project Manager and discharge him if Lender so desired. The bank account from which disbursements were made for the completion of the project was in the name of the Lender and the Project Manager. In other words, when the funds were disbursed by the Lender under its commitments, such funds were transferred to a bank account over which the Lender had absolute control. The construction superintendent had to be acceptable to the Lender and was subject only to the direction of the Project Manager and, by inference, subject to removal only by the Project Manager.

"The language in paragraph 18 of the agreement indicates that the only reason it was not signed by HHFA or the Administrator (Lender) was a doubt as to whether the law authorized such execution. The agreement did require written or oral approval by the Lender. The Lender gave written approval of the agreement. Outside of the terms and provisions of the completion agreement the evidence is overwhelming that the Lender in truth and in fact took over absolute control of and proceeded with the completion of the project.

"In my opinion the fact that the completion agreement was not signed by Lender is of no significance. Contractual liability under a written contract may be assumed without signing it. Girard Life Insurance & Trust Co. vs. Cooper, 162 U. S. 529; Laurent vs. Anderson, 6 Cir., 1934, 70 F.2d 819; First National Bank vs. Sleeper, 8 Cir., 1926, 12 F.2d 228; Commercial Standard Insurance Co. vs. Garrett, 10 Cir., 1934, 70 F.2d 969. In fact, the Lender in this case accepted the completion agreement in writing."

purports to discuss the terms of the completion agreement
However, it fails even to mention the most significant el
of that agreement as the same is involved in this action,
is, the fact that under the completion agreement the gove
assumed complete control of the Aleutian Homes project.
example, as the District Court indicated (supra, page 8),
was necessary that the project manager be acceptable to H
and the latter in turn was vested with full and exclusive
authority to take all necessary action in connection with
project, subject to the general direction of HHFA. HHFA
to approve subcontractors. It determined in what manner
ject funds were to be disbursed. This control gave rise
the fiduciary duty which the government owed appellant an
which is the basis of this lawsuit. Thus, the District C
found that (R. 108-109):

> "* * * the Lender took over full and com-
> plete control of such project and, in so doing,
> was acting in a fiduciary capacity with the
> plaintiff."

This is an additional instance of appellee's desire to av
facts which it finds distasteful.

Appellee is also in error in its discussion of
appellant's obligation relative to overhead expenses. Th
same was contained in the overhead agreement of April 24,
(Ex. 597/1-156), and was to "pay Overhead Expense, as her
defined, necessary to secure completion of Project and re

of Loan in such amount as may be required by Lender, which expenses are estimated to be, but shall not be limited to, $15,000 per month." The Aleutian Homes project was completed in October, 1954 (R. 61, 96), and appellant had then paid the Administrator $75,000 under the overhead agreement (R. 67, 100) There was no subsequent agreement indicating that appellant would pay further overhead expenses after the completion of the project.

Page 10. In discussing the payments made by appellan to The Bank of California, N. A., appellee does not give the full particulars. The bank was to have been paid $61,000 under stage 3 of the completion agreement and $89,000 under stage 4 (Ex. 583/1-140). However, the project manager did not see fit to pay those amounts. Consequently, it obtained payment from appellant under his guaranty, and he attempted to fulfill the obligation. Appellee's inference that appellant paid one creditor at the expense of others is highly improper.

Page 11. At page 11, appellee infers that permanent individual mortgages were not taken out and the FHA commitment expired for the reason that appellant did not pay additional overhead expenses. This is a patent absurdity. These events transpired, as the District Court found (R. 112), by reason of appellee's breach of its fiduciary duty to appellant.

Furthermore, appellee's observation is in direct contradiction to a letter prepared by HHFA, which reads as follows (R. 155):

"'The FHA and FNMA commitments will be
surrendered to avoid the expense of closing
permanent first mortgages and extension fees,
and if by October 31, 1955, it appears that
the project has a reasonable chance of financial
success, a refinancing plan looking toward long-
range amortization of the Administrator's loan
and repayment of other claims will be proposed
by the Housing and Home Finance Administrator.'
/206/"

Pages 11-12. It should be added to appellee's purported summary of the claims asserted by appellant that each
of said claims is based upon appellee's breach of its fiduciary
duty to appellant.

II

Appellee's alleged arguments are irrelevant and
unmeritorious.

Appellee's purported arguments may be summarized as
follows:

1. Appellant's claims are based on contract; and

2. Appellant's claims are within exceptions to the
Federal Tort Claims Act relating to

a. The exercise of a discretionary function,
or

b. Interference with contract rights.

These arguments arise from a misconception as to the basis of
appellant's claims, and as such should not be permitted to dive
attention from the real issue in this case, that is, whether

contract.

The underlying theory is set forth in a decision from the Eighth Circuit referred to by the District Court in its opinion in this case (R. 111).

> "'A relation subsisting between two persons
> in regard to a business, contract, or piece of
> property, * * * of such a character that each must
> repose trust and confidence in the other and must
> exercise a corresponding degree of fairness and
> good faith. Out of such a relation, the law raises
> the rule that neither party may * * * take selfish
> advantage of his trust, or deal with the subject-
> matter of the trust in such a way as to benefit
> himself or prejudice the other except in the exercise
> of the utmost good faith and with the full knowledge
> and consent of that other.'" (Emphasis added)

Farrow v. Dermott Drainage District
(CCA 8, 1944) 139 F2d 800, 805

Harper v. Interstate Brewery Co. (1942) 168 Or 26, 37-38, 120 P2d 757, 762-763

> "* * * it may be necessary for a plaintiff to
> show a contract between himself and the defendant
> in order to establish that the defendant has assumed
> a position, relationship or status upon which the
> general law predicates a duty independent of the
> terms of the contract but it does not necessarily
> follow that his only remedy is ex contractu. If
> from the position, contractually assumed, a duty
> be raised independent of the contract an action
> in tort may lie.

> "'* * * A mere breach of contract cannot be
> sued on as a tort, but for tortious acts, inde-
> pendent of the contract, a man may be sued in
> tort, though one of the consequences is a breach
> of his contract.' Stock v. City of Boston, 149
> Mass. 410, 21 N. E. 871, 14 Am.St.Rep. 430 (1889).

"Relationships of shipper and carrier, bailor
and bailee, physician and patient, and attorney and
client each originate in contract, express or implied;
yet for a breach of duties imposed by general law upon
persons assuming such relationship an action of tort
may lie. In this state an action in tort may even
arise directly out of contract if based on a fraudulent
promise which the promisor never had any intention of
fulfilling and which he successfully employed for the
purpose of deceiving the promisee."

As indicated in the <u>Harper</u> case, numerous contractual

relationships give rise to a fiduciary duty, the breach of whic

is tortious. These include attorney-client and physician-patie

A recent example may be found in

<u>Widing v. Jensen, Real Est. Com. (1962) 74 Or Adv Sh 1177</u>

in which it was held that the contractual relationship of a rea

estate broker and his client results in a fiduciary relationshi

between the two.

So, in the case at bar, the completion agreement gave

appellee full control of the Aleutian Homes project, and

appellee assumed such control (see findings of District Court,

supra, page 6). This in turn gave rise to a fiduciary duty

on the part of appellee not to exercise such control so as

improperly to affect those involved in the project, including

appellant. Thus, the District Court found that (R. 108-109)

"* * * the Lender ⎣appellee⎦ could legally
occupy the legal status of a fiduciary in
connection with the completion of the housing
project in question. Furthermore, I find and
hold that the Lender took over full and complete
control of such project and, in so doing, was
acting in a fiduciary capacity with the
plaintiff."

Appellant had an election to sue on the contract or to bring

Tort Claims Act.

Appellee's contention that appellant's claims are precluded by the discretionary function exception to the Federal Tort Claims Act is a patent absurdity. It may well be, as appellee suggests, that the Administrator exercised a discretionary function in entering into the negotiations which culminated in the execution of the completion agreement. It does not follow, and it is not true that he had discretion to breach the fiduciary duty arising from the relationship created by that agreement. See, for example,

Hatahley v. United States (1955) 351 US 173, 181, 100 L ed 1065, 1074

> "* * * Nor can the second portion of (a) exempt the Government from liability. We are here not concerned with any problem of a 'discretionary function' under the Act, see Dalehite v. United States (US) supra. These acts were wrongful trespasses not involving discretion on the part of the agents, and they do give rise to a claim compensable under the Federal Tort Claims Act."

Thus, the District Court found that appellee was not acting in the exercise of a discretionary function (R. 116):

> "I feel that the Lender, when it accepted the completion agreement and took over control of the project under which it was to provide long-term financing, was not acting in the exercise of a discretionary function. The Lender had an absolute obligation to furnish such long-term financing."

<u>exceptions to the Federal Tort Claims Act relative</u>

<u>to interference with contract rights, malicious</u>

<u>prosecution and abuse of process.</u>

In contending that appellant's claims are within the exceptions to the Federal Tort Claims Act relative to interference with contract rights, malicious prosecution and abuse of process, appellee has again misconstrued the basis of this action. Appellant seeks to recover damages sustained by reason of appellee's breach of its fiduciary duty, which is a tort entirely unrelated to interference with contract rights, malicious prosecution or abuse of process. If certain of the acts by which appellee breached its fiduciary duty did give rise to tort liability in these other categories, that fact would have no relevance. The fact is that appellee's acts constituted a breach of its fiduciary duty to appellant, and in delineating the issue in this case, the District Court so found (R. 112):

> "* * * I have already concluded that defendant could act as a fiduciary and was acting in a fiduciary or confidential capacity in assuming control over the completion of the project and the long-term financing. Assuming, arguendo, and I would so hold if I felt I had jurisdiction, that defendant in truth and in fact breached its duty in failing to provide, without justification, said long-term financing, is such breach of duty 'negligent or wrongful act or omission' within the meaning of the phrase as used in the Federal Tort Claims Act?"

At any rate, even if appellee's argument had some merit, the same could apply only to one claim asserted by appellant. Thus, he seeks to recover the following (see

fiduciary duty;

2. Sums advanced from his personal funds to pay expenses incurred during preparation for the project; and

3. The damage to and destruction of the equity of Aleutian Homes, Inc. in the Aleutian Homes project. Only the third could conceivably fall within the exception urged by appellee.

Appellee elected to base his action upon appellee's breach of fiduciary duty. Appellee's specious argument does not divert from this fact, and from the fact that the issue in this case is whether such breach of fiduciary duty is within the purview of the Federal Tort Claims Act.

Appellee suggests (page 29) that its tortious conduct was deliberate in character and consequently not covered by the Federal Tort Claims Act. In his opening brief, appellant fully demonstrated that breach of fiduciary duty is within the scope of the Act. Appellee's suggestion is not documented, and no further comment is required.

III

The judgment of the District Court must be reversed for the reason that breach of fiduciary duty is within the scope of the Federal Tort Claims Act.

Appellee states (page 30) that the District Court "was clearly correct in its conclusion that it lacked

case.

The District Court found that appellee could occupy the legal status of a fiduciary in connection with the completion of the Aleutian Homes project, and that it was acting in a fiduciary capacity with appellant (R. 108-109). It found th. appellee breached its fiduciary duty to appellant (R. 112). A: noted above (supra, page 12), it stated that the question was whether such breach of duty constituted a negligent or wrongfu act within the meaning of the Federal Tort Claims Act (R. 112, 113). The court held that breach of fiduciary duty was not within the purview of the Act (R. 113-114) and consequently that it did not have jurisdiction of appellant's claims (R. 11

Appellee urges (page 30) that the trial court did not make findings on this subject. Appellee denies the existe of a fiduciary duty and its breach. The court's opinion (R. 7' 117) expressly stands as its findings (R. 116, 117). Appellan accepts these findings and challenges only the court's conclusion. If appellee disputes the findings, this is the first time it has made that fact known. It did not move in the District Court to amend the findings under the provisions of Rule 52 (b), Federal Rules of Civil Procedure. Again, it did not file a cross-appeal in this court, and consequently its present protestations are not entitled to consideration.

<u>Harrington v. Empire Const. Co. (CCA 4, 1948) 167 F2d 389, 39</u>

> "With respect to the period after May 23, 1943,
> the District Judge in accepting the master's findings
> expressed the opinion that the most credible parts of
> the evidence showed that the defendant adopted the
> recommendation of the Wage and Hour Division as of
> that date and placed all of its field clerks on a 48-
> hour rather than a fluctuating hour basis. Since this
> finding was favorable to the plaintiff /appellant7,
> and the defendant has taken no appeal therefrom, we
> need not give it further consideration."

It indeed ill befits appellee to criticize the trial court's

findings at this point.

It should be noted that since appellant's opening

brief was filed herein, an additional case has been decided

demonstrating that the Federal Tort Claims Act constitutes a

waiver of governmental immunity from liability for all torts

except those expressly removed from such waiver.

<u>Winston v. U. S. (CA 2, June 28, 1962) 31 LW 2037</u>

> "'We adopt as our own the opinion of Judge
> Hincks, appearing at _____ F.2d _____ (1962),
> 30 LW 2434 * * * We think it desirable, by way of
> response to certain arguments raised in the course
> of our reconsideration of this matter, to analyze
> briefly several of the considerations which we
> believe lend additional support to the conclusion
> which we have reached. * * *

> "'The Act lists thirteen kinds of claims as
> to which immunity is not waived. None of these
> exceptions remotely relates to claims by persons
> who have suffered injury while being held in a
> federal prison (28 U. S. C. 2680 (1958)).* * *

> "'The care with which Congress detailed the
> express exclusion from the coverage of the Act of
> those situations in which the right of recovery was
> considered undesirable * * * leaves no room for the
> exception of additional situations which would other-
> wise be covered by the statute.* * *'"

one of the torts excluded from the operation of the Federal
Tort Claims Act; consequently, it is within the purview of
the Act.

The District Court's conclusion that it lacks
jurisdiction of this action under the provisions of the
Federal Tort Claims Act cannot be defended on the purported
grounds urged by appellee. The issue is whether breach of
fiduciary duty is cognizable under the Federal Tort Claims
Act. In his opening brief, appellant demonstrated that this
tort is within the purview of the Act. Appellee has not
even attempted to refute this fact. Unquestionably, the
judgment of the District Court should be reversed.

CONCLUSION

Appellant accepts the findings of the District
irt that under the facts presented by this case, appellee
s acting in a fiduciary capacity with him, and that appellee
eached the fiduciary duty it owed to him. Appellant
spectfully urges, however, that the District Court was in
ror when it held that breach of fiduciary duty is not within
e scope of the Federal Tort Claims Act.

For the reasons set forth hereinabove and in
pellant's opening brief, the judgment of dismissal of the
strict Court should be reversed.

Respectfully submitted,

KING, MILLER, ANDERSON, NASH & YERKE
NORMAN J. WIENER
JEAN P. LOWMAN
1200 American Bank Building
Portland 5, Oregon
Attorneys for Appellant

CERTIFICATE

I certify that, in connection with the preparation
is brief, I have examined Rules 18 and 19 of the United
s Court of Appeals for the Ninth Circuit, and that, in
inion, the foregoing brief is in full compliance with
rules.

NORMAN J. WIENER
Of Attorneys for Appellant

No. 17585

United States
Court of Appeals
for the Ninth Circuit

RAY B. WOODBURY,

Appellant,

vs.

UNITED STATES OF AMERICA,

Appellee.

Transcript of Record

**Appeal from the United States District Court
for the District of Oregon.**

Phillips & Van Orden Co., 4th & Berry, S. F , Calif —Rec 2/14/62—Printed 4/4/62

No. 17585

United States
Court of Appeals
for the Ninth Circuit

RAY B. WOODBURY,

Appellant,

vs.

UNITED STATES OF AMERICA,

Appellee.

Transcript of Record

**Appeal from the United States District Court
for the District of Oregon.**

Phillips & Van Orden Co , 4th & Berry, S F., Calif —Rec 2/14/62—Printed 4/4/62

INDEX

[Clerk's Note: When deemed likely to be of an important nature errors or doubtful matters appearing in the original certified record are printed literally in italic; and, likewise, cancelled matter appear ing in the original certified record is printed and cancelled herein accordingly. When possible, an omission from the text is indicated by printing in italic the two words between which the omission seems to occur.]

PAGE

ii

INDEX

NAMES AND ADDRESSES OF ATTORNEYS

KING, MILLER, ANDERSON, NASH &
  YERKE;
NORMAN J. WIENER,
JEAN P. LOWMAN,
    1200 American Bank Building,
    Portland 5, Oregon,

        For Appellant.

SIDNEY I. LEZAK,
    Acting United States Attorney;
ROGER G. ROSE,
    Assistant United States Attorney;
MORTON HOLLANDER,
    Chief, Appellate Section, Civil Division,
        Department of Justice,
        Washington 25, D. C.,

        For Appellee.

The United States District Court
for the District of Oregon

Civil No. 9403

RAY B. WOODBURY,

Plaintiff,

vs.

UNITED STATES OF AMERICA,

Defendant.

COMPLAINT

For a first cause of action plaintiff alleges:

I.

Plaintiff is now and at all times herein mentioned was a citizen and resident of the state of Oregon. Aleutian Homes, Inc., is now and at all times herein mentioned was a corporation organized and existing under the laws of the state of Oregon. Plaintiff is the owner of 799 shares of common stock of said Aleutian Homes, Inc., out a total of 800 shares authorized, issued and outstanding.

II.

The Housing and Home Finance Administration, hereinafter referred to as HHFA, is an agency of the United States of America. The Housing and Home Finance Administrator, hereinafter referred to as Administrator, is the head of said agency and is responsible for the general supervision and co-ordination of the functions of the constituent agencies of the HHFA. During the year 1952, and until sometime in the year 1953, Raymond M. Foley was the duly appointed and acting Administrator. Albert M. Cole succeeded said Raymond M. Foley as Administrator and now is and at all times since has been the duly appointed and acting Administrator.

III.

The Federal Housing Administration, hereinafter referred to as FHA, is an agency of the United States of America. The Federal Housing Commissioner, hereinafter referred to as Commissioner, exercises all the powers of the FHA. FHA is a constituent agency of HHFA.

IV.

The Federal National Mortgage Association, hereinafter referred to as FNMA, is a body corporate created by the Congress of the United States and is a constituent agency of HHFA.

V.

This action is brought pursuant to the provisions of Title 28, U.S.C.A., Sections 1346(b) and 2671 through 2680. The matter in controversy, exclusive of costs, exceeds the sum of $3,000.

VI.

In 1951 and 1952, the Secretary of Navy expressed interest in securing, as an aid to national defense, the construction of a housing project for naval personnel in the Kodiak, Alaska, area to relieve an acute shortage of housing facilities then existing.

VII.

In 1952 the Secretary of Navy requested the construction of such housing project be undertaken and requested that the FHA extend appropriate mortgage insurance commitments to cover said project in the total amount of $4,700,000.

VIII.

Subsequent to said request and on or about February 29, 1952, plaintiff caused Aleutian Homes, Inc., to be incorporated under the laws of Oregon. Said Aleutian Homes, Inc., was incorporated for the purpose of owning, constructing and operating said housing project in Kodiak, Alaska. In order to induce Aleutian Homes, Inc., to construct said housing project, FHA, acting on the request of the Secretary of Navy, issued firm commitments for mortgage insurance covering the houses in said project.

IX.

Further in order to induce Aleutian Homes, Inc., to construct said project, FNMA issued commitments to purchase the FHA insured mortgages in the total amount of $4,700,000.

X.

In order to induce Aleutian Homes, Inc., to construct said project so that housing facilities would be available to naval personnel in the area of Kodiak, Alaska, and in order to further the declared policy of Congress to assure the maintenance of industrial capacity for the production of pre-fabricated houses and house components so that such capacity might be available for the purpose of national defense, the HHFA agreed to loan Aleutian Homes, Inc., the sum of $4,230,000, which constituted 90 per cent of the amount of said FHA and FNMA commitments. Said loan from HHFA was intended as interim financing for said project, which loan was to be repaid out of the proceeds of the mortgage financing pursuant to the FHA and FNMA commitments hereinabove set forth. An actual total of $4,192,717.10 was advanced by HHFA for the construction of said project.

XI.

On or about April 27, 1953, said loan authorization, together with all other required contracts and documents, was executed by Aleutian Homes, Inc.

XII.

Pursuant to the aforementioned commitments and loan authorization, construction of said housing project commenced in 1953.

XIII.

By reason of certain difficulties unforeseen by plaintiff and Aleutian Homes, Inc., but anticipated and known to HHFA, its agents and employees, construction of said project fell behind schedule and by the end of 1953 only a portion of the construction of said project was completed.

XIV.

Because lien claimants and other creditors threatened to prevent the completion of said housing project urgently needed by naval personnel and because HHFA, FHA and FNMA desired to complete said project in the interest of national defense, on or about February 26, 1954, HHFA formulated and entered into a completion agreement with plaintiff, Aleutian Homes, Inc., creditors and other interested parties in which HHFA undertook to pay all creditors then existing, to take whatever steps were necessary to complete the construction of said project, and to operate said project until permanent financing arrangements were completed.

XV.

Pursuant to said completion agreement, HHFA assumed complete and exclusive control over the construction of said project, including complete and exclusive control over the conduct of Aleutian Homes, Inc., and all other aspects and phases of the construction and operation of said project. In carrying out said completion agreement HHFA selected a project manager, to be located in Portland, Oregon, who was subject to the complete and exclusive authority and direction of HHFA. All disbursements of funds and receipts of moneys were directed and controlled exclusively by HHFA. Said complete and exclusive control over the construction and operation of said project by HHFA was exercised continuously from February 26, 1954, until on or about June 14, 1957, at which time

HHFA secured an order from the United States
District Court for the District of Alaska appointing a receiver to take full control of said project.

XVI.

On or about October 26, 1954, actual construction of said project was completed. From July 1,
1954, until June 14, 1957, HHFA collected and reserved to its own use, rents from said housing project in the sum of $1,114,800.20.

XVII.

In entering into said completion agreement and
in reliance thereon plaintiff was induced to advance and did advance during the year 1954, to the
aforementioned project manager the sum of $75,000
to be used as overhead to complete said project,
which said sum upon the completion of the project
was to be repaid to plaintiff out of the mortgage
funds to be advanced by FNMA.

XVIII.

In entering into said completion agreement and
in assuming complete and exclusive control over the
construction and operation of said project in the
interest of national defense, HHFA entered into
and occupied a fiduciary relation with respect to
plaintiff, Aleutian Homes, Inc., creditors and other
interested parties to said completion agreement.

XIX.

In approximately May, 1955, HHFA, in exercising said complete and exclusive control over the

construction and operation of said project, in undertaking the payment of creditors and in the carrying out of said completion agreement, permitted the then existing commitments of FHA and FNMA, with respect to permanent long-range financing of said project, to terminate and lapse in order to effectuate alternative long-range financing of said project.

XX.

In breach of its fiduciary obligation to secure permanent long-range financing for said project, in lieu of financing in accordance with the commitments of its constituent agencies, FHA and FNMA, the HHFA, its agents and employees, carelessly and negligently failed and neglected or deliberately and willfully refused to secure such financing, and in breach of said fiduciary duties and obligations on or about May 28, 1957, did seize the bank account of Aleutian Homes, Inc., compelling the payment from it of $122,300, and on or about June 11, 1957, in the United States District Court for the District of Alaska, Third Judicial Division, Anchorage, commenced foreclosure proceedings in the name of the United States of America against Aleutian Homes, Inc., a corporation; Pacific Alaska Contractors, Inc., a corporation; Alex B. Carlton, doing business as Carlton Lumber Company, City of Kodiak, a municipal corporation of the Territory of Alaska; James C. Dougherty, Trustee under the Will of Hugh Dougherty; Lee Bettinger, Jack Hinckel; M. Justin Herman and David Oliver, as Trustees; Lindley R. Durkee and Melvin Frazier, as Trustees; and "Also all other persons or parties unknown claiming any right, title, estate, lien or interest in the real estate described in the complaint herein," defendants, Civil No. A-13,484, to collect the balance of moneys due on the interim loan used for the construction of said project and to foreclose the interest of plaintiff, Aleutian Homes, Inc., the unpaid creditors and other parties interested in said project and in the assets thereof.

XXI.

By reason of the negligent and wrongful acts and omissions of the employees of the Government of the United States of America as hereinabove set forth, plaintiff has suffered damages in the amount of $75,000.

For a second cause of action plaintiff alleges:

I.

Incorporates herein paragraphs I through XVI of the first cause of ction.

II.

To be paid out of the funds to be advanced by FNMA for the purchase of permanent mortgages were claims of The Bank of California, N.A., for $150,000, together with interest thereon from September 21, 1953. By reason of the failure of HHFA to pay said claim and by reason of his liability as an accommodation indorser to the note which represented said claim of The Bank of California, N.A., plaintiff has paid interest thereon in the amount of $14,594.80 and has paid principal in the amount of $150,000, no part of which has been repaid to plaintiff from any source. Said payments of interest and principal were made by plaintiff upon the following dates in the following amounts:

Date of Payment	Amount Paid	Credited to
Feb. 18, 1954	$ 1,083.33	Interest
June 2, 1954	1,875.00	Interest
Aug. 20, 1954	1,875.00	Interest
Dec. 6, 1954	1,895.83	Interest
May 18, 1955	3,750.00	Interest
May 18, 1955	41,455.00	Principal
May 18, 1955	14,526.43	Principal
June 13, 1955	2,352.75	Principal
July 11, 1955	2,352.75	Principal
Aug. 12, 1955	890.56	Interest
Sept. 13, 1955	285.31	Interest
Sept. 13, 1955	2,063.69	Principal
Sept. 28, 1955	658.25	Principal
Oct. 10, 1955	653.27	Interest
Oct. 10, 1955	25,591.13	Principal
June 11, 1956	787.92	Interest
July 6, 1956	1,499.58	Interest
July 6, 1956	61,000.00	Principal

III.

Incorporates herein paragraphs XVII through XX of the first cause of action.

IV.

By reason of the negligent and wrongful acts and omissions of the employees of the Government of the United States of America as herein above set forth, plaintiff has suffered damages in the amount of $164,594.80.

For a third cause of action plaintiff alleges:

I.

Incorporates herein paragraphs I through XVI of the first cause of action.

II.

To be paid out of the funds advanced by FNMA for the purchase of permanent mortgages was a claim by the General Casualty Company of America for $28,750.85, together with interest thereon at the rate of 6 per cent per annum from June 9, 1953, until paid. By reason of the failure of HHFA to pay said claim and by reason of the personal guaranty on the part of plaintiff given as an accommodation, judgment for the amount of said claim, together with interest, expenditures, attorneys' fees and costs was entered against plaintiff in the United States District Court for the District of Oregon on June 24, 1956. On September 18, 1956, said judgment was paid and satisfied by the payment by plaintiff of the sum of $33,542.09. In the defense of said action plaintiff incurred legal fees and other necessary expenses in the sum of $2,412.93.

III.

Incorporates herein paragraphs XVII through XX of the first cause of action.

IV.

By reason of the negligent and wrongful acts and omissions of the employees of the Government of the United States of America as hereinabove set forth, plaintiff has suffered damages in the amount of $35,955.02.

For a fourth cause of action plaintiff alleges

I.

Incorporates herein paragraphs I through XVI of the first cause of action.

II.

Commencing in 1951 and until the execution of the loan authorization and other documents on April 27, 1953, plaintiff had advanced out of his own personal funds necessary expenses incurred in the preparation for said project the sum of $150,-000. In order to place the priority of said claims of plaintiff behind the claims of other creditors and to delay repayment of said moneys, 1,500 shares of preferred stock of Aleutian Homes, Inc., at $100 per share par value, were authorized for issuance to plaintiff to be fully paid for by the cancellation of the claims represented by said cash advances. Said shares were to be redeemed by Aleutian Homes, Inc., at the completion of the project out of the funds to be advanced by FNMA for the purchase of permanent mortgages.

III.

Incorporates herein paragraphs XVII through XX of the first cause of action.

IV.

By reason of the negligent and wrongful acts and omissions of the employees of the Government of the United States of America as hereinabove set forth, plaintiff has suffered damages in the amount of $150,000.

For a fifth cause of action plaintiff alleges:

I.

Incorporates herein paragraphs I through XVI of the first cause of action.

II.

Subsequent to the completion agreement and during the years 1954, 1955 and 1956, plaintiff advanced and paid on behalf of Aleutian Homes, Inc., to satisfy various claims and charges in addition to those set forth in the first, second, third and fourth causes of action herein, the net sum of $9,297.04. Said disbursements and advances were made by plaintiff with the full knowledge of the HHFA and with the understanding and intention that plaintiff would be reimbursed for said disbursements and advances out of the funds to be advanced by FNMA for the purchase of permanent mortgages.

III.

Incorporates herein paragraphs XVII through XX of the first cause of action.

IV.

By reason of the negligent and wrongful acts and

omissions of the employees of the Government of the United States of America as hereinabove set forth, plaintiff has suffered damages in the amount of $9,297.04.

For a sixth cause of action plaintiff alleges:

I.

Incorporates herein paragraphs I through XVI of the first cause of action.

II.

The present fair market value of said housing project exceeds $5,800,000. The claims to be paid under the completion agreement, which were to be paid out of the funds made available from permanent long-range financing, including the redemption of the 1,500 shares of preferred stock held by plaintiff in the amount of $150,000, are in the total sum of $5,370,805.97. The equity in said project held by Aleutian Homes, Inc., which equity is in the process of being foreclosed by the HHFA in the action now pending in the United States District Court for the District of Alaska, as hereinabove set forth, exceeds the sum of $429,194.03. By reason of the negligent and wrongful acts and omissions of the employees of the government, as hereinabove set forth, the equity held in said project by Aleutian Homes, Inc., has been damaged and destroyed, so that said equity is of no present value. Plaintiff now owns 799 shares of common stock of said Aleutian Homes, Inc., out of a total of 800 such shares authorized, issued and outstanding. The damage to and destruction of said equity of Aleutian Homes, Inc., has injured plaintiff to the extent of 799/800 of the value of said equity.

III.

Incorporates herein paragraphs XVII through XX of the first cause of action.

IV.

By reason of the negligent and wrongful acts and omissions of the employees of the Government of the United States of America hereinabove set forth, plaintiff has suffered damages in the amount of $428,127.

Wherefore, plaintiff demands judgment against defendant as follows:

1. With respect to the first cause of action, the sum of $75,000.

2. With respect to the second cause of action, the sum of $164,594.80.

3. With respect to the third cause of action, the sum of $35,955.02.

4. With respect to the fourth cause of action, the sum of $150,000.

5. With respect to the fifth cause of action, the sum of $9,297.04.

6. With respect to the sixth cause of action, the sum of $428,127.

7. For his costs incurred herein.

> KING, MILLER, ANDERSON,
> NASH & YERKE,
>
> /s/ NORMAN J. WIENER,
>
> /s/ PAUL R. MEYER,
> Attorneys for Plaintiff.

[Endorsed]: Filed September 30, 1957.

[Title of District Court and Cause.]

MOTION TO DISMISS AND IN THE ALTERNATIVE FOR SUMMARY JUDGMENT

Comes now the United States of America, defendant herein, appearing by C. E. Luckey, United States Attorney for the District of Oregon, and respectfully moves the Court that the above-entitled cause be dismissed on the following grounds:

1. The Complaint does not state facts to constitute a claim upon which relief can be granted.

2. The Complaint shows on its face that the alleged tortious act occurred in "approximately May, 1955" and the records of this Court show that the action was not filed until September 30, 1957, and thus the action has been tolled by Title 28, United States Code, Section 2401.

3. The acts complained of as allegedly tortious are not within the provisions of the Federal Tort

Claims Act because they allegedly arose under circumstances showing the exercise of a discretionary function incognizable under the Federal Tort Claims Act by reason of Title 28, United States Code, Section 2680(a).

4. That the acts complained of may not subject the defendant to damages as an interference with contract relations by reason of Title 28, United States Code, Section 2680(h).

5. Particularly referring to plaintiff's sixth cause of action, defendant moves to dismiss the said cause of action because the plaintiff has alleged no facts giving him standing to sue.

6. Particularly referring to plaintiff's sixth cause of action, defendant moves to dismiss the said cause of action because the plaintiff has failed to join Aleutian Homes, Inc., an indispensable party to said cause of action.

In the alternative the defendant respectfully moves the Court that summary judgment be entered in favor of the defendant pursuant to Rule 56, Federal Rules of Civil Procedure, because the United States of America was not a party to the completion agreement complained of in the complaint, a copy of which is hereto attached as Exhibit A, and the parties to the agreement waived any rights against the Housing and Home Finance Agency arising from actions taken by and under the agreement.

Respectfully submitted,

/s/ C. E. LUCKEY,
United States Attorney for the District of Oregon,
of Attorneys for Defendant.

Affidavit of service by mail attached.

[Endorsed]: Filed February 14, 1958.

———

[Title of District Court and Cause.]

ORDER DENYING MOTION TO DISMISS

This matter coming on for hearing on April 28, 1958, upon defendant's motion to dismiss and in the alternative for summary judgment, and the court having heard argument thereon, and briefs having been submitted thereon by both parties hereto, and the defendant at said hearing having withdrawn its alternative motion for summary judgment, and the court being fully advised in the premises, now, therefore, it is hereby

Ordered that defendant's motion to dismiss be and the same hereby is denied with leave to defendant to renew said motion at the time of pretrial.

Dated this 28th day of April, 1958.

/s/ GUS J. SOLOMON,
Judge.

[Endorsed]: Filed April 28, 1958.

[Title of District Court and Cause.]

ANSWER

United States of America, Defendant, answering the complaint herein, respectfully shows this court as follows:

First Cause of Action

I-IV.

Defendant admits the allegations of Paragraphs I, II, III, and IV.

V.

Answering Paragraph V, defendant admits that this action purports to be brought under Title 28, USCA, Secs. 1346(b) and 2671 through 2680, but denies that such provisions confer jurisdiction upon this Court as the cause of action alleged herein is not cognizable under those sections of the law. The Government admits that the matter in controversy, exclusive of costs, exceeds the sum of $3,000.00.

VI.

Answering Paragraph VI, defendant is uninformed as to whether in 1951 and 1952 the Secretary of the Navy "expressed interest" in securing the construction of a Housing Project at Kodiak, Alaska, and therefore denies said allegation.

VII.

Defendant denies each and all of the allegations in Paragraph VII.

VIII.

Defendant admits the first two sentences of Paragraph VIII. Defendant admits that FHA in accordance with Section 203 of the National Housing Act, as amended, issued commitments to Brice Mortgage Company, an approved FHA mortgagee, to insure mortgages on the 344 dwellings to be built in the housing project, provided such mortgages were in conformity with the law and with the rules, regulations and requirements of FHA. Defendant denies that FHA in issuing said commitments acted upon the request of the Secretary of the Navy and denies that in issuing said commitments FHA did so in order to induce Aleutian Homes, Inc., to construct said housing project.

IX.

Defendant admits that Federal National Mortgage Association ("FNMA") issued commitments to Brice Mortgage Company to purchase at par such FHA insured mortgages as might be executed on the dwellings in the housing project, provided that such insured mortgages were in conformity with the requirements of FNMA. Defendant denies that FNMA in issuing said commitments did so in order to induce Aleutian Homes, Inc., to construct said project.

X.

Defendant admits that HHFA agreed to lend to Aleutian Homes, Inc., the sum of $4,230,000 in accordance with the provisions of the Loan Authorization dated Januray 15, 1953, as amended, a copy of which is annexed hereto as Exhibit 1. Defendant admits that said loan was intended as interim financing for said project and alleges that it was a condition to the granting of said loan and to the disbursement thereof that Aleutian Homes, Inc., should provide permanent financing. In accordance with such requirement Aleutian Homes, Inc., entered into a certain take-out agreement dated June 2, 1953, as amended, a copy of which and copies of the amendments to which are annexed hereto as Exhibits 2, 3, and 4. Defendant admits that HHFA advanced $4,192,717.10 for the construction of the project. Except as so admitted, the allegations of paragraph X are denied.

XI.

Answering Paragraph XI, defendant denies that Aleutian Homes, Inc., on or about April 27, 1953, executed a Loan Authorization. Defendant admits that on or about April 27, 1953, the said Aleutian Homes, Inc., executed various instruments, contracts and other documents, among others being the following:

(a) Note dated April 27, 1953, in the principal amount of $4,230,900.00 with interest at 5% per annum, payable to defendant and due December 31, 1953, the maturity of which was extended to become due October 31, 1955.

(b) Deed of Trust conveying and mortgaging the Housing Project, real estate and appurtenances to Trustees as security for the payment of the aforesaid note.

(c) Building Loan Agreement dated April 27, 1953, executed by Aleutian Homes, Inc., pursuant to which the said Aleutian Homes, Inc., agreed to construct said Housing Project with the proceeds of the aforesaid loan, such construction to be completed by October 31, 1953, the date of completion being later extended to September 24, 1954.

(d) Take-out Agreement dated June 2, 1953, as amended, executed by Brice Mortgage Company and Aleutian Homes, Inc., and plaintiff (hereinafter called "Woodbury"), in accordance with which Brice Mortgage Company, at the instance of Aleutian Homes, Inc., and Woodbury, agreed, in conformity with the requirements of the Loan Authorization, to furnish permanent financing for the Housing Project.

XII.

Answering Paragraph XII, defendant admits that construction of said Housing Project commenced in 1953.

XIII.

Answering Paragraph XIII, defendant admits that the construction of such Project did fall behind schedule, and that by the end of 1953 only a portion of the construction of said Project was completed. Defendant denies, that such failure in maintaining the schedule of construction was due to difficulties unforeseen by Woodbury and Aleutian Homes, Inc., but anticipated and known to defendant, and alleges that certain of the difficulties, including the submission to defendant of false and misleading applications for payment, were known to plaintiff and concealed from defendant. Defendant admits that work on said Housing Project came to a halt in November 1953, with the Project in an incomplete state of construction, and mechanics' liens and other claims were filed or asserted by various creditors, alleging that moneys due them for work, materials and services supplied or furnished by them remained due and unpaid.

XIV.

Defendant denies (except as otherwise stated herein) each and all of the allegations in Paragraph XIV and alleges that Woodbury and Aleutian Homes, Inc., following the abandonment of construction, desired to salvage whatever equity said Aleutian Homes, Inc., possessed in the said Housing Project, and to pay off the claims relating thereto. In the interest of doing so, said Aleutian Homes, Inc., and Woodbury and other persons formulated among themselves and presented to the Administrator of HHFA an Agreement contemplating the completion of the Housing Project, the disbursement of the balance of the proceeds of the government loan, and the payment, to the extent feasible, of claims and debts relating to said Housing Project, which said Agreement Aleutian Homes, Inc., and Woodbury urged the Administrator to sign and accept. The Administrator declined to sign any such Agreement but agreed to offer no objection thereto, and, accordingly, Aleutian Homes, Inc., Woodbury and others entered into and executed a certain Completion Agreement dated April 24, 1954, a true and correct copy of which is attached hereto and made a part hereof as Exhibit 5. As appears from said Completion Agreement, neither the Administrator nor the defendant undertook any obligation whatsoever to complete the said Project or to obtain permanent financing or to operate said Project until permanent financing arrangements were completed. The obligation to furnish permanent financing remained incumbent upon Aleutian Homes, Inc.

XV.

Defendant admits that by reason of the default in payment of the obligation of Aleutian Homes, Inc., evidenced by its Note, it instituted proceedings for the foreclosure of the mortgage security and the collection of the debt in a certain proceeding filed in the United States District Court for the District of Alaska, sitting at Anchorage, in a cause entitled United States of America v. Aleutian Homes, Inc., et al., wherein the Court appointed a Receiver to take possession and custody of the mortgaged Housing Project and the collateral security for the indebtedness of said Aleutian Homes, Inc., to the United States. Except as so admitted, defendant denies the allegations of Paragraph XV. Defendant alleges that the complete control, direction and management relating to the completion and operation of the Housing Project was vested in a certain Project Manager appointed, named and designated by said Aleutian Homes, Inc., as its Agent, in a certain Agreement (herein called "Project Management Agreement") dated April 24, 1954, executed by said Aleutian Homes, Inc., and approved in writing by Woodbury, a copy of which is annexed hereto as Exhibit 6.

XVI.

Answering Paragraph XVI, defendant admits that the actual construction of said Project was completed during the latter part of 1954. Defendant denies that HHFA collected and reserved to its own use rental from said Housing Project in the sum of $1,114,800.20. Defendant alleges that all such rentals and revenues were collected by Aleutian Homes, Inc., and placed to its credit and account in the United States National Bank, Portland, Oregon, in Special Account No. 3, under Depository Agreement dated May 6, 1954, permitting the disbursement of such funds by said Aleutian Homes, Inc., from said special account, but only for authorized and legitimate purposes upon the counter-signature of the Administrator or his designee.

XVII.

Defendant denies each and all of the allegations of Paragraph XVII. Defendant alleges that Woodbury, for the purpose of inducing the defendant to disburse the balance of the proceeds of the Government loan, executed a certain Overhead Agreement dated April 24, 1954, a true and correct copy of which is annexed hereto as Exhibit 7. Under the terms of said Agreement, Woodbury obligated himself to pay to the Government the sum of $15,000 a month for overhead expenses in connection with the completion and operation of said Project. Woodbury made such payments for a period of five months, aggregating $75,000.00, but failed and refused to pay the monthly installments of $15,000 due thereafter, and said default continues to this date.

XVIII.

Defendant denies each and all of the allegations of Paragraph XVIII, and specifically denies that it entered into any fiduciary relationship with Woodbury, Aleutian Homes, Inc., or others, and denies that the Completion Agreement establishes or purports to establish any such relation.

XIX.

Defendant denies each and all of the allegations of Paragraph XIX, and alleges that it was the obligation of Aleutian Homes, Inc., to furnish permanent financing to pay the interim loan made by the Government to said Aleutian Homes, Inc., and that it was the obligation of Aleutian Homes, Inc., to meet all requirements and conditions of FHA and FNMA for the issuance of commitments and for maintaining in full force and effect any and all FHA and FNMA commitments with respect thereto, including the Take-out Agreement, as amended, of Brice Mortgage Company. Notwithstanding such obligation, the said Aleutian Homes, Inc., and Woodbury, determined that the costs of meeting the

conditions required to maintain said FHA and
FNMA commitments in full force and effect were
too high and the said Aleutian Homes, Inc., and
Woodbury requested the defendant, in writing, for
leave for said Aleutian Homes, Inc., to permit such
commitments to lapse. A true and correct copy of
such written request is attached hereto as Exhibit
8. The defendant offered no objection thereto, and
Aleutian Homes, Inc., and Woodbury caused such
commitments to lapse and terminate.

XX.

Defendant denies each and all of the allegations
of Paragraph XX, except that it admits that foreclosure proceedings were filed in the United States
District Court for the District of Alaska, in the
proceedings entitled United States of America v.
Aleutian Homes, Inc., et al., and except that the
defendant admits that it caused $122,300.00 to be
withdrawn from Special Account No. 3 held in the
United States National Bank, Portland, Oregon, in
accordance with the provisions of the Depository
Agreement dated May 6, 1954, relating to such Special Account. The Depository Agreement expressly
provides that upon the default by Aleutian Homes,
Inc., in the payment of its indebtedness, the Administrator may withdraw the funds in such Special
Account for application on the amount due the
defendant. Defendant alleges that it never assumed
the obligation to secure for Aleutian Homes, Inc.,
permanent financing; this was the express obligation of Aleutian Homes, Inc.

XXI.

The defendant denies each and all of the allegations of Paragraph XXI.

Second Cause of Action

I.

Answering Paragraph I, defendant realleges Paragraphs I to XVI inclusive, of its Answer to the first cause of action.

II.

Answering Paragraph II, defendant denies the allegations thereof for lack of knowledge and information sufficient to form a belief as to their truth.

III.

Answering Paragraph III, defendant realleges Paragraphs XVI to XX, inclusive, of its Answer to the first cause of action.

IV.

Defendant denies the allegations of Paragraph IV.

Third Cause of Action

I.

Answering Paragraph I, defendant realleges Paragraphs I through XVI, inclusive, of its Answer to the first cause of action.

II.

Answering Paragraph II, defendant denies the

allegations thereof for lack of knowledge or information sufficient to form a belief as to their truth.

III.

Answering Paragraph III, defendant realleges Paragraphs XVII through XX, inclusive, of its Answer to the first cause of action.

IV.

Defendant denies the allegations of Paragraph IV.

Fourth Cause of Action

I.

Answering Paragraph I, defendant realleges Paragraphs I to XVI, inclusive, of its Answer to the first cause of action.

II.

Defendant denies the first sentence of Paragraph II for lack of knowledge or information sufficient to form a belief as to its truth, and denies that any agreement exists that shares of preferred stock, owned by Woodbury, were to be redeemed by Aleutian Homes, Inc. Any such redemption of such shares of preferred stock (a) would be unlawful and in fraud of creditors until all debts of Aleutian Homes, Inc., including its indebtedness to defendant, are first paid; (b) if made, should be paid in cash to defendant as the pledgee of such shares of preferred stock, and in accordance with the assignment to defendant in the Standby Agreement dated April 27, 1953, executed by Woodbury.

III.

Answering Paragraph III, defendant realleges Paragraphs XVII through XX, inclusive, of its Answer to the first cause of action.

IV.

Defendant denies the allegations of Paragraph IV.

Fifth Cause of Action

I.

Answering Paragraph I, defendant realleges Paragraphs I through XVI, inclusive, of its Answer to the first cause of action.

II.

Answering Paragraph II, defendant denies each and every allegation thereof.

III.

Answering Paragraph III, defendant realleges Paragraphs XVII through XX, inclusive, of its Answer to the first cause of action.

IV.

Defendant denies the allegations of Paragraph IV.

Sixth Cause of Action

I.

Answering Paragraph I, defendant realleges Paragraphs I through XVI, inclusive, of its Answer to the first cause of action.

II.

Defendant denies each and all of the allegations of Paragraph II. Defendant alleges that the present fair market value of said Housing Project is substantially less than the amount now due and owing defendant. Defendant further alleges that the 799 shares of common stock in the name of Woodbury were heretofore pledged, assigned and delivered to defendant as security for the indebtedness of Aleutian Homes, Inc., and the obligations of said Woodbury, and the said Woodbury has no right, title or interest in said shares until the indebtedness and obligations due defendant are paid and discharged in full.

III.

Answering Paragraph III, defendant realleges Paragraphs XVII through XX, inclusive, of its Answer to the first cause of action.

IV.

Defendant denies the allegations of Paragraph IV.

Second Defense

The Complaint fails to state a claim upon which relief can be granted.

Third Defense

The Complaint is not cognizable under the Federal Tort Claims Act, and the Court is therefore without jurisdiction of the subject matter thereof.

Fourth Defense

The claims asserted by Plaintiff are barred by the Statute of Limitations.

Fifth Defense

The alleged Agreement as set forth in the Complaint, by an officer or employee of the United States with Aleutian Homes, Inc., to find, obtain, and cause some third party to discharge the indebtedness of Aleutian Homes, Inc., to the United States, is void and not binding upon the United States and cannot give rise to a cause of action against the United States.

Wherefore, defendant prays that the Complaint herein be dismissed, with costs.

/s/ C. E. LUCKEY,
United States Attorney.

[Endorsed] Filed June 2, 1958.

———

[Title of District Court and Cause.]

PRETRIAL ORDER

On the 15th day of July, 1960, the above-entitled action came on for pretrial before the undersigned judge of the above-entitled court; plaintiff appeared by and through King, Miller, Anderson, Nash & Yerke, Norman J. Wiener, and Paul R. Meyer, of his attorneys, and defendant appeared by C. E. Luckey, United States Attorney for the District of Oregon, of attorneys for the defendant. Thereupon, the following proceedings were had.

Statement of the Case

Plaintiff has commenced this action alleging jurisdiction pursuant to the Federal Tort Claims Act (Title 28, USCA, §§ 1346(b) and 2671 through 2680). Plaintiff filed the complaint on September 30, 1957, alleging Oregon residence and ownership of 799 of 800 shares of stock of a total of 800 issued of Aleutian Homes, Inc.

Plaintiff alleges that after the Secretary of the Navy had expressed interest in securing housing for naval personnel at Kodiak, Alaska, the Federal Housing Administration issued firm commitments for mortgage insurance for a housing project to be owned, constructed and operated by Aleutian Homes, Inc., and that Federal National Mortgage Association issued firm commitments to purchase the Federal Housing Administration insured mortgages in the total amount of $4,700,000. Plaintiff further alleges that in furtherance of a policy to maintain prefabricated house production capacity, and support the needs of naval personnel, the Housing & Home Finance Agency agreed to lend Aleutian Homes, Inc., $4,230,000 constituting 90% of the amount of the FHA and FNMA commitments, as an interim loan, and that HHFA advanced a total of $4,192,717.10 for the construction of the project, and that loan documents for said loan were executed on or about April 27, 1953.

Plaintiff alleges that unforeseen difficulties delayed the construction schedule, and that completion was threatened by lien creditors and claimants and that HHFA formulated and entered into a completion agreement with plaintiff, Aleutian Homes, Inc., creditors and others, by which HHFA undertook to pay existing creditors, cause completion of the project and operate it until permanent financing arrangements were completed. Plaintiff alleges that pursuant to the completion agreement, HHFA assumed complete control of the project from February 26, 1954, until about June 14, 1957, when HHFA allegedly secured an order from the U. S. District Court for Alaska appointing a receiver. Plaintiff further alleges completion of the project, about October 26, 1954, and that HHFA collected and reserved to its own use, rents from the project amounting to $1,114,800.20.

Also, that plaintiff, under the completion agreement, advanced $75,000 as overhead to complete the project, to be repaid from FNMA mortgage purchase.

Plaintiff alleges that HHFA entered into the completion agreement and occupied a fiduciary relationship to the plaintiff, Aleutian Homes, Inc., creditors, and other interested parties thereto, and complains and alleges that in approximately May 1955, HHFA permitted the commitments of FHA and FNMA to lapse, and carelessly and negligently or deliberately and wilfully refused to secure long-range financing, seized the bank account of Aleutian Homes, Inc., and commenced foreclosure proceedings against the project in the name of the United States of America against named parties and others claiming interest in the real estate described in the complaint, being Civil A-13484, Third Judicial District, Anchorage, Alaska.

Plaintiff thereafter complains that he was damaged in the amount of $75,000 and adding an allegation that among the claims to be paid out of the FNMA mortgage purchase was a claim of $150,000 to the Bank of California, NA, which plaintiff was obliged to pay with interest as an accommodation endorser, totaling $164,594.80, for which sum plaintiff asserts a second cause of action.

As a third cause of action, plaintiff alleges that he was compelled to pay a bond premium by reason of a personal guaranty, together with costs incident to the defense of the claim and interest, which plaintiff alleges was also to be paid from the FNMA funds. Plaintiff seeks $35,955.02 on this count, including $2,412.93 legal fees.

As a fourth cause of action, alleging that he was to be paid therefor, from FNMA funds, plaintiff claims $150,000 for preferred stock shares exchanged for initial advances which the plaintiff alleges were to be redeemed by Aleutian Homes, Inc., from FNMA funds by the mortgage purchasers.

A fifth cause of action has been abandoned by plaintiff for unidentified disbursements claimed.

A sixth cause of action contends that Aleutian Homes, Inc., has an equity in the project based upon an asserted fair market value of $5,800,000 against alleged claims payable under the completion agreement in the total amount of $5,370,805.97, and plaintiff claims damage for 799/800ths of the difference, or $428,127.

Defendant filed a motion to dismiss, which the court denied, with leave to renew at pretrial. Defendant renews the motion.

In the motion, defendant moves dismissal on grounds: (1) The complaint fails to state facts to constitute a claim upon which relief can be granted; (2) that the complaint shows on its face that the alleged tortious act occurred in "approximately May 1955," and the records of this court show that the action was not filed until September 30, 1957, and is barred by 28 USC 2401; (3) that the complained of acts would not be actionable because they involve the exercise of a discretionary function under 28 USC 2680(a); (4) that the acts complained of could not subject the defendant to damages, as an interference with contract relations, by reason of 28 USC 2680(h); (5) that as to plaintiff's sixth cause of action, he has alleged no facts giving him standing to sue; (6) that as to plaintiff's sixth cause of action, he has failed to join Aleutian Homes, Inc., an indispensable party.

Defendant has also filed an answer and counterclaim and amended counterclaim.

In its answer, defendant denies that the allegations of the complaint are cognizable under the Federal Tort Claims Act, admits the incorporation of Aleutian Homes, Inc., for the purposes of owning, constructing and operating the project, and alleges that FHA issued commitments to Brice Mortgage Company, an approved FHA mortgagee, to under Section 203 of the National Housing Act, as amended, insure mortgages on the 344 dwellings to be built in the housing project, provided the mortgages conformed with FHA requirements.

Defendant asserted that FNMA issued commitments to Brice Mortgage Company to purchase at par, such FHA-insured mortgages as might be executed on the dwellings in the housing project, provided the insured mortgages conformed with the requirements of FNMA.

Defendant admits that HHFA agreed by an amended loan authorization attached as an exhibit to the answer, to lend Aleutian Homes, Inc., $4,230,900 in accordance therewith, as interim financing, conditioned upon Aleutian Homes, Inc.'s providing permanent financing, and that in accordance with such requirement, Aleutian Homes, Inc., entered into take-out agreements, copies of which are attached as exhibits, by which Brice Mortgage agreed to disburse mortgage loans on FHA-insured dwellings in the project, the proceeds to apply on the HHFA loan until it be paid in full.

Defendant denies plaintiff's allegation that plaintiff executed a loan authorization and alleged that among other documents, Aleutian Homes, Inc., on or about April 27, 1953, executed a note dated April 27, 1953, in the principal amount of $4,230,900, with interest at 5% per annum, payable to defendant and due December 31, 1953, the maturity of which was thereafter extended to October 31, 1955, a deed of trust as security for payment of the note, a building loan agreement, pursuant to which Aleutian Homes, Inc., agreed to construct said project with the proceeds of said loan by October 31, 1953, later extended to September 24, 1954, and the take-out agreement by which Brice Mortgage Company agreed with Aleutian Homes, Inc., in conformity with the loan authorization, to furnish permanent financing for the housing project.

The defendant admits that construction fell behind schedule, but alleges that the difficulties were unknown to defendant and the submission of false and misleading applications for payment were known to the plaintiff and concealed from the defendant and that thereafter liens and claims halted construction. Defendant denies that HHFA formulated and entered a completion agreement following abandonment of construction, and alleges that plaintiff Woodbury and Aleutian Homes, Inc., desired to salvage any possible equity in and pay off the claims relating to the project, and formulated among themselves and presented to the Administrator of HHFA an Agreement, contemplating completion of the Housing Project, the disbursement of the balance of the proceeds of the government loan, and the payment to the extent possible of claims and debts relating to said Housing Project, which Agreement Aleutian Homes, Inc., and Woodbury urged the Administrator to sign and accept. Defendant asserts that the Administrator declined to sign any such Agreement but agreed to offer no objection thereto, and accordingly Aleutian Homes, Inc., Woodbury, and others, entered into and executed a certain Completion Agreement, dated April 24, 1954, of which a copy was attached as an exhibit to the Answer. Defendant asserts that under the Completion Agreement neither the Administrator nor the defendant undertook any obligation to complete the project or obtain permanent financing or to operate the project until permanent financing arrangements were completed—but that the obligation to furnish permanent financing remained incumbent upon Aleutian Homes, Inc.

Defendant admits institution of foreclosure proceedings and that the Court appointed a receiver to take possession of the mortgaged Housing Project and the collateral security of the said Aleutian Homes, Inc., to the United States. Defendant further asserts that the complete direction and management relating to the completion and operation of the Housing Project was vested in a Project Manager appointed by Aleutian Homes, Inc., as its agent in a "Project Management Agreement," dated April 24, 1954, executed by Aleutian Homes, Inc., and approved in writing by plaintiff Woodbury, a copy of which is attached to the Answer.

Defendant denies HHFA collected rents and reserved them to its use. Defendant asserts that the rentals were collected by Aleutian Homes, Inc., and placed to its account in a special account under Depository Agreement, dated May 6, 1954, permitting disbursement for authorized purposes upon countersignature of Administrator or his designee.

Defendant further asserts that to induce the defendant to advance the balance of the proceeds of the loan plaintiff executed an overhead agreement on April 24, 1954, copy being annexed as an exhibit to the Answer, by which it is alleged Woodbury obligated himself to pay $15,000 per month for overhead expenses in the completion of the project, but after five months, defaulted on future due installments.

Defendant specifically denies entering into any fiduciary relationship and denies that the Completion Agreement establishes or purports to establish such relationship.

Defendant alleges that it was the obligation of Aleutian Homes, Inc., to furnish permanent financing to pay the interim loan made by the government, to meet all requirements of FHA and FNMA for commitments, and their remaining in force, including the take-out agreement with Brice Mortgage Company, but that Aleutian Homes, Inc., and Woodbury determined that the costs of maintaining the commitments of FHA and FNMA in force were too high and Aleutian Homes, Inc., and Woodbury made a written request for leave for Aleutian Homes, Inc., to permit the commitments to lapse. A copy of the request was attached as an exhibit to the Answer.

Defendant admits that it caused $122,300 to be withdrawn from the rental deposit account in accordance with the provisions of the Depository Agreement dated May 6, 1954, which expressly authorized the Administrator in event of default to withdraw said funds and apply them on the debt due defendant. Defendant alleges it never assumed the obligation to secure permanent financing but that this was the express obligation of Aleutian Homes, Inc.

Defendant generally denies other allegations of Count I of the Complaint.

Defendant generally urges the same answer to the plaintiff's second and third causes of action.

Defendant generally urges the same answer to the plaintiff's fourth cause of action but in addition alleges that redemption by Aleutian Homes, Inc., of Woodbury's shares of preferred stock would be unlawful and in fraud of creditors until all debts of Aleutian Homes, Inc., including those to defend- ant are first paid, and if redeemed should be paid to defendant in cash as the pledgee of such shares and in accordance with the assignment to the de- fendant in the Standby Agreement dated April 27, 1953, executed by plaintiff Woodbury.

Defendant generally urges as to Count VI of the Complaint the answer to Count I and further alleges that the present fair market value of the housing project is substantially less than the sum due and owing to defendant and that the 799 shares of common stock in the name of Woodbury were pledged and assigned and delivered to defendant as security for the indebtedness of Aleutian Homes, Inc., and the obligation of Woodbury, and Woodbury has no right, title or interest in the shares until the indebtedness due defendant be paid in full.

As additional defenses the defendant alleges:

As a second defense that the Complaint fails to state a claim upon which relief can be granted, as a third defense the Complaint is not cognizable under the Federal Tort Claims Act and that the Court is therefore without jurisdiction of the subject matter of the action, for a fourth defense that the claims of the plaintiff are barred by the statute of limitations, and as a fifth defense that the alleged agreement to find, obtain and cause some third party to discharge the indebtedness of Aleutian Homes, Inc., to the United States is void and not binding on the United States and cannot give rise to a cause of action against the United States.

* * *

In addition to reasserting the defenses pleaded in this pretrial order (pages 3 to 7, inclusive herein), the defendant asserts by contention as additional defenses to the complaint:

1. The defendant's motion to dismiss the Complaint should be allowed.

2. That the United States can be made a fiduciary only by its express consent, and no such consent has been given herein.

3. That the plaintiff, not having sought relief in the foreclosure proceedings of which he complains, the results of which alone can determine the worth of Aleutian Homes, Inc., stock, should be estopped and barred from his asserted causes of action herein, or in the alternative the proceedings under the Complaint in this action should be abated until conclusion of the proceedings in Civil A-13484, Third Judicial District of Alaska.

4. That by reason of paragraphs 13 and 18 of the Completion Agreement, the Borrower's Request dated April 23, 1954, the Standby Agreement executed April 27, 1953, and by other collateral documents and writings executed by plaintiff, he is estopped to assert the action herein.

5. That the statutory authority alleged by plaintiff as a basis for suit against the Administrator of HHFA, not made a party herein, does not waive the immunity of the United States, defendant herein.

6. That the decisions of the Administrator to not advance further funds to extend the FHA and FNMA commitments, and to foreclose were discretionary functions and not actionable under 28 USC 2680(a).

7. That insofar as plaintiff appears to rely on allegations that the Administrator or other officials of the defendant misrepresented circumstances relating to occupancy, long-term finance or other expectations or conditions, such allegations give rise to no cause of action by reason of 28 USC 2680(h).

8. That plaintiff has failed to allege any negligent or wrongful act or omission of defendant proximately causing the damages complained of, the defendant committed no negligent or wrongful act, and no negligent or wrongful act or omission of defendant was the cause of the damages asserted by plaintiff.

The parties, subject to the approval of the Court stipulate and agree that the issues raised by defendant's motion to dismiss, and the controverted issue of alleged fiduciary status of the defendant be segregated from and heard in advance of the other issues raised.

The parties further stipulate and agree that the pleadings insofar as they are enlarged by the contentions of the parties herein shall be deemed amended to conform to this pretrial order.

It is further agreed by the parties that:

(1) Plaintiff makes no contention that the plaintiff executed a Loan Authorization.

(2) Plaintiff makes no contention as to Count I of the Amended Counterclaim that the defendant is not the real party in interest.

(3)   Plaintiff makes no contention that Aleutian Homes, Inc., did not duly execute an Assignment of Claims dated April 23, 1954, a copy of which is attached to the Amended Counterclaim.

Agreed Facts

The following agreed facts shall be considered as evidence for all purposes, subject only to objections as to relevancy.

I.   Government Agencies Involved

A.   Housing and Home Finance Agency and Housing and Home Finance Administrator.

HHFA was created by the Reorganization Plan No. 3 of 1947 (61 Stat. 954, 5 U.S.C.A., Section 133y-16). Under this plan the various functions of the government relating to housing were consolidated within HHFA. At present, HHFA consists of five constituent agencies or units dealing with various aspects of the national housing program:

(1)   Federal Housing Administration (hereinafter referred to as "FHA"), an agency created by the President pursuant to authorization by Congress, which engages in programs of mortgage insurance.

(2)   Federal National Mortgage Association, a statutory corporation (hereinafter referred to as "FNMA"), which provides a secondary market for the purchase and discounting of mortgages.

(3) Urban Renewal Administration, an agency concerned with programs of urban renewal and slum clearance.

(4) Public Housing Administration, an agency which deals with programs relating to federally financed housing.

(5) Community Facilities Administration (hereinafter referred to as "CFA"), an agency which engages in a variety of programs relating to housing and community facilities not covered by the other four constituent agencies. CFA was formerly called the Community Facilities and Special Operations branch (CF&SO), but the change in its name did not affect its functions or authority. Among the programs administered by CFA were those related to Alaska housing and prefabricated housing.

The agencies related to Urban Renewal and Public Housing had no connection with the Aleutian Homes project.

The Housing and Home Finance Administrator (hereinafter referred to as "Administrator") is the head of HHFA and is responsible for the general supervision and coordination of the statutory functions of the constituent agencies of HHFA.

1. Prefabricated Housing Program

The original interest of the government in prefabricated housing was contained in the Veterans Emergency Housing Act of 1946, 60 Stat. 207, Chapter 268, Section 12(a). The government functions relating to this program of prefabricated housing were, at that time, vested in the Reconstruction Finance Corporation, a corporation (hereinafter referred to as "RFC"). The powers of RFC which were applicable to its functions in the field of prefabricated housing were set out in 15 U.S.C.A., Section 603. The powers and functions of RFC which related to prefabricated housing were transferred to HHFA by Reorganization Plan No. 23 of 1950 (64 Stat. 1279; 5 U.S.C.A., Section 133z-15), as limited by statute. By Title 12 U.S.C. Section 1723(d) the functions of HHFA under Section 2 of Reorganization Plan No. 22 of 1950 were transferred to FNMA August 2, 1954.

Provisions for the making of loans for prefabricated housing were added as Section 102a of the Housing Act of 1948 (62 Stat. 1268) by the Critical Defense Housing Areas Act of 1951 (65 Stat. 293; 12 U.S.C.A., Section 1701g-1).

The powers given the Housing and Home Finance Administrator with respect to prefabricated housing, set forth in 12 U.S.C.A., Section 1701g-2, include the following:

(A) All the powers and functions transferred to him by Reorganization Plan No. 23 of 1950.

(B) The powers, functions and duties set forth in 12 U.S.C.A., Section 1749a, except subsection (c)(2) thereof.

(C) The power to "take any and all actions determined by him to be necessary or desirable in making, servicing, compromising, modifying, liquidating, or otherwise dealing with or realizing on loans thereunder. Such powers, functions, and duties may be exercised in the several States, the District of Columbia, and the Territories and possessions of the United States.''

Included in the powers of the Administrator, set forth in Section 1749(c) to which reference is made in Section 1701g-2(B) as being applicable to the prefabricated housing program, are the following:

''(3)   sue and be sued;

''(4)   foreclose on any property or commence any action to protect or enforce any right conferred upon him by any law, contract, or other agreement, and bid for and purchase at any foreclosure or any other sale any property in connection with which he has made a loan pursuant to this subchapter. In the event of any such acquisition, the Administrator may, notwithstanding any other provision of law relating to the acquisition, handling, or disposal of real property by the United States, complete, administer, remodel and convert, dispose of, lease and otherwise deal with, such property: Provided, That any such acquisition of real property shall not deprive any State or political subdivision thereof of its civil or criminal jurisdiction in and over such property or impair the civil rights under the State or local laws of the inhabitants on such property;

''(5)   enter into agreements to pay annual sums in lieu of taxes to any State or local taxing authority with respect to any real property so acquired or owned;

"(6) sell or exchange at public or private sale, or lease, real or personal property, and sell or exchange any securities or obligations upon such terms as he may fix;

"(7) obtain insurance against loss in connection with property and other assets held;

"(8) subject to the specific limitations in this subchapter, consent to the modification, with respect to rate of interest, time of payment of any installment of principal or interest, security, or any other term of any contract or agreement to which he is a party or which has been transferred to him pursuant to this subchapter; and;

"(9) include in any contract or instrument made pursuant to this subchapter such other covenants, conditions, or provisions as he may deem necessary to assure that the purposes of this subchapter will be achieved."

2. Independent Offices Appropriation Act of 1955

The Independent Offices Appropriation Act of 1955 passed on June 24, 1954, as Ch. 359, 68 Stat. 272 (83rd Cong. 2 Sess., Public Law 428) established as of June 30, 1954, a revolving fund with which the Administrator could account for all assets and liabilities in connection with various programs, including

"* * * functions transferred under Reorganization Plan No. 23 of 1950 (5 U.S.C. 133z-15, note), or authorized under Sections 102, 102a, 102b, and 102c of the Housing Act of 1948, as amended (12 U.S.C. 1701g-1701g-3 [Prefabricated Housing Program]); * * * notes or other obligations purchased pursuant to the Alaska Housing Act, as amended (48 U.S.C. 484(a)); * * *"

It was further provided

"That said fund shall be available for all necessary expenses (including administrative expenses) in connection with the liquidation of the programs carried out pursuant to the foregoing provisions of law, including operation, maintenance, improvement, or disposition of facilities, and for disbursements pursuant to outstanding commitments against moneys herein authorized to be credited to said fund, repayment of obligations to the Treasury, and refinancing and refunding operations on existing loans * * *"

After non-payment of its note, the Aleutian Homes, Inc., project was included in the liquidating program administered by HHFA under the revolving fund established by this Act.

B. Federal Housing Administration.

FHA was established in 1934 with powers as codified in 12 U.S.C.A., Section 1702. It was transferred as a constituent agency to HHFA by Reorganization Plan No. 3 of 1947 (61 Stat. 954, 5 U.S.C.A., Section 133y-16). The powers to insure conventional mortgages on individual houses are contained in Title II, Section 203, of the National Housing Act of 1934 (48 Stat. 1248, Chapter 847, 12 U.S.C.A. 1709). That section was amended by the Housing Act of 1954 (68 Stat. 591) to change the value ratio of loans which FHA is authorized to insure thereunder.

Under the provisions of the Alaska Housing Act, FHA was given authority to insure mortgages in Alaska in a dollar amount up to 50 per cent higher than its authority with respect to mortgages on property located in the United States. Further it gave FHA authority to insure mortgages in Alaska without the requirement, applicable to housing in the states, that the commissioner find the project to be economically sound or an acceptable risk (63 Stat. 57, 65 Stat. 315, 12 U.S.C.A., Section 1715d).

C.   Federal National Mortgage Association

The creation of FNMA and the establishment of its powers is set out in 12 U.S.C.A., Sections 1716 through 1723d.

FNMA was transferred from the jurisdiction of RFC to HHFA to be "administered subject to the direction and control" of HHFA by Reorganization Plan No. 22 of 1950 (64 Stat. 1277, 5 U.S.C.A., Section 133z-15, as limited by statute. By Title 12 U.S.C. Section 1723(d) and functions of HHFA under Section 2 of Reorganization Plan No. 22 of 1950 were transferred to FNMA August 2, 1954.

V. Development of Project

A. Original Interest

Commencing in 1949, the possibility of securing additional housing for naval and civilian personnel connected with the Kodiak Naval Base in Alaska was discussed among Navy officials, officials of the Alaska Housing Authority, officials of the City of Kodiak and officials of FHA. The possibility of securing housing under the Wherry Act (Title VIII of the National Housing Act, as amended) was considered and rejection and studies were then made with respect to the possibility of construction of an off-base project of some 350 to 400 houses using conventional FHA assistance under Title II, Section 203, of the National Housing Act, as amended.

During 1950-1951, arrangements were made to secure, as a site for this project, certain land belonging to the federal government under the control of the Bureau of Land Management of the Department of Interior. Arrangements were made to transfer this land to the Alaska Housing Authority for reconveyance to the City of Kodiak for use for a project to be built by a sponsor selected by the City of Kodiak. Subsequently, in accordance with law, the Alaska Housing Authority conveyed the land directly to the approved sponsor. It was determined that the City of Kodiak would provide streets, the city and Department of Interior through Alaska Public Works would provide water and sewer facilities and schools and the local REA would provide power. During 1951, the City of Kodiak received a commitment from the Alaska Public Works program for money to construct the sewer and water facilities in connection with the proposed project.

During 1950 and 1951 considerable surveying of the site and engineering was carried on on behalf of the City of Kodiak and a Raymond Lewis of Los Angeles who was a proposed sponsor for the project. In late 1951, Mr. Lewis abandoned interest in sponsorship of the proposed project.

During 1951, plaintiff became interested in the promotion of a house panel invented by an architect, S. C. Horsley. In late 1951, plaintiff financed a trip by Horsley, R. A. Blanchard and G. K. Gosling to Alaska to investigate the possibility of selling the Horsley panel for use in houses in Alaska. In the course of this promotion, Lee C. Bettinger, the Mayor of Kodiak, was contacted by Gosling and commenced to interest plaintiff to become sponsor of the proposed project in the place of Raymond Lewis.

B.   Formation of Aleutian Homes, Inc.

In February 1952, Aleutian Homes, Inc., was incorporated under the laws of the State of Oregon and in February or March 1952, the City of Kodiak approved Aleutian Homes, Inc., as the sponsor of the proposed housing project. Thereafter, the Alaska Housing Authority conveyed the land selected for the site to Aleutian Homes, Inc.

C.   Financi

(a)   Indi

The prop under the p National Ho gram, a priv ual long-ter the project. Brice Mortg the permane

(b)   Insu

In order t sell the mor each of the l for Brice M ment from H

In accord spect to the diak, Alaska respect to R respect to A (1) the crit family units sonnel at th nency of th ability of s pay rentals $130 and $1

C. Financing of Project

1. Long-term Financing

(a) Individual Mortgages by Private Company

The proposed project was intended to be financed under the provisions of Title II, Section 203, of the National Housing Act, as amended. Under this program, a private mortgage agency takes out individual long-term mortgages on each house included in the project. With respect to the Kodiak project, Brice Mortgage Company was selected to act as the permanent mortgagee.

(b) Insurance of Private Mortgage by FHA.

In order to enable Brice Mortgage Company to sell the mortgages which it intended to obtain on each of the houses in the project, it was necessary for Brice Mortgage Company to obtain a commitment from FHA to insure said mortgages.

In accordance with FHA requirements with respect to the insurance of a project located in Kodiak, Alaska, the Secretary of Navy in 1951, with respect to Raymond Lewis and again in 1952 with respect to Aleutian Homes, Inc., certified to FHA (1) the critical urgent need of the Navy for 385 family units for use by military and civilian personnel at the Kodiak Naval Base, (2) the permanency of the Kodiak Naval Base, and (3) the ability of such military and civilian personnel to pay rentals for such units in the amount of $100, $130 and $150 for small two, large two and three bedroom units, including garage and kitchen equipment.

In 1952, FHA appraised the value of a 344 unit project at $5,904,250 and in April 1952, issued for a stated period its conditional commitment to Brice Mortgage Company to insure long-range individual mortgages on each home in a total amount of $4,706,400, which amount was based on 80 per cent of the FHA appraised value.

(c) Purchase of FHA Insured Mortgages by FNMA.

Also in 1952, FNMA issued its commitment to Brice Mortgage Company to purchase at par the individual long-range mortgages as they were obtained by Brice Mortgage Company and insured by FHA.

The $4,706,400 to be received from the long-term financing was to be used by Aleutian Homes, Inc., for

(1) repayment of the construction loan from HHFA $4,230,900; (2) payment of costs of taking out the permanent individual mortgages; and (3) any balance remaining as capital.

2. Short-term Interim Loan for Construction

Purposes from HHFA

During 1952, Aleutian Homes, Inc., and Brice Mortgage Company found it impossible to secure from private sources the financing required for the construction of the project prior to the obtaining of the long-range financing as set forth above, and sought assistance from HHFA.

During 1952, negotiations were had between Brice Mortgage Company, acting on behalf of Aleutian Homes, Inc., and the Community Facilities and Special Operations Branch of HHFA for the purpose of securing an interim loan for construction purposes. A final application was made by Aleutian Homes, Inc., late in 1952 and approved in January, 1953. This interim construction loan by HHFA was in the sum of $4,230,900, which constituted 90 per cent of the amount of the FHA and FNMA commitments with respect to the permanent long-range financing, the application indicating the difference between the projected costs and the loan amount applied for would be provided for by the Sponsor, Aleutian Homes, Inc.

The loan was authorized by a Loan Authorzation signed by the Administrator, and carried into effect by documents required by a Building Loan Agreement, including a guaranty of the Loan Agreement and the guaranty of the construction contract by R. B. Woodbury, and a promissory note and deed of trust. Procedures for disbursement under the loan were provided for in a Loan and Disbursement Agreement executed by R. B. Woodbury as President, Aleutian Homes, Inc., April 27, 1953. The construction contracts and stock of Aleutian Homes, Inc., were assigned to the Administrator. A Standby Agreement was executed by R. B. Woodbury, President, Aleutian Homes, Inc., and R. B. Woodbury, individually. Performance bonds run to Aleutian Homes, Inc., and the Administrator.

D. Contractual Arrangements for Construction of Project.

Contractual arrangements for the construction of the project under the interim loan from HHFA were signed in Seattle, Washington, on April 27, 1953. In general they provided as follows: Aleutian Homes, Inc., as the owner entered into a "general contract" with Kodiak Construction Co., for the construction of the housing project for the payment of the sum of $4,230,900 (the total maximum amount of the HHFA loan). Kodiak Construction Co., as general contractor in turn contracted with three subcontractors, plus a freight company, the total payment under which subcontracts, plus freight, similarly equaled the sum of $4,230,900 (the maximum total amount of the HHFA loan). These subcontracts were as follows:

1. A "supply contract" entered into with Alex B. Carlton, doing business as Carlton Lumber Company, for the purchase of the prefabricated housing packages.

2. A "site construction contract" entered into with Pacific Alaska Contractors, Inc., for preparation of the site.

3. A "construction contract" entered into with Leo S. Wynans Co., Inc., for the erection of the prefabricated houses on the prepared sites.

4. A cont portation of materials f Alaska.

VI. Const:

During th arose in the versy develop speaking th Pacific Alask controversy further work Construction proceeded to under the sit

In Octo cult ies arose the project. Alaska Cont against the Thereupon, the project

VII. Fo

When con fall of 195 considered of the proj on Ray B.

4. A contract with Coastwise Line for the transportation of prefabricated house packages and other materials from Portland, Oregon, to Kodiak, Alaska.

VI. Construction of Project to November, 1953

During the summer of 1953, certain difficulties arose in the preparation of the site and a controversy developed between Kodiak Construction Co., speaking through Leo S. Wynans, its agent, and Pacific Alaska Contractors, Inc. At the time of this controversy Pacific Alaska Contractors, Inc., ceased further work on the site preparation and Kodiak Construction Co., under the direction of Wynans proceeded to furnish labor and materials required under the site construction contract.

In October and November, 1953, financial difficulties arose in connection with the construction of the project, and, on November 6, 1953, Pacific Alaska Contractors, Inc., filed a claim of lien against the project for the sum of $150,504.43. Thereupon, construction came to a standstill with the project approximately 75 per cent completed.

VII. Formation and Adoption of Completion

Agreement

When construction came to a standstill in the late fall of 1953, several possibilities of action were considered. These included foreclosure, completion of the project by the surety companies, demand on Ray B. Woodbury for performance, introduction of additional money in the project in conjunction with Aleutian Homes, Inc., or in substitution of Aleutian Homes, Inc., sponsorship, or completion of the project based upon a completion agreement.

In November, 1953, demand was made on Ray B. Woodbury under his guarantee. Woodbury failed to comply with the demand.

In January, 1954, a completion agreement was formulated in substantially the form in which it became effective on April 23, 1954. The period from the end of January through April 23, 1954, was devoted to securing the necessary consent to placing the completion agreement in operation.

In general, the completion agreement provided for the completion of the construction of the project and the payment order of claimants, creditors and completion costs in four Stages. To carry out this program, Aleutian Homes, Inc., Kodiak Construction Co., and Leo S. Wynans Co., Inc., agreed to vest in a Project Manager exclusive authority to take any and all action in connection with the project that they would be authorized to take, subject to rights of HHFA defined therein.

VIII. Completion of Project

Under the completion agreement the project manager (Harry M. Langton) was appointed with certain prescribed duties and responsibilities and authority with respect to completion of the construction and payment of the claims against the project. Similarly a construction superintendent (Scott J. Cross) was selected to take charge of the physical completion of the project. Under this arrangement, the construction of 343 houses was completed on October 26, 1954. The 344th house was not erected because the lot provided therefor was found unsuitable for building.

By April 12, 1955, 341 out of the 343 houses constructed had passed FHA final inspection. The remaining two at that time were unacceptable for reasons relating to their foundations. Under the completion agreement, all claims listed in Stages 1 and 2 were paid, while only some of the claims in Stages 3 and 4 were paid.

IX. Abandonment of Existing Long-Term Financing Commitments

The permanent individual mortgages were not taken out on any of said 341 houses and during June, 1955, the FHA commitments to insure such mortgages and the FNMA commitments to purchase such mortgages at par expired.

X. Occupancy of Project

The occupancy of the Kodiak project in terms of number of houses rented and percentage of number of houses rented to the number of houses available for each of the months commencing in 1954 is as follows:

Date	Number of Houses Available	Number of Houses Rented
July, 1954	35	32
August, 1954	203	91
September, 1954	235	125
October, 1954	343	142
[From this date on]		
November, 1954		151
December, 1954		161
January, 1955		168
February, 1955		182
March, 1955		191
April, 1955		209
May, 1955		219
June, 1955		233
July, 1955		247
August, 1955		256
September, 1955		267
October, 1955		281
November, 1955		288
December, 1955		294
January, 1956		288
February, 1956		291
March, 1956		285
April, 1956		205
May, 1956		294
June, 1956		285
July, 1956		286
August, 1956		288
September, 1956		307
October, 1956		318
November, 1956		322
December, 1956		318
January, 1957		315
February, 1957		313
March, 1957		317
April, 1957		306
May, 1957		295
June 20, 1957		289
July, 1957	342	290

Date	Number of Houses Available	Number of Houses Rented	Percentage of Occupancy
August, 1957		296	87
September, 1957		299	88
October, 1957		287	85
November, 1957		279	82
December, 1957		278	82
January, 1958		283	83
February, 1958		284	83
March, 1958		285	84
April, 1958		287	84
May, 1958		275	81
June, 1958		275	81
July, 1958	339	263	77
August, 1958	339	257	75
January, 1959	339	238	70
February, 1959		238	70
March, 1959		227	66
April, 1959		224	66
May, 1959		217	64
June, 1959		216	63
July, 1959		215	63
August, 1959		204	60

The Navy determined that the cost in renting and the cost of utilities to occupants of Aleutian Homes, Inc., was more than the personnel and civilian employees could pay, and increased the rental allowance to military personnel living in the Aleutian Homes project in the amount of $37.50 a month for enlisted men and $36.00 a month for officers. This occurred ....

During the summer of 1957, the Navy indicated service personnel was to be reduced by 10 per cent and civilian personnel by approximately 33⅓ per cent.

XI. Payments Made and Received by Government
Agencies With Respect to Project

A. HHFA made advances to or for the benefit
of Aleutian Homes, Inc., for project construction
costs in the total amount of $4,192,717.10 as follows:

1. Prior to the completion agreement (from
June 25, to November 24, 1953), $3,330,062.68 (out
of the total authorized loan of $4,230,900).

2. Subsequent to the completion agreement,
$862,654.42 to the Aleutian Homes on requisition
of the Project Manager.

The difference between this total amount advanced by HHFA ($4,192,717.10) and the total loan
authorized ($4,230,900) of $37,282.90 was withheld
by reason of the one house not built and the two
houses which by April, 1955, had not passed final
FHA inspection.

In March, 1955, HHFA authorized advances in
an amount not to exceed $160,000 (in addition to
the original loan of $4,230,900) to be made to Aleu-
tian Homes, Inc., to be spent for the care and preservation of its security. HHFA advanced to Aleutian Homes, Inc., on March 15, 1955, $56,239.19,
which amount was repaid to HHFA on May 5, 1956,
together with $3,966.01, representing 7 per cent in-
terest on said sum from March 15, 1955, to May 5,
1956.

3. Interest under the note has been accruing at

the rate of
interest clai
was $211,10
interest clai
was $384,756

B. HHF.
half of Aleu
of $909,675.5

1. Prior
to October 3

2. After
project mana

3. Immed
withdrew fr
Aleutian H
tional $122,3

4. From

C. FHA
insure, and
$22,360.

D. FNM
purchase, a
422.77.

XII. R

From Ju
Aleutian H

the rate of 5 per cent. As of June 30, 1957, accrued interest claimed by HHFA to be due and unpaid was $211,105.65. As of December 31, 1959, accrued interest claimed by HHFA to be due and unpaid was $384,756.43 together with the principal balance.

B. HHFA received payments made by or on behalf of Aleutian Homes, Inc., in the total amount of $909,675.58 as follows:

1. Prior to the completion agreement (June 25, to October 31, 1953) $35,134.14.

2. After the completion agreement, from the project manager $402,241.44.

3. Immediately prior to foreclosure HHFA withdrew from bank accounts maintained by the Aleutian Homes, Inc., Project Manager an additional $122,300.

4. From the court appointed receiver $350,000.

C. FHA received fees for its commitments to insure, and extension thereof, the total sum of $22,360.

D. FNMA received fees for its commitments to purchase, and extension thereof, the sum of $106,-422.77.

XII. Rentals Received by Project Manager
Prior to Foreclosure

From July 1, 1954, through June 14, 1957, the Aleutian Homes, Inc., project manager received rentals from the project in the total amount of $1,-114,800.20, and disbursed said funds as indicated in the records he maintained of the project. Most of said funds were disbursed.

XIII. Payments Made by Plaintiff Ray B. Wood-
    bury Subsequent to the Formulation of the
    Completion Agreement.

During 1954, 1955 and 1956, plaintiff paid to The Bank of California, N. A., the following sums of money on the following dates in payment of the claim of The Bank of California, N. A., as set forth in the completion agreement:

Date of Payment	Amount Paid	Credited to
Feb. 18, 1954	$ 1,083.33	Interest
June 2, 1954	1,875.00	Interest
Aug. 20, 1954	1,875.00	Interest
Dec. 6, 1954	1,895.83	Interest
May 18, 1955	3,750.00	Interest
May 18, 1955	41,455.00	Principal
May 18, 1955	14,526.43	Principal
June 13, 1955	2,352.75	Principal
July 11, 1955	2,352.75	Principal
Aug. 12, 1955	890.56	Interest
Sept. 13, 1955	285.31	Interest
Sept. 13, 1955	2,063.69	Principal
Sept. 28, 1955	658.25	Principal
Oct. 10, 1955	653.27	Interest
Oct. 10, 1955	25,591.13	Principal
June 11, 1956	787.92	Interest
July 6, 1956	1,499.58	Interest
July 6, 1956	61,000.00	Principal

During 1954, plaintiff paid Brice Mortgage Company $35,000 in settlement of all claims of Brice Mortgage Company and Brice Realty Company against the project for alleged work done and services performed prior to the execution of the completion agreement.

During 1954, plaintiff paid $75,000 to the Administrator for use under a requirement to pay overhead under the overhead agreement and completion agreement that Ray B. Woodbury pay overhead therein described. Defendant made demands for additional overhead payments which Ray B. Woodbury did not make.

September 18, 1956, plaintiff satisfied the judgment obtained by General Casualty Company on July 24, 1956, for the unpaid premium on the bond issued on behalf of Kodiak Construction Co., together with expenses relating thereto by the payment to General Casualty Company of the sum of $33,542.09. In the defense of said action R. B. Woodbury incurred legal fees and other expenses in the sum of $2,412.93.

XIV. Foreclosure Suit

HHFA on or about June 11, 1957, in the United States District Court for the District of Alaska, Third Judicial Division, Anchorage, commenced foreclosure proceedings in the name of the United States of America against Aleutian Homes, Inc., a corporation; Pacific Alaska Contractors, Inc., a corporation; Alex B. Carlton, doing business as Carlton Lumber Company; City of Kodiak, a municipal corporation of the Territory of Alaska;

James C. Dougherty, Trustee under the Will of Hugh Dougherty; Lee Bettinger; Jack Hinckel; M. Justin Herman and David Oliver, as Trustees; Lindley R. Durkee and Melvin Frazier, as Trustees; and "Also all other persons or parties unknown claiming any right, title, estate, lien or interest in the real estate described in the complaint herein," defendants, Civil No. A-13,484.

On June 14, 1957, upon the motion of plaintiff, the court appointed M. G. Gebhart receiver of the mortgaged property until further order of the court.

On or about June 20, 1958, the court authorized the payment by the receiver to HHFA of $200,000 out of proceeds from operation of the project, and said $200,000 was paid to HHFA.

On or about September 12, 1958, plaintiff amended its complaint by adding as defendants the Territory of Alaska, Kodiak Construction Co., a corporation, Leo S. Wynans Co., Inc., a corporation, and United States of America.

On or about April 10, 1959, pursuant to request of receiver, the court authorized the payment by the receiver to HHFA of $150,000 out of proceeds from operation of the project and said $150,000 was paid to HHFA.

Plaintiff's Contentions

With respect to plaintiff's complaint

1. Plaintiff denies defendant's contentions.

2. HHFA participated in the formulation of the completion agreement dated 4/23/54 and accepted the same, under the terms of which plaintiff (a) agreed to become a standby creditor as to his then existing claims, (b) agreed to advance further substantial sums of money, and (c) agreed to relinquish any further control and direction of the project.

3. The construction and operation of the project subsequent to April 24, 1954, was under the control of HHFA, and plaintiff did in fact advance substantial funds to the project.

4. In entering into the completion agreement and in assuming control over the construction and operation of the project, HHFA and the Administrator entered into and occupied a fiduciary relationship with respect to plaintiff, Aleutian Homes, Inc., creditors and other interested parties to the completion agreement.

5. HHFA, its agents and employees, carelessly and negligently or deliberately and wilfully breached said fiduciary relationship by refusing to adopt a permanent long-range program of amortizing the Kodiak project in a manner which considered the claims of all the parties interested in the

completion agreement and instead by proceeding to satisfy and prefer its own interest as a creditor from the assets of the project to the exclusion of the interests of said other persons.

6. By reasons of said breach of fiduciary obligation, plaintiff has suffered damages in the amount of $75,000 as set forth in his first cause of action.

7. By reason of said breach of fiduciary obligation, plaintiff has suffered damages in the amount of $164,594.80 as set forth in his second cause of action.

8. By reason of said breach of fiduciary obligation, plaintiff has suffered damages in the amount of $35,955.02 as set forth in his third cause of action.

9. By reason of said breach of fiduciary obligation, plaintiff has suffered damages in the amount of $150,000 as set forth in his forth cause of action.

10. By reason of said breach of fiduciary obligation, plaintiff has suffered damages in the amount of $428,127 as set forth in this sixth cause of action.

* * *

Defendant's Contentions

I.

Defendant denies Plaintiff's Contentions.

II.

Defendant further contends:

A. That Defendant's Motion to Dismiss Plaintiff's Complaint should be granted.

B. That the complaint does not state facts to constitute a claim upon which relief can be granted.

C. That the complaint is barred by the statute of limitations, 28 U.S.C. §2401.

D. That the acts complained of in plaintiff's complaint arose in the exercise of discretionary functions and the Court has no jurisdiction thereof by reason of 28 U.S.C. §2680(a).

E. That the acts complained of may not subject defendant to damages as an interference with contract relations by reason of 28 U.S.C. §2680(h).

F. That plaintiff has failed to allege facts in his complaint giving him standing to sue.

G. That plaintiff has failed to join Aleutian Homes, Inc., an indispensable party to the action.

H. That the allegations of the complaint are not cognizable under the Federal Tort Claims Act, and the Court is therefore without jurisdiction of the subject matter of plaintiff's complaint.

I. That redemption of stock as demanded by Plaintiff's Fourth Cause of Action would be unlawful and in fraud of creditors until all debts of Aleutian Homes, Inc., including those to defendant are first paid, and if redeemed, the redemption proceeds should be paid to defendant in cash as pledgee of such shares and in accordance with the Standby Agreement dated April 27, 1953, executed by plaintiff.

J. That the present fair market value of the housing project is substantially less than the sum due and owing to defendant, and that the 799 shares of common stock in the name of Woodbury were and are pledged, assigned and delivered to defendant as security for the indebtedness of Aleutian Homes, Inc., and the obligation of Woodbury, and plaintiff has no right, title or monetary interest in the shares until the indebtedness due defendant be paid in full.

K. That the alleged agreement as set forth in the complaint, by an officer or employee of the United States with Aleutian Homes, Inc., to find, obtain and cause some third party to discharge the indebtedness of Aleutian Homes, Inc., to the United States is void and not binding upon the United States and cannot give rise to an action against the United States.

L. That the United States can be made a fiduciary only by its express consent, and no such consent has been given herein.

M. That the plaintiff, not having sought relief in the foreclosure proceedings of which he complains, the results of which alone can determine the worth of Aleutian Homes, Inc., stock, should be estopped and barred from his asserted causes of action herein, or in the alternative the proceedings under the complaint in this action should be abated until conclusion of the proceedings in Civil A-13484, Third Judicial District of Alaska.

N.   That by reason of paragraph 13 and 18 of the Completion Agreement, the Borrower's Request dated April 23, 1954, the Standby Agreement executed April 27, 1953, and by other collateral documents and writings executed by plaintiff, he is estopped to assert the action herein.

O.   That the statutory authority alleged by plaintiff as a basis for suit against the Administrator of HHFA, not made a party herein, does not waive the immunity of the United States, defendant herein.

P.   That insofar as plaintiff appears to rely on allegations that the Administrator or other officials of the defendant misrepresented circumstances relating to occupancy, long-term finance or other expectations or conditions, such allegations give rise to no cause of action by reason of 28 U.S.C. §2680(h).

Q.   That the rights and obligations of the plaintiff were defined by the loan document, and plaintiff is bound thereby.

R.   That plaintiff has failed to allege any negligent or wrongful act or omission of defendant proximate cause of the damages complained of, the defendant committed no negligent or wrongful act, and no negligent or wrongful act or omission of defendant was the cause of the damages asserted by plaintiff.

S.   That plaintiff should take nothing by reason of his complaint, and defendant should have costs and disbursements herein.

Issues

With respect to plaintiff's Complaint

1.   To what extent, if any, did HHFA enter into or accept the Completion Agreement?

2.   To what extent, if any, did HHFA assume control over the construction and operation of the project subsequent to April 24, 1954?

3.   Under the facts and law, did HHFA and the Administrator enter into and occupy a fiduciary relationship with respect to plaintiff, Aleutian Homes, Inc., creditors and other interested parties to the Completion Agreement?

4.   Did HHFA, its agents and employees, carelessly and negligently or deliberately and willfully breach said fiduciary relationship, if any?

5.   As a proximate result of said breach of fiduciary obligation, if any, did plaintiff suffer damages in the amount of $75,000 or any other amount as set forth in his first cause of action?

6.   As a proximate result of said breach of fiduciary obligation, if any, did plaintiff suffer dam-

ages in the amount of $164,594.80 or any other amount as set forth in his second cause of action?

7. As a proximate result of said breach of fiduciary obligation, if any, did plaintiff suffer damages in the amount of $35,955.02 or any other amount as set forth in his third cause of action?

8. As a proximate result of said breach of fiduciary obligation, if any, did plaintiff suffer damages in the amount of $150,000 or any other amount as set forth in this fourth cause of action?

9. As a proximate result of said breach of fiduciary obligation, if any, did plaintiff suffer damages in the amount of $428,127 or any other amount as set forth in his sixth cause of action?

With respect to defendant's defenses to plaintiff's Complaint

1. Should the defendant's Motion to Dismiss the complaint be allowed or denied?

2. Does the Complaint state a claim upon which relief can be granted (defendant's second defense to plaintiff's complaint)?

3. Does the Court have jurisdiction of the subject matter of the Complaint under the Federal Tort Claims Act (defendant's third defense to plaintiff's Complaint)?

4. Are the claims asserted by plaintiff barred by the statute of limitations (defendant's fourth defense to plaintiff's Complaint)?

5. Under the facts and law, is plaintiff estopped or barred from asserting the complaint herein because of failure to seek relief in the foreclosure action in Alaska?

6. Is plaintiff estopped to seek relief because of the documents and writings executed by him in evidence in this case?

7. Were the alleged acts complained of by the plaintiff relating to surrender of commitments and foreclosure discretionary functions within 28 USC §2680(a)?

8. Were the alleged acts complained of excepted from the consent given in the Federal Tort Claims Act by reason of 28 USC §2680(h)?

9. Could the defendant or the HHFA as an agent of the defendant enter into a fiduciary relationship absent its express consent?

10. Did the defendant or HHFA as an agency of the defendant enter into a fiduciary relationship to the plaintiff?

11. If defendant or HHFA as an agency of the defendant entered into a fiduciary relationship to plaintiff, did defendant or HHFA as an agency of the defendant breach such relationship?

12. If defendant or HHFA as an agency of the defendant breached a fiduciary relationship to plaintiff, was such breach, if any, the proximate cause of any damage to plaintiff?

13. Was the fair market value of the project at the time of a breach, if any, more or less than the sum of outstanding on the promissory note?

14. Is Aleutian Homes, Inc., an indispensable party to the action not joined?

Conclusion

The parties hereto agree to the foregoing Pretrial Order, and the Court being fully advised in the premises,

Now Orders that this case shall proceed before the Court without a jury, and

Orders That the defendant's Motion to Dismiss shall be segregated and first heard and that if the Complaint be not dismissed on the basis of said Motion, the Court shall proceed to try as a segregated issue the question of whether or not the United States or HHFA as an agency thereof became a fiduciary as to the plaintiff, and upon determination of said issues any remaining questions shall be tried; and it is further

Ordered that the foregoing pretrial order shall not be amended except by consent of the parties or to prevent manifest injustice; and it is further

Ordered that upon trial of this cause no proof shall be required as to matters of fact hereinabove found to be admitted, but that proof upon the issues between the plaintiff and defendant as hereinabove

stated shall be heard except insofar as said issues
may be determined by the aforesaid agreed facts.

Dated at Portland, Oregon, this 15th day of July,
1960.

/s/ JOHN F. KILKENNY,
District Judge.

Approved:

KING, MILLER, ANDERSON, NASH &
YERKE,

/s/ NORMAN J. WIRNER,
Of Attorneys for Plaintiff.

/s/ C. E. LUCKEY,
United States Attorney, District of Oregon, Of
Attorneys for Defendant.

[Endorsed]: Filed July 15, 1960.

———

[Title of District Court and Cause.]

ORDER

This matter coming on now to be heard upon
the defendant's motion to dismiss, or in the alternative, for a summary judgment under the provisions
of Rule 12(b)(6) and Rule 56, FRCP, and the
Court having considered such motion and the briefs
submitted by counsel, and being now advised in
the premises,

It Is Ordered that a decision on such motion be
and the same is hereby reserved.

It Is Further Ordered that the issue created by the pretrial order on whether defendant was or could be a fiduciary be and the same is hereby segregated from the other issues and that a trial be held on such issue on Monday, December 12, 1960, at 9:30 a.m.

Dated this 4th day of November, 1960.

/s/ JOHN F. KILKENNY,
District Judge.

Affidavit of Service by Mail attached.

[Endorsed]: Filed November 4, 1960.

[Title of District Court and Cause.]

OPINION

Kilkenny, J:

Plaintiff claims the right to recover $853,676.82 from defendant under the Federal Tort Claims Act (Title 28, U.S.C.A. §§1346(b) and 2671 through 2680). The claim grows out of the plaintiff's interest in a housing development at Kodiak, Alaska, which development involved the plaintiff and several governmental agencies. In order to fully understand the issues, it is necessary to have a clear picture of the agencies involved.

Housing and Home Finance Agency and Housing and Home Finance Administrator (hereinafter called HHFA) was created by the Reorganization

Plan No. 3 of 1947 (61 Stat. 954, 5 U.S.C.A. §133y-16). Under this plan the various functions of the government relating to housing were consolidated within HHFA. At present, HHFA consists of five constituent agencies or units dealing with various aspects of the national housing program:

(1) Federal Housing Administration (hereinafter referred to as "FHA"), an agency created by the President pursuant to authorization by Congress, which engages in programs of mortgage insurance.

(2) Federal National Mortgage Association, a statutory corporation (hereinafter referred to as "FNMA"), which provides a secondary market for the purchase and discounting of mortgages.

(3) Urban Renewal Administration, an agency concerned with programs of urban renewal and slum clearance.

(4) Public Housing Administration, an agency which deals with programs relating to federally financed housing.

(5) Community Facilities Administration (hereinafter referred to as "CFA"), an agency which engages in a variety of programs relating to housing and community facilities not covered by the other four constituent agencies. CFA was formerly called the Community Facilities and Special Operations branch (CF&SO), but the change in its name did not affect its functions or authority. Among

the programs administered by CFA were those related to Alaska housing and prefabricated housing.

The agencies related to Urban Renewal and Public Housing had no connection with the Aleutian Homes project.

The Housing and Home Finance Administrator (hereinafter referred to as "Administrator") is the head of HHFA and is responsible for the general supervision and coordination of the statutory functions of the constituent agencies of HHFA.

The original interest of the government in prefabricated housing was contained in the Veterans Emergency Housing Act of 1946, 60 Stat. 207, Chap. 268, §12(a). The government functions relating to this program of prefabricated housing were, at that time, vested in the Reconstruction Finance Corporation, a corporation (hereinafter referred to as "RFC"). The powers of RFC which were applicable to its functions in the field of prefabricated housing were set out in 15 U.S.C.A. §603. The powers and functions of RFC which related to prefabricated housing were transferred to HHFA by Reorganization Plan No. 23 of 1950 (64 Stat. 1279; 5 U.S.C.A. §133z-15), as limited by statute. By Title 12 U.S.C. §1723(d) the functions of HHFA under Section 2 of Reorganization Plan No. 22 of 1950 were transferred to FNMA August 2, 1954.

Provisions for the making of loans for prefabricated housing were added as §102a of the Housing

Act of 1948 (62 Stat. 1268) by the Critical Defense Housing Areas Act of 1951 (65 Stat. 293; 12 U.S. C.A., Section 1701g-1).

The powers given the Housing and Home Finance Administrator with respect to prefabricated housing, set forth in 12 U.S.C.A. §1701g-2, include the following:

(A) All the powers and functions transferred to him by Reorganization Plan No. 23 of 1950.

(B) The powers, functions and duties set forth in 12 U.S.C.A. §1749a, except subsection (c)(2) thereof.

(C) The power to "take any and all actions determined by him to be necessary or desirable in making servicing, compromising, modifying, liquidating, or otherwise dealing with or realizing on loans thereunder. Such powers, functions, and duties may be exercised in the several States, the District of Columbia, and the Territories and possessions of the United States."

Included in the powers of the Administrator, set forth in §1749(a) to which reference is made in §1701g-2(B) as being applicable to the prefabricated housing program, are the following:

"(3) sue or be sued;

"(4) foreclose on any property or commence any action to protect or enforce any right conferred upon him by any law, contract, or other agreement, and bid for and purchase at any foreclosure or any other sale any property in connection with which he has made a loan pursuant to this subchapter. In the event of any such acquisition, the Administrator may, notwithstanding any other provision of law relating to the acquisition, handling, or disposal of real property by the United States, complete, administer, remodel and convert, dispose of, lease and otherwise deal with, such property: Provided, that any such acquisition of real property shall not deprive any State or political subdivision thereof of its civil or criminal jurisdiction in and over such property or impair the civil rights under the State or local laws of the inhabitants on such property;

"(5) enter into agreements to pay annual sums in lieu of taxes to any State or local taxing authority with respect to any real property so acquired or owned;

"(6) sell or exchange at public or private sale or lease, real or personal property, and sell or exchange any securities or obligations upon such terms as he may fix;

"(7) obtain insurance against loss in connection with property and other assets held;

"(8) subject to the specific limitations in this subchapter, consent to the modification, with respect to rate of interest, time of payment of any installment of principal or interest, security, or any other term of any contract or agreement to which he is a party or which has been transferred to him pursuant to this subchapter; and;

"(9) include in any contract or instrument made pursuant to this subchapter such other covenants, conditions, or provisions as he may deem necessary to assure that the purposes of this subchapter will be achieved."

The Independent Offices Appropriation Act of 1955 passed on June 24, 1954, as Ch. 359, 68 Stat. 272 (83rd Cong. 2d Sess., Public Law 428) established as of June 30, 1954, a revolving fund with which the Administrator could account for all assets and liabilities in connection with various programs, including:

"* * * functions transferred under Reorganization Plan No. 23 of 1950 (5 U.S.C. 133z-15, note), or authorized under Sections 102, 102a, 102b, and 102c of the Housing Act of 1948, as amended (12 U.S.C. 1701g-1701g-3 [Prefabricated Housing Program]); * * * notes or other obligations purchased pursuant to the Alaska Housing Act, as amended (48 U.S.C. 484(a)); * * *"

It was further provided:

"That said fund shall be available for all necessary expenses (including administrative expenses) in connection with the liquidation of the programs carried out pursuant to the foregoing provisions of law, including operation, maintenance, improvement, or disposition of facilities, and for disbursements pursuant to outstanding commitments against moneys herein authorized to be credited to said fund, repayment of obligations to the Treasury, and refinancing and refunding operations on existing loans * * *''

After non-payment of its note, the Aleutian Homes, Inc., project was included in the liquidating program administered by HHFA under the revolving fund established by this Act.

FHA was established in 1934 with powers as codified in 12 U.S.C.A., §1702. It was transferred as a constituent agency to HHFA by Reorganization Plan No. 3 of 1947 (61 Stat. 954, 5 U.S.C.A., §133y-16). The powers to insure conventional mortgages on individual houses are contained in Title II, Section 203, of the National Housing Act of 1934 (48 Stat. 1248, Chapter 847, 12 U.S.C.A. §1709). That section was amended by the Housing Act of 1954 (68 Stat. 591) to change the value ratio of loans which FHA is authorized to insure thereunder.

Under the provisions of the Alaska Housing Act, FHA was given authority to insure mortgages in Alaska in a dollar amount up to 50 per cent higher than its authority with respect to mortgages on property located in the United States. Further it gave FHA authority to insure mortgages in Alaska without the requirement, applicable to housing in the states, that the commissioner find the project to be economically sound or an acceptable risk (63 Stat. 57, 65 Stat. 315, 12 U.S.C.A., §1715d).

The creation of FNMA and the establishment of its powers is set out in 12 U.S.C.A. §§1716 through 1723d.

FNMA was transferred from the jurisdiction of RFC to HHFA to be "administered subject to the direction and control" of HHFA by Reorganization Plan No. 22 of 1950 (64 Stat. 1277, 5 U.S.C.A., §133z-15, as limited by statute. By Title 12 U.S.C. §1723(d) the functions of HHFA under Section 2 of Reorganization Plan No. 22 of 1950 were transferred to FNMA August 2, 1954.

Likewise, it is necessary to know the names of the non-Federal government agencies and private organizations involved or in some way connected. They are:

A. Alaska Housing Authority. Agency of the Territory of Alaska concerned with housing problems in Alaska.

B. City of Kodiak, Alaska. The city through its officials, principally Mayor Lee C. Bettinger, took active interest in promoting a housing project for the City under private sponsors, and provided tax concessions for streets and other support for the project.

C. Hubbell and Waller. An engineering firm cooperating with the City for soil tests, street layout, etc.

D. Ray Lewis and associates. A firm which negotiated with the City with view to sponsoring construction of project.

E. Pacif[...]
Oregon, in [...]
interested w[...]
houses.

F. Aleut[...]
tion formed[...]
principal s[...]
Homes proje[...]

G. Brice[...]
Portland, O[...]
firms. Brice[...]
Homes, Inc.[...]
the project a[...]
FHA insure[...]
to FNMA. E[...]
ments from I[...]
the mortga[...]

H. Kodia[...]
tion organiz[...]
for the pur[...]
for the cons[...]

I. Pacifi[...]
ton corpora[...]
Kodiak Co[...]
foundations.

J. Carl[...]
Carlton whi[...]
furnish the[...]

E. Pacific Structures, Inc. A firm in Portland, Oregon, in which R. B. Woodbury and others were interested which planned to produce prefabricated houses.

F. Aleutian Homes, Inc. An Oregon corporation formed by R. B. Woodbury as President and principal stockholder to sponsor the Aleutian Homes project and become the owner thereof.

G. Brice Mortgage Co., and Brice Realty Co. Portland, Oregon, mortgage brokers and realty firms. Brice Mortgage Co. agreed with Aleutian Homes, Inc., to arrange permanent financing for the project as mortgagee under a proposed loan for FHA insured mortgages and sale of the mortgages to FNMA. Brice applied for and received commitments from FHA to insure and FNMA to purchase the mortgages on stated conditions.

H. Kodiak Construction Co. An Oregon corporation organzied with R. B. Woodbury as President for the purpose of being the General Contractor for the construction of the project.

I. Pacific-Alaska Contractors, Inc. A Washington corporation which had a sub-contract from Kodiak Construction Co., for site preparation and foundations.

J. Carlton Lumber Co. A firm owned by A. B. Carlton which had a sub-contract from Kodiak to furnish the prefabricated house packages.

K.   Leo S. Wynans Co., Inc. An Oregon corporation having a sub-contract from Kodiak to erect the houses on-site.

L.   Coastwise Steamship Lines. Had agreement to transport houses from Portland, Oregon, to Kodiak, Alaska.

M.   North Pacific Supply Co. A partnership at Portland, Oregon, in which R. B. Woodbury, Fred Miller and Jack Crawford were partners, as electrical equipment wholesalers.

N.   Columbia Supply Co. A partnership at Swan Island, Portland, Oregon, composed of R. B. Woodbury and Lucille Woodbury, his wife.

O.   Smith Q McMenamin. A Portland, Oregon, accounting firm employed by Woodbury as accountants on behalf of Columbia Supply Co., Aleutian Homes, Inc., and Kodiak Construction Co.

P.   General Casualty Co. A bonding company providing performance bond as surety for general contract performance by Kodiak Construction Co.

Q.   United States Fidelity & Guaranty Co. A bonding company providing performance bond as surety for site improvement contract of Pacific-Alaska Contractors, Inc.

R.   United National Indemnity Co. and The Fidelity & Casualty Co. of New York. Bonding companies providing performance bond as sureties on the house package contract of Alex B. Carlton.

S. United Pacific Insurance Co. Bonding company providing performance bond for construction contract of Leo S. Wynans, Inc.

Commencing in 1949, the possibility of securing additional housing for naval and civilian personnel connected with the Kodiak Naval Base in Alaska was discussed among Navy officials, officials of the Alaska Housing Authority, officials of the City of Kodiak and officials of FHA. The possibility of securing housing under the Wherry Act (Title VIII of the National Housing Act, as amended) was considered and rejected and studies were then made with respect to the possibility of construction of an off-base project of some 350 to 400 houses using conventional FHA assistance under Title II, Section 203, of the National Housing Act, as amended.

During 1950-1951, arrangements were made to secure, as a site for this project, certain land belonging to the federal government under the control of the Bureau of Land Management of the Department of Interior. Arrangements were made to transfer this land to the Alaska Housing Authority for reconveyance to the City of Kodiak for use for a project to be built by a sponsor selected by the City of Kodiak. Subsequently, in accordance with law, the Alaska Housing Authority conveyed the land directly to the approved sponsor. It was determined that the City of Kodiak would provide streets, the city and Department of Interior through Alaska Public Works would provide water and sewer facilities and schools and the local REA would provide power. During 1951, the City of Kodiak received a commitment from the Alaska Public Works program for money to construct the sewer and water facilities in connection with the proposed project.

During 1950 and 1951 considerable surveying of the site and engineering was carried on on behalf of the City of Kodiak and a Raymond Lewis of Los Angeles who was a proposed sponsor for the project. In late 1951, Mr. Lewis abandoned interest in sponsorship of the propsed project.

During 1951, plaintiff became interested in the promotion of a house panel invented by an architect, S. C. Horsley. In late 1951, plaintiff financed a trip by Horsley, R. A. Blanchard and G. K. Gosling to Alaska to investigate the possibility of selling the Horsley panel for use in houses in Alaska. In the course of this promotion, Lee C. Bettinger, the Mayor of Kodiak, was contacted by Gosling and commenced to interest plaintiff to become sponsor of the proposed project in the place of Raymond Lewis.

In February, 1952, Aleutian Homes, Inc., was incorporated under the laws of the state of Oregon and in February or March, 1952, the City of Kodiak approved Aleutian Homes, Inc., as the sponsor of the proposed housing project. Thereafter, the Alaska Housing Authority conveyed the land selected for the site to Aleutian Homes, Inc.

The proposed projejct was intended to be financed under the provisions of Title II, Section 203, of the National Housing Act, as amended. Under this program, a private mortgage agency takes out individual long-term mortgages on each house included in the project. With respect to the Kodiak project, Brice Mortgage Company was selected to act as the permanent mortgagee.

In order to enable Brice Mortgage Company to sell the mortgages which it intended to obtain on each of the houses in the project, it was necessary for Brice Mortgage Company to obtain a commitment from FHA to insure said mortgages. In accordance with FHA requirements with respect to the insurance of a project located in Kodiak, Alaska, the Secretary of Navy in 1951, with respect to Raymond Lewis and again in 1952 with respect to Aleutian Homes, Inc., certified to FHA (1) the critical urgent need of the Navy for 385 family units for use by military and civilian personnel at the Kodiak Naval Base, (2) the permanency of the Kodiak Naval Base, and (3) the ability of such military and civilian personnel to pay rentals for such units in the amount of $100, $130 and $150 for small two, large two and three bedroom units, including garage and kitchen equipment. In 1952, FHA appraised the value of a 344 unit project at $5,904,250 and in April 1952, issued for a stated period its conditional commitment to Brice Mortgage Company to insure long-range individual mortgages on each home in a total amount of

$4,706,400, which amount was based on 80 per cent of the FHA appraised value.

Also in 1952, FNMA issued its commitment to Brice Mortgage Company to purchase at par the individual long-range mortgages as they were obtained by Brice Mortgage Company and insured by FHA.

The $4,706,400 to be received from the long-term financing was to be used by Aleutian Homes, Inc., for (1) repayment of the construction loan from HHFA, $4,230,900; (2) payment of costs of taking out the permanent individual mortgages; and (3) any balance remaining as capital.

During 1952, Aleutian Homes, Inc., and Brice Mortgage Company found it impossible to secure from private sources the financing required for the construction of the project prior to the obtaining of the long-range financing as set forth above, and sought assistance from HHFA. In said year, negotiations were had between Brice Mortgage Company, acting on behalf of Aleutian Homes, Inc., and the Community Facilities and Special Operations Branch of HHFA for the purpose of securing an interim loan for construction purposes. A final application was made by Aleutian Homes, Inc., late in 1952 and approved in January, 1953. This interim construction loan by HHFA was in the sum of $4,230,900, which constituted 90 per cent of the amount of the FHA and FNMA commitments with respect to the permanent long-range financing, the application indicating the difference between the projected costs and the loan amount applied for would be provided for by the Sponsor, Aleutian Homes, Inc. The loan was authorized by a Loan Authorization signed by the Administrator, and carried into effect by documents required by a Building Loan Agreement, including a guaranty of the Loan Agreement and the guaranty of the construction contract by R. B. Woodbury, and a promissory note and deed of trust. Procedures for disbursement under the loan were provided for in a Loan and Disbursement Agreement executed by R. B. Woodbury as President, Aleutian Homes, Inc., April 27, 1953. The construction contracts and stock of Aleutian Homes, Inc., were assigned to the Administrator. A Standby Agreement was executed by R. B. Woodbury, President, Aleutian Homes, Inc., and R. B. Woodbury, individually. Performance bonds run to Aleutian Homes, Inc., and the Administrator.

Contractual arrangements for the construction of the project under the interim loan from HHFA were signed in Seattle, Washington, on April 27, 1953. In general they provided as follows: Aleutian Homes, Inc., as the owner entered into a "general contract" with Kodiak Construction Co. for the construction of the housing project for the payment of the sum of $4,230,900 (the total maximum amount of the HHFA loan). Kodiak Construction Co., as general contractor, in turn contracted with three subcontractors, plus a freight company, the total payment under which subcontracts, plus freight, similarly equaled the sum of $4,230,900, (the maximum total amount of the HHFA loan). These subcontracts were as follows:

1. A "supply contract" entered into with Alex B. Carlton, doing business as Carlton Lumber Company, for the purchase of the prefabricated housing packages.

2. A "site construction contract" entered into with Pacific Alaska Contractors, Inc., for preparation of the site.

3. A "construction contract" entered into with Leo S. Wynans Co., Inc., for the erection of the prefabricated houses on the prepared sites.

4. A contract with Coastwise Line for the transportation of prefabricated house packages and other materials from Portland, Oregon, to Kodiak, Alaska.

During the summer of 1953, certain difficulties arose in the preparation of the site and a controversy developed between Kodiak Construction Co., speaking through Leo S. Wynans, its agent, and Pacific Alaska Contractors, Inc. At the time of this controversy Pacific Alaska Contractors, Inc., ceased further work on the site preparation and Kodiak Construction Co., under the direction of Wynans, proceeded to furnish labor and materials required under the site construction contract.

In October and November, 1953, financial difficulties arose in connection with the construction of the project, and, on November 6, 1953, Pacific Alaska Contractors, Inc., filed a claim of lien against the project for the sum of $150,504.43. Thereupon, construction came to a standstill with the project approximately 75 per cent completed.

When construction came to a standstill in the late fall of 1953, several possibilities of action were considered. These included foreclosure, completion of the project by the surety companies, demand on Ray B. Woodbury for performance, introduction of additional money in the project in conjunction with Aleutian Homes, Inc., or in substitution of Aleutian Homes, Inc., sponsorship, or completion of the project based upon a completion agreement. In November, 1953, demand was made on Ray B. Woodbury under his guarantee. Woodbury failed to comply with the demand. In January, 1954, a completion agreement[1] was formulated in substantially the form in which it became effective on April 23, 1954. The period from the end of January through April 23, 1954, was devoted to securing the necessary consent to placing the completion agreement in operation. In general, the completion agreement provided for the completion of the construction of the project and the payment order of claimants, creditors and completion costs in four stages. To carry out this program, Aleutian Homes, Inc., Kodiak Construction Co. and Leo S. Wynans Co., Inc., agreed to vest in a Project Manager exclusive authority to take any and all action in connection

---

[1]See Appendix A.

with the project that they would be authorized to take, subject to the rights of HHFA defined therein.

Under the completion agreement the project manager (Harry M. Langton) was appointed with certain prescribed duties and responsibilities and authority with respect to completion of the construction and payment of the claims against the project. Similarly a construction superintendent (Scott J. Cross) was selected to take charge of the physical completion of the project. Under this arrangement, the construction of 343 houses was completed on October 26, 1954. The 344th house was not erected because the lot provided therefor was found unsuitable for building.

By April 12, 1955, 341 out of the 343 houses constructed had passed FHA final inspection. The remaining two at that time were unacceptable for reasons relating to their foundations. Under the completion agreement, all claims listed in Stages 1 and 2 were paid, while only some of the claims in Stages 3 and 4 were paid.

The permanent individual mortgages were not taken out on any of said 341 houses and during June, 1955, the FHA commitments to insure such mortgages and the FNMA commitments to purchase such mortgages at par expired.

The Navy determined that the cost in renting and the cost of utilities to occupants of Aleutian Homes, Inc., was more than the personnel and civilian employees could pay, and increased the rental allowance to military personnel living in the Aleutian Homes project in the amount of $37.50 a month for enlisted men and $36.00 a month for officers.

During the summer of 1957, the Navy indicated service personnel was to be reduced by 10 per cent and civilian personnel by approximately 33⅓ per cent.

HHFA made advances to or for the benefit of Aleutian Homes, Inc., for project construction costs in the total amount of $4,192,717.10 as follows:

1. Prior to the completion agreement (from June 25 to November 24, 1953) $3,330,062.68 (out of the total authorized loan of $4,230,900).

2. Subsequent to the completion agreement, $862,654.42 to the Aleutian Homes on requisition of the Project Manager. The difference between this total amount advanced by HHFA ($4,192,717.10) and the total loan authorized ($4,230,900) of $37,-282.90 was withheld by reason of the one house not built and the two houses which by April, 1955, had not passed final FHA inspection.

In March, 1955, HHFA authorized advances in an amount not to exceed $160,000 (in addition to the original loan of $4,230,900) to be made to Aleutian Homes, Inc., to be spent for the care and preservation of its security. HHFA advanced to Aleutian Homes, Inc., on March 15, 1955, $56,239.19, which amount was repaid to HHFA on May 5, 1956, together with $3,966.01, representing 7 per cent interest on said sum from March 15, 1955, to May 5, 1956.

3. Interest under the note has been accruing at the rate of 5 per cent. As of June 30, 1957, accrued interest claimed by HHFA to be due and unpaid was $211,105.65. As of December 31, 1959, accrued interest claimed by HHFA to be due and unpaid was $384,756.43, together with the principal balance.

HHFA received payments made by or on behalf of Aleutian Homes, Inc., in the total amount of $909,675.58 as follows:

1. Prior to the completion agreement (June 25 to October 31, 1953) $35,134.14.

2. After the completion agreement, from the project manager, $402,241.44.

3. Immediately prior to foreclosure HHFA withdrew from bank accounts maintained by the Aleutian Homes, Inc., Project Manager an additional $122,300.

4. From the court appointed receiver, $350,000.

FHA received fees for its commitments to insure, and extension thereof, the total sum of $22,360.

FNMA received fees for its commitments to purchase, and extension thereof, the sum of $106,422.77.

From July 1, 1954, through June 14, 1957, the Aleutian Homes, Inc., project manager received rentals from the project in the total amount of

$1,114,800.20, and disbursed said funds as indicated in the records he maintained of the project. Most of said funds were disbursed.

During 1954, 1955 and 1956, plaintiff paid to The Bank of California, N.A., the following sums of money on the following dates in payment of the claim of the Bank of California, N.A., as set forth in the completion agreement:

Date of Payment	Amount Paid	Credited to
Feb. 18, 1954	$ 1,083.33	Interest
June 2, 1954	1,875.00	Interest
Aug. 20, 1954	1,875.00	Interest
Dec. 6, 1954	1,895.83	Interest
May 18, 1955	3,750.00	Interest
May 18, 1955	41,455.00	Principal
May 18, 1955	14,526.43	Principal
June 13, 1955	2,352.75	Principal
July 11, 1955	2,352.75	Principal
Aug. 12, 1955	890.56	Interest
Sept. 13, 1955	285.31	Interest
Sept. 13, 1955	2,063.69	Principal
Sept. 28, 1955	658.25	Principal
Oct. 10, 1955	653.27	Interest
Oct. 10, 1955	25,591.13	Principal
June 11, 1956	787.92	Interest
July 6, 1956	1,499.58	Interest
July 6, 1956	61,000.00	Principal

During 1954, plaintiff paid Brice Mortgage Company $35,000 in settlement of all claims of Brice Mortgage Company and Brice Realty Company against the project for alleged work done and service performed prior to the execution of the completion agreement.

During 1954, plaintiff paid $75,000 to the Administrator for use under a requirement to pay overhead under the overhead agreement and completion agreement that Ray B. Woodbury pay overhead therein described. Defendant made demands for additional overhead payments which Ray B. Woodbury did not make.

On September 18, 1956, plaintiff satisfied the judgment obtained by General Casualty Company on July 24, 1956, for the unpaid premium on the bond issued on behalf of Kodiak Construction Co., together with expenses relating thereto by the payment to General Casualty Company of the sum of $33,542.09. In the defense of said action R. B. Woodbury incurred legal fees and other expenses in the sum of $2,412.93.

HHFA on or about June 11, 1957, in the United States District Court for the District of Alaska, Third Judicial Division, Anchorage, commenced foreclosure proceedings in the name of the United States of America against Aleutian Homes, Inc., a corporation; Pacific Alaska Contractors, Inc., a corporation; Alex B. Carlton, doing business as Carlton Lumber Company; City of Kodiak, a municipal corporation of the Territory of Alaska; James C. Dougherty, Trustee under the Will of Hugh Dougherty; Lee Bettinger, Jack Hinckel, M. Justin Herman and David Oliver, as Trustees; Lindley R. Durkee and Melvin Frazier, as Trustees, and "Also all other persons or parties unknown claiming any right, title, estate, lien or interest

in the real estate described in the complaint herein,"
defendants, Civil No. A-13,484. On June 14, 1957,
upon the motion of plaintiff, the court appointed
M. G. Gebhart receiver of the mortgaged property
until further order of the court. On or about June
20, 1958, the Court authorized the payment by the
receiver to HHFA of $200,000 out of proceeds from
operation of the project, and said $200,000 was paid
to HHFA. On or about September 12, 1958, plaintiff amended its complaint by adding as defendants
the Territory of Alaska, Kodiak Construction Co.,
a corporation; Leo S. Wynans Co., Inc., a corporation, and United States of America. On or about
April 10, 1959, pursuant to request of the receiver,
the Court authorized the payment by the receiver to
HHFA of $150,000 out of proceeds from operation
of the project and said $150,000 was paid to HHFA.

Plaintiff's Contentions

Generally speaking, the plaintiff's contentions are:

1. That HHFA participated in the formulation
of the completion agreement dated 4/23/54 and
accepted the same, under the terms of which plaintiff, (a) agreed to become a standby creditor as to
his then existing claims, (b) agreed to advance further substantial sums of money, and (c) agreed to
relinquish any further control and direction of the
project.

2. That the construction and operation of the
project subsequent to April 24, 1954, was under
the control of HHFA, and plaintiff did in fact
advance substantial funds to the project.

3. That in entering into the completion agreement and in assuming control over the construction and operation of the project, HHFA and the Administrator entered into and occupied a fiduciary relationship with respect to plaintiff, Aleutian Homes, Inc., creditors and other interested parties to the completion agreement.

4. That HHFA, its agents and employees, carelessly and negligently or deliberately and wilfully breached said fiduciary relationship by refusing to adopt a permanent long-range program of amortizing the Kodiak project in a manner which considered the claims of all the parties interested in the completion agreement and instead by proceeding to satisfy and prefer its own interests as a creditor from the assets of the project to the exclusion of the interests of said other persons.

5. That by reason of the alleged breaches of the alleged fiduciary obligation plaintiff was damaged in a substantial sum.

Defendant's Contentions

That the Federal Tort Claims Act (Title 28, U. S. C. A. §1346(b) and §§2671 through 2680) is not applicable to the factual situation in this case and, consequently, the Court has no jurisdiction to proceed, in that:

(a) The alleged breach of duty is not a "negligent or wrongful act or omission" under the Tort Claims Act; and

(b)   The acts of which plaintiff complains were in the exercise of a discretionary function and therefore not actionable under the express terms of the exceptions of the Tort Claims Act, Title 28, U. S. C. A. §2680.

In view of my ultimate decision, it is not necessary to mention other points raised by defendant.

The testimony is clear and convincing that the defendant, acting by and through the Navy Department, was vitally interested in the construction of housing for Navy personnel at Kodiak. Likewise, the testimony clearly shows that plaintiff, through his corporations and individually, was interested in the construction from an investment viewpoint. All parties entered into the original agreements in entire good faith.

After Brice Mortgage Company was unable to arrange for long-term financing, it became a certainty that such financing could be obtained only through defendant's agencies. In my opinion the evidence is conclusive that no housing project would ever have been commenced at Kodiak if long-term financing had not been contemplated by defendant's agencies. If there ever was any doubt on the subject of long-term financing, that doubt was removed when financial difficulties arose and construction ground to a halt in the fall of 1953.

A large scale housing project in Kodiak, Alaska, such as here contemplated, could not be successful unless supported by Navy personnel. That the Navy was vitally interested is clearly shown by the certificate of the Secretary of the Navy made in 1952 in which he certified to FHA the critical need of the Navy for 385 family units for use by military and civilian personnel at Kodiak Naval Base, the permanency of the Kodiak Naval Base and the ability of such military and civilian personnel to pay rentals as indicated on page 10 of this Opinion. Defendant was even more deeply involved in October and November, 1953, when certain liens were filed against the project. Construction came to a standstill when the project was approximately 75 per cent complete. Prior to the signing of the completion agreement, defendant, through HHFA, advanced $3,330,062.28 on the project. When we look at this agreement in light of the huge investment in the project then held by defendant, we can readily understand why defendant's agency wanted absolute control removed from the hands of plaintiff and his organizations and placed in the hands of defendant's agency.

The evidence is undisputed that HHFA played a major part in all of the negotiations leading up to the signing of the completion agreement on April 23, 1954. Certainly, defendant's agency is not to be criticized for attempting to save an investment of approximately three and one third million dollars. If the project was not completed, the investment would be worthless. In my opinion this agency, under the facts then existing and under the powers granted by Congress, had full right and authority

to complete the project, if it so desired. All parties
concluded that it was for the best interests of everyone concerned to proceed with the construction under the direction of a Project Manager. It is true
that neither HHFA nor the Administrator signed
the completion agreement. However, it is crystal
clear that all parties to the agreement anticipated
that HHFA would formally accept such obligations
as it had under the terms of this agreement. I am
not attempting to distinguish between HHFA and
the Administrator. The agreement refers to the
Administrator as the "Lender," and he will be
herein referred to as "Lender." Under its terms
certain promises were made in order to induce
Lender to disburse further proceeds of the loan.
The parties agreed to sign all documents required
by the Lender. All income from the project and
other proceeds were to be assigned to the Lender.
Plaintiff agreed to provide certain overhead expenses required by the Lender estimated at $16,000
per month. The Project Manager had to be acceptable to the Lender and was vested with full and
exclusive authority to take all action necessary in
connection with the project, subject to the general
direction of the Lender. Any and all subcontractors
had to be approved by the Lender. The Project
Manager was subject to removal on the request of
the Lender. In truth and in fact, the Lender had
an absolute right to designate the Project Manager
and discharge him if Lender so desired. The bank
account from which disbursements were made for
the completion of the project was in the name of

the Lender and the Project Manager. In other words, when the funds were disbursed by the Lender under its commitments, such funds were transferred to a bank account over which the Lender had absolute control. The construction superintendent had to be acceptable to the Lender and was subject only to the direction of the Project Manager and, by inference, subject to removal only by the Project Manager.

The language in paragraph 18 of the agreement indicates that the only reason it was not signed by HHFA or the Administrator (Lender) was a doubt as to whether the law authorized such execution. The agreement did require written or oral approval by the Lender. The Lender gave written approval of the agreement. Outside of the terms and provisions of the completion agreement the evidence is overwhelming that the Lender in truth and in fact took over absolute control of and proceeded with the completion of the project.

In my opinion the fact that the completion agreement was not signed by Lender is of no significance. Contractual liability under a written contract may be assumed without signing it. Girard Life Insurance & Trust Co. vs. Cooper, 162 U.S. 529; Laurent vs. Anderson, 6 Cir., 1934, 70 F.2d 819; First National Bank vs. Sleeper, 8 Cir., 1926, 12 F.2d 228; Commercial Standard Insurance Co. vs. Garrett, 10 Cir., 1934, 70 F.2d 969. In fact, the Lender in this case accepted the completion agreement in writing. The validity and construction of contracts through

which the United States is exercising its constitutional functions, their consequences on the rights
and obligations of the parties and the titles or liens
which they create or permit present questions of
federal law not controlled by the laws of any state.
United States vs. Allegheny County, 322 U.S. 174,
182; S.R.A., Inc. vs. Minnesota, 327 U.S. 558, 564;
United States vs. Jones, 9 Cir., 1949, 176 F.2d 278.

Defendant argues that under well established
legal principles defendant cannot occupy the position of a fiduciary. Restatement of the Law, Trusts
2d, §95; United States vs. Waylyn Corp., D.P.R.,
1955, 130 F. Supp. 783, aff'd Waylyn Corp. vs.
United States, 1 Cir., 1956, 231 F.2d 544, cert. den.
352 U.S. 827. Those authorities are not in point.
Lender was delegated broad general powers by the
Congress to go forward with prefabricated housing
and in particular with housing in Alaska. 15 U. S.
C. A. §603; 12 U. S. C. A. §1749(a); 12 U. S. C. A.
§1701g-(2); Federal Housing Administrator vs.
Burr, 1939, 309 U.S. 242.

If the United States Government, or any branch
thereof, enters into a contract with an individual,
natural or corporate, and does so in its private or
business capacity and not as a sovereign, it submits
itself to the same rules of law which govern the
construction of contracts between individuals.
S.R.A., Inc. vs. Minnesota, supra; Reading Steel
Casting Co. vs. United States, 268 U.S. 186; Lynch
vs. United States, 292 U.S. 571. In a case such as
this, where the governmental agency is acting in a

commercial field, with the full authority and consent of Congress, that agency should not be less amenable to the ordinary rules of law than would be a private enterprise under like circumstances. Keifer & Keifer vs. Reconstruction Finance Corp., 1938, 306 U.S. 381; Federal Housing Administrator vs. Burr, supra.

Defendant forcefully argues that United States vs. Waylyn Corp., supra, is authority for its proposition that defendant could not be a fiduciary under the circumstances of this case. In that case the United States instituted a suit to foreclose a loan. Defendant corporation counterclaimed for damages on a theory that the United States breached a certain fiduciary relationship in not doing certain things to enable defendant's apartment buildings to become self-supporting and self-liquidating. Plaintiff's motion to dismiss the counterclaim was allowed. The Court, in passing on the coverage of the counterclaim under the Federal Tort Claims Act, stated that the acts complained of and on which the counterclaim was based were obviously an exercise of a discretionary function and would fall within the exception contained in §2280(a). The case does not hold that the government cannot occupy a fiduciary relationship.

I am of the opinion that the Lender could legally occupy the legal status of a fiduciary in connection with the completion of the housing project in question. Furthermore, I find and hold that the Lender took over full and complete control of such project and, in so doing, was acting in a fiduciary capacity with the plaintiff. A more detailed statement of the evidence in support of this conclusion is neither necessary nor desirable.

The completion agreement was accepted by the Lender by letter dated April 27, 1954. The identical resolutions of Kodiak Construction Co. and Aleutian Homes each authorizing the signing of the completion agreement also turned complete control of the project over to a Project Manager who had to be acceptable to the Lender. The Lender designated the Manager's powers, duties, compensation and tenure. The same sort of an arrangement was made by resolution of each corporation in connection with the appointment of a Construction Superintendent acceptable to Lender. The Lender had full charge and control of the powers, duties, compensation and tenure of such Superintendent. In part the resolution read:

"* * *

"Now, Therefore, in order to indice Lender to accept Completion Agreement and in order to comply with the provisions thereof, this corporation does hereby:

"* * *

"2. Authorize the employment and appointment of a 'Project Manager' sho shall be vested with full and complete authority to do every act and thing which this corporation could do by its regularly

elected directors and officers in connection with any
manner or thing connected with said Project, and
this corporation does further authorize the officers
of this corporation to appoint such person and any
successor thereto as may be acceptable to Lender
to enter into an agreement with such person or
persons designating his powers, duties, compensation and tenure, such agreement to be in accordance
with the terms and conditions of such Completion
Agreement and subject to the approval of the
Lender;

"* * *"

It is clear from all pertinent parts and provisions
of the completion agreement, taken together and
considered in light of the facts and circumstances
surrounding the transaction at the time of execution,
and the actions of the parties subsequent thereto,
that the obligation of the Lender to furnish long-
term financing was within the contemplation of the
parties and was necessary to carry their intentions
into effect. In such case the obligation will be implied and enforced. Stern vs. Dunlap Co., 10 Cir.,
1955, 228 F.2d 939; Northeast Clackamas County
Electric Co-op vs. Continental Casualty Co., 9 Cir.,
1955, 221 F.2d 329; Sacramento Navigation Co vs.
Salz, 273 U.S. 326; Hudson Canal Co. vs. Pennsylvania Coal Co., 75 U.S. 276.

A person in a fiduciary relation to another is
under a duty to act for the benefit of the other as
to matters within the scope of the relation. Such

relation is defined in Black's Law Dictionary, 4th
Ed., 753; Farrow vs. Dermott Drainage District,
8 Cir., 1944, 139 F.2d 800, 805:

"A relation subsisting between two persons in
regard to a business, contract, or piece of property,
* * * of such a character that each must repose trust
and confidence in the other and must exercise a corresponding degree of fairness and good faith. Out of
such a relation, the law raises the rule that neither
party may * * * take selfish advantage of his trust,
or deal with the subject-matter of the trust in such
a way as to benefit himself or prejudice the other
except in the exercise of the utmost good faith and
with the full knowledge and consent of that other."

Already I have mentioned that the only source
of long-term financing in the area was through the
federal loan agencies. In my opinion an agreement
to provide such long-term financing was as much a
part of the completion agreement as if it had been
specifically mentioned. The providing of such financing was one of the duties of the Lender when it
moved in and took complete control of the project.
The Lender did not provide this long-term financing.
On the other hand, it commenced foreclosure proceedings.

Likewise, the fact that the completion of the
project required a larger expenditure of funds than
was anticipated at the time of execution of the completion agreement is something which must have
been within the contemplation of the parties and

an implied agreement on the part of the Lender
should be read into the contract to provide long-
term financing for such additional funds.

Whether the Lender, under the evidence in the
case, was justified in refusing to go forward with
the long-term financing is a question which I need
not decide. I have already concluded that defendant
could act as a fiduciary and was acting in a fiduciary
or confidential capacity in assuming control over
the completion of the project and the long-term
financing. Assuming, arguendo, and I would so hold
if I felt I had jurisdiction, that defendant in truth
and in fact breached its duty in failing to provide,
without justification, said long-term financing, is
such breach of duty "negligent or wrongful act or
omission" within the meaning of the phrase as used
in the Federal Tort Claims Act?

I now approach the vital question of jurisdiction
under the Tort Claims Act. The hearings before the
Committee on the Judiciary, House of Representatives, 77th Cong., 2d Sess. on the pending Tort
Claims Act quite conclusively show that Congress
did not contemplate waiver of the government's
immunity for all tortious conduct.[2] Mr. Justice

---

[2]Statement to the Committee by Francis M. Shea:
"If enacted, H.R. 6463 would broaden the existing
authority to make administrative adjustment of tort
claims, extending it to include claims for personal
injury and death as well as for property loss or
damage. It would also remove an existing inequality
in our law which permits suit to be brought against
the United States for certain types of tort claims,

Reed, author of the opinion in the important case of Dalehite vs. United States, 346 U.S. 15, in commenting on this legislative history, said:

"* * * Uppermost in the collective mind of Congress were the ordinary common-law torts. Of these, the example which is reiterated in the course of the repeated proposals for submitting the United States to tort liability is 'negligence in the operation of vehicles'. * * *"

Assuming that the violation of a duty imposed by the fiduciary relationship created in this case is tortious conduct, Restatement of the Law, Torts, §874; Harper vs. Interstate Brewery Co. (1942), 168 Or. 26, 120 P. 2d 757, does such violation fall

---

such as admiralty and maritime torts, and yet precludes suit on the ordinary common-law type of tort, such as personal injuries or property damage resulting from negligent operation of an automobile. * * *

"* * *

"The past 85 years have thus witnessed a steady encroachment upon the doctrine of sovereign immunity. Yet there remains a large and important category of wrongs for which there is as yet no satisfactory remedy—the ordinary common-law type of torts, such as personal injury or property damage caused by negligent operation of an automobile by a government employee in the course of his employment. * * *

"* * * It is neither desirable nor intended that the constitutionality of legislation, the legality of regulations, or the propriety of a discretionary administrative act should be tested through the

within the provisions of the Tort Claims Act? I
think not. The Restatement, in Chap. 43, classifies
the violation of a fiduciary duty as tortious under
rules applicable to certain types of conduct. Negligence is treated in an entirely separate and distinct
volume of such work. In construing the Tort Claims
Act the courts have uniformly held that immunity
was not waived as to all torts. Immunity was not
waived for conduct amounting to a nuisance. Dalehite vs. United States, supra. The Act does not impose absolute liability for the ownership and operation of a dangerous instrumentality. United States
vs. Ure, 9 Cir., 1955, 225 F.2d 709; Porter vs. United
States, 128 F. Supp, 590, aff'd 228 F.2d 389. The

medium of a damage suit for tort. The same holds
true of other administrative action not of a regula-
tory nature, such as the expenditure of Federal
funds, the execution of a federal project, and the
like." * * *

"* * *

"Memorandum for use of the Committee on the
Judiciary:
"The survival of government irresponsibility in
the field of common-law torts is an anachronism,
founded upon no sounder reason than a historical
prejudice against tort claims. No acceptable justification has ever been cited for this immunity and
in an area of steadily growing government activity,
involving considerable use of automobiles and other
mechanical equipment capable of causing damage to
person and property, the absence of a satisfactory
procedure for redressing such wrongs becomes a
grave defect in our social policy." (Emphasis
added.)

act does not impose liability without fault. Harris
vs. United States, 10 Cir., 1953, 205 F.2d 765.
Although fraud and deceit may constitute tortious
conduct, such conduct does not fall within the provisions of the Act. United States vs. Gill, (1957)
W.D. Pa., 156 F. Supp. 955. The courts, by inference, in construing the language "negligent or
wrongful act or omission" have applied the well-
known rule of ejusdem generis. Under this rule
the general words in a statute (or wrongful act
or omission) are confined to the class which it has
specifically described (negligent) and may not be
used to enlarge the meaning of such word. Cleveland
vs. United States, 329 U.S. 14; Fourco Glass Co vs.
Transmirra Products Corp., 353 U.S. 222; Haili vs.
United States, 9 Cir., 1958, 260 F.2d 744; In Re
Application of Rogers, 9 Cir., 1956, 229 F.2d 754.

It is true that the Courts have construed the
language to cover certain acts which are not strictly
negligent in nature. However, the wrongful acts
in such cases were closely related to negligence. For
example, the Court in Hatahley vs. United States,
351 U.S. 173, 181 (1956), held that a trespass, in
the confiscation of horses, was such a wrongful act
as was contemplated. Likewise, in Aleutco Corp. vs.
United States, 3 Cir., 1957, 244 F.2d 674, it was
recognized that the wrongful conversion of certain
property by the United States constituted a com-
pensable wrongful act. United States vs. Ein Chem-
icals Corp., D.C. N.Y., 1958, 161 F. Supp. 238, supports Aleutco's holding that the wrongful conversion

of property is such tortious conduct as is covered by the language in question. Plaintiff urges that under the plain language of the Act the defendant is liable if a private person would be liable. Clearly, this language must be read and construed with the other language of the Act. The test would be whether a private person would be liable to the plaintiff for "negligent or wrongful act or omission" of a government employee as defined and limited by the legislative history and Court decisions construing the Act.

I feel that the Lender, when it accepted the completion agreement and took over control of the project under which it was to provide long-term financing, was not acting in the exercise of a discretionary function. The Lender had an absolute obligation to furnish such long-term financing.

I express no opinion on the statute of limitations nor the legal effect, if any, of the indemnity agreements executed by plaintiff.

I conclude that I have no jurisdiction under the Tort Claims Act and that this cause must be dismissed without prejudice. No testimony was taken on defendant's counterclaim and that issue is not before the Court. If the government decides to proceed in this Court on such counterclaim, a trial date will be assigned.

This opinion shall stand as my findings and conclusions on plaintiff's claims. An appropriate judgment of dismissal without prejudice shall be prepared and presented.

Dated this 8th day of February, 1961.

/s/ JOHN F. KILKENNY.
District Judge.

[Endorsed]: Filed February 8, 1961.

———

United States District Court
District of Oregon

Civil No. 9403

RAY B. WOODBURY,

Plaintiff,

vs.

UNITED STATES OF AMERICA,

Defendant.

JUDGMENT OF DISMISSAL

Kilkenny, J.:

The findings of fact and conclusions of law found by the Court in the opinion filed in the above cause on the 8th day of February, 1961, be and the same are hereby adopted as the findings of fact and conclusions of law in this cause, and based on the conclusion that the Court has no jurisdiction of plaintiff's claims under the Tort Claims Act,

It Is Ordered And Adjudged that plaintiff's complaint and the causes therein set forth be and the same are hereby dismissed, without prejudice.

Dated this 24th day of February, 1961.

/s/ JOHN F. KILKENNY,
District Judge.

[Endorsed]: Filed February 24, 1961.

————

[Title of District Court and Cause.]

NOTICE OF APPEAL

Notice is hereby given that Ray B. Woodbury, plaintiff above named, does hereby appeal to the United States Court of Appeals for the Ninth Circuit from the judgment of dismissal entered in this action on February 24, 1961.

KING, MILLER, ANDERSON, NASH & YERKE,

/s/ NORMAN J. WIENER

/s/ PAUL R. MEYER,
Attorneys for Plaintiff.

[Endorsed]: Filed April 11, 1961.

[Title of District Court and Cause.]

BOND FOR COSTS ON APPEAL

Bond No. B-87629

Know All Men By These Presents

That we, Ray B. Woodbury, as Principal, and United Pacific Insurance Company, a corporation organized under the laws of the State of Washington, having an office and usual place of business in the City of Portland, County of Multnomah, State of Oregon, as Surety, are held and firmly bound unto the United States of America, defendant above named, in the sum of Two Hundred Fifty Dollars ($250), lawful money of the United States of America, for which payment well and truly to be made unto said United States of America, we bind ourselves, our heirs, legal representatives, successors and assigns, jointly and severally, firmly by these presents.

Whereas, in an action pending in the United States District Court for the District of Oregon between said Ray B. Woodbury, as plaintiff, and United States of America, as defendant, a judgment of dismissal was rendered against Ray B. Woodbury, as plaintiff, on February 24, 1961, and Ray B. Woodbury having filed a notice of appeal from said judgment of dismissal to reverse said judgment of dismissal on appeal to the United States Court of Appeals for the Ninth Circuit,

Now Therefore, the condition of this obligation is such that, if Ray B. Woodbury shall pay all costs if the appeal is dismissed or if the judgment of dismissal is affirmed, or such costs as the appellate court may award if the judgment of dismissal is modified, then the above obligation shall be void; otherwise it shall remain in full force and effect.

In Witness Whereof Ray B. Woodbury, as Principal, has hereunto set his hand and seal and United Pacific Insurance Company, as Surety, has caused its name to be subscribed hereto by its representatives thereunto duly authorized and its corporate seal to be hereunto affixed by its attorney-in-fact, this 11th day of April, 1961.

/s/ RAY B. WOODBURY,
Principal.

[Seal]   UNITED PACIFIC INSUR-
ANCE COMPANY,

By /s/ C. H. WERTON, JR.,
Attorney-in-Fact.

Countersigned:

D. K. MacDONALD & COMPANY,
Oregon, Inc.,

By /s/ C. O. TATE,
Resident Agent.

[Endorsed]: Filed April 11, 1961.

[Title of District Court and Cause.]

CERTIFICATE AND ORDER

Whereas the court entered its judgment of dismissal in the above-entitled action on February 24, 1961, dismissing plaintiff's complaint and the cause therein set forth, and

Whereas defendant's counterclaim herein is still pending before the court, and

Whereas the court in entering said judgment of dismissal on February 24, 1961, intended to make said judgment of dismissal final pursuant to the requirements of Rule 54(b) F.R.C.P.; now, therefore, the above-entitled court hereby makes the following

Finding

There is no just reason for delay in the entry of final judgment on plaintiff's complaint and the following

Direction

An entry of final judgment on plaintiff's complaint shall be made herein.

Based upon the foregoing finding and direction it is hereby

Ordered and Adjudged that said judgment of dismissal be and the same hereby is made final, and it is further

Ordered and Adjudged that this certificate and order be entered nunc pro tunc to appear of record as of February 24, 1961, which is the date when said judgment of dismissal was originally made and entered.

Dated this 21st day of April, 1961.

/s/ JOHN F. KILKENNY,
District Judge.

[Endorsed]: Filed April 21, 1961.

———

United States District Court
District of Oregon

Civil No. 9403

RAY B. WOODBURY,

Plaintiff,

vs.

UNITED STATES OF AMERICA,

Defendant.

Before: Honorable John F. Kilkenny,
District Judge.

Appearances:

MESSRS. NORMAN J. WIENER and
PAUL R. MEYER,
Of Attorneys for Plaintiff.

MR. C. E. LUCKEY,
> United States Attorney, District of Oregon, Appearing in behalf of the United States of America, and

MR. GEORGE W. PRYOR,
> Appearing in behalf of Housing and Home Finance Agency.

TRANSCRIPT OF PROCEEDINGS

December 12, 1960

The Court: Gentlemen, I will ask you to give your ideas here on how we would proceed this morning. Then I will try to outline procedure for you, just so we get your thoughts on that.

Mr. Wiener: If the Court please, I might bring the Court up to date on a conference Mr. Luckey and I have had in the past few days to attempt to give to you what we think the procedure is.

We recognize the complexities of this case, and I am sure the Court in view of the voluminous file has recognized many of the complex problems. In view of that, it would appear to both counsel for the Government and ourselves that the difficulty in this case is transmitting to the Court in some abbreviated form facts which have taken some three years to develop.

We have, therefore, gone through the chronological listing contained in the pre-trial order, in numerous instances gone through the chronological listing of the pre-trail order which contains some

1180 different chronological items starting from 1949 and going into 1958. We have taken from the files of the Government, primarily from the Government, these eleven hundred and some-odd items, and they are now in a file drawer before Mrs. Mundorff's desk. So out of the voluminous files the first thing we have done, we have abstracted those. [2*]

In a further attempt to bring this in focus, counsel for plaintiff—that is, myself and Mr. Meyer—have numbered the particular documents which we think bring into focus the issues that are involved in this case. I believe Mr. Luckey has done the same thing.

With respect to those, I would say that we have approximately 150 out of eleven hundred some-odd items which we think bring into focus the issue that is before this Court on this segregated issue. So from the plaintiff's standpoint it would appear that there are three phases to the trial on this issue. One is to present to this Court almost some 150-odd exhibits, part of the records of the Government. That is the first phase.

The second phase, your Honor, would be short oral testimony which will add some to the exhibits but are primarily for the benefit of putting certain witnesses before the Court so that the Court may ask questions that he may have.

Those witnesses are Mr. Woodbury, the plaintiff in this case seated at my left, Mr. Herbert Hardy, attorney, who is not in the courtroom but

---

*Page numbering appearing at top of page of original Reporter's Transcript of Record.

who is available upon telephone call, and Mr. Harry Langton sitting in the far corner over here in the front of the Bench, who was the Project Manager from the period of 1954. The oral testimony would not, in my opinion, take very long.

The third phase of it, and we have discussed it [3] with Mr. Luckey, is the reading into the record from depositions of the testimony of witnesses of the United States; that is, various employees of various agencies involved here, which was done over the course of several years in pretrial proceedings.

Now, I believe, your Honor, that that would be the extent, certainly the extent of the plaintiff's case. I think Mr. Luckey intends to do the same thing, and I think that his procedure is the same. I will let Mr. Luckey speak for himself on that phase of it.

The Court: Mr. Luckey?

Mr. Luckey: I think our procedure, your Honor, would follow the same general pattern. Of course, we would point out that there are some documents that are here from Mr. Woodbury's files, Columbia Supply's files and Aleutian Homes' files. There are some numerous depositions that have been taken both of the parties on both sides, and as to Government's witnesses as well, we of course with reference to Government's witnesses will necessarily be guided very largely, because we believe it is a documentary case primarily, upon what the witnesses for plaintiff may testify. We would not have more than two or three witnesses, your Honor. [4]

Mr. Wiener: Thank you.

We have prepared, your Honor, a chart for the sole purpose of assisting the Court in identifying the various agencies and various parties involved in this case.

First of all, it is my understanding of why we are here this morning is that the Court by its order of November 4th directed that this case proceed to trial on the segregated issues of, one, whether or not the Government could be a fiduciary, and, two, whether or not the Government, [8] assuming it is under the facts of this case, was a fiduciary.

On the first question, it would appear to us that this is a question of law which we have amply raised and searched in various briefs heretofore submitted to the Court, so I will not attempt to argue the law unless the Court specifically requests. [9]

The Court: You may call your first witness or start with your first exhibit, Mr. Wiener.

Mr. Wiener: I assume it is perfectly all right to introduce these exhibits without the necessity of having a witness on the witness stand?

The Court: That is correct.

Mr. Wiener: At this time, your Honor, we have already stipulated, Counsel and I have already stipulated that certain exhibits may be introduced

in the trial, but for the record we will now introduce or offer into evidence Exhibits 1 to 1176
of the two file drawers that are in front of the
Bench. They are numbered; the exhibits have been
marked. We now offer those in evidence pursuant
to the stipulation.

The Court: I would ask now, before Counsel
responds to that, whether on this issue there is any
claim, and I understand differently, but I want to
get it straight here. Is there any claim that all of
these exhibits have relevancy or materiality in so
far as this issue is concerned?

Mr. Wiener: No; from the standpoint of the
plaintiff [63] the answer is No.

The Court: Then I would suggest this: I would
suggest that you offer in evidence only those at
this particular time. Now if you want to offer them
just for the purpose of what may happen later in
the trial, we can do that, but as to the exhibits
which you feel are relevant and material, only
those should be offered at this time. I do not want
to have just a blanket offer, something that might
be binding on the Court, something that someone
might pick out on a question of appeal on either
side if my decision on this issue would be appealed.
Are you in a position to do that now?

Mr. Wiener: Yes, your Honor. I would like the
record to show that I have already stipulated things
that can be done, but, of course, that is subject to
the Court's approval. As far as I am concerned,
we will have picked out the documents which we
think have relevancy.

I might point out that it has been agreed that the chronological statement which is the basis for these 1176 documents has been agreed upon as chronological.

The Court: That is correct. That is in the pre-trial order.

Mr. Wiener: That is in the pre-trial order, and, in addition to that, there are some agreed facts in the pre-trial order which I have attempted to summarize.

The Court: That is true. I have read the [64] Agreed Facts, not once but twice. I do not pretend to remember them all, however; but if you would proceed that way, Mr. Wiener, that will be fine.

Mr. Weiner: Thank you. At this time, your Honor, I would then like to introduce as—or offer into evidence as Exhibit 1177, which has not yet been marked and merely, your Honor, for the purpose of assisting the Court, not for conclusion—that is, the document is no evidence in and of itself but merely as an aid to the Court, the chart which I referred to in opening statement.

* * *

The Court: Is there any objection, Mr. Luckey?

Mr. Luckey: No objection, your Honor, for that [65] purpose.

The Court: Those numbers will be assigned to those exhibits, and the exhibits are admitted.

(Chart previously referred to and marked as as Plaintiff's Exhibit 1177 for Identification

and photograph from Kodiak Mirror dated November 26, 1960, previously marked Plaintiff's
Exhibit 1178 for Identification, were thereupon received in evidence.)

Mr. Wiener: Another point which Counsel and
I have discussed which perhaps should be brought
up at this time, there are again numerous interrogatories and requests for admissions and answers,
and so on, which are part of the Court's files. It
is my understanding of the practice that for this
to become a part of the transcript of the record
they should be offered in evidence. I have discussed
it with Counsel as to whether or not we are concerned with any of them. They may become part
of the transcript of the record of this case, and
we now offer all the interrogatories and requests
for admissions and the answers to the interrogatories, all the answers and admissions. There are
seven in number.

The Court: Then I assume if they are to be
received that the Court's attention will be directed
to that portion [66] of those interrogatories and
the answers that may have relevancy or materiality
on this issue. Otherwise, I do not want to fill the
record with that material. [67]

* * *

Mr. Wiener: On Page 70, the fourth date,
March 31, 1952, from the Secretary of the Navy
Whitehair——

The Court: If you would read the number off,
we can get that.

Mr. Wiener: 115, and it is Whitehair to Richards, Whitehair being the Secretary of the Navy and Richards being the Commissioner of FHA. This is replying to prior correspondence mentioned from Bettinger indicating that a new sponsor was in the picture and reaffirming prior certifications by the Navy that they need these houses up here and that conditions have not changed since 1951 and, well, reaffirming the need for this project at least as far as the Navy saw it.

Mr. Luckey: No comment, your Honor.

The Court: Admitted.

(Document above referred to, [79] previously marked Plaintiff's Exhibit 115/48 for Identification, was thereupon received in evidence.) [80]

Mr. Wiener: The next document is the following one dated June 12th, a memorandum from Morse to Seward.

I might comment that, since Counsel has mentioned it, Mr. Morse was employed by HHFA. Brice Mortgage was in this picture. Mr. Morse at about this time resigned from HHFA or apparently decided to resign from HHFA to go to work for Brice. He prepared a full document apparently just setting forth his position and why he was going to work for Brice.

The only thing we claim, the reason we think it is important here is because he reviewed in minute detail the basis for this loan, the interest of the Government in it, the fact that—the whole history of it in 1951 and '52, what led to its signing, the fact that in his opinion this loan was perfectly justified under all proper procedures. He points out that the loan conditions are more strict than any of those approved by the Administrator under the Alaska Housing program.

The purpose of this is not to justify Mr. Morse one way or the other. It doesn't have anything to do with that, but he set forth in some chronological order what had happened, what had developed and what had transpired during these three years.

This man, incidentally, was the man closest [96] to the project as far as HHFA was concerned up until the change in administration here. You see, we had a new President come in in 1952, which made changes in this over-all program. This is No. 289.

Incidentally, Morse had nothing to do with this project after he went to work with Brice. That was a condition of his leaving this agency, that he not participate in Brice's participation.

Mr. Luckey: No comment, your Honor. It speaks for itself.

The Court: Admitted.

> (Document above referred to, previously marked Plaintiff's Exhibit 289/A2 for Identification, was thereupon received in [97] evidence.)

Mr. Wiener: Next page, 125, letter of January 27, 1954, the second January 27th, from Hazeltine to Cake, Jaureguy & Hardy—just to deviate from what has been now brought before the Court, and I do not think there is any dispute about it— this Completion Agreement was drafted prior to January 27th in Washington, D. C. We won't go into who drafted it or what the terms are, but, anyway, it was drafted, which led to a letter on January 27th from Hazeltine to Mr. Hardy who has now for the first time been brought into this picture, which says, "The attached Completion Agreement * * * has been the subject of negotiation between Aleutian Homes, Inc., and representatives of this Agency during the past week.

"The terms of this Agreement appear generally acceptable to us; however, prior to formal submission for approval by the Administrator it will be necessary for you to obtain the following: —" Now this was on January 27, 1954, and these are some of the larger things of the items; that Woodbury can put up funds in the approximate sum of $60,-000 for overhead; that evidence be produced that the [112] Completion Agreement will not render the permanent first mortgages uninsurable by the FHA, in other words, that they won't take the FHA out of this picture; and that also satisfactory evidence that this Completion Agreement will not adversely affect the sale of the permanent first mortgages to FNMA.

So Hazeltine's concern is at this time that Woodbury put up $60,000 for overhead and that the long-term commitments not be affected adversely one way or the other by this document.

Mr. Luckey: We think that is significant, your Honor, because if HHFA was going to keep these commitments alive or reasonably to keep them alive, they would not have been concerned about providing overhead funds for that.

The Court: Admitted.

(Document above referred to, previously marked Plaintiff's Exhibit 512/4 for Identification, was thereupon received in [113] evidence.)

Mr. Wiener: The next document is quoted in full on page 134. It is April 5, 1954, Hazeltine to Cole.

This is a note from the second in command to the No. 1 man, Exhibit 562.

This document provides a resume of the action that has been taken up to this particular time, obviously attempting to inform the top man as to what has happened; sets forth an analysis of the complete projects; suggests modification of certain documents; analyzes the costs of completion, analyzes the method of taking out the interim loan by the long-term loan, and makes a recommendation as to what is to be done; points out that,

"If the proposed Completion Agreement is placed in operation, Woodbury will withdraw from all active participation. A Project Manager and a Project Superintendent will be selected satisfac-

tory to the Agency, and they will be [128] responsible for all operations until our loan is repaid. In
addition, Woodbury is required to pay all overhead expenses, including extraordinary expense of
HHFA personnel, and there is now in the hands
of Mr. L. R. Durkee, Area Representative, a cash-
ier's check covering funds supplied by Woodbury
in the amount of $60,000 for these purposes.''

I am reading that from this document.

This, from our viewpoint, represents this particular—well, the Agency's views on this matter at
this particular time, and we can see a recommendation which is acted upon here in a few documents
later.

Mr. Luckey: This is an internal memoranda,
your Honor. Mr. Wiener calls him second in command. Actually, he was not second in command.
Mr. Cole was the Administrator. Mr. Hazeltine was
the Administrator of the Community Facilities Administration. To say he was a different type of
administrator as being second in command—he had
the command function of delegated authorities in
connection with this particular project, but he was
writing to his superior who had not delegated the
authority to authorize the further disbursements
under the loan after default, and the memorandum
points out that there are many conditions related
to the proposed further disbursements and that it
was worked out [129] with Mr. Herbert Hardy who
contacted the Agency in January, presenting plans
which, after some revision and conference with this

office, appeared to be workable. That is the substance of the memorandum.

It is significant to note here the understanding of the plan by Mr. Hazeltine:

"The plan also provides that, subsequent to the repayment of our loan, the remaining non-lienable creditors together with R. B. Woodbury and yourself will agree upon a Trustee who will be appointed to supervise liquidation of all other creditor claims remaining."

It indicated after HHFA's loan was paid there would be still other creditors, and other creditors and Woodbury would have to get together and name a Trustee if this plan were carried to completion.

The Court: Admitted.

    (Document, Memo from Cole to Hazeltine, April 5, 1954, previously marked Plaintiff's Exhibit 562/A-4 for Identification, was received in evidence.) [130]

* * *

Mr. Wiener: Now, your Honor, we come to the Completion Agreement itself. We are finally there on page 142, and this document 583/1-140, and this is the signed document. [136]

I am sure we could make many comments on these. I call the Court's attention—you do not have this in front of you, but I call the Court's attention——

Mr. Meyer: Here are two copies.

The Court: There is a copy attached.

Mr. Meyer: Which is the original which can be handed up to the Clerk.

Mr. Wiener: The Government is referred to in this document as the Lender, top of page 2. They refer to the "Housing and Home Finance Administrator, hereinafter called 'The Lender.'" The document is not signed by the Housing and Home Finance Administrator.

The Court: There is no place for the signature?

Mr. Wiener: There is no place for the signature.

The Court: The parties have a paragraph in there which shows the rather definite intention that it was to be signed. It was never so intended that they were to sign; is that correct?

Mr. Wiener: Well, that would be my interpretation of that language, that it was not contemplated that the Housing and Home Finance Administrator would be signatory, would sign this.

The Court: Or any other governmental agency, such as the FHA or the FNMA?

Mr. Wiener: I agree with the [137] interpretation.

The document provides that the Lender shall do certain things (bottom of page 4) including the deferment of collection of interest due under his loan. I call to the Court's attention that the language used in Paragraph 11(c)——

The Court: How do you construe that language there, Mr. Wiener?

"This Agreement is subject to compliance with the following conditions by Lender "——:

Mr. Wiener: How do I construe it?

The Court: Yes. I have this question: The Lender, does that indicate to you in any way that the Lender didn't have to do it; that he might do it, but that he could back away from the agreement at any time, or he didn't have to go ahead with the agreement as such?

The language is so peculiar, "This Agreement is subject to compliance with the following conditions by Lender." Even though the Lender is not a party, it does not say, "The Lender shall," or "The Lender will."

Now in the subdivisions that language is used, but in the general condition there, "This Agreement is subject to compliance with the following conditions by Lender," well, if the Lender didn't do that, then what happened to the agreement? I know we are not going to argue that out now, but that is one of the principal things here, but if you [138] have something, it would seem to me all the way through that this is rather peculiar language in the agreement.

Mr. Wiener: You have asked my opinion, have I, and I will just briefly state it.

The Court: Yes.

Mr. Wiener: My opinion, this was a document which, for all practical purposes, was a contract between everybody that is stated here, including the Lender. This is my opinion. It is true that this document was not signed—there is no question about that—by the Government, but it was accepted in that language by a letter which we will shortly come to. It speaks in the traditional form of an obligation on the part of a party to a document.

The Court: That particular language, that is what I am inquiring about. To me, it seems that that language actually modifies or is a modification of what is the language which is usually customarily used in order to bind a person.

"This Agreement is subject to compliance with the following conditions by the Lender." Let us look at it this way just for the moment: Suppose that we were not in the position that we are in there, but we are attempting to secure financing from some other source, and suppose we are getting that financing from a bank rather than from the Government and then we had that language, "This Agreement is subject to compliance with the following conditions by [139] the Bank," and you had mentioned the name of the bank.

What is running through my mind is what that language would mean when you apply it, the circumstances there, if you were starting on a new agreement. Would you then feel that there was an obligation of the bank to go ahead and comply with (a) and through the others there? That would be (a), (b), (c) and (d).

Mr. Wiener: Well, my answer, as I would understand it, would be that this language that you have just quoted, "This Agreement is subject to compliance," is another way for saying that this agreement is subject to being accepted by the bank in your hypothetical upon the ground that it will do certain things or, stating it a little differently, that this agreement will have no effect unless the bank in your hypothetical agrees that it will in exchange for the rights it has got herein, will agree to these other items which are spelled out, (a), (b), (c) and (d). In other words, I think——

The Court: In other words, you think, Mr. Wiener, that actually in construing the whole transaction here that there is something missing from the agreement as such?

Mr. Wiener: Well, I would say with all due— I would think that it is not carefully drafted in the sense that it expresses fully what the parties intended at this time, but I think this is in the nature, your Honor—that these [140] people who have signed—it is in effect an offer, in legal effect, in effect an offer to the Government which, for reasons which are not clear in the record—I don't know why they didn't sign this because they signed the Building Loan Agreement. They signed the Disbursing Agreement. I mean, the Housing and Home Finance Administrator signed——

The Court: I might be advised on this better if I reviewed the briefs again. It is some time since I have been over them.

I know it is indicated in some of the correspondence here some place that as a matter of law the Government felt they couldn't sign such an agreement.

Mr. Wiener: I think it is indicated somewhere in here that they felt they couldn't sign it.

The Court: That is in the last paragraph of the agreement as such.

Mr. Wiener: Yes, your Honor, but that then becomes a question of law whether they could in fact sign at all. It appears from our reading of the various housing statutes under which they are authorized, that they had authority to do anything they wanted. They had a revolving fund set up. They did have authority, but they maybe felt that one of the Government attorneys advised them they couldn't sign this document—I don't know—but the legal effect is—and I cannot emphasize this too strongly—that we believe this [141] document created a status whether it in fact—we are not suing here for breach of contract—it created a status, and whether in fact or not there was a binding legal contract for which we could sue for the breach is not—we have not raised the question because what did happen here, as I say, it created a status which was acted upon by the subsequent acts here which indicated a certain position or a certain relationship or duty on the part of the Government. It is an attempt to bring this all up to date and is certainly what finally happened.

I think if the question was whether there was a breach of contract, that our position would be that this was an offer to the Government which was supported by a letter of about May 21st which we will be coming to very shortly, which in fact thereby made the Government, whether they signed it or not, a party to the contract, and this is not foreign to the law at all, because in lots of Court of Claims cases where these contract cases generally arise, the Courts clearly say—I mean the Court of Claims has said in many cases that you can have an implied contract in law whether in fact there is an express contract, but I don't think we have to reach that—at least from our theory we do not have to reach the problem of whether in fact this was a binding legal contract. We do think it created a status, a relationship which the Government operated under [142] thereafter, assumed certain rights, obtained certain rights including the payment of moneys, which created certain duties. I mean, that is our position.

The Court: I understand your position.

Mr. Wiener: In any event, this document does provide that the Construction Superintendent shall be appointed and acceptable to Lender.

There is discussion in here as to the overhead agreement. I started out to point out that the, that at the top of page 4 of the Completion Agreement Woodbury agrees to execute and deliver to Lender an agreement to provide necessary overhead expenses for the completion of the project. Now, the language, "for the completion of the project," has been the subject of a great deal of interpretation by a lot of people, but I do call then for the Court's attention paragraph 11(c), your Honor, on page 5, where, "Lender will defer collection of interest due under loan until completion of project."

Now, that is an ambiguous term, but I think that the only proper and fair interpretation of it, looking at the status of the parties in April, 1953—

April, 1954, they expected to complete this project in October of 1954. This was the estimated completion date. The interest was to be held until October, 1954. The overhead was not to be paid until October, 1954. [143]

Now, why I emphasize this and I point out that the same language was used for both of these paragraphs is because there is much reference in 1955 and in 1956 to the fact that Woodbury in the year 1956 has not paid $15,000 for his overhead. This was in 1956, and the Government's position apparently was at that time that the $15,000 obligation continued until the loan was recast.

I emphasize this, that could not have been within the contemplation of the parties on either side because when they use the term, "completion of agreement," they must have been contemplating the physical completion of the project, not the recasting of the loan or the taking out of the loan, and much of the problem that developed here, as you will subsequently see, is because of the fact that somebody in the Government got mad at Woodbury because he didn't put up $15,000 for overhead in the year 1956, which we do not think can be read into the documents.

In any event, this is an important document, there is no question about it, and it has problems of construction that we differ on.

We would offer that in evidence, 583/1-140.

Mr. Luckey: If this be an offer, your Honor, which creates a status on the part of the Administrator, I certainly submit that the built-in safeguards of the offer to induce the Lender to make further disbursements cannot be read out [144] of the document and the agreement.

Paragraph 13 says that the obligations of any party signatory hereto shall not be released, discharged, or in any way affected.

If it is the position of the plaintiff that a party signatory by some operation other than signing this paragraph, this paragraph there mentions, "* * * or in any way affected, nor shall claimants or other parties signatory have any rights or recourse against Lender," and by a built-in provision the Lender is really deemed a signatory, and this should be influential in determining our obligation as Lender, "* * * shall have any rights or recourse against Lender by reason of any action Lender may take or omit to take under the foregoing powers; nor by reason of any action taken by Lender which in its opinion may be necessary to keep said project free from liens."

And Paragraph 14 is particularly significant as setting the stage for the early documents, the context in which this inducement was made:

"All provisions and requirements of loan documents executed in connection with loan by Lender to Owner shall remain in full force and effect, except as expressly modified;"

Now, the express modification concerned the extension of maturity dates, deferment of interest, and [145] things of that kind, and all the provisions of the trust deed would remain in force; all the provisions of the Loan Agreement, all of the

provisions of guarantees, and, as I pointed out in
the letter that has previously been introduced here
within the last few minutes, the Lender would not
accept any other situation in the language of the
letter to Mr. Durkee, concerning the Pacific-Alaska
Contractors. The objection that there should not be
any recourse against the Lender, that is what they
are talking about right here.

Then in paragraph 18 the Court has pointed out
and is aware, "No provision has been made for
execution of this document by the various Federal,
State and Territorial Agencies who are Claimants
or by the Bank of California since the national
banking laws and laws and regulations affecting
such agencies do not authorize the execution of such
Agreement."

There is no ambiguity in that language on the
part of, in the first instance, the people who are
offering this inducement to discuss disbursement of
loan procedures. "It is understood that either a
written or oral approval of this Agreement will
be obtained from them, if possible."

Mr. Wiener suggests there is a lot of power on
the part of the HHFA to do a lot of things here
with reference to signing an agreement, and so
forth. I suggest if there were any power of that
nature it would be vested in [146] the Administrator, and any writing in that type of situation
would be directed all the way by citing clause of
the statute with regard to an Administrator, but
that does not bind the United States which in this
situation would not be a party defendant properly.

If there can be read into these paragraphs any fiduciary situation or acceptance of a fiduciary obligation by the Government expressly, I fail to see how any party, be it the Government or otherwise your Honor, can by agreement protect itself against the imposition of a fiduciary obligation upon it. It couldn't be clearer that this was not the intent of the HHFA, not the intent of the United States, and in the absence of overreaching or undue imposing of evidence that shows attributes of a fiduciary relationship, it escapes me how in the face of these particular clauses in this Completion Agreement it can be asserted in good faith here that there was a fiduciary obligation in the contemplation of the HHFA here.

Now, if it is by operation of law, certainly there has been nothing in the pleadings to show or to suggest any overreaching, any unfair action, or anything of that kind. The only thing that has been alleged here is that we favored ourselves as a creditor by taking this foreclosure action really, and that, of course, is in the contemplation of the entire Completion Agreement. [147]

The Lender in order to disburse this additional loan, had to have certain safeguards and, certainly, a lender in protecting himself in that manner in disbursing the balance of the loan couldn't by that alone, even though he had some safeguards against disbursements, become a fiduciary.

Everybody understood. All the creditors, all the signatories to this document which Mr. Woodbury saw on several occasions and his attorney, Mr.

Hardy, understood that the Lender was not abro-
gating its original security documents and not accepting any responsibilities over and above that
that they did have originally, which would affect
their security documents before.

I think that the agreement is important. I think
it is a critical document in the entire case. There
are others to support it, but they were the same
type of exculpatory language so far as the Administrator is concerned, and they go right through
supporting the proposition that there was not any
fiduciary relationship.

The Court: The exhibit is admitted.

(Document, Completion Agreement, previously marked Plaintiff's Exhibit 583/1-140 for
Identification, was thereupon received in evidence.) [148]

Mr. Wiener: On page 175, the middle of the
page, January 31, 1955, a letter from Cole, the top
man in HHFA, to the Secretary of Navy.

Now a comment is made in our brief about [180]
this particular point so I call it to the Court's attention. This was, in effect, a statement from one
top Government agency to another one offering, as
we see it, to sell this project to the Navy. The comment is made that the project was constructed in
compliance with certain FHA requirements at a
cost of approximately five and a half million dollars and FHA has placed an appraised valuation
of $5,892,800 on the completed project.

I mentioned this in the course of opening statement. The comment is made that this would be advantageous to the Government to permit this agency to further its program of orderly liquidation of its investments in Alaska if the Navy would be interested in purchasing for its own use this housing project.

The Court: This was before a default was declared, or was there a default at this time?

Mr. Wiener: In the interim loan?

The Court: Yes.

Mr. Wiener: No, there was no default at this particular time, and the FHA and Fanny Mae commitments were in full force and effect at this particular moment, but its release of commitments is June 1, 1955, your Honor, so we are talking about now in January.

Mr. Luckey: There was always a default, your Honor, under the theory of the United States, in the HHFA—— [181]

The Court: I know your theory on this, that the default continued even under the Completion Agreement.

Mr. Luckey: That is right, and, as pointed out here by the Project Manager and his attorneys in the previous document that is in here, there was a $394,000 deficit plus $328,000 principal that they couldn't meet, so the Completion Agreement was not in a position to be at that time—it couldn't be consummated, and this is only an explanatory letter to examine details under which a transfer might be accomplished. It does not offer the property. It talks about the possibility of sale.

Mr. Wiener: Well, my comment on Mr. Luckey's comments is that the terms of this short-term note were extended on two different occasions, once for six months and once for four months, beyond the due date on the short-term note, and I do not understand Counsel's comments that the note for a short-term loan was in default at this particular time because the record indicates clearly that there were two extensions of due date on that note.

Mr. Luckey: They did extend it from time to time, your Honor; that is true.

The Court: 802 is admitted.

> (Letter to Secretary of the Navy from Housing and Home Finance Agency, January 31, 1955, previously marked [182] Plaintiff's Exhibit 802/65 for Identification, was thereupon received in evidence.) [183]

* * *

Mr. Wiener: The next exhibit, your Honor, is probably one of the key documents in the case. It is from anybody's standpoint. It is on the bottom of page 179, Document of March 7, 1955. It is from Hazeltine, who is now head of the CFA, to his superior, Cole, the head of HHFA, and this document is quoted in full in this pre-trial order. The posture of this letter must be considered that at this particular time FHA had denied the application for the increase in commitment. Just a short three weeks prior to this date, this same Hazeltine had said, "We are now going to proceed with the recasting and taking out of the mortgages," long-term [195] mortgages, which on this particular date the commitments were still in existence. So, of course, as Mr. Luckey says, this document speaks for itself, but we believe that this led to the decision to abandon the commitments for whatever valid reason might have been set forth therein.

I call particular reference to the Court's observation of the language quoted on page 182, the middle of the page, beginning with the paragraph, "This recommendation——"

The Court: Yes.

Mr. Wiener: The conclusion and recommendation is based upon the statement there that it is superfluous for one agency under the same head to go to the trouble and expense of transferring this short-term loan over to the long-term loan despite the legal commitments that were then in existence.

Now this decision, your Honor, is in the Government files. It is no knowledge out here to Langton, no knowledge to Woodbury or to Aleutian Homes, but this was the decision that was reached, and at a subsequent date here it was approved by Cole and thereafter followed.

As a matter of fact, this original document that I have in my hand here signed by Hazeltine has penciled or in ink on the bottom of it, 3-21-55 the date, "O.K. to follow recommended procedure using first alternative plan above described." And the first alternative plan above described [196] is that at Paragraph 1 on the bottom of page 182 which says,

"Continuation for a period of approximately six months of the present operation, whereby Aleutian Homes, Inc., is continued as a corporation but under complete control and supervision of the Administrator. Should this seasoning period develop the fact that the project has possibilities of normal payout a repayment program could be worked out and congressional enactment requested to transfer either to FNMA or FHA. There is a further possibility that the Navy's interest in this project might materialize in the form of an outright purchase."

I do not want the Court to misunderstand or Mr. Luckey. We do not question either the good or bad faith. It appeared to be perhaps a sensible procedure at this particular time to do this, but, nevertheless, this was the decision that was made and which was followed, carried out, as we will point out by subsequent correspondence.

Mr. Meyer: May I make one comment about where this document comes from, your Honor. You will notice at the end of the description in the pre-trial order it refers to having come originally from Exhibit 1, Document 207.

Exhibit 1 of the pre-trial order was what [197] was called a collateral file, and your Honor will note that all the contract documents from the loan authorization, the note, the deed of trust, the various construction contracts, all the contract documents are kept by the Government in what they call the collateral file.

This was considered apparently by the Government of sufficient importance as a contract document in the fact that this was placed and numbered in that collateral file, and that is where it was found. It is Document No. 207 in Exhibit 1 to the pre-trial order, which was this collateral file.

Mr. Luckey: I think it will be an unusual day when the file clerk will determine the course of litigation of this kind, your Honor. However, the document itself is concerned with whether there should be foreclosure at this time or some further attempt to work out a financing structure that will prevent foreclosure.

There is a lot of language in here that Mr. Hazeltine used, words of control, and so forth, to influence the Administrator who, you will recall in the early documents, didn't exactly, wasn't exactly happy about this loan when it was found in the office, but he anyway continued to carry this project without foreclosure, and that is the context in which the Commissioner of Community Facilities who had been close to this project came to [198] completion under the direction of the Project Manager who was representative of Aleutian Homes in Kodiak, trying to influence his superior to adopt this course of continued extension of loan.

The Court: 832/A-1-207 is admitted. [199]

* * *

Mr. Wiener: Page 185, second from the top, March 28, 1955, memorandum from Tyler of

FNMA to the files, in which this Loan Manager of Fanny Mae indicated he had had meetings with various representatives or with the representative of the HHFA to discuss this over-all thing. The comments on the discussion are contained in this memorandum.

One of the comments is made that the question was asked if Fanny Mae and FHA would be willing to refund any part of their fees. You see, by this time extensive commitment of fees had been paid to Fanny Mae and FHA, and his comment was as indicated there in the middle:

"This question was posed on the basis that the HHFA Administrator might elect to hold his blanket mortgage."

Our comment is that at this time with the increase in commitment of FHA funds having been denied, there was [201] discussion at the Washington level of the possibility of making the short-term loan a long-term blanket mortgage, which would permit the orderly retirement of its payment as distinguished from default status that it was about to be under.

Mr. Luckey: Just a discussion, your Honor, not binding on anyone.

Mr. Wiener: On the same page, the next document——

The Court: No. 849/49-4 is admitted.

(Memorandum re Aleutian Homes, Inc., dated March 28, 1955, from A. C. Tyler, Loan Manager, previously marked Plaintiff's Exhibit 849/49-4 for Identification, was thereupon received in evidence.)

Mr. Wiener: The next document is March 28, 1955, a correspondence now from Hazeltine in Washington to Langton out here in Portland. Discussion is had with respect to proposed individual mortgages, and he advised that it would be desirable to notify the creditors that the commitments were to be abandoned, and it contains a proposed form of letter to be sent under Langton's signature as Project Manager to the various creditors, including Woodbury.

This particular letter I have here of Exhibit 850 contains this proposed letter to be sent by Langton to these creditors. [202]

At this particular time, your Honor, the decision had been made to abandon the commitments.

Mr. Luckey: This is a proposal for a letter to the creditors indicating that the commitments might be abandoned under certain conditions, and that if certain conditions exist as of a particular time certain action might follow. There is no commitment of positive action in that letter.

The Court: No. 850/20 is admitted.

(Letter to Harry M. Langton from Hazeltine, March 28, 1955, with attached enclosures, previously marked Plaintiff's Exhibit 850/20 for Identification, was thereupon received in evidence.)

Mr. Wiener: On page 186, March 29, 1955, from Hazeltine to Cole. It goes into the details of the

Bank of California loan which was listed on the Completion Agreement, your Honor, at $150,000. As I recall, it was to be paid in two of four stages.

This letter comments that the bank appears in the Completion Agreement among "Stage 3" creditors. The comment is made that the bank was not signatory to the Completion Agreement.

The comment is made to Cole by Hazeltine that a letter for issuance to creditors by the Project Manager has been forwarded to Portland. [203]

Mr. Luckey: No comment.

The Court: That is No. what?

Mr. Wiener: 851.

The Court: It is admitted.

> (Memorandum of March 29, 1955, Hazeltine to Cole, previously marked Plaintiff's Exhibit 851/A-20 for Identification, was thereupon received in evidence.) [204]

Mr. Wiener: Page 187 at the bottom of the page, No. 859, Langton to Hazeltine, in which he says he has now reviewed this draft of this proposed letter that came to him from Hazeltine, and he has got a comment; Langton's comment is that an addition be made to the end of the letter which would indicate—in which he forwards a draft of a revised letter which he suggests he be authorized to forward out to [205] creditors. We will see the final form as it comes out in a few minutes.

Mr. Wiener: The principal change on this was the addition of certain language in the last paragraph which has to do with the commitments.

This was a proposed letter to the creditors of this project:

"The FHA and FNMA commitments will be surrendered to avoid the expense of closing permanent first mortgages and extension fees, and if by October 31, 1955, it appears that the project has a reasonable chance of financial success, a refinancing plan looking toward long-range amortization of the Administrator's loan and repayment of other claims will be proposed by the Housing and Home Finance Administrator." [206]

Now we emphasize that because this was suggested, that this language be added. It was approved and it was sent out in that form which, at least to our minds, indicates that all through this period of time here it was contemplated by everybody concerned that this so-called refinancing plan would be by the HHFA if these commitments are released. It was known by everybody at this particular time that there wasn't any other alternative; only the Government would be in a position to refinance a project in Kodiak, Alaska, of this magnitude.

The application for a loan that had been filed in November, 1952, indicated every private source of funds had been exhausted. Everybody knew, at least it is our claim everybody knew if there was going to be any refinancing done, it had to be done

through a proposal made by the Washington offices of our Government.

Mr. Meyer: May I just clarify one minor point.

On page 186 of the pre-trial order, going back
to the last paragraph of what is Exhibit 850, starting on the former page, this is the draft which
Hazeltine prepared, sent to Langton and said, "send
this to the creditors," and at the last paragraph as
set forth in the pre-trial order it contains this
paragraph which Mr. Wiener just read, and your
Honor will note that it concludes with the language
that, "* * * a refinancing plan looking toward long-
range [207] amortization of the Administrator's
loan and repayment of other claims would be proposed," what Mr. Langton added, and if your
Honor will then turn to page 188 to the paragraph
set forth about Line 23, at the end of that he added
the phrase, "by the Housing and Home Finance
Administrator."

That was the significant change that Mr. Langton made in the draft of the letter with respect to
that.

Mr. Luckey: If the Court please, that certainly
is not a commitment in the absence of a circumstance that never arose.

It was if by a certain date, October of 1955, October 31, 1955, it appears that the project has a
reasonable chance of financial success, so that
everybody realized there was a serious question
about its reasonable chance of financial success.

This letter was written to Woodbury and the

others. I mean the letter was sent, the attachment was sent to Mr. Woodbury and to others pointing out the cost of taking out these individual mortgages. The question was whether the project would justify the money, and Woodbury in the Overhead Agreement, of course, was not putting up money. The Administrator would have had to put up funds of his own in order to accomplish because of the financial condition of the project at that time.

The Court: 859/20 is admitted. [208]

(Letter from Hazeltine to Langton, April 7, 1955, previously marked Plaintiff's Exhibit 859/20 for Identification, was thereupon received in evidence.) [209]

Mr. Wiener: The next exhibit is page 193, top of the page, June 6, 1955, No. 891. It is a memorandum from the San Francisco office, Herman, where he requests authority to [219] make payment to one of the creditors, Copenhagen.

The purpose of this is to show that decisions were being made in Washington with respect to various payments of creditors.

Mr. Luckey: No comment. [220]

The Court: Have I admitted 888, 891 and 894?

The Clerk: It is 891 and 894 and then 863, the telegram, that have not been received.

The Court: They are now admitted.

(Office Memorandum, Herman to Hazeltine, June 6, 1955, previously marked Plaintiff's Exhibit 891/A-21 for Identification, was thereupon received in evidence.) [222]

Mr. Wiener: The same page, November 22, 1955, No. 983 has been assigned, and it is a letter from Hazeltine to [239] Langton in which Hazeltine on this date says, "I am interested in recasting this loan on a permanent basis with provision for amortization of principal and interest and orderly retirement of other claims."

Mr. Meyer: Your Honor, I would like to make just one comment here.

In this letter he says to Langton, "I am in agreement with your recommendation and am requesting our Division of Law to prepare the necessary documents." Now this is with respect to the four-month extension. Now this is what appears in these top letters that we have seen in which he states, "I told Langton to resubmit his proposal to four months instead of six months." Then on the surface he comes back and says on the surface, "I am not accepting your proposal." But the proposal as shown in the first instance, all the way through, is initiated by himself telling Langton, "Propose this to me, and I will accept it."

Mr. Luckey: I saw a letter from Mr. Langton saying how about continuing the situation in a status not in default, something of that kind, and to extend the maturity date under the blanket mortgage, or something. Then it will be noted in this, your Honor, Mr. Hazeltine says, "It will be appreciated if, shortly after the first of the year, you submit any ideas that you may have to meet this objective," that is, of recasting the loan on a permanent basis. **[240]**

The Court: No. 983 is admitted.

(Carbon copy of letter of November 22, 1955, Hazeltine to Langton, previously marked Plaintiff's Exhibit 983/21 for Identification, was thereupon received in evidence.) **[241]**

* * *

Mr. Wiener: The next document on the next page, 205, is from Herman to Hazeltine in which Herman now in San Francisco again makes an analysis of the operating statement, and he uses an estimated occupancy of 90 per cent.

The Court: This is on what page?

Mr. Wiener: Excuse me, on page 205, your Honor.

The Court: Herman?

Mr. Wiener: It says Emmert, but that is apparently a typographical error.

The Court: January 3rd?

Mr. Wiener: January 6th.

The Court: That should be Herman?

Mr. Wiener: That should be Herman, yes. The document I have in my hand indicates Herman rather than Emmert. It is signed by Herman also. It is Document No. 997. He makes **[244]** certain

forecasts in this document and suggests a proposed
plan. It is a three-page document and somewhat in
detail. He asks for Mr. Hazeltine's reaction to the
proposed new workable plan.

Mr. Luckey: No comment, your Honor.

The Court: No. 997 is admitted.

> (Office Memorandum of January 16, 1956,
> Herman to Hazeltine, previously marked
> Plaintiff's Exhibit 997/A-22 for Identification,
> was thereupon received in evidence.) **[245]**

* * *

Mr. Wiener: The next document is on the bottom of the page, April 4, 1956, from Hazeltine to
Herman in San Francisco in which he tells him they
are going to be out to Portland in the week of April
9th "in connection with the recasting of the present
mortgage of Aleutian Homes, Inc."

Mr. Luckey: This just gives plans and itinerary.

The Court: No. 1019 is admitted.

> (Carbon copy of letter of April 4, 1956,
> Hazeltine to Herman, previously marked Plaintiff's Exhibit 1019/22 for Identification, was
> thereupon received in evidence.)

Mr. Wiener: The next document is on page 210.
It is the document quoted in full dated April 5, 1956,
and No. 1021 has been assigned to it, and it is from
Hazeltine to Cole.

Now several times earlier I have indicated what
I consider to be certain key documents. This, your
Honor, is one of them, and the reason why it is set

out in full. This is a document which provides the
basis for certain action that was taken. It is tied
in with the memo that we discussed a few moments
ago from Herman in San Francisco where he had
provided certain information about the finances of
the project. Mr. Hazeltine comments to his superior with respect to the Completion Agreement,
what happened during the course of the Completion Agreement, the fact that if they [251] foreclosed, the claims of certain creditors who relied
upon the Completion Agreement would be eliminated. He points out if they foreclose, legal action
by the creditors to enforce their rights under the
Completion Agreement undoubtedly would follow.
In that event, the Court might find for the creditors
in view of the assurances given to the creditors in
the Completion Agreement which was accepted by
the Administrator.

Now here is somebody talking to the Administrator and the question—although I don't think it is
material, your Honor—I mean I don't think it is
determinative. I think it is material but not determinative as to whether in fact this was a binding
contract as far as the HHFA is concerned, but
certainly it would indicate by one of the top people,
the man who was actually making all the decisions,
Hazeltine here, that in his opinion on April 5, 1956,
this particular document had been accepted by his
agent.

He points out in this memo to his superior that,
"The control of the project and all funds is under
my jurisdiction and handled through the Project

Manager." He points out that the income from the project has been utilized to pay certain operating expenses. He says, "The financial condition of the project indicates that "We," "We," should look to recasting the present loan to provide principal payments to the Administrator in addition to interest. In order to accomplish this, an agreement will have to be reached with [252] all or a majority of the creditors listed."

So he comes up with two alternate proposals. They are both set forth there.

One of them suggests that the creditors be paid out of income after payment of operating expenses. He indicates that will take ten years to pay out in full.

The second one is that they tried to settle this with the creditors on the basis of 30-40 per cent, roughly $160,000.

He believes that the best course of action is the latter, that they try to settle these claims of creditors by paying 30 to 40 per cent, and he says that he has an opinion from legal counsel, HHFA legal counsel, that an increased loan can be authorized for this purpose.

He attaches to his memorandum an indication of the financial status of this corporation which indicates on his letter to his superior, Mr. Cole, that the income exceeds the outgo on a yearly basis by $19,344 after the payment of $282,456 to amortize the long-term loan plus interest and a service charge.

So his conclusion at this particular date apparently was that the financial status of this project was sufficient to justify doing this; that a long-term loan was feasible; that there was sufficient income from this project to pay not only that but to pay operating expenses and still [253] have an annual excess of some $19,000.

Mr. Luckey: That is on the basis, your Honor, that the memorandum proposes that they try to settle with creditors at 30-40 per cent for $160,000 and to get the principals' release of any interest or claim that they might hold against the project, which would be the claims of Woodbury, Wynans and the others, so it was just a proposal that again didn't reach any ultimate determination.

The Court: 1021/A-22 is admitted.

(Carbon copy of letter of April 5, 1956, Hazeltine to Cole, previously marked Plaintiff's Exhibit 1021/A-22 for Identification, was thereupon received in evidence.) [254]

* * *

Mr. Wiener: The next item would be on page 212.

The Court: Page 212?

Mr. Wiener: Page 212, the bottom, April 16, 1956, [255] again a significant memorandum in the interim here, oral testimony, and it is at the bottom of page 212. That will be No. 1025, in our opinion a very significant memorandum in this case. Between the April 5th memorandum and this memorandum Hazeltine had visited Portland, and we will present testimony as to what happened at that meeting.

Mr. Hazeltine makes his report on his return from this trip to his superior, which ultimately led then to the final decision in this case to foreclose.

He reports that he visited Portland; that he conferred with Woodbury; that he thereafter, after the conference with Woodbury, learned that the Bank of California had obtained certain collateral from Woodbury which was—which the Bank was using to satisfy the obligation to it which was set forth in the Completion Agreement; that from this collateral assignment, or from this assignment of collateral, the Wynans obligation to the Bank had been cut, reduced from $150,000 to $60,000, and the Bank expected to be paid in full from this source.

Now you recall that the April 5th meeting, your Honor, had been—a proposal had been made and approved by Cole that all the creditors, including the Bank of California, be paid 35-40 per cent or whatever percentage figures were there. So he now he comes and reports that the Bank of California, as far as it is concerned, it has made other [256] arrangements to get its payment, and so he concludes, "When I assured myself personally by contact with the Bank on this matter that any relief which the Government might afford the Bank would result in actual cash dollar improvement of the position of Woodbury, the sponsor of Aleutian Homes, I broke off all further negotiations.

"It seemed to me a matter of principle that no positive action should be taken at the expense of the Government which might tend to enrich the sponsor of Aleutian Homes when his former actions still

jeopardize the position of the Government even
though such an action might in some intangible way
improve the future position of the project from the
Government's standpoint.''

His conclusion is that various types of litigation
can now no longer be avoided.

Our comment on this particular document is that
from this stage forward, from this date forward,
the Government moved toward those ultimate steps
which were culminated in June of 1957 by the foreclosure, that this was the basis, apparently, when
they found that they didn't have to make arrangements to pay off the Bank of California, they decided to avoid any possibility of working this out
in any way, basis, and to go back to their position
that they had prior to the Completion Agreement.

Mr. Meyer: I would like to make a brief comment, your [257] Honor, that this appears from our
knowledge of the files to be the first indication that
the Government, or at least Mr. Hazeltine in charge,
was approaching the long-range settlement of the
project with the idea that Mr. Woodbury, who was
listed in Stage Four, and some of these other creditors who were on Stage Three and Four, should
not, and if he had anything to do about it, would
not receive any consideration in the ultimate determination or liquidation of the project.

I might state that this appears to be the first time
when he takes this position, stating that he is going
to take it even if it is to the disinterest of the Government or even if it is going to be disadvantageous

to the Government, the Government's interest, to
take it, they are going to take it anyway.

It will be tied up with oral testimony, your
Honor, that the first indication the plaintiff had
that this position had been taken is when they received foreclosure papers that were served a year
later, in June.

Mr. Luckey: I think that plenty of latitude has
been taken with the memorandum, your Honor. The
memorandum must be considered in the light of the
previous request that Mr. Hazeltine made to the
Administrator to have a basis that he could go out
and try to compose the creditors with. In that
memorandum he represented to the Administrator
that the [258] 30-40 per cent settlement with the
creditors would not be made unless the principal or
major contractors would release any interest or
claim they might hold against the project. It was on
that basis that the Administrator committed the
fund for that purpose, and then when Mr. Hazeltine got to Portland and discovered that the claim
that was involved with the Bank of California was
one that Woodbury interests were satisfying, anything that was given Woodbury on creditor claims
as distinguished from ultimately coming out through
a sponsorship, if the project would eventually be
beneficial and they should ultimately finance it in
some way as distinguished from that, he had a position that would not jeopardize the interests of the
Government and other creditors who would still be
having money owed to them while Woodbury by

sponsor has under his guaranty received some benefits to him.

The Court: Exhibit 1025 is admitted.

(Carbon copy of letter of April 16, 1956,
Hazeltine to Cole, previously marked Plaintiff's Exhibit 1025/A-32 for Identification, was
thereupon received in evidence.) [259]

Mr. Wiener: The next item is the middle of
page 220, December 11, 1956. 1098 is the number—
excuse me, it is at the bottom of the page, 219. I
skipped one. Bottom of page 219, second from the
bottom, November 27, 1956, correspondence between
HHFA General Counsel in Washington and the
Cake firm in Portland. It is No. 1091. It comments
on the case of Dougherty vs. Aleutian Homes pres-
ently pending at that time.

Mr. Luckey: It says, "* * * note the legal position you intend to adopt * * *."

The Court: 1091 is admitted.

(Carbon copy of letter of November 27,
1956, [266] Oakley Hunter to Cake, Jaureguy
& Hardy, previously marked Plaintiff's Exhibit
1091/22 for Identification, was thereupon received in evidence.) [267]

Mr. Wiener: The next item is the one on May
21, 1957, where Cole writes to the U. S. National

Bank and, in effect, withdraws $122,300 from the funds of the Project Manager.

The Court: Is the Depository Agreement part of the record here?

Mr. Wiener: It is a part of the various documents, but it is not one that I have introduced. I mean it is one of these documents down here, your Honor. It certainly is part of the over-all picture. It is No. 1144.

The Court: Admitted.

> (Carbon copy of letter of May 21, 1957, from Cole to United States National Bank, Portland, Oregon, previously marked Plaintiff's Exhibit 1144/23 for Identification, was thereupon received in evidence.)

Mr. Wiener: The next document is May 28, 1957, in the middle of the page, a transcript of a telephone conversation between Abell and Hazeltine, No. 1150, in which Hazeltine confers with Abell and says he talked to Holbrook to be the appraiser on this project, and Holbrook advised him he was going to make an appraisal for the receivership. He makes the comment about the fact that Langton will have to resign [274] and Abell says, "I thought Langton might become the receiver."

Hazeltine says, "That is O.K., but he would have to resign as Project Manager."

Abell says, "Well, we understand that."

And Hazeltine says, "He would be out no matter what happens unless the Court makes him the receiver.

"The minute he is out," Hazeltine says, "the books and files are all lying there for anybody to pick up and it would not be a good idea for them to fall into Aleutian Homes' hands. Discussed this very thoroughly with Hunter and find out if we should ask the Court for the files or what, but be sure somebody immediately gets hold of them and not Aleutian Homes—seal them up and hand them to the Court. Because if there is no action someone might get in ahead of us. Get on this right away."

Well, at least, as we see that, your Honor, one of the points we have set forth in our memorandum with the Government takes the position that, O.K., Langton was in fact Aleutian Homes, and, of course, our position is the other.

The Court: The Government does not take that position?

Mr. Wiener: The Government takes the position the reverse of ours, that Langton was Aleutian Homes and that they were in a different position.

Now, if, in fact, Langton was Aleutian Homes, and that is their official position at that time, then it seems [275] they would be concerned about these records. If they belong to Aleutian Homes, they belong to Aleutian Homes, but this seems to me consistent with their approach that they took during this period of time that in fact this was their project and these were records they wanted to make mighty sure that they do not get over to the corporation, which right now in this courtroom they take the position that this was—that Langton was Aleutian Homes, not the Government. That is our theory anyway.

Mr. Luckey: This memo points out that they wanted to get the books in the hands of the Court so that they will be preserved, your Honor, rather than lost.

Mr. Wiener: That is No. 1150.

The Court: 1150 is admitted.

(Document, transcript of telephone conversation between Hazeltine and Abell, May 28, 1957, previously marked Plaintiff's Exhibit 1150/A-32 for Identification, was thereupon received in evidence.) [276]

Mr. Wiener: I am going to object again. I am going to object further, now, your Honor, on the question that my understanding of this case, of this segregated issue, is that we are talking about whether the Government had any control in this case—excuse me—as to whether the Government was a fiduciary in this case, and at least I don't see how this bears on that particular question at this particular time.

The Court: I do not see it either, Mr. Luckey.

Mr. Luckey: The only thing is, your Honor, Mr. Woodbury brought it out in his direct examination by saying in his conversation with Mr. Hazeltine back there it was mentioned and that he wanted to clear it up.

The Court: I think it is a matter that is not relevant [625] or material on the issue which we are trying here, and if it was developed on direct I didn't pay attention to it as having anything to do with the issue here. [626]

Mr. Luckey: Your Honor, under Rule 41 of the Federal Rules of Civil Procedure, I would respectfully submit to your Honor that the plaintiff has completed the presentation of its evidence and that the defendant is entitled to dismissal on the ground that, upon the facts and the law, the plaintiff has shown no right to relief.

Of course, I submit to your Honor first of all that the United States cannot be a fiduciary in this situation. I think, of course, the Restatement of the Law of Trusts is indicative of the Federal law in that regard. Certainly there is not a case here that Counsel has cited that would impose upon the Government any fiduciary responsibility in a case of this kind.

Now, I am sure your Honor has researched the problem and has a view on it so that further remarks or advice that I might make would be superfluous, and I will not burden the Court's time unless the Court feels in addition to our memoranda there are some questions or explanations that might be called for.

With reference to whether or not we were a fiduciary in this situation, I think it is important to note [705] here that the United States was in the position only of a debtor-creditor with relationship to the debtor and that does not give rise to a fiduciary relationship. There is no allegation here and there is no proof of any overreaching. There is no proof of the United States assuming the obligation of a fiduciary, and under all the facts of this case there is no satisfactory establishment of the strong burden that one has in asserting fiduciary relationship on someone else, to establish the burden.

A fiduciary relationship is an equitable concept arising out of an assumption of the obligation to look out for another or in a position in equity, people being put in a position where the Court will say in the situation this party was one party, was to look out for his interest.

Now, there is nothing in these documents—in fact, to the contrary in the evidence, your Honor—that the Lender would not have continued to disburse those funds had he been in a position to lend under the original contract. That letter that Mr. Hazeltine wrote to Mr. Hardy who was dealing with these people out here, and Mr. Woodbury, indicates, and the Completion Agreement shows clearly that the Administrator would not have gotten into any situation that would have required him ever to respond as a fiduciary.

In addition to that, the Project Manager was the man through whom all these things were being done, and while [706] his action could be vetoed and he could be removed by the Administrator, he was the party that was acting by actual delegation formally and properly, I submit, your Honor.

There may be some question in your mind about that with Aleutian Homes. He was delegated particular duties of disbursement nature, and it was a matter of seeing that these funds were properly accounted for in the balance of the loan. The creditors, the bonding companies, and people of that kind would not have stood still, as they did, for the extension by written agreement unless there was someone in whom they had confidence to incur continuation of the disbursement.

Certainly the HHFA on the one hand in the position to disburse the balance of the loan to the project and the creditors on the other hand coming to them and employing them to help complete this project should not be placed equitably in the position of a fiduciary and release Mr. Woodbury of all his guaranties, all that sort of thing, in a situation of this kind where they go to the Government, the HHFA, and ask that these funds be further disbursed.

Finally, I would like to say that there is a serious question, I believe, on the matter of jurisdiction, and that is a matter that I submit is before the Court at all times because the plaintiff here is relying upon matters and documents that they assert impose upon the Administrator a contractual [707] obligation.

If this action is in contract, the jurisdictional limit of this Court is exceeded by the claim, and

their action is here, apparently, under the Tort
Claims Act. I suggest it is a tortious attempt to
bring something that is based upon contract by all
their presentation and theory of the case here under
the Tort Claims Act. If the Court is without jurisdiction, this matter should proceed no further.

I am sure your Honor appreciates that they talk
about our acceptance of the Completion Agreement.
They say, "We did nothing wrong when we abandoned the commitment that Mr. Woodbury didn't
provide overhead funds." He had an overhead fund
obligation in connection with the employment of
the Project Manager and his Overhead Agreement.

All those things, I submit to your Honor, impose
upon the Court in this situation a problem as to
whether or not they are actually attempting to proceed for a breach of contract, attempting to build
something that is not supported by the Restatement
or any other authority that I can find, and impose a
fiduciary relationship. When the project goes sour
as a result of contract obligations that cannot be
met by the original lender is not something that will
bring it within the Tort Claims Act. [708]

Mr. Luckey: I understand it may not have been
physically introduced here, your Honor. As I understand it, by stipulation all the documents in the
chronological listing were stipulated as admitted
with the right of either party to read them in full.

Now this letter is described in the context of this deposition.

The Court: Mr. Luckey, when we started just about a week ago I said all that we were going to consider here, after you asked me to take this mass of material and let that go probably to the Appellate Court, that we were going to try out these particular things, and you would introduce those matters that you felt were of importance at this stage. I do not think there could have been a misunderstanding on that. [838]

Mr. Luckey: That would complete our evidence on this segregated issue.

The Court: Is there any rebuttal? [873]

Mr. Wiener: That concludes our case on this segregated issue, your Honor.

The Court: I have a few questions to ask, more in the nature of——

Mr. Wiener: One other thing: I don't know if you still want to ask Mr. Woodbury questions.

The Court: No. I have given consideration to that.

I want to get Counsel's thinking now on what we have tried here. I rather feel that we have tried at least one issue beyond what I had actually intended, but that may not be true.

Now that the Court has placed itself in the position of the parties, it may seem that such position would have little, if anything, to do, and I would

agree, with one of the primary questions here; that
is the question of jurisdiction.

There were certain denials in the pretrial order
of certain contentions that I was of the belief might
raise an issue of fact—as to what actually occurred
and as to what actually transpired—and I believe
that it was necessary to proceed with the trial of
these issues, the principal one which we have here.
That is whether under these circumstances the Government could be a fiduciary.

On the Number 2, and that is: Was the Government in fact a fiduciary? Is there any other evidence
—and I [874] think that this is important and you
might want to consider it for a while—is there any
other evidence that either one of the parties might
want to offer on this particular subject, and that is
if there was a breach of fiduciary relationship.

Now it seems to me that you have explored it.
We have gone into rather thoroughly from both
sides, although I would say in truth and in fact in
rereading my order I am not sure that it was broad
enough to cover that feature.

First of all, I would like to hear the plaintiff on
the point.

Mr. Wiener: I think in our considered opinion,
your Honor, our opinion would be that we probably
have placed in evidence before this Court at this
time, either through the records or through the
agreed facts, not only the issue that you asked
about—that is, the issue of whether our evidence
bears on the question of a breach—but also to the
agreed facts, the question of damages.

The Court: I would say this: If you would go along with the one point there and say what you want on the question of breach, that that is as far as I would want to go right at this particular moment.

Mr. Wiener: We know of no other evidence in this case that bears on that. I think we have got all the facts before the Court, as far as we know them, anyhow. [875]

The Court: That is fine.

Now, Mr. Luckey, what is your position on that?

Mr. Luckey: I think with the record as it stands, your Honor, and our motion on the jurisdiction, that at least at the moment we would have nothing further to add.

The Court: That would be on the question of breach either, if it would happen to be found. You would have nothing more to offer on the question of breach?

Mr. Luckey: Maybe I misunderstood your Honor. But I understood where the question of jurisdiction the matter of breach——

The Court: Well, now, the two things I mentioned, jurisdiction first, Mr. Luckey: Now, then, the other question was that if the Government could be a fiduciary then was it in fact a fiduciary; if in fact a fiduciary, was there a breach of the relationship?

After all, we are taking this in its logical order here. It would seem to me, and that is why the question came to my mind, it would seem to me

there has been just as much evidence offered on the
question of breach here, or possible breach, if there
is such relationship, as there was on the question of
whether there was a fiduciary relationship.

Does the Government have any more testimony
that it might want to offer on the question, if there
was a breach [876] of the fiduciary relationship?

Mr. Luckey: Well, on the breach, as I understand it, your Honor, I think that we could be confronted with a lot of matters as to whether or not it
was reasonable under all the circumstances. I think
we have most of the material in, anyway, that would
be involved with that, Mr. Langton's deposition, and
so forth, which covers the point rather thoroughly.
We have not attempted to document that thoroughly
beyond Mr. Langton's deposition. I think, however,
that with the documents in evidence that that would
substantially be in a position to be presented to the
Court.

Ths Court: What I believe is this: It has taken
us a week now or approximately a week in this trial.
I think it would be a very foolish thing for the
Court now to adjourn, since we have gone ahead so
far on it, if there was any other evidence to be offered on the question of breach. We have to get this
case moving along. It has been here for a number
of years, and I personally would prefer, since we
have gone this far, to go ahead. I won't decide the
question of damages. I would reserve that question,
if I would ever get to it; I would reserve that question because that is something that could be threshed

out later. But I do believe that we are down to the point where if the case goes on appeal the Court on appeal at least will have before it everything with the exception of damages. [877]

Mr. Wiener: Yes.

Mr. Luckey: I think that the evidence is sufficient before the Court. There could be additional documentation, but I don't think——

The Court: I would say this then, and of course under the circumstances I would be extremely liberal, that if before the opinion of the Court is announced, and that will probably be some time, if either one of the parties feel they have something on this last matter which I have mentioned, the first question of a breach of this relationship, that I certainly would be inclined to hear any evidence that might be proper.

Mr. Wiener: All right.

The Court: And that would be either one of the parties.

Mr. Luckey: I can say this. I think any evidence that we would have on that would be purely a submission of documents, your Honor.

The Court: You have each submitted a trial memorandum. Should I hear plaintiff on whether we have additional briefs or memorandums which you would like to submit now before we speak of the argument of the case here?

Mr. Wiener: Your Honor, I think that with the full and constant attention this Court has given for five days and the thousands of—not thousands but

the many briefs that have been submitted and I am
sure are in the Court's file, that [878] unless the
Court would request further analysis of any particular phase of it I just don't know how we could
supplement it any more. I just don't know what the
Court would have in mind, and so far as we are
concerned, I recognize our trial memorandum is
very short, but my answer to your question is unless
the Court desires further briefing I don't know
what we can add for the Court's thinking on this
matter or to assist the Court unless the Court asks
us to, and of course then——

The Court: What is your thinking on oral argument, if you want oral argument? I would say this,
Gentlemen, that my time on account of the fact
that we have taken extra work here, that we may
have some difficulty on that in lining up that feature except possibly during the early part of the
Christmas week.

What is your thinking on it now, if you would
care for oral argument? Do you think there is
anything?

Mr. Wiener: I have thought about this before,
and it appeared to me that it might be of benefit
to the Court if—I realize that a lot of documents
have been put in here—after you have taken a
look at those documents perhaps that you would
like to have us present our views.

The Court: You may be assured that I will do
that if I feel that way; I will call you. I have not
hesitated in doing that in other cases, and if I

feel I would like some [879] points straightened out I certainly will call on you.

Mr. Wiener: The thing that disturbs me, I feel we have not apparently put over our theory of this case to our opposing counsel after three years because he indicated something here—if we haven't convinced him in three years what our theory is I certainly would like to have the opportunity to at least expand our theory to the Court. Maybe the Court has got our theory.

The Court: I think I understand your theory.

Mr. Wiener: If the Court understands our theory, fine.

The Court: I think I understand your theory. Now that is, first, without making any commitment at this time; No. 1 on the jurisdictional question or on the question if in fact there has been a fiduciary relationship established, that certainly I understand that theory.

Mr. Wiener: All right, if the Court then understands our theory, whether rightly or wrongly, then I would say that we could benefit the Court only if the Court feels we could be of benefit, and I personally—we have expanded this at great length here on the same basis of the brief. So far as the evidence is concerned, if the Court feels he would like to hear us expand it—if not, we would not want a further argument.

The Court: Mr. Luckey?

Mr. Luckey: If the Court please, I don't think it is [880] so much a case of our inability to under-

stand their theory as it is to be able to get us to
agree to it, but, at any rate, it is not in my mind
to take any different position with reference to the
argument than Mr. Wiener has stated. I think we
have filed brief on top of brief so that your Honor
already has a considerable burden in reading those
briefs, unless there is some point that your Honor
has that Counsel has neglected. I think in view of
the voluminous documentation here that, again if
the Court feels it has anything that it would like
to inquire of Counsel, we would all be better advised after that.

The Court: Then I will take it to be under advisement. Of course, if I feel that you gentlemen
can assist me on anything that may arise, I won't
hesitate to call you back.

Mr. Wiener: May I make one inquiry, your
Honor: I assume from what the Court has said
that there still has not been a decision on the question of the jurisdiction of this Court under the
Tort Claims Act.

The Court: No; that is true; that is true.

Mr. Wiener: I am hesitating because I am not
quite sure how to frame this question, but I hope
the Court and Counsel will indulge me.

If in fact we have a cause of action against the
United States which may not be cognizable in this
Court, that cause of action may still be cognizable
in the United [881] States Court of Claims. My
understanding of the law applicable to the Court
of Claims is that if a case is pending against the

United States in another court, then it is grounds for dismissal in the Court of Claims.

Why I am hesitating to say this is perhaps obvious, but the statute of limitations would run against the plaintiff in this case and my client, Mr. Woodbury, sometime probably during the year 1961 or at the earliest, I would say, sometime during the year 1961. I am only struggling for words, but what I am trying to say is that if this case is going to be decided on the jurisdictional question we still have a remedy elsewhere. Of course, if you decide on the merits that ends it one way or the other. I am merely calling up—perhaps the Court is cognizant of the fact that we had an alternate choice, but we selected this forum because this was proper, and if the Court——

The Court: I would say this, Mr. Wiener: Of course, anything that I would say now would be at a point where I have not decided on the jurisdiction, but, certainly, I would feel this way about it, that with so much money as your client has obviously involved here, if the Court felt there were some rights and those rights could be saved, the Court would be inclined to do that.

Mr. Wiener: All right, I just wanted to call the Court's attention to that fact.

(Trial Concluded.)

[Endorsed]: Filed October 9, 1961. [882]

In the United States District Court
for the District of Oregon

CERTIFICATE BY CLERK

United States of America,
District of Oregon—ss.

I, Keith Burns, Clerk of the United States District Court for the District of Oregon, do hereby certify that the foregoing documents consisting of Complaint; Defendant's motion to dismiss and in the alternative for summary judgment; Defendant's memorandum on motion to dismiss, etc.; Defendant's reply brief re motion to dismiss, etc.; Order denying motion to dismiss; Answer; Reply to counterclaim; Order that answer and counterclaim of defendant be stricken, etc.; Motion to file certain documents; Defendant's motion that defendant's answer and counterclaim heretofore stricken be reinstated; Order reinstating defendant's answer and counterclaim; Defendant's request for admissions; Plaintiff's answer to request for admissions; Plaintiff's amended answer to request for admissions; Amended counterclaim; Reply to amended counterclaim; Plaintiff's interrogatories; Plaintiff's request for admissions; Defendant's answers to plaintiff's interrogatories; Defendant's replies to plaintiff's request for admissions; Order on defendant's objections to request for admissions and defendant's objections to plaintiff's interrogatories; Answer to plaintiff's in-

terrogatory No. 20 (b)(1); Pre-trial order; Order
reserving decision on motion to dismiss; Stipulation re depositions; Opinion of Judge John F.
Kilkenny; Judgment of dismissal; Notice of appeal by plaintiff; Bond for costs on appeal; Designation of contents of record on appeal; Statement
of point; Defendant's motion to set counterclaims
for trial, etc.; Certificate and order; Defendant-
appellee's designation of contents of record on
appeal; Supplementary designation of contents of
record on appeal; Order denying motion for con-
solidation; Motion and order extending time to
docket appeal; Order denying motion to vacate;
Supplemental pre-trial order re amended counterclaim; Stipulation and order removing case from
calendar and Transcript of docket entries constitute the record on appeal from a judgment of dismissal of said court in a cause therein numbered
Civil 9403, in which Ray B. Woodbury is the plaintiff and appellant and United States of America
is the defendant and appellee; that the said record
has been prepared by me in accordance with the
designations of contents of record on appeal filed
by the appellant and appellee, and in accordance
with the rules of this court.

I further certify that there is being forwarded
under separate cover the reporter's transcript of
proceedings in four volumes. The exhibits are to
be retained in this office until further order of the
Court of Appeals or until ten days before the date
set for argument on this appeal.

I further certify that the cost of filing the Notice of Appeal, $5.00 has been paid by the appellant.

In Testimony Whereof I have hereunto set my hand and affixed the seal of said court in Portland, in said District, this 10th day of October, 1961.

[Seal]   KEITH BURNS,
Clerk;

By /s/ THORA LUND,
Deputy.

————

[Endorsed]: No. 17585. United States Court of Appeals for the Ninth Circuit. Ray B. Woodbury, Appellant, vs. United States of America, Appellee. Transcript of Record. Appeal from the United States District Court for the District of Oregon.

Filed and Docketed: October 13, 1961.

/s/ FRANK H. SCHMID,
Clerk of the United States Court of Appeals for the Ninth Circuit.

In the United States Court of Appeals
for the Ninth Circuit

No. 17,585

RAY B. WOODBURY,

                                 Appellant,

vs.

UNITED STATES OF AMERICA,

                                 Appellee.

STATEMENT OF POINT

The point on which appellant intends to rely on this appeal is that the United States District Court for the District of Oregon committed error when it concluded as a matter of law that it did not have jurisdiction of appellant's claims under the Tort Claims Act and thereupon dismissed appellant's complaint and the causes of action set forth in said complaint.

KING,   MILLER,   ANDERSON,   NASH   &   YERKE,

         /s/ NORMAN J. WIENER,

         /s/ JEAN P. LOWMAN,

                Attorneys for Appellant.

[Endorsed]:   Filed October 30, 1961.

———

[Title of Court of Appeals and Cause.]

STIPULATION AND ORDER

Whereas the record herein includes approximately 309 exhibits, many of which are voluminous in size, and

Whereas it is not feasible or economic to include said exhibits in the printed record on appeal

Now, Therefore, it is hereby stipulated by and between the parties hereto through their attorneys that subject to the approval of the court an order may enter

1. That the exhibits in the above-entitled cause need not be included in the printed record on appeal; and

2. That the original exhibits herein shall be made a part of the record on appeal.

Dated this 31st day of October, 1961.

/s/ NORMAN J. WIENER,
Of Attorneys for Appellant.

ROGER G. ROSE,

By /s/ SIDNEY I. LEZAK,
Assistant United States Attorney, of Attorneys for Appellee.

It Is So Ordered: Nov. 1, 1961.

/s/ RICHARD W. CHAMBERS,
United States Circuit
Court Judge.

[Endorsed]: Filed November 1, 1961.

17586

No. 17~~~2~~

United States

COURT OF APPEALS

for the Ninth Circuit

LEON DUDLEY NOAH,

Appellant,

v.

UNITED STATES OF AMERICA,

Appellee.

*Upon Appeal from the Judgment of the United States
District Court for the District of Oregon*

BRIEF FOR THE APPELLEE

SIDNEY I. LEZAK
   Acting United States Attorney
   District of Oregon
DONAL D. SULLIVAN
   Assistant United States Attorney

MAR

STEVENS-NESS LAW PUB. CO., PORTLAND, ORE.·   3.8.62—40

_LE
ldin
nue
ι

· S.

INDEX

Page

ii

INDEX (Cont.)

18 U.S.C. §
21 U.S.C. §
26 U.S.C. §
26 U.S.C. §
28 U.S.C. §
28 U.S.C. §

Rule 30, Fed
Rule 37(a),
Rule 52(b),

....

Agnew v. U.
   17 S. Ct.

Ambrose v
   F.N. 8

Bridges v. U

Buford v U
   Cert. De:

Chicago v. F
   101 F.2d

Coupe v. U.

Finn v. Woc

Glasser v. U
   86 L. Ed

Hass v. U.S

Herzog v. U

Holt v. U.S
   54 L. Ed

Kiger v. U.

STATUTES

CASES CITED

CASES CITED (Cont.)

F

No. 17692

United States
COURT OF APPEALS
for the Ninth Circuit

LEON DUDLEY NOAH,

Appellant,

v.

UNITED STATES OF AMERICA,

Appellee.

Upon Appeal from the Judgment of the United States District Court for the District of Oregon

BRIEF FOR THE APPELLEE

OPINION BELOW

The judgment of the District Court was rendered without an opinion.

JURISDICTION

Jurisdiction of the District Court is conferred by 18 USC § 3231. Jurisdiction of this Court to review the judgment of the District Court is conferred by

28 USC §§ 1291 and 1294(1) and Rule 37(a), Federal Rules of Criminal Procedure.

STATUTES

Title 26 USC 4704 (a)

"It shall be unlawful for any person to purchase, sell, dispense, or distribute narcotic drugs except in the original stamped package or from the original stamped package; and the absence of appropriate tax paid stamps from narcotic drugs shall be prima facie evidence of a violation of this subsection by the person in whose possession the same may be found."

Title 26 USC 4705 (a)

"It shall be unlawful for any person to sell, barter, exchange, or give away narcotic drugs except in pursuance of a written order of the person to whom such article is sold, bartered, exchanged, or given, on a form to be issued in blank for that purpose by the Secretary or his delegate."

Title 21 USC 174

"Whoever fraudulently or knowingly imports or brings any narcotic drug into the United States or any territory under its control or jurisdiction, contrary to law, or receives, conceals, buys, sells, or in any manner facilitates the transportation, concealment, or sale of any such narcotic drug after being imported or brought in, knowing the same to have been imported or brought into the United States contrary to law, or conspires to commit any of such acts in violation of the laws of the United States, shall be imprisoned not less than five or more than twenty years and in addition may be fined not more than

$20,000. For a second or subsequent offense, the offender shall be imprisoned not less than ten or more than forty years and, in addition, may be fined not more than $20,000.

Whenever on trial for violation of this section the defendant is shown to have or to have had possession of the narcotic drug, such possession shall be deemed sufficient evidence to authorize conviction unless the defendant explains the possession to the satisfaction of the jury."

Federal Rules of Criminal Procedure, Rule 30, 18 USCA

"Instructions

At the close of the evidence or at such earlier time during the trial as the court reasonably directs, any party may file written requests that the court instruct the jury on the law as set forth in the requests. At the same time copies of such requests shall be furnished to adverse parties. The court shall inform counsel of its proposed action upon the requests prior to their arguments to the jury, but the court shall instruct the jury after the arguments are completed. No party may assign as error any portion of the charge or omission therefrom unless he objects thereto before the jury retires to consider its verdict, stating distinctly the matter to which he objects and the grounds of his objection. Opportunity shall be given to make the objection out of the hearing of the jury."

Federal Rules of Criminal Procedure, 52 (b), 18 USCA

"Plain errors or defects affecting substantial rights may be noticed although they were not brought to the attention of the court."

.LE]
lding
nue
a

, S.

STATEMENT OF THE CASE

Although defendant's statement of the case is substantially correct, it is felt that certain additions and clarifications should be made.

Transaction of October 3, 1960

Special employee Love had made prior arrangements with the defendant to purchase narcotics on the mentioned date (Tr. 78) in front of the Oregon State Liquor store at 3532 Northeast Union Avenue in Portland. At about 5:15 - 5:30 P.M. Love met elsewhere with Narcotics agents Gooder and Windham and Portland City Officers, Putnam and Schafer (Tr. 2, 41, 56, 64). Love was supplied with a special 1952 Studebaker automobile (Tr. 38, 54, 64) which had been used by the officers in previous narcotics investigations (Tr. 54). The automobile and special employee were searched (Tr. 3, 22, 26, 56, 76), afterwhich Gooder concealed himself in the trunk of the car in such a manner as to enable him to observe the interior through an opening formed by the lowering of the back seat (Tr. 3, 15, 16, 55, 65, 68).

Love, who had been supplied with government funds, then proceeded to the roundevous at the liquor store followed by Windham and Schafer in one automobile and Putnam in another. At about 5:40 P.M. (Tr. 3, 14, 41, 57) defendant, who was visible to Gooder for 15 to 20 feet (Tr. 3, 18), was hailed by Love with "Hi partner. What's doing?" (Tr. 4). Defendant responded by inquiring as to what was going on, and whether Love was "ready" (Tr. 77). Defendant leaned through the window, took a rubber fingerstall (rubber finger protector) from his mouth and passed it to Love who in turn paid him $80 00 (Tr. 4, 18, 77).

Defendant then walked into the liquor store (Tr. 27, 57, 65, 77). Windham and Schafer observed defendant approach and leave from their car stationed at a vantage point estimated to be 200 to 300 feet away (Tr. 41, 42, 60). Putnam also observed and identified defendant from a distance which does not appear to be in the record. After the special employee's Studebaker and the automobile containing Windham and Schafer had left, Putnam remained and observed defendant enter a two-tone gray 1952 Pontiac with a temporary license sticker on the windshield. Putnam drove around the block twice and left while defendant was still seated in the Pontiac (Tr. 65-66).

Subsequent analysis of the contents of the fingerstall revealed a narcotic derivative.

Defendant produced a Pasco, Washington automobile dealer named Jeffries who testified that he saw defendant sometime during the day of October 3 in Pasco, Washington, 230-240 miles away (Tr. 90). Defendant himself testified that he had arrived in Pasco by train from Portland at about 2:00 on the morning of October 3, 1960, and had been picked up by Jeffries at his home at about 10:30 - 11·00 A.M. (Tr. 112-114).

6

Transaction of November 23, 1960:

On the morning of November 23, 1960, special employee Love met with agents Windham and Gooder, and officer Bisenius at a north Portland location. After searching Love's person and automobile and after furnishing him with $50.00 government funds (Tr 30, 79), Love, under the surveillance of Windham and Gooder (Tr. 30, 70) drove to the Kienow Grocery store parking lot.

After parking in the lot, Love waited a few minutes in his automobile and then crossed the street to a service station telephone booth to place a call to defendant for the purpose of completing arrangements for the sale (Tr. 70, 30, 79). He was informed that defendant had already departed. Upon return to his automobile and after speaking to Windham, who had followed on foot (Tr. 31, 80), Love moved his automobile to a better point within Gooder's observation (Tr. 31. 80).

At about 11:30 (Tr. 8-9) defendant walked out of the rear door of Kienows and entered Love's car. Love asked him why he couldn't get "spoons" (1/16 ounce narcotic). Defendant replied that he had run short, and that possibly later he could obtain more for him. At that time the defendant handed Love a cellophane wrapper containing five capsules in exchange for $50.00 (Tr. 80). After completing this transaction, both participants departed, and Love returned, with Windham and Bisenius following, to the original meeting place (Tr. 31, 9, 71). The capsules were delivered to Windham who searched Love and his vehicle again (Tr. 31, 50).

Defendant, in defense, testified that at about 10:00 - 10:30 A.M. on November 23, 1960, he went to the Kienow lot to deliver a message for "Joe" to the effect that "Joe" could not meet Love at a designated time. Love was alleged to have alighted from his car and the message was delivered while both were standing at the back door of the store (Tr. 119-121). Defendant returned to "Joes" and later boarded a plane for Pasco, Washington. During the course of testifying, defendant volunteered that he made his living as a professional gambler (Tr. 111)

Defendant has assigned three specifications of error:

"1. The trial court erred in its refusal to allow defendant's witness to show the color motion films of the scene of the alleged transaction on October 3, 1960 on the ground of objection that 'it is immaterial, irrelevant, incompetent, and remote in time and place as to the alleged transaction'. (TR. pg. 104)

"2. The trial court erred in the refusal to grant defendant's motion for judgment of acquittal and directed verdict as to the alleged transaction of November 23, 1960.

"3. The trial court erred in its instructions to the jury as the sum total of such instructions, through omission and commission, was highly beneficial to the prosecution and prejudicial to the defendant."

ARGUMENT

I. The Trial Court Did Not Err in Its Refusal to Allow Defendant's Witness to Show the Color Motion Films of the Scene of the Alleged Transaction of October 3, 1960.

As grounds for the admission of the color films, defendant's counsel urged that, although taken at a later date, the films would show that *because of traffic conditions* and *light conditions,* the view of the scene of the October 3, 1960 transaction was severely limited (Tr. 102). Since the films were taken on March 2, 1961 (Tr. 101), the Court on further interrogation brought out that defendant had hoped to recreate the same light conditions on film by shooting movies at the scene on a winter Oregon day that had approximately the same sunset as the fall Oregon day in question (Tr. 103-104). The court announced that it would sustain an objection to the film but would permit the photographer to testify to what he could observe. After this ruling, the government objected on the grounds that the proposed exhibit was "immaterial, irrelevant, incompetent, and remote in time and place as to the alleged transaction" (Tr. 104). No formal offer of proof was made nor was the film made a part of the record.

Although questionable, it will be assumed that there is sufficient material in the record to enable this Court to review the specification of alleged error.

A. *The Question of Admissibility of Color Motion Films Is a Matter Within the Discretion of the Court Which Discretion Was Properly Exercised.*

A reading of the photographer's testimony (Tr. 101-110) will show that the film was not offered for the purpose of showing what could be seen at the scene by way of physical character or obstructions to view, but was offered for the purpose of showing that because of light conditions, and distance, the facial features of a colored man could not be readily recognized by the human eye from certain vantage points.

In order to permit such a film in evidence, the court would have had to satisfy itself as to two necessary parts of the required foundation:

(1) Whether the exposure of a scene through the "regular lens" at "normal" setting of a Revere 8-millimeter camera counld produce a negative on Kodak Kodachrome daylight film (Tr. 102) which when flashed through a projector of unknown description on a large screen in a darkened room would produce two-dimensional light color and distance impressions similar to the impressions available to a human eye viewing the scene.

(2) Whether the conditions at the scene at the time filmed on March 2, 1961, were sufficiently similar to the conditions existing at the same place on October 3, 1961, to be of aid to the jury.

In the first part of the foundation, the question raised is whether a camera is an appropriate medium

.LE.
lding
nue
a

· S.

to demonstrate light, color, and distance. The court in the light of the evidence adduced in qualifying a lawyer as a photographer could easily conclude that the failure of the film to register sufficient features of a person under certain conditions of light, color, and distance would be irrelevant on the question of whether the human eye could adequately distinguish those features under the same conditions. No attempt was made to present testimony, expert or otherwise, to lay this foundation.

In *Sprinkle* v. *Davis* (C.A. 4th, 1940), 111 F.2d 925, moving pictures were offered in an automobile damage case to show how far from a particular point at an intersection a car approaching from another direction could be seen. In approving the lower court's rejection of this evidence, the appellate court said:

> "Whether a physical situation can be correctly portrayed by moving pictures is a question which must be left to the sound judgment and discretion of the trial judge."

In *Chicago* v. *Robinson* (C.A. 8th, 1939), 101 F.2d 994, films taken along a railroad track were admitted in a personal injury case for the purpose of showing the visibility to a train crew of a person lying on the tracks. Objection was interposed to the effect that there was no showing that the human eye could have seen as easily and plainly as the camera registered. The jury was instructed that the lense and film of the camera were not necessarily the real test of what the human eye would have seen. In view of this instruction, the appellate court held that the

admission
tion of the

Other ⱥ
missibility
discretion ꞏ
8th, 1931).
4th, 1959).
1950), 178
19 ALR 2d

In rega
foundation.
the conditi
at the time
ing conditi
denied bein
tion, had n
time and lᵢ
therefore h
ment witne

Gooder
could see ꞌ
that the lig
(Tr. 41), a
to take pi
Murry test
films were
sporadicalꞌ
assuming t
stantially
support th

admission of the films was within the sound discretion of the court.

Other authorities upholding the rule that the admissibility of moving pictures is within the sound discretion of the court are: *Stone* v. *Chicago* (C A. 8th, 1931), 53 F. 2d 813, *Willis* v. *Pennsylvania* (C.A 4th, 1959), 269 F.2d 549; *Finn* v. *Wood* (C.A 2d, 1950), 178 F.2d 583; Annotations 62 ALR 2d 686; 19 ALR 2d 877; 9 ALR 2d 921.

In regard to the second part of the necessary foundation, defendant had the burden of showing that the conditions of light, distance, and traffic existing at the time of filming were similar to the corresponding conditions on October 3, 1960. Defendant, who denied being present in Portland on the date in question, had no witness to identify the conditions at the time and location of the alleged crime His reliance therefore had to shift to the testimony of the government witnesses to establish the foundation.

Gooder testified that it was daylight and that he could see "very good" (Tr. 14). Windham testified that the light was good, that he could see "quite well" (Tr. 41), and that probably the light was good enough to take pictures (Tr. 43). In contrast to this, McMurry testified that on March 2, 1961, the date the films were taken, the sky was overcast, although sporadically the sun was visible (Tr. 101, 107). Thus, assuming that the sunsets on both days were substantially at the same time, the record would not support the conclusion that the light conditions as

‚LE
ldin
nue
ı

· S.

influenced by the clouds were also substantially the same.

In regard to traffic conditions, there was no testimony describing the traffic situation on October 3, 1960. Consequently, the record would not support the conclusion that traffic conditions on the date of the film were similar.

On the basis of the foregoing, the trial court correctly decided that the films were inadmissible. Such ruling is in accord with the decisions holding that the sufficiency of the *foundation* for the introduction of films is within the discretion of the trial judge. See *Martin* v. *Klein* (D.C. Mass. 1959), 172 F. Supp. 778; *Coupe* v. *U.S.* (C.A. D.C. 1940), 113 F.2d 145; *Stone* v. *Chicago* (C.A. 8th, 1931), 53 F.2d 813; *Millers* v. *Wichita* (C.A. 10th, 1958), 257 F.2d 93.

In summary, the showing of a film taken on March 2, 1961, wherein the scene did not register on the film sufficiently to identify facial features was properly within the discretion of the trial judge. Also, the total lack of evidence in the record of light and traffic conditions on the day of the alleged crime would not permit a decision to the effect that March 2, 1961, was comparable to October 3, 1960.

B. *The Exclusions of the Films Did Not Prejudice the Rights of the Defendant.*

Although the trial judge excluded the films, he did permit the photographer to testify that at roughly 300 to 350 feet it was difficult to discern the features

or appearance of persons (Tr 106) Such testimony
was admitted in spite of the fact that it was relevant
only for the purpose of discrediting the ability of
Windham and Schafer to identify defendant at a distance estimated to be 200 to 300 feet (Tr. 41, 42, 60).
If relevant at all, the films would have been merely
cumulative to the testimony of the photographer and
would have emphasized his testimony far beyond its
probative importance. See *U. S.* v. *Hall* (C A. 2d,
1953), 200 F.2d 957, where the court held that in a
marijuana prosecution any error in rejection of a
business record was harmless because the witness was
allowed to read the record while testifying. See also:
Sprinkle v. *Davis,* supra; *Meurling* v. *County* (C.A.
2d, 1956), 230 F.2d 167.

It should also be noticed that defendant was identified by *five* witnesses, and that the films would have
served only to attack the testimony of Windham and
Schafer who did not actually witness the transaction.
Unscathed, there remained Love and Gooder who
were in the Studebaker, and Putnam who remained
at the scene after the sale and who actually approached the defendant while driving around the
block (Tr. 66).

In *Kiger* v. *U. S.* (C.A. 6th, 1960), 281 F.2d 551,
the defendant, who was charged with bank robbery
attempted to refute the identification of nine witnesses by the introduction of a photo of himself showing discoloration and marks of a fight that occurred
a day prior to the robbery. The court held that al-

LE
din
nue
a

S.

14

though the photographs should have been admitted, their refusal was not prejudicial in view of the failure to otherwise impair the validity of the identification. In the case at hand, the testimony of the five identifying witnesses was in no way impaired. Thus, the court's refusal to allow the showing of the movies could not produce error.

II. The Trial Court Did Not Err in Refusing to Grant Defendant's Motion for Judgment of Acquittal as to the Transaction of November 23, 1960.

A. *In View of the Evidence, Defendant's Attack on Its Sufficiency Is Frivolous.*

Special employee Love whose person and automobile was searched prior to the November 23, 1960, sale (Tr. 79, 69, 45, 51, 30) testified that while waiting in the Kienow Store lot for defendant, he left his automobile, followed by Windham, to make a phone call for the purpose of completing final arrangements (Tr. 79) for the sale. Upon return to the lot, he moved his car to provide better surveillance for Windham, Gooder and Bisenius who were stationed at other vantage points. He further testified that defendant entered his automobile and after some discussion regarding future transactions handed him five capsules in exchange for $50.00 (Tr. 79-81). The capsules were later identified as containing heroin.

Agent Windham and Officer Bisenius observed the defendant enter and leave Love's automobile from one vantage point (Tr. 29-31, 44-51, 69-75), while Gooder observed (Tr. 7-11) from another. Although they did not witness the actual transfer of the narcotics, their testimony corroborated Love's identification of defendant at the scene of the crime.

In the appellant's brief, it has been asserted that Love may have obtained the narcotics, exhibit 2, from the telephone booth prior to the alleged sale at the Kienow parking lot. Such an assertion not only presumes that Love fabricated the entire transaction but is manifestly against the weight of the corroborating evidence. In this respect, the evidence shows that Windham followed Love to the telephone booth (Tr. 79, 8, 30, 70) and searched him and the vehicle after the transaction (Tr. 50, 31). The failure to find the $50.00 government advance funds in Love's possession after the alleged sale is strong corroboration of Love's testimony regarding the sale.

The reviewing court is not concerned with weighing the evidence or judging the credibility of the witness but must accept the government's evidence in its strongest light for the purpose of judging its sufficiency. See: *Glasser* v. *U.S.* (1942), 315 U.S 60, 80, 86 L. Ed. 680, 62 S. Ct. 457; *Buford* v. *U.S* (C.A. 9th, 1959), 270 F.2d 721, Cert. Den. 362 U S 937; *Bridges* v. *U.S.* (C.A. 9th, 1953), 199 F.2d 811. Nor may a reviewing court reject the unimpeached testimony of an informer-accomplice. See: *Hass* v. *U.S.* (C.A. 9th, 1929), 31 F.2d 13; *Ambrose* v. *U.S.* (C.A. 9th, 1960), 280 F.2d 766, F.N. 8.

The foregoing assertion which should have been argued to the jury has been foreclosed by the jury verdict as a matter of law.

III. Defendant Is Not Entitled to a Review of the Trial Court's Instructions, Nor Do the Instructions, as a Whole or Individually, Contain Prejudicial Error.

A. *Failure to Except, as a Rule, Forecloses a Review of the Instructions.*

In *Herzog* v. *U.S.* (C.A. 9th, 1956), 235 F.2d 664, this court in the majority opinion construed Rule 30 of the Federal Rules of Criminal Procedure requiring exceptions to instructions as being complimentary to Rule 52(b) of the Federal Rules of Criminal Procedure relating to "plain error." However, this court in the mentioned case also laid down ground rules for the application of Rule 52(b) and commented upon its past use:

> "This court has not gone overboard in its application of rule 52(b) to situations as here presented, and it does not propose to do so now. In the great bulk of the cases in which counsel have sought to have us consider claims of error in instructions not objected to at the trial we have declined to do so. More than once we have stressed the salutary nature of Rule 30 and the vitally important part it plays in the administration of justice. . . .
>
> In determining whether the giving or the failure to give an instruction warrants a reversal, *the courts are not to consider the instruction in isolation. They are obliged to examine the charge as a whole in light of the factual situation disclosed by the record.*" (Emphasis supplied.)

In the language of Judge Chambers' concurring and dissenting opinion to the cited decision, defendant is attempting to utilize a "shotgun 'plain error'" attack on the instructions. This approach should not be per-

mitted. Tak
ant's failure
fair.

B. *Failu*
to E
Waive

Defendan
such an ins
In *Mims* v.
court settled
the absence
the weight c
ing the quest
(C.A. 9th, 1
(C.A. 7th, 1
in the instruc

C. *In Vie*
Court
cence

The instr

"Nov
a presu
this pres
out the
ever arr
your sa
The pre
effect o
must co
presum
sufficier
sumptio

mitted. Taken as a whole and in the light of defendant's failure to except, the instructions were manifestly fair.

 B. *Failure to Request an Instruction on the Weight to Be Given to an Informer's Testimony Waived Error, If Any, in Not So Instructing.*

Defendant in his brief concedes that a request for such an instruction was not made (Ap. Br. p. 12). In *Mims* v *U.S.* (C.A. 9th, 1958), 254 F.2d 654, this court settled any doubt, if there ever was doubt, that the absence of a request for an instruction regarding the weight of an informer's testimony precluded raising the question on appeal. See also: *Zamlock* v. *U.S.* (C.A. 9th, 1952), 193 F.2d 889, 892; *U.S.* v. *Ginsburg* (C.A. 7th, 1938), 96 F.2d 882. This allegation of error in the instructions is patently without merit.

 C. *In View of the Trial Court's Entire Charge, the Court's Instruction on Presumption of Innocence Was Correct.*

The instruction given was (Tr. 29):

> "Now, I have told you that this defendant has a presumption of innocence in his favor, and *this presumption of innocence continues throughout the trial and up until such time, if that time ever arrives,* where the defendant is convicted to your satisfaction and beyond a reasonable doubt. The presumption of innocence has the weight and effect of evidence in favor of the accused. You must consider the evidence in the light of this presumption. The presumption of innocence is sufficient to acquit a defendant unless the presumption is outweighed by evidence satisfying

‑LF
ldin
nue
‑

· S.

18

the jury beyond a reasonable doubt of the defendant's guilt." (Emphasis supplied.)

Defendant apparently complains in his brief that the above instruction carried the connotation that the burden of proof would shift *during the trial* at such point that the jurors believed in his guilt. Construing the words of the instruction reasonably and as a whole, the words must be taken by the jury to mean that the accused is presumed innocent during the trial and *beyond* the trial until such time during their deliberation that they are convinced of guilt beyond a reasonable doubt.

In *Las Vegas* v. *U.S.* (C.A. 9th, 1954), 210 F.2d 732, 749, this court approved the following instruction:

"The defendants and each of them are presumed to be innocent at all stages of this trial, *unless that time arrives,* if its does arrive—it may not arrive—*that the evidence in the case should convince the jury,* or a member of the jury, that one or all of the defendants is guilty. . . ." (Emphasis supplied.)

See also: *Agnew* v. *U.S.* (1897), 165 U.S. 36, 51, 17 S. Ct. 235, 41 L. Ed. 624; *Holt* v. *U.S.* (1910), 218 U.S. 245, 253, 31 S. Ct. 2, 54 L. Ed. 1021.

Based upon the foregoing authorities and a reasonable construction of the trial judge's instruction, defendant's complaint amounts to frivolous nit-picking.

D. *The Court's Charge Regarding Alibi Was Correctly Given.*

The defendant in quoting the court's instruction on alibi (Ap. Br. 44) has again left out the complete instruction which appears as follows (Tr. 44-45):

> "If you find that he was in Pasco, Washington, at the time that he is alleged to have made this sale in Portland, Oregon, then of course you should find him not guilty. But *he does not have to prove that he was in Pasco, Washington* It is sufficient if, after all the evidence is in, you have a reasonable doubt as to whether he was present at the time and place of the alleged transaction It is not up to him to prove it beyond a reasonable doubt, or he doesn't have to prove it by a preponderance of the evidence He merely has to show you by evidence that there is a reasonable doubt that he was there at that time and place." (Emphasis supplied.)

In spite of the fact that the court specifically charged that the defendant "does not have to prove that he was in Pasco, Washington," the defendant has argued that the instruction might be construed by the jury to mean that defendant must prove that he was in Pasco, Washington Again, defendant's complaint is frivolous.

Finally, in regard to alibi, defendant asserts that he was entitled to such an instruction in regard to the November 23, 1960, transaction described in the remaining three counts.

A study of defendant's testimony will show that he admitted meeting Love at the Kienow parking lot at *approximately* the time in question on November

23, 1960 (Tr. 119-121). In view of this testimony he was not entitled to an instruction on alibi as to the latter counts in the indictment.

CONCLUSION

Appellee respectfully prays the court to affirm the judgment of the District Court.

Respectfully submitted,

SIDNEY I. LEZAK,
 Acting United States Attorney,
 District of Oregon,
DONAL D. SULLIVAN,
 Assistant United States Attorney,
 Of Attorneys for Appellee.

IN THE

UNITED STATES COURT OF APPEALS

FOR THE NINTH CIRCUIT

JOHN M. SHUBIN and PETER S. SHUBIN,

Petitioners,

vs.

THE UNITED STATES DISTRICT COURT FOR
THE SOUTHERN DISTRICT OF CALIFORNIA,
CENTRAL DIVISION; THE HONORABLE
WILLIAM M. BYRNE, Judge of the United States
District Court for the Southern District of California,
Central Division, and S. VINCEN BOWLES, INC.,

Respondents.

REQUEST FOR

RECONSIDERATION AND REHEARING

WILLIAM DOUGLAS SELLERS
510 Citizens Bank Building
16 North Marengo Avenue
Pasadena 1, California

Attorney for Petitioners
John M. Shubin and Peter S. Shul

IN THE

UNITED STATES COURT OF APPEALS

FOR THE NINTH CIRCUIT

JOHN M. SHUBIN and PETER S. SHUBIN,

                Petitioners,

vs.

THE UNITED STATES DISTRICT COURT FOR
THE SOUTHERN DISTRICT OF CALIFORNIA,
CENTRAL DIVISION; THE HONORABLE
WILLIAM M. BYRNE, Judge of the United States
District Court for the Southern District of California,
Central Division, and S. VINCEN BOWLES, INC.,

                Respondents.

REQUEST FOR

RECONSIDERATION AND REHEARING

WILLIAM DOUGLAS SELLERS
510 Citizens Bank Building
16 North Marengo Avenue
Pasadena 1, California

Attorney for Petitioners
John M. Shubin and Peter S. Shubin

IN THE

UNITED STATES COURT OF APPEALS

FOR THE NINTH CIRCUIT

JOHN M. SHUBIN and PETER S. SHUBIN,

                      Petitioners,

    vs.

THE UNITED STATES DISTRICT COURT FOR
THE SOUTHERN DISTRICT OF CALIFORNIA,
CENTRAL DIVISION; THE HONORABLE
WILLIAM M. BYRNE, Judge of the United States
District Court for the Southern District of California,
Central Division, and S. VINCEN BOWLES, INC.,

                Respondents.

REQUEST FOR
RECONSIDERATION AND REHEARING

To the Honorable, The Chief Judge and Associate Judges

the United States Court of Appeals for the Ninth Circuit:

The petitioners in the above matter respectfully request t

Honorable Court to reconsider its decision of January 31, 1963,

after remand by the Supreme Court, upon the Shubin petition for

writ of mandamus or other relief, and to grant rehearing upon th

following grounds:

Ground 1:   The Court of Appeals has twice denied the Shubins

petition for writ of mandamus, once before the granting of certio

by the Supreme Court and once after. According to this Court's

own statement its consideration was directed to different subject

matter in the two decisions. According to this Court's own state

its consideration, did not face or determine the issue of whether petitioners were entitled to a jury trial upon the issues raised by the complaint for declaratory relief and the answer thereto alone, a jury trial having been properly demanded, and whether if that right did exist, it was waived by the filing of a compulsory counterclaim.

This Court did not pass upon that question, yet it is the basic issue raised.

According to its own statements the issues considered in the two decisions were as follows:

First decision dated December 29, 1961 (par. 1):

"Before us is a petition for Mandamus to require the district court to grant petitioners a jury trial on certain issues raised by a proposed amended counterclaim."

Second decision dated January 31, 1963:

"This is a petition for Writ of Mandamus requiring the District Court to grant petitioners a jury trial on certain issues raised by an existing, and a proposed amended, counterclaim." (Decision, par. 1).

and

"Petitioners' second position is that they are entitled to a jury on the issue raised by the complaint and the original counterclaim already on file." (Decision, par. 2).

The basic issue was never "issues raised by a proposed

2.

amended counterclaim', as stated in the first decision. That proposed counterclaim had not been filed. The proposal to file that
"amended counterclaim" raised only the issue of petitioners' right
to file it. The basic issue of petitioners' right to a jury trial upon
the issues raised by the filed complaint and answer remained no
matter what happened to the "proposed amended counterclaim".
That question was ignored by the first decision though clearly
raised in the petition.

The second decision, that following remand by the Supreme
Court and dated January 31, 1963, and as quoted above, states the
issues to be "certain issues raised by an existing, and a proposed
amended, counterclaim" and "the issue raised by the complaint and
the original counterclaim", is closer by far than the alleged issues
stated in the first decision but still misses the point.

Not the issues raised by "existing" or "proposed amended,
counterclaim", not the issues raised "by the complaint and the
original counterclaim", but: Is the right to a jury trial as to issues
raised by a complaint for declaratory relief and the answer lost by
the filing of a compulsory counterclaim?

That is the issue. This Court has not faced that issue
squarely and it is the basic issue presented. It should, in order that
the Supreme Court will know its position clearly, for the importance
of the rights involved will of necessity cause this matter to be
resubmitted there.

Ground 2:   The decision of this Court upon remand holds that a

a. It ignores the law that a declaratory judgment action is neither legal nor equitable; and

b. It ignores the basic rule that a jury trial properly demanded is to be denied only under "imperative circumstances".

c. It ignores the basic concept that the filing of a compulsory counterclaim cannot be considered as a waiver of a right of jury with respect to issues raised in other pleadings as to which a jury has been properly demanded.

Ground 3: The decision of this Court upon remand is incompatible with the spirit and the law of Beacon Theatres and Dairy Queen which recognize the right to a jury trial properly demanded upon jury issues is to be denied only under "imperative circumstances", and in accepting as "imperative circumstances" circumstances which are in no sense "imperative" comprising:

a. The presence of a compulsory counterclaim;

b. The request for an accounting in the compulsory counterclaim when everyone admits there is nothing to account for;

c. The request for an injunction in the compulsory counterclaim which also clearly is not needed for the same reason the accounting is not needed.

Ground 4: The decision of this Court upon remand ignores the fact the issues of validity and infringement are suitable for a jury under United States v. Esnault-Pelterie, 299 U.S. 201, 205, that a jury trial was demanded as to those issues raised by the complaint and answer, and that the filing of a compulsory counterclaim does

4.

ot effect a waiver of that demand.

Ground 5:   This Court obviously erred in holding that there "can

e no adequate remedy at law" (penultimate paragraph of decision)

n the present case where the remedy at law is fully adequate as to

ne complaint and answer for which a jury trial has been demanded.

For each of the above reasons or grounds, this Court is

espectfully requested to reconsider and rehear this case.

Respectfully submitted,

/s/ W. D. SELLERS

WILLIAM DOUGLAS SELLERS

Attorney for Petitioners
John M. Shubin and Peter S. Shubin

CERTIFICATE

I hereby certify that in my judgment the foregoing Request

r Reconsideration and Rehearing is well founded and is not inter-

osed for delay.

/s/ W. D. SELLERS

WILLIAM DOUGLAS SELLERS

IN THE

UNITED STATES COURT OF APPEALS

FOR THE NINTH CIRCUIT

JOHN M. SHUBIN and PETER S. SHUBIN,

                                  Petitioners,

vs.

THE UNITED STATES DISTRICT COURT FOR THE
SOUTHERN DISTRICT OF CALIFORNIA, CENTRAL
DIVISION,

                                  Respondent,

THE HONORABLE WILLIAM M. BYRNE, Judge of
the United States District Court for the Southern
District of California, Central Division,

                                  Respondent,

and

S. VINCEN BOWLES, INC.,

                                  Respondent.

**PETITIONERS' BRIEF UPON REMAND
BY THE SUPREME COURT**

FILED

OCT 3 0 1962

FRANK H. SCHMID, CLE

WILLIAM DOUGLAS SELLERS
510 Citizens Bank Building
16 North Marengo Avenue
Pasadena 1, California

Attorney for Petitioners
John M. Shubin and
Peter S. Shubin

IN THE

UNITED STATES COURT OF APPEALS

FOR THE NINTH CIRCUIT

JOHN M. SHUBIN and PETER S. SHUBIN,

Petitioners,

vs.

THE UNITED STATES DISTRICT COURT FOR THE
SOUTHERN DISTRICT OF CALIFORNIA, CENTRAL
DIVISION,

Respondent,

THE HONORABLE WILLIAM M. BYRNE, Judge of
the United States District Court for the Southern
District of California, Central Division,

Respondent,

and

S. VINCEN BOWLES, INC.,

Respondent.

PETITIONERS' BRIEF UPON REMAND
BY THE SUPREME COURT

WILLIAM DOUGLAS SELLERS
510 Citizens Bank Building
16 North Marengo Avenue
Pasadena 1, California

Attorney for Petitioners
John M. Shubin and
Peter S. Shubin

TOPICAL INDEX

TABLE OF AUTHORITIES

Cases

Statutes

JOHN M. SHUBIN and PETER S. SHUBIN,

Petitioners,

vs.

THE UNITED STATES DISTRICT COURT FOR THE
SOUTHERN DISTRICT OF CALIFORNIA, CENTRAL
DIVISION,

Respondent,

THE HONORABLE WILLIAM M. BYRNE, Judge of
the United States District Court for the Southern
District of California, Central Division,

Respondent,

and

S. VINCEN BOWLES, INC.,

Respondent.

_____

PETITIONERS' BRIEF UPON REMAND
BY THE SUPREME COURT

_____

To the Honorable, the Chief Judge and Associate Judges of

the United States Court of Appeals for the Ninth Circuit:

STATEMENT OF CASE

1. The facts of the case prior to the filing of the Peti-

tion for Writ of Mandamus or Other Writ or Relief in this Court are

1.

set forth in the Brief filed with that Petition at pages 10-13, inclusive, and are also set forth in the decision of this Court at 299 F. 2d 47.

2. This Court, by its decision cited above, denied petitioners' request for a writ of mandamus to compel the District Court to grant a jury trial and allow a motion to amend petitioners' counterclaim.

3. Petition was made to the Supreme Court of the United States for a Writ of Certiorari to the United States Court of Appeals for the Ninth Circuit.

4. The Supreme Court, as stated above, granted certiorari and on May 14, 1962, per curiam, vacated judgment.

5. The Supreme Court remanded the case for reconsideration in light of Dairy Queen, Inc. v. Wood, 369 U.S. 469, 82 S. Ct. 894.

THE QUESTION NOW PRESENTED

In petitioners' original brief for mandamus, two questions were presented on pages 9-10 and they read as follows:

"Question 1: Is a party entitled under the Constitution to a jury trial in a case in which the complaint and the answer raise only jury issues but a counterclaim raising the same issues seeks equitable relief?

"Question 2: Does the District Court violate judicial discretion by refusing to grant leave to file an amended counterclaim which eliminates prayers for equitable relief when discovery proceedings have disclosed the absence of irreparable harm and that the legal remedy would be adequate?"

In view of the action by the Supreme Court and its emphasis the Dairy Queen case, the question now posed may be stated as llows:

Is a party entitled, under the Constitution and applicable statutes, to a jury trial in a case in which the complaint and the answer raise only jury issues, but a compulsory counterclaim, raising the same issues, seeks relief which may be viewed as equitable?

THE FACTS

The facts involved in this case are fully presented in petioners' original brief before this Court, and reference is made to iges 10-13 of that document.

SUMMARY OF ARGUMENT

In addition to the statements made in petitioners' original

ARGUMENT

In petitioners' original brief it was stated in essence that
the Supreme Court had, by its opinion in the case of Beacon
Theatres, Inc. v. Westover, 359 U. S. 500, 79 S. Ct. 948, 3 L. Ed.
2d 988, affirmed the constitutional right under the Seventh Amendment of a party to obtain a jury trial as to legal issues in an action
where both equitable and legal causes were joined, except under
the most imperative circumstances.

The presence of equitable issues in an action cannot auto-
matically be the basis for a holding that there is an abandonment
of the right to a jury trial, especially under the Declaratory Judgment Act and the Federal Rules which expand the legal remedies
and consequently restrict the scope of equity. As the Supreme
Court said in Scott v. Neely, 140 U. S. 106, 109-110, 11 S. Ct. 712,
714, 35 L. Ed. 358:

> "In the federal courts this (jury) right cannot be dis-
> pensed with, except by the assent of the parties entitled
> to it, nor can it be impaired by any blending with a
> claim, properly cognizable at law, of a demand for
> equitable relief in aid of the legal action or during
> its pendency. " (Parenthetical matter added.)

In the case of Dairy Queen, Inc. v. Wood (1962), 82 S. Ct. 894, 369 U. S. 469, 8 L. Ed. 2d 44, which was especially referred to by the Supreme Court in remanding the present case for reconsideration, it was emphasized that legal issues are entitled to jury determination where a party asserts his right thereto in a timely and proper manner despite the fact that these legal issues have been characterized as "incidental" to the equitable issues involved. Justice Black, speaking for the Court, stated that the adoption of the Federal Rules of Civil Procedure in 1938, 28 U. S. C. A., and especially Rule 18(a) permitting the joinder of legal and equitable claims in a single action, was not intended to change the basic holding of Scott v. Neely that the right to trial by jury of legal claims must be preserved. In fact, Rule 38(a) expressly reaffirms that constitutional principle.

In the Dairy Queen case, the Supreme Court said that in view of the Beacon Theatres case the sole question was "whether the action now pending before the District Court contains legal issues". By stating such a proposition, the Court impliedly reaffirmed the premise that the Seventh Amendment and federal statutes guaranteeing a jury trial on legal claims is inviolate for all practical purposes where timely and proper demand has been made.

The facts in the Dairy Queen case involve an alleged breach of a licensing contract where the licensor sought an injunction against continued use of the licensed trademark as well as an

said that regardless of the words used, where the complaint requested a money judgment, it presented legal issues, whether the action was for a debt under a contract or damages based upon the charge of trademark infringement. And in any case:

> "The necessary prerequisite to the right to maintain a suit for an equitable accounting, like all other equitable remedies, is, as we pointed out in Beacon Theatres, the absence of an adequate remedy at law."

The burden of showing the necessity of equitable relief is upon the person opposed to a trial by jury where the cause of action is one cognizable at law. The Court added that in view of the availability of masters to assist the jury "the burden of such a showing is considerably increased and it will indeed be a rare case in which it can be met".

In the present case where the original complaint and answer thereto raise the issues of validity and patent infringement, it is submitted that these are issues which justify a jury trial whether or not the counterclaim raises any equitable questions. To allow the District Court to hear the entire case in equity proceedings amounts to a substantial denial of the petitioners' rights to a jury trial. It would appear that the Supreme Court was also of the opinion that closer attention should be paid to a possible denial of these rights regardless of the decision by the District Court judge on other matters of questionable discretion in refusing leave to amend the counterclaim. Even if it is conceded that the purpose of amending the counterclaim is to eliminate the obvious

areas where equity may act, still equitable procedures should not
be forced upon the party theoretically to be benefited by their
employment, especially when the involved party has made no such
request and has, in fact, fought against such procedure. This
action by the interested party should not be interpreted as having
sustained the burden of showing irreparable injury and/or inade-
quacy of legal remedies.

CONCLUSION

In addition to the conclusions included in petitioners'
original brief at pages 24-25, it may also be stated that the right
to a jury trial exists though there may be areas in which equity
might act when it can be shown that there are legal claims present
also, the determination of which a party desires and properly
requests be made by a jury.

Dated: October 29, 1962.

Respectfully submitted,

/s/ WILLIAM DOUGLAS SELLERS
WILLIAM DOUGLAS SELLERS

Attorney for Petitioners
John M. Shubin and Peter S. Shubin

No. 17591

IN THE

United States Court of Appeals

FOR THE NINTH CIRCUIT

STANLEY E. HENWOOD, RICHARD I ROEMER, LEWIS M POE,
individually, as members of the UNITED INDUSTRIAL CORPORA-
TION STOCKHOLDERS' PROTECTIVE COMMITTEE and as
proxies of said Committee, JAMES V ARMOGIDA, ROBERT G.
BALLANCE, FRED A BERSHARA, NATHANIEL R DUMONT,
JOE L. FOSS, WILLIAM D LAWRY, ELMER M LUTHER, JR,
EDWARD H. McLAUGHLIN, CHARLES SODERSTROM; JOHN
A. STEEL, CLARENCE L SUMMERS, RO L WILLIAMS,
LOUIS W WULFEKUHLER, ALFRED T ZODDA, individually
and as members of the UNITED INDUSTRIAL CORPORATION
STOCKHOLDERS' PROTECTIVE COMMITTEE, BERNARD F.
GIRA and HERBERT J. PETERSEN,

Appellants,

vs.

SECURITIES AND EXCHANGE COMMISSION and UNITED IN-
DUSTRIAL CORPORATION,

Appellees.

Opening Brief of Appellants Bernard F. Gira and Herbert J. Petersen.

KENDRICK, SCHRAMM & STOLZY,
ELWOOD S. KENDRICK,
JOHN P. SCHOLL,
JACK CORINBLIT,

   612 South Flower Street,
   Los Angeles 17, California,

     Attorneys for Appellants.

FILED

DEC 1 1961

FRANK H. SCHMID, CLERK

Parker & Son, Inc., Law Printers, Los Angeles. Phone MA. 6-9171.

TOPICAL INDEX

IV.

V.

VI.

The mandatory injunction requiring appellants Gira and Petersen to file amended schedules 14B is erroneous because:

TABLE OF AUTHORITIES CITED

STATUTES

No. 17591

IN THE

United States Court of Appeals

FOR THE NINTH CIRCUIT

STANLEY E HENWOOD, RICHARD I ROEMER, LEWIS M POE, individually, as members of the UNITED INDUSTRIAL CORPORATION STOCKHOLDERS' PROTECTIVE COMMITTEE and as proxies of said Committee, JAMES V ARMOGIDA, ROBERT G BALLANCE, FRED A BERSHARA, NATHANIEL R. DUMONT, JOE L FOSS, WILLIAM D LAWRY, ELMER M LUTHER, JR, EDWARD H McLAUGHLIN, CHARLES SODERSTROM, JOHN A. STEEL, CLARENCE L SUMMERS, ROY L WILLIAMS, LOUIS W WULFEKUHLER, ALFRED T ZODDA, individually and as members of the UNITED INDUSTRIAL CORPORATION STOCKHOLDERS' PROTECTIVE COMMITTEE, BERNARD F. GIRA and HERBERT J PETERSEN,

Appellants,

vs

SECURITIES AND EXCHANGE COMMISSION and UNITED INDUSTRIAL CORPORATION,

Appellees

Opening Brief of Appellants Bernard F. Gira and Herbert J. Petersen.

Jurisdictional Statement.

This is a proxy contest case. Appellee Securities and Exchange Commission (hereinafter referred to as SEC) filed a complaint in the United States District Court for the Southern District of California naming as defendants the appellants named in the caption and one Herman Yaras and Eugene Schaefer doing business as Schaefer and Company and Appellee United Industrial Corporation. The complaint charged that appellants Bernard F. Gira and Herbert J. Petersen had solicited proxies in violation of Securities and Exchange

Regulation 14a-9, 17 C. F. R. 20.14a-9 which had been adopted by appellee SEC pursuant to Sections 14(a) and 23(a) of the Securities and Exchange Act of 1934, 15 U. S. C. 78n(a) and 78w(a).

Jurisdiction of the trial court was based upon 15 U. S. C. 78u(e) and 15 U. S. C. 78u(f). Final judgment in the trial court was entered on October 17, 1961 and appellants filed their notice of appeal herein November 14, 1961. Jurisdiction of this court is based upon 18 U. S. C. Sections 1291 and 1294.

Statement of the Case.

The Questions Involved.

Question 1—The final judgment below enjoined appellants Gira and Petersen from soliciting proxies unless Gira and Petersen affirmatively stated the following:

> "Defendants Bernard F. Gira and Herbert J. Petersen were instrumental in initiating and organizing the UIC Stockholders' Protective Committee and in formulating on behalf of said committee a slate of directors for membership on the Board of Directors of UIC in opposition to the slate of directors formulated by the management of UIC."

and

> "Defendants Bernard F. Gira and Herbert J. Petersen have participated with representatives of the Stockholders' Protective Committee and aided and abetted said committee and its representatives in conducting proxy solicitations in opposition to the management of UIC." [C. T. ....]

The rule of law upon which the court relied in entering this judgment was Conclusion of Law 2 which reads as follows:

"The evidence convincingly establishes that Bernard F. Gira and Herbert J. Petersen have been 'participants' in the contest for control of United Industrial Corporation within the meaning of Rule 14a-11(b)(3) Regulation 14, 17 C.F.R. 240.14a-11(b)(3). The definition encompasses not only the acknowledged members of the Committee but all those who, even indirectly, initiate, direct, finance, or otherwise seek to advance the objectives of a Committee contending for control of a corporation." [C. T. ....]

Was the court's judgment contrary to law when the record below establishes:

1. The definition of "participant" applied by the court in examining the facts is not contained in Rule 14a-11(b)(3), as adopted, and is in fact contrary to that rule.

2. A showing of "participation" within the meaning of Rule 14a-11(b)(3), as adopted, required a showing of either membership in a proxy solicitation committee or the exercising of leadership in the organization, direction, or financing of such a proxy solicitation committee. The trial court found named individuals to be members of the stockholder protective committee, *excluding appellants Gira and Petersen.* The trial court *failed to find* that appellants Gira and Petersen exercised leadership in the organization, direction, or financing of the proxy committee.

3. If the findings actually made were intended to infer "membership" or that these appellants exercised leadership in the organizing, directing or financing of the Stockholders Protective Committee, then to that extent they were not supported by any substantial evidence, and were clearly erroneous.

Question 2—Insofar as Findings of Fact 6, 12, and 15 suggest an agreement or agreements between appellants, Gira and Petersen, and Brandlin to secretly, jointly organize a proxy solicitation committee, are such findings clearly erroneous when the undisputed evidence shows:

1. The only communications between Brandlin and appellants Gira and Petersen were to the direct effect that if Brandlin ever participated in a proxy contest involving UIC it would be with an independent committee, organized, directed, and financed independently of and with no commitments to appellants, Gira and Petersen.

2. The acts, as well as the words, of Brandlin and the members of the committee completely covered all aspects of organization, direction, and finance and were done independently of any direction or control of appellants, Gira or Petersen.

Question 3—Finding of Fact 24 entered by the court reads as follows:

"The Committee's proxy statement and its other three communications soliciting the proxies of stockholders of UIC have been mailed to some 15,000 shareholders. The Committee admits that its solicitations have been conducted through the mails and instrumentalities of interstate commerce. As Gira and Petersen initiated the Committee and have participated, directly and indirectly in directing and advancing its objectives, the Committee's use of the jurisdictional facilities is attributable to them."

Is Finding 24 clearly erroneous when the undisputed and indisputable evidence shows that:

1. The Stockholders' Protective Committee was initiated by the law firm of Vaughan, Brandlin & Baggot through attorneys Joseph J. Brandlin and Richard I. Roemer on behalf of and with the individual members of the Stockholders' Protective Committee and that these persons exercised, in fact, all of the leadership in connection with the organization, direction, and financing of the Stockholders' Protective Committee including designation and recruitment of the slate of nominees for the Committee, conceiving, drafting, clearing, and mailing of all proxy literature and all of the financing of every step of the proxy contest.

Question 4—Was a mandatory injunction directing appellants, Gira and Petersen, to file corrected Schedules 14B "concerning their participation in the solicitation of proxies in respect of the common and preferred stock of UIC" contrary to law when the record established:

1. No findings of fact were made by the court as to the respects in which said Schedules 14B's were insufficient.

2. The Schedules 14B filed by appellants Gira and Petersen, with the caveat that they were not participants, were in compliance with the applicable rules and statutes.

Description of the Complaint and Final Judgment.

The complaint in this action filed by the Securities and Exchange Commission alleged in Count I thereof that appellants Gira and Petersen violated Rule 14a-9 of the Securities and Exchange Commission. That Rule provides:

> "No solicitation subject to this regulation shall be made by means of any proxy statement, form of proxy, notice of meeting, or other communication, written or oral, containing any statement which, at the time and in the light of the circumstances under which it is made, is false or misleading with respect to any material fact, or which omits to state any material facts necessary in order to make the statements therein not false or misleading or necessary to correct any statement in any earlier communication with respect to the solicitation of a proxy for the same meeting or subject matter which has become false or misleading."

The complaint alleged that appellants Gira and Petersen solicited proxies which were false and misleading in that these particular proxy solicitations *ommited* to make certain statements and *affirmatively made* other statements which made the proxy solicitations false and misleading. The particular solicitations against which the charge was laid consisted of four reports or letters identified as *Plaintiff SEC's Exhibit 13* and *Defendant Stockholders' Protective Committee Exhibit A*. These mailings were admittedly carried out by the Stockholders' Protective Committee, found by the trial court to consist of seventeen named individuals [Finding 4], other than appellants Gira and Petersen. A final judgment was entered against appellants Gira and Petersen, only upon the grounds that, for reasons to be hereinafter discussed, the solicitations made by the Stockholders' Protective Committee were "imputable" to Gira and Petersen. [C. T. ....]

The four proxy solicitation letters affirmatively state that appellants Gira and Petersen gave certain specific assistance to the Stockholders' Protective Committee including a stockholders list and information about the United Industrial Corporation as well as detailed statements concerning any prior contact or familiarity by members of the Stockholders' Protective Committee with Gira and Petersen. These appellants testified as to all of these facts before the Securities and Exchange Commission in March 1961. [Pltf. Exs. 33, 34.]

The judgment below, as to appellants Gira and Petersen, requires that as a condition of "further solicitation" (which these appellants did not and do not desire to carry on) that appellants *state* that they were instrumental in initiating and organizing the Protective Committee and formulating a slate of directors for that Committee and that they participated with and aided and abetted proxy solicitations by the Committee. They are further *enjoined* from stating that they are neither members or are participating with the Protective Committee in soliciting proxies.

In addition, the Judgment directed, by a mandatory injunction of the trial court, that appellants correct Schedule 14B filed with the Securities and Exchange Commission in July 1961, and set forth additional but undesignated information "concerning their status as participants in the proxy controversy."

It is appellants contention that the statements required by the trial court's judgment to be made concerning appellants are not true and that the findings of fact, conclusions of law, and judgment which require such statements to be made are unsupported in fact and unsupportable in law. It is appellants contention that the Schedules 14B filed by them comply with the rules and that the findings, conclusions of law, and judgment to the contrary are unsupported in fact and unsupportable as a matter of law.

The Background in Which the Questions Are Raised.

In this proxy contest the attacks by both the Stockholders' Protective Committee and management upon each other created an issue involving appellants Gira and Petersen. The issue as stated by the Stockholders' Protective Committee was that present management, including Gira and Petersen, were responsible for certain adverse results in connection with United Industrial Corporation. The attack by management was that the Stockholders' Protective Committee was a "front" for appellants Gira and Petersen and that they alone had been responsible for the economic adversity of UIC.

Because this issue was raised even prior to the first release of any proxy solicitation material by either side, the Securities and Exchange Commission permitted extensive comments by both sides concerning appellants. The Commission also made its own investigation in March 1961.

From the outset it was stated to the Securities and Exchange Commission and to 15,000 stockholders that Messrs. Gira and Petersen had sought the advice of Mr.

Brandlin, later counsel for the Committee wherein Messrs. Gira and Petersen stated they were *not* interested in waging a proxy contest; that Gira and Petersen had made available to the firm of Vaughan, Brandlin & Baggot a stockholders list; that they had given information to one of the slate of nominees concerning United Industrial Corporation; and that another of the members of the Committee, Mr. Williams, was an uncle of Gira. The Stockholders' Protective Committee distributed literature to the stockholders which made reference to every possible contact within a period of many years that Messrs. Gira and Petersen had ever had with any of the members of the Committee.

From the outset it has been clear that these appellants have been used by both sides as political punching bags in a struggle for control, although management material has been much more violent. The solicitation material of management went so far as to attack the honesty and integrity of these appellants and management was sued for libel. [Gira and Petersen Ex. II.] It is in this context that both the history and the present status of this controversy must be examined. Appellants Gira and Petersen have at all times asserted their own honesty and integrity. They are owners collectively of 100,000 shares of the stock of United Industrial Corporation, having purchased much of that stock at its highest price and having retained the ownership of that stock throughout this controversy. Their life savings are embroiled here. They have the opinion that present management will not likely protect their investment.

The charges levelled by the Securities and Exchange Commission here are *not* that Gira and Petersen, or the Stockholders' Protective Committee for that matter, failed to reveal the matters detailed above concerning contacts between them. The charges levelled by the Securities and Exchange Commission here are *not* that appellants Gira and Petersen have doubts concerning present management. *The charge is to the effect that these appellants secretly organized the Stockholders' Protective Committee and in substance still secretly control it.* These charges are the basis upon which the Securities and Exchange Commission seeks to "impute" to appellants Gira and Petersen the proxy solicitation material mailed by the Stockholders' Protective Committee: these charges are the basis upon which the Securities and Exchange Commission sought a judgment in this action *requiring*, in effect, that appellants *admit* their guilt; these charges form the basis upon which the Securities and Exchange Commission obtained a judgment below requiring appellant to amend their schedules 14B filed with the Securities and Exchange Commission, again admitting to the conclusions as seen by the Securities and Exchange Commission. It is these charges upon which the judgment now before this court is based which, it is submitted, these claims are completely without foundation.

The Manner in Which the Questions Are Raised.

At the trial below, at the end of SEC's evidence motions were made by all of the defendants to dismiss under F. R. C. P. 41(b). [C. T. ....] The motions were denied except as to defendant Herman Yaras. That defendant, the record established, had discussed with counsel for the Protective Committee a proxy contest; had sold to Richard I. Roemer, one of the attorneys for the Committee, 2,000 shares of UIC stock which

Roemer used in part to resell to members of the slate of the Stockholders' Protective Committee. Moreover, Yaras had sent Elmer N. Luther, Jr., who later became a member of the Stockholders' Protective Committee, to Brandlin. The court below granted the motion of Yaras to dismiss and found that these facts did not establish that Yaras was a "participant" within the meaning of 14a-11(b)(3) and did not constitute him "a solicitor of proxies" and did not permit the proxy solicitation of the Stockholders' Protective Committee to be "attributed" to him. [C. T. ....]

At the close of all the evidence, appellants renewed their Motions to Dismiss, which were denied; appellants objected to the Findings of Fact and Conclusions of Law, all of which objections were denied; appellants moved for a new trial and a new judgment under F. R. C. P. 59 and these motions were denied. [C. T. ....]

Specifications of Error.

The district court erred as a matter of law in entering the judgment appealed from and in denying appellants motions to dismiss and appellants motion for a new trial and for a new and different judgment because:

1. The court erroneously adopted and applied a rule of law that the acts of aid admitted by appellants and disclosed and known to the Securities and Exchange Commission and all of the stockholders constituted appellants "participants" within the meaning of Rule 14a-11(b)(3).

2. The court erroneously made no findings as to whether appellants exercised "leadership—initia-

tive" in organizing, directing, or financing the Stockholders' Protective Committee, which findings were essential to support any judgment under Rule 14a-11(b)(3).

3. To the extent that the findings actually entered can fairly be construed as a finding of "leadership—initiative" in organizing, directing, or financing the Stockholders' Protective Committee, there is no substantial evidence to support such findings.

4. Findings of Fact 6, 12, and 15 insofar as they find existence of agreements between appellants and Brandlin concerning a proxy contest are erroneous as a matter of law since there is no substantial evidence in the record to support them.

5. The following findings of fact in the respects indicated are erroneous as a matter of law for the reason that there is no substantial evidence to support them:

A. Findings 7 and 11 to the extent that it is stated therein that a stockholders list was surreptitiously removed or stolen.

B. Finding 17 to the effect that it states that Gira and Petersen *inspired* the formation of the Commitee.

C. Finding 18 to the extent that it suggests any relationship between the information given to Henwood by Gira and Petersen and Henwood becoming Chairman of the Committee.

D. Finding 19 to the extent that it is asserted that counsel for the Committee suggested a libel suit to Gira and Petersen.

E. Finding 20 to the extent that it states that Gira and Petersen took active roles as participants by reason of a letter sent to the SEC by counsel for Gira and Petersen but which letter was never sent to any shareholder.

F. Finding 21 to the extent that it characterizes a press release, plaintiff Exhibit 23, and to the extent it alleges that Gira and Petersen caused the press release to be "issued to the press."

G. Finding 22 to the extent that it alleges that Gira and Petersen were "true sponsors" of the Stockholders' Protective Committee and sought to supress their contacts with the Committee.

H. Finding of Fact 24 to the extent that it states that because "Gira and Petersen *initiated* the Committee, and have "participated directly and indirectly, in directing and advancing its objectives, the Committee's use of the jurisdictional facilities is attributable to them."

I. Findings on the affirmative defenses No. 2 to the extent that it states that Gira and Petersen "caused" a press release to be issued or intended to conduct a proxy contest behind a seemingly independent Committee.

6. Appellants hereby incorporate by reference the objections to the findings of fact made by the Stockholders' Protective Committee appellants at pages .... through .... of their brief as though fully set forth herein.

ARGUMENT.

I.

Additional Factual Background.

The statement of facts made by the Stockholders' Committee appellants in their brief, pages ...... to ......, accurately states the material facts in this matter and they are adopted herein so as to avoid unnecessary repetition in this brief. The following additional matters are set forth to supplement this statement of facts.

A. Gira and Petersen Leave UIC.

In 1960 United Industrial Corporation, a Delaware corporation, commenced doing business, having come into existence as a result of a merger of Topp Industries, Inc., a Delaware corporation, and United Industrial Corporation, a Michigan corporation. Bernard F. Gira, one of the appellants herein was a vice-president of Topp Industries, Inc., and had been a director and president of that corporation and its successor corporation since 1955. Appellant Herbert J. Petersen was one of the founders of Topp Industries, Inc. He had been a director of that corporation since 1951 and Executive Vice President since 1955. After the merger the company had a number of subsidiaries engaged in various aspects of the electronics business and other fields. [Deft. Gira and Petersen's Ex. LL, pp. 14 and 15.]

From January 1960 to January 1961, for many reasons, the stock of UIC declined from a high of $11. to a low of below $5.

By reason of the determination in late 1960 to recognize certain losses and to write-off research and development assets which, as of the end of 1960 no longer had value, and by reason of the fact that such write-off was in the magnitude of $7,000,000., a substantial policy crises was created in UIC. At a meeting in early January 1961 appellants Gira and Petersen resigned. [C. T. ....]

The announcement of the write-off and the timing thereof caused the stock to be suspended by the New York Stock Exchange and other national exchanges and by the Securities and Exchange Commission. Immediately upon leaving UIC, Gira and Petersen learned of intentions on the part of some of new management, particularly one Bernard Fein, to institute litigation against them.

B. Brandlin's "Independent Committee" Statement.

Gira and Petersen consulted with Roemer and Brandlin concerning their problems in the corporation. Gira and Petersen expressly stated that they would not engage in a proxy contest with respect to United Industrial Corporation. [R. T. 229, 1247, 1272.] Brandlin expressly stated that if he ever took on a proxy contest involving UIC it would only be with a committee of outstanding and independent individuals and particularly independent of Gira and Petersen. [R. T. 1247, 1248, 1269-1273.]

C. Gira and Petersen Do Not Organize the Committee.

Brandlin and Roemer began and continued the organization of what became the Stockholders' Protective Committee by recruiting nominees for the slate and they were joined in this program of recruitment by one of their first choices, Mr. Henwood. [R. T. 234-235, 1340-1341.] While Summers had been told by Petersen that Vaughan, Brandlin & Baggot might need a public relations man and Summers stated that this was his interest in the potential proxy contest, at a later date he joined the Committee as a member. [R. T. 1222-1223, 2112-2117, 2182.] The testimony was that *all* of the activities in the organization of the Committee were carried out entirely by attorneys Brandlin and Roemer with the help of Summers insofar as Dumont was concerned and Henwood insofar as Zodda was concerned. [R. T. 234-235, 1340-1341.] These activities, the record without any question established, were without the knowledge, consent, approval, or disapproval requested or obtained of Gira or Petersen. [R. T. 321, 323, 339.]

D. Gira and Petersen Do Not Direct the Proxy Contest.

Thereafter the proxy contest which involved the activities of drafting proxy material, submitting it to the SEC, redrafting and mailing, all were carried out by the Committee and particularly Brandlin and Roemer. [R. T. 236.] Again no evidence was submitted or findings of fact submitted to the contrary.

When it was rumored that management was charging that the Committee was a "front" for Gira and Petersen, Brandlin, in a discussion with Gira and Petersen stated he would send a wire threatening action at such a charge and asked Gira and Petersen to do the same. [R. T. 1261-1263.] Gira and Petersen did not send such a wire or any wire.

After management's literature came out attacking the integrity of Gira and Petersen, their attorney Kendrick sent the SEC a letter that was being considered by Gira and Petersen as a method of fighting back at the charges of misfeasance made by management. That letter was *not* sent to any stockholder. [R. T. 428, 467, 529.]

E. The Libel Suit.

Subsequently in July, Gira and Petersen filed a libel suit against management by reason of the direct charge of dishonesty made in a management mailing. A press release on this libel suit was independently prepared by a friend and public relations man, one Lewis, and was submitted to the SEC by Kendrick for approval. [R. T. 94, 95, 634, 469.] The only authority Lewis had to release the press release was upon approval by Kendrick, which approval was in turn conditioned on the approval of the SEC. [Pltf. SEC Ex. 25; R. T. 95, 631.] When the SEC disapproved the release and belatedly informed Kendrick of that disapproval, Kendrick contacted Lewis to direct him not to issue the release. However, contrary to prior express authority Lewis had permitted the release to be delivered to some news outlets. [Pltf. SEC Ex. 21; R. T. 631.] He testified that he "took a chance", contrary to express authority, upon his belief that the SEC would approve the release.

In fact,

> (a) The release was stopped in Los Angeles except for one minor article in the "Examiner". [Pltf. SEC Ex. 25; Deft. Gira and Petersen Ex. HH.]

(b) The release in the form prepared never appeared, in any publication. [Pltf. SEC Ex. 19; Defts. Gira and Petersen's Exs. AA, BB, CC, DD, HH.]

(c) In the form in which *part* of the material appeared, it was aboslutely sterile and innocuous.

(d) The release was not charged to be false and misleading and was therefore not encompassed within the issues submitted by the complaint.

(e) The release was never found to be false and misleading and is therefore not an issue in this case.

The SEC upon the basis of the issuance of that release (without any proof that any stockholder had been solicited or affected by it in any way) demanded that Gira and Petersen file Schedules 14B presumably upon the grounds that by reason of that act Gira and Petersen fell under 14a-11(b)(6) [not 14a-11(b)(3)] as of the time of the release. Gira and Petersen under protest filed such Schedules 14B. [Deft. Gira and Petersens' Ex. FF.] They contained a statement concerning the press release which, under Rule 14a-11(b)-(6), was all that was required.

On July 21, 1961 the complaint herein was filed by the Securities and Exchange Commission which charged appellants and others with violating Rule 14a-9.

II.

Findings of Fact Which Are Clearly Erroneous Cannot Support a Judgment Under Rule 52 of the Federal Rules of Civil Procedure. Moreover Rule 52 Has No Application Where the Law Applied Is Incorrect.

The rules of law applicable to appellate examination of findings by a trial court cannot be in dispute. Rule 52(a) provides that they may not be reversed unless they are clearly erroneous. The corollary is that if findings are clearly erroneous they cannot be used to support a judgment. However, it is established law both in courts of appeal and in the United States Supreme Court that where the question is whether the district court applied the *proper standard* the rejection of findings is a question of law and Rule 52(a) has no application.

> *United States v. Parke Davis & Company,* 362 U. S. 29, 80 S. Ct. 503 (1960) ;
>
> *Interstate Circuit v. United States,* 306 U. S. 208, 59 S. Ct. 467;
>
> *United States v. John J. Felin & Company,* 334 U. S. 624, 68 S. Ct. 1238;
>
> *Great Atlantic and Pacific Tea Company v. Supermarket Equipment Corporation,* 340 U. S. 147, 71 S. Ct. 127.

As Justice Frankfurter stated in *Baumgartner v. United States,* 322 U. S. 665, 64 S. Ct. 1241, "the conclusiveness of a finding of fact depends on the nature of the materials on which a finding is based.

The finding even of a so-called 'subsidiary fact' may be a more or less difficult process varying according to the simplicity or subtlety of the type of 'fact' in controversy. Finding so-called ultimate 'facts' more clearly implies the application of standards of law. And so the 'finding of fact' even if made by two courts may go beyond the determination that should not be set aside here."

See also:

> Chandler v. United States, 226 F. 2d 403;
>
> Sears, Roebuck & Company v. Johnson, 219 F. 2d 590;
>
> Hunter Douglas Corporation v. Lando Products, 215 F. 2d 372 (C. C. A. 9, 1954);
>
> Irish v. United States, 225 F. 2d 3 (C. C. A. 9 1955).

III.

The Conclusion of Law Below Finding Appellants, Gira and Petersen, to Be "Participants" Within the Meaning of Rule 14a-11(b)(3) of Regulation 14 Is Erroneous Because (1) It Is Based Upon the Application of Erroneous Standards, (2) There Are No Express Findings to Support It, and (3) the Indirect Findings Relating to the Issue Are Unsupported by the Evidence and Are Clearly Erroneous.

The Court below entered the following Conclusion of Law No. 2:

> "The evidence convincingly establishes that Bernard F. Gira and Herbert J. Petersen have been 'participants' in the contest for control of United Industrial Corporation within the meaning of Rule 14a-11(b)(3) of Regulation 14, 17 C.F.R. 240.

14a-11(b)(3).[7] The definition encompasses not only the acknowledged members of a committee, but all those who, even indirectly, initiate, direct, finance or otherwise seek to advance the objectives of a Committee contending for control of a corporation."

Rule 14a-11(b)(3), to which Conclusion of Law 2 refers, reads as follows:

"(b) *PARTICIPANT OR PARTICIPANT IN A SOLICITATION*. For purposes of this rule the term 'participant' and 'participant in a solicitation' include the following:

. . . (3) Any Committee or group which solicits proxies, any member of such Committee or group and any person whether or not named as a member who, acting alone or with one or more other persons, directly or indirectly, take the initiative in organizing, directing or financing any such Committee or group."

Parenthetically, it should be noted that the Court's Conclusion of Law is based expressly upon Rule 14a-11(b)(3) and no other provision of 14a-11. Thus, for example, the Court did *not* conclude that Gira and Petersen were participants under 14a-11(b)(4), (5) or (6). Thus, the Court did *not* conclude that Gira or Petersen solicited proxies (14a-11(b)(6)). Thus, the Court did *not* conclude that Gira and Petersen had lent money or entered into any arrangement or understanding with another participant for the purpose of financing or otherwise inducing the purchase, sale, holding or voting of securities of the Issuer by the participant or any other person (14a-11(b)(6)). The

Court did *not* conclude that Gira and Petersen had financed or joined with another to finance the solicitation of proxies (14a-11(b)(4)).

It is immediately apparent that the second sentence of Conclusion of Law 2, "is" without any warrant in the language of the Rule itself, distorts what the Rule says and expands the Rule's application far outside its boundary lines as written.

(a) The words "or otherwise seek to advance the objections of a committee contending for control of a corporation" simply is not in the Rule at all.

(b) The words "initiate, direct, or finance" in the court's language is, in the Rule itself "takes the initiative in organizing, directing, or financing."

It can immediately be seen that the rule as written excludes from the definition of the term participant, and as we shall show deliberately, those who aid, assist, advise or recommend in connection with a proxy contest. Moreover, "the initiative in organizing, directing, or financing" has reference to a finite group of those who exercise leadership in these activities. The emphasis is on those who take leadership action in the organizational activities or the activities of directing or financing the proxy contest.

The significance of the trial court's erroneous expansion of 14a-11(b)(3) is crucial in this case because if the rule had been applied as written the court must necessarily have found that the kind of assistance which appellants Gira and Petersen in fact gave could not make them participants in a proxy contest.

A. Gira an[...]
holders' [...]
14a-11(b[...]

An analy[...]
ings of Fa[...]
Petersen w[...]
holders' Pr[...]
pants" with[...]

Finding [...]
poration S[...]
sociation c[...]
neither Gir[...]
named in th[...]

Finding [...]
have met v[...]
casions tha[...]
mittee" also[...]
is evidenced[...]

Virtually [...]
bers of the [...]
rectly or by [...]
that they l[...]
[R. T. .....]

Althoug[...]
the Proxy [...]
lary terms [...]
been establ[...]
preme Cou[...]
S. Ct. 14[...]
planation [...]
indicating [...]

"

A. Gira and Petersen Were Not "Members" of the Stockholders' Protective Committee Within the Meaning of 14a-11(b)(3).

An analysis of the Conclusions of Law and Findings of Fact seem to concede that neither Gira nor Petersen were found to be "members of the Stockholders' Protective Committee" and thereby "participants" within that portion of Rule 14a-11(b)(3).

Finding of Fact 4 states that United Industrial Corporation Stockholders' Protective Committee is an association composed of seventeen named individuals and neither Gira nor Petersen are among the members named in that Finding of Fact.

Finding 22 which states that "Brandlin and Roemer have met with Gira and Petersen on many more occasions than they have met with members of the Committee" also supports this conclusion. The same result is evidenced by Conclusion of Law No. 3.

Virtually all of the seventeen (17) admitted members of the Committee testified at the trial, either directly or by deposition, and every one of them testified that they had no agreements with Gira or Petersen. [R. T. ....]

Although the term "membership" is not defined in the Proxy Rules the definition of analogous and corollary terms, as applied to group relationships, has long been established by the Supreme Court. Thus, the Supreme Court in *Bridges v. Wixon,* 326 U. S. 135, 65 S. Ct. 1443, accepted with approval the following explanation of the term "affiliation", admittedly a term indicating weaker ties than the term "membership":

". . . 'In the corporate field its use embraces not the casual affinity of an occasional similarity of objective, but ties and connections that, though less than that complete control which parent possesses over subsidiary, are nevertheless sufficient to create a continuing relationship that embraces both units within the concept of a system. In the field of eleemosynary and political organization the same basic idea prevails.' . . . 'Persons engaged in bitter industrial struggles tend to seek help and assistance from every available source. *But the intermittent solicitation and acceptance of such help must be shown to have ripened into those bonds of mutual cooperation and alliance that entail continuing reciprocal duties and responsibilities before they can be deemed to come within the statutory requirement of affiliation. . . .*" Emphasis supplied.)

As the court later commented in *Bridges v. Wixon, supra,* affiliation imports "less than membership but more than sympathy." The key distinction is agreement by all parties and performance of the duties required by all parties. Thus, in *Fisher v. United States,* 231 F. 2d 99, at 107, the court said "membership is composed of a desire on the part of the person in question to belong to an organization and acceptance by the organization." In this case, the evidence established that neither Gira nor Petersen desired or requested to be a member of the Stockholders' Protective Committee and that the seventeen individuals named as members did not and would not agree to accept Gira and Petersen as members. Certainly the testimony established that all of the duties of membership and particularly financing were carried on by those persons found by the court to be members and no one else.

We are, of course, not referring at this point to such advocate's labels as are represented by phrases like "not openly participants in the contest" [Finding 12]; "inspiring the formation" [Finding 17]; "closely related to the Committee" [Finding 19]; "true sponsors of the Committee's objectives" [Conclusion of Law 3]; and "defacto participation". [Conclusion of Law 3.] These adjectives, it is apparent, are deliberately short of the "Proxy Committee Membership" requirement and their use is therefore not inconsistent with what we believe to be a conceded fact—that the Securities and Exchange Commission did not contend nor did the Court find Gira or Petersen to be members of the Stockholders' Protective Committee under Rule 14a-11(b)(3).

B. Gira or Petersen Did Not Take Organizing, Directing or Financing Initiative With Respect to the Committee.

The remaining portion of Rule 14a-11(b)(3) which should be considered is what we will term here the "organizing initiative" provision of that Rule. Thus, although one is not a *member* of a Proxy Solicitation Committee, one may still be a participant because this rule also applies to "any person whether or not named as a member who, acting alone or with one or more other persons, *directly or indirectly, takes the initiative in organizing, directing or financing any such Committee or group.*" (Emphasis supplied.)

It is significant to note that the Securities and Exchange Commission *did not* propose and the trial court *did not* enter a finding that Gira or Petersen did "directly or indirectly take the initiative in organizing, directing or financing" the Stockholders' Protective

Committee. One finds the descriptive, but off point language, such as "closely related" [Finding 19]; "true sponsors" [Finding 22]; "instigated and inspired" [Conclusion of Law 3]; and "defacto participation" [Conclusion of Law 3], but never the simple direct fact as laid down by the rule.

The closest language, but still far off mark, is in the form of an introductory phrase to Finding of Fact 24. That entire Finding of Fact reads as follows:

"The Committee's proxy statement and its other three communications soliciting the proxies of stockholders of UIC have been mailed to some 15,-000 shareholders. The Committee admits that its solicitations have been conducted through the mails and instrumentalities of interstate commerce. *As Gira and Petersen initiated the Committee and have participated directly and indirectly in directing and advancing its objectives, the Committee's use of the jurisdictional facilities is attributable to them.*"

As a matter of legal clarity it is perfectly apparent that "initiating a committee" is substantially different than "taking the initiative in organizing a committee." Again, "directing and advancing its objectives" is a substantially different matter than "taking the initiative in directing or financing a committee." The language of the rules requires a showing of primary leadership in those activities which have to do with organizing, directing, or financing a committee. The difference is significant as will be hereinafter shown.

1. The record in this case shows that Gira and Petersen gave to the attorneys for the Stockholders'

Protective Committee a stockholders list which was ultimately used by the Committee to solicit proxies; Gira and Petersen met with Mr. Henwood, the subsequent Chairman of the Committee and gave him information about the financial history and prospects of United Industrial Corporation; a public relations employee, Summers, was referred to counsel for the Committee by Petersen and that this employee later became a member of the Committee; Williams, a complaining stockholder and Gira's uncle, talked with Gira about Williams' complaint as to his shares and that Gira told him that Mr. Roemer of the firm of Vaughan, Brandlin & Baggot was investigating the matter. Thus, the record could support a finding as to this kind and extent of aid to the Committee. If Rule 14a-11(b)(3) said that one is a participant "if one aids or assists a proxy committee in any manner", the record would be material at this point but the rule does not so provide. (This is one of the basic errors in Conclusion of Law 2 adopted and employed by the court.) [C. T. ....]

2. In fact, Rule 14a-11(b(3) by its terms, supports the proposition that one may aid, assist, support, counsel, advise, sponsor, advance objectives, instigate or inspire a proxy soliciting Committee and one is not a participant—unless all of the facts show "organizing-initiative, directing-initiative or financing-initiative." Presumably this is the reason that such oblique language was used by the Securities and Exchange Commission in its proposed and adopted Findings. The facts in the record do not support the *required* factual showing. Substituted adjectives which suggest corollary but distinguishable standards do not cure the defect.

3. The statutory and administrative history of Rule 14a-11(b)(3) overwhelmingly supports the proposition that organizing, directing or financing initiative required by that Rule must be evidenced by leadership in these activities. To sustain a finding of initiative in organization, it must be shown *that Gira and Petersen undertook to establish the Committee as fully able to accomplish its purposes.*

Rule 14a-11 was adopted on January 26, 1956 (17 C. F. R. 240.14a-11). This rule is the so-called proxy contest rule, that is it is applicable only when there is opposition in a contest to obtain proxies. Before its adoption, in *any* proxy solicitation the first informational document filed with the Commission and sent to the stockholders was the so-called "proxy statement," Schedule 14A, which was required by Rule 14a-3. In the pre-1956 proxy statement, Schedule 14A, Question 3b required that there be designated the "names of the person on whose behalf it (the proxy solicitation) is made" (see 17 C. F. R. 240.14a(3) 1949 edition).

When Rule 14a-11 was adopted the following changes, among others to be later discussed, were made:

1. The new Rule 14a-11 applied only to proxy *contests.*

2. There were still required to be filed and sent to the stockholders the "proxy statements," Schedule 14A, but in proxy contest Question 3b was changed, and renumbered to Item 3(b)(2), so that in that event the question to be answered was "state *by whom* the solicitation is made. . . ." Rule 14a-11, Schedule 14A (17 C. F. R. 240.14a-11. Schedule 14A).

As noted, this was a substitute for the prior requirement to state the "names of persons *on whose behalf
the proxy solicitation was being made.*"

3.   It was provided that a new form, 14B, was to be
filed covering information concerning "participants," as
that term was defined in Rule 14a-11.   The deliberate
and recognized purpose of all these changes was to narrow and more critically define the *persons* as to whom
information was required, to *leaders and persons and
groups primarily engaged in and responsible for the conduct of the proxy solicitations.* Thus, Chairman J. Sin-
clair Armstrong of the Securities and Exchange Commission issued the following statement at the time the
rules were adopted:

> "The proxy rule revision as proposed for public
> comment in August applied to all proxy contests,
> including not only those for election of directors,
> but for other types of contested corporate action
> for which shareholders votes are required.   The
> proposed revision called for more information in
> detail with respect to the background, interests and
> activities of the participants in the contest.   In
> the proposal, as now modified, the rules would make
> most of the new provisions applicable only to con-
> tests for control of Management, that is, for elec-
> tion or removal of directors and not to other types
> of proxy contests.
>
> In addition the definition of a 'participant' in
> proxy contests has been more precisely defined and
> narrowed to apply only to *persons and groups pri-
> marily engaged in and responsible for the conduct
> of the proxy solicitation and not to persons only*

incidentally involved." (Emphasis supplied) (C.-C.H. Federal Securities Law Reporter, 52 to 56 Decisions, Paragraph 76,376.)

Professor Loss, in his major work "Securities Regulations" observes that disclosure is now required *"of persons who were leaders in the Committees formation although not technically members."* (Loss Securities Regulation Vol. II, p. 884, Note 119.)

Moreover, the requirement for active leadership is graphically demonstrated by the fact that even the chief executive officers of the Issuer are excluded from the definition of the term "participant," by virtue of their office alone. Thus, the President of a corporation or any other chief executive officer, engaged in a proxy contest, who would obviously be the chief source of information, guidance, advice, aid and assistance, *is not a participant.* When Rule 14a-11 was first proposed "an officer who designates or who is authorized to designate a nominee" was to be included in the term "participant"—*even this was eliminated by the final rule as adopted* (See 20 Fed. Register, p. 3657).

The derivation of the "initiative" provisions of Rule 14a-11(b)(3) may have been 17 C. F. R. 240.12b-2(O) which includes in the term "promoter" the following definition:

> "Any person who, acting alone or in conjunction with one or more other persons, directly or indirectly takes initiative in founding and organizing the business or enterprise of an issuer."

Note that insofar as the "initiative" provisions of Rule 14a-11(b)(3) have a relationship to the "promoter" definition, the 14a-11(b)(3) definition is narrower and less inclusive. It excludes those who take initiative "in founding" a group and includes only initiative "in organizing" a Committee or group. Moreover, the term used in Rule 14a-11(b)(3) is *"the initiative" while* the "promoter" definition in 17 C. F. R. 240.12b-2(O) would have included "any initiative." Here too, therefore, there is a restrictive tightening of the definition to make specific the requirement for active leadership in the organizational activities of the Committee.

In this very action the court recognized that even substantial aid and assistance does not constitute "participation." Thus, it was shown with respect to the defendant Herman Yaras that

1. He sent committee member Luther to Brandlin.

2. He discussed with Brandlin a proxy contest but Brandlin rejected Yaras' participation therein for various reasons.

3. He sold to committee member Roemer 2,000 shares of stock when it was not otherwise available, which Roemer used to resell to some of the nominees so that shareholder stakes would be established.

Yet on the record and at the end of plaintiff's case defendant Yaras was found to be *not* a participant, *not* a solicitor of proxies, and the activities of the Proxy Commiteee were not *"attributed"* to him. *Preliminary discussions which end in a refusal to permit a joint committee and, aid or assistance which is short of organizational initiative is not included in the confines of* Rule 14a-11(b)(3).

The common sense of this construction is consistent
with the public purpose of the rule which, if it cannot
be sensibly administered, is positively harmful to the administration of the Securities and Exchange Act. It
should be recalled that Rule 14a-11 provides that *no
solicitation* of proxies in a proxy contest may be made
unless Schedules 14B are filed for every participant.
If proxy contests are commenced and Schedules 14B
are not filed for true participants, the solicitors are subject to *criminal penalties, civil injunction,* and possible
invalidation of proxies. This risk, of course, is almost
entirely upon dissenters, that is those who are seeking
to upset entrenched management. If the designation
"participant" is not carefully defined, and precisely administered, then the rule is a trap to destroy effective
opposition.

Moreover, Schedule 14B demands and properly so,
detailed exposure of many facts. Those who, directly
or indirectly, take the initiative in organizing, directing, or financing a proxy committee can answer, and
should properly be called upon to answer these questions. But the class of persons falling within the "aid
and assistance catagories" will be so large as to make
impossible the obtaining of 14B Schedules.

Commissioner Armstrong struck the proper balance
when he stated that Schedule 14B statements were to be
required *only* of persons and groups "primarily engaged in and responsible for the conduct of the proxy
solicitation. . . ."

In the light of the foregoing it is clear that Gira and
Petersen were not participants in the proxy contest
within the provisions of 14a-11(b)(3).

IV.

If the Judgment Below Was Based on a Holding That Gira and Petersen "Indirectly," i.e., Secretly, Took the Initiative in Organizing, Directing, or Financing the Stockholders' Protective Committee Such a Holding Is Contrary to Law Because There Are No Findings of Fact to That Effect and Such Findings Are Unsupported by Evidence in the Record.

As has been demonstrated in discussion under Section II, *supra,* the actions of Gira and Petersen, as established by the record, could not support a holding that Gira or Petersen were "participants" within Rule 14a-11(b)(3). Did the trial court hold that Gira and Petersen *secretly* agreed with Brandlin that they would jointly take the initiative in organizing, directing, or financing a committee to solicit proxies in opposition to management?

Again the record does not expressly state this to be the holding and there is no substantial evidence to support such a finding. The complaint charges directly and unambiguously that Gira and Petersen made false and misleading proxy solicitations. There is no charge in Count I of the complaint, which is the only count directed against Gira and Petersen, that they agreed or conspired to solicit proxies or to organize a committee or to become participants in a proxy contest. There is no allegation in the complaint that these solicitations were false and misleading because Gira and Petersen had secretly agreed or conspired to become participants in a proxy contest.

There is no Conclusion of Law or Finding of Fact to this effect. Therefore, any judgment based upon such an unalleged and unadjudicated conclusion must fall.

Certainly Finding of Fact 6 does not state that Gira and Petersen entered into a secret agreement with Brandlin to jointly take the initiative in organizing a proxy committee and to keep secret Gira and Petersen's participation therein. But since the word "agree" and the word "assurance" appear in Finding of Fact 6 that finding and the evidence on the subject matter contained therein should be examined.

The following is a brief summary of that finding:

1. "It was agreed" that a proxy contest was one way to combat the expected UIC lawsuit (note no finding was made as to who "agreed" and the record established only that a proxy contest was mentioned by Brandlin).

2. Gira and Petersen "agreed" that they could not be "openly identified" with a proxy committee. (Note, no finding is made as to whether Gira and Petersen agreed with each other only or agreed with someone else.) The record establishes only that *no one* used the word or the idea that *secret membership* was in order.

3. That Gira and Petersen were "given assurances" that if "seemingly" independent stockholders and prominent nominees and a suitable public relations consultant could be arranged and a stockholders list obtained, they, Brandlin and Roemer, would undertake a proxy contest. (There was not one word of evidence that anyone assured anyone of anything.)

It should be recalled that at the time of these discussions Gira had a serious physical illness and both Petersen and Gira were emotionally upset by reason of the attacks of management. They believed and do now believe in their own integrity with respect to their stewardship as officers of UIC. One member of the management group particularly involved in the attacks on Gira and Petersen was Bernard Fein, an old discredited hand at corporate raiding. [Pltf. Ex. 20.]

Having met with Brandlin to obtain advice as to their corporate interests, Brandlin mentioned the possibility of a proxy fight. Any lawyer would have mentioned that possibility. But Brandlin then stated, in sworn testimony, that he told Gira and Petersen that he would not represent them in a proxy contest. Gira and Petersen were advised by Brandlin that their only defense to the impending charge by management was to defend when the charges were made and the threatened litigation by management commenced.

But a successful proxy contest involving UIC was evident so that any blind man could see it. The dramatic drop in the price of the stock, the suspension of trading, the so-called write-down of assets in the amount of $7,000,000—any able lawyer would see the possibilities. Therefore, Brandlin told Gira and Petersen that if he, Brandlin, ever undertook a proxy contest involving UIC it would only be with an independent slate, owing no obligation whatsoever to Gira or Petersen. Why would a lawyer make that kind of a statement, if he wanted the men listening to him to secretly agree or join in initiating the organization of a proxy committee.

This is the key logical discrepancy which, together with the total absence of any other evidence, belies even an argued finding of a secret agreement. Brandlin testified in so many words directly that he would accept no agreement with Gira or Petersen to organize a

proxy committee. Gira, Petersen, Brandlin, and Roemer all testified that there was no agreement. The
slate of nominees testified that there was no agreement. The independence of this slate of nominees and
the independence of Brandlin in running the contest
with their help all demonstrate no agreement. The evidence is overwhelming on this point. Even self interest belies such a conclusion because an uncommitted
slate of nominees would do nothing for Gira or Petersen.

Since indirect participation through a secret agreement was neither charged nor found nor could it be
supported by the record, a judgment based upon such
a holding is erroneous as a matter of law.

V.

**Since Neither Gira nor Petersen Made or Partici-
pated in the Four Proxy Solicitations Which
Were the Subject of the Suit Below and Were
Not Members of or Organizers, Directors, or
Financers of the Stockholders' Protective Com-
mittee, the Judgment of the Court Which
Would Require Statement to the Contrary to
Be Made Is in Error. Moreover the Commit-
tee's Use of the Jurisdictional Facilities Cannot
Be Attributed to Gira or Petersen.**

It follows from the arguments made, *supra,* that a
judgment which would require Gira and Petersen or
anyone to include in proxy solicitation material statements concerning the relationship of Gira and Petersen
to the proxy contest which are untrue could not be justified under the law. Rule 14a-9 precludes only false
and misleading facts.

Moreover the true contacts between Gira and Petersen and the Stockholders' Protective Committee as discussed earlier certainly would preclude any holding that the action of the Stockholders' Protective Committee is "attributable" to Gira or Petersen.

In the court below the SEC relied upon *Securities and Exchange Commission v. May,* 134 Fed. Supp. 247, affirmed 229 F. 2d 124. In that case it was held that an opposition committee violated Rule 14a-9 by withholding information concerning one Bernard Frankel. The court recited the following evidence concerning the hidden activities of Bernard Frankel.

1. Frankel discussed with a member of the committee the advisability of acquiring shares and as a result the member of the committee bought shares.

2. Frankel and the member of the committee jointly discussed with the officers of the issuer corporation the problems of management. He did this on numerous occasions over a period of three years.

3. A second member of the committee acquired shares in the issuer as a result of conversations with Frankel. That second member of the committee and Frankel conferred with the issuer concerning company business.

4. It was shown that Frankel also contacted another individual, who had contributed $5,000 to the committee and whom the court subsequently held was one of the soliciting group. This individual, one Weismann, conferred with the issuer's president and stated that Frankel was one of the dissident group.

5. Frankel interested another individual, one Becker in the contest. The court found that Becker through Frankel made a large number of contacts for the committee. Thereafter, following suggestions of Frankel, Becker himself contacted many individuals concerning the purchase of stock in the issuer to assist the committee in bringing about a change in management.

6. Frankel and another member of the committee decided the location of the committee's offices in New York.

7. The court held that Frankel "was at least as active and had as much to say as any of the other avowed committee members."

8. The court found that Frankel was a member of the group soliciting proxies.

No more dramatic demonstration of the unsoundness of the SEC's position in this case and the erroneous character of the judgment, findings of fact, and conclusions of law can be demonstrated than by reference to *SEC v. May, supra*. The key to the *May* case is the factual demonstration that the hidden member of the committee was "at least as active and had as much to say" as any of the admitted members of the committee. The *May* case was a true case of joint control in which Frankel participated. The control and the intent to control the committee is evidenced by the activities whereby shares are acquired, conferences are held with management, representations are made that Frankel is a member of the group, contacts are made by Frankel expressly on behalf of the group, the location of the committee's offices is decided by Frankel. All the indicia indicating control are present to evidence the true relationships.

But a case in which control of a committee was found with factual findings to support that finding is no support for a case in which *no control* is either *found* or *supported by the record.*

It should be noted that in the *May* case the court found that Frankel was a "member" of the soliciting group, while in this case the SEC was unwilling even to propose such a finding. The only finding entered was one that "attributed" the activities of the committee to Gira and Petersen upon basis which we have argued before were unsound.

Findings of Fact 7 and 11 Are Clearly Erroneous to the Extent That It Is Stated Therein That a Stockholders List Was Surreptitiously Removed or Stolen From UIC. There Is No Substantial Evidence in the Record to Support Such a Finding.

When the complaint was filed in this action, the SEC did not allege that any provision of the United States Code or any Rule of the Securities and Exchange Commission had been violated by reason of any alleged misappropriation of a stockholders list. Objection was made at the trial to the admissability of evidence as to such an issue since it was neither pleaded nor was it relevant or material to the issues raised by the complaint. The objections were sustained as to the appellant Stockholders' Committee but overruled as to Gira and Petersen, with one exception. [R. T. 54.] When one witness testified that Robert Gira (the brother of appellant Bernard F. Gira) had asked him to remove a copy of a stockholders list the objection was overruled as to Petersen but not as to Bernard F. Gira. [R. T. 54.] This latter ruling was classical hearsay; no attempt was made by counsel for the SEC or the court to explain how an alleged statement made by a non-party to an interested party outside the presence of any party would be admissible against anyone. The same unrestrained disregard of the elementary rules of evidence was continued when the Securities and Exchange Commission proposed and the court signed a finding, Finding 11, which recited this hearsay evidence. The evidence should have been excluded.

With this evidence eliminated the rest of the testimony is nothing but speculation and conjecture. It was the SEC's burden to establish the facts concerning the stockholders list at the trial. The essence of Petersen's testimony was that a stockholders list was in his effects when he left the premises of UIC on January 14, 1961, which list was returned by Brandlin on January 29, 1961. [R. T. 60-76, 1250.] The only witness called by the SEC on this point was Donald Hanmer who testified that there were a number of stockholders lists on the premises and that a December 1960 list arrived on January 14, 1961. [R. T. 159, 160, 163, 187.] *The crucial point as to the number of lists on the UIC premises from and after January 14, 1961 was never established;* that is to say that it is perfectly consistent that a December 1960 list was on the premises and another December 1960 list was in Petersen's effects when all of his belongings were removed from the UIC premises on January 14, 1961.

Of course it is apparent that not one relevant inference or finding turns upon this question. The information contained in the stockholders list, *i.e.,* the names and addresses of stockholders of UIC cannot be appropriated or stolen by anyone. They belong to all the stockholders. The Delaware law, the UIC state of incorporation, like the general law makes it clear that any stockholder has a right to such information (Delaware Corporation Law, Section 219).

It follows from what has been said that a finding of "surreptitious removal" or "theft" is both immaterial and unsupported by the evidence and is therefore clearly erroneous.

VI.

The Mandatory Injunction Requiring Appellants Gira and Petersen to File Amended Schedules 14B Is Erroneous Because:

1. **No Specific Findings of Fact Were Entered Setting Forth the Extent to Which Said Schedule 14B Was Incomplete.**

2. **Under Rule 14a-11(b)(6) the Schedules 14B Actually Filed Were Completely Correct.**

There is not a single finding of fact or conclusion of law stating the respects in which Schedules 14B filed by Messrs. Gira and Petersen [Exs. 10 and 12] are incorrect or incomplete.

One can speculate that the intention may have been to find that

1. Appellants Gira and Petersen were secret participants or members of the Stockholders' Protective Committee, and

2. Appellants failed to set forth such an alleged secret participation or membership in Schedules 14B.

As heretofore argued, such a holding has no warrant in the evidence, findings of fact, or conclusions of law. A mandatory injunction may not require appellant to make statements which are not supported by the record.

It should be recalled that there was no allegation, finding of fact, conclusion of law, or judgment to the effect that appellants Gira and Petersen were "participants" within the meaning of Rule 14a-11(b)(6). This portion of the rule holds that a participant is "one who solicits proxies." However, it was contended at the trial and a finding of fact was made to the effect that a press release which announced the filing of a libel suit by appellants Gira and Petersen against the management of UIC in July of 1961 was a proxy solicitation. [See Pltf. Ex. 19.]

The record without dispute established that

1. The release was delivered without any authority of appellants Gira and Petersen and contrary to their express direction and therefore simply was not their act. [Pltf. SEC's Ex. 25; R. T. 95, and 631.]

2. The release in the form prepared never appeared, insofar as the evidence is concerned, in any publication. [Pltf. SEC's Ex. 19; Defts. Gira and Petersen's Exs. AA, BB, CC, DD, and HH.]

In the form in which part of the material appeared, it was absolutely sterile and innocuous.

Dispite this fact and out of an abundance of caution, plaintiffs Gira and Petersen filed Schedules 14B and set forth the facts concerning this press release. Since there is no contention or finding the facts set forth concerning the manner in which the schedules are incomplete or incorrect the mandatory judgment directing appellants Gira and Petersen to correct said Schedules 14B are without any warrant in the law.

Conclusion.

It is respectfully submitted that the judgment below be reversed.

Respectfully submitted,

KENDRICK, SCHRAMM & STOLZY,
ELWOOD S. KENDRICK,
JOHN P. SCHOLL,
JACK CORINBLIT,

By JACK CORINBLIT,

Attorneys for Appellants.

APPENDIX "A".

Regulation 14(a)-9 Under the Securities and Exchange Act of 1934.

Rule 14a-9.   False or Misleading Statements.

No solicitation subject to this regulation shall be made by means of any proxy statement, form of proxy, notice of meeting, or other communication, written or oral, containing any statement which, at the time and in the light of the circumstances under which it is made, is false or misleading with respect to any material fact, or which omits to state any material fact necessary in order to make the statements therein not false or misleading or necessary to correct any statement in any earlier communication with respect to the solicitation of a proxy for the same meeting or subject matter which has become false or misleading.

Note.   The following are some examples of what, depending upon particular facts and circumstances, may be misleading within the meaning of this rule:

(a) Predictions as to specific future market values, earnings, or dividends.

(b) Material which directly or indirectly impugns character, integrity or personal reputation, or directly or indirectly makes charges concerning improper illegal or immoral conduct or associations, without factual foundation.

(c) Failure to so identify a proxy statement, form of proxy and other soliciting material as to clearly distinguish it from the soliciting material of any other person or persons soliciting for the same meeting or subject matter.

(d) Claims made prior to a meeting regarding the results of a solicitation.

Regulation 14(a)-11 Under the Securities and Exchange Act of 1934.

Rule 14a-11. Special Provisions Applicable to Election Contests.

(a) Solicitations to which this rule applies.

This rule applies to any solicitation subject to this regulation by any person or group of persons for the purpose of opposing a solicitation subject to this regulation by any other person or group of persons with respect to the election or removal of directors at any annual or special meeting of security holders.

(b) Participant or Participant in a Solicitation.

For purposes of this rule the terms "participant" and "participant in a solicitation" include the following:

(1) the issuer;

(2) any director of the issuer, and any nominee for whose election as a director proxies are solicited;

(3) any committee or group which solicits proxies, any member of such committee or group, and any person whether or not named as a member who, acting alone or with one or more other persons, directly or indirectly, take the initiative in organizing, directing or financing any such committee or group;

(4) any person who finances or joins with another to finance the solicitation of proxies, except persons who contribute not more than $500 and who are not otherwise participants;

(5) any person who lends money or furnishes credit or enters into any other arrangements, pursuant to any contract or understanding with a participant, for the purpose of financing or otherwise inducing the pur-chase, sale, holding or voting of securities of the issuer

by any part
in opposition
do not includ
dinary cours
orders for t
is not otherw

(6) any (
vided, howev
person or or
ticipant to s
merely trans
ministerial c
by a particip
or advertisin
whose activi
duties in th
person regul
the issuer o
wise a parti
or any pers
ticipant, if
otherwise a

(c) Filing
14B.

(1) No s
by any pers
unless at lea
shorter per
showing o
with the C
exchange u
and regist

by any participant or other persons, in support of or in opposition to a participant; except that such terms do not include a bank, broker or dealer who, in the ordinary course of business, lends money or executes orders for the purchase or sale of securities and who is not otherwise a participant;

(6) any other person who solicits proxies: *Provided, however,* That such terms do not include (i) any person or organization retained or employed by a participant to solicit security holders, or any person who merely transmits proxy soliciting material or performs ministerial or clerical duties; (ii) any person employed by a participant in the capacity of attorney, accountant, or advertising, public relations or financial adviser, and whose activities are limited to the performance of his duties in the course of such employment; (iii) any person regularly employed as an officer or employee of the issuer or any of its subsidiaries who is not otherwise a participant; or (iv) any officer or director of, or any person regularly employed by, any other participant, if such officer, director, or employee is not otherwise a participant.

(c) Filing of Information Required by Schedule 14B.

(1) No solicitation subject to this rule shall be made by any person other than the management of an issuer unless at least five business days prior thereto, or such shorter period as the Commission may authorize upon a showing of good cause therefor, there has been filed, with the Commission and with each national securities exchange upon which any security of the issuer is listed and registered, by or on behalf of each participant

in such solicitation, a statement in duplicate containing the information specified by Schedule 14B.

(2) Within five business days after a solicitation subject to this rule is made by the management of an issuer, or such longer period as the Commission may authorize upon a showing of good cause therefor, there shall be filed, with the Commission and with each national securities exchange upon which any security of the issuer is listed and registered, by or on behalf of each participant in such solicitation, other than the issuer a statement in duplicate containing the information specified by Schedule 14B.

(3) If any solicitation on behalf of management or any other person has been made, or if proxy material is ready for distribution, prior to a solicitation subject to this rule in opposition thereto, a statement in duplicate containing the information specified in Schedule 14B shall be filed by or on behalf of each participant in such prior solicitation, other than the issuer, as soon as reasonably practicable after the commencement of the solicitation in opposition thereto, with the Commission and with each national securities exchange on which any security of the issuer is listed and registered.

(4) If, subsequent to the filing of the statements required by subparagraphs (1), (2), and (3) above, additional persons become participants in a solicitation subject to this rule, there shall be filed, with the Commission and each appropriate exchange, by or on behalf of each such person a statement in duplicate containing the information specified by Schedule 14B, within three business days after such person becomes a participant, or such longer period as the Commission may authorize upon a showing of good cause therefor.

(5) If any material change occurs in the facts reported in any statement filed by or on behalf of any participant, and appropriate amendment to such statement shall be filed promptly with the Commission and each appropriate exchange.

(6) Each statement and amendment thereto filed pursuant to this paragraph (c) shall be part of the official public files of the Commission and for purposes of this regulation shall be deemed a communication subject to the provisions of Rule 14a-9.

(d) Solicitations Prior to Furnishing Required Written Proxy Statement.

Notwithstanding the provisions of Rule 14a-3 (a), a solicitation subject to this rule may be made prior to furnishing security holders a written proxy statement containing the information specified in Schedule 14A with respect to such solicitation, *Provided* That—

(1) The statements required by paragraph (c) of this rule are filed by or on behalf of each participant in such solicitation.

(2) No form of proxy is furnished to security holders prior to the time the written proxy statement is required by Rule 14a-3 (a) is furnished to security holders: *Provided, however,* That this subparagraph (2) shall not apply where a proxy statement then meeting the requirements of Schedule 14A has been furnished to security holders.

(3) At least the information specified in Items 2 (a) and 3 (a) of the statement required by paragraph (c) to be filed by each participant, or an appropriate summary thereof, is included in each communication sent or given to security holders in connection with the solicitation.

(4) A written proxy statement containing the information specified in Schedule 14A with respect to a solicitation is set or given security holders at the earliest practicable date.

(e) Solicitations prior to furnishing required written proxy statement—Filing Requirements.

Three copies of any soliciting material proposed to be sent or given to security holders prior to the furnishing of the written proxy statement required by Rule 14a-3 (a) shall be filed with the Commission in preliminary form, at least five business days prior to the date definitive copies of such material are first sent or given to security holders, or such shorter period as the Commission may authorize upon a showing of good cause therefor.

(f) Application of this rule to Annual Report.

Notwithstanding the provisions of Rule 14a-3 (b) and (c), three copies of any portion of the annual report referred to in Rule 14a-3 (b) which comments upon or refers to any solicitation subject to this rule, or to any participant in any such solicitation, other than the solicitation by the management, shall be filed with the Commission as proxy material subject to this regulation. Such portion of the annual report shall be filed with the Commission in preliminary form at least five business days prior to the date copies of the report are first sent or given to security holders.

(g) Application of Rule 14a-6.

The provisions of paragraphs (c), (d), (e), (f) and (g) of Rule 14a-6 shall apply to the extent pertinent, to soliciting material subject to paragraphs (e) and (f) of this Rule 14a-11.

(h) Use of reprints or reproductions.

In any solicitation subject to this rule, soliciting material which includes, in whole or part, any reprints or reproductions of any previously published material shall:

(1) State the name of the author and publication, the date of prior publication, and identify any person who is quoted without being named in the previously published material.

(2) Except in the case of a public official document or statement, state whether or not the consent of the author and publication has been obtained to the use of the previously published material as proxy soliciting material.

(3) If any participant using the previously published material, or anyone on his behalf, paid, directly or indirectly, for the preparation or prior publication of the previously published material, or has made or proposes to make any payments or give any other consideration in connection with the publication or republication of such material, state the circumstances.

Section 26, Securities and Exchange Act of 1934.

Unlawful Representations

Section 26. No action or failure to act by the Commission or the Board of Governors of the Federal Reserve System, in the administration of this title shall be construed to mean that the particular authority has in any way passed upon the merits of, or given approval to, any security or any transaction or transactions therein, nor shall such action or failure to act with regard to any statement or report filed with or examined by such authority pursuant to this title or rules and regulations thereunder, be deemed a finding by such authority that such statement or report is true and accurate on its face or that it is not false or misleading. It shall be unlawful to make, or cause to be made, to any prospective purchaser or seller of a security any representation that any such action or failure to act by any such authority is to be so construed or has such effect.

Fifth Amendment to the United States Constitution.

No person shall be held to answer for a capital, or otherwise infamous crime, unless on a presentment or indictment of a Grand Jury, except in cases arising in the land or naval forces, or in the Militia, when in actual service in time of War or public danger; nor shall any person be subject for the same offense to be twice put in jeopardy of life or limb; nor shall be compelled in any criminal case to be a witness against himself, nor be deprived of life, liberty, or property, without due process of law; nor shall private property be taken for public use, without just compensation.

Judgment

This actio
a trial on the
ber 22, 196:
evidence an
entered a de
man Yaras
defendant N
having enter
Law, as to
tion ("UIC
and the me
Bernard F.
fect that th
entitled to a
joining the
Stockholder
wood, Richa
bers of and
Committee,
sen from e:
Section 14
15 U.S.C.
thereunder,
solicitation
stock of U
nard F. Gi
Rule 14a-1
and direct:
further a:
stockholde:
the resolu:

APPENDIX "B".

Judgment, Findings of Fact, and Conclusions.

JUDGMENT

This action came on for hearing before the Court as a trial on the merits between July 26, 1961, and September 22, 1961, and the Court having considered all the evidence and the arguments of counsel, and having entered a decree of dismissal as to the defendant Herman Yaras and a final decree by consent as to the defendant N. Eugene Shafer, d/b/a Shafer & Co., and having entered Findings of Fact and Conclusions of Law, as to the defendants United Industrial Corporation ("UIC") Stockholders' Protective Committee and the members thereof, and as to the defendants Bernard F. Gira and Herbert J. Petersen, to the effect that the Securities and Exchange Commission is entitled to a permanent injunction restraining and enjoining the defendants United Industrial Corporation Stockholders' Protective Committee, Stanley E. Henwood, Richard I. Roemer, and Lewis M. Poe as members of and proxies for said Stockholders' Protective Committee, and Bernard F. Gira and Herbert J. Petersen from engaging in acts and practices in violation of Section 14(a) of the Securities Exchange Act of 1934, 15 U.S.C. §78n(a), and Rule 14a-9 of Regulation 14 thereunder, 17 C.F.R. 240.14a-9, in connection with the solicitation of proxies as to the common and preferred stock of UIC, and commanding the defendants Bernard F. Gira and Herbert J. Petersen to comply with Rule 14a-11 of Regulation 14, 17 C.F.R. 240.14a-11, and directing the defendant UIC to arrange for the further adjournment of the annual meeting of its stockholders for a sufficient length of time to allow for the resolicitation of proxies heretofore given to the defendant Stockholders' Protective Committee, which proxies by the terms of this decree are invalidated, as demanded by the Securites and Exchange Commission, and it appearing that the Court has jurisdiction of the parties hereto and the subject matter hereof—

I.

IT IS ORDERED, ADJUDGED AND DECREED

that the defendants United Industrial Corporation Stockholders' Protective Committee, Stanley E. Henwood, Richard I. Roemer, and Lewis M. Poe, individually and as members of and proxies for said Stockholders' Protective Committee, all members, associates, substitutes, agents, employees and attorneys of said Stockholders' Protective Committee, and the defendants Bernard F. Gira and Herbert J. Petersen, their agents, employees, and attorneys, and all persons acting in conceit or participation with any of said defendants, be and they hereby are permanently restrained and enjoined from, directly or indirectly, making use of the mails or any means or instrumentality of interstate commerce or of any facility of any national securities exchange to solicit or to permit the use of their names to solicit any proxy in respect of the common or preferred stock of UIC, or otherwise soliciting any such proxy, by means of any proxy statement, form of proxy, notice of meeting or other communication, written or oral, containing any statement which at the time and in the light of the circumstances under which it is made is false and misleading with respect to any material fact, or which omits to state any material fact necessary in order to make the statements therein not false or misleading, or necessary to correct any statement in an earlier communication with respect to the solicitation of a proxy which has been or has become false or misleading, including the following:

(i) omitting to state that the defendants Bernard F. Gira and Herbert J. Petersen were instrumental in initiating and organizing the UIC Stockholders' Protective Committee and in formulating on behalf of said Committee a slate of directors for membership on the board of directors of UIC in opposition to the slate of directors formulated by the management of UIC;

(ii) omitting to state that the defendants Bernard F. Gira and Herbert J. Petersen have participated with representatives of the Stockholders' Protective Committee and aided and abetted said Committee and its representatives in conducting proxy solicitations in opposition to the management of UIC;

(iii) stating that the defendants Bernard F. Gira and Herbert J. Petersen are not members of the Stockholders' Protective Committee;

(iv) stating that the defendants Bernard F. Gira and Herbert J. Petersen are not participating with the Stockholders' Protective Committee in soliciting proxies in opposition to the management of UIC;

(v) stating that the formation of the Stockholders' Protective Committee was initiated solely as a result of complaints of the defendants Elmer M. Luther, Jr. and Roy L. Williams;

(vi) stating that certain losses sustained by UIC and diminution of stockholders' equity occurred during the time that Bernard F. Fein was Chairman of the Executive Committee; or voting any proxy of any stockholder of UIC now held by the defendants UIC Stockholders' Protective Committee, Stanley E. Henwood, Richard I. Roemer or Lewis M. Poe as proxies for said Committee, or any substitute for any such defendant, or voting any such proxy which is not received pursuant to a solicitation made subsequent to the entry of this decree, in accordance with Section 14(a) of the Securities Exchange Act of 1934, 15 U.S.C. §78n(a), and Regulation 14, 17 C.F.R. 240.14.

II.

IT IS FURTHER ORDERED, ADJUDGED AND DECREED that the defendants Bernard F. Gira and Herbert J. Petersen shall and they hereby are commanded to comply with Rule 14a-11 of Regulation 14, 17 C.F.R. 240.14a-11, by filing with the Securities and Exchange Commission and with each national securities exchange upon which the common or preferred stock of United Industrial Corporation is registered a corrected statement in duplicate containing the information specified by Schedule 14B of Regulation 14, concerning their participation in the solicitation of proxies in respect of the common and preferred stock of UIC.

III.

IT IS FURTHER ORDERED, ADJUDGED AND DECREED that the defendant United Industrial Corporation, its officers, directors, employees, and attorneys, and each of them, be and they hereby are restrained and enjoined from holding any meeting of stockholders of United Industrial Corporation, except for the purpose of adjournment, until November 21, 1961.

IV.

IT IS FURTHER ORDERED, ADJUDGED AND DECREED that this action be and the same is hereby dismissed, without prejudice, as to the defendants James V. Armogida, Robert G. Ballance, Fred A. Beshara, Nathaniel R. Dumont, Joe L. Foss, William David Lawry, Elmer M. Luther, Jr., Edward H. McLaughlin, Charles Soderstrom, John Autry Steel, Clarence L. Summers, Roy L. Williams, Louis W. Wulfekuhler and Alfred T. Zodda, individually and as members of the United Industrial Corporation Stockholders' Protective Committee.

II.

FINDINGS OF FACT

A. Summary of Facts

1. United Industrial Corporation is a Delaware corporation. The securities of UIC are widely distributed among some 15,000 shareholders. The common and preferred stocks of UIC are listed and registered on the New York Stock Exchange and the Pacific Coast Stock Exchange. Warrants for common stock are listed and registered on the American Stock Exchange and the Pacific Coast Stock Exchange. The warrants carry no voting rights.

2. UIC commenced operations in 1960 as the product of the merger between Topp Industries Corporation and United Industrial Corporation, a Michigan corporation. Gira and Petersen, who had been the principal executive officers of Topp Industries, became the president and executive vice-president, respectively, of UIC. They also served as members of the board of directors. Bernard F. Gira owns 58,000 shares of the common stock of UIC, 5,000 shares of preferred

and 52,000 warrants. Herbert J. Petersen owns 38,500 shares of common stock, 5,000 shares of preferred and 38,500 warrants.

3. Late in 1960, it became apparent to the board of directors that the assets of UIC would be subjected to write-downs and adjustments totaling approximately $7,000,000. One such adjustment would change a profit previously reported by Topp Industries into a substantial loss. The board of directors of UIC met on January 12, 13 and 14, 1961, to consider what action was necessary because of the impending write-downs and adjustments. In the course of these meetings Gira and Petersen resigned as officers and directors of UIC. On January 16, 1961, the New York Stock Exchange suspended trading in the securities of UIC. The Pacific Coast Stock Exchange also suspended trading in the securities. The SEC entered an order under Section 19a(4) of the Act, 15 U.S.C. Sec. 78s(a)(4), suspending trading in the securities. The effect of this order was to bar trading in the over-the-counter market as well as on the exchange.[3]

4. The United Industrial Corporation Stockholders' Protective Committee is an association composed of the defendants Stanley E. Henwood, Richard I. Roemer, Lewis M. Poe, James V. Armogida, Robert G. Ballance, Fred A. Beshara, Nathaniel R. Dumont, Joe L. Foss, William D. Lawry, Edward H. McLaughlin,

---

[3]On September 22, 1961, the SEC removed its bar against trading after the management of UIC and the Committee had made announcements to the Court concerning their intentions with respect to buying or selling securities of UIC in the event trading was allowed. The action of the SEC allows trading only in the over-the-counter market. The exchange suspensions remain in effect.

Charles Soderstrom, John A. Steel, Clarence L. Summers, Louis W. Wulfekuhler, Alfred T. Zodda, Elmer M. Luther, Jr., and Roy L. Williams. With the exception of Williams and Luther, the members of the Committee comprise the slate of fifteen which the Committee seeks to have elected as directors of UIC. Henwood, Roemer and Poe are named as the proxies for the Committee. Henwood is the Committee's chairman.

5. Shortly before he resigned as an officer and director of UIC, Bernard F. Gira had been negotiating to retain Richard I. Roemer as counsel for UIC.[4] Roemer is a partner in the Los Angeles law firm of Vaughan, Brandlin & Baggot.[5] Shortly after he resigned, Gira conferred with Roemer and J. J. Brandlin, a senior partner of the firm. At this time he sought advice as to what action he and Petersen might take to combat litigation which they expected the management of UIC to institute against them arising out of the substantial write-downs in the assets of UIC, and the suspension of trading in UIC's securities.

6. Gira was joined by Petersen during subsequent conferences with Brandlin and Roemer. From the commencement of these conferences, it was agreed that one effective way of combating the charges of misfeasance which UIC's management intended to bring against

---

[4] Roemer had been house counsel for U. S Science, a subsidiary of UIC, from early 1959 until late in December, 1960 Robert Gira, who is Bernard F. Gira's brother, was president of U. S. Science. He and Roemer have been friends for many years

[5] The firm name is now Vaughan, Brandlin, Baggot, Robinson & Roemer. The firm organized the Committee, and has served as its counsel throughout the proxy controversy. The firm has made substantial cash advances to defray the expenses of the Committee, and has estimated its contingent fees for legal service, exclusive of litigation fees, at $75,000.

Gira and Petersen would be for them to regain control of UIC through a proxy contest.[6] But it was also apparent that Gira and Petersen would have little chance of success in a proxy contest in which they were identified as participants with an insurgent committee, for the reason that they were the principal officers and in managerial control when the events leading to the disastrous write-downs in UIC's assets occurred. Gira and Petersen agreed that they were not in a position to be openly identified with any group intending to conduct a proxy contest. They were given assurances, however, that Brandlin and Roemer would be willing to undertake a proxy contest if it could be arranged that other seemingly independent stockholders would urge that such a contest be undertaken, if a slate of individuals of prominence could be assembled for election to the board of directors, if the services of a suitable public relations consultant could be arranged, and if a list of UIC's stockholders could be secured for the use of the opposition group. These conversations occurred during two weeks of the time Gira and Petersen were ousted from the management of UIC. There was also some discussion of a stockholders' derivative suit by Gira and Petersen but that unrealistic suggestion was discarded at once.

7. It is uncontradicted in the record that after Brandlin and Roemer made it clear that a successful proxy contest could not be mounted without a current stockholders' list, Robert Gira, who remained as President of U. S. Science for a short time after his brother,

---

[6]UIC has sued Gira and Petersen in Delaware for damages based on their asserted misconduct while they were officers and directors.

Bernard Gir
to "steal" th
holders' list a
to UIC fro:
duplicate of
refused to c
December 3
the execut:
Friday, Jan:
offices of cc
was made b,
without advi
had the lis:
offices on :
the time the
other than (
for the Con:

8. The :
to counsel i
candidates :
among stoc
mailing out
after the Cc

9. Late
the Commi
came its fir
rogated tr:
and was as
under whic
UIC stock:
was turne
F. Gira d:
in Malibu

Bernard Gira, had resigned, asked an employee of UIC to "steal" the stockholders' list for him. A new stockholders' list as of December 30, 1960, had been delivered to UIC from New York on January 14, 1960. No duplicate of this list existed at this time. The employee refused to do so. Shortly thereafter, the list as of December 30, 1960, was removed surreptitiously from the executive offices of UIC, and was delivered late Friday, January 27, 1961, by Gira and Petersen to the offices of counsel for the Committee where a duplicate was made by the law firm at its own expense. Then, without advising the management of UIC that his firm had the list, Brandlin returned it to UIC's executive offices on Sunday afternoon, January 29, 1961. At the time the list was duplicated no stockholder of UIC other than Gira and Petersen had approached counsel for the Committee to discuss a proxy contest.

8. The stockholders' list was of the utmost value to counsel for the Committee in assembling a slate of candidates for election to the board of directors from among stockholders unfriendly to management, and in mailing out the proxy solicitation material disseminated after the Committee was organized.

9. Late in March, 1961, in the course of examining the Committee's preliminary proxy statement which became its first mailing to stockholders, Roemer was interrogated under oath by members of the SEC's staff and was asked, *inter alia,* to describe the circumstances under which the Committee came into possession of the UIC stockholders' list. Roemer testified that the list was turned over to Brandlin and himself by Bernard F. Gira during an evening conference at Gira's home in Malibu when the three first discussed a proxy con-

test. This was about ten days after Gira had resigned as president and a director of UIC. Roemer testified that he and Brandlin examined the list briefly, and that when the conference ended took the list with them. Roemer did not disclose to the SEC's staff that his law firm had duplicated the list, nor did he disclose the strange circumstances under which the list had been returned to UIC's offices on a Sunday afternoon. Rather, when asked who the list belonged to, Roemer stated he supposed it was Gira's. When asked why Gira had the list in his possession after he had resigned, Roemer testified that he did not know. At a later date Roemer attempted to correct this and similar testimony which he had given in the course of a deposition in *UIC v. Henwood* by sending a letter to the staff of the SEC to the effect that the stockholders' list had been delivered by Gira and Petersen to the law offices of counsel for the Committee, and that it had not been obtained at Gira's home in Malibu.

10. Gira and Peterson also were asked by the staff of the SEC to describe the circumstances under which they turned the list over to counsel for the Committee. Both Gira and Peterson testified that the list had been included among effects which they took with them on January 14, 1961, the day they resigned as directors of UIC. They testified that they delivered the list to counsel for the Committee on Friday, January 27, 1961.

11. The evidence establishes beyond question that, without the knowledge or consent of management, the stockholders' list was removed from the executive offices of UIC during the week ending January 28, 1961 (probably on Friday, January 27), delivered by Gira and Petersen to counsel for the Committee late Friday,

January 27, 1961, duplicated during the week-end, and
returned on Sunday afternoon, January 29, 1961. Indeed, the record sustains the contention of the SEC that
the stockholders' list was stolen.

12.   It was also essential that counsel for the Committee represent, at least ostensibly, some stockholders
of UIC before setting about to organize an insurgent
Committee.   It had already been decided that Gira
and Petersen could not openly participate in the contest with the Committee and they could not be held
out as clients of the law firm.   Gira and Petersen
then communicated with Roy L. Williams and Elmer
M. Luther, Jr.

13.   Roy L. Williams, an uncle of Bernard F. Gira,
at one time had been employed by Gira as an employee
of Topp Industries.   As a holder of 400 shares of
UIC stock, Williams became concerned about the suspension in trading and the fall in the market price of
his stock.   Gira suggested to Williams that he get in
touch with Roemer.   Williams, who was led to believe
that Roemer was conducting an investigation into the
situation, telephoned him and complained about his investment in UIC.   Williams did not, however, authorize
the bringing of a proxy contest in his behalf.   He was
merely seeking information concerning his investment.

14.   Elmer M. Luther, Jr. previously had been an
employee of UIC.   His services were terminated in
December 1960, shortly before Gira and Petersen resigned.   Prior to his employment with UIC, Luther
had been an employee of Topp Industries.   As an
owner of 250 shares of stock in UIC, he, like Williams, was concerned with the suspension of trading in
the stock.   He discussed the situation with Petersen

who suggested that he communicate with Roemer. Luther called Roemer and complained about the status of his investment in UIC, but did not authorize Roemer to initiate a proxy contest. Neither Luther nor Williams paid Vaughan, Brandlin and Baggot any retainer. Both of them, however, at Roemer's request, did sign Schedules 14B under Regulation 14 which he had prepared for them and which identified them as participants in the proxy contest. Notwithstanding this and even after it had been publicly announced that the Committee had been formed, Williams and Luther considered themselves neither members of the Committee nor clients of counsel for the Committee. Their telephone calls to Roemer were seized upon by counsel for the Committee as a mandate to organize an expensive proxy contest. The assertion in the Committee's proxy statement that counsel for the Committee started the organization of the Committee on behalf of Luther and Williams is seriously misleading.

15. Having supplied counsel for the Committee with the stockholders' list needed to organize and conduct a proxy contest, Gira and Petersen continued to aid in the formation of the Committee. To ascertain the distribution of the larger stockholdings, Gira and Petersen again met with counsel for the Committee to canvass the names on the list, and agree upon the approach to be made to stockholders with significant holdings.

16. Petersen sent Clarence L. Summers, who became a member of the Committee, to Brandlin. Summers also agreed to serve as public relations consultant to the Committee. Summers had served UIC as public relations consultant in the past. He also sought out

Nathaniel R. Dumont, who became a member of the Committee's slate.

17. Having inspired the formation of the Committee, Gira and Petersen continued to meet with Brandlin and Roemer to supply needed information, including a summary outlining the operations of UIC's subsidiaries and divisions, and confidential reports containing derogatory comments about members of the management.

18. Late in February, 1961, Gira and Petersen, Elwood S. Kendrick, who had been retained by them to defend the litigation brought by the management of UIC, Brandlin, Roemer and Stanley E. Henwood, who was than a potential member of the Committee, met to discuss the affairs of UIC. At this meeting, Gira and Petersen outlined the operations of UIC and its subsidiaries. Significantly, on the day after this meeting, Henwood became chairman of the Committee.

19. Gira, Petersen, Brandlin and Roemer met again in April, 1961, in Kendrick's law offices to decide what action they could take to counteract the charges in management's proxy material that Gira and Petersen were closely related to the Committee. Counsel for the Committee suggested that Gira and Petersen institute a libel suit against the management.

20. It was with events occurring in July, 1961, that Gira and Petersen assumed even more active roles as participants in the proxy contest, although they continued to disclaim participation. Early in July counsel for Gira and Petersen indicated to members of the staff of the SEC that in his opinion they had been libeled by statements in management's proxy material and that his clients intended to communicate with the

stockholders of UIC to deny the alleged defamatory statements. Shortly thereafter, a proposed letter addressed to stockholders by Gira was delivered to the SEC so that members of its staff could comment on it as solicitation material. This letter, although headed "THIS IS NOT A PROXY SOLICITATION," was unmistakably solicitation material. While the letter was never mailed to stockholders, it evidences the fact that Gira and Petersen were vitally interested in unseating the management slate.

21. On July 12, 1961, Gira and Petersen filed a $2,000,000 damage suit in the Superior Court of Los Angeles County alleging that the proxy material which management was circulating to the stockholders of UIC defamed them. A few hours before this suit was filed, counsel for Gira and Petersen telephoned the SEC's staff to seek advice in connection with an announcement which had been prepared for release to news services announcing the filing of the suit. This press release described not only the filing of the libel suit, but also included a discussion of the proxy contest and named each member of the Committee's slate. The staff was urged to "clear" the release in time to make the afternoon editions of certain newspapers on the East Coast. Although counsel was advised that such a release would constitute a "solicitation" within the definition of that term in Rule 14a-1 of Regulation 14, the statement, nevertheless, was issued to the press. The text of the release makes it evident that it was in fact intended to influence stockholders of UIC to vote their proxies for the Committee and in opposition to management. The libel suit was filed two weeks before the scheduled annual meeting of stockholders, and at about

the time that the Committee's fourth and last solicitation material was sent to stockholders.

22. The Committee has never actually functioned as an association; all of its members have never been assembled together at one time. Since its formation there has been only one meeting, and that one involved several, but not all, of the Committee's members. Brandlin and Roemer have met with Gira and Petersen on many more occasions than they have met with members of the Committee. The Committee is merely an imposing "letterhead" association, most of whose members were selected by and agreed to serve as an accommodation to counsel for the Committee. Many of them were not even stockholders of UIC until Roemer purchased 2,000 shares of the stock from Herman Yaras and distributed 1,000 shares among the non-stockholder members so they could appear to have an interest in the enterprise. Yaras had been financial consultant for UIC and was a close associate of Gira and Petersen. Such a seemingly independent group was necessary as Brandlin and Roemer knew that stockholder support would not be forthcoming if Gira and Petersen, the true sponsors of the Committee, participated openly as members.

23. The Committee's proxy material also was misleading in stating that certain losses sustained by UIC and diminution of stockholders' equity occurred where Bernard F. Fein was Chairman of the Executive Committee of UIC. Fein did not become Chairman of the Executive Committee until after Bernard F. Gira and Herbert J. Petersen had resigned. The Committee contends that by inadvertence the statement was not removed from one paragraph of the Com-

mittee's last mailing to stockholders although it was removed from other paragraphs, and that in any event
it was not of great significance. The statement, however, was not so innocuous as the Committee suggests.
In the context in which it was made it clearly implied,
contrary to fact, that Fein, Gira and Petersen shared
executive and managerial responsibility in UIC during
the critical period in question.

24. The Committee's proxy statement and its
other three communications soliciting the proxies of
stockholders of UIC have been mailed to some 15,000
shareholders. The Committee admits that its solicitations have been conducted through the mails and instrumentalities of interstate commerce. As Gira and
Petersen initiated the Committee, and have participated, directly and indirectly, in directing and advancing
its objectives, the Committee's use of the jurisdictional
facilities is attributable to them.

B. Affirmative Defenses

1. In addition to denying that Bernard F. Gira and
Herbert J. Petersen were undisclosed sponsors of the
UIC Stockholders' Protective Committee, the Committee interposed certain affirmative defenses to the
SEC's action. The first such defense asserted by the
Committee is that, in the course of the examination of
its proxy material by the staff of the SEC, all material facts concerning Gira's and Petersen's connection
with the Committee were disclosed to stockholders as
early as April, 1961, when the Committee first began
circulating its solicitation material. The Committee
contends, therefore, that the SEC should be estopped
from contending that the Committee's proxy material is
false and misleading.

2. The Committee's assertion is contrary to the facts. Significant events establishing the close identification of Gira and Petersen with the Committee occurred subsequent to the time the Committee first began soliciting the proxies of stockholders. As recently as July, 1961, Gira and Petersen instituted the libel suit against management, and at the same time caused a press release designed to influence votes in the election contest to be issued. Other disclosures in the Committee's proxy material are wholly inadequate in the light of facts not known to the staff when the material was commented upon. For example, it was disclosed in the proxy material that Gira and Petersen had given the Committee a stockholders' list, but the circumstances under which the list was obtained and turned over to counsel for the Committee, which, as discussed above, are highly significant in evidencing the intention of Gira and Petersen to conduct a proxy contest behind the facade of a seemingly "independent" Committee, were not disclosed. Even if the facts were as the Committee contends this defense is legally insufficient because as against the SEC the doctrine of estoppel is not available. *N. Sims Organ & Co. v. SEC,* ....F. 2d........ (C. A. 2, 1961); *SEC v. Culpepper,* 270 F. 2d 241 (C. A. 2, 1959); *SEC v. Morgan, Lewis and Bookins,* 209 F. 2d 33 (C. A. 3, 1953); *SEC v. Torr,* 22 F. Supp. 602 (S.D.N.Y, 1938). See also Section 26 of the Securities Exchange Act, 15 U.S.C. 78z, which specifically provides that the failure of the SEC to act "with regard to any statement or report filed with or examined by such authority pursuant to this title or rules and regulations thereunder [may not] be deemed a finding by such authority that such statement or report is true and accurate on its

face or that it is not false or misleading." With respect to proxy solicitation material filed with the SEC, in addition to settled general principles, the statute makes it explicit that staff examination of solicitation material in no sense constitutes approval thereof, or bars a suit by the SEC to protect the public from further untrue or misleading solicitations.

3. The Committee misconstrues the effect of the examination of the Committee's preliminary proxy material by the staff of the SEC. The staff examines and, if necessary, comments upon all preliminary proxy statements and other communications intended for distribution to stockholders. This is an administrative procedure developed by the SEC to assist all contestants in a proxy controversy to comply with the proxy rules and to avoid untrue, misleading or exaggerated claims in their communications to stockholders. In nearly all proxy controversies the basic and essential facts are peculiarly within the knowledge of the contestants. It is the inescapable obligation of the contestants themselves to make certain that all material facts are set forth in their communications to stockholders in a straightforward and understandable manner. This obligation cannot be shifted to the SEC or to its staff. C. Subin v. Goldsmith, 224 F. (2d) 753 (C. A. 2, 1955), certiorari denied 350 U. S. 883.

4. The second affirmative defense asserted by the Committee is that the SEC should be denied relief in equity because in bringing this action to invalidate the Committee's proxies, the SEC comes before this Court with "unclean hands." The Committee has charged that the SEC's decision to institute this proceeding was unduly influenced by the management of UIC. The

record is barren of any evidence sustaining the accusation, and it is completely unwarranted. Indeed, in his summation, counsel for the Committee, in effect, withdrew this and other accusations that the SEC and its staff were not acting in good faith.

5. In any event, the decision to institute suits such as this is committed by statute to the discretion of the SEC. Section 21(e) of the Securities Exchange Act, 15 U S.C. 78u(e). Again, as noted in the Court's Memorandum Decision, the record shows SEC brought this action with due regard for the voting rights of stockholders of UIC and in the public interest.

6. The defendants have also stressed that management of UIC from the beginning of its solicitation has stated that the Committee was "fronting" for Gira and Petersen and that, therefore, the stockholders are fully aware of all the facts. Such charges by management are not, however, a substitute for disclosure by the insurgents of the facts which stockholders are entitled to know when they execute proxies for the election of directors. Clearly, management's accusation is no substitute for, nor does it relieve, the insurgents from the duty to make the affirmative disclosures required by the proxy regulations.

III.
CONCLUSIONS OF LAW

1. This Court has jurisdiction of this proceeding under Section 27 of the Securities Exchange Act of 1934, 15 U.S.C. §78aa.

2. The evidence convincingly establishes that Bernard F. Gira and Herbert J. Petersen have been "participants" in the contest for control of United Indus-

trial Corporation within the meaning of Rule 14a 11(b)(3) of Regulation 14, 17 C.F.R. 240.14a-11(b)(3).[7] The definition encompasses not only the acknowledged members of a committee, but all those who, even indirectly, initiate, direct, finance or otherwise seek to advance the objectives of a committee contending for control of a corporation.

3. The submission by the Committee of a list of nominal members, however distinguished, is all the more misleading when, as here the stockholders whose proxies are solicited, and even the members of the Committee themselves, are shielded from knowledge of the true facts concerning the origin of the Committee, and the extent to which Gira and Petersen instigated and inspired the formation of the Committee and by various means have sought to advance the Committee's objective to obtain control of UIC. While the statement in the Committee's proxy material that "nor are Gira and Petersen members of the Committee" may be correct in a formal sense, in the light of the evidence before the Court, it is clear that the omission to disclose their *de facto* participation constitutes an abuse of the solicitation process, in direct violation of Rule 14a-9 of Regulation 14, 17 C.F.R. 240.14a-9. See *S.E.C. v. May*, 134 F. Supp. 247 (S.D.N.Y., 1955), *affirmed* 229 F. 2d. 124 (C. A. 2, 1956).

4. The SEC is entitled to a decree (1) enjoining the defendants UIC Stockholders' Protective Commit-

---

[7] The Rule defines a "participant" to include "any Committee or group which solicits proxies, any member of such Committee or group, and any person whether or not named as a member who, acting alone or with one or more other persons, directly or indirectly, take the initiative in organizing, directing or financing any such Committee or group."

tee, Stanley E. Henwood, Richard I. Roemer and Lewis M. Poe individually and as members of and proxies for said Committee, and the defendants Bernard F. Gira and Herbert J. Petersen from violations of Section 14(a) of the Act, 15 U.S.C. §78n(a), and Rule 14a-9 of Regulation 14, 17 C.F.R. 240.14a-9 thereunder, in the solicitation of proxies in respect to the common or preferred stock of UIC to be voted at the adjourned annual meeting of stockholders; and (2) invalidating all proxies of stockholders of UIC now held by them; and (3) enjoining them from voting any such proxy which is not received pursuant to a solicitation made subsequent to the entry of the final decree in the action, in accordance with Section 14(a) of the Act, 15 U.S.C. §78n(a), and Regulation 14 thereunder, 17 C.F.R. 240.14.

5. As stated in the Court's Memorandum Decision, it is not the intention of the Court to cause any stockholder of UIC to lose his voting rights. It is within the equitable power of the Court, in enforcing the statutory prohibition against unlawful proxy solicitations, not only to invalidate proxies which have been obtained by means of misleading solicitations, but also to mold its decree to avoid such an eventuality. *SEC v. May,* 134 F. Supp. 247, *supra* and *SEC v. O'Hara Reorganization Committee,* 28 F. Supp. 523 (D. Mass. 1939). See also *SEC v. Trans American,* 163 F. 2d 511, 518 (C. A. 3, 1947), *certiorari denied* 332 U.S. 847.

6. Accordingly, the decree will provide for adjournment of the annual meeting of stockholders of UIC to a date not earlier than November 22, 1961, to allow time for the further solicitation of new proxies (in

accordance with the proxy rules) by management, the Committee, or any other committee, group, or individual, whether favoring or opposing management.

7. For the reason given in the Memorandum Decision, the circumstances do not require that the remaining members of the Committee be enjoined. Accordingly, the action will be dismissed, without prejudice, as to those defendants.

8. The SEC is also entitled to a decree directing the defendants Bernard F. Gira and Herbert J. Petersen to comply with Rule 14a-11 of Regulation 14, 17 C.F.R. 240.14a-11, by filing corrected statements containing the information required by Schedule B, concerning their status as participants in the proxy controversy.

APPENDIX "C."

Index of Exhibits.

Exhibits	Description	Marked for Identification		Admitted in Evidence	
		Date	Page	Date	Page
1	Schedule 14-B of Petersen	7/26–27	94		
2	Diagram of Building			7/26–27	158
				9/21–22	2206
3	Invoice of shareholders' list			7/26–27	162
4	Letter of transmittal on shareholders' list			7/26–27	163
5	Emery Freight Bill	7/26–27	167		
6	Receipt executed by Hamner covering stockholder list from Chemical Bank at the foot of letter heretofore received as Exhibit 4 Receipt dated 1-18-61.			8/1	189
7	Work papers of UIC relative to the stockholder list and a report to Ohio			8/1	192
8	Letter to State of Ohio dated 1-26-61			8/1	193
9	Emery Air Freight receipt			8/1	199
10	Certified copy of 14-B of Gira			8/1	201
11	Certified copy of 14-B of Yaras			8/1	202
12	Certified copy of 14-B of Yaras				
13	Copies of mailings #1, #2 and #3			8/1	205
14	Management material	8/1	207	8/1	207
				8/15	675
14-A	Definitive interim report to shareholders			8/15	676
15	Preliminary material submitted by the Stockholders' Protective Committee—certified copies	8/1	210	8/22	1016
16	Affidavit of Clerk of Chemical Bank				
17	Letter from Roemer to SEC dated 5-16-61			8/1	267
18	Papers on collateral loan for Yaras, etc.			8/2	391
19	Press release re libel suit			8/2	414
20	Letter from Gira to stockholders	8/2	417	8/2	429
21	Cohen letter of July 14			8/3	443

Exhibits	Description	Marked for Identification		Admitted in Evidence	
		Date	Page	Date	Page
22	Affidavit of Gordon	8/3	444		
23	Press release	8/15	633	8/15	63!
24	Copy of Wall Street Journal (Jan 17, 1961)	8/15	633	8/15	635
25	Affidavit of Bud Lewis			8/15	676
26	Roemer letter of 6-13			8/17	948
27	26th annual report of SEC	8/17	951		
28	Transcript of Luther	8/22	1017	9/12	1454
29	Transcript of Williams	8/22	1018	9/12	1454
30	Transcript of Ballance	8/22	1018	9/12	1454
31	Transcript of Wulfekuhler	8/22	1018	9/12	1454
32	Transcript of Lawry	8/22	1019	9/12	1454
33	Transcript of Gira	8/22	1019	9/12	1454
34	Transcript of Petersen	8/22	1019	9/12	1454
35	Transcript of Yaras	8/22	1019	9/12	1454
36	Transcript of McLaughlin	8/22	1020	9/12	1454
37	Transcript of Soderstrom	8/22	1020	9/12	1454
29-A	Transcript of Williams	8/22	1020	9/12	1454
28-A	Transcript of Luther	8/22	1020	9/12	1454
38	Transcript of Henwood	8/22	1021	9/12	1454
39	Transcript of Roemer	8/22	1021	9/12	1454
38-A	Transcript of Henwood	8/22	1021	9/12	1454
39-A	Transcript of Roemer	8/22	1021	9/12	1454
40	Affidavit of Risk	8/23	1132	8/23	1154
41	Affidavit of Cohen	8/23	1133	8/23	1154
42	Order of SEC directing an investigation and designating an officer to take the testimony in matter of UIC	8/23	1162	8/23	1169
43	Statement of assets and disbursements of the Stockholders' Protective Committee			9/12	1414
44	Article from Wall Street Journal			9/12	1415
45	Affidavit of Roy L Williams			9/12	1424
46	Minutes of meeting of 1-13-61			9/12	1443
47	Testimony of Dumont			9/12	1454
48	Testimony of Hugh E. McColgan			9/12	1454
49	Affidavit of Landau			9/13	1582
50	Deposition of Manuel Cohen			9/21	2207

Exhibits	
A	Mailing
B	Bishop's
C	Order fo
D	Letter t dated M:
E	Documer chase 19
F	Letter fr
G	Telegran
H	Diagram
I	Letter i 6-16
J	Affidavi
K	Transm
L	UIC file
M	Letter f
N	Deposit
O	Weinm:
P	Docume sheets
Q	Pencil 1961
R	Press r
S	Notes were to depositi
AA	Release
BB	Release
CC	Release
DD	Release
EE	Kendri:
FF	Letter 7/18
GG	Unedit
HH	Article 7/13 e examin
II	Affidav
JJ	Affidav
KK	Copy c

hibits	Description	Marked for Identification		Admitted in Evidence	
		Date	Page	Date	Page
A	Mailing #4			8/2	322
B	Bishop's Report on Fein	8/2	329	8/2	342
C	Order for Xerox machine			8/2	331
D	Letter to SEC from Brandlin dated March 24, 1961			8/2	381
E	Documents in BSF stock purchase 1959	8/2	431	9/22	2279
F	Letter from Cohen			8/16	787
G	Telegram from Cohen	8/17	905	8/17	905
H	Diagram on Board	8/17	972		
I	Letter from Brandlin to Risk, 6-16	8/24	1302	8/24	1303
J	Affidavit of Luther			8/24	1315
K	Transmittal letter of Affidavit			8/25	1331
L	UIC file by reference			8/25	1366
M	Letter from Risk			8/25	1386
N	Deposition of Sharon Clay Risk			9/14	1655
O	Weinman	9/15	1847	9/15	1883
P	Documents consisting of five sheets	9/15	1883	9/22	2279
Q	Pencil notes of November 12, 1961			9/19	1937
R	Press release			9/22	2279
S	Notes of Commission staff that were to be marked during Risk deposition	9/22	2280	9/22	2280
AA	Releases in newspaper	8/3	482	8/3	488
BB	Releases in newspaper	8/3	482	8/3	488
CC	Releases in newspaper	8/3	482	8/3	488
DD	Releases in newspaper	8/3	482	8/3	488
EE	Kendrick's sec'y letter to SEC	8/3	513	8/3	514
FF	Letter from Kendrick to Cohen 7/18	8/3	513	9/22	2282
GG	Unedited material of management	8/3	543	9/22	2281
HH	Article about libel suit from the 7/13 edition of the Los Angeles examiner	9/19	1949	9/22	2281
II	Affidavit of Petersen				
JJ	Affidavit of Gira				
KK	Copy of libel complaint			9/20	2100

Exhibits	Description	Marked for Identification		Admitt Evide
		Date	Page	Date
LL	Financial reports	9/21	2111	9/21
MM	Proxy statement mailed to the shareholders of Topp Industries Corporation	9/21	2111	
NN	Monthly report (financial statement)	9/21	2111	
AAA	Correction letter from Yaras	8/17	975	8/22
BBB	Intercompany correspondence of	9/14	1738	9/14
CCC	NIC from Gira to M. Bonner received on or about 9/19/60 concerning Permachem Corp.	9/14	1738	9/14
DDD	Press release	9/14	1764	

TOPICAL INDEX

I.

The court erred by purporting to impose an injunction against
    the appellants Armogida, Ballance, Beshara, Dumont, Foss,
    Lawry, Luther, McLaughlin, Soderstrom, Steel, Summers,
    Williams, Wulfekuhler and Zodda at the same time that the
    judgment dismissed said appellants from the action. That
    portion which purports to grant an injunction against said
    appellants is void.. 40

II.

That portion of the judgment which purports to impose an
    injunction against all the appellants soliciting further prox-
    ies unless under certain specified conditions is not sup-
    ported by the court's own findings of fact and conclusions
    of law 42

TABLE OF AUTHORITIES CITED

No. 17591

IN THE

United States Court of Appeals

FOR THE NINTH CIRCUIT

STANLEY E. HENWOOD, RICHARD I. ROEMER, LEWIS M POE, individually, as members of the UNITED INDUSTRIAL CORPORATION STOCKHOLDERS' PROTECTIVE COMMITTEE and as proxies of said Committee, JAMES V ARMOGIDA, ROBERT G. BALLANCE, FRED A. BESHARA, NATHANIEL R DUMONT, JOE L FOSS, WILLIAM D LAWRY, ELMER M LUTHER, JR, EDWARD H. McLAUGHLIN, CHARLES SODERSTROM, JOHN A STEEL, CLARENCE L. SUMMERS, ROY L WILLIAMS, LOUIS W WULFEKUHLER, ALFRED T ZODDA, individually and as members of the UNITED INDUSTRIAL CORPORATION STOCKHOLDERS' PROTECTIVE COMMITTEE,

Appellants,

vs

SECURITIES AND EXCHANGE COMMISSION,

Appellees

Appeal From the United States District Court for the Southern District of California, Central Division.

OPENING BRIEF OF APPELLANTS.

JURISDICTION.

This action was brought by the Securities and Exchange Commission (hereinafter referred to as "SEC") for alleged violations on the part of the Appellants of Section 14, subsection (a) of the Securities and Exchange Act of 1934, 158 USC 78 n., subsection (a) and of Regulation 14, 17 CFR 248.14 promulgated thereunder.

The plaintiff SEC requested an injunction against the Appellants, pursuant to Section 21, subparagraph (e) and (f) of the Securities and Exchange Act of 1934, enjoining them from any future violations of the Act.

The jurisdiction of the United States District (
was based upon Section 27 of the Securities and
change Act of 1934, 15 USC 78, subsection (a

From a judgment in favor of the plaintiff SE(
against the Appellants James V. Armogida, Brig
General Robert G. Ballance, Fred Beshara, Natl
R. Dumont, Joe J. Foss, Stanley E. Henwood,
liam David Lawry, Elmer M. Luther, Edward H.
Laughlin, Lewis M. Poe, Richard I. Roemer, Cl
Soderstrom, John Autry Steel, Clarence L. Sum
Roy L. Williams, Louis Wulfekuhler and Alfre
Zodda, permanently enjoining the Appellants from
tain acts, the Appellants have appealed. The judg
was entered on the 18th day of October, 1961,
these Appellants filed their Notice of Appeal on the
day of October, 1961.

This Court has jurisdiction to review the judg
and the findings of fact and conclusions of law i
the United States Judicial Code. (65 Stat. 92(
USC 1291, and 65 Stat. 727; 28 USC 1294.)

Applicable Statutes, Regulations, Rules an Constitutional Provisions.

The basic statutes, regulations, rules and Con
tional provisions which will become pertinent in
matter are Rule 14(a)9 and Rule 14(a)11; all of I
lation 14 promulgated under the Securities and
change Act of 1934 and Fifth Amendment to
United States Constitution. Inasmuch as such sta
regulations, rules and Constitutional provisions
lengthy they are set down verbatim in the Appendi
tached hereto and made a part of this brief.

STATEMENT OF THE CASE.

Preliminary Statement.

Briefly stated, the action which this Court is asked to review centers around a proxy contest in a corporation known as United Industrial Corporation, a Delaware corporation. In this proxy contest the Appellants, known as the Stockholders' Protective Committee, consisted of two small stockholders of United Industrial Corporation, Elmer M. Luther, Jr., and Roy A. Williams, and 15 other members who are known as the "slate" (and who own an aggregate of 25,830 shares). The slate which is running for election to the Board of Directors of United Industrial Corporation (hereinafter referred to as "U.I.C.") consists of James V. Armogida, Canton, Ohio, Director of Perry Rubber Company, and past President of Stark County, Ohio, Bar Association; Brigadier General Robert G. Ballance (retired 1959) United States Marine Corps; Santa Monica, California; Fred Beshara, Youngstown, Ohio, General Director and President of B & B Construction Company; Nathaniel R. Dumont, Beverly Hills, California, President of Dumont Engineering Company and Dumont Aviation Associates; Joe J. Foss, Sioux Falls, South Dakota, Commissioner of the American Football League and former Governor of South Dakota; Stanley E. Henwood, New York, New York, Executive Secretary of the International Poliomyelitis Foundation, and Chairman of the Stockholders' Protective Committee; William David Lawry, Los Angeles, California, President and Director of Tork-Link Corporation; Edward H. McLaughlin, Los Angeles, California, President of Union Hardware and Metal Company; Lewis M. Poe, Colorado Springs, Colorado, Secretary and General Attorney for Colorado Interstate Gas Company; Richard I. Roemer, Los Angeles, California, attorney, and partner in the firm of Vaughan, Brandlin & Baggot; Charles R. Soderstrom, San Pedro, California, automobile and utilities executive; John Autry Steel, San Francisco, California, insurance executive and owner of Steel & Company, Clarence L. Summers, Los Angeles, California, Public Relations Executive and Management Consultant and President of Pete Summers, Inc.; Louis Wulfekuhler, Los Angeles, California, President and Director of Lockheed Air Terminal, Inc.; and Alfred T. Zodda, New York, New York, Vice-President of Olin Mathieson International Corporation, and Vice-President and Director of Olin Mathieson Chemical Corporation. [Ex. 13; C. T. ....] It is contesting the present management of U.I.C. for election to the Board of Directors at the annual meeting of the stockholders for 1961.

The Stockholders' Protective Committee had accumulated votes sufficient to constitute a majority of the number of votes likely to be cast at the annual meeting set for July 27, 1961. [R. T. 1292-1293.] The management of U.I.C. and the Appellants were engaged in litigation against each other over mutual claims of false and misleading statements alleged to be in each other's proxy solicitation material, when the Securities and Exchange Commission intervened in the contest. [R. T. 17a-18a.] It filed a separate complaint charging the Stockholders' Protective Committee with making false and misleading statements to the stockholders in their proxy solicitation material. [C. T. ....] Thereafter the case was tried before the Honorable Thurmond Clarke from time to time between the dates of

July 25, 19(
in the follow:

(a) A fin
the Stockho
dividuals of

(b) A fur
these perso
Stockholder
of any kno
false or mis
of United Ir

(c) A ju
to all of the
Committee,
authority to

(d) A si
against the
dating the
Stockholder

(e) A fur
the same D
joining th
proxies to
Corporation
include cer
ing the St
statements
evidence p
tradictory
the Court.

While A
the Appella
Foss, Law

July 25, 1961, and September 22, 1961, and resulted in the following:

(a) A finding by the Court that the members of the Stockholders' Protective Committee were individuals of distinction in industry and finance.

(b) A further finding by the Court that in effect these persons of distinction, as members of the Stockholders' Protective Committee, were innocent of any knowledge of, or participation in, making false or misleading statements to the stockholders of United Industrial Corporation.

(c) A judgment of dismissal from the action as to all of the members of the Stockholders' Protective Committee, except the three members who hold the authority to vote the proxies at the meeting.

(d) A simultanous order in the same judgment against the same DISMISSED defendants invalidating the proxies theretofore obtained by the Stockholders' Protective Committee.

(e) A further order in the same judgment against the same DISMISSED defendants permanently enjoining them from making any solicitation of proxies to the stockholders of United Industrial Corporation, unless the solicitation material shall include certain statements and allegations concerning the Stockholders' Protective Committee which statements and allegations are unsupported by the evidence presented to the trial judge, and are contradictory to some of the Findings of Fact made by the Court. [C. T. ....]

While Appellants will argue that the dismissal against the Appellants Armogida, Ballance, Beshara, Dumont, Foss, Lawry, Luther, McLaughlin, Soderstrom, Steel,

Summers, Williams, Wulfekuhler, and Zodda makes a nullity of the purported injunction against them, they, nevertheless, have an interest in the appeal from this judgment for the reason that the judgment purportedly invalidates their proxies, and is based upon Findings of Fact and Conclusions of Law, substantial portions of which are not supported by the evidence or are superfluous to the issues, but which if disseminated to the stockholders of U.I.C. without being corrected to conform to the evidence will unjustly impugn the reputations and images these appellants to the extent that they will be unable effectively to solicit new proxies.

Pleadings and Parties.

The complaint in the action below brought before the trial court four separate groups of parties defendant on three separate theories or grounds.

One party defendant is the group making up the Stockholders' Protective Committee, heretofore mentioned, and who are the Appellants herein.

The second party defendant is the U.I.C. Management.

The third party defendant group consisted of Bernard F. Gira, Herbert J. Petersen and Herman Yaras.

The fourth party was Eugene Shafer, doing business as Shafer & Co.

The main thrust of the complaint as it pertains to the Appellants Stockholders' Protective Committee is that the Committee has solicited proxies from the stockholders of U.I.C. by means of false and misleading statements, and, with more particularity, that these false and misleading statements consisted of omitting to state that Gira, Petersen and Yaras had organized the Committee and its slate of directors, and had solicited proxies on behalf of the Committee; by affirmatively denying that Gira, Petersen and Yaras were members of the Committee.

The theory of the complaint against the defendant United Industrial Corporation management was that they were joined as nominal defendants for the purpose of giving the Court jurisdiction over the adjournment of the annual stockholders' meeting.

The main thrust of the complaint as it applied to the defendants Gira, Petersen and Yaras was that even though they had previously filed a so-called Schedule 14-B pursuant to Regulation 14(a)11 under the Securities Exchange Act of 1934, they should be required to file corrected Schedules 14-B containing additional information and acknowledge that they had participated in the proxy contest.

The main thrust of the complaint against the defendant Shafer, doing business as Shafer & Co., was that Shafer had violated Rule 14(a)11 of Regulation 14 by soliciting proxies (*on behalf of the management of the U.I.C.*) from stockholders of United Industrial Corporation, without first submitting his proxy soliciting material to the Securities and Exchange Commission, and further, without having filed a Schedule 14-B as required by Rule 14(a)11 of Regulation 14.

Since the "participation" of Gira, Petersen and Yaras, if any, as well as the "participation" of Shafer & Co., if any, is not necessarily to be imputed either to the Stockholders' Protective Committee or U.I.C.

management, therefore, in this brief, the Appellants will concern themselves with those areas of the pleadings, evidence and substantive law which relate to the charges made against the Appellants, to-wit: *the solicitation of proxies by false and misleading statements of material facts.*

Statement of Facts.

United Industrial Corporation is a Delaware corporation. The securities of United Industrial Corporation are widely distributed among some 15,000 shareholders. The common and preferred stock of United Industrial Corporation was, until January 16, 1961, listed and registered on the New York Stock Exchange and the Pacific Coast Stock Exchange. United Industrial Corporation commenced operation in January of 1960, as the result of a merger of Topp Industries Corporation, a Delaware corporation, and United Industrial Corporation, a Michigan corporation. The surviving corporation, Topp Industries Corporation, thereafter changed its name to United Industrial Corporation.

Bernard F. Gira and Herbert J. Petersen, who had been the principal officers of Topp Industries Corporation, were elected by the Board of Directors of the merged corporation as President and Executive Vice-President, respectively. They served as members of the Board of Directors during the year 1960.

Late in 1960 it became apparent to the Board of Directors that the assets of United Industrial Corporation would be subjected to certain write downs and adjustments totalling several millions of dollars. The Board of Directors of United Industrial Corporation met on January 12, 13 and 14, 1961 to consider the handling of the impending write downs which the auditors were having difficulty in estimating due to some alleged improper accounting practices. The closest estimate at this date was in the vicinity of $6,000,000.00 to $7,000,000.00. During the course of these meetings it was suggested by other members of the Board of Directors to Gira and Petersen that the necessary report of the impending write downs which was to be made to the various stock exchanges and the Securities and Exchange Commission could be made more favorably if the principal officers, under whose management the problems had developed, were no longer holding that position. In response to this suggestion, Gira and Petersen tendered their resignations as President and Executive Vice-President, which were accepted by the Board of Directors. Thereafter, and at the culmination of the three day meeting, January 14, 1961, they volunteered their resignations as Directors of the corporation.

On about January 16, 1961, the report of the write down was made to the New York Stock Exchange and to the Securities and Exchange Commission. The New York Stock Exchange, Securities and Exchange Commission and the Pacific Coast Stock Exchange immediately suspended trading in the securities of United Industrial Corporation. By this time the market value of the common stock had dropped to an all time low of $4-7/8. Approximately one year before, in January 1960, the market price had been $11-7/8. [Ex. 13.]

Several days after the suspension of trading, Gira telephoned Richard I. Roemer, an attorney with the firm of Vaughan, Brandlin & Baggot. [R T. 214-215.] Gira had become acquainted with Roemer during the preceding year in which Roemer had done legal work for one of the subsidiaries of United Industrial Corporation, namely, U. S. Science [R. T. 211-212], which had been under the management of the brother of Bernard F. Gira, namely, Robert Gira, before Robert Gira was transferred to a different division. [R. T. 212-213.] Bernard Gira had been sufficiently impressed with Roemer's ability that he had previously offered Roemer a job as general counsel for United Industrial Corporation in October of 1960. Roemer never accepted the offer, however. At Gira's request, Roemer and his partner, J. J. Brandlin, met with Gira at Gira's home approximately a week after the suspension of trading had taken place. [R. T. 214, 1241-1242.]

At this meeting Gira advised Brandlin and Roemer that he and Petersen had a combined investment of close to 100,000 shares of stock in the company, and that this investment represented a major part of their personal assets, and that he was very concerned over the future prospects of their investment. He expressed dissatisfaction with the practices of certain members of the Board of Directors who had assumed apparent leadership of the present management. He expressed the view that the financial future of the corporation was in jeopardy. He also indicated that he had heard rumors that the management might be taking legal action against Petersen and him, and that there was a possibility of an investigation by the Securities and Exchange Commission concerning the suspension of trading.

Gira asked Brandlin and Roemer for suggestions as to his future course. Brandlin and Roemer listened and then suggested several things, including the possibility of a proxy contest. [R. T. 217.] Gira indicated that he was not interested in engaging in a proxy contest nor in returning to the management of the affairs of U.I.C., he indicated that he was in very poor health, and might have to undergo major surgery in the near future. Brandlin and Roemer then stated that they were in no position to advise him properly on such short notice, and suggested that he come in to their office after they had had time to give the matter more thought. [R. T. 215-217, 1242-1244.]

There followed a meeting in Brandlin's office a couple of days later, with only Gira present, and at this time the three were in accord that both Gira and Petersen should be primarily interested in clearing their names from any stigma resulting from the newspaper articles commenting on their resignations and the recent suspension of trading in stock; that there was nothing to be done about the impending lawsuits except to await their filing and then concentrating their efforts on defending themselves, *but that they should not engage in any proxy contest.* [R. T. 1246-1248.] Gira stated definitely that he and Petersen were not interested in engaging in a proxy contest. Gira had already received calls from stockholders who were dissatisfied and asking for advice, and he then told Brandlin that if the law firm were interested in handling a proxy contest for other stockholders, they would refer any such calls to the law firm. [R. T. 1248-1249, 1372-1375; Ex. 33, pp. 192-193.]

At this time, Brandlin indicated that the firm might be interested in handling a proxy contest for other interested stockholders who might approach him, but indicated that it would be dependent upon whether or not he would be able to organize an outstanding slate of businessmen who would be definitely independent of any other faction connected with United Industrial Corporation, including Gira and Petersen. Brandlin also indicated that if the firm went into any proxy contest that it would need a stockholders' list, and would probably need the services of a qualified public relations man. Gira indicated that he and/or Petersen had possession of a stockholders' list, and that they would let Brandlin use it. [R. T. 1248-1250.] At this time Gira gave Brandlin the name of Pete Summers as being a public relations man who had previously worked for United Industrial Corporation, and was familiar with its operation. [R. T. 1223, 1254.]

Approximately two days later, on Friday, January 27, 1961, Gira and Petersen came back to the office of Brandlin and Roemer and delivered a stockholders' list to Roemer who indicated that the firm intended to make a duplicate copy of it. Gira and Petersen also told Roemer the names of some of the more substantial stockholders of the company. Then Petersen asked Roemer to transmit the list to the headquarters of United Industrial Corporation when the firm had finished duplicating it. [R. T. 79-81.] Thereafter, on Sunday, the 29th of January, 1961, immediately after the list had been duplicated, Brandlin personally delivered the list to the headquarters of United Industrial Corporation. [R. T. 220-227, 1250-1251.]

During the trial, the Securities and Exchange Commission sought to prove that the stockholders' list had been stolen from United Industrial Corporation's headquarters, either by or at the request of Gira and/or Petersen. Petersen, however, testified that the list had been accidentally included among certain other books, papers and personal effects which had been transported from his United Industrial Corporation offices, probably on the day he left. [R. T. 69-72.] However, it may have been on another occasion a few days thereafter. [R. T. 194.]

The evidence offered by the Securities and Exchange Commission in support of their contention that the list was stolen was objected to by the Appellants, and the objection was sustained as to all of the Appellants, Stockholders' Protective Committee. [R. T. 54, 58, 162, 164, 189, 192, 200.]

As of the time the law firm had received the stockholders' list they had also received a telephone call from Herman Yaras, then owner of approximately 15,000 shares of United Industrial Corporation [R. T. 1202] (a defendant who was dismissed on judgment of nonsuit). [R. T. 1517.] Yaras indicated that he was interested in seeing new management on the Board of Directors of United Industrial Corporation, and indicated his intention to come to the law firm's offices to discuss the matter. [R. T. 1204.] At approximately the same time the firm received a telephone call from Pete Summers, who had been told by Petersen that the firm might need the services of a public relations man. [R. T. 1222-1223.] Summers indicated he was seeking a possible job handling public relations for any proxy contest which the firm might engage in. During the course of this conversation, Summers indicated to Roemer that he knew Nathaniel Dumont well and thought Dumont, owner of 5,100 shares, might be interested in engaging in a proxy contest, and told Roemer he would make an inquiry of Dumont. [R. T 2179-2184.] Shortly thereafter, and before the date on which the stockholders' list was duplicated, Dumont transmitted a telephone message to the law firm, through Summers, to the effect that he was interested in discussing a proxy contest, and wanted an appointment with either Brandlin or Roemer. [R. T. 1594, 2181.] Within a few days after the stockholders' list had been duplicated, Brandlin had already talked in person to Dumont who indicated a willingness to explore a proxy contest, to serve on any committee that was organized, and pledged funds in support of a contest if Brandlin decided to undertake it. [R. T. 1213, 1231.] Brandlin also talked personally to Yaras who encouraged him to take steps to organize a proxy committee, but indicated his personal reluctance to serve on any committee which might be formed. [R. T. 1232.] Within a day or so of his discussion with Dumont, Brandlin sounded out Henwood, a friend and client, whether he might be interested in serving on a slate of directors if the firm went into a proxy contest. [R. T. 1210.] During this same few days, Roemer received telephone calls from stockholders Elmer Luther and Roy Williams, both of whom authorized the law firm to take whatever steps it thought necessary to oppose the management of United Industrial Corporation. [R. T. 229-232, 1315-1318; Exs. 28, J.] Immediately thereafter, Brandlin and Roemer commenced organizing a committee to oppose management which subsequently was called the Stockholders' Protective Committee. [R. T. 232-233.]

The selection of the Stockholders' Protective Committee was made primarily by attorneys Brandlin and Roemer. Brandlin selected Armogida, Beshara, Henwood, Lawry, McLaughlin, Poe, Summers and Wulfekuhler. Roemer selected Foss and Soderstrom, and also received the initial calls from Williams and Luther; and Summers selected Steel and Henwood selected Zodda. [R. T. 234-235, 1340-1341.] Other people were contacted, such as John Roosevelt, son of former President of the United States; Jerome Teggeler, partner of Dempsey, Teggeler & Co.; Gilbert Van Camp, Sr.; Rosalind Tripp; Edward Baruch; W. J. Alford; Jules Schubot, long time stockholders of U.I.C. or its predecessor. For various reasons those people declined to serve. [R. T. 324-328, 1341-1342.]

The original selections where made on a tentative basis with the understanding that each prospective member was to have the opportunity to ratify the entire make up of the slate before making the final acceptance. [R. T. 330.] It was also understood by all members of the slate that the law firm would not have a permanent commitment to go forward unless and until it was satisfied that the slate had a reasonable chance to win the contest. [R. T. 330, 1262, 1340.]

During the course of the organization of the slate, several of the prospective slate members inquired about acquiring shares of stock in the corporation. Roemer contacted Yaras and purchased 2,000 shares from the pledgee of Yaras' stock and, in turn, resold at his cost 1,000 shares among prospective members of the slate. [R. T. 244-246.]

Sometime in late February, 1961, Henwood had a conference with Gira and Petersen together with Brandlin and Roemer and attorney Kendrick, representing Gira and Petersen, at which time Gira and Petersen, at the request of Henwood and Brandlin, outlined the operations of the various subsidiaries of the United

Industrial Corporation so that Henwood and Brandl
would have a better understanding of the corporatio
[R. T. 288, 291-295, 1264-1265, 1668-1669.] On a
other occasion, Brandlin met with Gira, Petersen a1
their attorney and indicated to them that the Prote
tive Committee intended to send a *telegram* to the ma
agement of U.I.C. warning the Management that stat
ments to the effect that the Protective Committee w
a "front" for Gira and Petersen were libelous, a1
Brandlin urged that Gira and Petersen *send a simil
telegram.* Brandlin does not know whether Gira a1
Petersen ever sent such a telegram. [R. T. 1263-126
1425-1427.]

The first step in the contest taken by the Comm
tee was to prepare proxy soliciting material. This m
terial was prepared primarily by the attorneys who su
mitted preliminary drafts to each member of the Cor
mittee for their perusal and comment before the dra
was submitted on March 13, 1961, to the Securities a1
Exchange Commission for their clearance. [R. T. 27
278, 302.] Upon the submission of the initial dra
Mr. Sharon Risk, who was in charge of the staff gro1
handling the matter for the Securities and Exchan,
Commission, indicated that the staff was not in a p
sition to clear the material until they had more infc
mation concerning the "genesis" of the Stockholde1
Protective Committee. [R. T. 1797-1798.] At tl
time the SEC Staff indicated that they wanted to ta
the testimony of various members of the Committ
and other persons, both in Washington, D.C., and
Los Angeles. [R. T. 1275-1277, 1799-1800.] The a
torneys for the Committee agreed to make the me1
bers of the Committee available. [R. T. 1277-127£

Thereafter the Securities and Exchange Commission pursuant to an order of Section 21 (a) of the Securities and Exchange Act of 1934 took the testimony of Henwood, Roemer, McLaughlin, Wulfekuhler, Williams, Luther, Dumont, Ballance, Soderstrom, Lawry, Gira, Petersen and Yaras for the stated purpose of *"determining the adequacy and accuracy of the proxy solicitation material of the Stockholders' Protective Committee."* [R. T. 1166-1169; Exs. 29-39; 42.] These proceedings ran concurrently in Washington, D.C., and Los Angeles and took a period of approximately five days, commencing on the 27th day of March and ending on the 31st day of March, 1961. [R. T. 1279.] After the Securities and Exchange Commission staff had completed the examinations of the various witnesses, and had received other oral and documentary information from the attorneys for the Committee, the staff then consulted with Roemer in Washington, D.C., and outlined what, in their opinion, should be included in the proxy soliciting material. [R. T. 1820-1829.] *This was in line with their stated policy of giving assistance to those who seek their counselling in attempting to comply with the Regulations.* [R. T. 547.] The attorneys for the Committee had not been present at the taking of the testimony of the various witnesses except in the case of Roemer and Henwood [R. T. 1277], and did not have copies of any of the transcripts, but nevertheless redrafted the material in conformity with the suggestions of the staff of the SEC and then resubmitted it. There was then held a final conference between Roemer and various members of the staff of the Securities and Exchange Commission who made additional comments and recommended changes

in certain words and phrases, all of which Roemer com
plied with. [R. T. 303, 1280-1281, 1829.] The Stoc
holders' Protective Commitee finally received a clea
ance for the mailing of their first proxy solicitati
material on the 6th day of April, 1961. [R. T. 302
Thereafter, on the 13th day of April, 1961, the pr
posed second mailing was transmitted to the staff
the SEC and was cleared on the 23rd day of Apr
1961. [R. T. 309.] Again in this instance the sta
of the Securities and Exchange Commission suggest
a considerable portion of the language of the accor
panying letter which was used by the Committee. [
T. 309.] The third prospective mailing was transmitt
to SEC on or about the 14th day of May, 1961, ai
was cleared on the 25th day of May, 1961. [R.
310.] There were but a few changes suggested
the SEC for this mailing. The proposed fourth maili
was sent to the SEC on the 3rd day of July, 1961, and
this occasion a staff member of the Securities and E
change Commission dictated the changes over the te
phone to Roemer who took them down on or about Ju
11, 1961. [R. T. 311, 1983-1984, 2027.] All of the ma
ings of the Stockholders' Protective Committee appe
in Exhibits 13 and A, and some of the passages whi
became relevant in this case are as follows:

From Mailing No. 1:

"The formation of the Stockholders' Protecti
Committee started after Richard I. Roemer, a mer
ber of the Committee, a nominee for director, a:
a partner in the law firm representing the Cor
mittee, received complaints from stockholders F
mer M. Luther, Jr., a former employee of a su
sidiary of the company, and Roy L. Williams, B.

Gira's uncle, who own respectively 250 and 400 shares of the common stock of your company. They complained about the decrease in market value of the stock, its suspension from trading, and the apparent internal conflict within the board of directors. These two stockholders requested Mr. Roemer to take whatever steps were necessary to form a new slate of directors and provide your company with new management. This was done by contacting men whom the organizers of the slate considered to be leaders in industry, business and the professions. The selection was made with the qualifications of the individual as the primary consideration and, secondly, his stockholdings in the company. Those men who did not then own stock could not purchase it in the usual manner, since trading had been suspended. As a result, Mr. Roemer purchased 2,000 shares of the company's common stock from Mr. Herman Yaras who in the past had been a financial consultant to the company. Mr. Yaras still owns 10,000 shares of the common stock of the company. Of the shares purchased by Mr. Roemer, 1,000 were sold in 100 share lots to ten members of the slate at no profit. Mr. Roemer retains the remaining 1,000 shares."

"Prior to the foregoing, Mr. Roemer and one of his partners, J. J. Brandlin, conferred with B. F. Gira and H. J. Petersen, the former president and executive vice president, respectively, of the company, concerning Gira's and Petersen's investments in the company. Together, Messrs. Gira and Petersen own in excess of 95,000 shares of the common stock of the company. They stated that

they were not interested in waging a proxy c(
test, but they did furnish the Committee with
formation concerning the company including
stockholders list. The law firm of Vaugh
Brandlin & Baggot, in which Messrs. Brandlin a
Roemer are partners, does not represent Mess
Gira and Petersen, nor are Messrs. Gira and Pet
sen members of the Committee."

"This Protective Committee, its' agents and
employees, and anyone else directly or indirec
connected with it, have no contracts, arrangeme
or understandings of any kind whatsoever, dir
or indirect, with Messrs. Luther, Williams, G
and/or Petersen, concerning future employment,
nancing of this proxy contest, or any other re
tionship with your company."

From Mailing No. 3:

"Management, in its recent so-called 'Inter
Report' and perhaps in ensuing proxy statemer
apparently hopes to confuse you by attempting
link this Protective Committee with Mr. Gira a
Mr. Petersen. Management has brought a la
suit to void all of the blue proxies which you ha
given this Committee. Management claims in t
lawsuit (and has claimed in this proxy conte
that we and our slate of directors are the age
of Messrs. Gira and Petersen. Our Proxy Sta
ment, which you received about April 11, 19
disclosed that Gira and Petersen helped the Cc
mittee. In addition, they are the owners of cl
to 100,000 shares of common stock of U.I.
and we hope to receive their proxies. As p
viously stated, they gave us the help indica

in our Proxy Statement, and we welcomed that help just as we welcome the help and support of *all* stockholders. We appreciate the confidence in our slate of directors expressed by each of you who has sent us a BLUE PROXY."

"Management claims that our slate is a 'front' for Gira and Petersen, so let's look at the facts! Messrs. Wulfekuhler, Armogida, Beshara, and General Ballance know Gira and Petersen primarily as the former president and executive vice president of the company in which they all are substantial stockholders. Armogida and Beshara were formerly large stockholders of Perry Rubber Company, now a valuable subsidiary of U.I.C., and dealt with Gira and Petersen during its acquisition by U.I.C. Mr. Foss met Mr. Gira and Mr. Petersen about two years ago, and they have met two or three times since then on matters not related to this proxy contest. Mr. Henwood met and talked with Gira and Petersen once late in February, 1961, for the purpose of obtaining information about U.I.C. Mr. Dumont owns an interest in some unimproved land in which Mr. Gira, among others, has a 10% interest. Mr. Dumont met Gira and Petersen during World War II when their business interests were in allied fields (not related to U.I.C. or its subsidiaries). They have had various business dealings between 1945 and about 1953, none of which were related to U.I.C. or its subsidiaries, and they have met socially on a few occasions. Our original Proxy Statement discusses the acquaintance of Messrs. Roemer and Summers with Gira and Petersen. The remaining members of the slate, Messrs. Steel, Zodda, Lawry, Soderstrom and

McLaughlin, have never met or communicated in any way with Messrs. Gira and Petersen. We understand Mr. Petersen remembers meeting Mr. McLaughlin during World War II, but Mr. McLaughlin has no recollection of this."

"The attorneys for the Committee and to a lesser extent, members of the slate of directors themselves, have obtained the participation of fine business and professional men who have agreed to serve as directors of your company. They did not perform these services for Petersen and Gira, or anyone else not named in our soliciting material."

"We do not feel that it should be necessary to repeat that this Committee and its slate of directors have no obligation, contracts, arrangements, or understandings of any kind whatsoever with Gira, Petersen, any member of the slate, or anyone else. *THAT IS THE FACT!* Study the records of the members of our slate and we think you will agree that men of their ability and integrity do not 'front' for anyone."

"The only commitment our slate members have made to ANYONE is to use their best ability to restore confidence in U.I.C. and give the company the best management possible with the hope that profit will result to all of the stockholders along with sound growth. WE MAKE THIS COMMITMENT TO EACH AND EVERYONE OF YOU!"

Again From Mailing No. 1:

"None of the aforementioned nominees for director, except as hereinafter stated, has heretofore been a director of the company or has had, or now has, any material interest, direct or indirect, in any material transaction of the company except as a stockholder. James V. Armogida and Fred A. Beshara have the right to receive additional stock of the company based upon the net pre-tax profits of Perry Rubber Company, a subsidiary of the company, during the next four years, under a contract dated March, 1960. Vaughn, Brandlin & Baggot, of which Richard I. Roemer is a partner, rendered legal services to the company and its subsidiaries during the last 18 months and received fees amounting to $18,465. Pete Summers, Inc., public relations consultant, of which Clarence L. Summers is president, had an agreement with the company to conduct a products survey over a 90-day period for a fee of $15,000. It has received $5,000 to date under this agreement. Mr. Summers, in December, 1960, proposed to the company that he be paid a finder's fee in the event prospective acquisitions which he might locate would be purchased by the company. This proposal was not accepted by the company, and Mr. Summers has received no payments and makes no claims thereunder. Mr. Summers has authorized the Committee to state that he waives all rights he might have, if any, under such proposal. Each of the nominees has advised the Committee that he is not a party to any contracts, arrangements, or understandings with any person with respect to any securities of the company, and that neither he nor any of his associates has any contracts, arrangements, or understanding with any person with respect to any future employment by the company or any of its affiliates or with respect to any future transaction to which the company or any of its affiliates will or may be a party."

"Should the Protective Committee be successful in electing a majority of the directors of the company, counsel for the Committee, Vaughan, Brandlin & Baggot, and the Committee's public relations consultant, Pete Summers, Inc., feel that in the ordinary course of events the board of directors will consider the use of their services in the future as counsel and public relations consultant, respectively. However, no contracts, understandings, commitments, or arrangements, written or oral, express or implied, exist with respect to these matters. There are no contracts, arrangements, or understandings with any person with respect to any future sale, purchase, merger, acquisition, or other transaction of any kind or character with respect to which the company or any of its affiliates are or may be a party."

From Mailing No. 4:

"WE ARE CRITICAL!

"DEAR FELLOW STOCKHOLDERS:

"For Management to say that this Committee is not critical of Mr. Gira and Mr. Petersen is ridiculous. Mr. Huntington, who signed Management's proxy material dated June 26th, or whoever wrote that document, apparently chose to ignore the fact that we have consistently criticized the Directors who served during 1960, which includes Gira and Petersen."

"We are critical of Gira and Petersen and we are equally as critical of Huntington, Fein, Goodman and all the other Directors who served during 1960, and who are now asking for your vote. The Directors running for re-election who served during 1960 and 1961 are FEIN, GOODMAN, HUNTINGTON, HUFTY, MANN, WEIL and BARBER."

"In our opinion, these men, including Gira and Petersen, and Mr. Huntington, who was Chairman of the Board during 1960 and 1961, and Mr. Fein, who is now Chairman of the Executive Committee, must and will bear the responsibility for the chaotic condition of United Industrial Corporation. The seven Directors now asking for your vote, *led by Fein, Huntington and Goodman,* disavow any responsibility for your company's problems. They claim their confidence in Gira and Petersen was 'misplaced'. *We charge that the confidence that the stockholders placed in all of the Directors was misplaced."*

"LET'S CLEAR THE AIR ON GIRA AND PETERSEN—ONCE AND FOR ALL

"Management's so-called 'Interim Report' of May 15, 1961, again in Huntington's letter of June 1, 1961, and now in their latest report dated June 26, 1961, charges that this Committee is a 'front' for Gira and Petersen. *This is false!* Study our list of nominees and their backgrounds, and *we believe you will agree that men of their caliber do not 'front' for anyone."*

"WE REPEAT: We have *no* commitment of any kind to or from Gira or Petersen. They are

not 'motivating' this Committee. A vote on the Blue Proxy will *not* be a vote for 'Gira and Petersen' or anyone else not disclosed to you. Gira and Petersen *are not and cannot* use this Committee as a 'medium' to seize control of the company. We had told you of the assistance we had from Gira and Petersen long before you received the 'Interim Report.' We repeated our position in Report #3 and state it again above. We suppose, however, that *Management* will continue to harp on the subject of Gira and Petersen because they have nothing else to say, and they *must* '*pass the buck.*' Certainly there is little they can say that will justify or even explain the results for 1960, except to point at Gira and Petersen and attempt to link this Committee with them. *We don't believe you will be misled by Management's tactics.*"

"These 'results' were 'achieved' during the time that Gira was President, Petersen was Executive Vice President, Huntington was Chairman of the Board, Fein was Chairman of the Executive Committee, and they were all Directors, along with Weil, Mann, Barber, Hufty and Goodman. *ALL OF THESE MEN, EXCEPT GIRA AND* PETERSEN, ARE ASKING YOU TO PUT *THEM BACK IN OFFICE.*"

"Can Fein, Huntington, Goodman, Barber, Mann, Weil and Hufty disassociate themselves from these 'results' by simply pointing to Gira and Petersen? If, as they indicate, they knew nothing about what really happened during 1960 then certainly they were derelict in their duty and should

be replaced. *Do they claim that all these liquid
assets, cash and marketable securities, were spent
without their knowledge, or that the bank debt
was increased without their knowledge?* This is the
implication in their mailing of June 26th. Even
assuming that they are correct and that they didn't
know anything about these things, *would you want
them in office for another year so that more can
go on without them knowing about it?"*

On or about April 25, 1961, Management filed a
lawsuit in the United States District Court, Western
District of New York, in Buffalo, New York, naming
the Stockholders' Protective Committee and Gira and
Petersen as defendants. The main theme of this complaint, the same as used in their proxy solicitation material, was that the Stockholders' Protective Committee
had made false and misleading statements by denying
Management's charges that the Stockholders' Protective Committee were acting on behalf of Gira and
Petersen and were the agents and representatives of
Gira and Petersen. This action was transferred to
the Southern District of California in July of 1961,
after a motion for change of venue by the defendants.
At this time a counterclaim was filed by the Stockholders' Protective Committee charging Management
with false and misleading statements in their proxy
solicitation material in that they had accused the Committee of "fronting" for Gira and Petersen, and indicating that a vote for the Protective Committee would
be "a vote for Gira and Petersen." *A member of
the staff of the SEC had repeatedly urged the
attorneys for the Committee to file such a counterclaim.* [R. T. 1347-1349.] In this action, known as

U.I.C. v. Henwood, No. 747-61-TC, each side sought similar orders against the other based, primarily, upon identically opposite and mutually exclusive charges.

From the date on which the SEC staff cleared the initial solicitation material of the Stockholders' Protective Committee, the attorneys for the Protective Committee had complied with every request of the SEC.[1] [R. T. 311-312, 1347.] The SHPC had a strong motive to comply with anything the SEC staff requested because there were much ahead in the proxy contest and didn't want any friction to develop with the SEC. [R. T. 1295.] Their conduct was described by the SEC staff member who had charge of the proxy contest up to July 12, 1961, Mr. Sharon Risk, as "cooperative". [R. T. 2016-2017.] On July 11, 1961, when the same member of the staff of the SEC requested the attorneys for the Committee to cause to be filed a Schedule 14-B by Herman Yaras on the ground that the SEC staff had suddenly decided that he had been active as a "participant" on behalf of the Stockholders' Protective Committee, said attorneys indicated that, although they did not represent Mr. Yaras, they would contact his attorney and do what they could to induce him to file a 14-B. [R. T. 285-286.] Thereafter, they immediately contacted Yaras and his attorney and persuaded him to file a 14-B. Four business days later, on Monday, July 17, 1961, the at-

---

[1]Excepting one instance in which the attorneys had accidentally omitted to make a change in a piece of literature This was in reference to Bernard Fein being described as the "Chairman of the Executive Committee" as of a certain date instead of describing him as a "Member." The SEC staff member called this error to the attention of Roemer, who corrected it in several places in the literature, but inadvertently failed to correct it in one place. [R T. 311]

torneys for the Committee telephoned the SEC in Washington, D. C., and advised them that Mr. Yaras' 14-B was in the mail, but on the next day, July 18, 1961, the staff of the SEC recommended to the Commission that the action against the Protective Committee be brought. [R. T. 903-907.] (The trial court in the case at bar subsequently dismissed the case as to Mr. Yaras and held that Mr. Yaras was *not* a "participant," and therefore was not required to file Schedule 14-B.) [C. T. ....]

On or about July 12, 1961, Gira and Petersen filed a libel action against the members of the Board of Directors of U.I.C [Ex. KK] charging them with making derogatory statements in their proxy material about Gira and Petersen's "ability and integrity." [R. T. 1950.] At this time, their attorney, Kendrick, submitted a proposed press release concerning the filing of the lawsuit to the SEC staff for their opinion as to whether such a press release would constitute a proxy solicitation. The SEC staff advised the attorney that the press release would constitute a proxy solicitation and requested that Gira and Petersen file a Schedule 14-B. [R. T. 1977-1978.] At this time, the attorney for Gira and Petersen stated that he would withdraw the press release and not issue it. [R. T. 474-475.] As it turned out, the press agent, without authorization, went ahead and issued the press release. [R. T. 630-631.] The form in which it was published in the papers was not the same as the press release and turned out to be only a statement of the fact of the filing of the lawsuit. [R. T. 1950, 486-488; Exs. AA, BB, CC, DD.] *No member of the Stockholders' Protective Committee, nor its attorneys had anything to do with the filing of this lawsuit or in the issuance of the press release.* [R. T. 296.]

The decision to recommend the filing of the SEC action against the Stockholders' Protective Committee was made by members of the staff who, until July 12th, had only been assisting Mr. Risk, and were not as familiar with the handling of proxy contests as was Mr. Risk. [R. T. 2081, 2084-2085.] One of them, Gordon, had never handled a contest before. The discussion among the staff members leading up to the decision to recommend the filing of a lawsuit commenced after July 11, 1961. [R. T. 1855, 2087-2088], when an attorney for Management was in the offices of the SEC and urged several of the members of the staff, namely, Gordon, Weinman and Risk [R. T. 875-877] to bring an action against the Stockholders' Protective Committee based on the alleged participation of Yaras, *"at the last minute in order to void their proxies."* [R. T. 877-878.] This same attorney for Management telephoned the SEC staff concerning the same subject matter on July 11, 1961 [R. T. 784-786], and, on the following day, after Mr. Risk, the staff member who had been in charge of the proxy contest, and who was the one most familiar with the volumes of transcript and other information which the SEC had collected throughout the proxy contest, had left on his vacation [R. T. 732], the other members of the staff began "thinking and talking" about the filing of the lawsuit. [R. T. 733-736.] There was no mention of a lawsuit while Risk was on duty. [R. T. 1855.]

Trial.

The case of U.I.C. v. Henwood, No. 747-61 TC, had commenced trial before the same trial judge on July 17, 1961; however, on the second day of trial, the Court announced from the bench that he had received a long distance telephone call from a Mr. Kennamer, the Chief Enforcement Officer of the Securities and Exchange Commission, who had advised him that the SEC was about to intervene in some manner in the lawsuit. [R. T. 17a.] The trial of the action of U.I.C. v. Henwood was then continued to July 25, 1961. Thereafter, and on July 25, 1961, the Court suspended the trial of the action of U.I.C. v. Henwood and granted a priority to the action which had been filed by the SEC on July 21, 1961, as an independent action. [R. T. 23a.] This action, while embodying generally similar claims as those made by management in U.I.C. v. Henwood, does not include the opposite side of the issue which was presented by the Stockholders' Protective Committee counterclaim in U.I.C. v. Henwood.

On the day that the SEC v. Henwood case was called for trial, the SEC asked the trial court to grant an immediate temporary restraining order against the Appellants [R. T. 26a] restraining them from soliciting proxies by means of alleged false or misleading statements with respect to the Committee's relationship to Gira and Petersen, and from voting proxies already obtained by them pending the hearing of the action on the preliminary injunction. This restraining order also included recitals to the effect that the Appellants had previously solicited proxies by means of false and misleading statements concerning the Appellants' relationship with Gira and Petersen. [C. T. ....] The affidavits filed in support of the application for a restraining order did not contain any allegation whatsoever concerning any act or threatened act of the Appellants with respect to the solicitation of proxies by false and misleading statements which in any way concerned Gira or Petersen or Yaras. [C. T. ....] This was pointed out to the Court during the proceedings on the first day of trial. [R. T. 34a-35a.] The court stated from the bench that he had had Mr. Kennamer, the SEC's Chief Enforcement attorney before him in another case for two years [R. T. 36a], and that the Court *and* Mr. Kennamer had been arrayed against approximately "eight attorneys" but that *"we* were affirmed on appeal and certiorari was denied, and *we* saved some people millions of dollars, and if they had paid attention to *us* two years ago, *we* would have saved them more money." [R. T. 77a, 116a-117a.] The Court further indicated that he could see no need for Appellants to resist the temporary restraining order because "Mr. Kennamer isn't going to hurt anybody with his temporary restraining order." [R. T. 76a.] The following day after considerable discussion, the Court signed the temporary restraining order over the objection of counsel for Appellants and made findings of fact, all without foundation in the affidavits submitted by the SEC, and then ordered the immediate hearing of the preliminary injunction [R. T. 131a], even though counsel for Appellants had had no opportunity to prepare for the hearing and was actually engaged in a trial in another case in the Superior Court of the County of Los Angeles. [R. T. 128a-130a.]

On this occasion the Court again indicated that it had the "greatest respect and admiration for Mr. Kennamer" [R. T. 116a-117a] and was "mad" at Mr. Robinson. [R. T. 119a.] During the latter stages of the trial, the Court openly admitted that he felt that he had been "championing" the rights of Mr. Kennamer and the SEC in this case. [R. T. 1180.] The Court in its Memorandum opinion signed October 3, 1961, also embodied the suggestions and exact phraseology suggested by Mr. Kennamer in his argument. [R. T. 2213, 2214.]

The Court also signed the exact Findings of Fact and Conclusions of Law and Judgment as drafted by Mr. Kennamer without changing a single word, and this was after a full hearing in open court at which time the counsel for the Appellants and the counsel for Gira and Petersen pointed out to the Court various and obvious errors in the proposed Findings of Fact and Conclusions of Law and Judgment. [R. T. 2289-2347; C. T. ....]

On this same occasion, the Court described the appellants, as a group, as the "worst people" that the Court had ever had in its courtroom [R. T. 2311], although in the Memorandum Opinion and the Findings of Fact the Court had indicated that these same appellants were outstanding and men of distinction.

During the trial, the Securities and Exchange Commission produced as witnesses on behalf of the SEC certain members of the staff who were not completely familiar with all of the information accumulated by the Securities and Exchange Commission during the proxy contest. The Appellants requested and received definite assurances in open court from the attorney representing the Securities and Exchange Commission that the member of the staff who had been in charge of the case from the beginning and who had the most knowledge of circumstances and information accumulated by the SEC, Mr. Risk, would also be produced. [R. T. 25-26.] However, as the trial continued week after week the attorney for the Securities and Exchange Commission kept postponing the production of the witness [R. T. 861, 865-872] and finally refused to produce the witness. At this time, the Court refused to grant the request of Appellants' counsel to order the production of the witness on the stated ground that the Court was powerless to make such an order. [R. T. 1128-1132, 1336.] Finally, the Appellants gave notice of taking of the witness' deposition in Washington and the attorney for the Appellants traveled to Washington, D. C., to take the deposition of the witness Risk and the witness Cohen. [R. T. 1400, Ex. 50, Ex. N.] In each of these depositions, the witnesses refused to answer certain questions which the Court had already ruled were proper and which the Court subsequently ruled as being proper. The Court refused to grant any sanctions against the Securities and Exchange Commission for this refusal. [R. T. 1601-1663.]

Judgment.

As previously stated, the judgment enjoins the Appellants, and each and all of them, from voting any proxy of any stockholder now held by the Stockholders' Protective Committee, or from voting any proxy which is not received pursuant to a future solicitation of proxies in accordance with the Rules and Regulations of the Securities and Exchange Act of 1934, and further enjoins the Appellants, and each and all of them, from soliciting any future proxies unless they include in their proxy solicitation material statements which were not supported by the evidence, and, among other things, include the statement to the effect that defendants, Gira and Petersen, are "members" of the Stockholders' Protective Committee which will, in the light of the circumstances surrounding the contest, imply that the Stockholders' Protective Committee is acting in this proxy contest on behalf of Gira and Petersen. At the same time that it enjoins them and invalidates their proxies, the judgment dismisses from the action the Appellants James V. Armogida, Brigadier General Robert G. Ballance, Fred Beshara, Nathaniel R. Dumont, Joe J. Foss, William David Lawry, Elmer Luther, Edward H. McLaughlin, Charles Soderstrom, John Autry Steel, Clarence L. Summers, Roy Williams, Louis Wulfekuhler, and Alfred T. Zodda. [C. T. ....]

Questions Presented on Appeal.

1. DID NOT THE TRIAL COURT ERR IN PURPORTING TO ENJOIN CERTAIN OF THE APPELLANTS WHILE AT THE SAME TIME DISMISSING SAID APPELLANTS "WITHOUT PREJUDICE," AFTER A TRIAL ON THE MERITS?

2. DID NOT THE COURT ERR IN HIS JUDGMENT BY PURPORTING TO IMPOSE AN IN—JUNCTION AGAINST ALL OF THE APPELLANTS WHICH WAS NOT SUPPORTED BY THE COURT'S OWN FINDINGS OF FACT AND CONCLUSIONS OF LAW?

3. WAS NOT THE EVIDENCE LEGALLY INSUFFICIENT TO SUSTAIN THE JUDGMENT IN THAT THERE WAS NOT SUBSTANTIAL EVIDENCE TO SUPPORT THE ESSENTIAL DETERMINATION THAT APPELLANTS HAVE MADE FALSE AND MISLEADING STATEMENTS OF MATERIAL FACTS, OR OMITTED TO STATE MATERIAL FACTS NECESSARY TO MAKE THEIR SOLICITATION STATEMENTS NOT FALSE OR MISLEADING?

This question was raised by appellants' motion for a judgment of dismissal under Rule 41-B, which was denied by the Court.

4. DID NOT THE COURT DENY THE APPELLANTS DUE PROCESS OF LAW AS GUARANTEED BY THE FIFTH AMENDMENT TO THE UNITED STATES CONSTITUTION BY THE MANNER IN WHICH IT APPLIED REG-

ULATION 14 OF THE SECURITIES AND EX-
CHANGE ACT OF 1934 TO THE FACTS IN
THIS CASE?

5. DID THE APPELLEE SEC SHOW ITSELF
TO BE ENTITLED TO THE EQUITABLE REM-
EDY OF AN INJUNCTION AGAINST THE AP-
PELLANTS AND AN ORDER INVALIDATING
APPELLANTS' PROXIES IN ANY EVENT?

6. DID NOT THE TRIAL COURT DENY THE
APPELLANTS A FAIR TRIAL BY FAILING TO
EXERCISE GENUINE JUDICIAL DISCRETION
AND JUDGMENT?

Specification of Errors.

I. The Court erred by purporting to impose an injunction against the appellants Armogida, Ballance,
Beshara, Dumont, Foss, Lawry, Luther, McLaughlin,
Soderstorm, Steel, Summers, Williams, Wulfekuhler and
Zodda at the same time that the Judgment dismissed
said appellants from the action. That portion which
purports to grant an injunction against said appellants
is void.

II. That portion of the Judgment which purports
to impose an injunction against all the appellants soliciting further proxies unless under certain specified
conditions* is not supported by the Court's own Findings of Fact and Conclusions of Law.

III. The trial court erred in not granting appellants'
motion to dismiss the action as to all of the appellants

---

*For a complete statement of that portion of the injunction,
see Appendix A.

and to enter Judgment in favor of all of the appellants on the grounds that upon the facts adduced and the law of the case, plaintiff was not entitled to relief; such dismissal should have been "with prejudice."

IV. The Court erred by making an unconstitutional application of Regulation 14 of the Securities and Exchange Act of 1934 to the facts of this case and appellants were thereby denied due process of law as guaranteed by the Fifth Amendment to the Constitution of the United States.

V. The Court erred by making certain Findings of Fact which are clearly erroneous and/or immaterial and inappropriate to the Judgment and/or are argumentative.

A. A portion of Finding No. 5 is clearly erroneous.*

B. A portion of Finding No. 6 is clearly erroneous.*

C. A portion of Finding No. 7 is clearly erroneous.*

D. A portion of Finding No. 9 is immaterial and inappropriate to the Judgment.*

E. A portion of Finding No. 11 is clearly erroneous.*

F. A portion of Finding No. 12 is clearly erroneous and is also argumentative.*

G. A portion of Finding No. 13 is clearly erroneous.*

H. A portion of Finding No. 14 is clearly erroneous.*

---

*The exact language of each Finding which is herein challenged is stated verbatim in the argument section of this brief, *infra.*

I. A portion of Finding No. 15 is clearly erroneous.*

J. A portion of Finding No. 17 is clearly erroneous and argumentative.*

K. A portion of Finding No. 19 is clearly erroneous.*

L. A portion of Finding No. 20 is argumentative.*

M. A portion of Finding No. 21 is clearly erroneous.*

N. A portion of Finding No. 22 is clearly erroneous.*

O. Finding No. 23 is immaterial.*

P. A portion of Finding No. 24 is clearly erroneous.*

VI. The Court erred by not denying the Appellee (SEC) the equitable remedy of an invalidation of appellants' proxies and of an injunction against appellants for the reason that Appellee (SEC) had denied appellants due process as guaranteed by the Fifth Amendment to the United States Constitution by the manner in which Appellee had administered the Securities and Exchange Commission Regulation of 1934 in this case.

VII. The Court erred by denying the appellants a fair trial as guaranteed by the due process clause of the Fifth Amendment in that the Court failed to exercise genuine judicial discretion and judgment.

---

*The exact language of each Finding which is herein challenged is stated verbatim in the argument section of this brief, *infra*

I.

The Court Erred by Purporting to Impose an junction Against the Appellants Armog Ballance, Beshara, Dumont, Foss, Lawry, ther, McLaughlin, Soderstrom, Steel, Summ Williams, Wulfekuhler and Zodda at the Sa Time That the Judgment Dismissed Said pellants From the Action. That Portion Wl Purports to Grant an Injunction Against S Appellants Is Void.

That portion of the judgment which purporrts to join the appellants Armogida, Ballance, Beshara, mont, Foss, Lawry, Luther, McLaughlin, Soderstr Steel, Summers, Williams, Wulfekuhler and Zodda members of the Stockholders' Protective Commit from soliciting proxies except under certain conditio [C. T. ....] is void for the reason that the s judgment dismisses said appellants from the case.

It is a well recognized rule of law in all juris tions that a court must have jurisdiction over the son in order to enjoin him from doing or to comm him to do certain acts. *Booth v. Clarke,* 58 U. S. 333; *Clarke v. Boysen,* 39 F. 2d at 815; *Hatahle United States,* 351 U. S. 173 at 183.

---

*"It is ordered, adjudged and decreed that the defenc United Industrial Corporation, Stockholders' Protective (mittee, Stanley E. Henwood, Richard I. Roemer and Loui Poe, individually and as members of and proxies of said S holders' Protective Committee, *all members, associates,* substit agents, employees and attorneys of said Stockholders' Prote Committee . . ." [C. T. ....].

When a court of equity renders a decision against a defendant, and enjoins him from certain acts, it impliedly retains jurisdiction over said person for the purpose of carrying out its decree; BUT WHEN A COURT DISMISSES A PARTY FROM AN ACTION, IT LOSES ALL JURISDICTION OVER THAT PARTY, IT IS AS THOUGH THE ACTION HAD NEVER BEEN BROUGHT. THE DISMISSAL CARRIES DOWN WITH IT EVERY PREVIOUS ORDER MADE THEREIN. *Bryan v. Smith,* 174 F. 2d 212; *A. B. Dick Co. v. Marr,* 197 F. 2d 498; *Trowbridge v. Love,* 50 Cal. App. 2d 746. A proceeding is nonetheless terminated because it is dismissed "without prejudice," and the Court is nonetheless without further jurisdiction. *Mitchell v. Bd. of Governors of Washington,* 145 F. 2d 827, where a cause has been regularly tried on its merits a dismissal of the defendant is *with prejudice* regardless of the fact that the judgment may say "without prejudice". *United States v. Bd. of Comm. of Grady County,* 54 F. 2d 593, 596.

Based upon the evidence that was before the Court, the Court properly entered a judgment of dismissal as to the appellants Armogida, Ballance, Beshara, Dumont, Foss, Lawry, Luther, McLaughlin, Soderstrom, Steel, Summers, Williams, Wulfekuhler and Zodda, and once having done so, lost all jurisdiction over them, and any attempt to enjoin them in the same judgment is a nullity.

II.

That Portion of the Judgment Which Purports to Impose an Injunction Against All the Appellants Soliciting Further Proxies Unless Under Certain Specified Conditions Is Not Supported by the Court's Own Findings of Fact and Conclusions of Law.

That portion of the judgment which, in effect, purports to impose an injunction against all of the appellants from soliciting proxies in the future by means of any proxy statement or other communication, written or oral, which omits to state:

1. That Bernard F. Gira and Herbert J. Petersen were *"instrumental* in *initiating* and organizing the Stockholders' Protective Committee and in *formulating* on behalf of said Committee a slate of directors";

2. That "Bernard F. Gira and Herbert J. Petersen have *participated* with representatives of the Stockholders' Protective Committee and *aided and abetted* said Committee and its representatives in conducting proxy solicitation";

3. That "Bernard F. Gira and Herbert J. Petersen are members of the Stockholders' Protective Committee";

4. That "Bernard F. Gira and Herbert J. Petersen are *participating* with Stockholders' Protective Committee in soliciting proxies"

IS WHOLLY UNSUPPORTED BY THE FINDINGS OF FACT AND CONCLUSIONS OF LAW, FOR THE REASON THAT THE FINDINGS OF FACT AND CONCLUSIONS OF LAW MENTION ONLY TWO PARTICULARS WHEREIN APPEL-

LANTS ARE ALLEGED TO HAVE MADE
FALSE AND MISLEADING STATEMENTS IN
THEIR PREVIOUS PROXY SOLICITING MA-
TERIAL.

The first such Finding occurs in the last sentence in
Finding No. 14 (App. B) which states as follows:

> "The assertion in the Committee's proxy state-
> ment that counsel for the Committee started the
> organization of the Committee on behalf of Luther
> and Williams is seriously misleading."

The second such Finding is in the sentence of Finding
No. 23 (App. B):

> "The Committee's proxy material also was mis-
> leading in stating that certain losses sustained by
> UIC and diminution of stockholders' equity oc-
> curred when Bernard F. Fein was Chairman of the
> Executive Committee of UIC."

In neither of these particulars is there any reference
to Gira or Petersen. THERE ARE NO OTHER
FINDINGS WHICH PURPORT TO "FIND"
THAT THE LITERATURE OF THE STOCK-
HOLDERS' PROTECTIVE COMMITTEE WAS
FALSE AND MISLEADING IN ANY PAR-
TICULAR.

Therefore, such portion of the injunction as has been
enumerated in 1, 2, 3 and 4 above is wholly gratuitous
and outside the scope of any of the Findings of Fact
and Conclusions of Law.

III.

The Trial Court Erred in Not Granting Appellants' Motion to Dismiss the Action as to All of the Appellants and to Enter Judgment in Favor of All of the Appellants on the Grounds That Upon the Facts Adduced and the Law of the Case, Plaintiff Was Not Entitled to Relief; Such Dismissal Should Have Been "With Prejudice."

While the judgment of dismissal as to the appellants Armogida, Ballance, Beshara, Dumont, Foss, Lawry, Luther, McLaughlin, Soderstrom, Steel, Summers, Williams, Wulfekuhler and Zodda does not specify the grounds upon which it is entered, it is apparent that it is on the ground that under the evidence and the law the plaintiff failed to sustain its burden of proof as to the appellants so dismissed. Although the Court purported to enter the dismissal "without prejudice" it would appear that a dismissal after a full trial on the merits is "with prejudice", and the characterization of the dismissal as "without prejudice" does not change the legal effect. (*Mitchell v. Bd. of Governors of Washington*, 148 F. 2d 827.)

As indicated in the Court's Memorandum Opinion, which was incorporated by reference as part of the Findings of Fact and Conclusions of Law, ALL of the members of the Stockholders' Protective Committee were found to be men of "distinction" who had been "shielded" from any knowledge of any of the material facts which it is alleged were omitted from the proxy soliciting material of the Committee. There is no distinction made in the Findings of Fact or Conclusions of Law or the Memorandum Opinion of the Court be-

tween any members of the Stockholders' Protective
Committee, including Henwood, Poe and Roemer, ex-
cept that Henwood, Poe and Roemer are the persons
who had the authority and power to vote the proxies
which had been solicited on behalf of the Committee.
Therefore, in order to invalidate the proxies of the
Committee, it was necessary to enjoin those three ap-
pellants from using their power and authority to vote
the proxies. However, if the other members of the
Stockholders' Protective Committee were entitled to a
Judgment of Dismissal on the merits, THERE IS NO
LOGICAL BASIS WHY THE APPELLANTS
HENWOOD, POE AND ROEMER WERE NOT
ALSO ENTITLED TO THE SAME JUDGMENT.

ALL THE MATERIAL FACTS HAVE BEEN TOLD TO THE STOCKHOLDERS.

Over and above the technical grounds asserted above,
there remains the basic point made on this appeal, and
that is that the evidence failed to show that any of the
appellants individually or as members of the Stockholders' Protective Committee had violated the Securities and Exchange Act of 1934, and particularly Rule
14(a)9 promulgated thereunder.

In plaintiff's Complaint each of the appellants, without distinction, is charged with soliciting proxies by
means of proxy soliciting material which contained
false and misleading statements as to material facts in
violation of Rule 14(a)9. The pertinent language of
Rule 14(a)9 is as follows:

> "Communications, written or oral, containing
> any statement which, at the time and in the light
> of the circumstances . . . is false or mislead-

ing with respect to any *material fact* or which omits . . . any *material fact* necessary to make statements . . . not false or misleading or . . . to correct any statement in any earlier communication . . ."* (Emphasis added.)

As specified in the Complaint, the alleged false and misleading statements of MATERIAL FACTS were divided into three distinct subject matters: (a) statements, or omissions to state, concerning the Stockholders' Protective Committee's relationship with Gira and/or Petersen and/or Yaras; (b) an alleged statement concerning Luther and Williams and the formation of the Committee; and (c) a statement concerning the corporate office held by Bernard Fein as of a particular time.

(a) Regarding Gira, Petersen and Yaras.

With respect to the first category, that is, the relationship, if any, among the Stockholders' Protective Committee and Gira and Petersen and Yaras, it is the appellants' position that AN EXAMINATION OF THE WRITTEN SOLICITING MATERIAL SENT TO THE STOCKHOLDERS MANIFESTLY SHOWS THAT ALL OF THE MATERIAL FACTS SURROUNDING THE RELATIONSHIP OF THE STOCKHOLDERS' PROTECTIVE COMMITTEE WITH GIRA AND PETERSEN AND YARAS HAVE BEEN STATED. [Exs. 13, A.]

First of all, it should be borne in mind that the material facts in this case are basically undisputed. There-

*See Appendix A for complete language of rule.

fore, this Appellate Court is in as good a position as was the trial court to make a judgment as to whether or not the proxy soliciting material was false and misleading in the light of the circumstances surrounding the particular proxy contest.

In order to make a valid judgment as to whether or not proxy soliciting material is false and misleading, as defined in Rule 14(a)9, it is necessary to know the standard by which one is measuring. In order to know the standard, it is necessary to define one's terms. The words "MATERIAL FACTS" in the regulation does not mean every minute detail which could have been stated, nor does it mean every possible fact that relates to a subject matter (*Shvetz v. Industrial Rayon Corporation*, D. C. South. Dist. of New York (1960), C. C. H. Fed. Securities Law Rep. par. 90958). Simple basic economics would preclude the stating of a biography of every person who is in some way connected with a proxy contest. The Securities and Exchange Commission itself and the courts have held that "material facts" are those facts which *in the light of the particular circumstances* can reasonably be calculated to influence the votes of the stockholders in general. Such facts should be included in the proxy soliciting material and should be stated fairly (*Phillips v. United Corp*, C. C. H. Fed. Securities Law Rep. par. 90395 (1947).

Assuming the foregoing to be the proper standard, the next question is to determine what were the pertinent "circumstances" which were casting the light within which the material facts are to be judged.

In this particular proxy contest the stockholders of United Industrial Corporation were primarily interested in reversing the poor financial condition to which the corporation had dropped during the previous year and in reversing the trend of the market value of their securities. There was considerable indication that the poor condition which the corporation found itself in had been the result of mismanagement. The incumbent board of directors was disclaiming responsibility for the condtion and, as their excuse, were pointing their fingers at Messrs. Gira and Petersen who had recently resigned as president and vice president [Ex. 14]. The incumbent board had accused the Stockholders' Protective Committee of "fronting" for, and acting on behalf of, Messrs. Gira and Petersen, and had even stated that a vote for the Protective Committee would, in effect, be a vote for Gira and Petersen. [Ex. 14.] The obvious implication of these charges was that Gira and Petersen were attempting to be restored to a position in management through the vehicle of the Protective Committee, or at the very least, had some other significant arrangement or understanding with the Committee.

In the foregoing "light" the MOST material fact which could be calculated to influence the vote of the general stockholders of United Industrial Corporation was the fact of whether or not any arrangements or understandings existed between a member or members of the Protective Committee and Gira and Petersen which would benefit the latter pair.

With respect to that material fact, the Protective Committee stated categorically in its literature that there was "no obligation, contract, arrangement or understanding of any kind whatsoever with Gira, Petersen or anyone else." [Exs. 13, A.] Such a statement could certainly be calculated to influence the vote of many stockholders. If this statement were untrue, there is absolutely no doubt that the soliciting material is false and misleading. Throughout the case, however, there was no evidence of any kind to disprove this statement, and, indeed, nowhere in the Findings of Fact and Conclusions of Law or in the Judgment is there any statement of fact which contradicts this statement. In fact, the Court states in its Memorandum Opinion which is incorporated into the Findings of Fact and Conclusions of Law that the members of the Protective Committee are persons of distinction.

In addition to this most material fact, the literature of the Stockholders' Protective Committee went further and stated a whole spectrum of facts, ranging from much less material than the MOST material fact down to miscellaneous data of a basically immaterial nature. Thus the stockholders were told:

1. That Gira and Petersen had conferred with counsel for the Protective Committee prior to the time that counsel for the Protective Committee had undertaken the proxy contest;

2. That Gira and Petersen had discussed the subject of a proxy contest with the law firm, but had indicated that they personally did not want to be involved;

3. That Gira and Petersen had helped the attorneys for the Committee and the Committee itself by providing a stockholders' list;

4. That Gira and Petersen had given information to the attorneys for the Committee;

5. That Gira and Petersen had had a conference with the Chairman of the Stockholders' Protective Committee and had supplied him with information regarding the corporation;

6. That Gira was the nephew of Roy Williams; that Gira and Petersen knew Wulfekuhler, Armogida, Beshara and General Ballance as a result of their former position with the corporation; that Mr. Foss knew Gira and Petersen; that Dumont owned an interest in some unimproved land in which Gira had an interest and that they had known each other through business dealings and socially since 1945, and that Roemer and Summers knew Gira and Petersen; and

7. That the Stockholders' Protective Committee welcomed the help that they had received from Gira and Petersen and hoped and expected to get their votes. [Exs. 13, A.]

WHAT OTHER FACTS COULD HAVE BEEN STATED TO THE STOCKHOLDERS WHICH COULD REASONABLY BE CALCULATED TO INFLUENCE THE VOTES OF THE STOCK-HOLDERS? WHEREIN HAVE THE STOCK-HOLDERS BEEN MISLEAD BY THE FACTS AS STATED?

The Court in its Judgment answers these questions by stating in effect that the Stockholders' Protective Committee should have stated "that Bernard F. Gira and Herbert J. Petersen were *instrumental* in *initiating* and *organizing* the Stockholders' Protective Committee and in *formulating* * * * a slate of directors," but this is not a statement of FACT. These are mere conclusions and characterizations which are purportedly taken from the facts previously stated. The Judgment says that the Stockholders' Protective Committee should have stated that Gira and Petersen "*aided and abetted* said Committee." The phrase "aided and abetted" is practically synonymous with the word "help." The literature of the Stockholders' Protective Committee literally states that Gira and Petersen "helped" the Committee. [Ex. 13.] The Judgment further states that the Stockholders' Protective Committee should have stated that Gira and Petersen are "members" of the Stockholders' Protective Committee and that they "participated" with the Stockholders' Protective Committee. However, even the Conclusions of Law of the Court state that Gira and Petersen are not members in a "formal sense", but that their membership is concluded "from their de facto participation." [C. T. ....; Appendix B.] Here again we do not have a statement of fact, but a conclusion from the facts which have been told to the stockholders.

This conclusion is also an erroneous conclusion because it (a) makes "participation" as defined in the Regulations equivalent to "membership", and (b) applies an erroneous definition of "participation" as defined by the Rules.

Rule 14(a)11, subsection (b)3 defines a *de facto* unnamed "participant in a solicitation" as "any person * * * who * * * takes the initiative in organizing, directing or financing * * *." The phrase "takes the initiative" in common parlance refers to "the power of overcoming one's own inertia, of originating something, and having the self-reliance or energy required to take the first step in making new undertakings." Reduced to simplicity it obviously refers to that person, or persons, who assume the promotional responsibility for "organizing, directing or financing" a committee or group. While the appellants have always admitted that Gira and Petersen have helped the Stockholders' Protective Committee in several ways, the evidence is clear and convincing that neither Gira nor Petersen took the leadership, promotional responsibility, first step, or any act [*ergo "initiative"*] to organize, direct or finance the Stockholders' Protective Committee. (This was obviously Brandlin and Roemer.) Therefore, Gira and Petersen are not participants as defined in Rule 14(a)11, subsection (b)3.*

Rule 14(a)11, subsection (b)3 read in its entirety clearly distinguishes the phrase "participant in a solicitation" from a "member" of a committee. While a member of a committee may also be a "participant" one may be or become a "participant in a solicitation" in many ways other than membership on a soliciting committee. A person who even though not named as a member of a committee takes the initiative in organizing, directing or financing such committee becomes a "participant".

There s nothing in the Rules or Regulations that make such "participation" the equivalent of "membership."

THE CONCLUSIONS AND CHARACTERIZATIONS REQUIRED TO BE MADE IN APPELLANTS' MATERIAL BY THE COURT'S JUDGMENT AGAINST THESE APPELLANTS ARE NOT FACTS AND ARE NOT REQUIRED TO BE STATED ACCORDING TO THE LANGUAGE OF RULE 14(a)9.

To show the difficulty of adhering to a standard which requires the statement of CONCLUSIONS rather than FACTS, it should be pointed out that during the same trial the substantial evidence showed that Herman Yaras [R. T. 959-1014.]

*For complete text of Rule 14(a)11, Appendix A.

1. Conta
Protective C
to handle the

2. Had 1
them, but ur
forward and
management

3. Person
ment formed
involved in

4. Refer
mittee to the

5. Had
the Commit
doing, sold 1
disseminated
tective Com

6. Had
10,000 vote
tee.

However
dismissed
separate Fi
[C. T. ....
Committee
ing or orga
on behalf c
had he "par
Committee
abetted" si
ducting pro

The only
material o

1. Contacted the attorneys for the Stockholders' Protective Committee before the attorneys undertook to handle the proxy contest;

2. Had not only discussed the proxy contest with them, but urged the attorneys for the Committee to go forward and to organize a slate of directors to oppose management;

3. Personally was interested in seeing a new management formed, although he did not personally wish to be involved in the proxy contest;

4. Referred one of the initial members of the Committee to the attorneys; (Luther.)

5. Had additional contact with the attorneys for the Committee during the proxy contest, and in so doing, sold shares of stock to Roemer, which was later disseminated to the members of the Stockholders' Protective Committee;

6. Had given his personal proxy for approximately 10,000 votes to the Stockholders' Protective Committee.

However, the Court at the end of plaintiff's case dismissed Yaras under Rule 41-B and held in the separate Findings of Fact and Conclusions of Law [C. T. ....] that he had not "aided and abetted" the Committee; that he had not been "instrumental in initiating or organizing" the Committee or in "formulating" on behalf of said Committee a slate of directors, nor had he "participated" with the Stockholders' Protective Committee or its representatives, nor had he "aided or abetted" said Committee or its representatives in conducting proxy solicitations.

The only reference to Yaras in the proxy soliciting material of the Committee is the statement that he was a former "financial consultant to the company" and that he sold 2000 shares of stock to Roemer, who disseminated it to the Committee. [Ex. 13.] Yet, the net effect of the Court's Judgment in favor of Yaras and the Findings of Fact and Conclusions of Law applicable thereto [C. T. ....] IS A JUDGMENT IN FAVOR OF THE APPELLANTS AS TO THE ALLEGATIONS OF THE COMPLAINT WHICH CLAIM THAT THE COMMITTEE MISSTATED OR OMITTED MATERIAL FACTS CONCERNING YARAS' RELATIONSHIP WITH THE COMMITTEE!

By the same standards as were used by the Court in judging the appellants' material as it pertained to Yaras, the appellants were entitled to a Judgment of Dismissal on the merits as to all of the allegations of plaintiff's Complaint.

(b) Regarding Williams and Luther.

With respect to the allegations in the Judgment concerning the Committee's statements regarding Williams and Luther above mentioned, this will be dealt with extensively in the portion of our Brief devoted to an attack upon the Findings of Fact and Conclusions of Law. However, suffice it to say that there is no evidence in the case that the Stockholders' Protective Committee ever stated that the formation of the Stockholders' Protective Committee was initiated *"solely* as the result of complaints of * * * Luther and * * * Williams." [Ex. 13.]

(c) Regarding Bernard F. Fein.

With respect to paragraph I, subsection VI of the Court's Judgment [C. T. ....] referring to the statements made by the Stockholders' Protective Committee regarding Bernard F. Fein, the evidence was clear that the material of the Stockholders' Protective Committee did state that Bernard F. Fein was *Chairman* of the Executive Committee at a time when certain losses were sustained by United Industrial Corporation. This was in error because at that time Bernard F. Fein was only a *member* of the Executive Committee. Nevertheless, the evidence was also clear and unrebutted that this error was an oversight on the part of the attorneys for the Committee and that the Stockholders' Protective Committee was never given an opportunity to make a retraction of this statement for the reason that the Securities and Exchange Commission brought this action before the Stockholders' Protective Committee could send out their next mailing and further solicitation was thereafter enjoined.

Under any circumstances, this statement does not appear to have great materiality.

IV.

The Court Erred by Making an Unconstitutional Application of Regulation 14 of the Securities and Exchange Act of 1934 to the Facts of This Case and Appellants Were to Be Denied Due Process of Law as Guaranteed by the Fifth Amendment to the Constitution of the United States.

The courts have, on rare occasions, considered the constitutionality of the Securities and Exchange Act of 1934 and the Rules and Regulations promulgated thereunder. The constitutional issues involved concerning the Securities and Exchange Act of 1934 involved primarily procedural due process and freedom of speech as guaranteed under the Fifth Amendment to the Constitution. The case of *Securities and Exchange Com-*

mission v. May, 134 Fed. Supp. 247 at 256-257 specifically upheld the constitutionality of Rule 14(a)9 of the Rules and Regulations under the Securities and Exchange Act of 1934. A similar holding was made in the case of *Halsted v. Securities and Exchange Commission,* 182 F. 2d 660 C. A. D. C. Appellants do not dispute this line of cases.

Appellants do contend, however, that the application of the Rules and Regulations as made by the trial court herein denied appellants fundamental due process of law as guaranteed by the Fifth Amendment to the United States Constitution.

This is so for the reason that the injunction issued by the Court against the appellants requires the individual appellants as members of the Stockholders' Protective Committee to state in any subsequent soliciting material substantially as follows:

That Gira and Petersen were *"instrumental* in *initiating* and organizing the ·Committee" and in *"formulating* the Committee's slate of directors"; that Gira and Petersen had *"participated* with representatives of the Stockholders' Protective Committee and with members of the Committee itself in soliciting" and that they had *"aided and abetted"* the Committee and that they are *"members"* of the Stockholders' Protective Committee. [C. T. ...., Appendix B.]

As has been demonstrated in the previous discussion under item III in this Brief, these statements concerning Gira and Petersen are not statements of fact as such, but are statements of conclusions which are purportedly taken from facts.

Leaving aside for the moment the question of whether or not the conclusions purportedly taken from the facts are lawful, the further question presented is whether, assuming that a proxy solicitation conveys to the stockholders all of the material facts surrounding a particular transaction or issue, CAN THE SOLICITOR NEVERTHELESS BE GUILTY OF MAKING FALSE AND MISLEADING STATEMENTS FOR THE SIMPLE FAILURE TO STATE THE CONCLUSIONS OR INFERENCES THAT MIGHT LOGICALLY BE TAKEN FROM THE FACTS STATED?

A similar question was presented to the Court in the case of *Doyle v. Milton,* 73 Fed. Supp. 281.

In that case, the Court, finding that a proxy statement was not misleading, indicated that if the proxy solicitor had stated to the stockholders sufficient data from which an inference of *"selfish motive"* might be inferred, the solicitation statement would not be declared false and misleading merely because it omitted "a confession of selfish motive."

The Fifth Amendment of the United States Constitution states, in pertinent part, as follows: "No person shall . . . be deprived of life, *liberty,* or *property,* without due process of law; . . ."

It is self-evident that the injunction in this case purports to deprive appellants of their property rights in the proxies given to them by stockholders of United Industrial Corporation; in addition, it can be demonstrated that a question of procedural due process is involved in this case.

It has long been established that an indispensable ingredient of procedural due process is the requirement that for one to be wrongfully charged with violation of a statute or other regulation he must have previous fair notice, actual or constructive, of what acts are prohibited. (*Winters v. State of New York* (1938), 330 U. S. 507.)

Rule 14(a)9 simply provides that a person must state the material FACTS necessary to make a proxy soliciting statement not misleading. There is no suggestion in the Rule or in the Regulation under which it is promulgated that one must state more than facts. Yet for the trial court in this case to invalidate the proxies of the appellants, and also to form the basis of its injunction against the appellants, it was necessary that the Court APPLY Rule 14(a)9 to the facts of the case to mean that appellants were guilty of making false and misleading statements for failure to state, IN ADDITION TO THE MATERIAL FACTS, CERTAIN CONCLUSIONS WHICH THE COURT HAS TAKEN FROM THE FACTS.

This is clearly a denial of procedural due process. The appellants had a constitutional right to rely upon the clear meaning of Rule 14(a)9 and should not be held accountable for an extension of the Rule by the trial court which is not clearly delineated in the Regulation or the Rules. An *application* of a statute or regulation which infringes upon rights guaranteed in the Bill of Rights is an unconstitutional application.

Since the appellants were deprived of fair notice that such an application of the regulation would or could be made, they have been denied procedural due process even if the conclusions embodied by the trial court in its injunction WERE ONES WHICH CAN BE LOGICALLY DEDUCED FROM THE FACTS.

V.
Argument on the Findings of Fact.

Appellants find it necessary to make a detailed attack upon the purported Findings of Fact and Conclusions of Law of the Court for the reason that these Findings of Fact and Conclusions of Law will in all probability determine the final attitude of the stockholders in the United Industrial Corporation election of directors. Therefore, the appellants are making a detailed attack on the Findings of Fact in order that the Appellate Court may make proper orders for the correction of those Findings which are either clearly erroneous, argumentative, or superfluous and inappropriate to the judgment.

The purpose of requiring findings of fact is to aid the appellate court by affording it a clear understanding of the basis of the decision of the trial court (*United States v. Horsfall* (C. A. 10th, 1959), 270 F. 2d 107; *Irish v. United States* (C. A. 9th, 1955), 225 F. 2d 3).

> "Another purpose of requiring Findings of Fact and Conclusions of Law is to make definite just what is decided by the case in order to apply the doctrine of estoppel and res judicata to future cases." [Nordbye, Improvements in Statement of the Findings of Fact and Conclusions of Law (1940), 1 F. R. D. 25.]

The requirement that Findings of Fact be made is intended to evoke care on the part of the trial judge. Ascertaining the facts is the most important function of such Findings. (*United States v. Forness* (C. A. 2nd, 1942), 125 F. 2d 928.) "Findings should represent the judge's own determination and not the long,

often argumentative, statements of successful counsel."
(*United States v. Forness, supra; United States v.
Crescent Amusement Co.* (1949), 323 U. S. 173.)

Findings and Conclusions which represent the independent judicial labors and study of the District Judge
are more helpful to the Court of Appeals. (*Kinnear
Weed Corp. v. Humble Oil and Refining Co.* (C. A.
5th, 1958), 259 F. 2d 398; *Edward Valves, Inc. v.
Cameron Iron Works* (C. A. 5th, 1961), 289 F. 2d
355.)

It is not proper for the trial court to adopt an opinion drafted by one of the parties and it has been held
that if the opinion is drafted by one of the parties
and adopted by the trial court without notice to the
other parties, it is a denial of due process of law.
(*Chicopee Mfg. Corp. v. Kendall Co.* (C. A. 4th, 1961),
288 F. 2d 719.)

Findings upon matters which are superfluous or immaterial or inappropriate to the decree should not be
made. (*In re Imperial Irrigation District* (D. C. Cal.,
1941), 38 Fed. Supp. 770; affirmed 136 F. 2d 539.)

With the above in mind, the appellants hereby set
forth their objections to the following purported Findings of Fact made by the trial court (set out at length
in Appendix B):

A. That portion of Finding No. 5 which reads:
    "Roemer had been house counsel for U. S.
    Science, a subsidiary of UIC, from early 1959 un-
    til late in December, 1960."

is clearly erroneous for the reason that there is no evidence to support the finding that Roemer had been
"house counsel," as that term is ordinarily used. The
only testimony concerning this subject is that of Roe-

mer, who testified that he had acted as attorney for
U. S. Science Corporation during 1960. [R. T. 211-
212.] Roemer has never been an employee, as such,
of either U. S. Science or UIC, but has been as-
sociated with his present law firm since his admission
to the Bar in 1954 and has been a partner for several
years.

B.   That portion of Finding No. 6 which reads:

"Gira was joined by Petersen during subsequent conferences with Brandlin and Roemer. From
the commencement of these conferences, it was
agreed that one effective way of combating the
charges of misfeasance which UIC's management
intended to bring against Gira and Petersen would
be for them to *regain control* of UIC through a
proxy contest." (Emphasis added.)

is clearly erroneous, because it is not supported by any
evidence in the case. There is not one iota of evidence
in the whole record to indicate: (a) that at any time
there was an "agreement" of any kind among Brandlin, Roemer, Gira and/or Petersen that one effective
way of combating threatened litigation would be for
Gira and Petersen to regain control of UIC through
a proxy contest; and (b) that at any time the four
persons concerned ever arrived at any "agreement" as
to what should be done about the "threatened litigation." There is also no testimony that Gira and Petersen were attempting to regain control of UIC through
this Committee. On the contrary, all of the evidence, and the Court's decision by inference [C. T.
..........], establish clearly that the slate of the Stockholders' Protective Committee was completely independent and had no agreement of any kind with Gira and/or
Petersen.

The testimony regarding meetings among the four persons (Gira, Petersen, Brandlin and Roemer), subsequent to the first meeting at Malibu, came from Brandlin, Roemer, Gira and Petersen. The evidence showed that there were only two subsequent meetings among Gira and/or Petersen and/or Roemer and Brandlin. One was during the middle of the week of January 24th and the other was on January 27th.

Brandlin's Testimony.

Brandlin testified that a few days before Gira and Petersen delivered the stockholders' list to the law firm, Gira, *alone,* had come in to see Brandlin and Roemer, at which time Brandlin advised Gira that he knew of nothing that could be done about any threatened litigation and that they would just have to wait and see what happened. Brandlin also advised Gira that he could see no reason for Gira or Petersen to become involved in a proxy contest. Gira stated that he was not interested in a proxy contest and had enough to do with other problems. [R. T. 1247, 1248.]

Roemer's Testimony.

Roemer did not testify concerning the aforementioned meeting with Brandlin, but testified that the next meeting that he recalled after the Malibu meeting was with Gira and Petersen on the 27th of January, at which time they delivered the stockholders' list, and that the meeting was quite short and that the only discussion at that time was concerning the names and locations of some of the larger stockholders who were included on the list. [R. T. 224, 227.]

Gira's and Petersen's Testimony.

Neither Gira nor Petersen was specifically questioned in the trial concerning the meeting testified to by Brandlin, but both testified to the meeting concerning the delivery of the stockholders' list in substantially the same terms as those discussed by Roemer. [R. T. 80, 81, 395.] In the SEC transcript of testimony of both Gira and Petersen there is some indication that at the meeting which Brandlin referred to with Gira, Petersen was also present but this testimony was not admitted as against the Stockholders' Protective Committee appellants and, therefore, is not part of the evidence on which a Finding against appellants can be predicated.

C. The statement from Finding No. 6 as follows:
"Gira and Petersen agreed that they were not in a position to be *openly identified* with any group intending to conduct a proxy contest." (Emphasis added.)

is a clearly erroneous and also inappropriate Finding. The clear innuendo from such a statement is that it was planned that Gira and Petersen were to be *covertly* or *clandestinely* identified with such a group. The only witness who testified directly concerning the conversations alluded to in this Finding was Brandlin who, in discussing the meeting which took place with Gira alone, in Brandlin's office, in between the Malibu meeting and the date on which the stockholders' list was delivered, testified that Gira had concurred with Brandlin that he *"was not interested in becoming a participant in a proxy contest."* [R. T. 1248.] It is interesting also to note that the attorney representing the plaintiff SEC indicated on more than one occasion that he thought that Brandlin's testimony was quite "candid" and that he believed it. [R. T. 1513, 2212.]

D.   The statement in Finding No. 6 that:

> "They were given *assurances,* however, that
> Brandlin and Roemer would be willing to under-
> take a proxy contest if it could be arranged that
> other *seemingly independent* stockholders would
> urge that such a contest be undertaken," (Emphasis
> added.)

is clearly erroneous, because it is directly contrary to
substantial evidence presented on the subject.   The
words "seemingly independent" imply *not truly* independent.   There is an innuendo of some type of fraudulent conspiracy.

The evidence is clear and unrefuted that many of the
slate of the Stockholders' Protective Committee either
did not know Gira and Petersen (Soderstrom, Mc-
Laughlin, Zodda, Steel, Poe and Lawry) or had only
a slight acquaintance with them (Henwood and Foss)
or did not care for their way of doing business (Beshara) [R. T. 9a, 1669, 1714, 2054, 2059-2060, 2070,
2190; Ex. 13.]   The innuendo in the court's Finding
No. 6 is completely without foundation in the evidence.

The statement that "they were given assurances" is
again contrary to the evidence.   The only testimony on
the meeting referred to in this statement was that of
Brandlin, and his testimony was that the law firm
"might" *be interested,* but it was dependent upon
certain contingencies which Brandlin would have to
personally ascertain.   Certainly there was no indication that Brandlin was *assuring* Gira and Petersen
that he would conduct a proxy contest in their interest.
[R. T. 1247-1250.]

E. The statement in Finding No. 7 that:

"at the time the list was duplicated no stockholders of UIC other than Gira and Petersen had
approached counsel for the Committee to discuss
a proxy contest."

is clearly erroneous, because it is contrary to the substantial evidence in the case.

Yaras testified that he had talked to Brandlin by
telephone concerning his interest in a change of Management of UIC several days before the date on which
the stockholders' list was duplicated. [R. T. 988.]
Brandlin testified that Yaras had contacted him personally by telephone and that Dumont had delivered a message through Summers before the date on which the
stockholders' list was duplicated. [R. T. 1232, 1594.]
Summers' affidavit [R. T. 2179-2184] confirms this and
Dumont testified substantially the same. [R. T. 1724.]

F. The statement in Finding No. 7 that:

"It is uncontradicted in the record that after
Brandlin and Roemer made it clear that a successful proxy contest could not be mounted without a
current stockholders' list, Robert Gira, who remained as President of U. S. Science for a short
time after his brother, Bernard Gira, had resigned,
asked an employee of UIC to 'steal' the stockholders' list for him. A new stockholders' list as
of December 30, 1960, had been delivered to
UIC from New York on January 14, 1960. (sic)
No duplicate of this list existed at this time. The
employee refused to do so. Shortly thereafter, the
list as of December 30, 1960, was removed sur-
repetitiously from the executive offices of UIC,
and was delivered late Friday, January 27, 1961,

by Gira and Petersen to the offices of counsel for the Committee where a duplicate was made by the law firm at its own expense."

is a clearly erroneous finding as to these appellants for the reason that it is completely without foundation in the evidence.

THE RECORD CLEARLY SHOWS THAT ALL TESTIMONY CONCERNING THE MANNER IN WHICH THE STOCKHOLDERS' LIST WAS TRANSFERRED FROM THE POSSESSION OF UIC HEADQUARTERS TO PETERSEN WAS RULED INADMISSIBLE BY THE TRIAL COURT AS TO THE APPELLANTS HEREIN. [R. T. 54, 58, 62, 164, 189, 192, 200.] The only testimony with respect to how the stockholders' list came into the possession of Petersen, which was admitted against the appellants, was the testimony of Petersen himself, who indicated that the list was included among certain books, papers and personal effects which were transferred from his offices at UIC to his home. [R. T. 67, 69, 70, 72.]

G. Finding No. 9 should be stricken in its entirety, because it is an improper finding in that it does not purport to "find" ultimate facts, but purports to recite portions of the testimony. While it may be proper for a court in evaluating testimony to come to a finding or conclusion of an ultimate fact based upon only a portion of testimony, which portion the court believes to be accurate as distinguished from other portions of the testimony, it is completely improper to purport to recite testimony (rather than reciting a finding of fact), but actually to leave out pertinent portions of the testimony in such a manner as to distort the meaning of such testimony.

The recital of testimony in this case is distorted for the reason that it fails to state that when Roemer was interrcgated by members of the SEC staff and asked where the list was first made available to him, his first answer was that this had been in his law office. [R. T. 264-268.] Later in his testimony, it is true that he did acquiesce in the suggestion of the questioner that he had received the list at Gira's house. [R. T. 261.] Several weeks later, he sent a letter to the SEC and advised them that he had checked his records and corrected his testimony to show that he had received the list at the office. [Ex. 17, R. T. 265-266.] Roemer explained to the court that he had become confused in his mind concerning the chronological order of the meeting in Malibu and the meeting in the offices of Vaughan, Brandlin & Baggot. [R. T. 267-268.]

The statement "that Roemer did not disclose to the SEC staff that his law firm had duplicated the list nor did he disclose the strange circumstances under which the list had been returned to UIC offices on a Sunday afternoon" is not only argumentative, but is misleading because no such questions were ever asked of Mr. Roemer by the SEC.

This whole finding is superfluous and inappropriate to the judgment. Its only efficacy would be to serve as proxy soliciting material. The basic fact of from *whom* the stockholders' list came was disclosed to the SEC and the UIC stockholders. [Ex. 13.]

    H.   Finding No. 11, which states:

        "The evidence establishes beyond question that without the knowledge or consent of management, the stockholders' list was removed from the executive offices of UIC during the week ending

January 28, 1961 (probably on Friday, January 27)"

and

"Indeed, the record sustains the contention of the SEC that the stockholders' list was stolen"

is clearly erroneous for the reason that it is UNSUP-PORTED BY ANY EVIDENCE WHICH WAS INTRODUCED AS AGAINST THESE APPEL-LANTS. All such evidence was objected to by the appellants and the objections were sustained as to them. [R. T. 54, 58, 162, 164, 189, 192, 200.]

I. The language in Finding 12 that:

"It was also essential that counsel for the Committee represent, *at least ostensibly,* some stockholders of UIC before setting about to organize an insurgent Committee" (Emphasis added.)

and the language that:

"It had already been decided that Gira and Petersen could not *openly participate* in the contest with the Committee and they could not be held out as clients of the law firm" (Emphasis added.)

is not only argumentative, but is entirely misleading and clearly erroneous in the light of the substantial evidence [R. T. 1248-1249] as pointed out in our discussion of Finding No. 6 in paragraph B.

J. The statement in Finding No. 12 that:

"Gira and Petersen then communicated with Roy L. Williams and Elmer M. Luther, Jr."

is completely contrary to the evidence and clearly erroneous. The only evidence on this subject came from the testimony of Yaras and the transcript of testimony before the SEC of Luther and Williams (which was only admitted as against the individual person involved in such transcript.) [R. T. 1029-1032.] The uncontradicted testimony of Yaras before the trial court [R. T. 966] and the transcript of testimony of Luther before the SEC [R. T. 1040] was that Luther had contacted *Yaras* (*not* Gira or Petersen) who referred Luther to the law firm. The transcript of testimony of Williams before the SEC [R. T. 1095] was that Williams *contacted* Gira, who referred Williams to the law firm.

K.   The language in Finding No. 12 that:

"It had already been decided that Gira and Petersen could not *openly participate* in the contest with the Committee and they could not be held out as clients of the law firm" (Emphasis added.)

is clearly erroneous because it implies that Gira and Petersen did participate *covertly* and *clandestinely* in the contest. The testimony regarding this subject was basically that of Brandlin. [R. T. 1248.] Neither Roemer, Gira nor Petersen contradicted Brandlin in this regard.

L.   The statement in Finding No. 13 that Williams "did not, however, authorize the bringing of a proxy contest in his behalf"

and the statement in Finding No. 14 that Luther

"did not authorize Roemer to initiate a proxy contest"

is clearly erroneous in the light of the clear weight of the substantial evidence. The testimony on this subject came from the transcript of testimony of Luther before the SEC [R. T. 1040, 1041], the transcript of testimony of Williams before the SEC [R. T. 1122] and the affidavits of Luther and Williams [Exs. 45, S] and the testimony of Roemer [R. T. 230], all of whom indicate, without doubt, that BOTH LUTHER AND WILLIAMS AUTHORIZED ROEMER TO TAKE WHATEVER STEPS WERE NECESSARY TO PROTECT THEIR INTEREST.

M. The language in Finding No. 14 to the effect that Luther

"discussed the situation with Petersen who suggested that he communicate with Roemer"

is clearly erroneous because it is completely without support in the evidence. The uncontradicted testimony of Yaras [R. T. 966] in the trial and of Luther in his transcript of testimony before the SEC [R. T. 1040] was that Luther contacted *Yaras* (*not* Petersen), who suggested that he communicate with Roemer.

N. The statement in Finding No. 14

"The assertion in the Committee's proxy statement that counsel for the Committee started the organization of the Committee on behalf of Luther and Williams is seriously misleading"

is a misleading statement in itself and finds no support in the evidence. There is no statement in the literature of the Committee or the testimony that the organization of the Committee was "on behalf" of Luther and Williams. The literature states that the organization of the Committee (slate) "started after" [Ex. 13] Luther and Williams had authorized the firm to take the necessary steps. It is self evident that Brandlin was purporting to act on behalf of the whole Stockholders' Protective Committee after it was formed.

O. The language in Finding No. 15 that

"Gira and Petersen again met with counsel for the Committee to . . . agree upon the approach to be made to stockholders with significant holdings"

is clearly err
dence. The
395], Peters
226] concer
a short cas
the names o
no testimon
mittee ever
proach to
holdings."

P. The l
"having
tee" (
is not only
that the un
1262] and F
lin was the
Committee
on his own

Q. The
"La
wood S
to def
ment
Henw
the Co
is clearly e
these men
testimony
that the m
and Brand
type of b
its subsidi

is clearly erroneous and wholly unsupported by the evidence. The uncontradicted testimony of Gira [R. T. 395], Petersen [R. T. 79-81] and Roemer [R. T. 223-226] concerning the meeting referred to is that it was a short *casual* meeting and the only thing discussed was the names of the larger stockholders in UIC. There is no testimony of any kind that counsel for the Committee ever discussed with Gira and Petersen an *"approach to be made to stockholders with significant holdings."*

P. The language in Finding No. 17 that
"having *inspired* the organization of the Committee" (Emphasis added.)

is not only argumentative, but is clearly erroneous in that the uncontradicted testimony of Brandlin [R. T. 1262] and Roemer [R. T. 228, 232-233] is that Brandlin was the first person to discuss the organization of a Committee and proceeded to so organize the Committee on his own terms.

Q. The language in Finding No. 18 that
"Late in February, 1961, Gira and Petersen, Elwood S. Kendrick, who had been retained by them to defend the litigation brought by the management of UIC, Brandlin, Roemer and Stanley E. Henwood, who was then a potential member of the Committee, met to discuss the affairs of UIC"

is clearly erroneous because there is no evidence that these men met to "discuss the affairs" of UIC. The testimony by all parties concerned in the meeting was that the meeting was called at the request of Henwood and Brandlin so that Henwood would learn about the *type of business* of United Industrial Corporation and its subsidiaries. The testimony clearly shows that the subjects discussed at this meeting were for the sole purpose of educating Henwood regarding the scope of business fields in the UIC subsidiaries and at no time were the "affairs" of UIC discussed. [R. T. 142, 144, 287-288, 291-295, 1264-1265, 1668-1669.]

R. Finding No. 19 that

"Gira, Petersen, Brandlin and Roemer met again in April, 1961, at Kendrick's law offices to decide what action they could take to counteract the charges in management's proxy material that Gira and Petersen were closely related to the Committee. Counsel for the Committee suggested that Gira and Petersen institute a libel suit against the management."

is clearly erroneous for the reason that the uncontradicted testimony of Brandlin [R. T. 1263-1264] was that the parties met in Kendrick's law office for the purpose of deciding what could be done to counteract charges that management was threatening to make in its proxy material that the Stockholders' Protective Committee was *"fronting"* for Gira and Petersen. Counsel for the Committee did not suggest that Gira and Petersen institute a *libel suit,* but suggested that Gira and Petersen *send a telegram* advising management that if they made such statements their statements could be libelous. This statement is further clearly erroneous in that there is no evidence that Roemer attended this meeting and, in fact, Roemer did not attend this meeting.

S. In Finding No. 20, the statement

"It was with events occuring in July, 1961, that Gira and Petersen assumed even more active roles as participants in the proxy contest."

is argumentative in that it assumes that Gira and Petersen have previously participated, and because it fails to distinguish that the libel suit which Gira and Petersen filed in July of 1961 was based on an entirely different set of circumstances than the threatened libelous statements referred to in Finding No. 19. [Ex. 20, R. T. 422-429, 1350-1351.]

T. The complete statement in Finding No. 20 and Finding No. 21 should be stricken as being clearly erroneous, immaterial and therefore prejudicial to the appellants herein for the reason that all of the evidence alluded to in Findings Nos. 20 and 21 was adduced on the testimony of Gira, Petersen and Lewis and Exhibit No. 19. In each instance a valid objection was made by appellants which was sustained by the trial court and such evidence was never admitted as to the appellants.

U. In Finding No. 22, the statement that:

"The Committee has never actually functioned as an association; all of its members have never been assembled together at one time. Since its formation there has been only one meeting, and that one involved several, but not all, of the Committee's members. Brandlin and Roemer have met with Gira and Petersen on many more occasions than they have met with members of the Committee. The Committee is merely an imposing 'letterhead' association, most of whose members were selected by and agreed to serve as an accommodation to counsel for the Committee . . . Such a *seemingly independent* group was necessary as Brandlin and Roemer knew that stockholder support would not be forthcoming if Gira and Petersen, the true *sponsors* of the Committee, participated *openly* as members." (Emphasis added.)

is clearly erroneous and cannot be supported by any evidence. The testimony did not purport to establish ALL the meetings, but the uncontradicted evidence showed there were at least two formal meetings on the west coast. [R. T. 1713.] There is no evidence that the Committee "is merely an imposing 'letterhead' association." This is obviously argumentative, an opinion, and a conclusion unsupported by the evidence. Each of these men is prominent in his field and the testimony of those members who testified evidenced an interest in the Committee and an uncontradicted independence of thought and conduct. "Most" of the members did not serve as an "accommodation to counsel". Certainly, long-time stockholders such as Armogida, Ballance, Dumont, Beshara and Wulfekuhler have a real interest; namely, their investment. [Ex. 14; R. T. 1725-1726, 1728, 1734-1735, 1740, 2040-2041, 2050, 2054-2058.] Poe [R. T. 2069], Foss [R. T. 2074-2075] and Henwood [R. T. 1673-1674] testified without contradiction that they are independent of thought and action and that they have an interest in this proxy contest. Mr. Soderstrom states that he heard from Mr. Brandlin "quite frequently" [R. T. 1700], that he would be interested in buying more UIC stock [R. T. 1706] and that he was completely independent. [R. T. 1715.] He also had various meetings with Roemer and discussed "many phases" about the company. [R. T. 1711]. As for Mr. Lawry, all parties, including the SEC, stipulated that he was "an honest and distinguished gentleman." [R. T. 2190.] Furthermore, Mr. Lawry was present in court virtually every day of the trial [R. T. 2191], and testified without contradiction as to his independence. [R. T. 2192-2193.] Summers testified by affidavit that he was instrumental in bringing Dumont to the Committee and that he would act independently of any outside influence. [R. T. 2180-2183.] Mr. McLaughlin, by affidavit, testified that he considered that this was "an opportunity to make a profit on the stock of United Industrial Corporation if said company was properly managed." He further stated that he became a member of the slate "upon the request of my son-in-law, J. J. Brandlin," but that he "agreed to serve as a member" after making an independent investigation. [R. T. 2185-2189.]

Roemer's participation in the proxy contest as a member of the slate is understandable, although there is no evidence on this subject. Lawyers usually consider it an honor and a business asset to serve on the Board of Directors of large corporations.

If it can be said that anyone "agreed to serve as an accommodation to counsel", it would have to be found in Henwood's testimony. [R. T. 47a—portion of deposition in *UIC v. Henwood*.] However Henwood did not finally agree to serve until after he had obtained more information about the company. This occurred approximately four weeks after the initial request to serve was made. [R. T. 1668-1669, 1673-1674.] Henwood agreed to serve as Chairman of the Committee. [R. T. 1668] His office in New York served as the Committee's New York office. [Ex. 13.] He voluntarily went to Washington, D. C., to testify before the SEC in March, 1961. [Ex. 38.] Even if we assume that Henwood served as an "accommodation to counsel", does one of fifteen men constitute "most" of the members of the Committee? We submit that Finding No. 22 is clearly erroneous and wholly unsupported by evidence. The evidence clearly establishes that the Committee was spread from coast to coast [Ex. 13], and that constant and frequent communication was had with all members of the Committee. Brandlin testified, without contradiction, that there were frequent telephone conversations and that over 100 letters and reports were mailed or delivered to the Committee during the course of the proxy contest [R. T. 1342-1344], in addition to the meetings referred to.

It is clearly erroneous to find that the Committee and slate were a "seemingly independent group" since this clearly implies that the Committee and slate were not independent; and there is no evidence of any kind to support such a finding. The evidence is all to the contrary. Each member of the slate who testified stated that he would act independently and that he had no contract, arrangement or understanding of any kind whatsoever with Gira and Petersen. There is likewise no evidence to support the finding that Gira and Petersen were "the true sponsors of the Committee" and that Brandlin and Roemer knew that Gira and Petersen could not "openly" be members of the Committee. There was never any effort by Brandlin or Roemer to *hide* from the stockholders the fact that Gira and Petersen were helpful to the Committee. [Exs. 13, A.]

V. Appellants have conceded that the error referred to in Finding No. 23 was made. [R. T. 271.] The testimony is uncontradicted that the SEC advised that Fein was not Chairman during 1960 and that references to this fact should be changed, but, through oversight, the Committee neglected to change the one reference referred to although other changes in this regard were made. [R. T. 311.] The statement, however, is innocuous and immaterial due to the fact that the evidence, uncontradicted, is that Fein was a *member* of the Executive Committee during 1960, as opposed to Chairman. [R. T. 270.] The erroneous statement is immaterial and could not have had any effect on the vote of the stockholders, nor was there any evidence that this admitted error was material in that it affected the vote of the stockholders. Since the Stockholders' Protective Committee had been "cooperative" with the SEC staff, the SEC staff should have asked for a retraction from the Committee instead of bringing action. This is the manner in which they handled a similar matter for one of management's mailings. [Ex. 14.]

W. In Finding No. 24 the statement that:

"As Gira and Petersen initiated the Committee, and have participated, directly and indirectly, in directing and advancing its objectives . . ."

is argumentative and clearly erroneous in that it assumes that Gira and Petersen have participated and there is no evidence to support the finding that Gira and Petersen had been "directing and advancing its (the Committee's) objectives." The evidence, as demonstrated above, is all to the contrary.

X. That portion of No. 6 under the heading "Affirmative Defenses", on page 20 of the Findings of Fact [C. T. ....] which states as follows (Appendix B):

"The defendants have also stressed that Management of UIC from the beginning of its solicitation has stated that the Committee was 'fronting' for Gira and Petersen and that, *therefore, the stockholders are fully aware of all the facts.*" (Emphasis added.)

is a clearly erroneous finding for the reason that appellants have never stated that Management's accusation that appellants were "fronting" for Gira and Petersen made the stockholders fully aware of all the facts. There is no statement or other evidence in the entire record to support this statement which was prepared by counsel for the SEC and adopted by the trial court.

VI.

The Court Erred by Not Denying to the Appellee (SEC) the Equitable Remedy of Invalidation of Appellants' Proxies and of an Injunction Against Appellants for the Reason That Appellee (SEC) Had Denied Appellants Due Process as Guaranteed by the Fifth Amendment to the United States Constitution by the Manner in Which Appellee Had Administered the Securities Exchange Act and the Regulations Promulgated Thereunder in This Case.

The substantial evidence was clear and uncontroverted that as early as March, 1961, the Securities and Exchange Commission had taken testimony of Williams, Ballance, Wulfekuhler, Lawry, McLaughlin, Soderstrom, Luther, Henwood, Roemer, Gira, Petersen and Yaras. [Exs. 29-39A.] In addition, they had other information from the attorneys representing the Stockholders' Protective Committee such as Brandlin's letter of March 24th. [Ex. D.] The stated purpose of this inquiry was for the purpose of determining "the adequacy and accuracy of the proxy solicitation material of the Stockholders' Protective Committee". [R. T. 1166, 1169; Ex. 42.] After this information had been obtained, the Securities and Exchange Commission "cleared" four mailings of the Committee.

The evidence clearly shows that the Stockholders' Protective Committee cooperated with the Securities and Exchange Commission on each mailing by making the changes requested or suggested by the Commission staff. [R. T. 300-302, 308-312.]

At no time did a staff member of the Securities and Exchange Commission ever request the Committee or its attorneys to include in its material the *conclusions* and *characterizations* which were set out in their complaint and which formed the basis of the court's injunction, although the evidence is uncontroverted that as early as March and not later than June of 1961 the Securities and Exchange Commission staff had in its possession all of the essential information upon which it now claims to base its conclusions.

What happened in this case would appear to be as follows: The Securities and Exchange Commission gathered information concerning the people involved in the proxy contest. Based upon this information, they "cleared" material of the Stockholders' Protective Committee which purported to state certain facts concerning the proxy contest and the persons involved. After having "cleared" the material on three separate occasions, including July 11, 1961, the SEC then brought an action against the appellants to invalidate their proxies and obtain an injunction against them on the grounds that the statements made by the Protective Committee, and "cleared" by the Securities and Exchange Commission, had not been couched in particular terminology or phraseology.

Assuming for the sake of argument, that the particular terminology or phraseology consisted of inexorably logical conclusions from the facts in possession of the SEC, the fact remains that at no time did the SEC ever request such terminology or phraseology from the Stockholders' Protective Committee.

The SEC has always claimed that Section 26 of the Securities and Exchange Act of 1934, which states in pertinent part as follows:

> "No action or failure to act by the Commission . . . in the administration of this title . . . with regard to any statement or report filed with or examined by such authority pursuant to this title . . . be deemed a finding . . . that such statement or report is true and accurate on its face or that it is not false or misleading. . . ."*

gives them the right to conduct themselves in this manner. It is submitted that Section 26 has no application to the situation involved herein. Section 26 merely means that if the SEC has "cleared" material, that they are not to be prevented from bringing an action if it is later determined that the material contains false and misleading statements as to *material facts*. That is considerably different from taking the position that the SEC can clear a particular statement of facts and then later complain because the same facts are not stated in particular words or phraseology. (*Hatahley v. United States*, 351 U. S. 173.)

---

*For complete terminology of this section, consult Appendix A.

VII.

The Court Erred by Denying the Appellants a Fair Trial as Guaranteed by the Due Process Clause of the Fifth Amendment in That the Court Failed to Exercise Genuine Judicial Discretion and Judgment.

It is not uncommon for persons aggrieved by a particular decision of a court of law or equity to feel that they have not been given a fair trial. Recognizing the subjective perspective any argument on this question must necessarily have, appellants request this court to examine the following enumerated portions of the Reporter's Transcript on appeal in order to make an objective appraisal of whether or not the trial court actually exercised genuine judicial discretion and judgment as is inherent in procedural due process. [R. T. 17a-41a, 72a-152a, 54-58, 199, 550-555, 848-849, 1180, 1456-1457, 1459-1460.]

VIII.
Conclusion.

Appellants believe they have fully demonstrated that the Judgment and Findings in the case at bar are unsupported by any evidence and are clearly erroneous. It is respectfully submitted that the judgment should be reversed and the cause remanded to the trial court with directions to enter a judgment for the appellants Stockholders' Protective Committee.

Respectfully submitted,

VAUGHAN, BRANDLIN, BAGGOT,
ROBINSON & ROEMER,
MARK P. ROBINSON,
Attorneys for Appellants.

APPENDIX "A".

Regulation 14(a)-9 Under the Securities and Exchange Act of 1934.

Rule 14a-9. False or Misleading Statements.

No solicitation subject to this regulation shall be made by means of any proxy statement, form of proxy, notice of meeting, or other communication, written or oral, containing any statement which, at the time and in the light of the circumstances under which it is made, is false or misleading with respect to any material fact, or which omits to state any material fact necessary in order to make the statements therein not false or misleading or necessary to correct any statement in any earlier communication with respect to the solicitation of a proxy for the same meeting or subject matter which has become false or misleading.

Note. The following are some examples of what, depending upon particular facts and circumstances, may be misleading within the meaning of this rule:

(a) Predictions as to specific future market values, earnings, or dividends.

(b) Material which directly or indirectly impugns character, integrity or personal reputation, or directly or indirectly makes charges concerning improper illegal or immoral conduct or associations, without factual foundation.

(c) Failure to so identify a proxy statement, form of proxy and other soliciting material as to clearly distinguish it from the soliciting material of any other person or persons soliciting for the same meeting or subject matter.

(d) Claims made prior to a meeting regarding the results of a solicitation.

Regulation 14(a)-11 Under the Securities and Exchange Act of 1934.

Rule 14a-11. Special Provisions Applicable to Election Contests.

(a) Solicitations to which this rule applies.

This rule applies to any solicitation subject to this regulation by any person or group of persons for the purpose of opposing a solicitation subject to this regulation by any other person or group of persons with respect to the election or removal of directors at any annual or special meeting of security holders.

(b) Participant or Participant in a Solicitation.

For purposes of this rule the terms "participant" and "participant in a solicitation" include the following:

(1) the issuer;

(2) any director of the issuer, and any nominee for whose election as a director proxies are solicited;

(3) any committee or group which solicits proxies, any member of such committee or group, and any person whether or not named as a member who, acting alone or with one or more other persons, directly or indirectly, take the initiative in organizing, directing or financing any such committee or group;

(4) any person who finances or joins with another to finance the solicitation of proxies, except persons who contribute not more than $500 and who are not otherwise participants;

(5) any person who lends money or furnishes credit or enters into any other arrangements, pursuant to any contract or understanding with a participant, for the purpose of financing or otherwise inducing the purchase, sale, holding or voting of securities of the issuer

by any participant or other persons, in support of or in opposition to a participant; except that such terms do not include a bank, broker or dealer who, in the ordinary course of business, lends money or executes orders for the purchase or sale of securities and who is not otherwise a participant;

(6) any other person who solicits proxies: *Provided, however,* That such terms do not include (i) any person or organization retained or employed by a participant to solicit security holders, or any person who merely transmits proxy soliciting material or performs ministerial or clerical duties; (ii) any person employed by a participant in the capacity of attorney, accountant, or advertising, public relations or financial adviser, and whose activities are limited to the performance of his duties in the course of such employment; (iii) any person regularly employed as an officer or employee of the issuer or any of its subsidiaries who is not otherwise a participant; or (iv) any officer or director of, or any person regularly employed by, any other participant, if such officer, director, or employee is not otherwise a participant.

(c) Filing of Information Required by Schedule 14B.

(1) No solicitation subject to this rule shall be made by any person other than the management of an issuer unless at least five business days prior thereto, or such shorter period as the Commission may authorize upon a showing of good cause therefor, there has been filed, with the Commission and with each national securities exchange upon which any security of the issuer is listed and registered, by or on behalf of each participant

in such solicitation, a statement in duplicate containing the information specified by Schedule 14B.

(2) Within five business days after a solicitation subject to this rule is made by the management of an issuer, or such longer period as the Commission may authorize upon a showing of good cause therefor, there shall be filed, with the Commission and with each national securities exchange upon which any security of the issuer is listed and registered, by or on behalf of each participant in such solicitation, other than the issuer a statement in duplicate containing the information specified by Schedule 14B.

(3) If any solicitation on behalf of management or any other person has been made, or if proxy material is ready for distribution, prior to a solicitation subject to this rule in opposition thereto, a statement in duplicate containing the information specified in Schedule 14B shall be filed by or on behalf of each participant in such prior solicitation, other than the issuer, as soon as reasonably practicable after the commencement of the solicitation in opposition thereto, with the Commission and with each national securities exchange on which any security of the issuer is listed and registered.

(4) If, subsequent to the filing of the statements required by subparagraphs (1), (2), and (3) above, additional persons become participants in a solicitation subject to this rule, there shall be filed, with the Commission and each appropriate exchange, by or on behalf of each such person a statement in duplicate containing the information specified by Schedule 14B, within three business days after such person becomes a participant, or such longer period as the Commission may authorize upon a showing of good cause therefor.

(5) If any material change occurs in the facts reported in any statement filed by or on behalf of any participant, and appropriate amendment to such statement shall be filed promptly with the Commission and each appropriate exchange.

(6) Each statement and amendment thereto filed pursuant to this paragraph (c) shall be part of the official public files of the Commission and for purposes of this regulation shall be deemed a communication subject to the provisions of Rule 14a-9.

(d) Solicitations Prior to Furnishing Required Written Proxy Statement.

Notwithstanding the provisions of Rule 14a-3 (a), a solicitation subject to this rule may be made prior to furnishing security holders a written proxy statement containing the information specified in Schedule 14A with respect to such solicitation, *Provided* That—

(1) The statements required by paragraph (c) of this rule are filed by or on behalf of each participant in such solicitation.

(2) No form of proxy is furnished to security holders prior to the time the written proxy statement is required by Rule 14a-3 (a) is furnished to security holders: *Provided, however,* That this subparagraph (2) shall not apply where a proxy statement then meeting the requirements of Schedule 14A has been furnished to security holders.

(3) At least the information specified in Items 2 (a) and 3 (a) of the statement required by paragraph (c) to be filed by each participant, or an appropriate summary thereof, is included in each communication sent or given to security holders in connection with the solicitation.

(4) A written proxy statement containing the information specified in Schedule 14A with respect to a solicitation is set or given security holders at the earliest practicable date.

(e) Solicitations prior to furnishing required written proxy statement—Filing Requirements.

Three copies of any soliciting material proposed to be sent or given to security holders prior to the furnishing of the written proxy statement required by Rule 14a-3 (a) shall be filed with the Commission in preliminary form, at least five business days prior to the date definitive copies of such material are first sent or given to security holders, or such shorter period as the Commission may authorize upon a showing of good cause therefor.

(f) Application of this rule to Annual Report.

Notwithstanding the provisions of Rule 14a-3 (b) and (c), three copies of any portion of the annual report referred to in Rule 14a-3 (b) which comments upon or refers to any solicitation subject to this rule, or to any participant in any such solicitation, other than the solicitation by the management, shall be filed with the Commission as proxy material subject to this regulation. Such portion of the annual report shall be filed with the Commission in preliminary form at least five business days prior to the date copies of the report are first sent or given to security holders.

(g) Application of Rule 14a-6.

The provisions of paragraphs (c), (d), (e), (f) and (g) of Rule 14a-6 shall apply to the extent pertinent, to soliciting material subject to paragraphs (e) and (f) of this Rule 14a-11.

(h) Use of reprints or reproductions.

In any solicitation subject to this rule, soliciting material which includes, in whole or part, any reprints or reproductions of any previously published material shall:

(1) State the name of the author and publication, the date of prior publication, and identify any person who is quoted without being named in the previously published material.

(2) Except in the case of a public official document or statement, state whether or not the consent of the author and publication has been obtained to the use of the previously published material as proxy soliciting material.

(3) If any participant using the previously published material, or anyone on his behalf, paid, directly or indirectly, for the preparation or prior publication of the previously published material, or has made or proposes to make any payments or give any other consideration in connection with the publication or republication of such material, state the circumstances.

Section 26, Securities and Exchange Act of 1934.

Unlawful Representations

Section 26. No action or failure to act by the Commission or the Board of Governors of the Federal Reserve System, in the administration of this title shall be construed to mean that the particular authority has in any way passed upon the merits of, or given approval to, any security or any transaction or transactions therein, nor shall such action or failure to act with regard to any statement or report filed with or examined by such authority pursuant to this title or rules and regulations thereunder, be deemed a finding by such authority that such statement or report is true and accurate on its face or that it is not false or misleading. It shall be unlawful to make, or cause to be made, to any prospective purchaser or seller of a security any representation that any such action or failure to act by any such authority is to be so construed or has such effect.

Fifth Amendment to the United States Constitution.

No person shall be held to answer for a capital, or otherwise infamous crime, unless on a presentment or indictment of a Grand Jury, except in cases arising in the land or naval forces, or in the Militia, when in actual service in time of War or public danger; nor shall any person be subject for the same offense to be twice put in jeopardy of life or limb; nor shall be compelled in any criminal case to be a witness against himself, nor be deprived of life, liberty, or property, without due process of law; nor shall private property be taken for public use, without just compensation.

Judgment

This actio
a trial on the
ber 22, 1961
evidence and
entered a dec
man Yaras
defendant N.
having enter
Law, as to t
tion ("UIC
and the mer
Bernard F.
fect that th
entitled to a
joining the
Stockholders
wood, Richa
bers of and
Committee. :
sen from en:
Section 14(a
15 U.S.C. §
thereunder,
solicitation c
stock of U'
nard F. Gir:
Rule 14a-11
and directin
further adj
stockholders
the resoluti

APPENDIX "B".

Judgment, Findings of Fact, and Conclusions.

JUDGMENT

This action came on for hearing before the Court as a trial on the merits between July 26, 1961, and September 22, 1961, and the Court having considered all the evidence and the arguments of counsel, and having entered a decree of dismissal as to the defendant Herman Yaras and a final decree by consent as to the defendant N. Eugene Shafer, d/b/a Shafer & Co., and having entered Findings of Fact and Conclusions of Law, as to the defendants United Industrial Corporation ("UIC") Stockholders' Protective Committee and the members thereof, and as to the defendants Bernard F. Gira and Herbert J. Petersen, to the effect that the Securities and Exchange Commission is entitled to a permanent injunction restraining and enjoining the defendants United Industrial Corporation Stockholders' Protective Committee, Stanley E. Henwood, Richard I. Roemer, and Lewis M. Poe as members of and proxies for said Stockholders' Protective Committee, and Bernard F. Gira and Herbert J. Petersen from engaging in acts and practices in violation of Section 14(a) of the Securities Exchange Act of 1934, 15 U.S.C. §78n(a), and Rule 14a-9 of Regulation 14 thereunder, 17 C.F.R. 240.14a-9, in connection with the solicitation of proxies as to the common and preferred stock of UIC, and commanding the defendants Bernard F. Gira and Herbert J. Petersen to comply with Rule 14a-11 of Regulation 14, 17 C F.R. 240.14a-11, and directing the defendant UIC to arrange for the further adjournment of the annual meeting of its stockholders for a sufficient length of time to allow for the resolicitation of proxies heretofore given to the defendant Stockholders' Protective Committee, which proxies by the terms of this decree are invalidated, as demanded by the Securites and Exchange Commission, and it appearing that the Court has jurisdiction of the parties hereto and the subject matter hereof—

I.

IT IS ORDERED, ADJUDGED AND DECREED

that the defendants United Industrial Corporation Stockholders' Protective Committee, Stanley E. Henwood, Richard I. Roemer, and Lewis M. Poe, individually and as members of and proxies for said Stockholders' Protective Committee, all members, associates, substitutes, agents, employees and attorneys of said Stockholders' Protective Committee, and the defendants Bernard F. Gira and Herbert J. Petersen, their agents, employees, and attorneys, and all persons acting in conceit or participation with any of said defendants, be and they hereby are permanently restrained and enjoined from, directly or indirectly, making use of the mails or any means or instrumentality of interstate commerce or of any facility of any national securities exchange to solicit or to permit the use of their names to solicit any proxy in respect of the common or preferred stock of UIC, or otherwise soliciting any such proxy, by means of any proxy statement, form of proxy, notice of meeting or other communication, written or oral, containing any statement which at the time and in the light of the circumstances under which it is made is false and misleading with respect to any material fact, or which omits to state any material fact necessary in order to make the statements therein not false or misleading, or necessary to correct any statement in an earlier communication with respect to the

solicitation of a proxy which has been or has become
false or misleading, including the following:

(i) omitting to state that the defendants Bernard F. Gira and Herbert J. Petersen were instrumental in initiating and organizing the UIC
Stockholders' Protective Committee and in formulating on behalf of said Committee a slate of directors for membership on the board of directors of
UIC in opposition to the slate of directors formulated by the management of UIC;

(ii) omitting to state that the defendants Bernard F. Gira and Herbert J. Petersen have participated with representatives of the Stockholders' Protective Committee and aided and abetted said Committee and its representatives in conducting proxy
solicitations in opposition to the management of
UIC;

(iii) stating that the defendants Bernard F.
Gira and Herbert J. Petersen are not members of
the Stockholders' Protective Committee;

(iv) stating that the defendants Bernard F.
Gira and Herbert J. Petersen are not participating
with the Stockholders' Protective Committee in
soliciting proxies in opposition to the management
of UIC;

(v) stating that the formation of the Stockholders' Protective Committee was initiated solely
as a result of complaints of the defendants Elmer
M. Luther, Jr. and Roy L. Williams;

(vi) stating that certain losses sustained by
UIC and diminution of stockholders' equity oc-
curred during the time that Bernard F. Fein was
Chairman of the Executive Committee; or

voting any proxy of any stockholder of UIC now held by the defendants UIC Stockholders' Protective Committee, Stanley E. Henwood, Richard I. Roemer or Lewis M. Poe as proxies for said Committee, or any substitute for any such defendant, or voting any such proxy which is not received pursuant to a solicitation made subsequent to the entry of this decree, in accordance with Section 14(a) of the Securities Exchange Act of 1934, 15 U.S.C. §78n(a), and Regulation 14, 17 C.F.R. 240.14.

II.

IT IS FURTHER ORDERED, ADJUDGED AND DECREED that the defendants Bernard F. Gira and Herbert J. Petersen shall and they hereby are commanded to comply with Rule 14a-11 of Regulation 14, 17 C.F.R. 240.14a-11, by filing with the Securities and Exchange Commission and with each national securities exchange upon which the common or preferred stock of United Industrial Corporation is registered a corrected statement in duplicate containing the information specified by Schedule 14B of Regulation 14, concerning their participation in the solicitation of proxies in respect of the common and preferred stock of UIC.

III.

IT IS FURTHER ORDERED, ADJUDGED AND DECREED that the defendant United Industrial Corporation, its officers, directors, employees, and attorneys, and each of them, be and they hereby are restrained and enjoined from holding any meeting of stockholders of United Industrial Corporation, except for the purpose of adjournment, until November 21, 1961.

IV.

IT IS FURTHER ORDERED, ADJUDGED AND DECREED that this action be and the same is hereby dismissed, without prejudice, as to the defendants James V. Armogida, Robert G. Ballance, Fred A. Beshara, Nathaniel R. Dumont, Joe L. Foss, William David Lawry, Elmer M. Luther, Jr., Edward H. McLaughlin, Charles Soderstrom, John Autry Steel, Clarence L. Summers, Roy L. Williams, Louis W. Wulfekuhler and Alfred T. Zodda, individually and as members of the United Industrial Corporation Stockholders' Protective Committee.

II.
FINDINGS OF FACT

A. Summary of Facts

1. United Industrial Corporation is a Delaware corporation. The securities of UIC are widely distributed among some 15,000 shareholders. The common and preferred stocks of UIC are listed and registered on the New York Stock Exchange and the Pacific Coast Stock Exchange. Warrants for common stock are listed and registered on the American Stock Exchange and the Pacific Coast Stock Exchange. The warrants carry no voting rights.

2. UIC commenced operations in 1960 as the product of the merger between Topp Industries Corporation and United Industrial Corporation, a Michigan corporation. Gira and Petersen, who had been the principal executive officers of Topp Industries, became the president and executive vice-president, respectively, of UIC. They also served as members of the board of directors. Bernard F. Gira owns 58,000 shares of the common stock of UIC, 5,000 shares of preferred

and 52,000 warrants. Herbert J. Petersen owns 38,500 shares of common stock, 5,000 shares of preferred and 38,500 warrants.

3. Late in 1960, it became apparent to the board of directors that the assets of UIC would be subjected to write-downs and adjustments totaling approximately $7,000,000. One such adjustment would change a profit previously reported by Topp Industries into a substantial loss. The board of directors of UIC met on January 12, 13 and 14, 1961, to consider what action was necessary because of the impending write-downs and adjustments. In the course of these meetings Gira and Petersen resigned as officers and directors of UIC. On January 16, 1961, the New York Stock Exchange suspended trading in the securities of UIC. The Pacific Coast Stock Exchange also suspended trading in the securities. The SEC entered an order under Section 19a(4) of the Act, 15 U.S.C. Sec. 78s(a)(4), suspending trading in the securities. The effect of this order was to bar trading in the over-the-counter market as well as on the exchange.[3]

4. The United Industrial Corporation Stockholders' Protective Committee is an association composed of the defendants Stanley E. Henwood, Richard I. Roemer, Lewis M. Poe, James V. Armogida, Robert G. Ballance, Fred A. Beshara, Nathaniel R. Dumont, Joe L. Foss, William D. Lawry, Edward H. McLaughlin,

---

[3]On September 22, 1961, the SEC removed its bar against trading after the management of UIC and the Committee had made announcements to the Court concerning their intentions with respect to buying or selling securities of UIC in the event trading was allowed The action of the SEC allows trading only in the over-the-counter market. The exchange suspensions remain in effect.

Charles Sode
mers, Louis '
M. Luther, J
ception of W
Committee co
mittee seeks t
wood, Roeme
the Committe

5. Shortly
rector of UI
to retain Ri
Roemer is a
Vaughan, Br
signed, Gira
a senior part
advice as to v
combat litiga
of UIC to i
substantial w
suspension of

6. Gira v
conferences v
mencement o
effective way
which UIC's

---

[4]Roemer ha
of UIC, from
Gira, who is
Science. He a

[5]The firm n
& Roemer. T
as its counsel
made substant
Committee, an
exclusive of 1

Charles Soderstrom, John A. Steel, Clarence L. Summers, Louis W. Wulfekuhler, Alfred T. Zodda, Elmer M. Luther, Jr., and Roy L. Williams. With the exception of Williams and Luther, the members of the Committee comprise the slate of fifteen which the Committee seeks to have elected as directors of UIC. Henwood, Roemer and Poe are named as the proxies for the Committee. Henwood is the Committee's chairman.

5. Shortly before he resigned as an officer and director of UIC, Bernard F. Gira had been negotiating to retain Richard I. Roemer as counsel for UIC.[4] Roemer is a partner in the Los Angeles law firm of Vaughan, Brandlin & Baggot.[5] Shortly after he resigned, Gira conferred with Roemer and J. J. Brandlin, a senior partner of the firm. At this time he sought advice as to what action he and Petersen might take to combat litigation which they expected the management of UIC to institute against them arising out of the substantial write-downs in the assets of UIC, and the suspension of trading in UIC's securities.

6. Gira was joined by Petersen during subsequent conferences with Brandlin and Roemer. From the commencement of these conferences, it was agreed that one effective way of combating the charges of misfeasance which UIC's management intended to bring against

---

[4]Roemer had been house counsel for U. S. Science, a subsidiary of UIC, from early 1959 until late in December, 1960. Robert Gira, who is Bernard F. Gira's brother, was president of U. S. Science. He and Roemer have been friends for many years

[5]The firm name is now Vaughan, Brandlin, Baggot, Robinson & Roemer. The firm organized the Committee, and has served as its counsel throughout the proxy controversy. The firm has made substantial cash advances to defray the expenses of the Commitee, and has estimated its contingent fees for legal service, exclusive of litigation fees, at $75,000.

Gira and Petersen would be for them to regain control of UIC through a proxy contest.[6] But it was also apparent that Gira and Petersen would have little chance of success in a proxy contest in which they were identified as participants with an insurgent committee, for the reason that they were the principal officers and in managerial control when the events leading to the disastrous write-downs in UIC's assets occurred. Gira and Petersen agreed that they were not in a position to be openly identified with any group intending to conduct a proxy contest. They were given assurances, however, that Brandlin and Roemer would be willing to undertake a proxy contest if it could be arranged that other seemingly independent stockholders would urge that such a contest be undertaken, if a slate of individuals of prominence could be assembled for election to the board of directors, if the services of a suitable public relations consultant could be arranged, and if a list of UIC's stockholders could be secured for the use of the opposition group. These conversations occurred during two weeks of the time Gira and Petersen were ousted from the management of UIC. There was also some discussion of a stockholders' derivative suit by Gira and Petersen but that unrealistic suggestion was discarded at once.

7. It is uncontradicted in the record that after Brandlin and Roemer made it clear that a successful proxy contest could not be mounted without a current stockholders' list, Robert Gira, who remained as President of U. S. Science for a short time after his brother,

---

[6]UIC has sued Gira and Petersen in Delaware for damages based on their asserted misconduct while they were officers and directors.

Bernard Gir;
to "steal" th
holders' list a
to UIC fron
duplicate of t
refused to c
December 3(
the executive
Friday, Janu
offices of co
was made by
without advi:
had the list,
offices on S
the time the
other than (
for the Com

8. The s
to counsel i(
candidates ;
among stock
mailing out
after the Co:

9. Late i
the Commit:
came its firs
rogated und
and was ask
under which
UIC stockh
was turned
F. Gira dur
in Malibu v

Bernard Gira, had resigned, asked an employee of UIC to "steal" the stockholders' list for him. A new stockholders' list as of December 30, 1960, had been delivered to UIC from New York on January 14, 1960. No duplicate of this list existed at this time. The employee refused to do so. Shortly thereafter, the list as of December 30, 1960, was removed surrepitiously from the executive offices of UIC, and was delivered late Friday, January 27, 1961, by Gira and Petersen to the offices of counsel for the Committee where a duplicate was made by the law firm at its own expense. Then, without advising the management of UIC that his firm had the list, Brandlin returned it to UIC's executive offices on Sunday afternoon, January 29, 1961. At the time the list was duplicated no stockholder of UIC other than Gira and Petersen had approached counsel for the Committee to discuss a proxy contest.

8. The stockholders' list was of the utmost value to counsel for the Committee in assembling a slate of candidates for election to the board of directors from among stockholders unfriendly to management, and in mailing out the proxy solicitation material disseminated after the Committee was organized.

9. Late in March, 1961, in the course of examining the Committee's preliminary proxy statement which became its first mailing to stockholders, Roemer was interrogated under oath by members of the SEC's staff and was asked, *inter alia,* to describe the circumstances under which the Committee came into possession of the UIC stockholders' list. Roemer testified that the list was turned over to Brandlin and himself by Bernard F. Gira during an evening conference at Gira's home in Malibu when the three first discussed a proxy con-

test. This was about ten days after Gira had resigned as president and a director of UIC. Roemer testified that he and Brandlin examined the list briefly, and that when the conference ended took the list with them. Roemer did not disclose to the SEC's staff that his law firm had duplicated the list, nor did he disclose the strange circumstances under which the list had been returned to UIC's offices on a Sunday afternoon. Rather, when asked who the list belonged to, Roemer stated he supposed it was Gira's. When asked why Gira had the list in his possession after he had resigned, Roemer testified that he did not know. At a later date Roemer attempted to correct this and similar testimony which he had given in the course of a deposition in *UIC v. Henwood* by sending a letter to the staff of the SEC to the effect that the stockholders' list had been delivered by Gira and Petersen to the law offices of counsel for the Committee, and that it had not been obtained at Gira's home in Malibu.

10. Gira and Peterson also were asked by the staff of the SEC to describe the circumstances under which they turned the list over to counsel for the Committee. Both Gira and Peterson testified that the list had been included among effects which they took with them on January 14, 1961, the day they resigned as directors of UIC. They testified that they delivered the list to counsel for the Committee on Friday, January 27, 1961.

11. The evidence establishes beyond question that, without the knowledge or consent of management, the stockholders' list was removed from the executive offices of UIC during the week ending January 28, 1961 (probably on Friday, January 27), delivered by Gira and Petersen to counsel for the Committee late Friday,

January 27, 1961, duplicated during the week-end, and
returned on Sunday afternoon, January 29, 1961. Indeed, the record sustains the contention of the SEC that
the stockholders' list was stolen.

12. It was also essential that counsel for the Committee represent, at least ostensibly, some stockholders
of UIC before setting about to organize an insurgent
Committee. It had already been decided that Gira
and Petersen could not openly participate in the contest with the Committee and they could not be held
out as clients of the law firm. Gira and Petersen
then communicated with Roy L. Williams and Elmer
M. Luther, Jr.

13. Roy L. Williams, an uncle of Bernard F. Gira,
at one time had been employed by Gira as an employee
of Topp Industries. As a holder of 400 shares of
UIC stock, Williams became concerned about the suspension in trading and the fall in the market price of
his stock. Gira suggested to Williams that he get in
touch with Roemer. Williams, who was led to believe
that Roemer was conducting an investigation into the
situation, telephoned him and complained about his investment in UIC. Williams did not, however, authorize
the bringing of a proxy contest in his behalf. He was
merely seeking information concerning his investment.

14. Elmer M. Luther, Jr. previously had been an
employee of UIC. His services were terminated in
December 1960, shortly before Gira and Petersen resigned. Prior to his employment with UIC, Luther
had been an employee of Topp Industries. As an
owner of 250 shares of stock in UIC, he, like Williams, was concerned with the suspension of trading in
the stock. He discussed the situation with Petersen

who suggested that he communicate with Roemer. Luther called Roemer and complained about the status of his investment in UIC, but did not authorize Roemer to initiate a proxy contest. Neither Luther nor Williams paid Vaughan, Brandlin and Baggot any retainer. Both of them, however, at Roemer's request, did sign Schedules 14B under Regulation 14 which he had prepared for them and which identified them as participants in the proxy contest. Notwithstanding this and even after it had been publicly announced that the Committee had been formed, Williams and Luther considered themselves neither members of the Committee nor clients of counsel for the Committee. Their telephone calls to Roemer were seized upon by counsel for the Committee as a mandate to organize an expensive proxy contest. The assertion in the Committee's proxy statement that counsel for the Committee started the organization of the Committee on behalf of Luther and Williams is seriously misleading.

15. Having supplied counsel for the Committee with the stockholders' list needed to organize and conduct a proxy contest, Gira and Petersen continued to aid in the formation of the Committee. To ascertain the distribution of the larger stockholdings, Gira and Petersen again met with counsel for the Committee to canvass the names on the list, and agree upon the approach to be made to stockholders with significant holdings.

16. Petersen sent Clarence L. Summers, who became a member of the Committee, to Brandlin. Summers also agreed to serve as public relations consultant to the Committee. Summers had served UIC as public relations consultant in the past. He also sought out

Nathaniel R. Dumont, who became a member of the Committee's slate.

17. Having inspired the formation of the Committee, Gira and Petersen continued to meet with Brandlin and Roemer to supply needed information, including a summary outlining the operations of UIC's subsidiaries and divisions, and confidential reports containing derogatory comments about members of the management.

18. Late in February, 1961, Gira and Petersen, Elwood S. Kendrick, who had been retained by them to defend the litigation brought by the management of UIC, Brandlin, Roemer and Stanley E. Henwood, who was than a potential member of the Committee, met to discuss the affairs of UIC. At this meeting, Gira and Petersen outlined the operations of UIC and its subsidiaries. Significantly, on the day after this meeting, Henwood became chairman of the Committee.

19. Gira, Petersen, Brandlin and Roemer met again in April, 1961, in Kendrick's law offices to decide what action they could take to counteract the charges in management's proxy material that Gira and Petersen were closely related to the Committee. Counsel for the Committee suggested that Gira and Petersen institute a libel suit against the management.

20. It was with events occurring in July, 1961, that Gira and Petersen assumed even more active roles as participants in the proxy contest, although they continued to disclaim participation. Early in July counsel for Gira and Petersen indicated to members of the staff of the SEC that in his opinion they had been libeled by statements in management's proxy material and that his clients intended to communicate with the

stockholders of UIC to deny the alleged defamatory statements. Shortly thereafter, a proposed letter addressed to stockholders by Gira was delivered to the SEC so that members of its staff could comment on it as solicitation material. This letter, although headed "THIS IS NOT A PROXY SOLICITATION," was unmistakably solicitation material. While the letter was never mailed to stockholders, it evidences the fact that Gira and Petersen were vitally interested in unseating the management slate.

21. On July 12, 1961, Gira and Petersen filed a $2,000,000 damage suit in the Superior Court of Los Angeles County alleging that the proxy material which management was circulating to the stockholders of UIC defamed them. A few hours before this suit was filed, counsel for Gira and Petersen telephoned the SEC's staff to seek advice in connection with an announcement which had been prepared for release to news services announcing the filing of the suit. This press release described not only the filing of the libel suit, but also included a discussion of the proxy contest and named each member of the Committee's slate. The staff was urged to "clear" the release in time to make the afternoon editions of certain newspapers on the East Coast. Although counsel was advised that such a release would constitute a "solicitation" within the definition of that term in Rule 14a-1 of Regulation 14, the statement, nevertheless, was issued to the press. The text of the release makes it evident that it was in fact intended to influence stockholders of UIC to vote their proxies for the Committee and in opposition to management. The libel suit was filed two weeks before the scheduled annual meeting of stockholders, and at about

the time that the Committee's fourth and last solicitation material was sent to stockholders.

22. The Committee has never actually functioned as an association; all of its members have never been assembled together at one time. Since its formation there has been only one meeting, and that one involved several, but not all, of the Committee's members. Brandlin and Roemer have met with Gira and Petersen on many more occasions than they have met with members of the Committee. The Committee is merely an imposing "letterhead" association, most of whose members were selected by and agreed to serve as an accommodation to counsel for the Committee. Many of them were not even stockholders of UIC until Roemer purchased 2,000 shares of the stock from Herman Yaras and distributed 1,000 shares among the non-stockholder members so they could appear to have an interest in the enterprise. Yaras had been financial consultant for UIC and was a close associate of Gira and Petersen. Such a seemingly independent group was necessary as Brandlin and Roemer knew that stockholder support would not be forthcoming if Gira and Petersen, the true sponsors of the Committee, participated openly as members.

23. The Committee's proxy material also was misleading in stating that certain losses sustained by UIC and diminution of stockholders' equity occurred where Bernard F. Fein was Chairman of the Executive Committee of UIC. Fein did not become Chairman of the Executive Committee until after Bernard F. Gira and Herbert J. Petersen had resigned. The Committee contends that by inadvertence the statement was not removed from one paragraph of the Com-

mittee's last mailing to stockholders although it was removed from other paragraphs, and that in any event it was not of great significance. The statement, however, was not so innocuous as the Committee suggests. In the context in which it was made it clearly implied, contrary to fact, that Fein, Gira and Petersen shared executive and managerial responsibility in UIC during the critical period in question.

24. The Committee's proxy statement and its other three communications soliciting the proxies of stockholders of UIC have been mailed to some 15,000 shareholders. The Committee admits that its solicitations have been conducted through the mails and instrumentalities of interstate commerce. As Gira and Petersen initiated the Committee, and have participated, directly and indirectly, in directing and advancing its objectives, the Committee's use of the jurisdictional facilities is attributable to them.

B. Affirmative Defenses

1. In addition to denying that Bernard F. Gira and Herbert J. Petersen were undisclosed sponsors of the UIC Stockholders' Protective Committee, the Committee interposed certain affirmative defenses to the SEC's action. The first such defense asserted by the Committee is that, in the course of the examination of its proxy material by the staff of the SEC, all material facts concerning Gira's and Petersen's connection with the Committee were disclosed to stockholders as early as April, 1961, when the Committee first began circulating its solicitation material. The Committee contends, therefore, that the SEC should be estopped from contending that the Committee's proxy material is false and misleading.

2. The Committee's assertion is contrary to the facts. Significant events establishing the close identification of Gira and Petersen with the Committee occurred subsequent to the time the Committee first began soliciting the proxies of stockholders. As recently as July, 1961, Gira and Petersen instituted the libel suit against management, and at the same time caused a press release designed to influence votes in the election contest to be issued. Other disclosures in the Committee's proxy material are wholly inadequate in the light of facts not known to the staff when the material was commented upon. For example, it was disclosed in the proxy material that Gira and Petersen had given the Committee a stockholders' list, but the circumstances under which the list was obtained and turned over to counsel for the Committee, which, as discussed above, are highly significant in evidencing the intention of Gira and Petersen to conduct a proxy contest behind the facade of a seemingly "independent" Committee, were not disclosed. Even if the facts were as the Committee contends this defense is legally insufficient because as against the SEC the doctrine of estoppel is not available. *N. Sims Organ & Co. v. SEC,* ....F. 2d........ (C. A. 2, 1961); *SEC v. Culpepper,* 270 F. 2d 241 (C. A. 2, 1959); *SEC v. Morgan, Lewis and Bookins,* 209 F. 2d 33 (C. A. 3, 1953); *SEC v. Torr,* 22 F. Supp. 602 (S.D.N.Y., 1938). See also Section 26 of the Securities Exchange Act, 15 U.S.C. 78z, which specifically provides that the failure of the SEC to act "with regard to any statement or report filed with or examined by such authority pursuant to this title or rules and regulations thereunder [may not] be deemed a finding by such authority that such statement or report is true and accurate on its

face or that it is not false or misleading." With respect to proxy solicitation material filed with the SEC, in addition to settled general principles, the statute makes it explicit that staff examination of solicitation material in no sense constitutes approval thereof, or bars a suit by the SEC to protect the public from further untrue or misleading solicitations.

3. The Committee misconstrues the effect of the examination of the Committee's preliminary proxy material by the staff of the SEC. The staff examines and, if necessary, comments upon all preliminary proxy statements and other communications intended for distribution to stockholders. This is an administrative procedure developed by the SEC to assist all contestants in a proxy controversy to comply with the proxy rules and to avoid untrue, misleading or exaggerated claims in their communications to stockholders. In nearly all proxy controversies the basic and essential facts are peculiarly within the knowledge of the contestants. It is the inescapable obligation of the contestants themselves to make certain that all material facts are set forth in their communications to stockholders in a straightforward and understandable manner. This obligation cannot be shifted to the SEC or to its staff. C. *Subin v. Goldsmith,* 224 F. (2d) 753 (C. A. 2, 1955), *certiorari denied* 350 U. S. 883.

4. The second affirmative defense asserted by the Committee is that the SEC should be denied relief in equity because in bringing this action to invalidate the Committee's proxies, the SEC comes before this Court with "unclean hands." The Committee has charged that the SEC's decision to institute this proceeding was unduly influenced by the management of UIC. The

record is barren of any evidence sustaining the accusation, and it is completely unwarranted. Indeed, in his summation, counsel for the Committee, in effect, withdrew this and other accusations that the SEC and its staff were not acting in good faith.

5. In any event, the decision to institute suits such as this is committed by statute to the discretion of the SEC. Section 21(e) of the Securities Exchange Act, 15 U.S.C. 78u(e). Again, as noted in the Court's Memorandum Decision, the record shows SEC brought this action with due regard for the voting rights of stockholders of UIC and in the public interest.

6. The defendants have also stressed that management of UIC from the beginning of its solicitation has stated that the Committee was "fronting" for Gira and Petersen and that, therefore, the stockholders are fully aware of all the facts. Such charges by management are not, however, a substitute for disclosure by the insurgents of the facts which stockholders are entitled to know when they execute proxies for the election of directors. Clearly, management's accusation is no substitute for, nor does it relieve, the insurgents from the duty to make the affirmative disclosures required by the proxy regulations.

III.
CONCLUSIONS OF LAW

1. This Court has jurisdiction of this proceeding under Section 27 of the Securities Exchange Act of 1934, 15 U.S.C. §78aa.

2. The evidence convincingly establishes that Bernard F. Gira and Herbert J. Petersen have been "participants" in the contest for control of United Indus-

trial Corporation within the meaning of Rule 14a
11(b)(3) of Regulation 14, 17 C.F.R. 240.14a-
11(b)(3).[7] The definition encompasses not only the
acknowledged members of a committee, but all those
who, even indirectly, initiate, direct, finance or otherwise seek to advance the objectives of a committee contending for control of a corporation.

3. The submission by the Committee of a list of
nominal members, however distinguished, is all the
more misleading when, as here the stockholders whose
proxies are solicited, and even the members of the
Committee themselves, are shielded from knowledge of
the true facts concerning the origin of the Committee,
and the extent to which Gira and Petersen instigated
and inspired the formation of the Committee and by
various means have sought to advance the Committee's
objective to obtain control of UIC. While the statement in the Committee's proxy material that "nor are
Gira and Petersen members of the Committee" may
be correct in a formal sense, in the light of the evidence before the Court, it is clear that the omission to
disclose their *de facto* participation constitutes an abuse
of the solicitation process, in direct violation of Rule
14a-9 of Regulation 14, 17 C.F.R. 240.14a-9. See
S.E.C. v. May, 134 F. Supp. 247 (S.D.N.Y., 1955),
affirmed 229 F. 2d. 124 (C. A. 2, 1956).

4. The SEC is entitled to a decree (1) enjoining
the defendants UIC Stockholders' Protective Commit-

---

[7]The Rule defines a "participant" to include "any Committee
or group which solicits proxies, any member of such Committee
or group, and any person whether or not named as a member
who, acting alone or with one or more other persons, directly or
indirectly, take the initiative in organizing, directing or financing any such Committee or group."

tee, Stanley E. Henwood, Richard I. Roemer and Lewis M. Poe individually and as members of and proxies for said Committee, and the defendants Bernard F. Gira and Herbert J. Petersen from violations of Section 14(a) of the Act, 15 U.S.C. §78n(a), and Rule 14a-9 of Regulation 14, 17 C.F.R. 240.14a-9 thereunder, in the solicitation of proxies in respect to the common or preferred stock of UIC to be voted at the adjourned annual meeting of stockholders; and (2) invalidating all proxies of stockholders of UIC now held by them; and (3) enjoining them from voting any such proxy which is not received pursuant to a solicitation made subsequent to the entry of the final decree in the action, in accordance with Section 14(a) of the Act, 15 U.S.C. §78n(a), and Regulation 14 thereunder, 17 C.F.R. 240.14.

5. As stated in the Court's Memorandum Decision, it is not the intention of the Court to cause any stockholder of UIC to lose his voting rights. It is within the equitable power of the Court, in enforcing the statutory prohibition against unlawful proxy solicitations, not only to invalidate proxies which have been obtained by means of misleading solicitations, but also to mold its decree to avoid such an eventuality. *SEC v. May,* 134 F. Supp. 247, *supra* and *SEC v. O'Hara Reorganization Committee,* 28 F. Supp. 523 (D. Mass. 1939). See also *SEC v. Trans American,* 163 F. 2d 511, 518 (C. A. 3, 1947), *certiorari denied* 332 U.S. 847.

6. Accordingly, the decree will provide for adjournment of the annual meeting of stockholders of UIC to a date not earlier than November 22, 1961, to allow time for the further solicitation of new proxies (in

accordance with the proxy rules) by management, the Committee, or any other committee, group, or individual, whether favoring or opposing management.

7. For the reason given in the Memorandum Decision, the circumstances do not require that the remaining members of the Committee be enjoined. Accordingly, the action will be dismissed, without prejudice, as to those defendants.

8. The SEC is also entitled to a decree directing the defendants Bernard F. Gira and Herbert J. Petersen to comply with Rule 14a-11 of Regulation 14, 17 C.F.R. 240.14a-11, by filing corrected statements containing the information required by Schedule B, concerning their status as participants in the proxy controversy.

hibits	De
1	Schedule 14
2	Diagram of
3	Invoice of s
4	Letter of 3 holders' list
5	Emery Fre
6	Receipt exec ering stockh ical Bank heretofore r Receipt date
7	Work pape the stockho to Ohio
8	Letter to 1-26-61
9	Emery Air
10	Certified co
11	Certified co
12	Certified cc
13	Copies of r #3
14	Managemer
14-A	Definitive i holders
15	Preliminar; by the S; Committee
16	Affidavit (Bank
17	Letter fro dated 5-16
18	Papers or Yaras, etc.
19	Press rele
20	Letter fro
21	Cohen lett

APPENDIX "C."

Index of Exhibits.

bits	Description	Marked for Identification		Admitted in Evidence	
		Date	Page	Date	Page
	Schedule 14-B of Petersen	7/26–27	94		
	Diagram of Building			7/26–27	158
				9/21–22	2206
	Invoice of shareholders' list			7/26–27	162
	Letter of transmittal on shareholders' list			7/26–27	163
	Emery Freight Bill	7/26–27	167		
	Receipt executed by Hamner covering stockholder list from Chemical Bank at the foot of letter heretofore received as Exhibit 4. Receipt dated 1-18-61.			8/1	189
	Work papers of UIC relative to the stockholder list and a report to Ohio			8/1	192
	Letter to State of Ohio dated 1-26-61			8/1	193
	Emery Air Freight receipt			8/1	199
	Certified copy of 14-B of Gira			8/1	201
	Certified copy of 14-B of Yaras			8/1	202
	Certified copy of 14-B of Yaras Copies of mailings #1, #2 and #3			8/1	205
	Management material	8/1	207	8/1	207
				8/15	675
A	Definitive interim report to shareholders			8/15	676
	Preliminary material submitted by the Stockholders' Protective Committee—certified copies	8/1	210	8/22	1016
	Affidavit of Clerk of Chemical Bank				
	Letter from Roemer to SEC dated 5-16-61			8/1	267
	Papers on collateral loan for Yaras, etc.			8/2	391
	Press release re libel suit			8/2	414
	Letter from Gira to stockholders	8/2	417	8/2	429
	Cohen letter of July 14			8/3	443

Exhibits	Description	Marked for Identification		Admitted in Evidence	
		Date	Page	Date	Page
22	Affidavit of Gordon	8/3	444		
23	Press release	8/15	633	8/15	63.5
24	Copy of Wall Street Journal (Jan. 17, 1961)	8/15	633	8/15	635
25	Affidavit of Bud Lewis			8/15	676
26	Roemer letter of 6-13			8/17	948
27	26th annual report of SEC	8/17	951		
28	Transcript of Luther	8/22	1017	9/12	1454
29	Transcript of Williams	8/22	1018	9/12	1454
30	Transcript of Ballance	8/22	1018	9/12	1454
31	Transcript of Wulfekuhler	8/22	1018	9/12	1454
32	Transcript of Lawry	8/22	1019	9/12	1454
33	Transcript of Gira	8/22	1019	9/12	1454
34	Transcript of Petersen	8/22	1019	9/12	1454
35	Transcript of Yaras	8/22	1019	9/12	1454
36	Transcript of McLaughlin	8/22	1020	9/12	1454
37	Transcript of Soderstrom	8/22	1020	9/12	1454
29-A	Transcript of Williams	8/22	1020	9/12	1454
28-A	Transcript of Luther	8/22	1020	9/12	1454
38	Transcript of Henwood	8/22	1021	9/12	1454
39	Transcript of Roemer	8/22	1021	9/12	1454
38-A	Transcript of Henwood	8/22	1021	9/12	1454
39-A	Transcript of Roemer	8/22	1021	9/12	1454
40	Affidavit of Risk	8/23	1132	8/23	1154
41	Affidavit of Cohen	8/23	1133	8/23	1154
42	Order of SEC directing an investigation and designating an officer to take the testimony in matter of UIC	8/23	1162	8/23	1169
43	Statement of assets and disbursements of the Stockholders' Protective Committee			9/12	1414
44	Article from Wall Street Journal			9/12	1415
45	Affidavit of Roy L Williams			9/12	1424
46	Minutes of meeting of 1-13-61			9/12	1443
47	Testimony of Dumont			9/12	1454
48	Testimony of Hugh E. McColgan			9/12	1454
49	Affidavit of Landau			9/13	1582
50	Deposition of Manuel Cohen			9/21	2207

Exhibits	
A	Mailing
B	Bishop'
C	Order i
D	Letter dated
E	Docume chase 1
F	Letter
G	Telegra
H	Diagra
I	Letter 6-16
J	Affidav
K	Transc
L	UIC fi
M	Letter
N	Deposi
O	Weinn
P	Docum sheets
Q	Pencil 1961
R	Press
S	Notes were t deposit
AA	Releas
BB	Release
CC	Release
DD	Release
EE	Kendr
FF	Letter 7/18
GG	Unedit
HH	Article 7/13 e examin
II	Affidav
JJ	Affida
KK	Copy

hibits	Description	Marked for Identification		Admitted in Evidence	
		Date	Page	Date	Page
A	Mailing #4			8/2	322
B	Bishop's Report on Fein	8/2	329	8/2	342
C	Order for Xerox machine			8/2	331
D	Letter to SEC from Brandlin dated March 24, 1961			8/2	381
E	Documents in BSF stock purchase 1959	8/2	431	9/22	2279
F	Letter from Cohen			8/16	787
G	Telegram from Cohen	8/17	905	8/17	905
H	Diagram on Board	8/17	972		
I	Letter from Brandlin to Risk, 6-16	8/24	1302	8/24	1303
J	Affidavit of Luther			8/24	1315
K	Transmittal letter of Affidavit			8/25	1331
L	UIC file by reference			8/25	1366
M	Letter from Risk			8/25	1386
N	Deposition of Sharon Clay Risk			9/14	1655
O	Weinman	9/15	1847	9/15	1883
P	Documents consisting of five sheets	9/15	1883	9/22	2279
Q	Pencil notes of November 12, 1961			9/19	1937
R	Press release			9/22	2279
S	Notes of Commission staff that were to be marked during Risk deposition	9/22	2280	9/22	2280
AA	Releases in newspaper	8/3	482	8/3	488
BB	Releases in newspaper	8/3	482	8/3	488
CC	Releases in newspaper	8/3	482	8/3	488
DD	Releases in newspaper	8/3	482	8/3	488
EE	Kendrick's sec'y letter to SEC	8/3	513	8/3	514
FF	Letter from Kendrick to Cohen 7/18	8/3	513	9/22	2282
GG	Unedited material of management	8/3	543	9/22	2281
HH	Article about libel suit from the 7/13 edition of the Los Angeles examiner	9/19	1949	9/22	2281
II	Affidavit of Petersen				
JJ	Affidavit of Gira				
KK	Copy of libel complaint			9/20	2100

Exhibits	Description	Marked for Identification		Admitted in Evidence	
		Date	Page	Date	Pag
LL	Financial reports	9/21	2111	9/21	2178
MM	Proxy statement mailed to the shareholders of Topp Industries Corporation	9/21	2111		
NN	Monthly report (financial statement)	9/21	2111		
AAA	Correction letter from Yaras	8/17	975	8/22	101:
BBB	Intercompany correspondence of	9/14	1738	9/14	173!
CCC	NIC from Gira to M Bonner received on or about 9/19/60 concerning Permachem Corp	9/14	1738	9/14	173!
DDD	Press release	9/14	1764		

Unite

STANLEY F
individually,
TION STO
of said Cor
FRED A.
WILLIAM
McLAUGH
CLARENC
KUHLER,
UNITED I
TECTIVE
PETERSE.

SECURI

APPEAL
Soi

BR

Of Counsel:
FRANK G.
JAMES O.
RALPH L.

United States Court of Appeals

For the Ninth Circuit

No. 17591

STANLEY E. HENWOOD, RICHARD I. ROEMER, LEWIS M. POE, individually, as members of the UNITED INDUSTRIAL CORPORATION STOCKHOLDERS' PROTECTIVE COMMITTEE and as proxies of said Committee, JAMES V. ARMOGIDA, ROBERT G BALLANCE, FRED A. BESHARA, NATHANIEL R DUMONT, JOE L FOSS, WILLIAM D LAWRY, ELMER M LUTHER, JR, EDWARD H McLAUGHLIN, CHARLES SODERSTROM, JOHN A STEEL, CLARENCE L SUMMERS, ROY L WILLIAMS, LOUIS W WULFE-KUHLER, ALFRED T. ZODDA, individually and as members of the UNITED INDUSTRIAL CORPORATION STOCKHOLDERS' PROTECTIVE COMMITTEE, BERNARD GIRA and HERBERT J PETERSEN,

Appellants,

vs

SECURITIES AND EXCHANGE COMMISSION and UNITED INDUSTRIAL CORPORATION,

Appellees

APPEAL FROM THE UNITED STATES DISTRICT COURT FOR THE SOUTHERN DISTRICT OF CALIFORNIA, CENTRAL DIVISION

BRIEF OF THE APPELLEE UNITED INDUSTRIAL CORPORATION

RAICHLE, MOORE, BANNING and WEISS,
10 Lafayette Square,
Buffalo 3, New York,
Attorneys for Appellee,
United Industrial Corporation.

Of Counsel
FRANK G. RAICHLE,
JAMES O MOORE, JR.,
RALPH L. HALPERN.

TABLE OF CONTENTS

CITATIONS.

Cases:

United States Court of Appeals

FOR THE NINTH CIRCUIT

No. 17591

STANLEY E. HENWOOD, RICHARD I. ROEMER,
LEWIS M. POE, individually, as members of the
UNITED INDUSTRIAL CORPORATION STOCK-
HOLDERS' PROTECTIVE COMMITTEE and as
proxies of said Committee, JAMES V. ARMOGIDA,
ROBERT G. BALLANCE, FRED A. BESHARA,
NATHANIEL R. DUMONT, JOE L. FOSS, WILLIAM
D. LAWRY, ELMER M. LUTHER, JR., EDWARD H.
McLAUGHLIN, CHARLES SODERSTROM, JOHN A.
STEEL, CLARENCE L. SUMMERS, ROY L. WIL-
LIAMS, LOUIS W. WULFEKUHLER, ALFRED T.
ZODDA, individually and as members of the UNITED
INDUSTRIAL CORPORATION STOCKHOLDERS'
PROTECTIVE COMMITTEE, BERNARD GIRA and
HERBERT J. PETERSEN,

Appellants,

vs.

SECURITIES AND EXCHANGE COMMISSION and
UNITED INDUSTRIAL CORPORATION,

Appellees.

BRIEF OF THE APPELLEE UNITED
INDUSTRIAL CORPORATION

Jurisdictional Statement

This is an action instituted by the Securities and Exchange Commission pursuant to the provisions of Section
21(e) and Section 21(f) of the Securities Exchange Act

of 1934, 15 USC § 78u(e) and § 78u(f). The jurisdiction of the Court below arises under Section 27 of the Securities Exchange Act of 1934, 15 USC § 78aa, and the jurisdiction of this Court is founded on United States Judicial Code, 28 USC §§ 1291, 1294.

The complaint recites that the defendants, other than the defendant United Industrial Corporation, have engaged or are about to engage in acts and practices in violation of Section 14(a) of the Securities Exchange Act of 1934, 15 USC § 78n(a) and of Regulation 14, 17 CFR § 240.14a, prescribed by the Securities and Exchange Commission to govern the solicitation of proxies in respect of any security registered and listed on any national securities exchange. The complaint charges that the appellants, individually and as members of the United Industrial Corporation Stockholders' Protective Committee, have solicited proxies for use at the 1961 Annual Stockholders Meeting of the Corporation by means of statements which were false and misleading with respect to material facts and which *omitted* to state material facts. It specifies the failure of such proxy statements to disclose the part played by the defendants Gira, Petersen and Yaras in the initiation and organization of the Committee and their participation in the proxy solicitation in opposition to the existing management of the Corporation.

Statement of the Case

United Industrial Corporation (hereinafter sometimes referred to as "United" or the "Company"), a Delaware corporation, is an industrial complex engaged in the operation of various businesses through wholly owned subsidiaries and divisions located throughout the United States. The Company resulted from the merger on De-

cember 31, 19
old line Michi
many years be
and Topp Ind
originally bee
1951 by the de
principally in
and assets of
corporation, w
ed by Topp In

Upon the co
the Company
Topp corpora
dent of both T
chief executiv
and the defen
both Topp co
dent of Unit
Directors was
executives of '
old United In
the Company,
outstanding, w
Exchange and
shares were
American Sto
the American
addition were
(Ex. LL).

After consu
gradually mo
Los Angeles,
ness of Topp

cember 31, 1959 of United Industrial Corporation, an old line Michigan corporation, the stock of which had for many years been listed on the New York Stock Exchange, and Topp Industries Corporation, a company which had originally been organized in the State of California in 1951 by the defendants Gira and Petersen and was engaged principally in the electronics industry. All of the business and assets of Topp Industries Corporation, a Delaware corporation, were prior to October, 1959, owned and operated by Topp Industries, Inc., a California corporation.

Upon the consummation of the merger the operation of the Company was vested in the former principals of both Topp corporations. The defendant Gira, the former president of both Topp corporations, became the president and chief executive officer of United Industrial Corporation and the defendant Petersen, the former vice-president of both Topp corporations, became the executive vice-president of United Industrial Corporation. The Board of Directors was divided between the former directors and executives of Topp Industries and former directors of the old United Industrial Corporation. The common stock of the Company, of which more than 2,000,000 shares were outstanding, was listed for trading on the New York Stock Exchange and the preferred stock, of which over 1,000,000 shares were outstanding, was listed for trading on the American Stock Exchange. Warrants were also listed on the American Stock Exchange. All these securities in addition were listed on the Pacific Coast Stock Exchange (Ex. LL).

After consummation of the merger Gira and Petersen gradually moved the executive offices of the Company to Los Angeles, which had been the principal place of business of Topp Industries, Inc., and thereafter the operations of the Company were conducted from these offices. For the year ending December 31, 1960, the first fiscal year of its operations, the Company showed an operating loss in excess of $6,000,000 (Ex. 13). Early in January of 1961 Arthur Young & Co., the Company's independent accountants, made a direct request to the Board of Directors that they be accorded an opportunity of appearing before the Board and disclosing information which had come to their attention requiring very substantial write-downs in the Company's assets, occasioned by material misstatements which had been made by officers of the Company in the interim financial statements and the evaluation by officers of the Company of certain inventories and deferred charges. A meeting of the Board of Directors was held in Los Angeles on January 12, 13 and 14, 1961. At the conclusion of this meeting the Board asked for and received the resignation of the defendants Gira and Petersen as officers and directors of the Company (R. 61, Ex. 33, p. 190)*. By order of the Board of Directors the preliminary findings of the independent accountants were made known to the Securities and Exchange Commission, the New York Stock Exchange, and to the financial institutions which had financed the Company. As a result of these disclosures trading in both the common and the preferred stock of the company was suspended. (Over-the-counter trading was resumed on September 22, 1961 pursuant to permission of the Securities and Exchange Commission. Trading of the Company's securities was resumed on the Pacific Coast Stock Exchange on November 16, 1961.)

As a consequence of these occurrences eight stockholders derivative actions have been instituted against the

---

*R refers to Volume II of the Transcript of the Record (Reporter's Transcript)

Company and
Courts of the
State of New
action in the (
and Petersen
Company is a
second Wedne
regulations of
require that t
the stockholde
is undertaken
Annual Meeti
As a result o
preliminary f
Arthur Young
audit and fur
after the date
ing to take ac
control of the
caused the for
tive Committ
in this action
proxy solicita
of the defend.
ters of this a

Early in A
complete and
and Exchang
the Company
holders list
the Company
statement, th
material fact

Company and its former and present directors in the Courts of the State of Delaware and the Courts of the State of New York. The Company has also instituted an action in the Courts of the State of Delaware against Gira and Petersen and others. The annual meeting of the Company is appointed by its by-laws to be held on the second Wednesday in May of each year. The rules and regulations of the Securities and Exchange Commission require that the Company's Annual Report be furnished the stockholders at or prior to the time proxy solicitation is undertaken by the management in connection with the Annual Meeting. Rule X-14A-3(b), 17 CFR 240.14a-3(b). As a result of the conditions which were reflected in the preliminary findings reported by the Company's auditors, Arthur Young & Co. was unable to complete the annual audit and furnish certified financial statements until long after the date appointed for the Annual Meeting. Seeking to take advantage of this circumstance and to regain control of the Company, the defendants Gira and Petersen caused the formation of the so-called Stockholders' Protective Committee whose members are named as defendants in this action. The information of this Committee, the proxy solicitation it has undertaken and the participation of the defendants Gira and Petersen form the subject matters of this action.

Early in April of 1961 the Committee, having filed incomplete and misleading statements with the Securities and Exchange Commission, mailed to the stockholders of the Company proxy solicitation material, using a stockholders list which had been surreptitiously taken from the Company by Gira and Petersen. The falsity of this statement, the misrepresentations it contained and the material facts which it omitted were fully developed upon

the trial of this action and treated of in a later portion
of this brief. Knowing full well that the management of
the Company was foreclosed from soliciting proxies by
virtue of the Securities and Exchange Commission's regulations and the unavailability of the audited Annual Report,
the Committee instituted an action in the Court of Chancery
for the State of Delaware to enjoin any postponement of
the Annual Meeting and thus to assure the success of
their attempt to regain control of the Company. The
Securities and Exchange Commission expressed its view
by letter to the Chancellor in this action on behalf of
United and voiced its objection to this attempted perver-
sion of its regulations. After a hearing on the merits,
the Delaware Court of Chancery denied the relief sought
by the Committee and sanctioned the necessary adjournment of the Annual Meeting.

Upon the dissemination of the false and misleading
proxy statement the Corporation acted promptly to protect the interests of its stockholders. On April 25, 1961,
some three months prior to the commencement of the
instant case, it instituted an action in the United States
District Court for the Western District of New York
against these same defendants, with the exception of the
defendants Yaras and Shafer. The complaint in the
corporate action, just as the complaint in the case at
bar, charged that the defendants were soliciting proxies
for use at the 1961 Annual Meeting by false and misleading statements with respect to material facts and by omitting in their proxy statements certain material facts. The
complaint in the corporate matter went on to specify
failure of defendants' proxy material to disclose the connection of Gira and Petersen with the solicitation and
their relationship with various members of the so-called

Stockholders' Committee and other participants in the solicitation. An injunction was sought to prevent the defendants from voting the proxies that they had obtained and from continuing to solicit proxies by false and misleading statements.

The defendants filed answers which were in effect general denials and the plaintiff corporation took immediate steps to progress the trial of the action by taking the depositions of the defendants Henwood and Roemer and noticed the depositions of substantially all of the other defendants. Thereupon the defendants made a motion to change the venue of the action to the United States District Court for the Southern District of California on the ground that the activities complained of were all centered in that district and the majority of the defendants resided therein. The United States District Court for the Western District of New York granted the defendants' motion and transferred the case to California. A day or two after the entry of the order transferring the case, the defendants served and filed amended answers which for the first time asserted a counterclaim alleging that an "Interim Report" issued by the management of the Company in response to the proxy solicitation of the Committee, together with a letter from the management of the Company which accompanied the Annual Report to the stockholders, were false and misleading and constituted an unlawful solicitation of proxies. The counterclaim went on to allege that the false and misleading character of the report and the letter consisted of statements connecting Gira and Petersen with the solicitation undertaken upon behalf of the Committee. A reading of the counterclaim makes clear that the transactions therein complained of emanated from the State of New York and that the convenience of all of the parties would best be served by a trial within the State of New York of the additional issues raised in the counterclaim. It is, therefore, apparent that the attorneys for the defendants saw fit to withhold from the United States District Court for the Western District of New York the true nature of the litigation until they had succeeded in removing it from the Court's jurisdiction.

The case came on for hearing before the United States District Court for the Southern District of California on July 17. Plaintiff moved for a transfer of the case back to the Western District of New York in the light of the changed circumstances brought about by the interposition of the counterclaim. After hearing both sides the Court reserved decision on this motion. Thereupon the Court heard argument on the plaintiff's motion for a preliminary injunction which was predicated on affidavits and on the depositions that had been taken of certain of the defendants. During the course of the argument the Court informed counsel that he had been advised by the Pacific coast counsel for the Securities and Exchange Commission that the Commission was filing an action in the United States District Court for the Southern District of California to restrain the Stockholders' Protective Committee from soliciting proxies in violation of the Securities Exchange Act of 1934. The argument on the motion for a preliminary injunction and the testimony of witnesses sworn on behalf of the defendants was not concluded on July 18, 1961 and the matter was adjourned to July 25, 1961.

On July 21, 1961 the present action was instituted. In addition to the final judgment enjoining defendants from using proxies obtained through the medium of false and misleading statements the plaintiff Securities and Exchange Commission sought a temporary restraining order and a preliminary injunction enjoining further solicitation of proxies by the Stockholders' Protective Committee and restraining the Company from holding the Annual Meeting until further order of the Court.

The hearing on the motion for a preliminary injunction in the Company's action was resumed on July 25, 1961. During the course of the hearing the action instituted by the Securities and Exchange Commission came before the Court and the attorneys for the Securities and Exchange Commission and the attorneys for the defendants appeared before the Court for the purpose of arguing the motion of the Securities and Exchange Commission for a temporary restraining order directed againt the Committee. In the course of the colloquy the attorney for the Stockholders' Committee stated that it would be proper for the Court, which was hearing the Corporation's case, to undertake the hearing of both cases (R. 18a).

On July 26, 1961 the Court entered a temporary restraining order enjoining the holding of the Annual Meeting and the further solicitation of proxies by both the Company and the Committee. The Company consented to this order but the other defendants objected to it and insisted that the Securities and Exchange Commission proceed immediately with its proof in the action that it had instituted (R. 151a). Thereupon the Court adjourned the hearing on the Company's application for a preliminary injunction and proceeded immediately to the taking of the testimony in the instant case. During the course of the trial it was stipulated by all of the parties that the Court should consider the trial to be on the merits rather than on an application for a preliminary injunction (R. 1570, 1573, 1574). The taking of testimony continued from day to day with adjournments to accommodate the business of the Court and was concluded on September 22, 1961. On October 3, 1961 the Court filed its decision and on October 18, 1961 the findings of fact and conclusions of law were filed and a final judgment was entered herein.

United was named as a defendant in this action solely for the purpose of enabling the Court to grant adequate relief by way of ordering an adjournment of the Annual Meeting of stockholders which was imminent at the time of the institution of the action. No other claim is made against the Company in this case (par. 5, Complaint; Appellants' Committee brief p. 7). Throughout this protracted litigation the Company has readily consented to successive adjournments of the Annual Meeting and although no such relief was prayed for in the complaint and it has not been charged with any wrongdoing in connection with the solicitation of proxies, the Company has also consented to the entry of orders prohibiting any further solicitation by Management while the restraining order against the Committee was still in effect (R. 19a, 20a). Consonant with its role as a nominal defendant the Company did not take an active part in the trial of the action. No proof was offered on its behalf and cross examination on its behalf was confined to clarification. This course was dictated in recognition of the paramount public interest represented by the Securities and Exchange Commission and by the further circumstances that as the trial developed it became apparent that the defense was founded in an attack upon the procedures and, indeed, the integrity of that Governmental agency (R. 883, 885, 893, 894, 1178).

Nonetheless the Company has a very vital interest in the outcome of this litigation because it profoundly affects private interests represented by the corporate business

and financial community and the fifteen thousand stockholders who own the company. It is these private interests
that the Company sought to protect when, three months
prior to the institution of the instant action, it commenced
the action in the United States District Court for the Western District of New York, which was subsequently transferred to the United States District Court for the Southern
District of California, and which is still pending. The
record in this case and the judicial determination that has
been made thereon in the public interest confirms the action
it has taken in protection of the private interests it has a
duty to represent.

ARGUMENT

POINT I

The record clearly supports the findings of fact.

The attacks upon the findings of fact by both sets of
appellants must be analyzed and assessed in the light of
the well established equitable rule of appellate review
which has been incorporated in the Federal Rules of Civil
Procedure, Rule 52(a):

> "* * * Findings of fact shall not be set aside unless
> clearly erroneous, and due regard shall be given to the
> opportunity of the trial court to judge of the credibil-
> ity of the witnesses . * * *"

In *Stacher v. U. S.,* 258 F. 2d 112 (9th Cir. 1958), this Court
said at page 116:

> "Further, the government was the prevailing party
> below, and hence we must take that view of the evi-
> dence most favorable to it. Appellee is entitled to the
> benefit of all favorable inferences from the facts prov-
> ed relative to the issue of residence. If, when so view-
> ed, there was substantial evidence to sustain the find-

ings, then the judgment may not be reversed by this Court unless against the clear weight of the evidence or unless influenced by an erroneous view of the law.'' See also *Joseph v. Donover*, 261 F. 2d 812 (9th Cir. 1958). It is the duty of this Court to accept the findings of fact made by the trial court once it has tested the record and found that there is credible evidence to support such findings. This is particularly true where, as in the case at bar, the record consists almost entirely of sworn testimony.

The line of cases cited by the appellants Gira and Petersen, such as *U. S. v. Parke Davis & Co.*, 362 U. S. 29 (1960), can have no application to the review of this record. In those cases the reviewing court relied on the well established power to review the application of legal standards and principles to factual situations which were virtually undisputed. In this case the judgment is predicated entirely on the determination by the trial court of disputed questions of fact and there is no substantial issue as to the legal consequences which must flow from the facts as determined by the court below.

The "clearly erroneous" test is not met by references to isolated words or phrases in particular findings. It involves an analysis of the record, the drawing of all inferences favorable to the prevailing party and an ultimate determination as to whether or not there is evidence which, if believed, would support the findings that have been made. The existence of a choice between permissible views of the weight of the evidence does not denote error. *U. S. v. Yellow Cab Co.*, 338 U. S. 338, 341 (1947).

Moreover, in the case at bar the record must be reviewed in the light of the circumstances that this litigation does not arise out of a controversy between interested private parties. On the contrary the case was commenced by the

Securities and Exchange Commission in the execution of its statutory duty under Section 21 of the Securities and Exchange Act of 1934 (15 U. S. C. § 78u). The determination of the Securities and Exchange Commission to institute this action was not made in a vacuum and represents the exercise of the expertise the agency has gained over a quarter of a century in the administration of this act of Congress. 2 Loss, Securities Regulation 784 (2d ed. 1961).

The appellants' criticisms of the findings of fact are fully met by a review of the record even without the favorable inferences to which appellees are entitled under the well established rule. See *Axelbank v. Rony*, 277 F. 2d 314, 316 (9th Cir. 1960). The strength of the record is emphasized by the fact that the great bulk of the testimony was adduced from the defendants themselves who were called as adverse witnesses.

a. Gira's Plan to Replace Directors

This contest for corporate control had its genesis during the period when Gira and Petersen were the chief executive officers of United Industrial Corporation. As early as December of 1960 the defendant Summers, who had been employed by Gira and Petersen as a public relations adviser of the corporation, prepared at the request of Gira a document outlining the procedure to be followed to replace certain unidentified directors (R. 2183).

b. Resignations of Gira and Petersen

This plan was forestalled by the forced resignations of Gira and Petersen as the chief executive officers and as directors of the Company at a meeting of the Board of Directors held on January 12, 13 and 14, 1961 (R. 61). This meeting was called at the request of the Company's inde-

pendent auditors, Arthur Young and Co., for the purpose
of informing the Board of a pattern of material misstate-
ments contained in the interim financial statements of the
Company which substantially affected the valuation that
had been placed on certain of the Company's assets. The
Board of Directors felt constrained by the terms and conditions of the Company's listing agreement with the New
York Stock Exchange, its loan agreement with the Bank of
America and the rules and regulations of the Securities
and Exchange Commission to report these facts to those
interested parties. Gira and Petersen obviously disagreed
violently with this decision and as a result their resignations were demanded (Brandlin Dep. 118, 119; R. 1206).

c. Discussions of Proxy Contest

Petersen and Gira did not waste any time in carrying
forward their plans. They both retained separate counsel
and had several discussions respecting the actions of the
other members of the Board, of whom they were very critical (R. 71, Brandlin Dep. 118, 119). Petersen discussed
the possibility of a proxy contest with the defendant Yaras
(R. 146, 147). On January 25, 1961, approximately ten
days after his resignation, Gira arranged a meeting at his
home in Malibu with the defendant Roemer and Brandlin
(R. 214, 215). He expressed dissatisfaction with the counsel he had retained and sought advice as to the steps that
should be taken to protect his interests.

One of the two courses of action discussed at the meeting
in Malibu was that of waging a proxy contest (R. 218, 260).
There is some confusion as to whether Gira was advised at
that time "that he as such should not engage in a proxy
contest" (R. 357) or whether this advice was given to Gira
by Brandlin and Roemer at a later date (R. 262, 263).

d. Stockholders List Stolen and Delivered to Brandlin for Duplication and to Wage Proxy Contest

In any event Gira and Petersen two days thereafter delivered to the offices of Brandlin and Roemer the Company's stockholders list (R. 78, 220, 221). The stockholders list was delivered by Gira and Petersen because they were advised that such list would be necessary to wage a proxy contest (R. 72, 221, 222). This stockholders list was the only list available to the Company (R. 169). Such list contained the stockholders at December 30, 1960 and was ordered for the purpose of advising certain states of the number of stockholders residing therein at such date as required by the pertinent statutes (R. 161). The list, which consisted of approximately 750 pages (R. 170, 171), was reproduced in the offices of Brandlin and Roemer during the weekend of January 28 and 29, 1961 (R. 117) for the avowed purpose of a proxy fight (R. 1200, 1201). Roemer testified that the list was duplicated for Gira and Petersen and at that time Roemer and Brandlin had no other client who was interested in a proxy fight (R. 280, 355).

There is a sharp conflict in the evidence with respect to the circumstances surrounding the obtaining of the list. It is firmly established that the list was first received by the Company on January 14, 1961 (R. 198; Ex. 4). It was placed in a locked file and receipted for on January 18, 1961 (R. 188; Ex. 6). The list was used by employees of the Company between the time of its receipt and January 26, 1961 to prepare a report for the Ohio Department of Taxation (R. 190-193; Exs 7 and 8).

Brantly, the Vice-President of U. S. Science. a United subsidiary, testified that during the week of January 16 Robert Gira, the brother of the defendant Bernard Gira, requested him to secure the stockholders list and to remove it from the plant. Robert Gira described the location of the list and told him where the key was located (R. 54-57). He also assured Brantly that the list would be returned after it had been duplicated (R. 56). Brantly quite properly refused to take part in any such activity and reported the matter to his superior (R. 57). This testimony is unimpeached and stands uncontradicted. No explanation has been made of the failure of the defendant Gira to call his brother as a witness. The defendant Petersen testified that on January 14, 1961, the day of his resignation, he loaded the personal effects that were in his office in his station wagon and took them to his home (R. 69, 70). The following day while he was unloading the station wagon he discovered that this twenty-pound, two-volume stockholders list had just happened to be included among his personal belongings (R. 71). In the face of the testimony of the employees of the Company and the documentary evidence Petersen maintained that this list remained in his possession until he and Gira delivered it, pursuant to the request of Brandlin, to the law offices of Brandlin and the defendant Roemer on January 27, 1961 (R. 72).

As we have noted above, the task of duplicating this 750-page list was undertaken on Saturday and Sunday, January 28 and 29. On Sunday, January 29, at a time when the offices of United were closed, Brandlin personally returned the list (R. 1250), driving a considerable distance out of his way (R. 1182-3). Although the facilities of the Company are subject to diligently applied Navy and Air Force security regulations (R. 88, 89), Brandlin testified that he walked right into the plant and left the list on a secretary's desk (R. 1251). The list contained no address, no letter of transmittal, nor any other indication, revealing that it had ever been taken from the plant (R. 1251, 1253-4). Moreover, although Brandlin realized that the list was the property of the Company, he did not conceive that it was incumbent upon him to advise the management of the Company that he had been in possession of it (R. 1251, 1252).

The fact that the list was surreptitiously removed from the premises of the Company—and in fact was stolen—becomes clear beyond peradventure when it is realized that Brandlin returned the list not to Gira or Petersen but to the Company after it had been duplicated.

e. Formation of so-called "Committee"

Within four days of the meeting at Malibu, Brandlin, spurred on by Gira, had determined to put together a slate to wage a proxy contest (R. 1201) and the stockholders list had been procured and duplicated (R. 1200). Gira had been advised that he "as such" should not wage a proxy contest (R. 357) and he agreed with Roemer's and Brandlin's analysis of the situation (Brandlin Dep. 33, 34, 35). Gira, however, inquired of Roemer and Brandlin whether they would be interested in handling the proxy contest if other stockholders came to them and requested that they set up an organization and conduct a contest for control of United (R. 1248, 1249). Roemer and Brandlin expressed an interest and at that point Gira advised them that he would make the stockholders list available (R. 1249, 1250).

Shortly thereafter the defendant Summers, who had formerly been Gira's public relations man and who was the author of the original plan to replace directors, called on Roemer and said that he had been advised by Petersen that the law firm was going to undertake a proxy contest and might require his services (R. 2181). Summers not only became a member of the Committee, but he also produced another Committee member, Dumont, a long standing friend and business associate of Gira's (R. 1726, 1727). Yaras, the financial consultant of Gira and Petersen, who had previously discussed a proxy contest with Petersen, next called on Brandlin and expressed interest in the undertaking (R. 1224). Yaras was eventually left off the Committee because of the fact that he had at one time been in bankruptcy (R. 1239).

Williams, Gira's uncle, was next referred to Roemer by Gira (R. 1095). Although he had never met Roemer, he called him on the phone with the suggestion of Gira and stated that he was interested in trying to find out what had happened to the stock (R. 1095, 1096). Until Williams received from Roemer Form 14-B which was required by the Securities and Exchange Commission, he didn't have any idea what was going on (R. 1103). He testified that he knew "absolutely nothing about the committee" and at no time authorized Roemer or anyone else to conduct a proxy contest on his behalf (R. 1115, 1120, 1121).

Elmer Luther, a discharged former employee of the Company and a personal friend of Petersen and Gira, was referred to Roemer by Yaras (R. 1037, 1039, 1040). In the course of his deposition he testified that he was not a member of the Committee and he did not know who was making the decisions for the Committee (R. 1036, 1047). Luther testified further that he never authorized Roemer to engage in a proxy contest on his behalf (R. 1075, 1076), and in fact had not contacted him until the first part of March (R. 1041). Parenthetically, it is noted that even as late as the trial of this action, neither Brandlin nor Roemer had ever seen either Luther or Williams (R. 372, 1278).

The Committee's proxy material (Ex. 13) carefully omits any reference to the direct connection of Gira and Petersen with the formation of the Committee and fails to disclose the peculiar circumstances under which the stockholders list was obtained. The Committee's initial proxy material contains the following statement:

> "The formation of the Stockholders' Protective Committee started after Richard I. Roemer, a member of the Committee, a nominee for director, and a partner in the law firm representing the Committee, received complaints from stockholders Elmer M. Luther, Jr., a former employee of a subsidiary of the company, and Roy L. Williams, B. F. Gira's uncle, who own respectively 250 and 400 shares of the common stock of your company. They complained about the decrease in market value of the stock, its suspension from trading, and the apparent internal conflict within the board of directors. These two stockholders requested Mr. Roemer to take whatever steps were necessary to form a new slate of directors and provide your company with new management.
>
> "This was done by contacting men whom the organizers of the slate considered to be leaders in industry, business and the professions. The selection was made with the qualifications of the individual as the primary consideration and, secondly, his stockholdings in the company."

Thus it appears from the foregoing passage of the Committee's proxy statement that Luther and Williams were the moving parties and that Gira and Petersen had nothing to do with the formation of the Committee. This impression is further sought to be created among the stockholders by the statement in the next paragraph of the Committee's proxy statement which reads in part as follows:

"They (Gira and Petersen) stated that they were not interested in waging a proxy contest but they did furnish the committee with information concerning the company including a stockholders list."

The failure to reveal the fact that Gira and Petersen made such statements if indeed they did, only after Gira had been advised that he "as such" was in no position to bring the proxy contest himself, makes the material clearly misleading under the proxy rules of the Securities and Exchange Commission (Reg. X-14A; 17 CFR §240.14a). Gira himself was obliged to admit that at the meeting at his home the subject of a proxy contest was discussed as one of a series of actions that might be instituted *in his behalf* (R. 394). The situation is further aggravated by the sentence in the Committee's proxy material that "the law firm of Vaughan, Brandlin & Baggot", in which Messrs. Brandlin and Roemer are partners, "does not represent Messrs. Gira and Petersen, nor are Messrs. Gira and Petersen members of the Committee". Certainly stockholders solicited to vote for the Committee were entitled to know that the lawyers who were organizing the Committee and were claiming to do so in behalf of Luther and Williams were the lawyers selected by the defendant Gira to advise him concerning a proxy fight and that they had advised him that it would not be wise for him "as such" to bring the proxy contest (R. 357).

The testimony and exhibits further establish the fact that the "Committee" exist in name only, that it held no meetings other than a social gathering attended by less than half of its members at the Los Angeles Country Club (R. 1710, 1711, 1713), has formulated no plans and exists only for the purpose of the proxy fight. Particular attention is invited to the testimony of the defendant Henwood

who was desc
material as t
said that the
or for any o
Committee. it
lack of them—
Industrial Co:
and which is
brief, as follo

In a teleph-
part of Janua
lin's and Roen
Brandlin said
a proxy fight
Brandlin did
volved and, ir
ed that he '
not" (Henwo
given a defi
the time cam
Henwood ind
dep. 13). In
he agreed to
Brandlin's c
knew nothing
Henwood's d
that time he
United Indu
one" (Henw
"know anyth
never receiv
statement (T
become a me

who was described in the Committee's proxy solicitation material as the chairman of the Committee. Henwood said that the Committee never met to elect him chairman, or for any other purpose. His amazing account of the Committee, its organization and activities—or, rather, the lack of them—given in his deposition testimony in United Industrial Corporation, *et ux.* v. Stanley E. Henwood, *et al.,* and which is designated part of the record herein, is, in brief, as follows.

In a telephone conversation with Brandlin, in the latter part of January, 1961 (evidently a few days after Brandlin's and Roemer's conversation with Gira at Gira's home), Brandlin said to Henwood, "How would you like to get into a proxy fight?" (Henwood dep. 9). Henwood testified that Brandlin did not mention the name of the company involved and, importantly, Henwood said that Brandlin stated that he "didn't know whether he had a client our not" (Henwood dep. 9). Henwood claims not to have given a definite answer at that time but later, when the time came that Brandlin told him "he had a client", Henwood indicated that he would join the fight (Henwood dep. 13). Importantly, Henwood testified that at the time he agreed to become a participant he didn't know who Mr. Brandlin's client was (Henwood dep. 15). He said that he knew nothing about United at the time (Henwood dep. 15). Henwood's deposition was taken on May 5, 1961 and as of that time he had "never seen a financial statement of United Industrial Corporation nor had he asked to see one" (Henwood dep. 16). As of that date, he did not "know anything about its assets or its liabilities". He had never received nor asked for a balance sheet or earning statement (Henwood dep. 17). At the time he agreed to become a member of the Committee, Henwood didn't know whether the Company was making or losing money (Henwood dep. 18) and further he did not know whether the Company had a "substantial net worth or whether it was insolvent" (Henwood dep. 18). Henwood said that he simply did a "favor for Brandlin" in "lending" his name to the Committee (Henwood dep. 19). He said the Committee had no plan or program, except to "win the proxy fight" (Henwood dep. 19). Henwood said that if the Committee should win the proxy fight, it will get together and see if it could get up a plan (Henwood dep. 20). Laconically, Henwood stated that "if any other member of either the Committee or the slate has any plans, they have not communicated them" to him (Henwood dep. 211).

It is significant that Henwood agreed to serve as chairman of the so-called Committee the day following his meeting with Gira and Petersen on February 27, 1961 (R. 287-293; 1674).

The defendants Armogida and Beshara had become stockholders in United by virtue of its acquisition of the Perry Rubber Company in which they had been large stockholders. Both of them were acquainted with Gira who had negotiated the merger (R. 2050, 2055). They were contacted by Brandlin who made a trip to Canton, Ohio for that purpose (R. 2050, 2052).

The defendant Ballance had been a stockholder in Topp Industries and was acquainted with Gira. He was also a stockholder in another company that had developed a product which Ballance was trying to sell to Perry Rubber Company, a United subsidiary. Gira had introduced Ballance to the Perry Rubber Company as his good friend (Exs. BBB, CCC). Brandlin contacted him to serve on the Committee.

The balance of the Committee was made up of persons recruited by Brandlin, Roemer, Henwood and Summers. None of them had ever held stock in United or had any other interest in the Company or any knowledge of its operations (Ex. 13).

f. Subsequent Activities of Gira and Petersen

The interest of Gira and Petersen in the proxy contest did not end upon the formation of the Committee. After they had furnished the stockholders list they met with Roemer and Brandlin on at least six occasions (R. 255, Brandlin dep. 48-68). In addition, there were numerous phone conferences (Brandlin dep. 67).

Early in February Gira and Petersen analyzed for Brandlin and Roemer the distribution of United stock and the larger stockholdings (R. 80, 372, 373; Brandlin dep. 48). At a later meeting Gira and Petersen advised Brandlin and Roemer on the details of the proposed sale by United to its subsidiary U. S. Semi-Conductor because it was felt that this transaction might be of importance in the Committee's solicitation of proxies (Brandlin dep. 49, 50). A further meeting was held with Gira, Petersen, Robert Gira and Kendrick, the lawyer whom Brandlin had recommended to Gira (Brandlin dep. 60, 66). At this meeting there was discussion of the action the Committee had instituted in Delaware to prevent the Company from adjourning the annual meeting pending the preparation of the auditors' reports (Brandlin dep. 60, 61). As we have noted above, this action was designed to take advantage of the restriction of proxy solicitation upon the part of Management until the Annual Report was available to stockholders.

A subsequent meeting was held to discuss the steps that should be taken to meet Management's claim that Gira and Petersen were connected with the Committee. At this meeting Brandlin first suggested to Gira and Petersen and their lawyer a libel suit and asked them to threaten the United Board of Directors with such an action (R. 1263, 1264; Brandlin dep. 64).

In the latter part of February Brandlin arranged a meeting between Gira and Petersen and the defendant Henwood at the Town House in Los Angeles (R. 288, 1264; Brandlin dep. 68). Brandlin had previously advised Henwood that Gira was a very high type man and had spoken well of his integrity and ability (Henwood dep. 47). At this meeting Gira gave Henwood a complete description of the Company's business and its prospects (R. 292; Brandlin dep. 68, 69). It is of some significance that the day after the meeting Henwood agreed to buy some United stock and serve on the Committee (R. 1674; Henwood dep. 54, 60, 61, 62).

The assistance rendered the Committee by Gira and Petersen was not limited to conferences. Early in February they retained Bud Lewis, a public relations consultant formerly employed by United, and issued a press release designed to answer a Wall Street Journal article on the suspension of trading of United stock (R. 632; Exs. 23 and 24). In the press release Gira and Petersen characterized the management of the Company as "interim" and expressed dissatisfaction with it (Ex. 23). Gira prepared for the Committee a comprehensive study of United (R. 400) and furnished the Committee with the so-called "Bishop reports" which purported to contain derogatory information on two of the present directors of United (R. 348; Brandlin dep. 119). In the midst of the proxy contest Gira and Peterson prepared a lengthy letter to the stockholders which was highly critical of the management of the Company (Ex. 20). Although this letter disclaimed their participation in the proxy contest, it was clearly a solicitation of proxies. The letter was not mailed when the Securities and Exchange Commission advised counsel for Gira and Petersen that it would be deemed a solicitation.

g. Timing of Libel Suit

Finally, fifteen days prior to the date of the adjourned annual meeting Gira and Petersen instituted the libel action which had originally been recommended by Brandlin at an earlier meeting (Ex. KK; R. 1263, 1264; Brandlin dep. 64). The action was not brought against the Directors of United who would have authorized the publication of the material claimed to be libellous but rather against the persons who comprised the management slate (Ex. KK). Prior to the filing of this lawsuit Gira and Petersen cleared a press release prepared by Lewis (R. 649). This release describes the proxy fight in detail and sets forth the names of the Committee's slate of directors (Ex. 19) and was designed and intended to offset the management proxy material (R. 651, 652). Although both Gira and Petersen had been advised that this press release could not be issued until it had been "cleared" with the Securities and Exchange Commission, it was in fact released by their public relations man, Lewis, without such S. E. C. clearance (R. 631).

h. Summary

The above-described activities of Gira and Petersen cannot be reconciled with the disclaimer in the Committee's proxy material (Ex. 13) of any connection with them.

Moreover, a comparison of the roles played by Gira and Petersen with the lack of interest evidenced by Luther and Williams belies the statement in the proxy material that they were the originators of this undertaking.

In keeping with the Company's status in this litigation as a nominal party, no attempt is made in this brief to make a point by point reply to the arguments advanced upon behalf of the appellants herein. An analysis of the record in the light of the appellants' contentions demonstrates that the Findings of Fact upon which the judgment is predicated are amply supported by the evidence and more than meet the standards adopted by the Federal Rules of Civil Procedure with respect to appellate review.

POINT II

Omissions from "Committee's" proxy material.

Appellants' argument that the proxy contest here involved should be considered akin to a political campaign (R. 1288) is entirely without merit. This motion has been laid to rest in a clear and succinct opinion by Chief Judge Clark of the Second Circuit in *S. E. C. v. May*, 229 F. 2d 123, 124 (2d Cir. 1956) where he stated:

> "Appellants' fundamental complaint appears to be that stockholder disputes should be viewed in the eyes of the law just as are political contests, with each side free to hurl charges with comparative unrestraint, the assumption being that the opposing side is then at liberty to refute and thus effectively deflate the 'campaign oratory' of its adversary. Such, however, was not the policy of Congress as enacted in the Securities Exchange Act. There Congress has clearly entrusted to the Commission the duty of protecting the investing public against misleading statements made in the course of a struggle for corporate control."

Rule X-14A-9 (17 CFR § 240.14a-9) of the S. E. C. provides:

> "No solicitation subject to this regulation shall be made by means of any proxy statement, form of proxy, notice of meeting, or other communication, written or oral, containing any statement which, at the time and in the light of the circumstances under which it is made, is false or misleading with respect to any material fact, or which omits to state any material fact necessary in order to make the statements therein not false or misleading or necessary to correct any statement in any earlier communication with respect to the solicitation of a proxy for the same meeting or subject matter which has become false or misleading."

The main thrust, of course, of the omissions is the failure of the Committee's proxy material to reveal the true relationship between Gira and Petersen on the one hand and the Committee and Brandlin on the other. This relationship has been developed in detail in Point I of this brief and will not be repeated here. However, we do set forth at this point a summary of the omissions. The uncontradicted testimony of Alan R. Gordon, a long time member of the staff of the Securities and Exchange Commission (R. 447), clearly and succinctly describes the patent violations of the above quoted Rule X-14A-9 (R. 693-709, 717, 761). He was asked by one of the counsel for the appellants to relate the areas of omission to disclose material facts necessary to make the statements made by the Committee not misleading (R. 693). In reply to such inquiry he testified in detail with respect to such omissions which we briefly set forth.

1. The *circumstances* under which the stockholders list was obtained by and furnished to the Committee was not disclosed (R. 695).

2. The statement in the Committee's proxy material (Ex. 13) concerning the origins of the contest states that two thousand shares of United stock had been obtained by the defendant Roemer from the defendant Yaras and that a thousand of those shares had been split among ten of the Committee's candidates. *It says that, but it says no more.* It does not state that Mr. Yaras had contacted the attorneys for the Committee as a complainant to inquire about the possibilities of a contest or other action prior to the formation of the Committee (R. 696).

3. The fact that Gira and Petersen issued a press release in February, 1961 through Mr. Lewis relating to the Company's affairs at about the time of the inception of the contest is not disclosed (R. 696).

4. The relationship between Messrs. Gira and Petersen and the law firm of Vaughan, Brandlin and Baggot is not adequately disclosed in accordance with the facts as previously outlined (R. 696, 697).

5. Roemer's close and intimate association with Gira and Petersen is omitted (R. 704).

6. The proxy statement of the Committee fails to disclose that the defendant Summers had been contacted by Petersen and referred to Vaughan, Brandlin and Baggot and that Summers in turn had suggested to the defendant Dumont to get in touch with such firm (R. 707).

7. Such proxy material should have disclosed that toward the end of February, 1961 a meeting was arranged by Brandlin between Henwood and Gira and Petersen. At the time Henwood was not yet the chairman of the Committee. The following day, however, he agreed to serve in that position, to buy stock in United and to provide funds for the waging of a proxy contest (R. 708).

8. The proxy statement should have disclosed that the steps or acts necessary to wage a proxy contest had been performed by the law firm of Vaughan, Brandlin and Baggot, namely, seeking out and finding persons to stand as members of the slate, arranging the financing of the contest, the payment of certain bills of the Committee, authorizing the solicitation material which was used by the Committee, and in general managing the contest (R. 708).

9. The proxy material should have further disclosed that the nominal chairman of the Committee, Mr. Henwood, had had little participation in these matters and even less knowledge of them; that the Committee, so-called, in actuality consists of the persons found or selected by others to stand as a slate for election to office plus two other individuals, Luther and Williams. The Committee, *as such*, had not itself conducted the contest (R. 708).

10. Not only does the Committee's material fail to disclose the circumstances surrounding the obtaining of the stockholders list but further fails to disclose how the law firm rid itself of the list (R. 761).

The foregoing touches but the highlights of the omissions. There are other and equally material omissions but for the purposes of this brief and the demonstration being made at this point, the examples that are enumerated make it sufficiently clear that there have not only been omissions but there has been a deliberate pattern of material omissions from the Committee's proxy material.

This case does not turn on the narrow line of whether Gira and Petersen are formal or acknowledged members of the Committee but on the question of whether they have materially contributed to or assisted in bringing about the proxy contest, whether they are admitted members of the

Committee or not. To say that Gira and Petersen are not participants in the proxy contest and have not made solicitations is merely to pervert the rules of the Securities and Exchange Commission. Each rule was adopted with a particular purpose in mind. One may not avoid the impact of the rule by becoming a secret or undisclosed member of a committee; nor may one avoid the duties that fall upon a participant by setting the committee in operation and then disavowing that fact and disavowing all further activities. *Central Foundry Co. v. Gondelman*, 166 F. Supp. 429 (S. D. N. Y. 1958).

Rule X-14A-11(b), 17 CFR § 240.14a-11(b) provides that a participant, among others, includes any member of a committee or group, and any person *whether or not named as a member* who, acting alone or with one or more other persons, directly or indirectly, takes the initiative *in organizing,* directing or financing any such committee or group and it also includes any person who solicits proxies. Rule X-14A-1, 17 CFR § 240.14a-1 includes within the definition of "solicit" and "solicitation" the furnishing of a communication to security holders under circumstances reasonably calculated to result in the procurement, withholding or revocation of a proxy. Gira's press releases of February 7, 1961 (Ex. 23) and July 12, 1961 (Ex. 19) were designed for the purpose of procuring proxies for the Committee and the withholding of proxies from Management (R. 641, 642). The seed from which the Committee sprouted was planted in Brandlin's office by Gira. Gira's press agent in this instance was one Bud Lewis who testified that both the February 7, 1961 press release referring to the management of United as "interim management" and the press release with respect to Gira's carefully timed libel suit of July 12, 1961 were both "cleared" by Gira (R. 637,

638, 649). Lewis further testified that the February 7th press release was an accurate statement of Gira's intention (R. 641, 642) and that at the time the release was issued Lewis desired to be employed by United. The only way that he could be employed by United was for Gira and the Committee to gain control of the Company. The press release was addressed to the stockholders of United with the avowed intent to offset Management's proxy solicitation (R. 651, 652). It is important to note that Gira's libel suit was timed in such a manner that the press release would be published fifteen days prior to the scheduled stockholders meeting. The complaint in such libel action is directed not against the incumbent members of the Company's Board of Directors who were the individuals who would have authorized the dissemination of the Company's proxy material, but instead the libel suit is directed against the nominees of Management (Ex. KK).

The fact that the suit is directed against the nominees, of course, serves the purpose of Gira very neatly, much more so than if it were directed against individuals who were not part of Management's slate but nevertheless were incumbent directors.

Appellants in order to comply with the proxy rules should have made the disclosures required of them.

POINT III

Trial Court granted appropriate relief.

The judgment of the trial Court contains four operative paragraphs which provide:

1. The Committee, its proxies, agents, employees and attorneys, Gira and Petersen are enjoined from directly

or indirectly soliciting proxies of stockholders of United unless certain specified omissions from earlier material are contained therein and unless certain specified misrepresentations in such earlier material are corrected (C. T. 238, 239)*, and from voting any proxies obtained prior to the entry of the decree (C. T. 239, 240).

2. Gira and Petersen are directed to file a corrected Schedule 14B as required by Rule X-14A-11, 17 CFR § 240.14a-11 (C. T. 240).

3. United, its officers, directors, employees and attorneys are enjoined from holding any stockholders meeting until 34 days after the entry of the decree** (C. T. 240).

4. The complaint is dismissed without prejudice as to the members of the Committee other than its proxies and Gira and Petersen (C. T. 240, 241).

It appears that the appellants have appealed from the first two operative paragraphs of the judgment; the preceding points of this brief have developed the violations of the Securities Exchange Act of 1934, 15 U. S. C. §78a, et seq. and the proxy rules promulgated thereunder. Reg. X-14A, 17 CFR 240.14a.

There is authority for the relief granted by the Court. In *Central Foundry Co. v. Gondelman*, 166 F. Supp. 429, 446 (S. D. N. Y. 1958) *mod. sub nom. S. E. C. v. Central Foundry Co.*, 167 F. Supp. 821 (S. D. N. Y. 1958), in consolidated actions brought against an insurgent committee by both management and the Commission, the Court declared the proxies void, adjourned the meeting to permit ample time for resolicitation, and spelled out precisely the

---

* C T refers to Volume I of the Transcript of the Record (Clerk's Transcript)

** This Court has enjoined the holding of such meeting until its further order

corrective statement to be included in the next piece of proxy material. The Court ordered that the opposition committee clearly state in the next piece of proxy material (1) that the resolicitation had become necessary because of the Court's determination in an action brought by the company and the 'S. E. C. that the committee's earlier solicitations, written and oral, had been materially misleading and unlawful, and (2) that the statements in an earlier letter of the management to the effect that a referee had recommended that the organizer of the committee be exonerated from his disbarment had been included because the S. E. C. had so insisted on the basis of false information given to it by the committee. The Court adopted this procedure after having rejected the procedure which would have permitted the defendant committee to merely distribute a correction. The Court thought that this was not the relief best calculated to protect investors, because it would place the onus on the stockholders to revoke their proxies. See also 2 Loss, Securities Regulation 956-960 (2d ed. 1961).

We note at this point that the Committee claims to have had approximately 1,100,000 votes after its third mailing (R. 1293), and as a result became, as they put it very cooperative with the Securities and Exchange Commission, and obeyed its rules. What the appellants fail to disclose in their testimony and argument are the facts that these proxies were solicited by the use of false and misleading proxy material and that, moreover, these proxies were obtained at a time when United had not commenced to solicit proxies nor had forms of proxies on behalf of management been mailed to its stockholders (Exs 13, 14). The form of proxy was not mailed by management until June 26, 1961 (Ex. 14), whereas the Committee had already at that time mailed its so-called report No. 1 dated March 27, 1961, its report No. 2, and its report No. 3 dated May 26, 1961 (Ex. 13). There were eligible 2,642,148 votes to be cast at the stockholders meeting (Ex. 14). Since management commenced its solicitation of proxies it has received substantially in excess of 1,200,000 and the proxies of the Committee have been substantially reduced by those running to management revoking the earlier ones held by the Committee.

Needless to say the proxy rules of the Securities and Exchange Commission must be meticulously followed, whether one has what it considers sufficient proxies to carry the day, or whether it is merely commencing its solicitation. In any event, it is amply demonstrated that the appellants have flagrantly violated the rules and the number of proxies they hold is of no consequence.

The relief formulated by the Court permitting the Committee to resolicit is a remedy that they cannot complain of. If all the facts are revealed to the stockholders and the Committee is given an opportunity to resolicit, they cannot be injured. As wrong-doers the relief granted accords to the appellants an opportunity that equity does not generally reserve for wrong-doers.

The trial Court in its decision (C. T. 186) stated its reason for dismissing the complaint without prejudice as to certain of the defendants. Such defendants, it stated, were "shielded from knowledge of the misleading nature of the solicitation materials distributed in their names." Although scienter is not a requirement under the S. E. C. proxy rules, the Court, sitting in equity, felt that in its discretion the relief sought by the Securities and Exchange Commission could be adequately accomplished by the restraint placed upon the Committee, its proxies, agents, employees and attorneys. Rule 65(d) of the Federal Rules of Civil Procedure of course provides that every order granting an injunction is binding upon "the parties to the action, their officers, agents, servants, employees, and attorneys, and upon those persons in active concert or participation with them who receive actual notice of the order." Thus it is clear that the parties with respect to whom the complaint was dismissed were not even indispensable parties at the commencement of the action but were merely proper parties. There is serious doubt whether such individuals have standing to make this appeal. *Bryan v. Smith,* 174 F. 2d 212, 214 (7th Cir. 1949).

CONCLUSION

It is submitted that the trial Court properly found that the Committee failed to make adequate disclosures under the proxy rules and as a result thereof the proxies heretofore obtained by the Committee were properly invalidated. There remains no doubt from a reading of the record that Gira and Petersen were the prime movers behind the Committee and they in fact planted its seed.

Counsel for the Committee have made the argument that Gira is not seeking re-employment by United. Whatever the fact may be in this regard, the Court's attention is invited to the fact that United has brought action against Gira and Petersen among other things to recover substantial sums of money as a result of alleged wrongdoing on the part of Gira and Petersen which it is claimed damaged United. Moreover, Gira and Petersen are named defendants in numerous stockholders derivative suits pending in both New York and Delaware for alleged wrongs committed against United. Accordingly, the defendants Gira and Petersen have motives more powerful than mere employment to see that management of United is in hands friendly to them. A reading of the Committee's proxy solicitation material will make clear that neither the Committee nor its slate has any disposition to vigorously assert the claims of United against the defendants Gira and Petersen.

For the foregoing reasons the judgment of the District Court should be affirmed.

Respectfully submitted,

RAICHLE, MOORE, BANNING AND WEISS,
*Attorneys for Appellee United Industrial
Corporation.*

FRANK G. RAICHLE
JAMES O. MOORE, JR.
RALPH L. HALPERN
Of Counsel

In The

United States Court of Appeals

For the Ninth Circuit

No. 17595

Alsco Storm Windows, Inc.,

Appellant

vs.

United States of America,

Appellee

Alsco Northwest, Inc.,

Appellant

vs.

United States of America,

Appellee

REPLY BRIEF FOR THE APPELLANTS

Joseph J. Lyman
1700 K Street, N.W.
Washington, D. C.
Attorney for Appellants

Hamblen, Gilbert & Brooke
Paulson Building
Spokane, Washington
Of Counsel

FILED

₁ ℣ 3 1 1962

Wilson · Epes Printing Co. · RE 7-6002 · Washington 1. D. C.

FRANK H. SCHMID, CLERK

INDEX

In The

United States Court of Appeals

For the Ninth Circuit

No. 17595

ALSCO STORM WINDOWS, INC.,
Appellant

vs.

UNITED STATES OF AMERICA,
Appellee

ALSCO NORTHWEST, INC.,
Appellant

vs.

UNITED STATES OF AMERICA,
Appellee

REPLY BRIEF FOR THE APPELLANTS

Analysis of Defendant's Cases

The defendant-appellee has raised no serious issue of law or fact in its brief. However, a brief discussion of some of the cases cited and relied upon is warranted.

It is an endless and unprofitable task to compare the details of one case with the details of another in order to establish that the conclusion of the evidence in one should be adopted in the other.

The defendant has cited a number of cases to support its contention that the installers, on the record facts and findings here, were employees under the statutes and regulations involved.

Particular emphasis was placed on the decision *Westover* v. *Stockholders Publishing Co.*, 237 F.2d 948 (CA-9) (Appellee's Brief p. 14). The category of workers involved "route district men" who handled subscription home deliveries of a newspaper in the city areas, and "dealers" who handled home deliveries and single copy sales distribution in suburban areas, rather than skilled mechanics in the building trades. Various factors of detailed control existed in *Westover* which compelled the conclusion that the workers concerned were "employees." Some of these were: (1) a written contract governed the relationship and set out the duties and obligations of each party; (2) the workers were required to canvas an area designated by the taxpayer with a frequency determined by the taxpayer; (3) the workers were required to be available at such times and places as the company designated to pick up papers brought to them; (4) carrier boys selected by the company helped the workers here; (5) they were required to maintain accurate and up-to-date lists of subscribers and their addresses which were to be available to the taxpayer on demand and not to be given to any other person; (6) they were constantly under the taxpayer's supervision concerning their activities; (7) the taxpayer could fix the prices the workers charged, and guaranteed them minimum weekly net earnings thus in effect supplying the floor and ceiling of their incomes; (8) the workers had no investment in the facilities for doing the work. None of these factors are evident with respect to the installers. The installers were masters of their own time; they could earn a great deal or little, depending on their desire to work; they had no obligation beyond the job at hand; upon completion of one job they could take another, take none, work elsewhere and later return to plaintiff without any impairment in the relationship. They had an investment in the tools and equipment necessary for the performance of the work, they were free to hire and control their own helpers without interference from the plaintiffs; they could combine with others or work alone as they chose and divide the earnings as they decided without interference from the plaintiffs. All this is indication of a freedom not even suggested in *Westover*.

The mere fact that the workers in *Westover* were not controlled as to the details of their work, standing alone, is not determinative as to their employment status. Control becomes an important and perhaps a deciding factor when the other elements such as freedom to select jobs, being master over one's own time, investment in the tools of performance, freedom to hire and direct helpers and freedom to work for others are also evident. In *Westover* these other elements were lacking. Want of direction and control in and of itself would not make an independent contractor out of an employee. The case at bar, however, has numerous elements depicting freedom of the worker in addition to plaintiffs' lack of control over the manner and means of his performance. The difference is essential. The difference makes *Westover's* workers employees and *Alsco's* independent contractors. Nor did *Westover, supra,* suggest that it had overruled the holding of this Court in *Broderick, Inc.* v. *Squire,* 163 F.2d 980 (CA-9), that real estate salesmen were independent contractors (see Appellant's Brief pp. 33, 39); nor did it overrule *Anglim* v. *Empire Star Mines, Ltd.,* 129 F.2d 914 (CA-9), which held miners to be independent contractors (see Appellants' Brief, pp. 39, 40). The differences in categories of workers compel different decisions on the same issue of law.

Great reliance is placed upon the Massachusetts District Court's decision in *Security Roofing & Construction Co.* v.

United States, 163 F. Supp. 794, because it is an "applicator" case, holding them to be employees. (See Appellee's Brief, p. 16) However, that decision did not propose to overrule four other "applicator" cases decided in the same Circuit but by different judges. They were *Metropolitan Roofing & Modernizing Co.* v. *United States,* 125 F. Supp. 670 (Mass.); *American Homes of N. E., Inc.* v. *United States,* 173 F. Supp. 857 (Mass.); *Jagolinzer* v. *United States,* 150 F. Supp. 489 (R.I.) and *Thorson* v. *United States,* 173 F. Supp. 65 (Mass.) aff'd. 282 F.2d 157 (CA-1). Only *Thorson* was decided subsequent to *Security.* The other three were prior. All were decided in favor of the taxpayers. The United States Court of Claims distinguished a Spokane, Washington, case, *Edwards* v. *United States,* 168 F. Supp. 955 (Ct. Cl.) from *Security* in holding "installers" to be independent contractors. Some of the distinguishing features in *Edwards* which are also evident in the case here were: (1) *Security's* mechanics all devoted years of work to the one company. Here the installers varied from two to thirty and only two at most were "regulars." (2) *Security's* men were specifically prohibited from doing any additional work of any kind for a customer, and could not resolve even a minor problem without consulting the taxpayer. Here there were no such restrictions ever contemplated. (3) There were strict requirements that *Security's* men refer business to the office, here there was no such requirement, but it was optional if they wanted to earn a small commission. (4) *Security* fixed the rate of pay regardless of difficulty, here there was some basis for negotiation in unusual matters which might arise on a job. (5) *Security* hired a number of inexperienced men which required a supervisor to be on the site constantly, here only experienced men were considered by the plaintiffs and no interference was anticipated unless the desired result was not forthcoming. (6) *Security* moved men about and split crews indiscriminately, here a man or crew usually finished a job before going to another, but there were rare occasions where the installers did go to other jobs and this was at the "request" of the plaintiffs. (7) In *Security* there was evidence of indiscriminate discharge, there was no evidence of it here and none was practiced as the arrangement was actually carried out. (8) The *Security* applicators felt compelled to take all jobs offered, good or bad, as a condition of employment, here the installers rejected unsuitable jobs without a hint of recrimination.

It is noteworthy that Judge Aldrich who wrote the opinion in *Security, supra,* as a District Court judge was later elevated to the First Circuit Court of Appeals. As an Appellate Court judge he concurred in the First Circuit's opinion in *United States* v. *Thorson,* 282 F.2d 157, which held applicators to be independent contractors on facts similar to those here. In *Thorson,* the *Security* case was readily distinguished.

The defendant seized upon isolated judicial phrases to sustain its position here. (Govt. Brief p. 16) The defendant cites *E. F. Williams* v. *United States,* 139 F. Supp. 875 (NDNY) at p. 878. ". . . it appears that the same can be only performed by an experienced roofer in a manner which is generally acceptable," and apparently concludes that this factor alone led Judge Brennan to find that *Williams'* "roofers" were employees. Those same words were used by the same judge in another applicator case where he held they were independent contractors, *Silver* v. *United States,* 131 F. Supp. 209 (NDNY). At p. 211 Judge Brennan stated:

> "It is further evidence that the work of the applicator was of such a nature that it could only, or at least most conveniently, be performed in a generally accepted manner."

The *E. F. Williams* case, *supra,* by no means overruled *Silver.* It comes as no surprise to the government that

Judge Brennan specifically distinguished *Williams* from *Silver*, although the isolated language in *Williams* deemed controlling by the government here was present in both cases. In *Williams, supra,* 139 F. Supp. at p. 887 the Court pointed out:

> "It would appear to be without profit to again discuss these statutes, regulations and decided cases which are referred to in the decision of *Silver* v. *U. S., supra.*
>
> The decision indicates in sufficient detail the guides to the conclusion to be made here.
>
> "Assuming that the *Silver* case was correctly decided and that the same general situation is involved, a similar decision does not necessarily follow because of factual differences."

The government here would torture the Findings of Fact of the Court below and reshape them to fit *E. F. Williams, supra,* in an effort to sustain its position. It's reliance on *Williams* means that the government would prefer that the Findings of Fact by the Court below should have been other than as found. It would seem that the government, as Appellee, is arguing the proposition that the facts found are "clearly erroneous." It is indeed an odd position for the prevailing party below to take on appeal. The government would suggest that the following facts in *Williams* be deemed controlling here: (1) The taxpayer furnished the equipment necessary for the performance of the work; (2) almost 50 per cent of the jobs were concerned with work paid at hourly rates necessitating a close watch on the time consumed in doing the work; (3) helpers were sent to the job by the taxpayer, who were paid at hourly rates fixed by the taxpayer and the roofer had no control over the helper; (4) Friday was "pay-day" with no exceptions. However, a loan might be negotiated out of time on request; (5) many of the jobs were flat-roofing, requiring only a mop and hot tar, pay being on an hourly rate; (6) all of the men had been with the company 24 to 27 years. None of these facts were found by the District Court below here.

Here, the two "regulars" had the longest stay, but all others, about 30 or so, came and went; all jobs here were paid on a job-to-job basis at piece-work rates with an insignificant co-mingling of hourly rate work; an installer here could pick up his earnings at any time or wait to the end of a week or two weeks if he desired; the installers hired and fired their own helpers and completely controlled their activities; the installers furnished all their own tools and equipment for the performance of the jobs. These factors and others found by the Court below clearly distinguish *E. F. Williams, supra,* from the case at bar. The single factor of control of details of the work was absent in both cases. That element standing alone would not make *Williams'* "roofers" independent contractors. But if those same roofers had the freedom of choice and movement together with an investment in the equipment, enjoyed by Alsco's installers, their status would have tended toward that of independent contractors.

Another applicator case relied upon by the government (Appellee Brief pp. 16-17) is *Ben* v. *United States,* 139 F. Supp. 883, aff'd 241 F.2d 127 (CA-2). This was also Judge Brennan's case. Again the government seized upon isolated language (Appellee Brief pp. 16-17):

> "The element of freedom from control in the manner of the performance of the work * * * loses much of its significance when the skill of the worker is relied upon in the accomplishment of the particular task."

In *Farm & Home Modernization Co., Inc.* v. *United States,* 138 F. Supp. 423 (NDNY), decided on the same day by the same judge, held "installers" to be independent contractors. As to freedom from control the same Court said at p. 426:

"No inspections of the work were made by the plaintiff. * * * The plaintiff appeared to rely upon a completion slip signed by the owner upon completion of the job to indicate a satisfactory performance thereof and also upon the experience of the applicator to insure the performance of the work in accordance with the contract."

Again Judge Brennan distinguished the *Silver* case while deciding that *Ben's* applicators were employees. In *Ben, supra,* 139 F. Supp. at p. 886:

"It would appear without profit to again discuss the statutes, regulations and decided cases which are referred to in the decision of *Silver* v. *U. S., supra.* They are referred to in that decision in sufficient detail to indicate the guide posts to the conclusion to be made here. Factually the two cases differ in several important aspects even though they may be considered as embodying the same general situation."

In *Ben,* the Court found that all applicators were expected to take any job offered to them as a condition of obtaining future work. A failure to accept any job offered resulted in cutting off work summarily. Any personal trait of *Ben's* applicators deemed offensive, apart from faulty work, was cause for dismissal. The continuous presence of the applicators was expected by *Ben,* which restricted their performances elsewhere. Here was also a high rate of co-mingling of unit price and hourly rates on many jobs performed. On appeal the Second Circuit affirmed *per curiam,* 241 F.2d 127, but felt compelled to say that the case was "a close one." (At p. 128) The case at bar shows none of the restrictions by plaintiffs on the installers that were imposed by *Ben* on its applicators.

In the case at bar, the Alsco installers could reject jobs without fear of recrimination; there was no co-mingling of unit pay and hourly rate pay and some 30 installers came and went indiscriminately except for one or two "regulars."

The case
v. *Higgins,*
here. (App'
signed cont
many provi:
and travele
of the contr
relationship

Walling v
is not in po
Labor Stand
to say in *W*
at p. 150:

" * * *

[Fair L
ployee e
under ot
[citing c
* * *

The definiti
Acts require

Bonded I.
131 F. Supp
bearing on i
to blow insi
the taxpaye
clock and w
supervised
on teaching

A number
F.2d 54 (C.
DC), *Unite*
Hearst Pul
are cited as

None of t
involved he

The case *Ringling Bros.-Barnum & Bailey Com. Shows*
v. *Higgins*, 189 F.2d 865 (CA-2) is readily distinguishable
here. (Appellee Brief p. 18) The circus performers had
signed contracts for a specified period which imposed
many provisions limiting their activities. They ate, slept
and traveled with the show as a unit during the period
of the contract. No such restrictions are apparent in the
relationship between the installers and the plaintiffs here.

Walling v. *American Needlecrafts*, 139 F.2d 60 (CA-6)
is not in point. (Appellee Brief p. 19) This is a Fair
Labor Standards Act case. The Supreme Court had this
to say in *Walling* v. *Portland Terminal Co.*, 330 U.S. 148
at p. 150:

> " * * * in determining who are 'employees' under the
> [Fair Labor Standards] Act, the common law em-
> ployee categories or employer-employee classifications
> under other statutes are not of controlling significance.
> [citing cases] This Act contains its own definitions,
> * * *."

The definition of "employee" under the FICA and FUTA
Acts requires more definite tests.

Bonded Insulation & Construction Co. v. *United States*,
131 F. Supp. 635 (N.J.) (Appellee Brief, p. 19) has little
bearing on the issue here. There the workers undertook
to blow insulation materials into existing houses by using
the taxpayer's machines and tools. They punched a time
clock and were paid on an hourly rate. Their work was
supervised constantly by a company official who insisted
on teaching the men how to do the work.

A number of other cases, *United States* v. *Kane,* 171
F.2d 54 (CA-8), *Grace* v. *Magruder,* 148 F.2d 679 (CA
DC), *United States* v. *Vogue,* 145 F.2d 609 (CA-4), and
Hearst Publications v. *United States,* 70 F. Supp. 666,
are cited as controlling in Appellee's Brief at pp. 18-19.

None of these cases concerned the category of workers
involved here. Also it is significant that these cases were

decided prior to the "1948 amendment" which re-affirmed
the congressional intent that the common law control test
should weigh heavily to decide who were "employees"
under the statutes. This legislation specifically rejected
the "economic reality" test as determinative of who are
"employees" under Sections 3121(d) and 3306(i), Internal
Revenue Code. It would seem that the pre-1948 cases
which recognized any test which expanded the definition
of "employee" beyond the common law control test are
without significance.

Conclusion

"The appetite for taxes is not so voracious, the com-
mands of the statute are not so inexorable, as to require
the doing of an injustice when there is open another
course, if followed, will lead neither to evasion by the
taxpayer nor extortion by the Government." *Hilpert* v.
Commissioner, 151 F.2d 929, 933 (CA-5, 1945).

In view of the foregoing, the Conclusions of Law and
Judgment of the District Court should be reversed.

Respectfully submitted,

JOSEPH J. LYMAN
1700 K Street, N.W.
Washington, D. C.
Attorney for Appellants

HAMBLEN, GILBERT & BROOKE
Paulson Building
Spokane, Washington
Of Counsel

No. 17595

United States
Court of Appeals
for the Ninth Circuit

ALSCO STORM WINDOWS, INC.,

Appellant,

vs.

UNITED STATES OF AMERICA,

Appellee.

ALSCO NORTHWEST, INC.,

Appellant,

vs.

UNITED STATES OF AMERICA,

Appellee.

Transcript of Record

Appeals from the United States District Court for the
Eastern District of Washington,
Northern Division.

Phillips & Van Orden Co., 4th & Berry, S F , Calif.—Rec 12/20/61—Printed 1/15/62

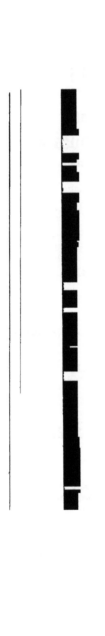

No. 17595

United States
Court of Appeals
for the Ninth Circuit

ALSCO STORM WINDOWS, INC.,

                                       Appellant,

vs.

UNITED STATES OF AMERICA,

                                       Appellee.

ALSCO NORTHWEST, INC.,

                                       Appellant,

vs.

UNITED STATES OF AMERICA,

                                       Appellee.

Transcript of Record

**Appeals from the United States District Court for the
Eastern District of Washington,
Northern Division.**

Phillips & Van Orden Co , 4th & Berry, S F , Calif —Rec 12/20/61—Printed 1/15/62

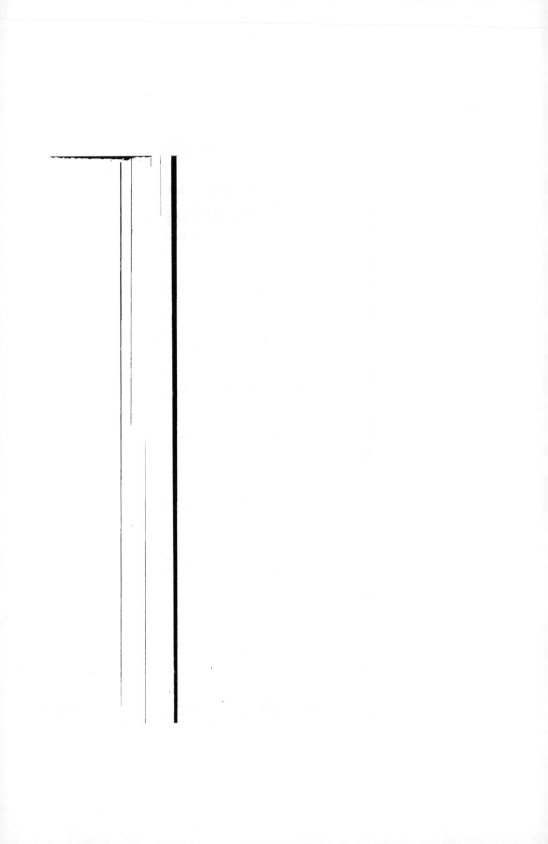

INDEX

[Clerk's Note: When deemed likely to be of an important nature, errors or doubtful matters appearing in the original certified record are printed literally in italic; and, likewise, cancelled matter appearing in the original certified record is printed and cancelled herein accordingly. When possible, an omission from the text is indicated by printing in italic the two words between which the omission seems to occur.]

INDEX

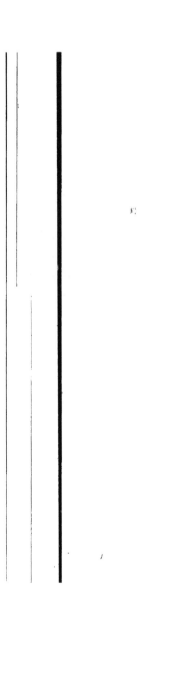

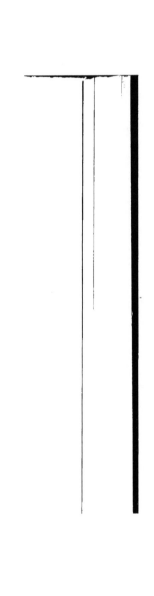

NAMES AND ADDRESSES OF ATTORNEYS OF RECORD

JOSEPH J. LYMAN,
Attorney at Law,
1700 "K" Street, N.W.,
Washington 6, D. C.;

FRED GILBERT,
HAMBLEN, GILBERT & BROOKE,
Attorneys at Law,
912 Paulsen Building,
Spokane, Washington,

Attorneys for Appellants.

FRANK R. FREEMAN,
U. S. Attorney,

CARROLL D. GRAY,
Asst. U. S. Attorney,
Room 334 Federal Building,
Spokane 10, Washington,

Attorneys for Appellees.

In the United States District Court for the Eastern
District of Washington, Northern Division

Civil Action No. 1882

ALSCO STORM WINDOWS, INC., for Its Own
Account, and as Transferee of the Assets of
Vent-Air Awnings, Inc., North 328 Fancher
Way, Spokane 62, Washington,

Plaintiff,

vs.

UNITED STATES OF AMERICA,

Defendant.

COMPLAINT FOR REFUND OF EMPLOY-
MENT TAXES ERRONEOUSLY PAID
AND COLLECTED

1. This Court has jurisdiction in this action
under the provisions of Section 1346(a)(1), Title
28, United States Code.

2. The plaintiff is a corporation doing business
in the State of Washington. The defendant is the
United States of America. Plaintiff, by this action,
seeks to recover federal employment taxes (federal
insurance contributions and federal unemployment
taxes) erroneously paid to and collected by the
defendant.

3. The plaintiff filed its Employer's Quarterly
Federal Tax Return (Treasury Department Form
941) with the Director of Internal Revenue at Se-

attle, Washington, and erroneously paid federal insurance contributions taxes on certain persons listed thereon.

4. The plaintiff filed its Annual Return of Excise Taxes on Employers of Four or More Individuals under the Federal Unemployment Tax Act (Treasury Department Form 940) with the Director of Internal Revenue at Seattle, Washington, and erroneously paid federal unemployment compensation taxes to the defendant on the aforesaid persons.

5. The persons upon whom the said taxes were erroneously paid were not employees within the meaning and coverage of Sections 3121(d) and 3306(i), Title 26, United States Code, in that, no employer-employee relationship existed between such persons and the plaintiff within the meaning of the aforesaid sections.

6. For many years, and particularly during 1955 through 1958, the period of this claim, the plaintiff in pursuing its home improvement business would obtain work orders from home owners and other individual property owners for the purpose of affecting certain structural improvements on their premises. The plaintiff corporation then contracted with various skilled mechanics or installers to perform the necessary structural improvement work. The plaintiff contracted with such installers and mechanics under circumstances and conditions where the relationship of employer and employee, as defined under the usual common law rules appli-

cable, did not in fact exist. The relation between the corporation and the mechanics or installers was that of principal and independent contractor.

7. The plaintiff having been informed that it was erroneously paying the aforesaid employment taxes on the earnings of the mechanics and installers, on April 8, 1958, April 28, 1958, and April 13, 1959, filed claims for refund of federal insurance contributions and federal unemployment taxes so erroneously paid. The claims were timely filed with the Director of Internal Revenue at Seattle, Washington, on Treasury Department Forms 843, in accordance with the provisions of Sections 6511(a) and 6513(c)(1), Title 26, United States Code. The reasons for allowing the claims were set out in detail, the substance being that the employment taxes were erroneously paid to the defendant on the mechancis' and installers' earnings though they were not, in fact, employees within the meaning of the provisions of Sections 3121(d) and 3306(i), Title 26, United States Code.

8. The Commissioner of Internal Revenue, through his duly authorized delegate, disallowed the claims for refund by letters, dated July 29, 1959, and in addition, plaintiff executed Treasury Department Forms 2297, Waiver of Registered Mail Notification of Disallowance, following the Commissioner's letters of disallowance. This action is timely filed in accordance with the provisions of Sections 6532(a) and 7422(a), Title 26, United States Code.

In any event, more than six months have expired since the initial filing of the aforesaid claims as provided in Section 6532(a), Title 26, United States Code.

9.   The plaintiff claims a refund of federal insurance contributions taxes erroneously paid for the period January 1, 1955, to December 31, 1958, in the amount of $986.53, or such greater amount as may be allowed by law.

10.   The plaintiff claims a refund of federal unemployment taxes for the years 1955, 1956 and 1958 in the respective amounts of $36.23, $37.94 and $16.59, making a total of $90.76, or such greater amount as may be allowed by law.

Wherefore, the plaintiff prays that judgment be granted in the total amount of $1,077.29, together with interest and statutory costs and such additional amounts as may be allowed by law.

/s/ WILLARD J. ROE,
Attorney for Plaintiff.

/s/ JOSEPH J. LYMAN,
Of Counsel.

[Endorsed]: Filed November 10, 1959.

In the United States District Court for the Eastern
District of Washington, Northern Division

Civil Action No. 1883

ALSCO NORTHWEST, INC., a Corporation,
North 328 Fancher Way, Spokane 62, Washington,

Plaintiff,

vs.

UNITED STATES OF AMERICA,

Defendant.

COMPLAINT FOR REFUND OF EMPLOY-
MENT TAXES ERRONEOUSLY PAID
AND COLLECTED

1. This Court has jurisdiction in this action
under the provisions of Section 1346(a)(1), Title
28, United States Code.

2. The plaintiff is a corporation doing business
in the State of Washington. The defendant is the
United States of America. Plaintiff, by this action,
seeks to recover federal employment taxes (federal
insurance contribution taxes and federal unemployment taxes) erroneously paid to and collected by the
defendant.

3. The plaintiff filed its Employer's Quarterly
Federal Tax Return (Treasury Department Form
941) with the Director of Internal Revenue at Seattle, Washington, and erroneously paid federal

insurance contributions taxes on certain persons listed thereon.

4. The plaintiff filed its Annual Return of Excise Taxes on Employers of Four or More Individuals under the Federal Unemployment Tax Act (Treasury Department Form 940) with the Director of Internal Revenue at Seattle, Washington, and erroneously paid federal unemployment compensation taxes to the defendant on the aforesaid persons.

5. The persons upon whom the said taxes were erroneously paid were not employees within the meaning and coverage of Sections 3121(d) and 3306(i), Title 26, United States Code, in that, no employer-employee relationship existed between such persons and the plaintiff within the meaning of the aforesaid sections.

6. For many years, and particularly during 1954, through 1958, the period of this claim, the plaintiff in pursuing its home improvement business would obtain work orders from home owners and other individual property owners for the purpose of affecting certain structural improvements on their premises. The plaintiff corporation then contracted with various skilled mechanics or installers to perform the necessary structural improvement work. The plaintiff contracted with such installers and mechanics under circumstances and conditions where a relationship of employer and employee, as defined under the usual common law rules appli-

cable, did in fact not exist. The relation between the corporation and the mechanics or installers was that of principal and independent contractor.

7. The plaintiff having been informed that it was erroneously paying the aforesaid employment taxes on the earnings of the mechanics and installers, on October 23, 1957, December 3, 1957 and April 14, 1959, filed claims for refund of federal insurance contributions and federal unemployment taxes so erroneously paid. The claims were timely filed with the Director of Internal Revenue at Seattle, Washington, on Treasury Department Forms 843, in accordance with the provisions of Sections 6511(a) and 6513(c)(1), Title 26, United States Code. The reasons for allowing the claims were set out in detail, the substance being that the employment taxes were erroneously paid to the defendant on the mechanics' and installers' earnings though they were not, in fact, employees within the meaning of the provisions of Sections 3121(d) and 3306(i), Title 26, United States Code.

8. The Commissioner of Internal Revenue, through his duly authorized delegate, disallowed the claims for refund by letters, dated July 29, 1959, and in addition, plaintiff executed Treasury Department Forms 2297, Waiver of Registered Mail Notification of Disallowance, following the Commissioner's letters of disallowance. This action is timely filed in accordance with the provisions of Sections 6532(a) and 7422(a), Title 26, United States Code. In any event, more than six months have expired since the

initial filing of the aforesaid claims as provided in Section 6532(a), Title 26, United States Code.

9. The plaintiff claims a refund of federal insurance contributions taxes erroneously paid for the period ending September 30, 1954, through March 31, 1958 in the amount of $3,053.37, or such greater amount as may be allowed by law.

10. The plaintiff claims a refund of federal unemployment taxes for the calendar years 1955, 1956 and 1957 in the respective amounts of $100.13, $138.17 and $89.92, making a total of $328.22, or such greater amount as may be allowed by law.

Wherefore, the plaintiff prays that judgment be granted in the total amount of $3,381.59, together with interest and statutory costs and such additional amounts as may be allowed by law.

/s/ WILLARD J. ROE,
Attorney for Plaintiff.

/s/ JOSEPH J. LYMAN,
Of Counsel.

[Endorsed]: Filed November 10, 1959.

———

[Title of District Court and Cause.]

Civil No. 1882

ANSWER

For an answer to plaintiff's complaint, **defendant** admits, denies and alleges as follows:

I.

Defendant admits the allegations contained in paragraph 1 of the plaintiff's complaint.

II.

Defendant denies each and every allegation contained in paragraph 2 of plaintiff's complaint.

III.

Defendant denies each and every allegation contained in paragraph 3 of plaintiff's complaint.

IV.

Defendant denies each and every allegation contained in paragraph 4 of plaintiff's complaint.

V.

Defendant denies each and every allegation contained in paragraph 5 of plaintiff's complaint.

VI.

Answering paragraph 6 of plaintiff's complaint, defendant does not have sufficient information to form a belief as to the truth of the allegations set forth in said paragraph 6 and therefore denies each and every allegation contained therein.

VII.

Defendant denies each and every allegation contained in paragraph 7 of plaintiff's complaint, except that defendant admits that a claim for refund was filed.

VIII.

Answering paragraph 8 of plaintiff's complaint, defendant does not have sufficient information to form a belief as to the truth of the allegations of said paragraph 8 and therefore denies each and every allegation contained therein.

IX.

Defendant denies each and every allegation contained in paragraph 9 of plaintiff's complaint and specifically denies that plaintiff is entitled to a refund in the sum of $986.53 or any other sum whatsoever.

X.

Answering paragraph 10 of plaintiff's complaint, defendant does not have sufficient information to form a belief as to the truth of the allegations of said paragraph 10 and therefore denies each and every allegation contained therein and specifically denies that plaintiff is entitled to a refund in the sum of $191.42 or any other sum whatsoever.

Wherefore Defendant Prays that judgment in its favor be entered herein, together with the costs allowable by law, and that plaintiff's complaint be dismissed with prejudice.

Dated this 7th day of January, 1960.

/s/ DALE M. GREEN,
United States Attorney.

Certificate of service by mail attached.

[Endorsed]: Filed January 7, 1960.

[Title of District Court and Cause.]

Civil No. 1883

ANSWER

For an answer to plaintiff's complaint, defendant admits, denies and alleges as follows:

I.

Defendant admits the allegations contained in paragraph 1 of the plaintiff's complaint.

II.

Defendant denies each and every allegation contained in paragraph 2 of plaintiff's complaint.

III.

Defendant denies each and every allegation contained in paragraph 3 of plaintiff's complaint.

IV.

Defendant denies each and every allegation contained in paragraph 4 of plaintiff's complaint.

V.

Defendant denies each and every allegation contained in paragraph 5 of plaintiff's complaint.

VI.

Answering paragraph 6 of plaintiff's complaint, defendant does not have sufficient information to form a belief as to the truth of the allegations set forth in said paragraph 6 and therefore denies each and every allegation contained therein.

VII.

Defendant denies each and very allegation contained in paragraph 7 of plaintiff's complaint, except that defendant admits that a claim for refund was filed.

VIII.

Answering paragraph 8 of plaintiff's complaint, defendant does not have sufficient information to form a belief as to the truth of the allegations of said paragraph 8 and therefore denies each and every allegation contained therein.

IX.

Defendant denies each and every allegation contained in paragraph 9 of plaintiff's complaint and specifically denies that the plaintiff is entitled to a refund in the sum of $3,053.37 or any other sum whatsoever.

X.

Answering paragraph 10 of plaintiff's complaint, defendant does not have sufficient information to form a belief as to the truth of the allegations of said paragraph 10 and therefore denies each and every allegation contained therein and specifically denies that the plaintiff is entitled to a refund in the sum of $328.22 or any other sum whatsoever.

Wherefore Defendant Prays that judgment in its favor be entered herein, together with the costs allowable by law, and that plaintiff's complaint be dismissed with prejudice.

vs. Uni

Dated this

Certificate (

[Endorsed]

[Title of Dist:

Civil

A pre-trial
entitled causes
ington. Judge
plaintiffs were
the defendant
son, their atto:
trial order h:
follows:

The followi:
parties and re-

1. The pla:
in the State (

2. The pla:
eral Tax Re
941) with the

Dated this 7th day of January, 1960.

/s/ DALE M. GREEN,
United States Attorney.

Certificate of service by mail attached.

[Endorsed]: Filed January 7, 1960.

———

[Title of District Court and Cause.]

Civil Action Nos. 1882 and 1883

PRE-TRIAL ORDER

A pre-trial conference was held in the above-entitled causes on May 19, 1960, at Spokane, Washington. Judge William J. Lindberg presided. The plaintiffs were represented by Willard J. Roe; and the defendant by Robert L. Fraser, Charles Magnuson, their attorneys of record. As a result, this pre-trial order has been formulated and settled as follows:

Nature of Proceedings
Admitted Facts

The following facts have been agreed upon by the parties and require no proof:

1. The plaintiffs are corporations doing business in the State of Washington.

2. The plaintiffs filed Employer's Quarterly Federal Tax Returns (Treasury Department Form 941) with the Director of Internal Revenue at Se-

attle, Washington, for the period 3/31/54 through 12/31/58 and paid FICA taxes stated thereon.

3. The plaintiff Alsco Storm Windows, Inc. filed its Annual Returns of Excise Taxes on Employees of Four or More Individuals under the Federal Unemployment Tax Act (Treasury Department Form 940) with the Director of Internal Revenue at Seattle, Washington, for the calendar years 1955, 1956 and 1958 and paid FUTA taxes stated thereon. The plaintiff Alsco Northwest, Inc., filed its returns (Treasury Department Forms 940) with the District Director of Internal Revenue at Seattle, Washington, for the calendar years 1955, 1956 and 1957 and paid the FUTA taxes stated thereon.

4. The plaintiffs filed timely claims for refund of the plaintiffs' portion of the federal insurance contributions (FICA) taxes only and the federal unemployment (FUTA) taxes paid to the defendant on the earnings of certain "installers" or "applicators" on the grounds, in substance, that these persons were not, in fact, employees within the meaning of the provisions of Section 3121(d) and 3306(i), Title 26, United States Code.

5. Plaintiffs' claims for refund filed as set forth herein, were disallowed by the Commissioner of Internal Revenue under date of July 29, 1959, and these instant suits were timely filed.

Plaintiffs' Contentions

1. That plaintiffs were not required to assume liability for the payment of federal insurance con-

tributions (FICA) and federal unemployment (FUTA) taxes and that any payments made by the plaintiffs were erroneous on the ground that the "installers" or "applicators" were not employees but were independent contractors.

2. The working arrangement between the plaintiffs and the "installers" or "applicators" was oral, there being no written contract setting out the duties and responsibilities of the respective parties. The working arrangements as actually carried out will disclose that the plaintiffs did not exercise that degree of direction and control over the manner and method in which the "applicators' " or "installers' " services were performed to permit a finding that the "installer" or "applicators" were employees under the common-law tests.

Defendant's Contentions

1. The payments of federal insurance contributions (FICA) and federal unemployment (FUTA) taxes made by plaintiffs were correct, since the "installers" or "applicators" were employees as defined under the Federal Insurance Contributions Act and the Federal Unemployment Tax Act, Sections 3121(d) and 3306(i), Internal Revenue Code of 1954.

2. The working arrangement between the plaintiffs and the "installers" or "applicators" was oral, there being no written contract setting out the duties and responsibilities of the respective parties. Testimony as to the working arrangements as actually

carried out, will disclose that the plaintiffs did exercise that degree of direction and control over the manner and method in which the "applicators'" and "installers'" services were performed to permit a finding that the "installers" or "applicators" were employees under the common-law tests.

Issue of Fact

1. Whether the "installers" or "applicators" listed on Forms 941(c), attached to the claims for refund, were employees of plaintiffs, or independent contractors.

Issue of Law

1. Whether the Commissioner was correct in determining that these "installers" or "applicators" were employees of plaintiffs, and therefore plaintiffs were liable for the payment of federal insurance contributions (FICA) and federal unemployment (FUTA) taxes.

Exhibits

The following exhibits may be received in evidence, if otherwise admissible, without further identification. It being stipulated that each is what it purports to be:

1. Plaintiffs' original tax returns, Forms 940 and 941;

2. Plaintiffs' claim for refund, Forms 843;

3. Forms 941-c, listing the names of the persons designated as "installers" or "applicators." (Attached to Forms 843)

Stipulation

It is stipulated and agreed between counsel for the respective parties hereto that the plaintiffs not be required to prove the amount of the refund due. In the event the Court enters a finding that the "installers" or "applicators" are independent contractors, then in that event the parties will compute the amount of refund due. Should the court enter a finding that the "installers" or "applicators" are employees then no computation would be required.

It is stipulated and agreed between counsel by the respective parties hereto that neither the plaintiff nor the defendant will call more than 2 installers each to testify as to the working arrangement that existed between them and the plaintiffs. Two or less installers are to be selected by the plaintiff and two or less installers are to be selected by the defendant. It is agreed that their testimony will represent the working arrangement that existed as to all installers.

It Is Hereby Ordered that the foregoing constitutes the pre-trial order in the above-entitled causes and that upon the filing hereof of the pleadings pass out of the case and are superseded by this order, which shall not be amended except by consent of the parties, or by order of the Court to prevent manifest injustice.

Dated December 16, 1960.

/s/ CHARLES L. POWELL,
United States District Judge.

The foregoing form of pre-trial order is hereby approved:

/s/ WILLARD J. ROE,
Attorney for Plaintiff.

/s/ ROBERT F. EWING,
Attorney for Defendant.

[Endorsed]: Filed December 16, 1960.

———

[Title of District Court and Cause.]

Civil Nos. 1882 and 1883

FINDINGS OF FACT AND CONCLUSIONS OF LAW

This matter having come on regularly for trial before the above-entitled court on the 30th day of March, 1961, plaintiffs being represented by Joseph J. Lyman and Willard J. Roe, its attorneys of record, and defendant being represented by one of its attorneys of record, Robert F. Ewing, Assistant United States Attorney for the Eastern District of Washington, the Court having heard testimony and arguments of counsel and having orally announced its decision, and being fully advised in the premises, makes the following

Findings of Fact

I.

The plaintiffs are corporations doing business in the State of Washington, and are primarily engaged in the business of contracting for the sale, application and installation of aluminum storm windows and siding.

II.

The plaintiffs filed Employer's Quarterly Federal Tax Returns (Treasury Department Form 941) with the Director of Internal Revenue at Seattle, Washington, for the period 3/31/54 through 12/31/58 and paid FICA taxes stated thereon.

III.

The plaintiff Alsco Storm Windows, Inc., filed its Annual Returns of Excise Taxes on Employees of Four or more individuals under the Federal Unemployment Tax Act (Treasury Department Form 940) with the Director of Internal Revenue at Seattle, Washington, for the calendar years 1955, 1956 and 1958 and paid FUTA taxes stated thereon. The plaintiff Alsco Northwest, Inc., filed its returns (Treasury Department Form 940) with the District Director of Internal Revenue at Seattle, Washington, for the calendar years 1955, 1956 and 1957 and paid the FUTA taxes stated thereon.

IV.

The plaintiffs filed timely claims for refund of the plaintiffs' portion of the Federal Insurance Contributions (FICA) taxes only and the Federal Unemployment (FUTA) taxes paid to the defendant on the earnings of certain installers on the grounds, in substance, that these persons were not, in fact, employees within the meaning of the provisions of Section 3121(d) and 3306(i), Title 26, United States Code.

V.

The plaintiffs' claims for refund filed as set forth herein were disallowed by the Commissioner of Internal Revenue under date of July 29, 1959, and these instant suits were timely filed and consolidated for trial.

VI.

Working arrangements between the plaintiffs and the installers were oral, there being no written contract setting out the duties and responsibilities of the respective parties.

VII.

The plaintiffs had the names of several qualified installers who would be contacted when there were jobs to be performed. In some instances installers would come to plaintiffs' office seeking work and at other times the plaintiffs would advertise through various media for experienced installers. Plaintiffs had some installers who worked regularly and for no one else in the period in qeustion, while other installers only worked periodically.

VIII.

When the plaintiffs were ready to commence work on a particular contract, the installer, if he agreed to do the job, was handed a work sheet which contained the name and address of the property owner

where the work was to be performed, a general description of the work, together with an approxima-
tion of the materials to be applied, or the number of
storm windows to be installed.

IX.

Generally, the relationship between the plaintiffs
and the installers was such that the installers were
free to accept or reject any proffered job. On at
least one occasion, however, two of the plaintiffs'
regular installers were called into the office of the
production manager of the plaintiffs for disciplinary reasons because they were seen at a competing
firm. Loyalty to the plaintiffs' firm was discussed on
this occasion. The two installers involved were not
doing a job for the plaintiffs at the time and were
driving their own trucks which contained no materials owned by the plaintiffs.

X.

On some occasions installers who applied for work
when no work was available were referred to competing firms, however, regular installers of the
plaintiffs, who had worked for plaintiffs over a
period of years, were not referred to a competitor
during those times when no work was available.

XI.

Contract materials such as storm windows were
furnished by the plaintiffs, but tools and installation
equipment, such as ladders, were generally fur-

nished by the installer himself, as was the transportation to and from the jobs. The installers paid their own transportation expenses and also their own expense for meals and lodging for jobs performed out of the local area.

XII.

The installers worked either alone or with an associate installer. On many occasions numerous work orders were picked up upon a single call to the office. Plaintiffs occasionally attached priority to these work orders and installers were instructed as to which jobs were to be done first, second, etc. Installers were free to, and did on occasion, employ helpers without the approval of the plaintiffs. The helpers were paid either by the installer or by the plaintiffs, at the specific direction of the installer, from the amount of compensation due from the plaintiffs to the installer on the specific job on which the helpers were employed. The helpers were under the control of the installers in the performance of their work and with respect to hiring, and discharge.

XIII.

Occasionally two installers would commence a job together and before it was finished one installer would be moved to another location and job at the request of the plaintiffs. The installer who was moved did not always return to the original job that he had commenced. Single installers were occasionally moved from one job to another at the request or direction of plaintiffs because of deadlines that

vs. Unite

had to be met, not always re started.

As a part of installers prese ing jobs for tl bearing the adv furnished to in the same. The v if the coveral pay.

The plaintiff to the installers within a work installers was p tion of a job t staller would g the home own F.H.A. jobs, t completion et Payments for company check

The installe the performan or reimbursem

The insta le generally had

had to be met, illness and weather. The installer was not always returned to the job he had originally started.

XIV.

As a part of plaintiffs' written policy to have the installers present a neat appearance while performing jobs for the plaintiffs, white coverall uniforms bearing the advertisement of Alsco on the back were furnished to installers who were requested to wear the same. The weekly charge for rental and cleaning of the coveralls was deducted from the installers pay.

XV.

The plaintiffs generally paid the prevailing rate to the installers on a per unit basis for jobs included within a work order. Any extra labor performed by installers was paid on an hourly basis. Upon completion of a job that was to be paid in cash, the installer would get the money in some instances from the home owner and turn it over to plaintiffs. On F.H.A. jobs, the installer was instructed to get a completion certificate signed by the home owner. Payments for all jobs to the installers were made by company checks.

XVI.

The installers paid all their expenses incident to the performance of the work without accounting to or reimbursement from the plaintiffs.

XVII.

The installers could not substitute materials and generally had no authority to change the contract.

However, in minor matters which would not involve any change in the increasing or decreasing of the money due on a particular job, the installer might consult with the customer and could proceed without prior consultation with the plaintiffs.

XVIII.

The installers did not hold themselves out to the public in any way, shape or form as being installers in business for themselves. None of the installers possessed contractors cards.

XIX.

Plaintiffs would advertise their products and business on the various jobs by placing placards at the job sites. They also advertised on the coveralls worn by the installers as heretofore mentioned. Plaintiffs did attempt to encourage the installers to advertise plaintiffs' business on the trucks owned by the individual installers, but such advertisement was rejected by the respective installers. Interested people passing by a job site were referred to the plaintiffs or a salesman working for the plaintiffs.

XX.

Plaintiffs did not hire supervisors as such to observe, instruct or direct the installers as the work progressed. Salesmen were supposed to look over jobs and did look over jobs. They occasionally offered suggestions or gave directions which were adhered to by the installers. The manager of the plaintiffs inspected jobs and gave both suggestions and directions, and, as he testified, he expected them to be followed. The manager had the power to instruct the installers as to the way a job should be done. The plaintiffs, through their manager and production manager, had the power to terminate a job with an installer during the course of a job as well as after a job was finished. If not satisfied with an installer's work, the plaintiffs removed him from a job in progress or did not offer him another work sheet upon completion of the job.

XXI.

Plaintiffs on occasion issued written bulletins to the installers which pointed out the way various aspects of a job was to be done. These bulletins also listed various things that the installers were not to do before, during and after performance of any particular job.

XXII.

The installers were not members of any labor union and plaintiffs' dealings with them were on an individual basis.

XXIII.

The installers were not required to start or finish work at any particular time but regulated their own work day. They were not promised work for any set period of time.

XXIV.

Upon completion of a job being financed by F.H.A., the installer was to get a completion slip signed by the customer which certified that the customer was satisfied with the job as done. If the customer did not sign the slip, as happened on occasion, the installer would find out the complaint and report it to the plaintiffs. If additional work was needed, generally the same installer would go back and complete the job. If it was due to the fault of the installer, the work would be done at the installer's own expense. The installer who performed the original job did not always return to complete the job in accordance with the complaint, although he was available, except for being assigned to another new job. At the completion of the job the installer performed his own clean up work without additional compensation.

From the foregoing Findings of Fact the Court makes the following

Conclusions of Law

I.

The Court has jurisdiction of the subject matter herein.

II.

The plaintiffs did exercise that degree of direction and control over the manner and method in which the installers performed their services to constitute the installers employees under the usual common-law tests.

III.

The payments of Federal Insurance Contributions (FICA) and Federal Unemployment (FUTA)

taxes made by plaintiffs were correct, since the installers were employees as defined under the Federal Insurance Contributions Act and the Federal Unemployment Tax Act, Sections 3121(d) and 3306(i), Internal Revenue Code of 1954.

IV.

The plaintiffs' complaints should be dismissed with prejudice.

V.

The defendant should have judgment for its costs herein incurred.

Dated May 18, 1961.

/s/ CHARLES L. POWELL,
United States District Judge.

Presented by:

/s/ ROBERT F. EWING,
Assistant United States
Attorney.

[Endorsed]: Filed May 19, 1961.

Alsco Storm Windows, Inc., et al.

United States District Court for the Eastern
District of Washington, Northern Division

Civil No. 1882

ALSCO STORM WINDOWS, INC., for Its Own
Account, and as Transferee of the Assets of
Vent-Air Awnings, Inc.,

Plaintiff,

vs.

UNITED STATES OF AMERICA,

Defendant.

Civil No. 1883

ALSCO NORTHWEST, INC., a Corporation,

Plaintiff,

vs.

UNITED STATES OF AMERICA,

Defendant.

JUDGMENT

This matter having come on regularly for trial
before the above-entitled Court on the 30th day of
March, 1961, and the Court having heard testimony
and arguments of counsel and having orally announced its decision and entered its finding of fact
and conclusions of law,

It Is Hereby Ordered, Adjudged and Decreed
that:

vs. Unit

1. The pla
dismissed wit!

2. The def
herein incurre

Dated May

Presented by

Approved as

[Endorsed]:

[Title of Distr

Notice is h
dows, Inc., th
peals to the U
Ninth Circuit
this action on

1. The plaintiffs' complaints be and are hereby dismissed with prejudice.

2. The defendant have judgment for its costs herein incurred.

Dated May 18, 1961.

/s/ CHARLES L. POWELL,
United States District Judge.

Presented by:

/s/ ROBERT F. EWING,
Assistant United States
Attorney.

Approved as to form:

/s/ JOSEPH J. LYMAN,

/s/ WILLARD ROE,
Attorneys for Plaintiffs.

[Endorsed]: Filed and entered May 19, 1961.

———

[Title of District Court and Cause.]

Civil No. 1882

NOTICE OF APPEAL

Notice is hereby given that Alsco Storm Windows, Inc., the plaintiff above named, hereby appeals to the United States Court of Appeals for the Ninth Circuit from the final judgment entered in this action on May 19, 1961.

Dated this 17th day of July, 1961.

HAMBLEN, GILBERT &
BROOKE,

By /s/ FRED W. GILBERT,

and

/s/ JOSEPH J. LYMAN,
Attorneys for Appellant.

Service of copy acknowledged.

[Endorsed]: Filed July 17, 1961.

———

[Title of District Court and Cause.]

Civil No. 1883

NOTICE OF APPEAL

Notice is hereby given that Alsco Northwest, Inc., the plaintiff above named, hereby appeals to the United States Court of Appeals for the Ninth Circuit from the final judgment entered in this action on May 19, 1961.

Dated this 17th day of July, 1961.

HAMBLEN, GILBERT &
BROOKE,

By /s/ FRED W. GILBERT,

and

/s/ JOSEPH J. LYMAN,
Attorneys for Appellant.

Service of copy acknowledged.

[Endorsed]: Filed July 17, 1961.

[Title of District Court and Cause.]

Civil Action No. 1882

Civil Action No. 1883

STIPULATION

It is stipulated by and between counsel for the respective parties that the above-captioned cases be, and they are, hereby consolidated for purposes of trial and appeal and such other procedures which may be warranted.

FRANK R. FREEMAN,
United States Attorney;

By /s/ CARROLL D. GRAY,
Ass't. United States Attorney,
Attorney for Defendant.

/s/ FRED W. GILBERT,

/s/ JOSEPH J. LYMAN,
Attorneys for Plaintiffs.

[Endorsed]: Filed July 28, 1961.

[Title of District Court and Cause.]

Civil No. 1882

Civil No. 1883

STATEMENT OF POINTS

Appellants set forth the following points on which they intend to rely in this appeal:

1. The Court erred in dismissing the Complaints;

2. The Court erred in holding that appellants had not sustained the burden of proof that the applicators were not employees within the meaning of Sections 3121(d) and 3306(i), Internal Revenue Code.

3. The Court erred in holding that the appellee sustained the allegations set out in the pre-trial order that the applicators were employees under the common-law tests.

4. The Findings of Fact and Conclusions of Law and Judgment of the District Court are unsupported by and contrary to the evidence of the record.

> Respectfully submitted,
>
>   /s/ JOSEPH J. LYMAN,
>
>   HAMBLEN GILBERT &
>   BROOKE,
>
>   By /s/ FRED W. GILBERT,
>   Attorneys for Appellants.

Receipt of copy acknowledged.

[Endorsed]: Filed August 10, 1961.

In the District Court of the United States for the Eastern District of Washington, Northern Division

Civil No. 1882

ALSCO STORM WINDOWS, INC., for Its Own Account, and as Transferee of the Assets of Vent-Air Awnings, Inc.,

Plaintiff,

vs.

UNITED STATES OF AMERICA,

Defendant.

Civil No. 1883

ALSCO NORTHWEST, INC., a Corporation,

Plaintiff,

vs.

UNITED STATES OF AMERICA,

Defendant.

Before: Honorable Charles L. Powell, Judge, without a jury

TRANSCIPT OF PROCEEDINGS
March 29, 1961

Appearances:

    For the Plaintiff:
        JOSEPH J. LYMAN,
           Attorney at Law.
        WILLARD J. ROE,
           Attorney at Law.

For the Defendant:
     DALE M. GREEN,
          United States District Attorney;
     ROBERT F. EWING,
          Assistant U. S. District Attorney.

MILTON L. LEE,

called and sworn as a witness on behalf of the
plaintiffs, testified as follows:

Clerk of the Court: Please state your full name
to the Court?

A.   Milton L. Lee.

Direct Examination

By Mr. Lyman:

Q.   What is your occupation, Mr. Lee? [6*]

A.   I am the manager of Alsco Northwest.

Q.   And that, also, includes a relationship similar to Alsco Storm Windows, Inc.?

A.   Yes. I have the same position in that corporation.

Q.   Now, I want to call your attention to the
period 1954 to 1958; what was your relationship
to the particular corporations at that time?

A.   I was the president and manager of each.

Q.   Now, in 1954 to 1958 where did you spend
a great deal of your time with respect to your
business?

─────
*Page numbering appearing at foot of page of original Reporter's
Transcript of Record.

(Testimony of Milton L. Lee.)

A. I spent about two-thirds of that period in Salt Lake City.

Q. Now, you have another corporation in Salt Lake City which has no connection with these two, is that correct, sir?

A. Well, it's the parent corporation, but they are independent of each other, yes.

Q. In other words, the payroll records with which we are concerned of the two plaintiff corporations were separate and apart from the Utah corporation?   A. Yes.

Q. Very well. Now, when did you come to this area and actively participate in the businesses of these two plaintiff corporations?

A. The early part of 1958. [7]

Q. But you were aware, were you not, of the business activity of these corporations even though you were in Utah?

A. Oh, yes, I made frequent trips through the area.

Q. All right, sir. Now what, essentially, is the business of these two plaintiff corporations during that time?

A. During that time we were in the business of manufacturing and selling storm windows, storm doors, and siding.

Q. And these are aluminum products, are they not?   A. They are all aluminum products.

Q. Now, how would you go about getting business for your company to make its profit?

A. Our business was secured through salesmen, mainly; we had dealers, also.

(Testimony of Milton L. Lee.)

Q. And what would these salesmen do?

A. The salesmen would contact the home owners and sell them our products on an installed basis.

Q. And then would you obtain a contract between the customer and your company?

A. Yes.

Q. All right. Now, these salesmen, what was their status insofar as Internal Revenue is concerned and these particular taxes are concerned?

A. They have been ruled to be independent agents not subject to withholding tax and social security tax. [8]

The Court: Does that answer your question?

Mr. Lyman: Yes, your Honor.

The Court: Well, that is hearsay.

Q. (By Mr. Lyman): No, I was going to ask him if he had any personal knowledge what the status was insofar as Internal Revenue is concerned in these taxes.

The Court: All right.

Mr. Lyman: I don't even know it is material, your Honor, but I just want to show you the status of these particular salesmen who deal later, with these applicators.

The Court: I don't understand from the pleadings and these interrogatories and pre-trial order that the salesmen deal directly with the applicators.

Mr. Lyman: Well, perhaps it is not material, your Honor, but they do, nevertheless; perhaps it is not material here.

Q. I will show you Plaintiffs' Exhibit 1 for iden-

(Testimony of Milton L. Lee.)

tification and ask you is this a typical contract that a salesman would enter into on behalf of your company with a customer (hands paper to witness)?

A. It's a copy of one.

Q. Now, I will ask you what is Plaintiffs' No. 2 for identification (hands paper to witness)?

A. This is a copy of a work order which is made up from this contract. [9]

Q. The contract being Plaintiffs' 1 for identification, is that correct?   A. Yes.

Q. All right, have you seen this, Mr. Ewing? Now, Plaintiffs' 3 for identification, is that also a contract similar to Plaintiffs' 1 for identification (hands paper to witness)?

A. Yes, that is a copy of a contract.

Q. And Plaintiffs' 4 for identification is a work order similar to Plaintiffs' 2 for identification (hands paper to witness)?

A. Yes, that is a copy of the work order made up from No. 3.

Q. Now, in other words, a contract and a work order are a set of documents relative to a job that is going to be done, is that correct, sir?

A. That is correct.

Q. And Plaintiffs' 5 for identification, is that a contract similar to the others I have shown you (hands paper to witness)?   A. Yes.

Q. And Plaintiffs' 6 is a work order pursuant to the contract of Plaintiffs' Exhibit 5 for identification?   A. Yes.

Q. All right, sir, and Plaintiffs' 7 for identifica-

(Testimony of Milton L. Lee.)

tion, [10] is that a contract between a customer and your company (hands paper to witness)?

A. Yes, it is.

Q. And Plaintiffs' 8 for identification, is that a work order pursuant to the contract which is Plaintiff's 7 (hands paper to witness)?

A. Yes, it is.

> (Counsel shows documents to defendant's counsel.)

Mr. Lyman: If the Court please, the plaintiff offers Exhibits 1 through 8 for identification in evidence. There is no objection on the part of the defendant?

Mr. Ewing: There is no objection, your Honor.

The Court: All right, they will be admitted as Plaintiffs' Exhibits 1 through 8, inclusive.

> (Whereupon, said documents were admitted in evidence as Plaintiffs' Exhibits Nos. 1 through 8, inclusive.)

Q. (By Mr. Lyman): Now, Mr. Lee, after the contract comes into the Company, who draws up the work order?

A. Specifically, no particular person. It may be done by the salesman himself or by somebody in the office.

Q. But it is done in your office?

A. Yes, it is.

Q. Now, other than these salesmen, what other categories [11] of persons do you have?

A. Well, we have two other categories, three, ac-

(Testimony of Milton L. Lee.)

tually. We have our office personnel, our shop personnel, and our subcontract personnel, the applicators and installers.

Q. All right. Now, the office personnel, there is no question but they are employees under this proceeding?   A. No question with me.

Q. Now, the shop personnel, how do they work?

A. They are regular full time employees, they punch a clock, subject to wages and hours law.

Q. They punch a clock, is that correct?

A. Yes.

Q. You determine their hours?   A. Yes.

Q. And you give them a place to work?

A. Yes.

Q. That is in your shop?   A. Yes.

Q. And do you have a supervisor in the shop?

A. We have several.

Q. And they supervise the work of these people?

A. Yes.

Q. And are these persons given various jobs to do, according to the will of the supervisor? [12]

A. Yes, they are.

Q. Now, their status is not in issue in this proceeding?   A. No.

Q. Now, this other category, installers and applicators you mentioned, whose status is in this proceeding, how do they work with respect to pay?

A. They work by the job on a piece work basis.

Q. And who determines their hours?

A. They determine them themselves.

Q. And who furnishes the equipment and the tools necessary for the performance of this work?

(Testimony of Milton L. Lee.)

A. They furnish their own.

Q. And do these applicators and installers have helpers?　　A. Some do.

Q. And how do they get these helpers?

A. They hire them.

Q. Well, does the Company have any part in the hiring of these hepers?

A. Not to my knowledge.

Q. Well, do they, as far as you know, Mr. Lee?

A. Well, they don't as far as I know, yes.

Q. And who pays these helpers, who determines their pay?

A. The pay is determined by the applicator or installer who hires them.

Q. And who determines the working conditions of these [13] installers?

A. The person who hires them.

Q. Does the Company in any way interfere with the relationship between your applicators and these helpers, as far as working conditions?

A. They never have, to my knowledge.

Q. Now, these work sheets which were identified, well, you have seen them in evidence, they are given, what is done with those with respect to these installers?

A. Well, those work sheets are turned over to our shop manager, factory manager.

Q. Who is that?

A. Who is Mr. Ralph Williams.

Q. All right.

A. He, in turn, prepares the windows and the

(Testimony of Milton L. Lee.)

doors for the siding necessary to go on the job, and then hands them, that is, the work orders and material, over to an installer or an applicator.

Q. All right, now what does the applicator do with that work sheet and these materials that he has picked up?

A. He takes them on his own equipment, delivers them to the job, puts the job on. When the job is finished, he comes in and gets paid for it.

Q. Now, do you have any written agreement with these applicators, or is it an oral situation? [14]

A. It's oral.

Q. Now, other than the writing on the work orders which you have identified, are there any other instructions given by the Company to these men as to how to do this work?

A. Specifically, how to do each job, do you mean, sir?

Q. Yes.   A. No.

Q. Do you have any supervisors to go out into the field and supervise the work of these men?

A. No.

Q. What is the average experience of these applicators during this period?

A. Oh, I would say the average experience must be at least two or three years.

Q. Now, do some of them have more than that?

A. Yes.

Q. Now, is there any kind of guarantee of compensation that these men get?

(Testimony of Milton L. Lee.)

A. No, except if they finish a job properly, they get paid for it.

Q. But I mean on the matter of the fact that they may put in time, does that feature in any way at all?   A. No.

Q. In other words, each of these work orders which you have [15] identified is a separate and complete job in itself?   A. That is correct.

Q. And the man's compensation is based upon that work order, is that correct?

A. That is accurate.

Q. Now, do you ever have a situation where you may have a window job or a siding job, incidentally, how are the siding applicators paid?

A. The siding applicators are paid the same way.

Q. Per square?   A. Per piece and per job.

Q. Per job? Now, do you ever have a situation where, in the course of making an installation, you may have some carpentry work which cannot be measured by the unit?

A. Yes, that often happens.

Q. Now, what happens there, as far as compensation to the men is concerned?

A. Well, he makes an extra charge on his work order, which he turns in and receives payment for it.

Q. Is there any particular basis for it with respect to windows and with respect to siding?

A. Generally it's based on the hours they spend on the extra work.

(Testimony of Milton L. Lee.)

Q. And who determines how many hours there are? A. The man, himself. [16]

Q. And does the Company ever question his added expense? A. We have.

Q. What happens then?

A. Well, it's a matter of dispute and negotiation. As a matter of fact, we question it; we sometimes require a fellow to produce evidence that he did what he said he did and spent the time he said he did on it. That is a rare situation, however.

Q. I see. Well, with respect to the installations which are paid on a piece work basis, percentage wise, if you can, how much is this extra work?

A. In the window and door business it might not exceed two or three per cent.

Q. I see, and what about siding?

A. With the siding business it might be considerably more, say, ten per cent or fifteen per cent, something like that.

Q. Now, on the siding when you find you have extra work to do, what happens then? How does the man go about doing it when it is not contemplated in the original contract?

A. He generally calls the company, and we would renegotiate the contract with the customer or decide to do it as part of the original contract or, in some cases, we have actually given up jobs because we don't feel that we can [17] renegotiate them and don't feel we can make a profit.

Q. Now, has a man to your knowledge ever been

(Testimony of Milton L. Lee.)

taken off a job while it was in progress or discharged from a job while it was in progress?

A.   You mean completely removed from the job,
permanently?

Q.   Yes.   A.   Yes.

Q.   And what would the reason be for such a
thing?

A.   Unsatisfactory performance of the application.

Q.   But other than that, there would be no indiscriminate firing?   A.   No.

Mr. Ewing: I object, your Honor, I don't understand what he means by "indiscriminate."

Q.   (By Mr. Lyman):   Well, let me ask you this,
then: What would be the basis of severing a relationship with an installer or applicator?

A.   There would probably be two main categories
of severing relationships. One would be unsatisfactory performance; the other would be a lack of
sufficient work to keep a man busy.

Q.   All right. Well, now, if you find that a man
has performed unsatisfactorily, how do you sever
that relationship; do you understand my question?

A.   Almost always the relationship between us
and an [18] applicator and installer takes place
after his job is completed or after we think it's
completed.

Mr. Ewing: I don't think that is responsive to
the question.

The Court: No, sustained.

Q.   (By Mr. Lyman):   Well, let me ask you this:

(Testimony of Milton L. Lee.)

How many applicators do you usually have working during the year, what is the highest number you have had?   A.   At one time?

Q.   Yes.

A.   In all our branches, probably 30.

Q.   And then what would be the least number that you would have?

A.   Oh, about eight or ten.

Q.   Now, of that eight or ten how many would you call, for want of a better term, regulars?

A.   Eight or ten.

Q.   And that is through all your branches?

A.   Yes.

Mr. Ewing: Your Honor, could I get a clarification of what counsel means by "regulars"?

The Court: I think if he doesn't' want to say, you can get it on cross.

Q.   (By Mr. Lyman):   Well, regulars; well, first, how many branches do you have? [19]

A.   At that particular time we were operating four.

Q.   Now, for instance, when you got to your slow periods, about how many would you have, of regulars?   A.   Two or three.

Q.   And would they be in the category of, what persons, if you can name them?

A.   The ones that come to my mind are George Aronson and Don Lewis.

Q.   All right. Now, when I say "regulars," do they work any differently than the people who come and go in your plant?

(Testimony of Milton L. Lee.)

A.   No, not any different than the installers.

Q.   I mean the installers that come and go through the company, these regulars, are they the persons—how is it that they seem to stay on and other persons seem to leave, can you explain that?

A.   Well, we continue to give contracts or work sheets to men who do satisfactory work and are dependable and we have mutual good will with them.

Q.   All right. If a situation arises where a man completes a job and even though work is available, you would not give him another work order?

A.   Yes.

Q.   What are those circumstances?

A.   The circumstances would be based upon unsatisfactory [20] performance on the job.

Q.   Under those circumstances you would not renew the relationship?

A.   We just wouldn't renew the relationship, that is right.

Q.   How do you go about getting applicators?

A.   Oh, we secure new applicators by telephone, by applications in person, by employment bureaus, by newspaper ads.

Q.   Is there anything in your arrangement with the applicators and installers which obligates the Company to give them work, any given number of jobs?

A.   No, we don't have any guarantee to any installer or applicator.

Q.   Is there anything in your arrangement where

(Testimony of Milton L. Lee.)
the installer has agreed that he would do a certain
number of jobs?

A. Not to my knowledge.

Q. Has there ever been a situation where work
was unsatisfactory and not performed in a workmanlike manner by any installer or applicator?

A. Yes.

Q. What happens there insofar as completing
that work is concerned?

A. We demand that the installer or applicator
who does the job go back on his own time and complete it or fix up [21] the deficiency.

Mr. Lyman: Will you indulge me a moment,
your Honor?

Q. What is the situation with respect to the
men taking off time when you may perhaps have
work orders in the shop to be applied?

A. They have always been free to take the time
off that they require.

Q. Do you have any specific examples of any
particular persons who took such time away from
these application jobs?

A. Yes, we specifically have difficulty keeping
our jobs going at the time of the year when the
hunting and fishing season is opened and the fellows
like to go hunting and fishing, and so they go.

Q. What arrangements, if any, are made?

A. Well, usually it's a gentlemen's agreement
between the fellows and Ralph Williams. They us-
usually tell him that they are going to go hunting,

Alsco Storm Windows, Inc., et al.

(Testimony of Milton L. Lee.)

and going to go at a certain time, and he is aware of the fact, and that is about what it amounts to.

Q. Well, what do you do with the jobs that you have in the shop that have to be applied?

A. Well, oh, we just do the best we can with what we have. We wait, usually, I mean, we get [22] behind.

Q. Did any of these installers that have performed services for you, and applicators as well, ever perform services for other companies, like competitors in this area?   A. Yes.

Q. And are these jobs performed between jobs that they perform for you?   A. Yes.

Q. Do you have any knowledge whether an installer who is performing a job for you may do some minor repair for a customer and be paid by the customer?

A. I think almost all of them have at one time or another.

Q. Is that a practice, or do you know?

A. Well, the practice, if you are asking me if it is the usual thing or it might happen, in the majority of jobs they put on, I would say no, but I still say I think almost everybody that has applied for us has done it at one time or another.

Mr. Lyman: I believe that is all for this witness, your Honor.

(Testimony of Milton L. Lee.)

Cross-Examination

By Mr. Ewing:

Q. Mr. Lee, you stated that you came to Spokane to work in 1958, is that correct, from Salt Lake?

A. Yes. [23]

Q. And during the period from 1954 to 1958, what was your relationship to Alsco Northwest and Alsco Storm Windows here?

A. I was the president.

Q. And being president, I assume that you were familiar with the work order procedure, even though you were not here?   A. I established it.

Q. And could you explain briefly, again, what that work order procedure was, who initiated the work order? Who initiated the work order?

A. Well, the work order was, generally speaking, a copy of our production order, it was made out by somebody in the office or a salesman or a dealer.

Q. Is that the work order was made out by the dealer or salesman or the purchase order?

A. The work order is a copy of the purchase order.

Q. And who made out the work order?

A. The person that made out the purchase order.

Q. The same person made out both orders?

A. It was a copy of the same thing, a carbon copy.

Q. When you had work to be done, how were these installers notified of such?

A. Well, there was no positively established pro-

(Testimony of Milton L. Lee.)

cedure. If we were behind in our application, we
would get on the [24] phone and contact new men.
If we were up on our application, why, the fellows
would be coming in at regular intervals, so it would
vary.

Q. As to your regular installers, using that word
in the sense in which you used it, your regular installers, they just simply came in and picked up
work orders and went out on the job without any
notification, I suppose, is that right?

A. Well, if you are asking if we have to notify
them between each group of jobs they got, no, that
is a distinguishing feature between them being regular and irregular.

Q. Did you keep a file for each installer and keep
his work order in that file, or just how did that
work?

A. Part of the time, part of this period we did
that, part we didn't.

Q. What do you mean by that?

A. Well, it is just a difference in establishing
procedures in the office. There is one part of the
time in this period we did keep a specific file for
each man and keep all of the work orders in it.
At another part of this period we didn't do it.

Q. Who handed the work orders out to the installers, did they go right to the file and get their
orders, or did somebody give them to them? [25]

A. Generally speaking, they were passed out
hand to hand by Mr. Williams or one of his assistants.

(Testimony of Milton L. Lee.)

Q. Was there any written agreement between your company and the installers other than the work order? Was that the only thing in writing as between you and the installers, that is, Alsco and the installers?

A. In the way of an agreement?

Q. Right. A. Not that I know of.

Q. Would the work order be the only thing that would indicate an agreement? Was there anything **else?** A. In writing?

Q. In writing. A. Yes.

Q. You say there was other things in writing?

A. No, that was the only thing that represented an agreement in writing.

Q. Were pay negotiations entered into at the time an installer picked up his work order?

A. Sometimes.

Q. Who set the prices, unit prices, as to which these installers would be paid?

A. Those prices were generally arrived at from a conference that all the installers and applicators that were interested would attend, and the management and production [26] department, we sat down and negotiated them, so to speak.

Q. As I understand your testimony as to work done in the work order they were paid by the unit price? A. Yes.

Q. As to extra work, it was a different pay system, is that correct?

A. No, not a different pay system, it's a different pay basis.

(Testimony of Milton L. Lee.)

Q. Well, they were not paid by the unit price for extra work, were they?

A. I don't understand you, by the "unit price"?

Q. Well, piecemeal; was it piecemeal. Was the basis of extra work paid on a piecemeal basis?

A. No, I have already stated I think in almost all cases the basis of extra work was the time spent on the extra work.

Q. And what would extra work be and what would be your definition of extra work?

A. Well, to a large extent extra work was not defined by us, it was defined by the installers, because in most cases we never saw it or had any particular interest in seeing it. It was a matter of judgment with them. If a man put up a storm window and he found out that he had to have blind stops, that isn't the usual thing, he [27] considered it extra, so he charged extra.

Q. And, as I understand, he listed the hours it took him to do that extra work and you paid him?

A. Sometimes he listed the hours and sometimes he didn't.

Q. Well, any hours that were listed, you paid him on the basis of what he says in his order?

A. Almost invariably we paid on what was on the work order.

Q. Were these installers free to accept or reject any work order that was offered to them?

A. Yes.

Q. In the event that a work order was offered to

(Testimony of Milton L. Lee.)

an installer and he turned it down, what would happen then, if anything?

A. Well, I don't know what you mean, what would happen?

Q. Well, was he given another work order, or if you offered a work order to one installer and he turned that one down, would he get another job, or just what would happen to it?

A. Well, yes and no, the circumstances would determine that.

Q. By "yes and no," you mean sometimes an installer would be given another job and sometimes he wouldn't?

A. It is still based on having turned one down?

Q. Right.

A. Well, I am not familiar with any situation like that [28] myself. I do know that installers turned down work orders because they had something else to do. They had a job of somebody else's to go on, or wanted to make a trip, or something. Well, as I say, except for unfinished work or bad performance, a fellow would get another job, yes.

Q. Do you know of your own knowledge of any work order which an installer turned down because he wasn't satisfied with the price or the money he was going to get on that job?   A. Yes.

Q. And as to that particular type of situation, what would happen to the installer, then?

A. Well, that particular type of situation would generally be referred to me and in every case that I can recall I negotiated with this particular ap-

(Testimony of Milton L. Lee.)

plicator or installer and worked out a satisfactory pay basis, that is my knowledge of it.

Q. Have there been times when an installer has applied for work with you, maybe one of your regular installers, and you haven't had a job for him at that time?

A. Yes, that frequently happens.

Q. Speaking of Alsco, have you referred him to a competitor in those cases?

A. Yes, I have referred a great many men to competitors. [29]

Q. Have there been jobs where more than one applicator was required on that particular job, in other words, two or more applicators worked on different jobs?   A. Yes.

Q. If a question came up in the performance of that job, which applicator's word would control as to what should be done?

A. Well, I am not in a position to answer that question.

Q. I think you stated on direct examination that there are times when an installer would hire a helper to help him?   A. Yes.

Q. And that installer was hired by the—helper was hired by the installer and discharged by the installer?   A. Yes.

Q. Now, did you keep the pay records of that helper at all?   A. Yes, we did, in some cases.

Q. You handled the money for the applicator, is that right?   A. In some cases.

(Testimony of Milton L. Lee.)

Q. Who furnished the materials that went into any particular job?

A. Are you speaking about any particular job, you mean one of our contracts?

Q. In general, who furnished the materials that went into these jobs? [30]

A. The Company did.

Q. Who delivered them to the job site?

A. The applicator and installer.

Q. Was anything else furnished by your company other than materials?

A. I don't know of anything, I don't quite follow the question.

Q. Did you ever loan out ladders, or anything like that?

A. Yes, we have loaned out tools which an installer wouldn't normally be expected to have.

Q. Did your company have supervisors or other personnel such as salesmen, that would go out on jobs when they were in the process of being completed and observe the job in progress and possibly make some instructions or suggestions to the installer?

A. We had no supervisors, we had no regular system of inspecting jobs, and if a salesman directed an installer, he did it on his own.

Q. Did any of the salesmen go out and look the jobs over?   A. Yes, it has been done.

Q. Were they supposed to go out and look the jobs over?

A. Well, I don't know what you mean by "sup-

(Testimony of Milton L. Lee.)

posed to." It's true that the Company would like to have every salesman go out and see a job while it's in the process of application, but, as a practical matter, it's more rare [31] than usual.

Q. Was it the policy of your Company that they were supposed to go out and look at jobs?

A. We encouraged them to do it, that is right.

Q. Did either the plant foreman, Mr. Williams, or you ever go out and look at a job?

A. Together?

Q. Well, not together, but either one of you?

A. Well, I can't speak for Mr. Williams, except that I think he did. As far as I am concerned, I have been out.

Q. And on these jobs that you have gone out to look at, have you ever made any suggestions to the applicators?

A. Specifically, I can't recall any directions I have given an applicator on a job that had to do with his work.

Q. You can't remember any?

A. No, I can remember a couple of instances in which changes in the contract or additions to the contract have been made and which I have told the man that instead of doing half a job that "We are going to do the whole job, or that we are going to add a little siding to the back of his house, or do a gable, or put an awning on," or something like that, which would actually amount to additional work; but as far as offering advice in a situation like that at a job, I don't recall ever having [32] done it.

(Testimony of Milton L. Lee.)

Q. You can't recall ever giving any directions to an applicator on a job?

A. Yes, if he wanted to know how to get to another job, I certainly would tell him.

Q. If what?

A. If he wanted to get from one job to another, I would tell him, sure.

Q. No, have you ever given any directions to an applicator on these jobs that you have gone out to look at, have you ever given them any directions as to that job?

A. Well, I just answered that question, no, not that I recall.

Mr. Ewing: May I have the deposition opened and published?

The Court: Do you want it published?

Q. (By Mr. Ewing): Do you recall when you were in my office on the 21st day of November of last year for me to take your deposition?

A. Yes.

Q. And were you present with an attorney at that time?   A. Yes.

Q. And after the deposition was taken, did you read it and sign it as being correct?

A. Yes. [33]

Q. Referring to page 16 of this deposition, line 22, this is testimony that was given at that time:

"Q. On these jobs that you have gone out to look at, have you ever made any suggestions?

"A. Surely.

"Q. And you expected them to be followed?

(Testimony of Milton L. Lee.)

"A. Well, if I made a suggestion, I certainly would.

"Q. Have you ever given any directions?

"A. To an applicator?

"Q. Yes?"

Q. (By Mr. Ewing): Now, is that true?

A. Well, you have asked me a series of questions in which you said have I ever given them any directions. Well, as I said here a few minutes ago, if we had an addition for a job, or a change in the procedure, why of course I would give them directions. You asked me if I would tell a man how to do a specific job at a specific time. I don't remember ever doing it.

Q. Now, I didn't ask you whether you told him how to do the whole job, I just asked you whether you have been out on jobs and ever given directions in reference to that job, maybe on only one particular point on that job?

A. I said I couldn't remember having done it.

Q. Well, is your testimony in the deposition correct, [34] referring to page 17, line 1:

"A. Well, if I made a suggestion, I certainly would." Indicating that you wanted them followed:

"Q. Have you ever given any directions?

"A. To an applicator?

"Q. Yes.

"A. If the occasion arose, I would, yes."

A. Yes, I think that is accurate.

Q. (By Mr. Ewing): Later on, on **the same page, and down** at line 17:

(Testimony of Milton L. Lee.)

"Q. Well, I am just speaking generally, not of any particular job, but just of all the jobs in general. You say you can't remember of your own knowledge when you ever have given any directions, is that right?

"A. Well, no, I don't.

"Q. But you had the power to give the directions? A. Yes.

"Q. And if those directions weren't followed, what, if anything, would happen to the applicator?

"A. Well, we would be inclined not to give him another job."

Q. (By Mr. Ewing): Is that about right? [35]
A. Yes.

Q. Has there ever been a time within your knowledge when an applicator has been put off a job during the course of that job? I think you have already testified on direct that you have discharged applicators during the course of the work for reasons, not doing satisfactory work, or something similar to that, is that right? A. Yes.

Q. Do you feel that you have the power to discharge a man during the course of a job?

Mr. Lyman: Objection, your Honor, when he says the question, "Do you feel that you have the power," that is getting into conjecture, that is for the Court to decide on the line of facts.

The Court: No, no, overruled.

Q. (By Mr. Ewing): The question is: Do you have the power to discharge a man off his job during the course of that job?

(Testimony of Milton L. Lee.)

A. For bad workmanship?

Q. Well, for any reason?   A. Yes.

Q. Would there be times when a home owner or customer would call into your office during the performance of the work and say he was dissatisfied with the work that that applicator was doing, does that ever happen? [36]   A. Yes.

Q. What would be done then in reference to that applicator, would he ever be taken off a job?

A. Well, I don't recall an instance in which a man was taken off a job for that reason under those circumstances.

Q. Again referring to the deposition, on page 22, line 23:

"Q. Would there be times when a home owner would call into your office during the performance of the work and say he was dissatisfied with the work?   A. Yes.

"Q. What would be done then?

"A. Well, on occasion the job would be taken away from the man that was doing it, and on other occasions the home owner would **probably be** educated as to why he was doing what he was, and some cases the home owner would complain about the work being done when maybe it was a matter of what he had to work with."

Skipping down to line 18 on page 23:

"Q. Would that be done strictly on the word of the home owner over the telephone?

"A. No.

(Testimony of Milton L. Lee.)

"Q. Somebody would go out and look at the job? [37]

"A. They don't do anything strictly on what a person might say, a snap judgment.

"Q. Somebody from your office then would go out and look the job over at that time?

"A. Surely.

"Q. And the person that went out from your office would inspect the job at that time and find out what the dissatisfaction was about, I assume, is that right?   A. Yes.

"Q. And if that representative from your office felt that the work was not being done in a satisfactory manner, then that person who went out from your office would excuse that applicator from that job?

"A. Yes, that is about the way it would work, yes."

Q. (By Mr. Ewing): Now, is that, as I have just read, correct?

A. That is essentially correct.

Q. Did the installers share in the profits or losses of your business at all?   A. No.

Q. Were there any occasions that you know of where an installer was taken off a job before it was completed and moved to another job? [38]

A. Oh, yes, there have been several occasions when installers have been asked to go from one job to another.

Q. Who were they asked by?

A. Well, usually Mr. Williams, I would say.

(Testimony of Milton L. Lee.)

Q. And if he asked them to go, I assume he meant what he was saying, they had better go, is that right?

Mr. Lyman: Objection, your Honor.

The Court: Sustained.

Q. (By Mr. Ewing): When Mr. Williams told a man to go to another job after he had started one, as a rule did these applicators go?

Mr. Lyman: Objection, your Honor, this is hearsay. Mr. Williams is here.

The Court: Sustained.

Q. (By Mr. Ewing): You say that there were occasions, however, when a man was taken off a job before it was completed and moved to another job?

A. Well, if I understand your question, sir, he was terminated on one job and put on a job.

Q. To your knowledge, was an installer ever taken off a job that he had originally started, was he ever taken off that job before it was finished and put on some other job?

A. Oh, I know of occasions when they have had two or three jobs running concurrently, yes. [39]

Q. Did the installer, do you know of your own knowledge whether the installer who was moved to the second job always returned to the first job?

A. I don't know of any situation when he didn't return to the first job.

Q. You don't know whether that has happened or not, is that correct?

(Testimony of Milton L. Lee.)

A. Well, I know that they always returned to their original jobs and finished them.

Q. Isn't it true, Mr. Lee, that you have always considered these installers that have worked for you to be contract employees?

Mr. Lyman: Objection, your Honor, this is a legal conclusion he is asking the witness.

The Court: Sustained.

Q. (By Mr. Ewing): Referring to the deposition, on page 27, beginning at line 3:

"Q. Will you state whether or not you felt that you could move the installers around from one job to another at your discretion?

"A. Well, the applicators and installers with us have always been considered to be contract employees."

Mr. Lyman: Objection, your Honor, the fact that it [40] is in the deposition doesn't cure anything. It is not an inconsistent statement and before counsel can use a deposition it seems to me he has to show, first, that there is an inconsistent statement which is inadmissible in evidence.

The Court: No, he can use the deposition for any purpose.

Mr. Lyman: Do I understand the Court correctly to say to make admissible what would ordinarily not be admissible?

The Court: No, that isn't what I had in mind. What is inadmissible about that, that is a statement by this witness against interest, isn't it?

Mr. Lyman: Well——

(Testimony of Milton L. Lee.)

Mr. Ewing: It's my understanding, your Honor, and I intend to do so after I finish questioning this witness, I intend to admit the entire deposition into evidence for substantive purposes, and I understand under Federal Rules of Civil Procedure, Points B and 27-F, that such a thing can be done in this type of a situation.

Mr. Lyman: Well, your Honor, I understand that the deposition is admissible if the witness is not present or to prove inconsistent statements which would be evidentiary.

The Court: Mr. Ewing, you mean Rules 27-B and 27-F? You had better get a better rule. [41]

Mr. Ewing: Excuse me, your Honor, 26, Rule 26. I am referring to 26-D 1 and 2, and 26-F.

The Court: If this were the president of the corporation or the managing agent, I would see no reason why D-2 wouldn't apply to him, do you?

Mr. Lyman: Sure, but my point was, your Honor, certainly it can be used for any purpose but not to make admissible what is obviously inadmissible evidence. For instance, if you asked him a legal conclusion which is inadmissible, which is objectionable, and the Court sustained it, it isn't cured by the fact that he might have asked it on a deposition.

The Court: That is true, the conclusion you are talking about is when he referred to his contract employees, I assume. I presume, however, since that particular question has reference to "contract employees" which would indicate it was calling for a

... *dours, Inc., et al.*

... ding, your Honor,
... ish questioning the
... ire deposition into
... and I understand
Procedure, Points 3
... done in this type

... r, I understand
... the witness is not
... statements which

... Rules 27-B and
... rule. [41]
... Honor, 26, Rule
... 2, and 26-F.
... president of the
... ent, I would see
... him, do you?
... int was, your
... any purpose but
... seriously inadmis-
... you asked him a
... ble, which is ob-
... it, it isn't cured
... it in a deposi-

... clusion you are
... to his contract
... wer, since that
... "contract em-
... fr..t

(Testimony of Milton L. Lee.)

legal conclusion, and so, therefore, the particular question might be sustained in that respect, but that doesn't make the deposition inadmissible. It can be used for more than impeachment, Mr. Lyman.

Mr. Lyman: Yes, I understand that.

The Court: And this particular question, I will sustain the objection on the ground it calls for a legal conclusion.

Mr. Ewing: As to the answer I would move that it [42] should be considered and can be considered based on the principle that it is an admission against interest.

The Court: Well, what do you mean by "contract employee"?

Mr. Ewing: Well, I don't know what he means, I am going to ask him that.

The Court: That was your question, though, you used the term, he didn't.

Mr. Ewing: Well, originally he used the term.

The Court: Well, you haven't read any place yet where he used the term.

Mr. Ewing: Well, I stated in his deposition his answer to a question was:

"A. Well, the applicators and installers with us have always been considered to be contract employees."

That is his answer to a question of mine.

The Court: What was your question, again?

Mr. Ewing (Reading):

"Q. Will you state whether or not you felt that

(Testimony of Milton L. Lee.)
you could move the installers around from one job to another at your discretion?''

The Court: You are not objecting to that question, are you, Mr. Lyman? [43]

Mr. Lyman: No, that question is all right.

The Court: All right. Then, the answer should be, likewise, admissible, shouldn't it?

Mr. Lyman: Well, it is not responsive here. I see what you mean, your Honor; it is not responsive here in the deposition.

The Court: Well, I wouldn't say it isn't responsive. I think from what Mr. Ewing just read it is responsive. You might not like the answer but it is still responsive.

Mr. Lyman: Oh, yes. If the Court please, in the next question Mr. Ewing says:

"Q. That wasn't the question——"

so he has disowned it, himself.

The Court: Well, that doesn't mean it is not admissible now, does it? He can ask him again twice or three times.

Mr. Lyman: Again, he said:

"Q. That isn't the question, Mr. Lee. The question was, if you can state whether or not you felt that you could move one installer from one job to another at your discretion?

"A. I don't feel that way, and I never have, no."

That is not a responsive question and answer because Mr. Ewing [44] has disavowed all these things before.

vs. Unit...

(Testimony of
The Court:
of the deposi
Mr. Lyman:
of the deposit
missible to en
answering to a
The Court:
stances since i
what the effe
let it stay in.
Q. (By Mr.
able experienc
it true that t
supervision?
A. Well, as
have never ha
Q. Isn't it
direct, that th
three years' ex
that correct?
A. No, I d
many years' e
time, and I s
perience, on a
Q. Well, t
years' experie
him closely in
a job properly
A. Well, w
turned in.
Q. What d

(Testimony of Milton L. Lee.)

The Court: His disavowal doesn't take them out of the desposition.

Mr. Lyman: His disavowal doesn't take them out of the deposition but I think it should not be admissible to cure a witness who is prohibited from answering to a legal conclusion.

The Court: Well, I think under the circumstances since it is his term, well, I am not saying what the effect of it would be, but I think I will let it stay in. I think I will permit the answer.

Q. (By Mr. Ewing): Taking, first, your reasonable experience in this type of work, Mr. Lee, isn't it true that the job can be done without close supervision?

A. Well, as I said before, it is being done, we have never had close supervision for it.

Q. Isn't it true, I believe you stated on your direct, that these installers usually have two or three years' experience in this type of work, isn't that correct?

A. No, I didn't answer that. I was asked how many years' experience they had in this period of time, and I said I thought about two years' experience, on an average.

Q. Well, taking an installer of two or three years' experience, would it be necessary to watch him closely in order to do this work, in order to do a job properly? [45]

A. Well, we would be more aware of what he turned in.

Q. What do you mean by that?

(Testimony of Milton L. Lee.)

A.   Well, I think we would be a little more cau-
tious about whether or not he brought in the payments when he finished the job, which they are supposed to do, and a man that had had more experience, and by that we would be guided.

Q.   Taking a man of five to ten years' experience,
would it be necessary, in your opinion, to watch him
closely in reference to him doing his job?

A.   I don't know what you mean by watching him
closely, I mean.

Q.   You state that you do not hire supervisors,
is that correct?   A.   That is right.

Q.   Now, what is your definition, what would you
term a supervisor?

A.   Oh, a man whose sole job it was to go around
and see that somebody else did a job.

Q.   And taking that job description which you
just gave, would a person like that be necessary
in this type of work? In other words, is it necessary to have somebody stand over that man, watching him all the time, in this type of work?

A.   No. [46]

Q.   And as pointed out in your deposition, you
have at times gone out and checked work, haven't
you?   A.   Yes.

Q.   And you have given suggestions before,
haven't you?   A.   Well, sure I have.

Q.   And you have given directions before, haven't
you?

A.   Well, what do you mean "directions"?

Q.   Yes or no.

(Testimony of Milton L. Lee.)

A. Direction? I have already testified that if I had a change in the job or a change in the procedure, I would give directions, of course.

Q. Has Alsco ever issued directives to installers, I will call them directives, or bulletins, or something to that effect?

A. Yes, we have issued bulletins.

Q. So there are things in writing other than just the work orders that are issued to the installers, is that correct?

A. Well, yes, there is more or less a general set of rules, there have been from time to time.

Q. What do you mean by "general set of rules"?

A. Well, they would outline procedures that we would like to have followed in the prosecution of a job.

Q. Who is "they" when you refer to "they"?

A. The bulletins. [47]

Q. They would outline the procedures which you would like to have followed?   A. Yes.

Q. Isn't it true that you expected them to be followed?

A. Well, I think that could be said, yes.

Q. As I understand your testimony on direct, when a job was completed the installer, if it was not a cash transaction, the installer was to get a completion slip signed by the home owner, is that correct?

A. We generally required one or the other, yes.

Q. Was an installer ever paid for that job before he got that completion slip signed?   A. Yes.

(Testimony of Milton L. Lee.)

Q. In full?   A. Yes.

Q. What is the necessity for the completion slip?

A. So the company can get its money.

Q. And who picks up the money if it is a cash transaction?

A. Well, it could be picked up at the time of completion of the job by the installer, it could be picked up then or later by a salesman, or it could be mailed into the company by the customer.

Q. If the installer picks up the money, he delivers it to one of Alsco's representatives, I assume?

A. Correct. [48]

Q. How is the installer paid, is he paid by check or is he paid out of the cash?

A. Paid by check.

The Court: Mr. Ewing, let us have a recess now for ten minutes.

(Whereupon, a recess was taken for a period of ten minutes.)

Q. (By Mr. Ewing): Mr. Lee, have there been instances within your knowledge when the home owner did not sign the completion slip?

A. Yes.

Q. And generally what would be done then, if he didn't sign the slip, if the customer did not sign the slip?   A. We would ask him why not.

Q. Would the installer bring that slip back to you and tell you what the complaint of the home owner was?   A. He could have, yes.

(Testimony of Milton L. Lee.)

Q. And assuming that there had to be some more work done on that job in order to satisfy the home owner, would that installer be returned to that job to do that work?   A. Yes.

Q. Would it always be that installer that went back to finish that job?

A. If he was still around, it would always be that installer, yes. [49]

Q. You are sure of that?

A. That is my knowledge.

Mr. Ewing: At this time, your Honor, I would move the admission of this deposition taken in November of 1960, of Milton Lee's, for substantive purposes.

Mr. Lyman: Your Honor, I don't understand that, the witness is here. If there is any inconsistency, certainly it's counsel's position to bring it out, but to put the whole deposition in as evidence, I think it's immaterial in the first place, and I object to it. [50]

The Court: I think that is what the rule says, so I will admit the deposition and consider it as evidence. I assure you that I will not consider the immaterial testimony as being binding upon you. [52]

"DEPOSITION OF MILTON L. LEE

Appearances:

> JOSEPH J. LYMAN,
>> Attorney at Law,
>>> 1001 Connecticut Avenue, N.W.,
>>> Washington 6, D. C., by
>
> WILLARD J. ROE,
>> For the Plaintiffs.
>
> DALE M. GREEN,
>> United States Attorney, Eastern District
>> of Washington, by
>
> ROBERT F. EWING,
>> Assistant United States Attorney,
>> For the Defendant.

Deposition of Milton L. Lee, taken on behalf of the defendant in the above-entitled causes, before Donald B. Oden, Notary Public, pursuant to stipulation of counsel, at 1:30 o'clock p.m. on the 21st day of November, 1960, Federal Building, Spokane, Washington.

Mr. Ewing: Let the record show that this deposition is being taken pursuant to agreement [53] between co-counsel for the plaintiffs, Willard J. Roe, and Robert F. Ewing, Assistants United States Attorney, pursuant to the Federal Rules of Civil Procedure.

Let the record also show that the plaintiffs are represented at the taking of this deposition by Willard J. Roe, co-counsel for the plaintiffs.

Anything further?

(Off the record discussion.)

Mr. Ewing: Yes, all objections will be deemed to be reserved until time of trial.

I will be asking most of the questions and answer as directly as you can.

"MILTON L. LEE

being first duly sworn, was examined on behalf of the defendant and testified as follows:

"By Mr. Ewing:

"Q. What is your name, please?

"A. My name is Milton L. Lee.

"Q. And your address?

"A. West 3236 Houston, Spokane, Washington.

"Q. And what is your occupation?

"A. I am the Manager of Alsco Northwest.

"Q. By Manager, you mean also President of Alsco Northwest? [54]

"A. Well, my present occupation is Manager.

"Q. What was your status with Alsco Northwest from 1955 through 1958?

"A. I was President.

"Q. That is with Alsco Northwest?

"A. Alsco Northwest, Incorporated.

"Q. And were you also President of Alsco Storm Windows, Inc.?   A. I was.

"Q. And were you President of that company from 1955 to 1958?   A. Yes.

"Q. And in your capacity as President of these

(Deposition of Milton L. Lee.)

two corporations, do you know what the process was for receiving work orders to be given to installers?   A. Yes, I do.

"Q. And what was that procedure? How did you receive the work orders?

"A. Well, we received the work orders from dealers and field representatives.

"Q. Were these dealers and field representatives employees of yours?   A. Sometimes.

"Q. And those who weren't employees, what was their [55] status in reference to your company?

"A. Well, they would be independent dealers, just buying from us.

"Q. And these are the people that you received work orders from; I mean, they got the orders for you?

"A. They made out the orders, as a rule, yes.

"Q. When you had a work order to be fulfilled, how were the installers notified of such?

"A. Well, they would be notified, or they were notified through our plant manager.

"Q. And what is his name?

"A. Ralph Williams.

"Q. And when Mr. Williams notified a particular installer that he had a work order for him, that installer would then come down to the plant?

"A. That's right.

"Q. Do you have a copy of a work order with you?   A. I do.

"Q. Would you be able to turn that over to me at this time?

(Deposition of Milton L. Lee.)

"A.   Uh-huh. (Document handed to Mr. Ewing.)

"Q.   This is a copy of a work order that has been processed or been used?

"A.   Yes, this copy was processed in 1956. Well, it was actually processed in '57· [56]

"Q.   Was there any agreement between your company and an installer other than the work order? Was there any agreement in writing between your company and an installer other than the work order?

"A.   No, there never was any written agreement, to my knowledge.

"Q.   The only written agreement between your company and the installers was this work order?

"A.   Well, there is no written agreement between us and the installer in the work order.

"Q.   This was the only thing in writing, the work order was the only thing that was in writing?

"A.   That's right.

"Q.   To your knowledge, were any of those installers members of any union?

"A.   Well, I wouldn't want to be specific as to that, but I think some installers have belonged to unions, yes.

"Q.   You didn't hire them on a union status?

"A.   No.

"Q.   In other words, preference call or anything like that?   A.   No.

"Q.   Were pay negotiations entered into upon the acceptance of a work order by an installer? [57]

"A.   Yes. As a matter of fact, we have had vari-

(Deposition of Milton L. Lee.)

ous meetings with these fellows and more or less outlined the pay arrangement, with the understanding that if there is anything that isn't specifically covered in this piece work schedule, it would be a matter of negotiation with us.

"Q. How were the installers paid? Were they paid by the hour?

"A. Oh, they are paid by the piece and by the job.

"Q. Was there any other talk between the installer and the representative of your company at that time, that you know of your own knowledge, other than just pay negotiations?

"A. Are you speaking of this meeting?

"Q. No, no. When an installer came in, I assume that somebody in your company, one of your representatives or you, asked the installer if he would accept this work order, is that right?

"A. Yes.

"Q. And was there any other conversation in reference to the particular job at that time?

"A. You are not speaking of this particular job?

"Q. No, not this particular one, but——

"A. Well, as a rule, no. On occasion, however, a job would be turned down by a fellow, and [58] then, of course, I would be called in to negotiate some kind of a settlement with him.

"Q. In the event that a work order was offered to an installer and he did turn it down, what happened then?

(Deposition of
"A. Well, '
"Q. And wl
that refused t
other?

"A. He wo
he would, mayb
because he turn
forfeit his rigt

"Q. Was h
turned down o

"A. Well, t
man.

"Q. Which
tion?

"A. Well, t
vary in degree
if you had a ¡
try to call in ¡
of doing it. If
ably go lookin
I say, that na
wouldn't forfe

"Q. Would
turned down a
as soon as ano

"A. Ordina
"Q. By his
wasn't laid off
"A. Well, :
body off.

"Q. Was t

(Deposition of Milton L. Lee.)

"A. Well, we usually called in another fellow.

"Q. And what happened to the particular fellow that refused the work order? Was he given another?

"A. He would wait to get another one, or maybe he would, maybe he wouldn't. I mean, he could. Just because he turned down a deal wouldn't necessarily forfeit his right to further jobs.

"Q. Was he offered another work order if he turned down one?

"A. Well, that would depend entirely on the man.

"Q. Which man, the installer or your organization?

"A. Well, the installer, yes, because these jobs vary in degree of skill they need to perform, and if you had a particularly difficult job, you would try to call in a man that you thought was capable of doing it. If he turned it down, you would probably go looking for somebody else to do it, but, as I say, that man wouldn't necessarily be out, he wouldn't forfeit his right to another job. [59]

"Q. Would you call that particular man that turned down a work order, would he be called back as soon as another work order came in?

"A. Ordinarily he would, yes.

"Q. By his refusing to accept a work order, he wasn't laid off any amount of time?

"A. Well, that kind of work, you don't lay anybody off.

"Q. Was there any disciplinary action so far

(Deposition of Milton L. Lee.)

as you were concerned as to an installer who refused to accept a work order?

"A. Well, I don't believe that issue has ever come up with me.

"Q. You don't know of any disciplinary action that has been taken against an installer who refused to accept a work order?

"A. No, I don't. Usually when a fellow turned down a work order, it was a matter of negotiation to figure out—it is usually because of price, that is what I am getting at.

"Q. Have there been installers come into your office, not having been called by you, but just come in looking for work?   A. Yes.

"Q. And if you didn't have a work order to give them [60] at that time, would you do anything?

"A. Well, we might try to make a note of the fact that the fellow is available.

"Q. Have you ever referred him to a competitor of yours who may have a work order?

"A. Yes, numerous times.

"Q. When you don't have work for them, you have referred them to some other competitor?

"A. Yes, yes, absolutely.

"Q. Have they taken that other job, do you know of your own knowledge?

"A. Oh, sure. Yes.

"Q. Is it your opinion that the installers were free to accept or reject any work order that was offered to them?

(Deposition of
"A. It has
they do it.
"Q. Were
one applicator
"Q. Gener:
ticular job? H
"A. Well, :
dow business,
very often hire
tice. If they n
themselves a he
"Q. Would
on a particular
installer interv
"Q. —I c
"A. No, I u
"Q. In the
on a particular
how that job s
tor's word wo:
"A. Well,
that I know of
"Q. Do th
"A. Yes, t
disagreed on
naturally nei-
money until the
refer it to the
"Q. You s
than the insta'
helpers?

(Deposition of Milton L. Lee.)

"A. It has always been a matter of practice that they do it.

"Q. Were there jobs which required more than one applicator?   A. Yes.

"Q. Generally, how many would work on a particular job? How many installers?

"A. Well, as a general rule in the storm window business, it is a one-man job. However, they very often hire helpers. That is the usual [61] practice. If they need more help, they go out and hire themselves a helper.

"Q. Would there be more than one applicator on a particular job, though? I use applicator and installer interchangeably, so——   A. Yes.

"Q. ——I don't want to confuse you.

"A. No, I understand. Well, there could be, yes.

"Q. In the event two applicators were working on a particular job and a question came up as to how that job should be performed, which applicator's word would control?

"A. Well, I wouldn't know. There is no rule that I know of.

"Q. Do they usually refer those matters to you?

"A. Yes, that would be a situation where, if they disagreed on how they could get the job done, naturally neither one of them would make any money until they got it settled, so they would usually refer it to the plant manager or myself.

"Q. You say on some jobs there would be other than the installers; in other words, there would be helpers?   A. Yes.

(Deposition of Milton L. Lee.)

"Q. Or apprentices?

"A. Frequently. [62]

"Q. And who would hire them?

"A. Well, from personal knowledge, I couldn't say, but I would assume that the applicator himself hired them.

"Q. You didn't?

"A. We didn't, no, the company didn't hire them.

"Q. Has there been any instance where a helper's work was unsatisfactory on a particular job and he had to be discharged?

"A. Oh, we wouldn't have any knowledge of that. If the work was unsatisfactory, it wouldn't be the helper we would go to, we would go to the applicator.

"Q. You didn't discharge any helpers?

"A. No, we wouldn't have any means of discharging a helper if he is hired by somebody else.

"Q. Did you handle the pay records of the helpers at all?

"A. Well, not as a rule, we didn't. We might have in particular instances where an applicator would ask us to pay the helper out of the gross proceeds, we might have done it, but as a rule we didn't pay helpers.

"Q. You say in some instances for the convenience of the installer you would handle the pay records [63] for that installer?   A. Yes.

"Q. Did you deduct taxes, and so forth, from the helper's checks?

"A. Without referring to them, I couldn't say,

(Deposition of Milton L. Lee.)

but presumably we handled them in the normal course of business, that is, like we would handle anybody else's. Of course, when you are speaking of helpers, I assume you mean the second man in a crew?

"Q. Well, somebody other than an installer.

"A. Yes. Well, they lots of times might team up and it wouldn't necessarily be an installer and a helper, might be just two fellows. As a crew, you might say.

"Q. You say the helper—we'll call him the helper—he was hired by the installer, is that right?

"A. I have already said that.

"Q. Would this require your approval?

"A. No. Not even my knowledge.

"Q. Who furnished the materials that went into any particular job?

"A. You mean who delivered them to the installer?

"Q. Well, the materials were purchased by your Company, were they not?

"A. As a rule, yes. If they were our contracts, we [64] certainly bought the materials.

"Q. Who delivered them to the job site?

"A. Well, it would depend on what they were and where they were obtained. Sometimes they were delivered to the job site by the company and sometimes the installer would deliver them to the job site.

"Q. Sometimes the installer would come to the company and pick up the materials and deliver them?

"A. As a rule, with windows and doors, that is

(Deposition of Milton L. Lee.)

what they do, they pick up the materials at the plant.

"Q. By 'they,' you mean installers?

"A. Installers, uh-huh.

"Q. Was anything else furnished by your company other than materials?

"A. Are you speaking of equipment, maybe?

"Q. Equipment?

"A. No, except on rare occasions we might loan out ladders, and so forth, but as a practice, we didn't furnish any tools.

"Q. As a practice, you didn't furnish anything other than materials, is that right?

"A. Yes, material, uh-huh.

"Q. In the event an installer broke one of his tools, who would pay to get him a new one? [65]

"A. He would.

"Q. Was he reimbursed?   A. No.

"Q. Did your company have any supervisors or other personnel that would go out on jobs that were in the process of being completed and observe them and give any instructions or suggestions?

"A. Not as a general rule, no. The plant manager might on occasion check a job, or if there is a complaint, we would send somebody out, but we didn't employ supervisors.

"Q. Did any of your salesmen go out and look the jobs over?

"A. Oh, as a matter of fact, they are supposed to, but as a rule, I don't think they ever go near a job.

(Deposition of Milton L. Lee.)

"Q. Well, there is nobody to watch the procedure of this work as it is going on at all from your office?   A. No.

"Q. In other words, the installer just went out and started a job and worked right on through, and when he was finished, came in and got another work order, and there was nobody from your office, no representative from your office, ever went out [66] to check the work at all?   A. No.

"Q. So if questions came up during the performance of the job, the installer would just contact your company?

"A. The installer usually contacted the plant foreman, and if he thought it was necessary, he would refer it to me.

"Q. Well, did either the plant foreman or you ever go out and look at a job?   A. Yes.

"Q. And when you got out to the job, would you make some suggestions based on what their problem was?   A. Surely.

"Q. And you expected those suggestions to be followed?

"A. I don't think I quite follow you.

"Q. If you went out and looked at a job and there was some dispute, say, as to the installer, that is the reason you were out there, would you make some suggestion to the installer in order to get the problem straightened out?

"A. Well, I am not aware of any situation that has come up where the installer has been in dispute with the company about how to do something. It

(Deposition of Milton L. Lee.)

is usually a situation where the homeowner, the [67] customer, has got some question that the installer just doesn't know enough or is not familiar with the contract so he can't settle it himself, so in a situation like that, they usually refer it back to the office and somebody contacts the customer. In other words, an effort is made to try to satisfy the customer and then, of course, the installer is advised as to that, and that is usually what it amounts to.

"Q. The installer is advised by you or one of your representatives?

"A. He would either be advised by one of us or the customer himself.

"Q. The installer was, I suppose, supposed to follow whatever instructions you gave him?

"A. Surely.

"Q. But you say the only instances when you went out to look at a job is when you were called about some question that came up on the job; in other words, if no questions arose during the performance of the work, nobody from your company would go out and look at a job?

"A. Well, I would say not necessarily.

"Q. What do you mean by that?

"A. Well, if you are asking me to say positively that [68] nobody ever went out to a job, I couldn't say. You started out to ask me if we had supervisors, if we employed supervisors, or make a practice of seeing these jobs in the course of construction. We don't. On the other hand, if there is a job going up across the street from me, I would obvi-

(Deposition of Milton L. Lee.)

ously take a look at it, maybe just out of my own curiosity, but we didn't supervise the applicators in the sense that you are talking about it.

"Q. On these jobs that you have gone out to look at, have you ever made any suggestions?

"A. Surely.

"Q. And you expected them to be followed?

"A. Well, if I made a suggestion, I certainly would.

"Q. Have you ever given any directions?

"A. To an applicator?

"Q. Yes.

"A. If the occasion arose, I would, yes.

"Q. And you expected him to follow those directions that you gave?

"Mr. Roe: I object. It is leading.

"Q. (By Mr. Ewing): You stated that there have been times when you have given directions to an applicator, is that right? [69]

"A. No, I didn't say that. You asked me if I would give them directions, and I said I would and if I gave them, I would expect them to be followed, yes. My day-to-day knowledge of these applications is not such that I would be in that position.

"Q. Well, I am just speaking generally, not of any particular job, but just of all the jobs in general. You say you can't remember of your own knowledge when you ever have given any directions, is that right?   A. Well, no, I don't.

"Q. But you had the power to give the directions?   A. Yes.

(Deposition of Milton L. Lee.)

"Q. And if those directions weren't followed, what, if anything, would happen to the applicator?

"A. Well, we would be inclined not to give him another job.

"Q. He would be discharged?

"Mr. Roe: I object. It is leading.

"Q. (By Mr. Ewing): If the installer didn't follow your directions, he just wouldn't be given any more work orders; is that what you are saying?

"Mr. Roe: I object. It is leading.

"Q. (By Mr. Ewing): What, if anything, would happen to an applicator if he didn't follow your [70] directions?

"A. Well, there have been times when an applicator hasn't done a job properly. We don't give him another one.

"Q. That is after the job is finished?

"A. Well, yes. Remember, I said that our contact with these jobs in progress hardly exists.

"Q. Has there ever been a time within your knowledge when an applicator has been, I won't say discharged, but put off the job during the course of that job?

"A. Well, I don't exactly remember the incidents, but I'm sure there have been, yes.

"Q. In that event, they just wouldn't get any more work orders?

"A. That's right. If we felt their work was not satisfactory on that job, we wouldn't be giving them another one.

"Q. Is it my understanding that you had the

(Deposition of Milton L. Lee.)

power to give directions; even though you may not have exercised it, you felt you had power to give directions as to how the job should be performed?

"Mr. Roe: Object. That question calls for a conclusion of the witness as to what the interrogator's understanding is.

"Q. (By Mr. Ewing): Assuming that you never gave [71] directions to an applicator, you state that you felt that you had the power to give directions to an applicator?

"Mr. Roe: I object. It is leading.

"Mr. Ewing: Why is it leading?

"Mr. Roe: Would you read it again?

"(Question read.)

"Mr. Ewing: I think he has already answered that once and I just wanted to make sure as to whether he has.

"(Off the record discussion.)

"Q. Did you have the power to give directions, Mr. Lee?

"A. Yes, in making a deal with an applicator to apply a job, at least I would assume that you would have the power of instructing him as to the way it should be done. Unwritten law in the business, you might say.

"Q. Did you, in fact, instruct installers as to how the job should be done?

"A. Oh, on occasion, yes.

(Deposition of Milton L. Lee.)

"Q. There were occasions during the performance of the job?

"A. No, no, I didn't say during the performance of it.

"Q. When were these instructions given, after the job [72] was finished?

"A. No, when this order was ready for delivery to an installer, if there were any specific information that the installer should need, such as taking out long ladders or roof jacks or ladder jacks or scaffolding or special tools or something that we had knowledge of that the installer should know about, why, naturally we would instruct him as to how to do it, what to take out.

"Q. Were there any directions given during the performance of the work?

"A. Oh, if an applicator called in and he needed some advice on the subject or on the application of it, I presume we would, yes.

"Q. Are you stating that the only time you intervened during the performance of a job was when an installer called you?

"A. No, but it would be necessitated by a call from the installer or a call from the customer, or both.

"Q. That is why I say, the only time that you gave directions or intervened during the performance of a job was when it was initiated either by the installer or the homeowner?

"A. As a rule, yes. [73]

"Q. Did you ever go out on the job during the

(Deposition of
performance o'
an installer or
"A. Oh, I
was no specific
spect the work
"Q. What v
"A. Oh, I
tomer, straight
"Q. As an
"A. Show a
or show a deal
of reasons.
"Q. But yo
over or inspec'
those type of v
"A. I didn'
"Q. Well, d
were there?
"Q. Did yo
that something
suggestion?
"A. I didn'
"Q. Well, y
numerous [74]
work?   A.
"Q. But v
said anything?
"Q. Were
tions or directi
that you had :
"Mr. Roe:

(Deposition of Milton L. Lee.)

performance of the work without being called by an installer or applicator?

"A. Oh, I have been on many jobs when there was no specific call, yes, but I wasn't there to inspect the work, necessarily.

"Q. What were you there for?

"A. Oh, I would be there to talk to the customer, straighten out the financing.

"Q. As an incident to that visit——

"A. Show another customer a job being installed or show a dealer a job being installed. There is lots of reasons.

"Q. But you say that you never looked the work over or inspected the work when you were out on those type of visits?

"A. I didn't state that.

"Q. Well, did you look the work over when you were there?   A. Sure.

"Q. Did you make any suggestions? If you felt that something wasn't right, did you ever make a suggestion?

"A. I didn't do that as a matter of practice, no.

"Q. Well, you just stated that there have been numerous [74] occasions when you did inspect the work?   A. That's right.

"Q. But you are saying that you very seldom said anything?   A. That is correct.

"Q. Were there times when you gave suggestions or directions during the performance of a job that you had gone out to look at?

"Mr. Roe: If you can recall.

(Deposition of Milton L. Lee.)

"A. I don't recall of any job where I have intervened with the installer, no.

"Q. (By Mr. Ewing): Do you know of your own knowledge of anybody else that represents your company has gone out to look at jobs and inspect them?   A. No.

"Q. You are the only one that does the inspecting?

"A. I know of my own knowledge that there would be others that would be in the same position I would that would be on the job, yes, but I have no knowledge as to whether they would intervene with the installer or whether they wouldn't.

"Q. In the event a homeowner was dissatisfied with the installer's work, what would be done then?

"A. Well, there is no general rule as to how you satisfy a homeowner. You do it the best way you can. [75]

"Q. Would there be times when a homeowner would call into your office during the performance of the work and say he was dissatisfied with the work?   A. Yes.

"Q. What would be done then?

"A. Well, on occasion the job would be taken away from the man that was doing it, and on other occasions the homeowner would probably be educated as to why he was doing what he was, and some cases the homeowner would complain about the work being done when maybe it was a matter of what he had to work with. I am speaking of the windows and the doors that he was installing or the

(Deposition of Milton L. Lee.)

opening that he was putting them on. I say there is no general rule as to how you take care of a complaint.

"Q. You stated that there were times when the homeowner would call and state that he was dissatisfied with the installer's work and you would take that installer off that job?

"A. Well, I can't remember that I ever did that, but I'm reasonably sure that it has happened.

"Q. Would that be done strictly on the word of the homeowner over the telephone?   A. No

"Q. Somebody would go out and look at the job? [76]

"A. They don't do anything strictly on what a person might say, a snap judgment.

"Q. Somebody from your office then would go out and look the job over at that time?

"A. Surely.

"Q. And the person that went out from your office would inspect the job at that time and find out what the dissatisfaction was about, I assume, is that right?   A. Yes.

"Q. And if that representative from your office felt that the work was not being done in a satisfactory manner, then that person who went out from your office would excuse that applicator from that job?

"A. Yes, that is about the way it would work, yes.

"Q. Were there any set hours that an installer would have to work?   A. None.

(Deposition of Milton L. Lee.)

"Q. There wasn't any time which he had to be there in the morning?   A.   No.

"Q.   Or leave in the evening?   A.   No.

"Q.   Did the installers share in the profits or losses of your business? [77]   A.   No.

"Q.   Were there any occasions that you know of where an installer was taken off one job before it was completed and put on another job?

"A.   Well, not to my knowledge, I don't know of the number of times when an installer would be taken off a job. They are few. As a matter of fact, I am not aware of one, although I'm sure in 15 years it could happen.

"Q.   You say that there were a number of times when an installer was taken off a job?

"A.   I say the **number of times would be few.** There were only a few occasions when that would ever come up, and I'm not aware of one.

"Q.   Are you aware of any instances where an installer was taken off a job before it was finished and put on another job? Say, for instance, you had a death?

"A.   I know of one particular instance where a man left a job before it was finished.

"Q.   That was of his own will, voluntarily?

"A.   Well, he was just gone for three or four days. We got somebody else to finish the job and then eventually he came back. Pretty upset that we had done it, but we did. [78]

"Q.   Were there certain deadlines to be met on some of these jobs?

(Deposition of Milton L. Lee.)

"A.　Of course. There is a deadline on every job.

"Q.　In that event, if an applicator was working on one job and your deadline was about to be met on another job, would that installer be taken off the job he had originally started and put on that one where the deadline had about run out?

"A.　Well, I am not familiar enough with the operation of these applicators as to moving from one job to another to say that. Applicators are usually given a certain amount of work to do. We are speaking of specific jobs. Sometimes he might be given a dozen contracts at one time. If the customer called up in the process of this load of windows he is installing and said, 'If you don't put my windows on, I'll cancel,' I imagine, as a matter of courtesy, the applicator would stop one job and start another, but that isn't being taken off one and put on the other, that is just a routine business transaction. I mean, you have emergencies like that. That is about the way you would handle it.

"Q.　In those instances, how would the installer be paid for that job that he went onto; in other [79] words, the second job?

"A.　Just exactly like he would have been paid if it hadn't happened that way.

"Q.　You mean he would be paid by the unit for the work on the second job?　　A.　Sure.

"Q.　And when he finished that job, he would go back to the job that he originally started?

"A.　Well, when he finished both jobs, he would bring them in and get paid for both of them, the same as if he did one and then he did the other.

(Deposition of Milton L. Lee.)

"Q. Will you state whether or not you felt that you could move the installers around from one job to another at your discretion?

"A. Well, the applicators and installers with us have always been considered to be contract employees.

"Q. That wasn't the question——

"A. As such, we treat them as individuals with a certain amount of ability.

"Q. That isn't the question, Mr. Lee. The question was, if you can state whether or not you felt that you could move one installer from one job to another at your discretion?

"A. I don't feel that way, and I never have, no.

"Q. As a matter of fact, you did move them when [80] somebody called, say, on one job and said, 'I've got storm windows I've got to get up,' and this particular applicator was working on another job, you could call him and send him to that other job, could you not?

"A. Well, only if he is willing to go.

"Q. But you would ask him to go, wouldn't you?

"A. I sure would.

"Q. What if he didn't go?

"A. You mean what would I do if he didn't go?

"Q. Yes.   A. I don't know. I don't know.

"Q. That has never arisen?

"A. Well, I don't think it has. I don't remember any instances like that when any applicators haven't been more than willing to co-operate. After

(Deposition of Milton L. Lee.)

all, they get paid for the same work that we would get paid for.

"Q. So as a general rule when you did ask them to go from one job to another, they went?

"A. They did, yes.

"Q. Taking a person of reasonable experience in this type of work, isn't it true that the job could be done without close supervision?

"A. Well, it is being done without close supervision, [81] yes.

"Q. And taking a man who is reasonably experienced in this type of work, isn't it true that he could do the job with little or no supervision?

"A. They are doing it.

"Q. Could an applicator substitute materials that were purchased by you for the job? In other words, could he use materials other than those which you delivered to this job site?

"A. Could he?

"Q. Yes.   A. That is possible.

"Q. Would this be with your approval or of representatives of your firm?

"A. Well, I guess I misunderstand. You say could he use somebody else's material. Well, he could. Well, if he could do it and we have no control over him, why, he would, wouldn't he? I mean, I don't quite follow what you——

"Q. I am not asking whether you have any control over him or not, I am asking you if the installer could use materials other than those which were delivered by you for a particular job? Would

(Deposition of Milton L. Lee.)

he have to use just those materials which were delivered by you? [82]

"A. He was supposed to use what is ordered to the job, yes, sir.

"Q. And if other materials were needed, could he go ahead and buy those other materials? What would be the situation there?

"A. The usual practice is that he would buy the other material and use it, yes.

"Q. You wouldn't buy the other materials?

"A. We would, yes, on occasion. It would depend on where the job was and how much the material cost and its availability and proximity to the job. A lot of things would enter into it. He would do that or sometimes we buy for him.

"Q. Could the installer substitute materials other than those that were in the work order without your approval?

"A. Well, I think you would have to be more specific than that.

"Mr. Ewing: Would you read the question back?

"(Question read.)

"Mr. Roe: I don't understand that question myself. If the materials aren't in the work order, why would he even have any need for them on the job? What kind of materials would he be [83] substituting?

"Q. (By Mr. Ewing): I assume that these materials that are on the work order, it doesn't always

(Deposition of Milton L. Lee.)

exactly work out that those are just the materials that are needed for that particular job. Are there times when other materials are needed other than those which are in the work order? A. Yes.

"Q. And as to those other materials, before the applicator put those other materials into the job, would he call you for your approval first?

"A. Not as a rule.

"Q. He would go ahead and purchase the materials out of money out of his own pocket?

"A. Yes, or if he didn't have it, he would probably call us up for permission to charge it to us.

"Q. The question I am asking you is, could he put those other materials into the job without prior approval from you?

"A. Well, I wouldn't answer that question plain yes or no. Sometimes he would and sometimes he wouldn't. It depends on the nature of these added materials. If it is a small item, he feels that the customer would accept it and it would be okay with us, he probably would take it upon himself to be the judge; if he felt he would be taking a chance he [84] wouldn't be reimbursed, he would probably come back to us.

"Q. If a homeowner desired repairs done which were outside of the work order, or if the homeowner desired any work to be done which was outside the work order, would the installer contact you before performing that work? A. Usually.

"Q. Was the installer free to negotiate with the homeowner as to work outside the work order?

(Deposition of Milton L. Lee.)

"A. Yes.

"Q. Do you know of any instance where that was done?   A. Yes.

"Q. Without your approval?   A. Yes.

"Q. In other words, you are saying that there have been jobs where the installer has entered into a separate contract with the homeowner?

"A. Well, there have been lots of jobs where the installers have entered into subsequent contracts with the homeowner that grew out of the contact that he made when they were working on the house, yes.

"Q. And that would be without your approval or knowledge?   A. Oh, sure. [85]

"Q. There wasn't any policy that those matters should be referred to you or your representatives?

"A. Only if they involved our material and our contracts.

"Q. When extra work was required to be done on a job, how was the applicator paid as to that extra work?

"A. If the work was performed on one of our contracts?

"Q. Yes.

"A. Well, he is usually paid on the basis of the request that the applicator would make. In other words, if he did work that he thought was worth $10, he asked for $10.

"Q. In other words, he wasn't paid by the unit price for extra work?   A. No.

"Q. He was more or less paid——

(Deposition of Milton L. Lee.)

"A. No such a thing. Probably his asking price for extra work was based on the number of hours he put in, as a rule, I would imagine, but there is no set figure on that.

"Q. So the work within the work order was paid on the unit price and work outside the work order or extra work was paid by the hour?

"Mr. Roe: I object as leading.

"A. Not paid by the hour, no. [86]

"Q. (By Mr. Ewing): Didn't you just say it was based, probably, on an hourly rate?

"A. No, I didn't.

"Q. Well, what did you say?

"A. I said I thought that the applicator doing extra work would probably determine his asking price based on the number of hours he put in, but he doesn't work by the hour, as far as we are concerned.

"Q. He wasn't paid by the unit price as to the extra work?

"Mr. Roe: I object. It is leading.

"A. I don't know what you mean by unit price.

"Mr. Roe: Well, he is telling you. I submit he should ask you.

"Q. (By Mr. Ewing): As to work within the work order, didn't you say it was paid by unit price; isn't that what you call unit price? Is that what you call it?

"A. The pay on contract jobs, which is the usual thing with us, is based on piece work.

"Q. I see. Now, the pay as to the extra work,

(Deposition of Milton L. Lee.)

was that based on piece work? In other words, you didn't use the same type of pay scale as to that work which was within the work order and that work which was outside of the work order? [87]

"A. No, it is a different plan of payment for extra labor.

"Q. Will you state whether or not an installer could make changes in a contract without your approval?

"A. No, the installer can't make changes in our contract.

"Q. That applies to any type of change, is that right?   A. Yes.

"Q. Could an installer do anything that you could not veto? Do you know what I mean by veto?

"A. No, I don't know what you mean by veto.

"Q. Well, in other words, you could put your arm down or hand down and say, 'You can't do that'? Could an installer do anything which you could say couldn't be done or could be done?

"Mr. Roe: Would you repeat that again?

"(Question read.)

"Mr. Roe: Could an installer do anything that you say could be done or could not be done?

"A. Yes, he can do many things that we don't have any veto power over.

"Q. (By Mr. Ewing): Will you state whether or not you provide or offer to provide workmen's compensation coverage for your installers?

vs. Unite

Deposition of

"Mr. Roe:

"Mr. Ewing

"Mr. Roe:

"A. I don'

"Q. (By N

men's comp. f

"A. That I

"Q. Who w

"A. The of

"Q. After a

for the instal o

homeowner?

"A. By ne

require him to

"Q. When

necessary for h

the homeowner

satisfied with th

"A. Yes, it

"Q. Pardo

"A. It was

"Q. In oth

work order to

pletion slip fr

"A. Oh, ye

"Q. An is s

order? [89]

"Q. Was i

paid to get a c

"Q. Well,

each job?

(Deposition of Milton L. Lee.)

"Mr. Roe: Object. It is irrelevant. [88]

"Mr. Ewing: Just one of the elements.

"Mr. Roe: Go ahead and answer.

"A. I don't know.

"Q. (By Mr. Ewing): Did you provide workmen's comp. for your installers?

"A. That I don't know.

"Q. Who would know?

"A. The office manager would know.

"Q. After a job was completed, was it necessary for the installer to get a completion slip from the homeowner?

"A. By necessary, what do you mean? Did we require him to do it?

"Q. When an installer finished a job, was it necessary for him to get any type of clearance from the homeowner signifying that the homeowner was satisfied with the work for your records?

"A. Yes, it was necessary.

"Q. Pardon?

"A. It was necessary, but it wasn't required.

"Q. In other words, you wouldn't issue another work order to an installer until he received a completion slip from the homeowner?

"A. Oh, yes, we would, and we did.

"Q. An installer could start out on another work order? [89]   A. Yes.

"Q. Was it necessary before that installer was paid to get a completion slip?   A. No, no.

"Q. Well, was the completion slip necessary on each job?

(Deposition of Milton L. Lee.)

"A. It was necessary, but it wasn't required.

"Q. And what did that slip signify?

"A. Completion slip?

"Q. Yes.

"A. It signified the work was done.

"Q. Did it signify it was done in a satisfactory manner?

"A. Well, not necessarily. It signified the customer signed a piece of paper that states that the work is done in a satisfactory manner.

"Q. Have there been instances within your knowledge when the howeowner didn't sign the slip?   A. Yes.

"Q. What would be done then?

"A. What would be done with the installer?

"Q. Yes.

"A. We would pay him off and give him another job.

"Q. Well, if the homeowner didn't sign the slip, would somebody from your office go out and ask why? [90]

"A. Yes, surely. Usually, the salesman went back to get it, mostly by prearrangement.

"Q. If something further was necessary to be done, another installer would come in and finish the job up?

"A. No, no, we sent back the same installer, if he was available.

"Q. And he finished the job up?

"A. Uh-huh.

"Q. If he wasn't available, somebody else would

(Deposition of
come and finis!

"Q. Do yo
whether any of
selves out to th

"A. Yes.

"Q. You n
paper?

"A. Are yo

"Q. Yes.

"Q. What i

"A. Most of
companies like
hold himself up
available, why,
known to comp

"Q. So far
the fact other t

"A. I don't
one way or the

"Q. Did yo
ever have a sig

"A. Yes, w

"Q. Did th
there advertisi

"A. I don't

"Q. You h
that has happe

"Q. Can y
going to be it.

"A. (No re

"Mr. Roe:

(Deposition of Milton L. Lee.)
come and finish it?   A. Surely.

"Q. Do you know of your own knowledge whether any of these installers have ever held themselves out to the public as being installers?

"A. Yes.

"Q. You mean they have advertised in the paper?

"A. Are you asking me if they advertised?

"Q. Yes.   A. I don't know that.

"Q. What is the basis of your 'yes' answer?

"A. Most of the application work goes through companies like ourselves, and when you said did he hold himself up to the public as being an applicator available, why, yes, he did. He made his skills [91] known to competitors of ours and took their jobs.

"Q. So far as you know, they never advertised the fact other than just going to those people?

"A. I don't know whether they have or haven't, one way or the other.

"Q. Did you ever advertise on a job? Did you ever have a sign out on the lawn advertising?

"A. Yes, we have done it, yes.

"Q. Did the applicator ever have a sign out there advertising that he was an applicator?

"A. I don't know of any, no.

"Q. You have never seen any instances where that has happened?   A. No.

"Q. Can you tell me who your witnesses are going to be in this case?

"A. (No response.)

"Mr. Roe: Tell him, if you know.

(Deposition of Milton L. Lee.)

"A.   I don't. Is this still on the record?

"Mr. Ewing: Yes.

"Mr. Roe: Yes.

"Q. (By Mr. Ewing): Your answer is you don't know?   A. I don't know.

"Q. Do you know approximately how many applicators were working for you between 1955 and 1958? [92]

"A. Total number in the two companies?

"Q. Right.

"A. I don't know, but I would estimate.

"Q. Approximately how many?   A. 30.

"Q. Was this seasonal work?

"A. I don't know what you mean by seasonal.

"Q. Did you work in the wintertime, too?

"A. Yes. We have work every season, but there is more in some seasons than others.

"Q. But the winter wouldn't prevent you from doing this type of work?   A. No.

"Mr. Ewing: I believe that is all. [93] .

MILTON L. LEE

Redirect Examination

By Mr. Lyman:

Q. You recall that counsel was reading certain questions and answers to you that you made on your deposition relative to the term "contract employee," do you recall that just now?   A. Yes.

(Testimony of :

Q. Now, w!
question was:

"Q. Will y
you could mo'
job to another

Do you rec:
Q. Do you 1

"A. Well, t
have always be
ees." [94]

A. Yes.

Q. Would y
tract employee:

A. I mean :

Q. And ther

"Q. If you (
could move on,
at your diseret

"A. I don't
Do you rem:

A. Yes, sir.

Q. Do you

"Q. As a 1
when somebod;
got storm win!
ticular applica
could call him
you not?"

Do you rem,

A. Yes,

Q. Do you

(Testimony of Milton L. Lee.)

Q. Now, when you answered that question, the question was:

"Q. Will you state whether or not you felt that you could move the installers around from one job to another at your discretion?"

Do you recall that question?   A. Yes.

Q. Do you recall making this answer:

"A. Well, the applicators and installers with us have always been considered to be contract employees." **[94]**

A. Yes.

Q. Would you tell us what you mean by "contract employees"?

A. I mean subcontractors.

Q. And then do you remember this question:

"Q. If you can state whether or not you felt you could move one installer from one job to another at your discretion?

"A. I don't feel that way and I never have, no."

Do you remember that answer?

A. Yes, sir.

Q. Do you remember this question:

"Q. As a matter of fact, you did move them when somebody called, say, on one job and said, 'I've got storm windows I've got to get up,' and this particular applicator was working on another job, you could call him and send him to that other job, could you not?"

Do you remember this question?

A. Yes.

Q. Do you remember this answer:

(Testimony of Milton L. Lee.)

"A. Well, only if he is willing to go."

A. Yes.

Q. Now, do you recall during this period, if you have any [95] recollection of your own, while you were there or during this period, whether or not the unit prices for windows and for siding were changed as a result of conferences between you and the applicators?   A. Yes, they were.

Q. And how did that come about, if you know, who started it off?

A. It started off by the applicators approaching me to have such a meeting and discuss the prices.

Q. And did the prices go up as a result of that meeting?   A. They did.

Q. Now, there was some question raised about the company loaning out tools. How often would you loan an applicator or an installer a tool?

A. Very, very seldom.

Q. And what sort of thing would it be?

A. It might be an extension ladder, a 40-foot extension ladder, or staging, or possibly if you had an extremely large unit you might loan him a truck to haul it out.

Q. That would be on a rare occasion?

A. Yes.

Q. Ordinarily the men had their own tools and their own equipment and their own trucks, isn't that true?   A. Right, sir.

Q. Now, was there any different rate that the men demanded [96] or negotiated for a job that was higher than the first floor?   A. Yes.

(Testimony of Milton L. Lee.)

Q. And how did that come about, if you know?

A. More or less the same way, they would just say, "I can't make any money on this kind of basis, I have got to have a better deal," so we would negotiate a better rate.

Q. And if the job was some distance away from the metropolitan center or the city center, would that have any effect on the amount the man would get?

A. Yes, the rates changed for that, too.

Q. Now, who would pay expenses for these installers, many of them had to stay overnight, isn't that so?   A. Yes.

Q. And they would go away for periods at a time?   A. Yes.

Q. And who would pay their expenses?

A. They paid their own.

Q. It would come out of the gross amount of their earnings?   A. That is right.

Q. Now, I believe the question was answered or asked, "Do you have power to discharge a man for bad performance," do you recall the question by Mr. Ewing?   A. Yes. [97]

Q. Well, I will ask you this question: If a man is not performing in a workmanlike manner and is not in keeping with the time of the customer, isn't that the time that you would exercise that power?

A. Yes.

Q. What was your interest in the performance of a job, what did you look for?

A. Our interest is in a complete performance of

(Testimony of Milton L. Lee.)

the work on a job. In other words, we gave a man a work order and said, "Do the job, bring it in complete," and then our interest was in the complete performance of the work on the job.

Q. Now, when a man would go out, what interest, if any, did you have in the manner or the method in which he went about the job?

A. We had no interest in that.

Q. Now, did you ever tell a man which side of the house to start on, for instance?   A. No.

Q. Or which windows to put up first?

A. No.

Q. Or which door to put on?   A. No.

Q. Who decided those details?

A. He decided those details for himself. [98]

Q. Now, when a customer would complain, you would usually have somebody from the shop or yourself would go out, isn't that correct?

A. Usually from the shop.

Q. Yes. Now, was that Mr. Williams, as a rule?

A. I think so.

Q. Now, what was his function?

A. Well, he was the manager of the production department and, as such, he passed out the work orders to the installers and applicators, too.

Q. Then he would go out on his customer complaint?   A. Yes.

Q. All right. Now, did he ever——

A. (Interposing): Not always; I mean, he went out on some of them.

(Testimony of Milton L. Lee.)

Q. Now, did he ever direct or show a man the details of how to perform his work on the job?

A. I can't say that.

Q. I see, all right. Now, counsel asked you several questions about leaving one job to go.,to another; when those things happened, whose job would a man leave to go to?

A. He would usually leave one of his own jobs to go to another of his own jobs. In other words, if he had a load of windows, he would have several work orders, in other words, if the occasion occasioned, he might [99] leave and go on to another job and then come back to the first one.

Q. Did these installers occasionally have more than one job going at the same time?

A. Yes, they frequently did.

Q. Did you ever have a situation when you would tell one man to go to work on another man's job and compel him to divide up the profit?

A. I have no knowledge of such a situation.

Q. Has it ever happened?

A. Not to my knowledge.

Q. Now, I believe counsel asked you, "Can't these jobs be done without somebody standing over and supervising," do you recall that question?

A. Yes.

Q. Isn't it a fact that you rely upon the experience of these men to do a satisfactory job in accordance with the contract?   A. Entirely.

Q. And it is this reliance that has caused you to dispense with supervisors, isn't that true?

(Testimony of Milton L. Lee.)

A. Yes. When you say "dispense," we never had supervisors.

Q. Well, I mean in the nature of the business that supervisors are not required, so you have never had the necessity for it? [100]

A. That is right.

Q. Now, I believe you answered questions on direct examination to the effect that there were no written agreements between the applicators and the company? A. That is correct.

Q. Now, I believe you were also, just to refresh your recollection, that other than the writing on the work orders which you identified, there were no other written directions or instructioins as to how to do the job? A. Specific job?

Q. Yes. A. No.

Q. Now, counsel has asked you if there were bulletins of some kind; what were the nature of these bulletins, what was their purpose?

A. Well, the purpose of the bulletins would be to lay out the general specifications of a good job; for instance, a suggested approach to do satisfactory work.

Q. Well, they were suggestive of an approach to a job?

A. Well, they were not signed contracts.

Mr. Lyman: No. I believe that is all, your Honor.

The Court: Mr. Ewing?

By Mr. Ewing

Q. In refer from one [101] that he would that correct?

Q. Referrir line 16:

"Q. As a when somebod 'I've got storm this particular job, you would job, could you:

"A. Well, (

"Q. But yo you? A.

"Q. What i

"A. You didn't go?

"Q. Yes.

Q. (By M right? A.

Q. Some of did they not?

Q. And ass for an installe point along th job, say in Pa that job whic

(Testimony of Milton L. Lee.)

Recross-Examination

By Mr. Ewing:

Q. In reference to this moving installers around from one [101] job to another, I believe you stated that he would go only if he was willing to go, is that correct? A. Yes.

Q. Referring to the deposition again, page 27, line 16:

"Q. As a matter of fact, you did move them when somebody called, say, on one job and said, 'I've got storm windows I've got to get up,' and this particular applicator was working on another job, you would call him and send him to that other job, could you not?

"A. Well, only if he is willing to go.

"Q. But you would ask him to go, wouldn't you? A. I sure would.

"Q. What if he didn't go?

"A. You mean what would I do if he didn't go?

"Q. Yes. A. I don't know. I don't know."

Q. (By Mr. Ewing): Does that sound about right? A. Yes.

Q. Some of these installers had out of town jobs, did they not? A. Yes.

Q. And assuming that you had a job in Yakima for an installer and you wanted him to stop at some point along the [102] way to Yakima to do another job, say in Pasco, now at that intermediate point at that job which that installer would do in Pasco,

(Testimony of Milton L. Lee.)

wasn't he paid by the hour on that job, his final destination being Yakima? In other words, he is going to do a job in Yakima, but there is another job that you asked him to do on the way, which we will say is in Pasco, his final destination is Yakima, isn't it true that as to that job in Pasco he would be paid by the hour for that job?

A. No, not if it is a regular installation job he wouldn't.

Q. And that has never happened that you know of?

A. Well, I am not aware of any hourly work having been done on that kind of a job, no. Now, if it is a matter of a complaint, or something like that, it could be, but you are talking about a job.

Q. Yes, a regular job.   A. A regular job?

Q. You don't know of anything like that?

A. I don't know of any.

Q. You stated that supervisors are not required, is that correct?   A. Required?

Q. Supervisors are not required in this type of work?   A. Not in our business.

Q. Yet you will recall in the deposition when I asked you [103] if you had been out on a job and if you had given suggestions and directions before, you stated you have, do you recall that?   A. Yes.

Q. And I believe you stated in your deposition that salesmen are supposed to go out and look at these jobs?   A. Yes.

Q. And isn't it true that the production manager, Mr. Williams, goes out and looks at these jobs now

(Testimony of Milton L. Lee.)

and then? A. He has done it.

Q. And hasn't Mr. McFarlane gone out and looked at these jobs? A. Yes.

Q. Who is Mr. McFarlane?

A. Well, he was the manager of the company prior to the time I came here.

Q. So even though there was nobody looking over this person's shoulder, the installer's shoulder, to every detail on the job, there were people going out and checking that work, were there not?

A. Every job?

Q. Well, not every job, I won't say every job.

A. There were people who check a few jobs, yes.

Q. Just a few? A. Yes. **[104]**

Mr. Ewing: That is all I have.

Redirect Examination

By Mr. Lyman:

Q. With regard to the last matter, when a salesman or Mr. Williams or Mr. McFarlane or yourself, you went out to look at a job or its progress, your interest, was it not, was to see that it conformed with the contract to the customer?

A. That is correct.

Q. Did you have any interest in which side of the house he began on? A. No.

Q. Or how he was going about doing the job?

A. No.

Mr. Lyman: That is all, your Honor.

The Court: I have a few questions: What is your residence, Mr. Lee?

(Testimony of Milton L. Lee.)

A. W. 3236 Houston, Spokane, Washington.

The Court: I thought you were living in Salt Lake City?

A. I lived in Salt Lake City until 1958.

The Court: Is Alsco Storm Windows a Washington corporation?   A. Yes.

The Court: It isn't so alleged in the [105] complaint. Is Alsco Northwest a Washington corporation?

A. It is, yes, sir.

The Court: Where were these returns filed that are involved here?

A. I think they were all filed in Tacoma, sir.

The Court: Now, your company, these two companies, had liability insurance, did they?

A. General liability, sir.

The Court: Yes.

A. Yes.

The Court: Was it a blanket liability policy?

A. General liability, yes, your Honor.

The Court: Who, in your organization, had charge of the liability insurance coverage?

A. Who is responsible for getting the contracts written?

The Court: Yes.

A. Those contracts were supervised by Mr. McFarlane.

The Court: Who is he?

A. He was the manager before I came.

The Court: Well, what about after you came?

A. Well, they were in force.

(Testimony of Milton L. Lee.)

The Court: Well, you don't have a continuous policy, do you? Don't you renew it annually?

A. Yes, sir, but the policy is the same.

The Court: Have you ever read the policy? **[106]**

A. Well, I think I am familiar with it, yes, sir.

The Court: Well, does it cover the operations of these installers and applicators?

A. Yes, sir.

The Court: Have you ever been sued by a customer because of any tortious act committed by an applicator or installer?   A. I don't think so.

The Court: Have you ever been sued?

A. Yes, sir.

The Court: For any tort liability? Do you know what I mean by "tort," any wrongful act, such as an automobile accident, or something like that?

A. No, sir, I don't think we have.

The Court: Where is the bulletin that you issued to these applicators or installers?

Mr. Ewing: May I answer that?

The Court: I was asking him.

Mr. Ewing: Well, I know.

The Court: Let me ask him, where is it?

A. We no longer use it, sir.

The Court: Have you got a copy here?

A. We couldn't get a copy.

The Court: You have got a lot of applicators, they must have some copies. **[107]**

A. Well, I understand that the defense has a copy.

(Testimony of Milton L. Lee.)

The Court: Do you have a copy, Mr. Ewing?

Mr. Ewing: Yes, I do.

The Court: All right. You talked about the unit price that you paid these applicators, what was the unit price?

A. In the storm window and door business it's based on windows, so much a window, so much a door.

The Court: It doesn't have anything to do with the size of the windows?

A. Not as much as the type of windows, sir.

The Court: What about the siding or roofing, is that by squares?

A. Siding and roofing is, generally speaking, based on so much per square.

The Court: When you say "generally speaking," that must mean that you must make a different rule for each case?

A. Well, there are certain parts of a siding job that you don't base on a square.

The Court: I see. Then you must have to make a different contract for each particular job, is that right?

A. It amounts to that, if the job involves different particular specifications.

The Court: Now, you stated on your **[108]** direct examination, as I recall, in answer to a question as to whether or not you removed men from the job if the installer and applicator did not perform correctly, that you would remove them from the job for unsatisfactory workmanship and you

(Testimony of Milton L. Lee.)

might sever your connection because of "lack of work to keep him busy," did you do that?

A. Yes.

The Court: Under what circumstances would you sever your connection with an applicator because of lack of work to keep him busy?

A. We had no work order to pass out to him so he had no job.

The Court: Well, you must have had some kind of an arrangement as to where you were going to find these men. Did you have them call at your office to report for work? How did they know when the work order was available?

A. Well, they sometimes called us. We frequently called them. The fellows are aware of the seasonal adjustment in our business, they sort of keep in touch.

The Court: Now, there might be times, then, when you would furnish enough work to keep an applicator busy continuously?

A. Yes, sir, we have had several applicators that have worked for several years.

The Court: For you and nobody else? **[109]**

A. Yes, sir.

The Court: Did you ever have a repeat business where these men go out and do work on the job?

A. I don't quite follow you, on the same job?

The Court: **Yes.**

A. Yes, sir.

The Court: You may have a contract with Mrs.

(Testimony of Milton L. Lee.)

John Doe for 1957, do you ever have a contract with her, for example, in 1960?

A. Yes, sir.

The Court: Now, you talked about the pad of work orders and purchase orders being the same and one a carbon of the other, do you have a pad of those work orders here?

A. No, sir.

The Court: You just give us the pink copy, what is that?

A. That is the copy we generally used for a work order.

The Court: I see. Well, what color are the others?

A. The original copy is white, the second copy is pink, and the third copy is yellow and the fourth copy is goldenrod, as I remember, sir.

The Court: And the customer, who keeps the fourth copy?

A. Well, to run through the series, this is about the way [110] they are handled: We keep a copy in the office, which is a file copy. We give a copy to the factory, which is the work order to the applicator. We usually send a copy to the dealer and salesman that turned it in, that is three. The fourth copy is a shop copy, which is used to manufacture the windows and it is filed in our factory.

The Court: Well, now, are they all printed differently?

A. No, it's the same form, different colored sheets.

(Testimony of Milton L. Lee.)

The Court: Does it say the same thing at the **top and the bottom?**

A. They are carbon copies.

The Court: Your contracts are signed by your representative salesmen, aren't they?

A. Yes.

The Court: And the purchase orders are signed by the same salesman?

A. He usually makes them out. The work order in the window business is generally made out by the man who measures the windows.

The Court: Who is that?

A. And that has generally been the salesman.

The Court: The purchase order has this notation: "Recheck all measurements. Positively no returns. Write **[111]** each order in quadruplicate. Mail original and duplicate to Alsco, Inc., Spokane 62, Washington. Retain duplicate in your files." Who are they referring to when they say "your files"?

A. The dealer.

The Court: Who is the dealer?

A. Well, the dealer might be an independent account, a dealer.

The Court: I will ask you to look at Exhibits 5 and 6, the dealer's name appears to be the customer who made the purchase. Does he keep the quadruplicate?

A. Well, sir, in this particular case of 6, the dealer's name was not written on it originally. They apparently had difficulty reading the customer's

(Testimony of Milton L. Lee.)

name, so they printed it on the left side, but the customer is not the dealer, no, sir, in this case.

The Court: You say that all these forms are always the same?

A. The purchase order and the work order, sir?

The Court: Yes.

A. Yes, sir, that is pretty generally the situation.

The Court: I will ask you to look at Exhibits 4 and 8 and compare them. They are not the same, are they (hands papers to witness)?

A. Well, no, sir. The difference is that this calls for [112] a specific type of window and in this case it's a door. We use different forms for different types of products.

The Court: Then you had different forms of purchase orders and work orders, didn't you.

A. Yes, sir.

The Court: Well, how many different forms did you have?

A. Well, I think we had two window and door forms, and a siding form; that would be three.

The Court: But these then are not, you don't have all of them here, then, do you?

A. I don't think we have any siding form, no, sir.

The Court: Weren't any of these purchase orders or work orders used by you that gave information as to where on the house the work was to be done?

A. The indication would be made by the number of the unit.

(Testimony of Milton L. Lee.)

The Court: Well, what does that have to do with it?

A. Well, we have a system of measuring the openings on a house, of numbering them, so when they are measured, why, we number them, and when a fellow goes out to put them on he knows where each unit goes.

The Court: Well, is that on the purchase order?

A. Yes, sir, it should be. In other words, Window No. 1 is a specific opening on a house. [113]

The Court: All right, that is all I have.

Mr. Lyman: If the Court please, I just want to make one objection, if I may.

The Court: To my questions? You certainly may. Do you want to move to strike it?

Mr. Lyman: I hesitated, but I have got to do it. The Court queried the witness on the question of liability insurance and I want to move an objection to the question as being immaterial in this type of case for the reason that for the purpose of a definition of employee under this particular statute the definition of employee in a particular state would have no relevance.

The Court: Would have no what?

Mr. Lyman: Would have no relevance. I refer to a case, a classic case, I think it's the 7th Circuit, Dimmett, and others.

The Court: Is it cited in your brief?

Mr. Lyman: No, your Honor.

The Court: I think you are correct about that. That is true, that the employee-employer relation-

(Testimony of Milton L. Lee.)

ship under the particular state law would not control as to the federal law, and the interpretations under the federal statutes, but, however, I had another question on the insurance matter and you don't have to answer this if you don't want to.

Mr. Lyman: I wouldn't know the answer. [114]

The Court: And so I think probably the question as to the interpretation of the liability policy would be immaterial because those other matters aren't controlling now, either. By that I mean the admissions at that time that they made when they withheld the tax and paid it over would not be controlling here, so if you want to make a motion to strike that part of the testimony on the grounds that my question is immaterial, I will grant your motion.

Mr. Lyman: Yes, your Honor.

The Court: All right.

Mr. Lyman: Thank you.

The Court: That is all, Mr. Lee.

(Witness excused.)

... Iuc., et al.

... haw would not con-
... the interpretations
... however, I had an-
... matter and you
... don't want to.
... the answer. [114]

... ably the ques-
... the liability policy
... other matters
... that I mean the
... made when they
... would not be con-
... make a motion to
... on the grounds
... I will grant your

RALPH E. WILLIAMS,

called and sworn as a witness on behalf of the plaintiffs, testified as follows:

The Clerk: Please state your name to the Court, please?

A. Ralph E. Williams.

The Clerk: Thank you, please be seated.

Mr. Ewing: I didn't catch that.

The Clerk: Ralph E. Williams. [116]

Mr. Lyman: Your Honor, we will endeavor not to be repetitious since it would serve no purpose.

Direct Examination

By Mr. Lyman:

Q. Mr. Williams, what is your present address?

A. N. 1502 Lewis, Spokane.

Q. Spokane? And what is your present occupation?

A. Production manager for Alsco Northwest, Inc.

Q. When did you first come with Alsco Northwest?   A. 1948.

Q. And how long have you been with the Spokane branch?   A. Continuously.

Q. From 1948?   A. That is right.

Q. All right, sir. Now, will you tell us how you go about getting applicators to do this work?

A. Well, some by reference, by newspaper ads, by telephone, and some, when we first started we broke them in from just green help.

(Testimony of Ralph E. Williams.)

Q. Now, in 1954 to '58, the period with which we are concerned, the men who were performing the service then were experienced in this work, were they not?   A. Most generally, yes.

Q. Now, may I have the work order, sir? I will show you Plaintiffs' Exhibits 2, 4, 6 and 8, and they are the [117] work orders, are they not, that you give the applicators when they go out on these jobs (hands papers to witness)?

A. That is right, we give them normally the pink copy.

Q. You give them normally the pink copy?

A. Normally, yes.

Q. Now, just so I get my colors straight, would Exhibits 2 and 4, which are not pink copies, would they be carbon copies of the pink copy which is in the file?

A. That is right, they are all in the same boat.

Q. In other words, I took the wrong one?

A. That is right. These are the copy that would go to the installer.

Q. But the information on Exhibits 2 and 4 would be the same on the pink copies?

A. Yes.

The Court: How about the printed matter?

Q. (By Mr. Lyman): How about the printed matter, would that be the same?

A. The printed matter would be the same unless it was a different type of windows, there would be four copies of this, and four of this (indicating).

Q. When you say different type windows, you

(Testimony of Ralph E. Williams.)

are referring to Plaintiffs' 8, but all of the colors of the various forms would have the same printed matter on it? [118]

A. The same thing, exactly.

Q. All right. Now then, I will ask you to look at the reverse side of each of the Exhibits 2, 4, 6 and 8, and tell us what is the purpose of the figuring on the reverse side?

A. Well, that is their pay scale, different type windows had a different price.

Mr. Lyman: Your Honor, I am not familiar with your procedure. May I stand here?

The Court: All right.

Q. (By Mr. Lyman): Now, for instance, we are looking at Plaintiffs' 8 in evidence, and there is certain writing on there, and what, essentially, is that writing, what does it mean?

A. The installer would write in there the number of windows and the price, and I would okay it, whether it would be paid or not, so the bookkeeper would know it was okay.

Q. All right. Now, based upon the computation on the rear side of the work order, that would comprise the pay, would it not, of an installer-applicator? A. Yes.

Q. And his pay was based upon each of these individual jobs? A. That is right.

Q. And each job was a separate [119] undertaking? A. That is right.

Q. Now, I notice in Plaintiffs' 6 in evidence, there are similar figures and there is some writing

(Testimony of Ralph E. Williams.)

"Extra labor for taking off plexiglass and stripping and one old screen door, $3.50." Now, what does that mean?

A. That means that he has entered into it with the customer to take that old stuff off before he puts that new on. We assume when they sold the windows there was a place for the window, and so that would be charged back to the job.

Q. All right. Now, he has the figure "$3.50" at the top of that computation, and then I am pointing to a line which says, "Charge extra labor $3.50."   A. That is right.

Q. Is that correct? Now, is there any indication there about hours of any kind?

A. No, no, just a specific amount of the job that he has done for the contract.

Q. Now, who decided that he gets $3.50, who arrived at that figure $3.50?

A. In this instance it was Gene, my foreman.

Q. Now, did the company arrive at $3.50 or does the man suggest the $3.50?

A. That is arbitrary with the salesman who sold the job. In other words, they check back with him and they [120] generally authorize that extra payment.

Q. In other words, the salesman who authorizes the extra payment, and it would come out of his commission?   A. That is right.

Q. All right, sir. Now, on Plaintiffs' 4 you have a similar computation in this block, and there is a

(Testimony of .
note, notation.
the significance
A. Well, th
in Portland by
has okayed to
that out of his
Q. In other
helper?   A
Q. And he
part of his gr
A. That is
one check to h
is directing the
Q. All right
tiffs' 2 in evide
and I notice
"$8.00," what
A. That wo
Q. And is t
there? [121]
Q. Do you
if you know?
A. No, it
copy by the sa
Q. All right
of these order-
installer?
Q. Now, h
A. Beg y
Q. How d
a number of j

(Testimony of Ralph E. Williams.)

note, notation, "Pay Dean Minton $3.00," what is the significance of that?

A. Well, this was an out-of-town job performed in Portland by I presume the installer Mr. Minton has okayed to pay Dean Minton, maybe his son, that out of his part of the contract.

Q. In other words, Dean Minton would be his helper? A. That is right.

Q. And he was directing the company to pay part of his gross proceeds to the helper?

A. That is right. In other words, making out one check to him, possibly, and one to him, and he is directing that they do that.

Q. All right, sir. Now, I will show you Plaintiffs' 2 in evidence. It has a block for computation, and I notice under the word "Other" it has "$8.00," what is that, if you know?

A. That would have been extra labor.

Q. And is there anything to indicate hours on there? **[121]** A. There is nothing.

Q. Do you know how that $8.00 was arrived at, if you know?

A. No, it would possibly be written up on a copy by the salesman.

Q. All right. In the shop you give out a number of these orders, do you not, sometimes to a single installer? A. That is right.

Q. Now, how does that work?

A. Beg your pardon?

Q. How does that work, why do you give them a number of jobs?

(Testimony of Ralph E. Williams.)

A. Well, maybe one job will have two doors on it and it is not enough to take out, and a lot of his time will be road time, and so we give him what he thinks it would be put on to satisfy and to put more jobs on in a given length of time.

Q. Now, you said "road time." He doesn't get paid for road time, does he?

A. No. I mean it would save him, he couldn't make enough money if he took out two units at a time, so we give him a load, and he could go any place he wanted and he could route it that way, save himself the road time.

Q. Who makes up the schedule when you give out a group of jobs? A. He would. [122]

Q. He decides which house he will do first and even if he wants to do two at the same time?

A. Once in a while we have a customer who is leaving town by a certain date, or going on a vacation, and asking if it is possible to have their job put on before they leave. If they are tied up with jobs, we would get another installer, possibly, who wasn't tied up, who was available to do the job.

Q. Now, if the installers are all out working and putting up their siding and windows and you have a new job coming in which is rush, this customer absolutely must have it right away, what do you do, as foreman there?

A. Well, we check and see who would be the most available and ask him if they could spare the time to do the job. If they said "no" then we

(Testimony of Ralph E. Williams.)

would have to shop around and get another one who would be available.

Q.   Then that would be his job, though?

A.   That is right.

Mr. Ewing: Just to clarify it a little bit here, you say the person who would be the most available, do you mean some installer who would not be working on a job at that time?

A.   Either that or if they all had jobs out, it would just be the one who could get off a job. Maybe it was a [123] mistake on the part of an order, maybe a couple of windows or doors. While that was being made up, he would go out and put the job on, but you wouldn't pull a man off a job to come in and do another job.

Q.   (By Mr. Lyman): Now, other than these work orders which you have seen and identified, are there any other directions or instructions that you give a man how to do the work?

A.   Only when we put an ad in the paper and maybe get some new installers.

Q.   No, I say are there any other instructions other than what is on here, to an installer as to how to do the work?   A.   No, oh, no.

Q.   You don't have supervisors that go out and direct them, is that correct?   A.   That is right.

Q.   And when you do go out, what is your purpose when you go out to look at a job, what do you look for?

A.   Well, I either ask for an opinion on them——

(Testimony of Ralph E. Williams.)

Q. (Interposing): Do you understand my question? A. Beg your pardon?

Q. Do you understand my question?

A. Maybe I didn't.

Q. Do you ever go out on a job to see the progress? [124]   A. No.

Q. Oh, you haven't?

A. No, not to see how, no.

Q. Is there anyone from the shop that might go out?   A. No one.

Mr. Ewing: Excuse me, what was the answer?

(Last answer read.)

Q. (By Mr. Lyman): Now, these applicators, do you know whether they hire helpers; I mean, do you have that knowledge?

A. Occasionally I would, a lot of times I wouldn't.

Q. But they do hire help?   A. They do.

Q. And the company doesn't interfere in any way with those helpers?   A. Not a bit.

Q. And the pay and the working conditions of those helpers are determined solely by the applicator?   A. That is right.

Q. Now, you have sometimes a rush of business and then sometimes it falls off, is that correct, during the particular year?   A. Yes.

Q. Now, in the Spokane office about how many men would you have at your peak time? [125]

A. Well, we would have about eight to ten men.

(Testimony of Ralph E. Williams.)

Q. And your slowest time, how many would you have?   A. Two or three.

Q. And usually who would those be, if you know?

A. Well, it would be the same men, at that period it was Don Lewis and George Aronson, would be the two.

Q. Yes. Now, did these other men who worked for Alsco from time to time, did they work for other companies performing similar businesses in this area?   A. Some of them, yes.

Q. And would they then come back to Alsco and do work for Alsco?   A. Yes.

Mr. Lyman: I believe that is all, your Honor, it would be repetitive to go into anything else.

Q. Oh, let me ask this: These applicators or installers with whom you work, are you familiar with the tools they have?   A. More or less, yes.

Q. Could you give us an estimate of what the investment or the cost they have to acquire these tools; or, put it this way: If they lost them suddenly, what would the replacement cost be?

A. Well, some of them have a portable power saw and hand tools, and then their own trucks; it could be—I [126] wouldn't have any idea—each one would be a little different investment. Some of them have more elaborate tools than others.

Q. Well, could you give an estimate, just so we have an idea?

A. Well, on the hand tools and saw. I imagine $100, $150.

(Testimony of Ralph E. Williams.)

Q. And what would the complete investment of a rig, truck and tools be for an average applicator, from your experience?

A. Well, it could be $2500 for the truck, and so forth.

Mr. Lyman: Yes.

Cross-Examination

By Mr. Ewing:

Q. Mr. Williams, I understand you have worked for Alsco here in Spokane since 1948, is that right?

A. Yes, sir.

Q. And what is the title of your job?

A. Well, I am in charge of production.

Q. In charge of production?

A. That is right.

Q. And how long have you held that job?

A. Since 1948.

Q. Will you describe the duties of that job, please, briefly? [127]

A. Well, I hire the people in the shop, supervise the shop employees, lay out the orders to fit the different windows on the orders that come in, purchase the material, and at that time when we had installers I was in charge of the installers, installation.

Q. Do you hire installers, is that part of your job?   A. I did, yes.

Q. Likewise, do you discharge installers?

A. Yes, sir.

(Testimony of Ralph E. Williams.)

Q. As to extra work on these jobs, what is the pay basis for extra work?

A. That varied in different, within different times, normally the extra labor would be for blind stopping.

Q. What is the pay basis, is it paid by unit, piecemeal?   A. No, it would be by the job.

Q. What do you mean "by the job"?

A. Well, if they had one things other than put on the windows it may be a number of hours, I imagine they would put it in on the labor contract.

Q. As to extra work, then, they are paid by the hour, is that correct?

A. Well, on the basis of that.

Q. Well, if the person has done three hours extra labor he has been paid a certain amount per hour for that job and I suppose it's three times that certain amount, is [128] that it?

A. That would be it, yes.

Q. So he is paid by the hour, is he not?

A. He is paid by the hour.

Q. Did I understand you to say as to this extra payment that would in some cases be due an installer for doing the extra work the salesman would authorize the extra payment and it would come out of his commission money?

A. Yes, sir, that is right, because he had contracted the job for so much and that would be it.

Q. This extra work money would not come out

A. I wouldn't be so sure on that because I am of Alsco funds?

(Testimony of Ralph E. Williams.)

in charge of production and I am not always sure.

Q. Isn't it true that extra work had to be approved by your office?   A. Yes.

Q. So if you approved it, I would assume that you pay it, don't you?   A. At that time, yes.

Q. When you had work to be done, how were these installers notified, again?

A. Well, generally, by, they would come into the plant ready for more work.

Q. As to your regular installers, did they need to be notified at all, wouldn't they just [129] come in?

A. Not, normally when they got the order they had out, they would come in for more work.

Q. Now, isn't it true that when work orders— well, I will ask you this first: Isn't it true that at times an installer was given as many as, say, eight or nine work orders at one time?

A. It could possibly be, yes.

Q. And isn't it true that when you gave those work orders to him you told him which job was to be done first, second, and so forth, you established the priority?

A. No, not unless there was maybe a priority on one job, they regulated their own jobs.

Q. If there was a job, you told him to do that job first?

A. No, if it was reasonable, if he could do it, we told him to get someone else.

Q. Pardon?

(Testimony of Ralph E. Williams.)

A. If it was reasonable for him to do it, if he could possibly do it.

Q. Well, if you gave an installer four or five orders any one of which he could start with, but you had a job that should be done right away, wouldn't you tell him to do this job first?

A. I would ask if he could, and if he said he couldn't, I would take the job back, the work order back, and give it to someone else. [130]

Q. Was there any agreement between Alsco, the company you represent, and the installers, in writing, outside of what may be included in the work order?

A. No, other than to outline in a bulletin the amount we pay for each window, each type window, each size, I mean, if there was a size differential and extra labor, what I mean is, if they went out on a 15-mile radius from town, they would get more per unit.

Q. The only written evidence of any agreement between you two, that is, between the installer and Alsco, would be the work order and these bulletins?

A. That is right, and the bulletin was just a bulletin that we gave any employee that came in, any installer, mostly for new installers.

Q. Were any pay negotiations entered into at the time the job was, an installer picked up a work order?   A. No.

Q. Who made the final determination as to what the price would be that would be paid to an installer?

(Testimony of Ralph E. Williams.)

A. Well, if there was any, if it wasn't according to the regular run or trend of prices that we had given them, it would be up to the manager, Mr. McFarlane.

Q. Do you have any knowledge of, say, you give a man two orders, one to do in Pasco and one to do in Yakima, Yakima being it's final destination point, do you know [131] of any jobs where a man when he stopped to do the Pasco job he would be paid by the hour for that job?

A. Not unless it would be a service job, or something like that.

Q. What do you mean, "a service job"?

A. Well, a complaint.

Q. He would just be redoing some other job?

A. That is right.

Q. You would never be negotiating a new job and he would be paid by the hour?   A. No.

Q. Were these installers free to accept or reject a work order that was offered them?

A. They were, occasionally they did.

Q. Do you know of any instances where an installer did not accept a work order?

A. Yes, when maybe they would find another job and refuse to take a job that was offered them.

Q. You mean they would start working for somebody else?   A. That is right.

Q. Well, if they start working for somebody else, they wouldn't be in to see you, would they?

A. Sometimes they would have a job before they came back in to see me. I would hand them a work

(Testimony of Ralph E. Williams.)

order and they would say, "I don't want to go there." And I would say, [132] "I don't have anything else for you right now."

Q. If somebody came in and you said, "I don't have any jobs for you now," would you refer them to any competitors?

A. Yes, I would. I mean, I might do that if it would help the boy.

Q. Did your company have any policy at all as to these installers working for other people?

A. No.

Q. And that applies to your regular installers, too?

A. It applies to all installers, because we couldn't keep them busy all the time, we shouldn't deprive them of doing work for somebody else if we didn't have jobs for them.

Q. As to these helpers, sometimes I think you stated that an applicator does hire a helper to help him?   A. Occasionally.

Q. Who keeps the pay records of the helper?

A. The applicator, the installer.

Q. Has Alsco ever kept any records for the helper?   A. Not to my knowledge.

Q. Well, isn't there on one of these exhibits that you testified to on direct examination, didn't you say that this fellow Minton, on the work order, Minton was the helper? [133]

A. Could I see the order, please?

Q. And he was directing you to pay the [134] helper?

RALPH E. WILLIAMS

recalled as a witness on behalf of the plaintiffs, resumed the stand and testified further as follows:

Cross-Examination
(Continued)

By Mr. Ewing:

Q. Mr. Williams, is Alsco now, at the present time, operating in substantially the same manner that they operated during the period 1954 to 1958?

A. No, we are wholesale, the department I am in now, only.

Q. Do they have installers?

A. I have no installers, no.

Q. Do installers work for Alsco at all, that you know of?

A. They put on doors once in a while on contract jobs, yes.

Q. Who does Mr. McFarlane work for now?

A. I think he is with a company of his own, AllState.

Q. Who furnished the materials that went into any particular job, any job in general? **[135]**

A. If it was Alsco window material, we furnished the material.

Q. And did you deliver them to the job site?

A. On occasion we have, where they weren't equipped to haul, we have delivered.

Q. And the other times the installer would pick them up at Alsco and take them out to the job himself?

(Testimony of Ralph E. Williams.)

A. We only deliver to assist the installer, the contractor.

Q. Was anything else furnished by Alsco other than material?   A. Not that I know of.

Q. Ladders, or anything like that?

A. We have loaned ladders, yes, we have loaned maybe a tool that wouldn't be a common tool to an installer.

Q. How about it, do you own any trucks, did Alsco own any pickup trucks?

A. We have had pickup trucks, yes.

Q. Were those used by installers at all?

A. They were just used for on delivery.

Q. You don't know of any instance where an installer used Alsco's own trucks?

A. In what period are you talking of, the very inception?

Q. Well, say the period between 1954 and 1958?

A. Oh, if one of their rigs broke down, we might have loaned them one, it would just be for the trip. [136]

Q. I believe you stated on direct examination that nobody went out and checked these jobs, was that your answer?   A. Not normally, no.

Q.. Were salesmen supposed to check these jobs?

A. No, the salesman generally doesn't know enough about the job to inspect the job.

Q. Did you hear Mr. Lee testify this morning through his deposition, which he admitted was true, that salesmen were supposed to check these jobs?

A. They do on occasion, but I didn't know that

(Testimony of Ralph E. Williams.)
they were supposed to, not from my department,
they were not supposed to.

Q. You don't know of your own knowledge
whether, in fact, they have checked jobs in the past?

A. No, I wouldn't know, because I am with production and not the sales.

Q. Did you hear Mr. Lee testify this morning
that he has been out on jobs and has given directions and suggestions on occasion?

A. I heard his statements this morning.

Q. How does that coincide with your statement
that nobody went out and looked at these jobs?

A. Nobody went out to inspect the jobs from
my department.

Q. What is your department?

A. Production and installation. **[137]**

Q. With reference to, I believe you stated you
do the hiring, or you did do the hiring?

A. Yes, I did do the hiring.

Q. And on occasion you hired, I suppose, new
applicators?   A. That is right.

Q. Is their work checked at all?

A. Normally, if we would get a complaint, we
would maybe go out and check a job on a complaint,
a customer's complaint.

Q. In other words, the man that you have never
known before has come in and would say he is an
installer, you would send him out to do a job and
not even check that job?

A. Sometimes we would send them out with another installer, a seasoned installer.

(Testimony of Ralph E. Williams.)

Q. Sometimes you would send them out with a seasoned installer?

A. Yes, if they have had experience with other companies.

Q. Was the other installer to check their work for you?

A. No, merely to, not for us, merely to help them.

Q. The installer was working for you, though, wasn't he?

A. He wasn't working for me, he was a contractor working for himself, putting on our product.

Q. You have never been out on any of these jobs, personally? [138]

A. Yes, I have been out on jobs where there has been complaints or trouble.

Q. And what would you do if a complaint arose and you went out and checked the job, what would be the procedure then?

A. Well, I would try to see if I could withhold the contractor's pay until he had finished the job, done a job satisfactory to the customer, like he had contracted for.

Q. Did you tell the installer what needed to be done in order to complete that job?

A. If I was out on the job.

Q. You have been out on jobs on occasion, then?

A. On occasion, just where there is customer complaints.

Q. You heard Mr. Lee testify this morning that

(Testimony of Ralph E. Williams.)

he had the power to give instructions to these installers, did you have that same power?

A.   I imagine I did.

Q.   I believe you stated on direct that there have
been times when directives or bulletins have been
issued by Alsco to installers, is that correct?

A.   We have made up bulletins to tell the contractors to more or less, it was how the job is to be,
we would like to have the job done so it would be
acceptable to the customer. [139]

Q.   What was your understanding of these bulletins, what was the purpose of them?

A.   The purpose of them was when we hire new
men in our peak season or busy season so they
would know what to do, what the job is on.

Q.   Were they only given to new men?

A.   Not necessarily, they were available to all of
them.

Q.   They were directed to all installers, isn't
that correct?

A.   To all installation contractors, I think it
reads.

Q.   And you wanted everybody to get them,
didn't you, all installers, not just the new ones,
isn't that true?   A.   Yes.

The Clerk: Marking Defendant's Identification
No. 11.

Q.   (By Mr. Ewing):   Showing you Defendant's
Identification No. 11, entitled "Important Informa-
tion to All Installers and Applicators;" issued by
Alsco Storm Windows, Inc., apparently signed by

(Testimony of Ralph E. Williams.)

Melvin McFarlane, Manager, dated May 9, 1960 (hands paper to witness), I will show you that and ask you if you are familiar with that?

A. No, sir, I have never, I have never seen that one before.

Q. You have never seen that one before?

A. No, I didn't. [140]

Q. It's entitled "Alsco Storm Windows, Inc.," is it not?   A. That is right.

Q. So it must have been issued by Alsco?

A. It could have been.

Q. You are not familiar with what is herein stated here?

A. No, because that doesn't apply to me.

Q. It does apply to applicators and installers, does it not?   A. It does, yes.

Mr. Ewing: I will ask the admission of this bulletin (shows document to plaintiffs' counsel).

Mr. Lyman: I haven't read it, your Honor, but we object to it simply on the date it is issued, May 9, 1960, which is more than two years after the period here involved. I, frankly, haven't read the contents, but on that basis I object to it.

Mr. Ewing: I would state as to that, your Honor, that it is directed to applicators and installers. I think it can be brought out that is what is stated herein was the same type of procedure that prevailed in 1954 to 1958.

The Court: I think you had better bring that out before this would be admissible, because if it speaks

(Testimony of Ralph E. Williams.)

as of the date it bears, prospectively, I would think it would be inadmissible.

Q. (By Mr. Ewing): Reading some of those items on there, one through seven, could you tell me whether **[141]** those things that are stated therein were applicable in 1954-1958; in other words, whether the same things applied although they were not reduced to writing at that time?

A. Like the rate of pay increase? I think you will find it in that bulletin.

Q. Were those things that are stated therein the same thing?

A. I will have to check them because I am not familiar with them. I will have to check against the other one, and that has been several years ago, yes.

Q. Do you want to check against the other one which I have (hands paper to witness)? There is a difference, isn't there?   A. Check material.

The Court: Is this off the record?

Mr. Ewing: Yes.

Q. Taking No. 1, isn't that about the same as this one here, 6?

A. No, this is, just a minute.

Q. No. 1 and No. 6, aren't they about the same?

A. They are about the same, yes.

Q. Now, as to No. 7, I am not interested in how much here, but wasn't this the policy in 1954?

A. This one isn't on here.

Q. No, it isn't, but wasn't this policy "No extra labor **[142]** will be paid except when authorized by office." Wasn't that the policy in 1954?

(Testimony of Ralph E. Williams.)

A. I don't know what they had in Mr. McFarlane's office at that time.

Q. You were the production manager?

A. I was the production manager.

The Court: Is this back on the record now?

A. "No extra labor will be paid except when authorized by office. The rate of pay is based on the schedule dated May 6, 1960."

Q. Referring to any of these things on this May 9, 1960, bulletin, were any of those things applicable in 1954?   A. Some of them were.

Q. Which ones were they?

A. Well, the caulking is similar, now that is not, flashing strip or casing trim, that applies to siding, whereas this one applies to windows only, no siding applied in this one, so that would be similar, and that one isn't in there. This is sidings, so that wouldn't be in this one.

Q. Was the same thing applicable in 1954, between 1954 and '58, even though it wasn't in writing at that time?

A. Well, we asked the boys to do their jobs, clean jobs, yes.

Q. Were these things, could these things be applied in [143] 1954?

A. Some of them could, yes.

Q. Well, will you tell me exactly which ones could?

A. Well, you could caulk around windows and doors, yes.

Q. Now, what else?

(Testimony of Ralph E. Williams.)

A. "Return all siding," it could have been siding and accessories, "to local office," because that was "No extra labor will be paid," yes.

Q. Here?   A. I think that should apply.

Q. Pardon?   A. That would apply.

Q. It did apply in '54 and '58?

A. Yes, I think he meant that to apply.

Q. It would have applied, wouldn't it?

A. It could apply.

Q. Now, referring to Defendant's Identification——

The Court: Back on the record?

Mr. Ewing: Yes, back on the record.

Q. Referring to Defendant's Identification No. 11, Mr. Williams, being a bulletin dated May 9, 1960, is it true that items 3, 4, 5, 6 and 7, although not reduced to writing between the period of 1954 to '58, were applicable at that time?

A. That would apply, yes. [144]

Mr. Ewing: I will move the admission, based on this testimony, of Defendant's Identification 11.

Mr. Lyman: Well, your Honor, I don't think that cures it, but I have no objection to its admissibility except for items 1 and 2, which have not been identified. Very well, no objection.

The Court: All right, it's admitted only as to Items 3 to 7, inclusive, right?

Mr. Ewing: That is correct.

The Court: All right, it will be admitted and although they don't need to be deleted, it's under-

(Testimony of Ralph E. Williams.)

stood that Items 1 and 2 are not to be considered as items applicable to the case, is that right?

Mr. Lyman: That is correct.

The Court: All right.

(Whereupon, said document was admitted in evidence as to Items 3 through 7, inclusive, as Defendant's Exhibit No. 11.)

Q. (By Mr. Ewing): Showing you Defendant's Exhibit No. 11, would you read No. 3 on that bulletin, please?

A. (Reading): "Keep yard and applied siding clean as work progresses. Pile scrap in neat pile." No. 3.

Q. In other words, in reference to No. 3 you are telling the applicators that they are to pile scrap in neat piles during the course of the job, and you are also [145] telling them to "Keep yard and applied siding clean as the work progresses," is that correct?

A. That is what that implies, yes.

Q. That is what it says, isn't it?

A. That is what it says.

Q. Would you read No. 4, please?

A. (Reading): "Make no suggestion to customer contrary to work order. If you question any item on the work order, consult salesman who sold the order or the local manager. Install according to company installation manual. We will only authorize payment for satisfactory work."

Q. Referring to this part that you just read, the

(Testimony of Ralph E. Williams.)
third sentence, "Install according to company installation manual," where is that manual; is it here today?

A. I don't know what manual, yes, do we have a manual here? I don't know, I am sure, this is for siding and there is a siding manual, applicators' manual.

Q. And from reading that sentence, it belongs to the company, it's a company installation manual, is that correct?

A. Yes, we give that to all customers, you know.

Q. To all customers?   A. Customers.

Q. How about installers?

A. That is the installing contractors, they should, if they [146] have put on siding, they should have one, yes.

Q. According to this sentence they are supposed to install according to that manual, are they not?

A. Well, there is only one way you can put the siding on, that is in a neat manner, yes.

Q. Would you read No. 5, please?

A. (Reading): "Return all siding and accessories to local office."

Q. And No. 6?

A. (Reading): "Caulk around all windows, doors, and other openings before installing sill, flashing strip or casing trim."

Q. In effect, you are telling the installers in No. 6 to caulk around all windows, doors and other openings before installing sill, flashing strip or casing trim, in other words, if there is more than

(Testimony of Ralph E. Williams.)

one way to do this job, you are instructing the installers to do it this way, in other words, to caulk the windows before installing the sill?

A. This was new to most of them and to keep from having expensive repairs it's customary for most any company to put out a bulletin telling them how to apply siding.

Q. Mr. Williams, in effect, aren't you telling these installers how to do the job, then?

A. I didn't write this. [147]

Mr. Lyman: Just a minute, I want to object to that. I think it's argumentative, and between this bulletin and the statements thus far I think the Court can draw a conclusion.

The Court: Sustained.

Q. (By Mr. Ewing): Will you read No. 7, please?

A. (Reading): "No extra labor will be paid except when authorized by office. The rate of pay is based on schedule dated May 6, 1960."

Q. Well, from the first sentence in No. 7 as to any extra work the installer was to get authority from the office first before proceeding, is that correct?   A. That is what it says, yes.

Q. Now, when you issued these bulletins to installers, I assume that you expected them to follow what is therein?

Mr. Lyman: Objection, your Honor, this is argumentative. It calls for a mental process.

The Court: Sustained.

Q. (By Mr. Ewing): Showing you Plaintiffs'

(Testimony of Ralph E. Williams.)

Identification No. 9, Mr. Williams, which is issued by Alsco Northwest, Inc., and Alsco Storm Windows, Inc., entitled "Code of Ethics and Cooperation," directed to all installation contractors, dated November 28, 1956, with no signature on it (hands paper to witness), I show you [148] that, are you familiar with that?   A. Yes, I am.

Q. Are you familiar with the contents therein?

A. Yes.

Q. And having been issued in 1956 I assume it was applicable from '56 on, at least?

A. Yes.

Mr. Ewing: I move the admission of Defendant's Indentification 9.

Mr. Lyman: No objection.

The Court: It will be admitted as Defendant's 9.

(Whereupon, said document was admitted in evidence as Defendant's Exhibit No. 9.)

Q. (By Mr. Ewing): With reference to Defendant's Exhibit No. 9, will you under the section called "AIM" will you read that paragraph, please?

Mr. Lyman: Objected to, your Honor. Your Honor, I am going to object to his reading it, it speaks for itself and I think it is unduly long and drags out the testimony.

The Court: Well, overruled.

Q. (By Mr. Ewing): Will you read it, please?

A. (Reading): "The installation contractor, who by his work must come in contact with the

(Testimony of Ralph E. Williams.)

customer, is in many instances a good-will ambassador, so to speak. [149] His appearance, actions, and work reflect directly back on whoever he is contracting for. By this token Alsco Northwest, Inc., has set forth the following Code of Ethics for your consideration.''

Referring to this code of contact, it says, ''Installers will be expected to present a neat appearance at all times.'' Could you elaborate on that a little bit, what do you mean by that?

A. Well, we have had coal heavers, and so forth, who have come and asked for jobs and we have given them jobs, and they were not exactly presentable.

Q. Isn't it true, Mr. Williams, that these installers were required to wear white coveralls?

A. No, not required to, they were preferred to wear them and if they paid for them themselves.

Q. You don't know what the policy of the company was?   A. On the coveralls, I wouldn't.

Q. Would you—who would know?

A. Because I never insisted that they all wear coveralls.

Q. Who would know whether they were required to wear them or not?

A. I will say they wouldn't be required, I wouldn't know.

Q. Who could I ask to find out?

Mr. Lyman: Objection, your Honor, I think this is imposing on the witness a question that he couldn't possibly [150] answer.

(Testimony of Ralph E. Williams.)

The Court: Well, he can say so if he can't answer it, overruled.

A. I cannot answer the question because I don't know.

Q. (By Mr. Ewing): In reference to some installers, then, did they wear white coveralls?

A. Yes, they did.

Q. Was there any inscription on these coveralls, was there anything stated on these coveralls, any advertisement or anything like that?

A. Some of them had "Alsco" on them, yes.

Q. "Alsco" was printed right on the coveralls?

A. On the coveralls.

Q. And was there anything else on there?

A. It might have been there initially, I don't know, I don't remember.

Q. Point No. 2 in this Code of Ethics, referring to Defendant's Exhibit 9, it says: "Your manner should be efficient and such as to impress the customer with your knowledge of the job to be done." Can you elaborate a little bit on what you mean by "efficient," "your manner should be efficient"?

A. Well, we have shown them jobs that were put on, on our samples, and so forth, that they should know how to do a job, and we expected a job that would be satisfactory [151] to the customer.

Q. And would you read No. 3, please?

A. (Reading): "Your attitude with the customer is to be one of cooperation, friendliness and cheerfulness."

(Testimony of Ralph E. Williams.)

Q. Now, referring to page 2 of this Code of Ethics entitled "Specific points to watch," isn't it true that it sets out seven points in there, six of which start out with the words "Do not"?

A. That is right.

Q. And would you read those, please?

A. (Reading): "Do not fail to caulk all units that should be caulked.

"Do not try to cover up defective product of work.

"Do not leave out any pilot screws in two lite windows for any reason.

"Do not fail to pick up completion or cash.

"Do not make any appointment with the customer you do not or cannot keep, as they may stay home from work to keep this appointment.

"Do not leave any windows or doors that are not cleaned thoroughly inside and out.

"Always check with customer to find out which way they want their doors to hang."

Q. In reference to No. 3, "Do not leave out any pilot screws [152] in two lite windows for any reason," that would be during the course of the work, would it not?

A. That is a part of the window, it is just like leaving off a headlight off a car.

Q. And No. 1, "Do not fail to caulk all units that should be caulked," would the caulking process be done during the course of the job?

A. That is part of the job.

Q. Do you know whether, of your own knowl-

(Testimony of Ralph E. Williams.)

edge, whether these installers ever advertised for themselves as being in the business of installers?

A. Yes, I have found ads in the paper and called them and called installers who have had ads in the paper.

Q. They have advertised themselves?

A. Yes.

Q. And yet some installers, when they worked for you, were wearing white coveralls with "Alsco" printed on the coveralls, is that correct?

A. Not the ones, no, but they were wearing coveralls.

Q. Do you know of your own knowledge whether Alsco has ever asked any installer to advertise for them?   A. Not to my knowledge.

Q. Has there ever been a time within your knowledge that an applicator or installer has been put off the job during the course of the job? [153]

A. No, I have had them walk off the job.

Q. Could an installer be put off the job by you during the course of the job?

Mr. Lyman: I want to object to that. Just a moment, that calls for a conclusion. I think you ought to find out if it has been done, and then what would be the circumstances.

Mr. Ewing: Mr. Lee testified this morning, and he heard Mr. Lee's testimony.

The Court: I think, Mr. Ewing, the thing to find out is this man's—if he had knowledge of the extent of his authority, if that is what you are asking him. I will overrule the objection on that

(Testimony of Ralph E. Williams.)

ground, but I think your question, you might re-frame your question.

Q. (By Mr. Ewing): Has any installer been removed from a job during the course of that job by you or at your direction?

A. Not to my knowledge, no.

Q. If a home owner supposedly upon completion of a job was dissatisfied with that work and called Alsco, would that call be directed to you?

A. Not normally, no; I mean, it might come down to me if they asked me to send someone out to do a repair job, or something.

Q. Have you ever received such calls from [154] that? A. Not from my office.

Q. Were there any occasions that you know of or within your own knowledge where an installer has been taken off a job that he originally started during the course of that job and moved to a second job?

A. Not unless he was willing to do so.

Q. That isn't the question, the question is: Has an installer been moved off a job which he started to do, a second job, before the first one was finished? A. I can't recite any one instance, no.

Q. You don't know, within your knowledge?

A. I don't know of a particular job, no.

Q. Taking a person of reasonable experience in this type of work, isn't it true that the job can be done without close supervision? A. Yes.

Q. What do you understand by the word "supervisor"?

(Testimony of Ralph E. Williams.)

A.   Oh, "supervisor," my definition?

Q.   Yes.

A.   Would be one who would control the type——

Q.   Control the what?

A.   (Continuing): ——the type of work and the quality of the work, and so forth.

Q.   One who would watch over somebody else's work?   A.   That is right. [155]

Q.   Based on that definition of a supervisor, would that type of person be necessary in this kind of an operation?

A.   Not necessary, it couldn't, distance being a factor, you couldn't follow even the installing crews around.

Q.   But I believe you have stated that you and Mr. Lee testified that he has gone out on the job and checked on occasion?

A.   I heard him say that, yes, sir.

Q.   And salesmen were supposed to go out and check them?   A.   He said that this morning.

Q.   And these directives were issued to installers, were they not?   A.   Installing contractors, yes.

Q.   Are there times, Mr. Williams, that the materials that are set out in a work order do not always, it doesn't always work out that those are exactly the materials that are needed for that job?

A.   That could happen, yes.

Q.   And that, therefore, a change has to be made?

A.   It could be, yes.

Q.   During the course of time it would take an

(Testimony of Ralph E. Williams.)

installer to make that change, how is he paid during that time?

A. We, at one time we, if they didn't have the material, if they had to come in, it was the fault of the factory [156] that the contractor didn't get the right material, we would pay him and make it worth his trip in.

Q. Well, Mr. Williams, if an installer has to make a change in a work order or in a job that he is doing during the time that it takes him to make that change, how is he paid?

A. There would have to be a different work order.

Q. Do you always issue work orders for changes?   A. Not always.

Q. How is the installer paid during that time, do you know?

A. That is one time, I think, we paid them on an hourly basis for coming in and picking up the material and going back out.

Q. You paid him on an hourly basis during the time it took him to make the change and when he got back on the regular job included within the work order, he was back on a regular piecemeal basis, is that correct?   A. That is right.

Q. There is a commingling, then, of per unit and per hour, and so forth, is that correct?

A. And the extra labor, why, we didn't want to see him out, yes.

Q. And, as I understand it from these directives,

(Testimony of Ralph E. Williams.)
any change that was to be made had to be made
from your [157] office, first.

A.   Not through my office, it would be sometimes
checked with the salesman or the manager and he
would direct me to send someone out.

Q.   As you stated in this directive of May 7
which you say was applicable between '54 and '58,
which states, "No extra labor will be paid except
when authorized by office," that would be, or that
would mean that all changes would have to be approved by the office, wouldn't it?

A.   That is right, before they would be paid.

Q.   If an installer was working on a cash job, in
other words, he was directed to pick up cash, I
assume he would, and he would take that down to
Alsco, is that correct?   A.   Yes.

Q.   You didn't pay him out of that cash, did you?

A.   I paid none of them, we had a payroll department that took care of the payroll.

Q.   Do you know how these installers were paid?

A.   I am positive they were paid by check.

Q.   But when a change had to be made in a job,
I assume that the installers would come down to the
office and report that complaint to Alsco's representatives to find out what the trouble was. Now, do
you know of your own [158] knowledge whether
that same installer always went back and finished
that job?

A.   Not always, no, generally, I mean, it was a
new contract, any additional work would be adding
to the contract that he would be working on.

(Testimony of Ralph E. Williams.)

Q. Are you saying that sometimes when there was a change in a contract or sometimes when an owner would not sign the certificate certifying satisfaction with the job, such fact would be reported to Alsco, but there were times when that same installer did not go back and finish that job up?

A. When it was a condition where there would be no danger and the installer was out of town and the applicator, we would wait until he got back to town to do his own service, because he is held responsible for the job, as the contractor.

Q. Do you know of your own knowledge where there have been occasions where another installer other than the one who started that job would come back and finish it?

A. If a contractor had quit and left the job unfinished, we would have to have someone else go back and finish the job.

Q. Would that be the only reason or purpose that you know of where that situation would happen?

A. That would be the only reason I know of. [159]

Mr. Ewing: That is all I have.

Redirect Examination

By Mr. Lyman:

Q. Mr. Williams, do you remember this morning before the recess counsel asked you if you hired the applicators, and I believe you answered "yes," do you recall that?   A. Yes.

(Testimony of Ralph E. Williams.)

Q. And I believe he asked you, did you discharge the applicators, and I believe you said "yes." Now, would you tell us what you meant by "discharge"?

A. Well, if a man didn't complete a contract, violated a contract, why, we wouldn't give him another contract.

Q. In other words, you considered each one of these work sheets as a separate undertaking?

A. As a separate contract.

Q. And if you would not give him another contract, that was not renewing the relationship, is that what you are trying to say?

A. That is right, that is what I am trying to say.

Q. Now, counsel was asking you whether you took anyone off a job during the course of the work, do you recall that?   A. Yes.

Q. You have to answer.   A. Yes. [160]

Q. Now, isn't it true that when there was an interruption in the work, in the course of the work, it was usually that the man himself, the applicator left the job?

A. That is right, we didn't pull him off the job.

Q. I don't believe I asked you who determines the hours that these applicators work?

A. Oh, they work as many hours as they wish.

Q. And are there any particular days that they are required to work?   A. No, sir.

Q. And they work on holidays, Sundays?

A. They can, yes.

Q. Do you know whether these men have done

(Testimony of Ralph E. Williams.)

work for customers and were paid directly by customers?

A. In some instances, yes, there have been.

Q. Now, from your understanding and your experience with Alsco during this period, how much of the work was done was considered this extra work that you paid by the hour, relatively how much?

A. Oh, golly, less than one per cent, I would say, I mean.

Q. Now, was there anything in the arrangement that you had with the applicators when you took them on that you would guarantee them a certain number of jobs? A. No.

Q. And did they ever promise to do a certain number of jobs [161] for you for certain favors?

A. No.

Q. Now, it's your intention, is it not, to remain in the shop, and you do have a shop there with tools and a regular sort of manufacturing the windows process, is that correct? A. That is correct.

Q. And you are the foreman or supervisor of those people who work in the shop, right?

A. That is right.

Q. Now, how does their, for instance, their vacation differ from the time taken off by the installers and applicators?

A. Well, shop workers who work by the time clock, they work one year, they get a week's vacation with pay, and then for each additional year up to, they get one day up to two weeks.

(Testimony of Ralph E. Williams.)

Q. And who determines the schedule when they go?   A. We do.

Q. The company does?

A. Yes, the company does.

Q. Now, tell me, when these installers and these applicators want to take time off from their work, how is that done?   A. They just took time off.

Q. When do they go, how many times a [162] year?

A. I wouldn't know, because I have no supervision over them. I mean, I was not out there with them.

Q. Well, do they go more than once a year, many of them?   A. Some did.

Q. During your busy seasons when you had your greatest number of contracts, would any of these installers leave for any reason to go hunting, for instance?   A. Oh, yes; yes, sir.

Q. Was that usual or unusual?

A. That was usual.

Q. Now, getting back to your particular duties, it wasn't your function particularly to go out on a job and supervise it, was it?   A. No, it wasn't.

Q. And it was only in the customer complaint department that you did go out?   A. Yes, sir.

Q. Did the company hire anyone for the purpose of overseeing the work of these installers, if you know?   A. No, sir.

Q. Now, counsel has shown you Exhibits 9. 10 and 11, isn't it a fact that those exhibits are suggestive of the way the work should be done (hands

(Testimony of Ralph E. Williams.)
papers to witness)？   A. Yes, sir.

Q. Now, when these bulletins were issued from time to time, [163] isn't it true that the customers still came in and complained？   A. Yes, sir.

Q. And did anyone, was anyone discharged as a result of these customer complaints？

A. I have a time or two refused to renew a contract, wouldn't give them any more contracts to take out, yes, until they got the jobs finished.

Q. Now, isn't it a fact that those bulletins really express that the work should be done in a workmanlike manner, isn't that all it says？

A. Yes, it's more or less a leader.

Mr. Ewing: I object, your Honor, as a conclusion of the witness.

The Court: It's an exhibit, isn't it？

Mr. Lyman: Yes, it speaks for itself, it's true.

Q. Well, let's put it this way: Was it your purpose in putting this out to remind them to do their work in a workmanlike manner？

A. That is right.

Q. Let me ask you this, sir, I notice you have the notice there, notice to contractor, and it is dated 1954. Do you notice that in Exhibit 9, I believe, all installation contractors, do you see that heading？

A. 1956？ [164]

Q. 1956, you are right. Yes, in 1956 you issued a bulletin to all installation contractors？

A. **Yes, sir.**

Q. That is Plaintiffs' 9？   A. Yes.

Q. Now, at the time you issued that bulletin did

(Testimony of Ralph E. Williams.)

you know of your own knowledge that Alsco was withholding taxes and social security taxes and withholding taxes from the earnings of these men?

A. I did not.

Q. As a matter of fact, when did you learn that during that period of '54 to '58 that such taxes had been withheld?   A. Today.

Q. In other words, you never had contacted the payroll end of it?

A. No, other than to okay for payment the contracts when they were returned to me.

Q. In all the years you were with Alsco you never got into a discussion of this particular problem with any of the front office, so to speak?

A. No.

Q. Nor any of the men? Did any of the men raise the question to you?   A. No, sir. [165]

Q. Now, as far as the bulletin, I think it's No. 11, where they make certain suggestions to the installers, isn't it a fact that these men took pride in their work?

A. The majority of them did, yes.

Mr. Lyman: I believe that is all, your Honor.

Recross-Examination

By Mr. Ewing:

Q. I will ask you again, Mr. Williams, do you know of your own knowledge whether an installer has ever been taken off a job at the direction of Alsco personnel during the course of the job?

A. I can't cite a specific instance, no.

(Testimony of Ralph E. Williams.)

Q. These installers don't move from one job to another at their own whim, do they?

A. They have that prerogative if they take out a group of contracts, to get those, that sometimes the customers are ill, they can't do their job, they will move to another contract.

Q. You don't know of your own knowledge whether they have ever been asked to move from one contract? A. Not to my own knowledge.

Q. As to this figure of less than one per cent of their own work.

A. I just picked it out of my own [166] knowledge.

Q. You don't know whether it is one per cent exactly?

A. No, I wouldn't say one per cent. [167]

DONALD E. LEWIS

called and sworn as a witness on behalf of the plaintiffs, testified as follows:

Clerk of the Court: Please state your full name.
A. Donald E. Lewis.
Clerk of the Court: Thank you, please be seated.
The Witness: All right.

Direct Examination

By Mr. Lyman:

Q. What is your present address, Mr. Lewis?
A. E. 8002 Shannon, here in the city, yes.

(Testimony of Donald E. Lewis.)

Q.   And what is your occupation?

A.   At the present time I am partner-owner of Capital Aluminum Company.

Q.   Now, taking you back to the years 1954 to 1958, were you performing services for Alsco Storm Windows and Alsco Northwest, Inc.?

A.   Yes, I was.

Q.   Or either of the two corporations?

A.   Yes.

Q.   And what was the nature of your [168] service?

A.   I worked as a window installer, windows, doors.

Q.   And during that period how were you paid, what was the basis of your compensation?

A.   It was on piece work, piece work basis, so much a unit.

Q.   And did you do any siding?   A.   No.

Q.   Yours was purely a window——

A.   I think I put on one siding job while I was there, or helped on that.

Q.   And you were paid per square?

A.   Per square, yes.

Q.   Now, when you would get one of these work orders, and I will ask you here, is this Exhibit 8, Exhibit 6, for example, are they typical of the work orders that you would receive?

A.   Yes, they are.

Q   And would you get more than one, sometimes, in the same day?

(Testimony of Donald E. Lewis.)

A. Generally, yes, we would get several at a time, sometimes, depending on how busy we were.

Q. And then you would take these work orders and you would go to the factory and load the windows, am I correct?

A. Yes, that is right; of course, we got the orders and the windows at the same time.

Q. And then you would proceed to the job site? [169]   A. Yes.

Q. Now, did you take anyone with you?

A. No, not necessarily.

Q. Did you ever hire a helper?

A. No, I never did, myself.

Q. Now, how would the company know when a job was finished?

A. Why, we would come back in, we were required to come in the same day that it was finished, but usually pay day was on a Friday, we would bring our orders in at that time.

Q. In other words, you might finish a job early in the week but you would save up these work orders and present them at one time?

A. That is right, generally.

Q. Were there times when you didn't report for, perhaps, two or even three weeks?

A. If we were out of town, that was true.

Q. Then you would bring them all in together?

A. We have done that, or we have mailed them in, either way.

Q. Have you ever had occasion to draw pay or

(Testimony of Donald E. Lewis.)

compensation against work that was not yet complete, you, personally?

A.   We used to make a draw all the time, most of us fellows, before we left, out of town trips, especially.

Q.   And that would be applied against [170] work?

A.   Against the work that we were taking out, yes.

Q.   And then you got the balance when you came in?   A.   Yes.

Q.   Did you ever have a situation where you hadn't completed a job on a Friday, but you would draw up to what you had done?

A.   Well, generally, if it was our own doing, if the job wasn't done, we didn't get paid until it was finished.

Q.   In other words, the job had to be completed before you were actually entitled to your pay?

A.   Unless it was like a salesman there, then they would pay us for what we had done.

Q.   Now, in this arrangement that you had with Alsco, did you have any understanding with them that you would be guaranteed any particular number of jobs?   A.   No.

Q.   And did you work out any arrangements with Alsco that you would do a certain number of jobs for them?   A.   Not in this business.

Q.   Yes. In other words, when you completed one of these work orders that you have in front of you, you came back for another one, as a rule?

(Testimony of Donald E. Lewis.)

A. Well, that is right, several, you know, like say maybe one, maybe several.

Q. Under the arrangements you were not required to come back **[171]** at all, were you?

A. Well, if we picked up a little cash, it would have been a good idea.

Q. No, but I·mean under the arrangements you could have taken none, or worked elsewhere, as you so desired?

A. Oh, yes, we probably could have.

Q. Now, I believe you were the one, or one of the gentlemen who were named by these witnesses that when the work was slow you got whatever work there was available, am I correct, did you work pretty steadily?   A. Yes, I was pretty steady.

Q. Do you know of your own knowledge that there were a number of installers for Alsco that came and went during the year?

A. Yes, several, several.

Q. And do you have any knowledge that some of these installers would work for other companies in between jobs for Alsco?

A. Well, I will tell you, I was usually so busy myself that I didn't pay too much attention on that kind of a deal, I don't really know on that; some came and left and would come back again eventually, but whether they worked in between orders or not, I don't really know.

Q. All right, sir. Now, when you would put on a window sometimes a salesman would mis-measure;

(Testimony of Donald E. Lewis.)

you would have [172] to put in a piece of wood of some kind, am I correct in that?

A. Yes, that is right.

Q. Now, that not being measurable by a unit, how would you be paid for that?

A. Well, that would fall into this extra labor class, hourly basis.

Q. Now, was there a time when you were with Alsco that you would just give them a flat price, rather than so much per hour?

A. Not to my knowledge.

Q. In other words, the hourly rate is what you thought the job was worth?   A. That is right.

Q. Now, no one ever checked your hours, did they?   A. Not on the job, no.

Q. They took your word for whatever you came back with?   A. Yes.

Q. If you thought the extra work was worth ten dollars, you would divide that into so many hours?

A. Well, we kept track of our time, we were expected to do that.

Q. Did you do that on the back of the sheet?

A. Well, on the orders we had to turn in, we were supposed to have on there how many hours you worked. [173]

Q. Are any one of these orders yours, particularly?   A. No.

Q. That is Mr. Aronson, that is George Aronson; Mr. Aronson, I believe, was named as one of the steady people?   A. Yes.

Q. Do you notice here "Charge extra labor,

(Testimony of Donald E. Lewis.)

$3.50,'' do you notice that?   A. Yes.

Q. Nothing about hours on there, is there?

A. No.

Q. So there wasn't a requirement that you list the number of hours?

A. No, actually there wasn't a requirement that we had to.

Q. Now, in doing these jobs, you provided your own tools, did you not, sir?

A. Yes, that is right.

Q. Now, tell me, can you give us a brief description of what these tools consisted of?

A. Well, most of us carried either a band saw or a bench saw, metal cutting blades, and hand tools, and that type of thing.

Q. Now, with your tools and equipment necessary to do this job, how much of an investment do you have in it, aside from your truck? [174]

A. Oh, I would say one-fifty, two hundred, in there somewhere.

Q. And then you have your own truck, is that correct, sir?   A. Yes.

Q. Maintain your own liability insurance?

A. That is right.

Q. And you maintained the truck as far as repairs are concerned, without reimbursement?

A. That is right.

Q. And when you go out of town for a number of days or a week, why, who pays the expenses incident to that?   A. We paid our own.

Q. Out of the gross amount?

(Testimony of Donald E. Lewis.)

A. Yes, that is right.

Q. Have you ever taken time off away from the company during the season when they had some work orders?   A. Oh, yes.

Q. And then you came back?

A. Yes, came back to work.

Q. And where would you go?

A. Well, I was one of these hunters they are talking about.

Q. Now, who fixed the hours of those installers, or your hours?

A. We set our own hours, actually.

Q. Did you work on holidays or Saturdays, Sundays? [175]

A. Yes, several times.

Q. Was there any guarantee of compensation here outside of the piece work rates?   A. No.

Mr. Lyman: I believe that is all.

Cross-Examination

By Mr. Ewing:

Q. Mr. Lewis, I think you stated you worked for Alsco during the period 1954 to 1958?

A. Yes, that is right,

Q. And that was as an installer?   A. Yes.

Q. Did you ever advertise that you were in the business of an installer at that time?   A. No.

Q. Did you have any advertising on your truck at all?   A. Nothing, no.

Q. Did you advertise in the paper at all?

(Testimony of Donald E. Lewis.)

A. Nothing.

Q. In reference to these white overalls, did you wear these white overalls? **A.** Yes, I did.

Q. Did you feel required to wear them?

A. No, I don't think there was any ruling out that we had [176] to wear them.

Q. Who paid the cleaning charges on them?

A. We paid those ourselves.

Q. And was there an advertisement with "Alsco" inscribed on the coveralls?

A. On the back, yes.

Q. Did they encourage you to wear them?

A. It presented a neat appearance, yes; they naturally wanted that at all times.

Q. Had Alsco ever approached you to advertise **for them in any other way** except this white uniform?

A. Oh, we were approached several times by Mr. McFarlane as to putting a sign on the truck, or something like that.

Q. Will you explain that, please?

A. Well, I mean he, as I say, several times he would come out and discuss about he would pay the charge if we would put a sign on the sides of our pickups.

Q. A sign advertising Alsco?

A. Advertising Alsco, yes.

Q. On your own trucks? **A.** Yes.

Q. Did you do that? **A.** No.

Q. Was there at the time you picked up these work orders, [177] was there any explanation given

(Testimony of Donald E. Lewis.)

to you by Mr. Williams at all on these work orders?

A. Nothing unless it was a special job.

Q. And what would be a special job?

A. Well, there happened to be some from a, oh, little carpentry work; in other words, it would fall back in this extra labor bracket again: I mean, something that we didn't know should be done until we got there.

Q. As I understand it, as to the extra work you were not paid by the unit?

A. No, not on extra work, no.

Q. Have you always figured your extra pay up based on hours? A. Oh, yes.

Q. Have you ever refused a work order?

A. No, none that I can think of.

Q. Do you feel that you are free to accept or reject work orders?

A. Well, that could be answered two ways; I mean, in most cases you didn't want to refuse them because it was your income.

Q. Could you have had any fear of rejecting a job and still keeping your job?

Mr. Lyman: Objection, your Honor. Now, we are getting into real conjecture here.

The Court: I think we are. Would you read the [178] question, Mr. Reporter?

(Last question read.)

Mr. Ewing: Did you sustain that?

The Court: Yes.

Q. (By Mr. Ewing): Did Alsco discourage you

(Testimony of Donald E. Lewis.)

at all from working for competitors when they had no work for you?

Mr. Lyman: I object to that, your Honor. There is no foundation laid for that, and that is, again, a conclusion and asks for a mental process.

The Court: Oh, the word "discourage" is used, I think he may answer; overruled.

A. What was the question, again?

(Last question read.)

Q. (By Mr. Ewing): The question was: Did Alsco discourage you at all from working for competitors when there was no work available?

A. When there was no work there, no, I wouldn't say that they did.

Q. Have you ever been called into Mr. McFarlane's office in reference to working for somebody else?

A. It was mentioned on an occasion or two, yes, when we were busy.

Q. And would you relate the incident, if it was an incident, or what? [179]

A. Well, yes, I mean, the one I recall is at the time he seen Mr. Busby's pickup and mine in front of a competitor's place, and called us both in and asked us, you know, what we were doing there, if we planned on quitting, or going to work for him, or just what we were doing.

Q. Mr. McFarlane called you into his office?

A. Into his office, yes.

Q. Did he see you out there, or something?

(Testimony of Donald E. Lewis.)

A.   Yes, he happened to go by while the trucks were setting there.

Q.   They were your trucks?   A.   Yes.

Q.   Were you doing a job for Alsco at the time?

A.   I wasn't doing anything right at the time.

Q.   What was the conversation between you and Mr. McFarlane in reference to it?

A.   Well, that is kind of hard to remember, Mr. Ewing, that far back.

Q.   Substantially.

A.   Well, one of Mel's favorite deals there was loyalty to company, you know, as far as going to work for someone else.

Q.   Mr. McFarlane mentioned or talked to you about loyalty to the company? [180]

A.   He has made that, used that phrase several times.

Q.   And yet you were not doing a job for Alsco at that time?

A.   Not right at that time; as far as having windows on the truck, or anything, I didn't, because that was one of the things that was brought up in the conversation between the three of us.

Q.   Were there times when changes had to be made in a work order?

A.   Yes, there would be.

Q.   During the time it took you to make the change during that period of time, how were you paid for that period of time?

A.   Well, now, that depends on what kind of a change you would mean. In other words, if it was

(Testimony of Donald E. Lewis.)

an error in measuring, or something like that, we would bring the order back in and write up the order for the new unit and then take out other work.

Q. Were you paid during the time it took you to do these things?

A. No, that part of it, no, we were paid for putting the units on, that was expected to go along with that.

Q. Have you been moved from one job to another at all; in other words, have you started one job and been moved to another job before the original job was finished?

A. I think most of the old fellows have at one time or [181] another been asked to do a rush job, or one that might be on the verge of cancellation, or something like that.

Q. You have been asked to go off that job and start another job?   A. To do another one, yes.

Mr. Ewing: I think that is all I have.

The Court: Would you go back to the first job when you did?

A. Yes, we were expected to go back on our original job.

Redirect Examination

By Mr. Lyman:

Q. In other words, both those jobs were yours?

A. Yes, that is right. Once the order was given to us it was considered our order.

Q. And if a customer canceled out, why, you would lose that pay, wouldn't you?

(Testimony of Donald E. Lewis.)

A.   We would just turn our pay back in, right.

Q.   That is one you lost, they didn't pay you for that at all?

A.   They might pay you for the trip out, I mean it wasn't your fault because it was canceled, or something like that, but that was all.

Q.   But on that, where there was faulty workmanship apart from the materials, were you required to go back and do [182] that on your own time?   A.   I never had that happen to me.

Q.   Well, now, that brings up a point in that incident in McFarlane's office, isn't it a fact that the reason he questioned you, he considered you the prime installer in his organization?

Mr. Ewing: I object, your Honor, this would be a conclusion of the witness.

The Court: Sustained.

Q.   (By Mr. Lyman):   Well, did he ever say anything about the nature of your work?

A.   Oh, yes.

Q.   Compliment you? Pardon?

A.   Yes, they have.

Q.   But in talking to you about that incident he didn't guarantee you any money, any salary, or anything?

A.   Oh, no, no, he didn't offer any raises.

Q.   Just, it was all conversation?

A.   Yes, that is right?

Q.   Are you a competitor today of Alsco?

A.   Oh, yes.

Mr. Lyman: That is all I have.

(Testimony of Donald E. Lewis.)

The Court: Don't you get your supplies from them?

A. Yes.

The Court: They wholesale, don't they? [183]

A. Yes, we also wholesale.

ALLEN L. GREEN

called and sworn as a witness on behalf of the plaintiff, testified as follows:

Clerk of the Court: Please state your name to the Court.

A. Allen L. Green.

Direct Examination

By Mr. Lyman:

Q. Where do you live, Mr. Green?

A. 620 W. Augusta.

Q. And what is your occupation?

A. Well, I am an installer, aluminum siding installer.

Q. And during the years 1954 to '58 and any particular year during that time, did you perform some, either carpentry or installation services for Alsco?

A. Yes, in '57, I believe it was, and '58.

Q. And did you install awnings, I mean, pardon me, windows as well as aluminum siding?

A. Yes. [184]

Q. What is the difference between the two in the work that you do?

(Testimony of Allen L. Green.)

A. Oh, there is quite a little difference, a window is a window, and siding sure isn't the same.

Q. Well, now, a window was a finished product that you could fit into a pre-arranged space?

A. Yes, in that sense of the word, yes.

Q. And the siding, on the other hand——

A. Each piece, practically, has to be cut and fit; not all of it, but a good share.

Q. Now, how were you paid for the windows?

A. A unit, by the unit.

Q. Then on the siding, then, how were you paid?

A. By the unit.

Q. Now, when you ran into difficulty on the siding job, let's say that you come to an unanticipated obstruction or rotten boards, what would happen then in regard to pay, what would you do?

A. Well, if it was extra work, some minor detail, I know in my case I just went ahead and did it and turned in my time and I was paid for it by the hour, but if it was something, if the company made the statement that he had been promised this or that, then I immediately referred it back to the higher-ups.

Q. And then what would you do, go back to the office and [185] discuss this contract with them?

A. Well, not particularly; usually, I guess that in most cases, if it is of any importance they discussed it with the salesman, as he was the one that would have to pay it, and then if they thought it was justified, they told me to go ahead, and I turned in my time by the hour on it.

(Testimony of Allen L. Green.)

Q. Now, on these siding jobs did you ever get paid for the extra work on any other basis than by the hour?   A. No, other than by the unit.

Q. By the unit? Now, comparing the amount of work that you were paid for per square, and the amount per hour, percentagewise, which was the greater?

A. Oh, a lot of variation with different days, there would be parts of houses that it would be slow on the siding, and then there would be other parts that would go fast, but taking it in my present work I do much better on the scale by the piece than I do by the hour.

Q. But in an ordinary siding job on a house, it's more per square unit rate than there is any other?

A. Oh, yes.

Q. In other words, the hourly rate, that would be the extra work, would be a minor part of it, am I correct, sir?   A. Oh, very.

Q. Now, did you ever do any work for a customer of a minor [186] nature where you dealt directly with the customer?

A. Well, blessed if I can think of any right offhand, particularly. It seems to me that I did hang one door that they paid me for extra, but I don't recall whether I was working for Alsco at that time, or another party by the name of Fred Storey.

Q. Well, that wasn't unusual in this business, to do this little extra work for customers, was it?

A. Well, it is unusual, yes, because in most cases

(Testimony of Allen L. Green.)

you are required to do, it was usually figured ahead of time, the contract was a set price.

Q. I was wondering if you ever got into a situation where a woman wanted some shelves in a basement for some preserves?   A. No, I never did.

Q. Now, did you ever do work for Alsco and then do work for someone else and then come back to Alsco?

A. Oh, yes, I started to work for Alsco in 1950, and then worked for them for several months, and then dropped out and went back to carpenter work, and then again went back to Alsco, I think it was four or five, maybe six times that I worked for others, and then for Alsco.

Q. And while you worked for Alsco, was there an occasion where you did a job on your own that was not necessarily in windows or siding, but it was in this nature of home [187] improvement?

A. Yes.

Q. Then you came back to work for Alsco after that?   A. Yes.

Q. And you had your own tools?   A. Yes.

Q. And your own truck? And who fixed your hours of work?   A. Myself.

Q. And are you one of these hunters, this group?

A. Well, no, I didn't happen to be particularly. I, on a couple of occasions, I took a couple of days off and went to the coast to see my daughter, and I didn't ask anybody about it, I figured it was my own business. I went over and saw her and didn't say anything about it.

(Testimony of Allen L. Green.)

Q. When you came back did you pick up some work orders?

A. Well, I still had some with me.

Q. Then you completed those and turned in a sheet?

A. I completed those, they were not too particularly busy at that time, they were not rushed, I wasn't hurting the company any.

Q. They didn't hire you?

A. That is right.

Q. Did you ever have a helper?

A. Well, from my standpoint I would only class it as a helper, as a working partner. [188]

Q. Well, you worked together with someone?

A. That is right, as I have heard this word used here of "hire." Well, in my own case I would usually contact somebody and just ask them if they wanted to go to work with me on a partnership basis. I would take out my operating expense and then we would split the difference.

Q. But Alsco wouldn't tell you how much to give this man?   A. No, oh, no.

Q. They would pay you?

A. Oh, no, out of courtesy to me, saving me on some bookkeeping, I would split it up and then they would write out checks for the other fellow, and mine, also.

Q. But you directed how the money should be split?   A. That is right.

Mr. Lyman: I believe that is all, your Honor.

(Testimony of Allen L. Green.)

The Court: May I ask him, did you belong to a union, Mr. Green?

A. Yes, I do, the Carpenters' Local.

The Court: Does Mr. Lewis belong to a union?

Mr. Lewis: No.

The Court: **Do you know?**

A. I don't know, I wouldn't say.

The Court: Were these always union jobs you went on? [189]

A. No, when you are working on your own, why, I ran into that quite often. I would go into, oh, like Moses Lake, Wenatchee, Ephrata, and, oh, possibly somebody would see me working out and they would question about whether I was a union man or not, and when I explained I was doing it on contract, there was nothing more said.

The Court: Do you have a certificate entitling you to purchase supplies without paying sales tax?

A. No, I don't, personally.

The Court: Then you are not actually operating as an independent contractor at all times?

A. Well, only when I bought anything. While I was working for Alsco I bought it under Alsco's name.

The Court: And used their tax number?

A. How is that?

The Court: And used their tax number?

A. No, I don't recall on that.

The Court: Well, did you pay a sales tax on it?

A. Yes, I think so, because it was only small items.

(Testimony of Allen L. Green.)

The Court: I think perhaps, Mr. Ewing, we might have a recess now, we have been going since two here. Ten minutes.

(Whereupon, a recess was taken for a period of ten minutes.) [190]

Cross-Examination

By Mr. Ewing:

Q. Mr. Green, when did you go to work for Alsco?

A. I think it was in 1950, the first time.

Q. And how many applicators did they have working for them at that time, if you know?

A. Well, I wouldn't know for sure, but I believe that here locally at that time that there was around four or five, something like that.

Q. And in that event did you go to the end of the list when you applied for a job out there; in other words, if they have four work orders and you are the fifth man you wouldn't get a job, is that correct?

A. Well, I suppose that if orders were gone, I wouldn't get a job, that was for sure.

Q. Have you ever gone out to Alsco at a time and asked for work when they didn't have any available for you?   A. Yes.

Q. And at that time you would go to work somewhere else?   A. That is right.

Q. In the course of working on particular work orders for Alsco, did anybody ever come out to look at the job on any of the jobs you have been on?

(Testimony of Allen L. Green.)

A.   Yes, the man that sold the job, to be honest, but the man that sold the job came by, and I think for no other [191] reason that to see if I might have picked up a lead, somebody that was interested in it, but the man that was with him was the salesman and he started to tell me how to do it. It didn't take me long to tell him that it was none of his business, and we soon settled that.

Q.   You didn't follow his directions at all?

A.   No.

Q.   Yes. Have you been moved at all from one job to another?

A.   I don't recall of it, other than in instances of where for some reason or other it was a question of being idle when I was waiting for some extra windows to be made or for some material to be shipped to me, or something of that nature, and then if I had other work, I went elsewhere; if I had another contract I would go elsewhere and work on that, and finish up when I got the extra windows or extra material.

Q.   Would you always return to the original job and finish it up?

A.   Oh, yes, we were required to do that, as far as that goes.

Q.   Showing you Defendant's Exhibit No. 9, which is a Code of Ethics and Cooperation, did you get a copy of that when you worked for Alsco?

A.   Well, it seems as I did, yes, I believe so.

Q.   Did you read it? [192]

A.   Well, that is about all I did do, was read it;

(Testimony of Allen L. Green.)

when I first went to work for Alsco it was during the slack time in the carpentry business, and I wasn't figuring on any particular steady employment with them, I just took it as a fill-in.

Q. You recall receiving this bulletin?

A. No, not personally.

Q. You never recall receiving that?

A. No, this part here, I had this, and then I had another sheet that was attached, because I believe I had some price lists on it, and that sort of thing, but to be honest, I don't particularly recall, I don't recall this one, of all these "do nots," I really don't.

Q. You don't recall receiving anything?

A. No, not on that one.

Q. As I understand, you didn't install windows, you installed aluminum siding?

A. Well, I started in with them on windows, and then later I switched over to siding when they started installing it.

Q. Are you working for Alsco now?

A. No.

Q. In reference to extra work, if it was something more than a minor detail, would you get that cleared through Alsco, first? [193]

A. If it was of any size, of any importance, yes; if it was just something that was minor, why no.

Q. If it involved any change in money at all, would you contact Alsco?

A. Yes, because I believe that it was up to the salesman to say whether he wanted to pay that

(Testimony of Allen L. Green.)
extra or not, or whether he wanted to talk the customer into paying it.

Q. I believe you stated you don't have a contractor's card or a tax card?   A. No.

Mr. Ewing: I think that is all.

Mr. Lyman: No further questions.

The Court: Just a moment. You paid workmen's compensation, industrial insurance?

A. How is that?

The Court: Did anyone pay industrial insurance or workmen's compensation on you and your associates?

A. Well, now, I don't recall. Usually while I was working for Alsco, I don't just remember in that sense about just how that worked out on that deal. Each time that I went to work for Alsco it was in the wintertime and carpenter work was slack as a rule, and I didn't question particularly about that, as I recall, to be perfectly honest.

Q. Were there any deductions in your **[194]** check?

A. There was at one time, and then of recent times, I believe in 1958, I believe it was, that there was not.

The Court: You don't know whether they deducted anything for industrial insurance?

A. No, I don't know; really, I can't really say on that, on the industrial insurance. No, I can't really say on that.

The Court: That is all.

(Witness excused.)

Mr. Lyman: No, no questions. Again if I may, your Honor, I object.

The Court: Sustained, strike it.

Mr. Lyman: I am sorry, your Honor. It always raises a red flag, a question like that. Your Honor, the plaintiff rests.

(Plaintiffs rest.) [195]

Defendants' Case in Chief

GEORGE ARONSON

called and sworn as a witness on behalf of the defendant, testified as follows:

Clerk of the Court: Please state your name to the Court.

A. George Aronson.

Clerk of the Court: Thank you, please be seated.

Direct Examination

By Mr. Ewing:

Q. Mr. Aronson, what is your address?

A. 4924 N. Stevens.

Q. And how long have you lived in Spokane?

A. Well, I have been in and around Spokane since 1937.

Q. Have you ever worked for Alsco Storm Windows, Inc., or [196] Alsco Northwest, Inc.?

A. I have worked for both of them.

Q. And who are you employed with at the present time?   A. AllState Aluminum.

(Testimony of George Aronson.)

The Court: Who, again?

A. AllState.

The Court: AllState what?

A. Aluminum Products.

Q. (By Mr. Ewing): And what years did you work for Alsco?

A. I worked for Alsco from about '48 on to about '58 or '59, I think, or later.

Q. You were working at Alsco between the periods of 1954 and 1958?　　A. Yes.

Q. Can you describe your duties; generally, what did you do for Alsco?

A. Why, I installed doors and windows.

Q. You were an installer?　　A. Yes.

Q. Was that in homes, did you make installations in homes?　　A. Yes.

Q. Was this continuous employment for you?

A. Yes, sir.

Q. Have you ever worked for anybody else during the period [197] that you worked for Alsco?

A. No, I haven't.

Q. They had continuous employment for you?

A. Always.

Q. How were you contacted when Alsco had a job to be performed?

A. Well, I would either be called at the house or I would go out to the plant and pick up my orders.

Q. Were there times when you picked up more than one order?　　A. Oh, yes, several.

Q. Yes, could you pick out orders you wanted to,

(Testimony of George Aronson.)

or did you have any discretion as to what orders you wanted to take?

A. No, they was issued to you.

Q. Did you accept all orders that were given to you? A. Yes, sir.

Q. Did you feel that you could accept or reject any order that was offered to you?

A. I probably could have but I didn't.

Q. You have never rejected an order, is that correct? A. No, sir.

Q. At the time you picked up your work orders, was there any conversation at that time between you and any of the representatives for Alsco in reference to those work orders that were picked up? [198] A. I didn't quite get you, sir.

Q. At the time certain work orders were issued to you, was there any conversation at that time between you and a representative from Alsco in reference to that work order?

A. No, sir, I don't believe so.

Q. In other words, you just picked up the work orders and went out to the job?

A. That is right.

Q. Who fixed the rates at which you were to be paid?

A. Well, it was a set price, yes, they made up the price list and that is what we went by.

Q. Did you share in discussions as to what you were to be paid?

A. I think there was one or two meetings that——

(Testimony of George Aronson.)

Q. That there were?

A. That they had, that we come to, what we was supposed to be paid.

Q. Do you share in the profits or losses of Alsco's business at all?   A. No.

Q. Have you ever advertised in the paper that you were an installer?   A. No, I never have.

Q. Do you ever advertise in any phone [199] book?   A. No, sir.

Q. How do you get to work, do you have your truck or pickup?   A. I have my own pickup.

Q. And did you have your own pickup at the time in question as between 1954 and 1958?

A. Yes, sir.

Q. Is there any advertisement on your truck indicating that you were an installer?

A. No, no advertising whatsoever.

Q. In other words, you have never held yourself out to the public as being engaged in business for yourself?   A. No, sir.

Q. Has Alsco ever asked you to advertise for them?

A. There was a couple of times, yes, they wanted us to put advertising on.

Q. Pardon?

A. There was a couple of times that they asked us to put advertising on our trucks.

Q. They wanted you to advertise Alsco on your trucks?   A. Yes, that is right.

Q. Did you do that?   A. No, we didn't.

Q. When you were performing jobs for Alsco,

(Testimony of George Aronson.)

that were based on these work orders issued to you, did you wear ordinary [200] clothing, or what?

A. Oh, we wore coveralls the biggest part of the time, yes.

Q. Are you referring to the white coveralls issued by Alsco?   A. That is right.

Q. As a rule, did all installers wear these?

A. Most all the boys did, yes.

Q. Were you encouraged to wear them?

A. Well, they wanted us to wear them, yes.

Q. And as I understand it, well, on the coveralls you wore was there any advertisement on it?

A. Well, there was the Alsco sign on the back, and then they had our name on the front.

Q. Who paid the rental and cleaning charges for these?   A. We did.

Q. Did you pay a certain amount each week, or what?   A. Yes, 72c a week.

Q. As I understand it, Alsco would purchase the materials that would go into a job?

A. That is right.

Q. And you furnished your own tools?

A. Own tools.

Q. On any jobs that you have been on, did Alsco furnish anything other than materials? [201]

A. Well maybe, yes, some tools that we didn't have and on certain jobs that we needed to have them.

Q. They furnished them?

A. We could get tools from Alsco, yes.

Q. Have you ever used any of Alsco's trucks?

(Testimony of George Aronson.)

A. Well, I did the first year or so I worked there.

Q. When was that?

A. Well, that was about '49 and '50, I think, that I used the company truck.

Q. And were you an installer at that time, too?

A. Yes, sir.

Mr. Lyman: Your Honor, I move that that be stricken, not being in the period involved.

The Court: No, I will let it stand.

Q. (By Mr. Ewing): As far as your pay is concerned, were you paid on any particular day?

A. No, you can get paid any time you finished orders.

Q. In other words, your pay was based on completion of a work order?   A. That is right.

Q. On a cash transaction were there some cash transaction jobs that you bid on?   A. Yes, sir.

Q. Did you collect the money from the customer upon completion of that job? [202]

A. That is right.

Q. Were you instructed to turn that money over to Alsco?   A. Yes, sir.

Q. How were you paid, by check?

A. By check, yes.

Q. On jobs that you have done for Alsco, has there been more than one applicator on that job on occasion?   A. There has at times, yes.

Q. Has Alsco ever split you applicators up and transferred one applicator to another job and retained one man on the original job?

(Testimony of George Aronson.)

A. I think there is one or two times that it has been done, yes.

Q. And you would complete the original job?

A. Either I would or the other fellow that was working on the same job would.

Q. So, of the two of you, one of you wouldn't finish that original job if you were transferred, is that correct?

A. Well, if we finished the other job first, we could go back on the one and help him finish up again.

Q. But say you and some other installer started a job, you stated at times Alsco split you up and one stayed on that job and the other one has gone to some other job? A. That is right. [203]

Q. Now, the one that went to the other job, did he ever return to the original job?

A. There is one occasion I remember, yes, we did.

Q. Has there been occasions when you already finished the original job and therefore there was nothing to return to as far as the second man was concerned? A. None that I can recall, no.

Q. In other words, the second man always returned to the original job?

A. Well, I couldn't rightfully say.

Q. But there were times when Alsco split you up? A. Yes, there has been several times.

Q. You say "several times"?

A. I think there is a couple of times that I can recall.

(Testimony of George Aronson.)

Q. Have you worked with new applicators at all, that is fellows that are new to that type of work?

A. They have sent guys out with me, yes, to learn the trade.

Q. Were you instructed to watch their work at all, or anything like that?　A. That is right.

Q. Were you to report the progress of their work or their efficiency back to Alsco?

A. I have at times, yes.

Q. Did Alsco ever have any salesmen or other personnel [204] come out and check any job that you have been on?

A. There has been occasions they have, yes.

Q. Who would these people be that would come out?

A. Well, I have had salesmen come out and I have had, well, the manager.

Q. By "the manager," do you mean Mr. Lee or Mr. McFarlane?　A. McFarlane.

Q. And when they were out there did they offer any suggestions or give any directions as to how the work should be done?

A. I believe that was a couple of times that that happened, yes.

Q. Would you follow those directions?

A. Yes, as close as possible.

Q. Did you feel that you were supposed to follow those directions?

Mr. Lyman: Objection, your Honor, there is entirely too much leading. I haven't objected up until now.

(Testimony of George Aronson.)

The Court: Sustained.

Q. (By Mr. Ewing): Now, these salesmen that came out and looked at your work, you say there have been times when they would tell you to do certain things?

A. They would suggest things, yes, to do.

Q. How would they frame their remarks to you, that is, what would they say to you? [205]

A. Well, now, that I couldn't rightfully remember, I mean.

Q. You say Mr. McFarlane has been out and checked jobs you have been on?

A. I think there is once or twice that he has, yes.

Q. Did he offer any comments or suggestions or directions?

A. Well, we tried to work out something that we could go ahead and do the job right, yes.

Q. Did you follow his directions?

A. I tried to, yes.

Q. Were you, as an applicator, ever taken off the job before it was finished and moved to another job?

A. There has been times, yes, I have.

Q. Have you always returned to the original job?   A. Yes.

Q. Have there been times when you have had to go back and re-do jobs that were started by other applicators?   A. Yes.

Q. What happened to that applicator who had originally done that job or part of that job?

A. Well, there is some of them that has stayed on, yes.

Q. Some of them that haven't?

(Testimony of George Aronson.)

A. Well, there might have been one or two, I wouldn't say for sure.

Q. Taking a person of reasonable experience as an installer, is it true that the job could be done with little supervision, [206] in other words, you have been with Alsco for some years, do you feel you can do your job without being told how to do it, for the most part?   A. I think so.

Q. Could you use materials other than the ones that were furnished by Alsco?

A. There was times we had to get material, yes, that was furnished by Alsco.

Q. Where would you get it from?

A. Well, we would get it at the lumber yard.

Q. Did you contact Alsco first?

A. At times I would, and then if it was just some minor thing, well, I would just go get a piece of lumber and do so.

Q. As to extra work, how were you paid for extra work, on what basis?

A. So much per hour.

Q. And for work which was included within the work order, how were you paid for that?

A. Piece work.

Q. If you had to make a change in a job during the time it took you to make the change, how were you paid during the interval?

A. That would be extra labor.

Q. And you were paid by the hour for [207] that?

A. By the hour.

(Testimony of George Aronson.)

Q. As to minor changes, what do you consider minor changes? Let me put it this way: If the change involved any transaction involving money, more money or less money, would you contact Alsco first?   A. Yes.

Q. Have you been on any jobs where the home owner required some additional work done which was not included within the work order?

A. No, I never did do any additional work unless it was on the work order.

Q. Have you ever been requested to do so by a home owner?

A. We have been asked to, but then we never, I never have.

Q. Was there any reason for that?

A. Well, I didn't want to get involved in it, I guess.

Q. Have you been on jobs where a change had to be made in the work order?

A. Well, if there was mismeasured windows, yes.

Q. In reference to that change, would you contact Alsco first, before making any changes?

A. Oh, we would take the material back and have it changed, yes.

Q. Did Alsco ever furnish signs advertising their firm or product, on jobs that you have been on?

A. The only signs I have seen was when the work was going [208] on they would probably place a sign with "Alsco" on the property, I mean, as some advertising.

(Testimony of George Aronson.)

Q. They would have a sign out on the lawn, or something like that?   A. Yes.

Q. Referring you to Defendant's Exhibit No. 9, which is a directive issued by Alsco on November 20, 1956, entitled "Code of Ethics and Cooperation," I will ask you, did you receive a copy of that (hands paper to witness)?   A. Yes, I think so.

Q. And did you read it?

A. Well, I probably read part of it.

Q. Do you try to follow those things that are set out in these things?

A. Yes, I try to follow them as close as possible.

Q. On this page one, I notice on page two of Defendant's Exhibit 11 it says, "Do not fail to caulk all units that should be caulked," did you try to follow that as close as possible?   A. Yes.

Q. And No. 2, "Do not try to cover up defective work product or work," did you try and do that as closely as you could?   A. That is right.

Q. No. 3 says, "Do not leave out any pilot screws in two [209] lite windows for any reason," did you try and follow that?   A. Yes, sir.

Q. As to the rest of them on here, 4, 5, 6 and 7, did you try and follow them as closely as you could?

A. Yes, I tried to follow everything that they had on there.

Q. Referring you to Defendant's Exhibit No. 11, which is another bulletin issued by Alsco, referring to Item 6 on this, it says, "Caulk around all windows, doors and other openings before installing sill, flashing strip or casing trim," did you do that?

(Testimony of George Aronson.)

A. Well, that is something I didn't have anything to do with, that comes under siding, I believe.

Q. That would be a siding installer?

A. That is right.

Q. Yes.   A. On strictly windows and doors.

Q. Would most of these things on here apply to a siding applicator, as opposed to——

A. That is right.

Q. (Continuing): ——as opposed to an installer?   A. That is right.

Q. After completing a job, say an **FHA** job, was it necessary for you to get a certificate signed by the home [210] owner certifying that he was satisfied with the job?

A. Yes, he would look the job over and if he was satisfied, he would sign the completion.

Q. Have you been on jobs where the owner has not signed the slip?   A. Yes, I have.

Q. And what would you do, then?

A. Well, I would bring it back into the office.

Q. And you would get the complaint straightened out with the office?

A. With the office and the customer.

Q. Did you always return to that job to finish it up?

A. Well, if there was something the customer didn't think he had gotten, well, we always went back and tried to get him satisfied so we could get our completion.

Q. I will ask you this: Have there been times when you have completed the work in the work

(Testimony of George Aronson.)

order and the customer has not signed it because
of some oral agreement, possibly, that has been
entered into between the salesman and the home
owner?   A.   That I have, yes.

Q.   And in reference to that work, did you have
to do it?

A.   Yes, we was compelled to do it, yes.

Q.   That work wasn't in the work order, however, it wasn't set out in the work order, was [211]
it?

A.   Now, I don't quite remember on that, if it
wasn't, then there probably was another order made
up on it, then.

Q.   How were you paid for that?

A.   Well, if there was any more material to go
on, why, it would be piece work or hourly wage.

Q.   In the event it wouldn't involve materials,
how would you be paid for it?

A.   I don't quite get you?

Q.   If this extra work that you had to do because
of the agreement between the salesman and home
owner did not involve any new materials but some
other work which didn't involve new materials, how
would you be paid for that work?

A.   That would be an hourly basis.

Q.   Do you have a contractor's card or tax
stamp?   A.   No, I haven't.

Mr. Ewing: That is all I have.

(Testimony of George Aronson.)

Cross-Examination

By Mr. Lyman:

Q. Mr. Aronson, I believe you said you worked in the early years of 1948 to 1959; I mean, from the early years 1948 to 1958 for Alsco, is that correct?

A. I worked for them just about ever since they started in. [212]

Q. And do you recall that in the early years there that when you were working piece work on these windows that you would have extra work involving some carpentry to fit the windows properly?

A. That is right.

Q. And wasn't it the fact that back in the early years they asked you to just name your own price but keep it low, and you used to give them a flat figure for it, isn't that true?

A. No, there was always a set wage.

Mr. Ewing: I would object, your Honor. I would like a clarification of what he means by "early years"—'54?

Mr. Lyman: Well, is it your best recollection, then, that they always had this question of computing it by the hour?

A. It was hourly wages, yes.

Q. Now, when the hourly rates seemed a little high the company would take exception sometimes, wouldn't they, not with you, but with some of the applicators?   A. That could be.

Q. You know of such instances, do you not?

(Testimony of George Aronson.)

A. It might have happened once or twice, I wouldn't say for sure.

Q. And then the applicator would negotiate with the company [213] or try to prove that he did put that time in?

A. Well, I don't know what the other guys have done.

Q. Did you ever hear about anything like that in all the years you were there?

A. Oh, I probably heard about it but never thought anything of it.

Q. Now, there was a time when you did leave Alsco, wasn't there?

A. Well, I left two weeks one time when my mother died.

Q. When what?

A. When my mother passed away.

Q. I don't mean that, sir, didn't you go into a gas station venture? A. No.

Q. Was that your brother, Walt?

A. That is my brother Walt, yes.

Q. Well, you were one of those persons that Mr. Lee and Mr. Williams said that was one of the regulars, you and I believe Lewis?

A. Yes.

Q. And when things were busy there would be a great influx of these installers that would come in, and applicators, is that correct?

A. That is correct.

Q. And they worked there under the same conditions that you [214] did? A. Yes, sir.

(Testimony of George Aronson.)

Q. Paid the same way? A. Yes.

Q. Had tools just like you did?

A. Yes, sir.

Q. And their hours were no different than yours?

A. Well, they kept their own hours.

Q. What I mean is that the company didn't tell them what time to start work and what time to quit?

A. They didn't tell any of us what time to start.

Q. And you who worked, as you say, steady, and they who worked intermittently, worked under the exact same conditions?

A. Well, when times were good and there was a lot to do, why, they hired more installers.

Q. What I am saying is that their conditions of work were the same as yours?

A. Yes, no different.

Q. Paid all the same?

A. Paid all the same.

Q. When you wanted to take off somewhere you certainly had a right to do it, without any question, didn't you?

A. When I wanted time off and they said "Yes," well, fine.

Q. I believe you said you were a person who never took a [215] vacation?

A. I never did.

Q. That is by your own choice?

A. That is right.

Q. Now, isn't it a fact that you put on literally hundreds of these jobs?

(Testimony of George Aronson.)

A. I put on a good many of them.

Q. And I believe you testified, it is true, is it not, that very few, in only a couple of instances, did somebody from the company come out?

A. Well, there has been a couple of instances that they have come out, yes.

Q. But in the great majority of these hundreds, or perhaps a couple of thousand cases, you have never seen anyone from the company?

A. Well, there has been salesmen out and looked them over, yes.

Q. Well, these salesmen have no technical knowledge of how to put on a window, do they?

A. Well, that could be.

Q. I am asking you, sir, do they?

A. Maybe they do.

Q. They never told you how to put on a window?

A. There is one guy that tried to tell me.

Q. But you didn't pay any attention to [216] him?

A. Well, I put it on the way he wanted it.

Q. Well, now, if a salesman came out and told you to put on a window the way you knew it was wrong——

A. If he wanted it on that way, I would put it on that way.

Q. Then you would have to go back and do it over?

A. At times, well, at his expense, yes.

Q. At whose expense?

A. At the salesman's expense.

(Testimony of George Aronson.)

Q. Supposing the salesman wouldn't pay you, then whose expense would it be?

A. Well, I wouldn't put it on.

Q. Well, in other words, if you knew as an applicator of many years experience that it was wrong to put it on that way?

A. No, but if the salesman requested it put on that way, I would put it on that way.

Q. Even though it was wrong?

A. Yes, sir.

Q. Do you know of any other applicator that would do that?

A. I think any of them would.

Q. Do you know of any other applicator that has done it? A. No, I don't.

Q. Have you ever knowingly put on a window wrong? A. No, not to my knowledge.

Q. And Mr. McFarlane has no technical knowledge of this [217] business at all, does he?

Mr. Ewing: I object, your Honor, as being a conclusion of the witness.

The Court: Just a moment, sustained.

Q. (By Mr. Lyman): As a matter of fact, Mr. McFarlane has no technical knowledge of any type of business, has he?

Mr. Ewing: I object again.

The Court: Sustained, how would he know?

Q. (By Mr. Lyman): Do you know whether he has any technical knowledge?

A. I imagine he does, he has been in it quite a while.

(Testimony of George Aronson.)

Q. Have you ever seen him put any windows on?   A. No, I haven't.

Q. Do you know of any supervisors that are hired for the specific purpose of going out and supervising the men?   A. No, I don't.

Q. You heard the testimony of the other applicators, Mr. Lewis and Mr. Green, are they correct when they said no one supervises them and tells them how to do the work?

Mr. Ewing: I object, your Honor, I don't think this witness knows what other installers might do.

The Court: Sustained.

Q. (By Mr. Lyman): Did you hear the testimony of Mr. [218] Green and Mr. Lewis?

A. Yes, I did.

Q. And did you hear them state that no one told them the manner and method in which these windows should be put on, do you recall them making the statement?

Mr. Ewing: I object, your Honor, I don't think he said that statement.

Mr. Lyman: I asked the question specifically.

The Court: Overruled.

Q. (By Mr. Lyman): Do you recall that?

A. No, I don't.

Q. You were sitting here during the proceedings, were you not, sir?   A. Yes, sir.

Q. These bulletins, do they tell you "Caulk around the windows and doors and other openings

(Testimony of George Aronson.)

before installing sill and flashing strip and casing trim," that is part of the job, isn't it?

A. Not in my windows, that is in a siding setup.

Q. Well, where counsel was asking, "Do not fail to caulk all units that should be caulked," would you leave them empty simply because you hadn't read this?   A. Oh, no.

Q. You would do it, anyway, wouldn't you?

A. Well, it's part of the windows. **[219]**

Q. In other words, you didn't need this written material to tell you to caulk where you should caulk?   A. I didn't need it, no.

Q. And if Alsco failed to print this and distribute it, you would caulk your openings, would you not?

A. That is what we was instructed to do when we first started putting the windows in.

Q. And that is the proper way to complete a contract, isn't it?

A. I imagine it would be.

Q. Well, isn't it a fact that the company's interests in this insofar as you were concerned was that you should complete this job in accordance with its contracts with the customer, isn't that true, they wanted a good, workmanlike job from you, isn't that true?   A. That is right.

Q. And no one came out there and told you which windows to put on first or which door to put on first, did they?

A. No, but it was wrote on the contract which

(Testimony of George Aronson.)

one was to be put on first, or second, or third, or fourth, which was the one.

Q. Well, couldn't you put a door on first if you wanted to?

A. I could have if I wanted to, if there was a door to be put on, yes.

Q. Let me understand you about these contracts, these [220] openings have numbers, is that correct?   A. That is right.

Q. And you can put any windows on first, could you not, it wouldn't make any difference?

A. The windows are numbered.

Q. Pardon?

A. The windows are numbered.

Q. And they are put in the truck in that order?

A. Oh, no, they are put on the house in that order.

Q. Would it make any difference whether you put a window on the side of the house or in the front of the house first?

A. Well, it probably wouldn't, but then we go by the numbers so that when the customer takes his windows out he knows which window goes back in again, for cleaning.

Q. Yes, I know that, the windows are numbered so that when they store them they can fit them back into the proper opening?

A. That is right.

Q. But as far as you are concerned, would it make any difference if you started on the second

(Testimony of George Aronson.)

floor and put the proper window in the proper hole, would it make any difference?

A. No, it wouldn't make no difference, no.

Q. And if the lady of the house was busy downstairs and [221] didn't want you downstairs, and told you to go upstairs and put the windows in up there first, well, you could do that, couldn't you?

A. Yes, we could.

Q. And you have done it, have you not, sir?

A. Well, I couldn't say for sure.

Q. It says, this bulletin, "Do not try to cover up defective product or work," well, you wouldn't do that anyway, would you?

A. Well, I would sure try not to.

Q. And you didn't need this printed matter here to tell you that, did you, you know better, isn't that true?   A. It could be.

Q. Well, sir, I would like to know, do you know better than to try to hide work?

A. Well, I hope so, yes.

Q. You clean your windows, do you not, before you install them?   A. That is right.

Q. Take pride in your work?

A. That is right.

Q. And you also make appointments with customers to see that they are going to be home?

A. Call them before I put the windows in, yes.

Q. And you get a group of orders from the shop, you are the [222] one that makes the appointments with the customers, are you not?

A. At times we do and at times we just take

(Testimony of George Aronson.)

off on a job and people are home and we go ahead with them, we don't necessarily have to call them.

Q. What I am trying to say is that the company doesn't line up the appointments and hand you a schedule which you have to follow?

A. They do pretty well.

Q. Pardon?

A. Yes, they line them out for us quite very much.

Q. Did Mr. Williams ever put a schedule out for you and tell you, "You have to take them in this order"?

A. Well, now, if there is an order that is rush, he will write "Rush" on that order and "To be put on first."

Q. You put that on first?

A. That is right.

Q. What about the second? Did Mr. Williams tell you which one you put on second?

A. I have had quite a few times that he has wrote which ones should be on first, second and third.

Q. And on up to the end, is that right?

A. That is right.

Q. Did you hear Mr. Williams testify here that you people make up your own schedule? [223]

A. I couldn't rightfully say I did.

Q. Well, you were here this afternoon?

A. That is right.

Q. Did he make up schedules for anyone else besides you?

(Testimony of George Aronson.)

A. Well, that is something I don't know, sir.

Q. You are the only one, as far as you know, that he makes up a schedule for?

A. He might have made a schedule up for others.

Q. Does he do this with every job, he schedules every job for you?

A. No, not unless it's rush.

Q. And let's say this is an ordinary group of orders and there is no rush involved at all, just a routine group of four orders.   A. Yes.

Q. Does Mr. Williams every time on these thousands of jobs that you have done, give you a list that you have got to follow in any particular order?   A. Not at all times, no.

Q. No. When there is a rush job he asks you to do this rush job first?

A. Yes, he will mark "Rush" on my order.

Q. Right, because a customer will cancel out and you will lose your earnings, won't you?

A. Right. [224]

Q. As a matter of fact, he doesn't care which job you do after that, does he?

A. No, I don't imagine he would.

Q. All right, here is a statement in this bulletin, it says, "Your attitude with the customers must be one of cooperation, friendliness and cheerfulness," you wouldn't be any other way, would you?

A. At least I try to be decent to people, yes.

Q. You don't need this bulletin to remind you

(Testimony of George Aronson.)

of that, do you?   A. No.

Q. It says, "Present a neat appearance at all times," you don't need Alsco to tell you that, do you?   A. I hope not.

Q. Now, Mr. McFarlane asked you to put a sign of Alsco on your truck and you said "No," isn't that true?   A. That is right.

Q. You still worked there, didn't you?

A. Yes.

Q. Pardon?   A. Yes, sir.

Q. Now, isn't it a fact that while you were at Alsco that the rates that were paid for these windows changed from time to time per unit?

A. There is one time that they have changed, as far as I know [225] now.

Q. You recall once? And that is at the request of the installers, was it not, they wanted more money?   A. Yes, I imagine it was.

Q. And you were among those installers?

A. Pardon?

Q. You were one of those installers?

A. Yes, but I don't think I ever sat in on the meeting, when they had the meeting I think I was out of town.

Q. When you came back you were getting more per unit?   A. Yes.

Q. Now, wasn't there a different amount that was paid if you went up above the first floor, for instance?

A. Yes, they did add a little bit to the second floor.

Q. Counsel questioned you about being split up,

(Testimony of George Aronson.)

the team being split up, who would the man be that you would usually go with?

A. Well, I have gone with Lewis, I have gone with Busby.

Q. And those would usually be good-sized jobs with a number of windows, wouldn't they?

A. Correct.

Q. And the purpose was that you could put more windows on more quickly if you had two men rather than one?

A. Yes, and then if we had to go up quite a ways with them, why, it would take two of [226] us.

Q. Yes, and then you were paid according to the number of units you put on?

A. That is right.

Q. Now, when you brought the sheet back, who would decide which ones got paid how much?

A. It was split down the center.

Q. You had your own tools, did you not?

A. Yes, sir.

Q. Furnished all your own tools and maintained your car?   A. That is right.

Q. Or your truck, that is, and you paid all your own expenses incident to this work out of your gross receipts?   A. That is right.

Q. Was there anything in your arrangement with Alsco that you were guaranteed a certain number of jobs?   A. No, sir.

Q. And did you ever at any time ever promise

(Testimony of George Aronson.)

them that you would do a certain number of jobs
a year?   A. No, sir.

Q. Pardon?   A. No, sir.

Q. Now, counsel asked you if all these jobs that
you did, whether you required supervision, I believe you answered you didn't, is that correct?

A. I think so. [227]

Q. And that is because you are experienced in
this work, isn't that true?   A. That is right.

Q. And the company relies upon your experience and your ability to do a workmanlike job,
isn't that right?   A. That is right.

Q. And you know when you come in with a
completion certificate or you tell them the job is
completed they are satisfied, isn't that true?

A. That is right, I hope so.

Q. And upon that representation to them, you
get paid, isn't that right?   A. That is right.

Q. Pardon?   A. That is right.

Q. So any contact that anyone from the office
had with you on these jobs concerned a customer
complaint, as a rule, did it not?

A. I don't rightfully know.

Q. Well, men would come out on the job because some customer complained, is that the reason
they came out?   A. Could be, yes.

Q. And it was the purpose of the company, was
it not, to create good customer relations, isn't that
true?   A. I reckon so. [228]

Q. And whenever the customer was critical, why
they tried to satisfy the customer by asking you

(Testimony of George Aronson.)

to do this particular work for the customer, wasn't that so?   A. That is right.

Mr. Lyman: I believe that is all, your Honor.

Redirect Examination

By Mr. Ewing:

Q. Referring to Defendant's Exhibit No. 9 again, "Code of Ethics and Cooperation," is it true that irregardless of what they say in here is right or wrong, did you try and follow what they say in here?

A. I tried to follow what they said, yes.

Q. Is there any connection between this presenting a neat appearance and wearing white coveralls? In other words, is it in your mind when you present a neat appearance you were to wear these coveralls furnished you?

A. Well, would I have to wear them or wouldn't I have to wear them?

Q. Well, they talk about presenting a neat appearance at all times in this Code of Ethics here, to you would that mean wearing these coveralls, and so forth?

A. Well, I reckon so, yes.

Mr. Ewing: That is all I have.

The Court: That is all, Mr. Aronson, step [229] down.

The Witness: Thank you.

Mr. Lyman: Oh, just one question, if I may, your Honor.

(Testimony of George Aronson.)

Recross-Examination

By Mr. Lyman:

Q. When you and Mr. Busby got into this job, wasn't it your selection of Mr. Busby or your selection of Mr. Lewis?   A. No.

Q. Or Mr. Lewis selected you or Mr. Busby selected you?   A. No.

Q. Well, how was it done?

A. We was asked by the company.

Q. And who asked you, if I may ask?

A. Well, now, I don't rightfully recall who asked us, but we was asked.

Q. Well, there are only two people who could ask you, either Mr. Lee or Mr. Williams; now which of those asked you?

A. I believe it was Mr. McFarlane.

Q. The man that is not here?   A. No.

Q. And you have worked with Mr. Busby on several occasions, have you not?

A. Yes, I worked with him. [230]

Q. And you worked with Lewis on several occasions, isn't that true?   A. I guess so.

Q. And isn't it a fact that after the first time, at least, it was the result of your own selection or his selection that you two got together?

A. Well, I haven't worked very much with anybody, I have been a lone wolf all the time, practically. [231]

CLARENCE LLOYD BUSBY,

called and sworn as a witness on behalf of the defendant, testified as follows:

Clerk of the Court: Please state your full name?

A. Clarence Lloyd Busby.

Clerk of the Court: How do you spell that Busby?

A. (Spells.) B-u-s-b-y.

Clerk of the Court: Thank you, please be seated.

Direct Examination

By Mr. Ewing:

Q. Mr. Busby, what is your address?

A. 711 S. Cowley, 7-1-1.

Q. And are you working at the present time?

A. No, between jobs. [232]

Q. Have you at any time worked for Alsco Storm Windows Co. or Alsco Company Northwest, Inc.? A. Yes.

Q. And when was that?

A. It was several times, you might say in and out from 1949.

Q. Since 1949? A. Since 1949.

Q. Up to what time?

A. Up to, oh, '59·

Q. In what capacity did you work for that company? A. As an installer.

Q. Generally working as an installer, what did you do?

A. Well, it was our place to take windows,

(Testimony of Clarence Lloyd Busby.)
doors and siding out and install it on the homes
where they directed.

Q. Was there any written contract between you
and Alsco that you know of?   A. No.

Q. Did you perform your work on the basis of
work orders?   A. Yes.

Q. And where were they picked up at?

A. They was picked up, generally, right at the
plant.

Q. Were there any conversations or negotiations entered into between you and the representative of Alsco at the time you picked up your work
orders?

A. Well, generally on how many jobs he is
going to take out [233] and such as that.

Q. Did Alsco give you the work orders?

A. Yes, we was handed a certain amount of
work orders.

Q. Well, were you free to accept or reject any
work order that was offered to you?

A. Well, I would say that you would be free to
object to any one.

Q. Have you ever rejected a work order given
you?   A. I have, yes.

Q. And what would follow after that rejection?

A. Well, generally a better working condition
due to the fact that the only reason I rejected it
was because of an area, or something like that,
which was generally seen, and after negotiation.

Q. Did Alsco ever give you more than one work
order at a time?   A. Oh, yes.

(Testimony of Clarence Lloyd Busby.)

Q.   Did they attach any priority to these orders ?

A.   Oh, quite often.

Q.   What do you mean by that, would they tell you which ones to do first and second, and so on ?

A.   Well, from two different ideas, one would be an order that was older than another order should naturally come first.

Q.   Would they tell you to do that first ? [234]

A.   Well, that would be a general—it would be an understood order, yes.

Q.   Has there been any times when you have gone to Alsco looking for work when they did not have a job for you?   A.   Oh, yes.

Q.   Not having a job for you at those times, did they refer you to a competitor?   A.   No.

Q.   Did Alsco discourage you at all from working for competitors when they did not have a job for you?

A.   I think that there was a definite feeling in that direction, yes.

Q.   Well, can you explain that?

A.   Well, if you should go to work for somebody else you was naturally set down.

Mr. Lyman: Objection, your Honor, this kind of testimony is conjectural.

The Court: I don't think it's responsive.

Mr. Lyman: Pardon me?

The Court: I don't think it's responsive.

Mr. Lyman: That is right.

The Court: Sustained.

(Testimony of Clarence Lloyd Busby.)

Q. (By Mr. Ewing): Has Mr. McFarlane ever called you into his office at all?

A. Oh, yes, I have been there quite often. [235]

Q. And what was that in reference to?

A. Well, several different things, at one time he seen our trucks, I was with Mr. Lewis, and he seen our trucks setting at a competitor's place, and he definitely told us that we wasn't loyal to the company.

Q. You were called into Mr. McFarlane's office as a result of somebody seeing your truck?

A. That is right.

Q. Were you doing a job for Alsco at that time?　　A. We were not.

Q. Did you have any Alsco materials on your trucks?　　A. We did not.

Q. Did you, as an installer, Mr. Busby, ever hold yourself out to the public as being in the business of an installer, have you ever advertised that you were in business?

A. No, no advertising.

Q. And you stated you did own a truck at the time in question?　　A. That is right.

Q. Did you advertise at all in the truck?

A. No.

Q. Or in papers?　　A. No.

Q. The phone book?　　A. No. [236]

Q. Were you at any time approached to advertise Alsco on your truck?　　A. Oh, yes.

Q. And would you relate that incident, please?

(Testimony of Clarence Lloyd Busby.)

A. Well, they asked us if we wouldn't allow an Alsco sign to be put on our trucks, and we refused.

Q. You refused?   A. Yes.

Q. Who furnished the materials for these jobs?

A. Alsco, the main plant.

Q. Have you ever used Alsco's trucks?

A. Oh, yes.

Q. On jobs you have done for them?

A. Yes.

Q. Have they ever furnished you anything else in the way of equipment?

A. Oh, quite often an extra long ladder for higher staging, or a saw, larger saw than what we was generally packing in our small tool kits, things of that kind.

Q. Have they ever furnished you any jacks?

A. No, generally we all had our own jacks.

Q. And have they ever furnished you any scaffolding?

A. Well, the ladders was used for scaffolding.

Q. In the event you broke a tool in the course of doing a job, who would replace that? [237]

A. Generally, we did.

Q. And were you reimbursed for that at all?

A. No, that was our own.

Q. As to work which was included within a work order, what was the basis for payment to you for that work?

A. Well, I would say piece work would be the ruling.

(Testimony of Clarence Lloyd Busby.)

Q. Were there times when you did extra work, that is, work outside of the work order?

A. Oh, yes.

Q. And how were you paid for that work?

A. Generally, by the hour.

Q. Have there been occasions when changes had to be made in the job?

A. Yes, there have been occasions of that.

Q. Could you make changes in a job without consulting Alsco first?

A. Very minor ones we could handle, but all the important ones had to be discussed with the office.

Q. Have you ever been moved off a job before it was finished, to another job at the direction of Alsco personnel?   A. Oh, yes.

Q. And you would then start a second job at a different location?   A. Yes.

Q. Were you always returned to the job that you started? [238]

A. Sometimes; sometimes, no.

Q. Are you saying that there have been times when you started a job, were removed to a second job and never returned to the job you originally started?   A. That is right.

Q. Who would finish the job you originally started?   A. Generally, another installer.

Q. And were you paid piecemeal for the work you had done on the first job, I mean, to the extent you went?

vs. United

Testimony of C

A. To the e:

piecemeal situat

Q. And ther:

unit basis on th

The Court:

mean piece wor

Mr. Ewing:

Q. (By Mr.

staller such as :

have close supe

Mr. Lyman:

leading, and ca:

The Court: :

Q. (By Mr.

without close st:

Mr. Lyman:

thing.

The Court:

ask [239] h m

Q. (By Mr.

working on a

Alsco come out

A. I would

Q. Who wi

A. In m st

dealer.

Q. Have th

jobs you have

given any dir

should be done

(Testimony of Clarence Lloyd Busby.)

A. To the extent you went, it was generally a piecemeal situation.

Q. And then, of course, you would be paid on a unit basis on the second job you went to?

The Court: When you say "piecemeal," you mean piece work?

Mr. Ewing: Piece work, or a unit price.

Q. (By Mr. Ewing): To an experienced installer such as you, Mr. Busby, was it necessary to have close supervision?

Mr. Lyman: Exception, your Honor, this is leading, and calls for a conclusion.

The Court: Sustained.

Q. (By Mr. Ewing): Could you do your work without close supervision?

Mr. Lyman: Objection, your Honor, the same thing.

The Court: It calls for a conclusion, you can ask [239] him what happened.

Q. (By Mr. Ewing): During the course of working on a job, would any representatives from Alsco come out to check that job?

A. I would have to say yes.

Q. Who were they, do you know?

A. In most cases it would be a salesman or a dealer.

Q. Have these salesmen that have been out on jobs you have been on made any suggestions or given any directions to you as to how the work should be done?   A. Oh, yes.

(Testimony of Clarence Lloyd Busby.)

Q. Would you explain that, what would they say to you?

A. Quite often it was a question as to the manner you were carrying your job on, if you really thought that was proper.

Q. Did you follow the directions or suggestions that these people gave you?

A. Absolutely.

Q. After a job was done, were you to get anything signed by the customer certifying that the job was done, that he was satisfied with the job?

A. Yes, it was either completion or cash.

Q. Have you been on jobs where the customer was not satisfied and would not sign the completion slip?   A. Oh, yes. [240]

Q. And what would be the reason for the customer not signing, any specific reason?

A. Oh, it was a matter of several things.

Q. And if a customer had a complaint, is it true that you would take that complaint to Alsco and tell them what the trouble was and why the customer would not sign the slip?

A. That is right.

Q. On those occasions have you always been returned to that job to finish up that job in accordance with what the customer wanted?

A. Not every occasion, no.

Q. Where would you go?

A. Generally, if we did not go back, we would go on other work.

(Testimony of Clarence Lloyd Busby.)

Q. In other words, you were available to go back to that job, but outside of the fact that——

Mr. Lyman (Interposing): Objection, your Honor, he hasn't said that.

The Court: Sustained.

Q. (By Mr. Ewing): Did you say that there have been times when you did not return to the job that you started after registering the complaint with Alsco?   A. That is right.

Q. When somebody else finished that job? **[241]**

A. Generally.

Q. Have you ever entered into a separate contract with the home owner arising out of some job that you were doing for Alsco?   A. No.

Q. In the course of your employment with Alsco were directives or bulletins ever issued to you?

A. Oh, yes.

Q. Referring you to Defendant's Exhibit No. 9, being a Code of Ethics and Cooperation, issued by Alsco on November 28, 1956, do you recall receiving that bulletin (hands paper to witness)?

A. Oh, yes, I believe I do.

Q. Did you read it when you got it?

A. Oh, yes.

Q. Referring to page two on this bulletin, at Point 1 here it says, "Do not fail to caulk all units that should be caulked," did you follow that?

Mr. Lyman: Objection, your Honor, as leading. He ought to ask him what he did with respect to these things and let the witness discuss it.

The Court: Sustained.

(Testimony of Clarence Lloyd Busby.)

Q. (By Mr. Ewing): In reference to No. 1 here, "Do not fail to caulk all units that should be caulked," have you followed that? [242]

Mr. Lyman: Objection, your Honor.

The Court: Sustained.

Q. (By Mr. Ewing): Will you state whether or not you have followed the directions set out in this Code?

Mr. Lyman: Your Honor, objection for the same reason.

The Court: I think I should sustain the objection, he can ask him what he did, but you are giving him the answer, Mr. Ewing. Sustain the objection.

Mr. Ewing: I can ask him, did he follow these directions, can I not?

The Court: No, you are asking him a leading question, you are giving him the answer. What you should do is, what did he do about those things, you can ask him that but you can't tell him what to answer, that is a classical leading question. He is your witness, counsel.

Mr. Ewing: Yes, sir.

Q. (By Mr. Ewing): Referring to Points 1 through 7 here on page 2 of this exhibit, what did you do in reference to those points that are set out in there?

A. Well, we definitely followed them because they was put there for our sake.

Q. Outside of this written bulletin that was issued to you, have there ever been any oral meetings at Alsco?   A. Oh, yes. [243]

(Testimony of Clarence Lloyd Busby.)

Q. And what was discussed at these meetings?

A. Mostly it would be arbitration on working conditions, pay raises, and, oh, it was just a general work program in some cases.

Q. Taking Exhibit No. 9 here, Point No. 1 here was, "Present a neat appearance at all times," what would you do in reference to that particular point?

A. Well, we tried to follow it. One of the ways we tried to follow it is by, it was a very dirty job, I mean aluminum is black, consequently a boy in the field could become very dirty very easily, and it was hard to keep your appearance up in a neat manner. Therefore, the biggest share of us found it was easier and better to wear white coveralls because they, in turn, even though they were dirty, they were still a neat, workable uniform.

Q. Were you requested to wear these overalls?

A. As a direct order, no.

Q. Did these coveralls have any advertising on them?   A. Yes.

Q. And what was inscribed on them?

A. Generally, "Alsco Northwest" on the back, and your first name on the front, above the left-hand pocket.

Q. You say they never gave you a direct order to wear these; I will ask you, did they ever request you to wear them? [244]

Mr. Lyman: Objection as leading, your Honor.

The Court: Sustained.

Q. (By Mr. Ewing): Who paid the rental and cleaning charges on these coveralls?

(Testimony of Clarence Lloyd Busby.)

A. We generally did, most of the time.

Q. Did you have a contractor's card or a tax stamp?   A. No, I did not.

Mr. Lyman: Your Honor, I want to object to that as immaterial as a matter of evidence because it has nothing to do with determining the definition of a master and servant in the common law sense.

The Court: Well, it has something to do with determining whether he is an independent contractor, he is either one or the other, isn't he? [245]

* * *

The Court: Did you want to strike the last answer?

Mr. Lyman: Yes, your Honor.

The Court: It's immaterial and hearsay.

Mr. Lyman: It's immaterial, I am sure that I can persuade the Court, and there is no question as far as the record is concerned.

The Court: If he did have a tax stamp and was an independent contractor and held himself out as such, don't you think he would be entitled to show that?

Mr. Lyman: I don't think it would make any difference.

The Court: Why not? That is exactly what you are trying to show that he is an independent contractor, aren't you?

Mr. Lyman: Well, yes, but we are trying to show that they are not employees within the master and servant doctrine.

(Testimony of Clarence Lloyd Busby.)

The Court: That is true, you don't take any one thing under the present cases, even all those cases that you have been in, as the general situation.

Mr. Lyman: That is correct, your Honor. In other [247] words, if you had a close situation where there were obvious elements of control where they had supervisors breathing down their necks, then I would say if you had a tax stamp that may weigh very heavily against the employer and employee relationship, but where we have this obvious freedom here which has come out so far, this tax stamp is evidently being sought by the Government as a strong point to overcome all of these factors.

The Court: I think probably you had better wait to argue the case until the testimony is all in, hadn't you?

Mr. Lyman: Very well, your Honor.

The Court: In view of your position that you say that this is not in any manner controlled by the state law and the tax stamp has no particular materiality, with which I am inclined to agree, which may apply, because we don't determine this by the statute, the law by the particular section of the statute involved, I will strike that portion of the testimony. Did you have something further?

Mr. Ewing: I am through with him.

Cross-Examination

By Mr. Lyman:

Q. Mr. Busby, these meetings that you just mentioned, that is, where the question was raised as to the situation that you were not getting enough money per unit, [248] per window, isn't that true, didn't they try to get more money per window at these meetings, the applicators?

A. That was part of it, yes.

Q. And you had some negotiations with the officers of the company and I believe you did get some increase in the unit rate, did you not?

A. That was part of it, yes.

Q. And then there were also discussions, were there not, that extra work was coming in a little too heavy and they wanted you to watch it, that perhaps all this extra work wasn't being done as you were claiming, wasn't that part of the discussion?   A. That is right, pro and con.

Q. And at these discussions the company said that, "We have no way of checking these hours that you give us," isn't that true, "We rely on you"?   A. That is right.

Q. And a lot of controversy arose because many installers were bringing in extra work in amounts which seemed a little unreasonable, wasn't that one of the complaints?

A. That was one of the complaints.

Q. So then the company decided "you had bet-

er prove the t
so that we can
that part of the
A. That was
Q. There w:
work?   A.
Q. Now, the
would normally
wouldn't you. I
A. I would
them, no.
Q. You mea
A. I think
swer that by s:
ers our income
can put a uni
things enter i
tear that down
them, on down
program of to
extent, that is t
Q. I see. A
ing, then, that
that tend to v
do a workman
A. I will b
say, a part of
Q. I see.
A. But th
money and w
Q. Because

Windows, Inc., et al.

(Busby.)

...ation

...s that you just
...stion was raised
...not getting enough
...m, isn't that true,
...per window at

...ations with the
I believe you did get
...did you not?

...discussions, were
...ming in a little
...watch it, that
...being done as
...part of the dis-
...and con.
...company said
...these hours
..."We rely on

...because many
...work in amounts
...wasn't that one

...se,
...] "you had bet-

(Testimony of Clarence Lloyd Busby.)

ter prove the number of hours you do, somehow, so that we can arrive at some fair result,'' wasn't that part of the conversation, [249] also?

A. That was, but it was very innocuous.

Q. There was a little emphasis on this extra work?   A. Yes, that is true.

Q. Now, these bulletins that were put out, you would normally do these things, anyway, on a job, wouldn't you, like caulk your windows?

A. I would have to say some of them, some of them, no.

Q. You mean you would leave a space in there?

A. I think that I would have to truthfully answer that by saying that since we was piece workers our income is based entirely on how fast we can put a unit in, and every other one of these things enter into the picture, has a tendency to tear that down, neat appearance would be one of them, on down the line, would definitely have a program of tearing your speed down to a certain extent, that is the way I would have to answer that.

Q. I see. All right, sir. Well then, you are saying, then, that you would omit caulking; wouldn't that tend to violate the contract that you had to do a workmanlike job?

A. I will have to omit the caulking on, like I say, a part of them.

Q. I see.

A. But the caulking one is a part of the efficiency and we [250] tried to do our work efficiently.

Q. Because if you don't you are going to have

(Testimony of Clarence Lloyd Busby.)
to go back and do it over again, and that is going
to be a bigger waste of time?

A. That is right, loss of money again.

Q. And you don't want to waste time on these
jobs?   A. That is right.

Q. So actually, when they tell you to do certain
things or remind you to do certain things which
are part of the job, anyhow, you would do them
without any written instructions, wouldn't you,
like caulking?

A. Caulking would be one of them, yes.

Q. I think they have one in here about "Don't
leave out a pilot screw in a two lite window for
any reason," do you know what that means?

A. I do, but I am afraid I cannot answer that
because it is too long a story.

Q. Well, if you left out a pilot screw, why you
wouldn't have completed your contract, would you?

A. In some cases I would have to say yes, in
some cases I would have to say no.

Q. You heard Mr. Williams say it is like leaving a headlight off a car.

A. That is right, but sometimes the headlight
left off the car is proper if the condition happens
to be right. [251]

Q. If you leave the headlight off the car and
you have paid for headlights, then you don't have
a complete car, do you?

A. That is very true.

Q. All right. And then when it says, "Pick up

(Testimony of Clarence Lloyd Busby.)

the completion or the cash,'' why, that is necessary anyhow, that is how you get paid, isn't it?

A. That was, I understood it that that was one of the ways that they could, in turn, pay us.

Q. All right. Did you ever get in a situation where a home owner might ask you to do some little thing, hang up a clothesline or build a shelf for her?   A. Well, not so much that, no.

Q. Well, I mean some minor work, I don't mean anything major.

A. They have asked considerable times about a thing that you have not mentioned, which I did not do.

Q. I don't know, what would that be; in other words, you didn't engage in any extra work with these home owners?   A. No.

Q. You wanted to get your job on and get away?

A. That is right.

Q. Now, you did a great number of jobs for Alsco during the time that you were in and out, did you not, sir?   A. Quite a few, yes. [252]

Q. And it was on very few occasions that a salesman would come out, haven't they, isn't that so?

A. Well, I would say that they was, more than fifty per cent of the time that there was a salesman there.

Q. All right. Now, this salesman would complain about the extra work that you were putting in, would he not, that would be his problem with you?

(Testimony of Clarence Lloyd Busby.)

A. Well, that didn't concern me near as much as his presence, being there, no.

Q. Well, did he ask you to look out for leads for him for other jobs?   A. Oh, yes.

Q. And he would develop customer relations with the customer, too, at the same time, wouldn't he?   A. That is right.

Q. And he was looking for other jobs in the neighborhood when he was talking to you?

A. That is right.

Q. And if he had mismeasured that job in any way and you had to do extra work, he saw he was going to lose part of his commission, isn't that true?

A. That is right.

Q. And that is where you would get in an argument with him sometimes, isn't that so?

A. Well, very seldom we ever got in an argument because we [253] generally knew more than he did about the work, very seldom would they give you an argument.

Q. In other words, he didn't have the technical knowledge of the work that you did?

A. No.

Q. You just listened and then would be pleasant about it?   A. That is about the size of it.

Q. And then when he said what he had to say and left, why, you were happy he left?

A. Yes.

Q. Now, this situation of moving from one job to another, now, let me understand that, sir. You

(Testimony of Clarence Lloyd Busby.)

would have a group of orders, say four or five, when you leave the shop, would you not, sir?

A. Yes, sir.

Q. And then you would start putting up some windows in a particular place, and then you may get a call that there is a rush order, somebody is going to cancel if we don't get it up today, did you get that, sir?

A. That is right, I am following you.

Q. I just wanted you to answer for the record.

A. Yes.

Q. Then that job would be yours, wouldn't it, the rush job?

A. The rush job that I am to be moved onto.

Q. That is right. [254]

A. After I picked it up that work order would be considered mine, right.

Q. And if your first customer was in no particular hurry, you could go back and finish that first one, could you not? A. That is right.

Q. And you often did?

A. Often we did.

Q. And then you had both of them, you were paid on both? A. Yes.

Q. Did you ever work with somebody, together, I don't believe you testified that you did, the two of you together on a job?

A. You mean, two installers working together?

Q. Yes. A. Quite often.

Q. Well, how many jobs would that be, a regular thing or an unusual thing?

(Testimony of Clarence Lloyd Busby.)

A. Well, I would say neither.

Q. That would be a larger job, would it not, like a hospital or apartment house?

A. A hospital, a larger unit deal, a real large window would cause a real rough condition on one man, consequently, it would become a very small problem with two different crews. [255]

Q. I see. So then two of you would go out and do this larger job, isn't that correct, sir?

A. That is right.

Q. And then you would decide between yourselves how the compensation or the pay should be divided?

A. Well, that would be generally understood, you know, before we left.

Q. I mean, you decided between yourselves?

A. Yes.

Q. Now, that little incident you discussed where I believe you and Lewis were called in by Mel McFarlane? A. Yes.

Q. That was during a rather busy time, was it not, Alsco had a lot of orders going?

A. No, at the time it wasn't too busy, I would say it was just a medium time.

Q. Well, Mel McFarlane said something about loyalty to the company, did he use that word?

A. That is the word he used.

Q. And he didn't offer you any pay or any incentive to stay with Alsco, did he?

A. No, definitely not.

Q. Just conversation at that time?

(Testimony of Clarence Lloyd Busby.)

A. It was conversation on his part as a boss, yes.

Q. Now, you didn't have any arrangement with Alsco that you [256] were going to do a certain number of jobs for them for a certain number of months or weeks, did you, nothing in your arrangement with them like that, was there?

A. No, neither written nor oral.

Q. And they didn't tell you they were going to give you a certain number, either? What I mean is, over a long period of time?

A. No, I would say not over a long period of time.

Q. In other words, you have got a group or one or two in a certain day, and that would be your work for that particular period, isn't that correct, sir?   A. That is right.

Q. And each of these work sheets that you received and this being a typical one which is in evidence here, Plaintiffs' Exhibit 6, is that typical of the work orders that you received (hands paper to witness)?

A. Yes, that is typical of one of the work orders.

Q. Now, you would be paid, would you not, on the basis of the work set out in that work order?

A. That is right.

Q. And if on the back you indicated you had some extras, why, you would indicate it on the back like that "Extra labor, $3.50," is that correct?

(Testimony of Clarence Lloyd Busby.)

A. That is right, except it was always my understanding that there would be no extra labor paid unless it was shown by [257] the hour.

Q. Okay, but that one is not by the hour, is it?

A. Possibly they just missed it there, or something, I can't say; this is not mine.

Q. Each of those work sheets determined your particular pay for that particular job?

A. That is right.

Q. And you work on a job basis for Alsco, did you not?   A. That is right.

Q. I believe you have testified that you came in and went out several times, did you work for other companies in similar businesses?

A. Not so much other companies as I did for the parent companies, dealers. I have more time in than any of the rest of the installers, I believe, in the parent companies' dealers.

Q. You would work with their dealers?

A. That is right, which is actually working for the company but is working for one of the dealers.

Q. But the dealer paid you?

A. The dealer paid me. In other words, I was working with the same identical material.

Q. But you were paid by a different person?

A. Paid by a different outlet.

Q. Then you would come back and work for Alsco Northwest, [258] and then go off again?

A. That is right.

Q. Now, let me ask you, you said a dealer would

(Testimony of Clarence Lloyd Busby.)

often come out to a job, did I understand you to say that? A. That is right.

Q. You mean, a dealer would come out to a job you were doing for Alsco?

A. No, no, a dealer would come out to the job that was his, let's put it that way.

Mr. Lyman: I believe that is all, your Honor.

Redirect Examination

By Mr. Ewing:

Q. You stated, Mr. Busby, that there has been jobs where more than two applicators were on that job? A. Yes.

Q. Two or more? A. Yes.

Q. Has Alsco ever split those installers up and sent one to one job and continued the other one on the original job?

A. Oh, I would say so, yes.

Q. Has that happened on jobs you have been on?

A. Well, I am sure it has, although I could not pinpoint any one instance. [259]

Q. I think you stated that less than 50% of the time that sometimes salesmen would come out on the job? A. Oh, yes.

Q. Would they ever tell you to do something?

Mr. Lyman: Objection, your Honor, as leading.

The Court: Overruled.

(Last question read.)

A. Well, quite often.

Q. (By Mr. Ewing): Would you do it?

A. In cases where I felt I was the controlling judge on it, I would do so.

Mr. Ewing: That is all I have.

Mr. Lyman: Nothing further, your Honor.

The Court: That is all, Mr. Busby.

(Witnessed excused.)

Mr. Ewing: I am through, your Honor.

The Court: Does the Government rest?

Mr. Ewing: The Government rests, your [260] Honor.

MILTON L. LEE,

recalled as a witness on behalf of the plaintiffs in rebuttal, resumed the stand and testified further as follows:

Direct Examination

By Mr. Lyman:

Q. Will you give your full name again, Mr. Lee?   A. Milton L. Lee.

Q. Mr. Lee, you recall the testimony of Mr. Aronson yesterday, do you recall his testimony?

A. Yes.

Q. Do you recall specifically he was asked whether or not he ever refused or rejected a job, do you recall that question being put to him?

A. Yes, I do.

Q. And do you recall his answer, that he said he hadn't, to his knowledge?

A. That is as I remember it.

(Testimony of Milton L. Lee.)

Q. Now, do you have any recollection of any different situation?

A. Yes, I do. I remember talking to George on several occasions at the time we were getting into the siding business, trying to induce him to take on combination [261] jobs where he would be putting on a little siding, maybe, and windows, too. At that time he specifically said that he would not be interested in putting on any siding, regardless.

Q. And yet he continued with the company?

A. Yes, he continued to install windows.

Q. Now, do you have any recollection of Mr. Aronson saying that when he was given an order by someone to do a rush job as a preference, why, he always did it; do you remember his testimony to that effect?   A. Yes.

Q. Now, do you have any specific recollection of any different situation occurring with reference to rush jobs? In other words, did you ask him at any time concerning a rush job?

A. Yes, I have had occasion to call George while he had work orders out and asked him to do a job that we considered to be quite important to us, and having been turned down.

Q. Well, what would he say, what reason would he give?

A. Well, George is a conscientious fellow, George would usually say, "No, I am tied up, I have got these other people I have committed myself to them, so I can't do it."

Q. And what would you do then? [262]

(Testimony of Milton L. Lee.)

A. We would get somebody else.

Q. Now, do you recall yesterday counsel was questioning Mr. Aronson, I believe he asked him questions to the effect if he ever had anyone else work for him, do you remember that question?

A. Yes, I do.

Q. And do you recall his answer was that he did not have anybody else work for him? A. Yes.

Q. Now, do you know of any situation that is contrary to that?

A. Yes, George has told me that he took out his brother.

Q. And do you know whether he ever told anybody else that he took out his brother?

A. Well, I read the same thing in his deposition.

Q. And that is on file in this court?

A. That is right.

Q. And that deposition was taken by the Government? A. Correct.

The Court: It is not offered, though.

Mr. Lyman: Well, for what it is worth, then, your Honor, I don't want to offer the whole deposition, I just don't think anything that loads the record is necessary.

Q. Now, do you recall that counsel was questioning Mr. Aronson about a situation where two men are put [263] together to do a large job, do you recall that? A. Yes.

Q. Now, what happens there, how do these two men get together?

(Testimony of M
A. Well, the
have a job that
that two men ea
Q. What kin
A. That wou
be a job requiri
material on it, l
Q. All right.
A. Two or t
fellows you know
will work toget
Q. When you
what happens t
A. Sometim
they will say,
fellow."
Q. All right
A. All right
Q. Now, you
to each other,
A. Well, ha
do the job tog
to split up the
take it out and
Q. Does th
how they want
A. None wl
Q. I think
taking one of t
him elsewhere,
A. Yes, I d

(Testimony of Milton L. Lee.)

A. Well, the process is very simple, when you have a job that you realize the conditions are such that two men can work efficiently more than one.

Q. What kind of a job would that be?

A. That would usually be a large job, it would be a job requiring staging or extra handling of the material on it, long ladders.

Q. All right, go ahead.

A. Two or three-story jobs, you usually get two fellows you know are competent and ask them if they will work together.

Q. When you ask them, will they work together, what happens there?

A. Sometimes they will say yes or no, sometimes they will say, "I don't like to work with that fellow."

Q. All right, what happens then?

A. All right, so you finally get somebody else.

Q. Now, you finally get two that are amenable to each other, then what happens?

A. Well, having found two fellows that would do the job together, why they decide how they want to split up the [264] proceeds of the job, and they take it out and do it.

Q. Does the company interfere in any way in how they want to decide to split up the proceeds?

A. None whatsoever.

Q. I think there was some mention there about taking one of those men off the big job and sending him elsewhere, do you recall that testimony?

A. Yes, I do.

(Testimony of Milton L. Lee.)

Q. Now, how often, in your connection with this company, did that happen?

A. I never heard of it happening.

Q. What would happen to the big job if only one man were left?

A. Well, that is just the point, you would almost have to discontinue working on the job until you could get them back together.

Q. Now, do you remember the testimony of Mr. Aronson about taking a new man out, yes, a new man, to show him some work, do you recall that testimony?   A. Yes.

Q. What was the situation with respect to that?

A. In the case of new men, usually, if they haven't had experience, you usually find a man that is doing that type of work and ask him if he will take them out and show them what the ropes [265] are.

Q. Now, do all your applicators take these men out, or how does that work?

A. No, they don't, some of them will have nothing to do with new men; others are very generous about it, they say, "I don't mind him watching me for a day or two," and so they take them out.

Q. Is there any pay arrangement for these new people?

A. Well, that is varied from time to time. The company, of course, assumes no obligation to pay them, but if a man going out on a job can use an extra man, sometimes they can, why, they take him along as a helper; otherwise, they just say, "He

vs. *United*

(Testimony of M

can go along, b

along as an obs

Q. Did you

sign and put it

his truck?

A. No, that

edge.

Q. Did you

A. Yes, we l

Mr. Lyman:

By Mr. Ewing:

Q. Did you

Mr. Aronson o

to move him

didn't go?

Q. What d

called Mr. Aron

where else and

A. Yes, I ha

work orders on

was particularl

Q. Do you

that time was

A. Well, as

sider any job t

priority to fin

whether the job

Q. In othe

(Testimony of Milton L. Lee.)

can go along, but I won't pay them,'' so they go along as an observer.

Q. Did you ever get any applicator to take a sign and put it on his truck or let you paint it on his truck?

A. No, that has never happened, to my knowledge.

Q. Did you ask them?

A. Yes, we have asked a lot of them.

Mr. Lyman: That is all, your Honor.

Cross-Examination

By Mr. Ewing:

Q. Did you state, Mr. Lee, that you have sent Mr. Aronson out on jobs and you have called him to move him to a different job and he [266] didn't go?   A. I didn't state that.

Q. What did you say? Did you say you have called Mr. Aronson on occasions to do a job somewhere else and he didn't go?

A. Yes, I have asked Mr. Aronson when he had work orders out if he would start another job that was particularly pressing at the time.

Q. Do you know whether the job he was on at that time was a rush job or not?

A. Well, as a matter of fact, we usually consider any job that is in process being pretty much priority to finish, I don't remember specifically whether the job he was on was rush, but it could be.

Q. In other words, the job he was on could

(Testimony of Milton L. Lee.)

have been rush just like the one you wanted to send him to?   A. That is right.

Q. That would be a pretty good reason for not leaving, then, wouldn't it?   A. Of course.

Q. Now, you stated that Mr. Aronson had somebody work for him for a time, which you didn't know about, but later found out about?

A. His brother?

Q. Was it your testimony that you later found out that Mr. Aronson had somebody working for him that you didn't [267] know about?

A. No.

Q. Well, what did you say in reference to that?

A. I was asked if I knew George Aronson had a helper at one time and I said "yes."

Q. And who was that?   A. His brother.

Q. Do you have any control over helpers?

A. No.

Q. Do you hire helpers?

A. No, I don't remember that we ever have.

Q. Do you discharge helpers at all?

A. I don't remember ever doing it.

Q. Is it your policy to want to know when an installer has a man working for him?   A. No.

Q. I believe that Mr. Lyman asked you if you knew of any instance within your own knowledge where you knew a worker had been taken off a job before it was finished and moved to some other job, and you stated that you never knew that happened.

A. The specific question was with regard to a

(Testimony of Milton L. Lee.)

large job, where two men were working on it at the same time, I don't remember that happening, no.

Q. You don't remember an installer, those installers, being [268] split up, is that what you mean? A. That is right.

Q. Do you know of your own knowledge whether one installer working on a job has ever been moved off that job to another job before it was finished?

A. I know of lots of cases where installers have been asked to go from one job to another before it was finished, yes.

Mr. Ewing: That is all I have.

Redirect Examination

By Mr. Lyman:

Q. With reference to the last question, Mr. Lee, does the particular installer who is asked this, does he have some discretion or say in the matter?

A. Yes, he does.

My. Lyman. That is all. That is all, your Honor, the plaintiffs rest. [269]

* * ˛

ORAL OPINION OF THE COURT

The Court: Gentlemen, I have reviewed these cases, while I haven't read them necessarily in detail, I am not nearly as familiar with them as Mr. Lyman is. I feel that I am as able now as I am at any time to make a determination in this case. I recognize the fact that I am not bound by any State court determination as to what is an employee. I am not to be influenced by the actions of the plain-

tiff before 1958 because the matter is to be viewed
as though we were making an initial determination
on the real estate when this matter comes up, and
this is, is there control, are the elements and all the
other elements in the definition given by the statute
such as to require a determination that this is an
employer-employee relationship, as defined by the
Act, because the Act says:

> "Section 3121(d) Employee. For the pur-
> poses of this chapter, the term 'employee'
> means:
>
> Subdivision 2. Any individual who, under the
> usual common law rules applicable in deter-
> mining the employer or employee relationship,
> has the status of an employee."

and the same definition in Section 3306.

So, we turn to the cases to find out what the rule
is before we apply it to the particular facts in our
particular case. Now, the amendments that I have
read, as I understand the statutes, were adopted in
1948, so, I don't know that the cases before 1948
have any particular bearing except as they may shed
some light upon what the common rule might be
with reference to what is an employer-employee relationship.

In U. S. v. Silk, decided in 1947, at 331 U. S. 704,
there were two classes of employees and the two
cases were consolidated. Unloaders of coal were paid
by the piece work, they were paid by the ton,
whereas, the unloaders of trucks were not employees
and, therefore, not covered.

Bartels v. Birmingham was a case involving proprietors of music halls and name band leaders, and it was held in that case the musicians were employees of the leaders and not proprietors. That was decided in 332 U. S., 126.

Now, in 1945 in 148 Fed. (2d), 649, Grace v. Magruder, coal hustlers were determined to be employees and it is said that the control wasn't all entirely essential.

Now, in 1943 in Radio City Music Hall v. United States - 135 Fed. (2d), 715, there was a degree of control of details and it was held in that case that the entertainers were employees.

And those, I think are most of the cases cited which were cited prior to the amendment.

I can't find any particular comfort in a lot of these cases, except as they may shed some light on the particular facts in our case, or as they may have facts that are similar. Now, there a number of cases, and I note and will note, in passing, the number of cases that Mr. Lyman has appeared in: Consolidated Housecraft v. United States in the Eastern District of New York - 170 Fed. Supp., 842, was a case in which Mr. Lyman presents the matter for the employer, or for the dealers, the plaintiff. It was held that where the salesmen got orders the corporation submitted to applicators the orders, which they could either accept or reject. If they were accepted, they had almost complete discretion and they fixed their own schedule and hired their helpers. Supervision was only superficial. They held they were independent contractors.

Mervis v. United States, decided last year in 187 Fed. Supp., 248, by J. Skelly Wright, the Judge in Louisiana, held almost the same thing, as did Silver v. United States in 1944 - 131 Fed. Supp., 209. That was a case in which Judge Brennan, to whom reference will be made later, decided the case.

Now, in United States v. Thorson, decided in 1960, in which Mr. Lyman participated - 282 Fed. (2d), 157, it held that there was no exercise of direct control over the applicators and, therefore, they were held to be independent contractors.

Now, I have notes on and I could refer to a number of other cases but, generally, there are a number of these particular type, this particular type of a case, that is, where a salesman would go out and get orders, where the applicators would go out, take a work order, and go out and do the work, and a number of them have held, and I think the majority of them, have held. that where there is no supervision, where there is no control, where there is nothing that is done to direct the work, the applicators are independent contractors.

Now, I refer to Edwards v. United States in the Court of Claims, in which Mr. Lyman participated - 168 Fed. Supp., 955, decided in 1958. That is the Spokane case to which reference is made, and Mr. Edwards was operating with Inland Roofing. In that case the Court, I think it was Judge Jones, Chief Judge Jones, said:

> "There was no supervision. The plaintiff did not know anything about the work."

He never took a man off the job, and that there was a complete lack of supervision, although the contractors could, that is, the applicators could, take jobs or refuse them, as they chose, and, apparently, the Inland Roofing Company withheld them, as they chose.

American Homes of N. E., Inc. v. United States, 1959 in Massachusetts - 173 Fed. Supp., 857, the applicators were not employees. And Jagolinzer v. United States - 150 Fed. Supp., 489, they were held not employees, as the right to control was that only of the result, and not of the means and method, both of which cases Mr. Lyman participated in.

In 1959 Fleeman v. United States - 175 Fed. Supp., 336, in Ohio, the case holds that there was no right to control of the means, only the right to control the result. The applicators were held to be independent contractors.

Now, we have a situation, also, in these cases that were referred to by counsel for the Government in his argument, Ringling Brothers is an old one, 1951 - 189 Fed. (2d), 865, and they were held to be employees, and I think probably, counsel, Mr. Lyman's description of the relationship between the Ringling Brothers' performers and the company is a different situation than we have here.

I come back to the problem, and I feel that Judge Brennan, in the Ben v. United States case - 139 Fed. Supp., 883, and Judge Aldritch, in Security Roofing & Construction Company v. United States in 163 Fed. Supp., 794, has given us the measure, because in the particular cases each case has to stand upon its own bottom. We have to have a situation where all of the circumstances are taken into consideration and not any particular one, and Mr. Lyman, in his argument, mentions the fact that these things show that these parties were independent contractors. There are just as many things, it seems to me, that show that they were classified as employees and since the burden of proof is on the plaintiff in a case of this kind, I feel that it is up to me to make the determination from the facts, whether they control or not, I mean, and determine whether they control or not.

Now, I will not detail by any means the notes that I have, but there are certain things that seemed to me to be present in this case that were not in some of the other cases, not particularly in the Inland Roofing case. and I will make reference now to Mr. Lee's deposition. What kind of control was exercised?

"Q. On these jobs that you have gone out to look at. have you ever made any suggestions?

"A. Surely.

"Q. And you expected them to be followed?

"A. Well, if I made a suggestion, I certainly would.

"Q. Have you ever given any directions?

"A. To an applicator?

"Q. Yes.

"A. If the occasion arose, I would, yes.

"Q. And you expected him to follow those directions that you gave?"

objection and, again, stating the question:

"Q. (By Mr. Ewing): You stated that there have been times when you have given directions to an applicator, is that right?

"A. No, I didn't say that. You asked me if I would give them directions, and I said I would and if I gave them, I would expect them to be followed, yes. My day-to-day knowledge of these applications is not such that I would be in that position."

bear in mind that one of the problems is not what kind of supervision was exercised, but whether the party has the right to exercise the supervision, whether it was exercised or not. Again, on page 19, line 18:

"Q. Did you have the power to give directions, Mr. Lee?

"A. Yes, in making a deal with an applicator to apply a job, at least, I would assume that you would have the power of instructing him as to the way it should be done. Unwritten law in the business, you might say.

"Q. Did you, in fact, instruct installers as to how the job should be done?

"A. Oh, on occasion, yes."

Again, on pages 22 and 23:

"Q. Would there be times when a home owner would call into your office during the performance of the work and say he was dissatisfied with the work?

"A. Yes.

"Q. What would be done, then?

"A. Well, on occasion the job would be taken

away from the man that was doing it, and on other
occasions the home owner would probably be educated as to why he was doing what he was, and in
some cases the home owner would complain about
the work being done when maybe it was a matter of
what he had to work with. I am speaking of the
windows and the doors that he was installing or the
opening that he was putting them on. I say, there
is no general rule as to how you take care of a complaint.''

And on page 24:

"Q. And if that representative from your office
felt that the work was not being done in a satisfactory manner, then that person who went out from
your office would excuse that applicator from that
job?

"A. Yes, that is about the way it would work,
yes.''

Now, it seems to me as though there is a decided
ability and recognized ability to control in this particular case and, therefore, it seems to me it doesn't
come within the Edwards case or a number of the
other cases, but it actually comes within the Ben
case, the Williams case, the Consolidated Security
Roofing case, and I call also attention to the testimony of Aronson, while I realize that that was not
at the instance of the plaintiff, it gives a direct
conflict to the testimony in reference to some of the
matters that are determined or testified to by the
plaintiff's witnesses, and I feel that under the circumstances there has not been, the burden of proof

has not been sustained and, accordingly, judgment will be for the defendant.

* * *

[Endorsed]: Filed August 21, 1961.

[Title of District Court and Cause.]

Civil Nos. 1882 and 1883

CERTIFICATE OF CLERK

United States of America,
Eastern District of Washington—ss.

I, Dorothy E. Moulton, Clerk of the United States District Court for the Eastern District of Washington, do hereby certify that the documents annexed hereto are the original documents filed in the above-entitled cause to wit:

Date Filed   Title of Document

11/10/59—Complaint for Refund of Employment Taxes Erroneously Paid and Collected (Civil No. 1882).

11/10/59—Complaint for Refund of Employment Taxes Erroneously Paid and Collected (Civil No. 1883).

1/ 7/60—Answer (Civil No. 1882).

1/ 7/60—Answer (Civil No. 1883).

12/16/60—Pretrial Order.

3/29/61—Deposition of Milton L. Lee (enclosed herewith but not attached hereto).

5/19/61—Findings of Fact and Conclusions of Law.

260   *Alsco Storm Windows, Inc., et al.*

Date Filed   Title of Document

5/19/61—Judgment.

5/29/61—Bill of Costs.

7/17/61—Notice of Appeal (Civil No. 1882).

7/17/61—Notice of Appeal (Civil No. 1883).

7/18/61—Bond for Costs on Appeal (Civil No. 1882).

7/18/61—Bond for Costs on Appeal (Civil No. 1883).

7/20/61—Consent to Substitution of Attorney (Civil No. 1882).

7/20/61—Consent to Substitution of Attorney (Civil No. 1883).

7/28/61—Stipulation.

8/10/61—Statement of Points.

8/10/61—Designation of Record.

8/16/61—Designation of Record.

8/18/61—Order Extending Time to Docket Record on Appeal.

8/21/61—Reporter's Transcript—Record of Proceedings at the Trial (enclosed herewith but not attached hereto).

Plaintiffs' Exhibits P-E-1—P-E-8 (enclosed herewith but not attached hereto).

Defendant's Exhibits D-E-9 and D-E-11 (enclosed herewith but not attached hereto).

and that the same constitute the record for hearing of the appeal from the judgment of the United States District Court for the Eastern District of

Washington, in the United States Court of Appeals for the Ninth Circuit, as called for in Appellants' Designation of Record, and Appellees' Designation of Record, and

I further certify that Exhibit D-10 requested in the Appellants' Designation of Record has not been included in this record on appeal as it was not offered or admitted.

In Witness Whereof, I have hereunto set my hand and affixed the seal of said District Court at Spokane in said District this 9th day of October, A. D. 1961.

[Seal]   /s/ DOROTHY E. MOULTON,
Clerk, United States District Court, Eastern District of Washington.

———

[Endorsed]: No. 17595. United States Court of Appeals for the Ninth Circuit. Alsco Storm Windows, Inc., Appellant, vs. United States of America, Appellee; Alsco Northwest, Inc., Appellant, vs. United States of America, Appellee. Transcript of Record. Appeals from the United States District Court for the Eastern District of Washington, Northern Division.

Filed October 11, 1961.

Docketed: October 25, 1961.

FRANK H. SCHMID

Clerk of the United States Court of Appeals for the Ninth Circuit.

Alsco Storm Windows, Inc., et al.

In the United States Court of Appeals
for the Ninth Circuit

No. 17595

ALSCO STORM WINDOWS, INC., for Its Own
Account and as Transferee of the Assets of
Vent-Air Awnings, Inc.,

Appellant,

vs.

UNITED STATES OF AMERICA,

Appellee.

No. 17595

ALSCO NORTHWEST, INC., a Corporation,

Appellant,

vs.

UNITED STATES OF AMERICA,

Appellee.

STATEMENT OF POINTS

Appellants set forth the following points on which
they intend to rely on appeal:

1.   The Court erred in concluding as a matter of
law that the applicators were employees under the
Federal Insurance Contributions Act, § 3121(d),
Internal Revenue Code, and the Federal Unemployment Tax Act, § 3306(1), Internal Revenue Code.

2.   The Court erred in drawing illogical inferences from undisputed facts, such inferences being

induced by an erroneous view of the applicable law.

3. The Court erred in making some findings of fact without evidentiary support in the record.

/s/ JOSEPH J. LYMAN,
Attorney for Appellants.

[Endorsed]: Filed October 20, 1961.

———

[Title of Court of Appeals and Cause.]

STIPULATION AS TO PRINTING OF THE RECORD

It is hereby stipulated and agreed, subject to the approval of the Court, that the parties may refer in their briefs and argument to any part of the certified record filed with the Court which has not been designated for printing, viz. Plaintiffs' Exhibits 1-8, inclusive, and Defendant's Exhibits 9 and 11.

/s/ JOSEPH J. LYMAN,
Counsel for Appellants.

/s/ LOUIS F. OBERDORFER,
Assistant Attorney General,
Counsel for Appellee.

Dated: October 17, 1961.

So Ordered: Oct. 19, 1961.

/s/ R. CHAMBERS,
Circuit Judge.

[Endorsed]: Filed October 20, 1961.

To be argued by:
Thomas A. Harnett

United States Court of Appeals

For the Ninth Circuit.

Docket No. 17609

ALBIN STEVEDORE COMPANY,
a Washington Corp.,

Appellant,

v.

CENTRAL RIGGING & CONTRACTING CORPORATION,

Appellee.

On Appeal from the United States District Court Western District
of Washington: Northern Division

BRIEF FOR PLAINTIFF-APPELLANT.

CLARKE, CLARKE, ALBERTSON & BOVINGDON,
Attorneys for Plaintiff-Appellant,
1118 Alaska Building,
Seattle 4, Washington.

WATTERS & DONOVAN,
Of Counsel,
161 William Street,
New York 38, New York.

SUBJECT INDEX.

CITATIONS.

CASES.

STATUTES.

RULES.

TEXTS.

... E. Co., Sup. Ct.

... Co., 22 Wend.

... 136, 184, 260

... M'ls, 257 App.
... 1939)

... S. 2d 776.
... Monogram Pre-
... App. 2d 12, 7

... yers (1855),

... 18,5

... AMERICAN

... itration &

... itration &

... Sec 27c, pp.

... ctice, Vol.
17,8

... : Practice,

United States Court of Appeals

FOR THE NINTH CIRCUIT.

Docket No. 17609

ALBIN STEVEDORE COMPANY, a Washington Corp.,

Appellant,

v.

CENTRAL RIGGING & CONTRACTING CORPORATION,

Appellee.

On Appeal from the United States District Court
Western District of Washington: Northern Division

BRIEF FOR PLAINTIFF-APPELLANT.

Statement.

This is an appeal by the Plaintiff-Appellant, Albin Stevedore Company (hereafter called Appellant) from the order of the United States District Court for the Western District of Washington, Northern Division granting summary judgment in favor of the Defendant-Appellee, Central Rigging & Contracting Corporation (hereafter called Appellee) and from each and every part of said order. [Transcript of Record,* p. 134, Order Granting Summary Judgment; p. 135, Notice of Appeal]

The District Court thus held that both the first and second causes of action set forth in the action before that

---

*(All references hereinafter are to the Transcript of Record and will be designated TR with a reference to the page number thereof and wherever possible to the line or paragraph on said page.)

Court had been submitted to the arbitrators appointed by the American Arbitration Association. This appeal brings before this Court these questions, i.e., the scope of the arbitration proceedings, the extent of the arbitrators' jurisdiction and the extent of the arbitrators' award. The Appellant contends that the District Court improperly entered an order granting summary judgment in favor of the Appellee and in denying the Appellant's motion for summary judgment.

This Action.

Appellant, a Washington Corporation, commenced this action in the Superior Court of the State of Washington, King County [TR p. 6]. The Appellee, a New York Corporation, removed this action from the Washington State Court to the United States District Court for the Western District of Washington—Northern Division. The removal was based on the parties' diversity of citizenship [TR p. 1-3 Petition for Removal].

THE PLEADINGS

a. Complaint

The complaint alleged two causes of action. The first cause of action sought the recovery of $6,000, the balance due on a written contract containing an agreed price of $14,000 for work, labor and services performed by the Appellant as a stevedore in the loading of specified cargo on board the vessel *"Despina C"*. The agreed price for the work was $14,000, $8,000 of which was paid during the progress of the work and the balance of $6,000 was to be paid upon the completion. The Appellant performed this work. The Appellee conceded the indebtedness but had only paid $8,000 and failed to pay the balance of $6,000 [TR p. 6, ¶ V of the First Cause of Action of the Complaint].

The second cause of action was for additional work that the Appellant was required to do at the request of the

Appellee and for this Appellant sought the recovery of $16,067.97 [TR pp. 6, 7, 8, ¶s I through and including IX, the Second Cause of Action of the Complaint].

b. Answer

The Appellee answered the complaint, denied that there was an agreed price to perform the work, denied the fact that the balance of the payment of $6,000 was due and owing to the Appellant by reason of the failure of the Appellant to tender to the Appellee an affidavit of receipt of full payment as a condition for receiving any balance due under the contract [TR p. 69, ¶ 5, Answer].

With regard to the second cause of action, the Appellant pleaded a general denial [TR pp. 67, 70]. In addition the Appellee alleged an affirmative defense that the Appellee was ready and willing to arbitrate pursuant to the Rules of the American Arbitration Association.

c. Motion of Appellee for a Stay of the Action

The Appellee moved in the District Court for a stay of the litigation pursuant to the provisions of 9 U. S. C. 3 [TR pp. 11-13]. The Appellant cross moved to enjoin the arbitration proceedings [TR pp. 40 through and including 72]. The Appellant's motion was denied and a stay of the litigation was granted Appellee, pursuant to 9 U. S. C. section 3 [TR p. 72, lines 11 through and including 20]. The Appellant served a notice to appeal that decision [TR p. 73]; the appeal was voluntarily dismissed [TR pp. 74, 75] and the dismissal was granted on February 7, 1961 [TR p. 76]. Thereafter the Appellee commenced arbitration proceedings [TR pp. 34-39 at 38, 39, Original Demand; TR pp. 85-87 at 86, Amended Demand].

ARBITRATION PROCEEDINGS

a. Appellee's Demand for Arbitration

On January 19, 1960, by an amended demand for arbitration, the Appellee demanded arbitration in accordance with Paragraph 22 of a written contract between the parties [TR pp. 85 through and including 87].

The Appellee specified the following demand for arbitration:

"II

Demand for Arbitration.

"Central Rigging & Contracting Corp. hereby demands arbitration on the following disputes which are subject to arbitration under the above quoted clauses, and designates New York City as the place of arbitration.

"Central Rigging & Contracting Corp. hereby disputes and contests a claim of Albin Stevedore Company for the sum of $22,067.97, and each and every part thereof, *to the extent that said claim exceeds the sum of $6,000.* Said claim has been made by Albin Stevedore Company against Central Rigging & Contracting Corp. for payment of work performed which was required by the aforesaid contract. *The said disputed claim of Albin Stevedore Company for sums in excess of $6,000* is based on the additional expense of Albin Stevedore Company in performing said contract caused by the alleged failure of Central Rigging & Contracting Corp. to furnish a ship with 45 ton boom and with other adequate loading equipment as allegedly required by the terms of the aforesaid contract . . ." [TR pp. 86, 87, Emphasis supplied].

b. Appellant's Answering Statement

By its answering statement Appellant acknowledged the Appellee's admission "that the sum of $6,000 is payable to Albin Stevedore Company for services rendered in loading and stowing of certain equipment on board the vessel 'Despina C'. Accordingly, Albin Stevedore Company hereby demands that the said sum of $6,000 be paid to it forthwith" [TR pp. 89-90].

And

> "In addition to the said $6,000 about which there is no dispute, Albin Stevedore Company is owed an additional sum of $16,067.97 . . ." [TR p. 90].

Thus the Appellant sought payment forthwith of the sum of $6,000 [TR p. 90] and an award in the sum of $16,067.97 together with interest at the rate of 6 per cent from September 3, 1959 [TR p. 92].

The arbitration was subject to the Commercial Arbitration Rules of the American Arbitration Association [TR p. 17 ¶ 11 incorporating by reference p. 14 ¶ 22]. These rules are set forth fully in the Transcript of Record and marked Exhibit A commencing at Page 84.

In the "Instructions for Proceeding Under These Rules" it stated that the demand for arbitration should include ". . . 3) Brief but specific statement of the dispute(s) to be arbitrated, amount claimed, if any, and the relief sought . . ." [TR p. 84, third page of Exhibit A].

Section 7, subdivision a, of the rules provides that the proceedings are initiated:

> ". . . a. By such party giving written notice to the other party which notice shall contain *a statement setting forth the nature of the dispute, the amount involved, if any, the remedy sought . . .*"

The Rules further provide as follows:

> "Section 8. CHANGE OF CLAIM—After filing the claim, an answer if any, if either party desires to make any new or different claim, such claim shall be made in writing with the Tribunal Clerk and a copy thereof mailed to the other party who shall have a period of seven days from the date of such mailing within which to file an answer with the Tribunal Clerk . . ." [TR p. 84, fifth page of Exhibit A, emphasis supplied].

It is the position of the Appellant that the effect of the demand for arbitration and the answer, provided for in the Commercial Arbitration Rules, governs the scope and extent of the controversy submitted to the arbitrators. Neither party sought or obtained a "Change of Claim."

c. The Arbitration Hearing, the Award and the Confirmation

Following a hearing and within the period prescribed by the rules, the arbitrators made the following award:

> "We the Undersigned Arbitrators have been designated in accordance with the Arbitration Agreement entered into by the above named parties and dated August 14, 1959, and having been duly sworn and having duly heard the proofs and allegations of the Parties, AWARD, as follows:
>
> 1) Central Rigging & Contracting Corp. hereinafter referred to as Central, shall pay to Albin Stevedore Company, hereinafter referred to as Albin, the sum of NINE THOUSAND FIVE HUNDRED DOLLARS ($9,500.00) plus interest at the rate of six per cent (6%) per annum from September 18, 1959, to the date of this award in *full settlement of all claims submitted to this arbitration* . ." [TR p. 95; emphasis is ours.]

Thereafter this award was confirmed in the Supreme Court of the State of New York (the site of the Arbitration and the law of which state governs the parties' rights as set forth in their contract). A judgment for $9,500 plus interest, covering the claims submitted to arbitration, was entered in the New York County Clerk's Office and has been satisfied.

The Post Arbitration Proceedings in the District Court.

(Motion and Cross Motion for Summary Judgment)

Following the arbitration, the award and the confirmation in the Supreme Court of the State of New York, the Appellant moved to vacate the stay in the District Court and for summary judgment in its favor on the first cause of action, i.e., for the sum of $6,000 on the ground that the first cause of action had not been submitted to the arbitrators because the demand for arbitration embraced solely a dispute of the *"claim of Albin Stevedore Company* *for the sum of $22,067.97 and each and every part thereof to the extent that said claim exceeds the sum of $6,000 * * *''* [TR p. 86, Emphasis supplied.]

The District Court denied Appellant's motion and granted summary judgment in favor of Appellee on its motion [TR p. 134].

Statement of Points on Which the Appellant Intends to Rely on in the Appeal.

1. Appellee's demand for arbitration and Appellant's answering statement were the source and definition of the authority exercised by the arbitrators.

2. The parties submitted to the arbitrators but one dispute, namely, Appellant's claim set forth in its Second Cause of Action, being the excess over and above the sum of $6,000.00 admitted to be due.

3. The arbitrators had no jurisdiction to consider anything except the subject of Appellant's Second Cause of Action, namely, the excess amount owing from Appellee to Appellant over and above the $6,000.00 admitted to be due.

4. The subject matter of Appellant's First Cause of Action, namely, the $6,000.00 admitted to be owing from Appellee to Appellant was not submitted to the Arbitrators for decision.

5. The Court erred in granting Appellee's motion for summary judgment.

6. The Court erred in refusing to grant Appellant's motion for summary judgment.

Appellant's Contentions.

1. The sole dispute that the Appellee submitted to arbitration was "the sum of $22,067.97 and each and every part thereof *to the extent that said claim exceeds the sum*

of $6,000.'' [Part II of the "Amended Demand for Arbitration Against Albin Stevedore Company". See TR p. 86.]

2. The power, jurisdiction and authority of the Arbitrators was limited to the dispute the parties submitted to them.

3. The Arbitrators' award was solely "in full settlement of all claims submitted to this arbitration" [TR p. 95].

4. In view of the fact that Appellee conceded that the sum of $6,000.00, the amount demanded in the first cause of action, was due and owing to Appellant, there was no issue of fact thereon and summary judgment for that amount should have been granted in Appellant's favor.

I.

The sole dispute that the appellee submitted to arbitration was "the sum of $22,067.97 and each and every part thereof to the extent that said claim exceeds the sum of $6,000.00"

Appellee's Demand for Arbitration and Appellant's Answering Statement Were the Source and Definition of the Authority Exercised by the Arbitrators.

The Appellee made the demand for arbitration and framed the issue on which it desired the arbitrators' action and decision. Appellee stated its dispute in precise language as follows:

"II

DEMAND FOR ARBITRATION

"CENTRAL RIGGING & CONTRACTING CORP. hereby demands arbitration on the following disputes which are subject to arbitration under the above quoted clauses, and designates New York City as the place of arbitration.

"CENTRAL RIGGING & CONTRACTING CORP. hereby disputes and contests a claim of Albin Stevedore

Company f
every part
exceeds the
by Albin S
ging & Con
formed whi
The said d
pany for s
additional
performing
failure of
furnish a
adequate l
the terms
86, 87, Em

By the terms
and the Appellee
govern the parti
nated site for the
the power of arb
submitted to th
authority the arb
Wait, Cyclopedia

Historically, th
from the nineteen
Welwood, 71 N.
state said:

"Arbitr
other cont
view of ar
general ru
Mr. Morse
'The Court
in its ever
whole, wil
reasonable
intended
should be
will be in
in the su
award d
mitted wi

Company for the sum of $22,067.97, and each and every part thereof, *to the extent that said claim exceeds the sum of $6,000.* Said claim has been made by Albin Stevedore Company against Central Rigging & Contracting Corp. for payment of work performed which was required by the aforesaid contract. *The said disputed claim of Albin Stevedore Company for sums in excess of $6,000* is based on the additional expense of Albin Stevedore Company in performing said contract caused by the alleged failure of Central Rigging & Contracting Corp. to furnish a ship with 45 ton boom and with other adequate loading equipment as allegedly required by the terms of the aforesaid contract . . ." [TR pp. 86, 87, Emphasis supplied].

By the terms of the written contract between Appellant and the Appellee, the law of New York was chosen to govern the parties' rights and New York was the designated site for the arbitration proceeding. In New York, the power of arbitrators is confined strictly to the matters submitted to them for determination and beyond that authority the arbitrators have no jurisdiction. 21 *Carmody-Wait, Cyclopedia of New York Practice,* Section 94, p. 495.

Historically, this view has been pronounced and repeated from the nineteenth century to date. Thus, in *Jones* v. *Welwood,* 71 N. Y. 208 (1877), the highest court of that state said:

"Arbitration contracts should be construed like other contracts, and the same rule applied with a view of arriving at the intent of the parties . . . The general rule, as now settled, is well expressed by Mr. Morse in his work on arbitration, page 342. 'The Court will look at the language of the submission in its every part and from a consideration of the whole, will determine the matter of intent. If the reasonable construction appears to be that the parties intended to have everything decided, if anything should be, then a decision of all matters submitted will be imperatively required; . . . but if anything in the submission indicates a contrary purpose an award determining a part only of the matters submitted will be sustained' " (71 N. Y. 208, at 213).

Some twenty-seven years later, an intermediate appellate court stated in *Cullen & Dwyer* v. *Shipway*, 78 App. Div. 130, 79 N. Y. S. 627; aff'd (no op.) 177 N. Y. 571, 69 N. E. 1122 (1904) as follows:

"* * *

"The rule seems to be well settled that the power of arbitrators is confined strictly to the matters submitted to them for determination and any award made on any other subject is void (*Dodd* v. *Hakes*, 114 N. Y. 263). In the case just cited the court said: 'The law is well settled that the power of arbitrators is confined strictly to the matters submitted to them, and if they exceed that limit, their award will in general be void.

"They cannot decide upon their own jurisdiction, nor take upon themselves authority by deciding that they have it but must, in fact have it under the agreement of the parties whose differences are submitted to them before their award can have any validity, and the fact of jurisdiction, when their decision is challenged, is always open to inquiry.'

"Here the arbitrators were not asked to construe contract No. 1 or determine its legal effect, and when the third arbitrator proceeded to do that he was doing what the parties had never agreed he should do, and as already stated, he therefore, acted without jurisdiction. His award was void and was properly so held by Special Term" (78 App. Div. 130, 132).

Likewise, in *Conway* v. *Roth,* 179 App. Div. 108, 166 N. Y. S. 108 (1st Dept. 1917), the court said:

"Parties to a statutory arbitration have no power to confer jurisdiction upon arbitrators over subject matters which they would not have under a written submission . . . The arbitrators sit as a court with no powers except those conferred by the written submission duly executed and acknowledged."

More recently, in 1946, in Supreme Court Special Term, New York County, in the *Matter of the Arbitration Between Transport Workers Union of America, CIO and 5th Avenue Coach Co.*, 187 Misc. 247, 63 N. Y. S. 2d 17 the Court relied on the authority of *Jones* v. *Welwood, supra,* and stated at p. 249:

> "The submission to arbitration clothed the arbitrator with jurisdiction to hear and determine the specific issues which the parties by their voluntary agreement, designated as the subjects to be determined by him. The submission is, at one and the same time, the source and definition of the authority to be exercised by the arbitrator."

At page 252, the Court further stated:

> "Apparently the arbitrator overlooked the force of the submission of February 14, 1946. The submission was a contract that was as binding upon him, upon qualifying as an arbitrator as it was upon the parties. *Whatever may have been the attitude of the parties in October, 1945, the submission plainly fixed the status of the dispute as it existed on February 14, 1946, and enumerated the items which were required to be adjudicated by the arbitrator.*"
> [Emphasis supplied.]

See also:

> *Matter of Wilkins,* (1902), 169 N. Y. 494, 496, 62 N. E. 575.

The law of New York, in this regard, was succinctly restated in a recent case involving the Appellee in this action, in fact in an arbitration proceeding that is collateral to this matter and was included in the original demand for arbitration of the matters under consideration [TR pp. 34-39, inclusive] *Matter of Central Rigging & Contracting Corp'n. (Howard International, Inc.),* [Supreme Court, N. Y. Co.—*New York Law Journal,* Oct. 14, 1961, p. 13, col. 4 (not yet otherwise reported)]. The Court stated:

> "Arbitration is a matter of agreement (*Lehman* v. *Ostrovsky,* 264 N. Y. 103). The agreement here was to arbitrate 'in accordance with the Rules of the American Arbitration Association' and the respondent was not called upon to arbitrate in any other manner . . .

"Likewise, the law is well established that the power of the arbitrator is limited by the terms of the submission and that an award which exceeds the scope of the submission will be vacated. The arbitrators may not write a new contract for the parties without such parties' consent nor may they assume authority by merely deciding that they have it (*Western Union Telegraph Co.* v. *Am. Communications Ass'n C. I. O.*, 299 N. Y. 177; *Dodds* v. *Hakes*, 114 N. Y. 260; *Halstad* v. *Seaman*, 82 N. Y. 27.)"

Basically speaking, this view is not peculiar to the law of the State of New York but appears to be the prevailing law throughout the United States since early times. The indications of this fact are demonstrated in opinions of the United States Supreme Court such as *McCormick* v. *Gray* (1851), 13 How. 26, 54 U. S. 26 at p. 38, 14 L. Ed. 36; *The York and Cumberland R. R. Co.* v. *Myers* (1855), 59 U. S. 246, 15 L. Ed. 380. In the latter case, at page 252, the Supreme Court said: "The law is well settled that by the reference of an action to arbitrators, nothing is included in the submission but the subject matter involved in it . . ."

The current weight of authority in this country is that an arbitrator's jurisdiction or authority to act is derived from and limited by the arbitration agreement or submission which forms the basis of their award and it is essential that the award conform to, and comply with, the arbitration submission or agreement. 6 C J S, *Arbitration & Award*, §80, pp. 219-220; 3 Am. Jur. 945-946, *Arbitration & Award*, §123. Moreover, the authority of the arbitrators is derived from the arbitration agreement and is limited to a decision of the matters submitted therein either expressly or by necessary implication. 6 C J S, *Arbitration & Award* §27 c, pp. 167-168.

See also:

> *Fortune* v. *Killebrew*, 86 Tex. 172, 23 S. W. 976;
> *Gulf Oil* v. *Guidry*, 160 Tex. 144, 227 S. W. 2d
> 406, 408;

Pancoast v. *Russell,* 148 Cal. App. 2d 909, 914,
307 P. 2d 719;

Crofoot v. *Blair Holding,* 119 Cal. App. 2d 156,
184, 260 P. 2d 156, 171.

As recently as 1960, a District Court of Appeal of the
State of California in *William B. Logan & Associates* v.
Monogram Precision Industries, 184 Cal. App. 2d 12; 7
Cal. Rptr. (West's) 212, decided a case which involved
language of a submission almost identical in form to that
now before this Court. In that case, the parties agreed
that they

"Submit to the American Arbitration Association, all rights and claims that they have in, to, and
concerning *the amount whereby the claim for the
period of May 13 through May 25 exceeds $2,400.00*
and the items covered *thereby* and all disputes concerning *the same,* including but not being limited to
the reasonableness and authorization *thereof,* and the
determination of all rights and claims they may have
in, to, and concerning the amount of $951.00 claimed
as traveling expenses ..." [Emphasis is the Court's]
184 C. A. 2d 14.

The Court, after setting forth this language said:

"The arbitrator awarded $3,000.00 in settlement
of the amount of fee in dispute and $610.50 for trav-
eling expenses. There is no issue concerning the
travel item and all of the issues arise out of the
arbitration agreement's meaning and effect insofar
as concerns item (2). [Set forth above]"

There the appellant contended that the contract was amenable but to one interpretation in that the quoted phrase
submitted to arbitration only the reasonableness of the
amount by which the claim of $4,675.00 exceeded $2,400.00
for services during the particular period including reasonableness and authorization of services included in such
excess. The theory was that the word "disputes" could
refer only to the claims recited because of the fact that all

other items had been separately settled. The respondent contended that "disputes" refers generally to "amount" and that reasonableness thereof can be in excess of the amounts originally claimed. It was argued that otherwise the contract would be ambiguous and unclear as to what "all disputes concerning the same" refers to in the agreement.

In evaluating and passing upon the contentions raised by the parties, the Court at 184 C. A. 2d 15 stated the generally recognized rules that if the language of a contract is clear and certain and there is no ambiguity, parol evidence is inadmissible to vary its meaning and that if it is in writing, such contract represents a complete integration of previous negotiations and the contractual understanding of the parties.

At 184 C. A. 2d 15, the Court stated:

> "In our opinion there is no ambiguity in the terms of the arbitration agreement. On its face, it is not fairly susceptible of two interpretations . . . nor is its meaning obscure . . . The agreement clearly reflects that there were only two items relating in the dispute between the parties. As concerns item (2) there is no ambiguity in the specific provision attached nor is it rendered uncertain by reference to any other portion of the agreement or to the surrounding circumstances . . ."

The Court said at 184 C. A. 2d 17 as follows:

> "There is, however, a fundamental distinction between cases wherein the act is equivocal and the evidence of the intent of the party is competent and relevant to establish its legal effect, and those cases where the *terms* of an agreement are set forth in writing and the words are not equivocal or ambiguous. In the latter cases . . . 'the writing or writings will constitute the contract of the parties, and one party is not permitted to escape from its obligation by showing that he did not intend to do what his words bound him to do.' *By the same token, neither will such party be permitted to reap more benefit from a contract than its language permits.*" [Latter emphasis is supplied.]

In concluding, the Court then stated the following rule which we assert is the rule to be followed here:

> "While every intendment of validity must be given an arbitration award (*Sampson Motors, Inc.* v. *Roland,* 121 Cal. App. 2d 491 [263 P. 2d 445]), it is well settled that an arbitrator derives his power from the arbitration agreement and he cannot exceed his derived power. (*Crofoot* v. *Blair Holdings Corp.,* 119 Cal. App. 2d 156 [260 P. 2d 156].) To confirm an award in excess of the powers granted by an arbitration agreement would destroy the very purpose of arbitration and be contrary to the sound policy of encouraging the settlement of private disputes by the voluntary agreement of the parties. Since the arbitrator here exceeded the express limitations of the agreement, the superior court must make an order vacating the award. (*Flores* v. *Barman,* 130 Cal. App. 2d 282 [279 P. 2d 81].)" [184 C. A. 2d 17]

The Appellant contends that the demand for arbitration and the answering statement are not ambiguous and are clear and precise and that only one question was submitted to the arbitrators by these parties, i.e., a dispute as to

> "The sum of $22,067.97 and each and every part thereof *to the extent that said claim exceeds the sum of $6,000.00."* [Part II of the "Amended Demand for Arbitration against Albin Stevedore Company.", TR p. 86; emphasis supplied.]

The Appellee and the Appellant never submitted to the arbitrators as a dispute the sum of $6,000.00 which is the demand in the first cause of action. The authority of the arbitrators never extended to the question of whether $6,000.00 was due to Appellant under the written contract and that sum could not validly be and was not embodied in any award rendered by the arbitrators.

The District Court had jurisdiction of the controversy set forth in the first cause of action and because that sum was admittedly due the Appellant the District Court should have granted summary judgment in the sum of $6,000.00

with interest from September 18, 1959, in favor of the
Appellant.

**The Arbitrators' Award was Solely "In Full Settlement of
All Claims Submitted to this Arbitration." Therefore,
There was No Decision by the Arbitrators Except as to
Matters Submitted to Them and in Dispute Before Them.**

In the District Court the Appellee maintained that both
the first and second causes of action were determined by
the award of the arbitrators. We contend that this position is not justified in the light of the facts and the law
applicable to the facts.

Initially, we respectfully point out that the award itself
states ". . . this award [is] in full settlement of all claims
submitted to this arbitration." [TR p. 95] Thus, the arbitrators chose simple language to show the extent of the
award, *i.e.,* the claim submitted to them. That claim was
"the sum of $22,067.97 and each and every part thereof
to the extent said claim exceeds the sum of $6,000." [Part
II of the "Amended Demand for Arbitration". TR pp.
86-87.]

When an arbitration award is free from corruption or
misconduct on the part of the arbitrators, the court indulges
every reasonable intendment and presumption (*Byers* v.
Van Deusen (1830), 5 Wend. 268, 269) so as to give effect
to the proceedings of the arbitrators and to favor the regularity and the integrity of their acts. Conversely, nothing
will be presumed for the purpose of overturning it. (*Nichols*
v. *Renssalaer Co. Mut. Ins. Co.,* 22 Wend. 125). Likewise, a court will not presume that arbitrators have decided
matters not in dispute. [21 *Carmody-Wait, Cyclopedia of
New York Practice,* Sec. 148, at pp. 548-550].

Also it has been stated that even if the words of an award
are so comprehensive that they may take in matters not
written in the submission, it is presumed that nothing
beyond it was awarded, unless the contrary is expressly
shown, or appears on the face of the record [*Carmody-
Wait, op. cit.* Vol. 21, Sec. 148, at pp. 549-550]. In other

words, it is a fundamental requisite of an award that it shall be coextensive with the submission. *Jones* v. *Welwood* (1877), 71 N. Y. 208; 10 *Carmody on New York Pleadings and Practice*, §1196-1198.

In *Fudicker* v. *The Guardian Mutual Life Ins. Co.* (1875), 62 N. Y. 392, the court stated the well settled principle governing arbitration, which should not be overlooked, namely that all reasonable intendments and presumptions are indulged in support of the award.

The award and decision of the arbitrators clearly reflects that the arbitrators concerned themselves solely with the "claims submitted to this arbitration".

The Appellant moved in the Supreme Court of the State of New York to confirm that award. Appellant's motion was granted on consent of the Appellee and without any opposition. The Court's decision reads:

> "Albin Stevedore Co. (Central Rigging & Contracting Corp.) Motion to confirm the award of the arbitrators is granted, there being no opposition. Since, however, the respondent was ready to pay the award and so informed the petitioner's attorneys, the petitioner should recover no costs in this proceeding to confirm. Settle order." [TR p. 115]

The moving papers submitted by the Appellant at the time of the motion fully apprised the New York Court of the position of the Appellant, which is the same here. In Paragraph "7" of the affidavit of Thomas A. Harnett, read in support of that Motion, the scope of the controversy submitted to arbitration was fully set forth therein with references made to the Respondent's Amended Demand for Arbitration and the Petitioner's Answering Statement in reply thereto. The scope of said Arbitration was clearly set forth in the moving papers and was succinctly stated therein, to wit,

> "A single controversy, to wit, the sum, if any, in excess of $6,000 due and owing to Albin for work and services performed in the loading of the DESPINA C . . ." [TR p. 126]

The New York Supreme Court did not determine substantively, by reason of the form of the order it signed, that the arbitration award embraced the two causes of action as the Appellee has contended in its moving affidavits on its motion for summary judgment [TR pp. 115-118]. The sole reason the Supreme Court, New York County, signed the counter-order submitted by the Appellee [TR pp. 98-99 and TR pp. 130-131] was that the form of the Appellant's order [TR pp. 123-124] was improper in that it contained a factual finding or decisional discussion. It is the practice in New York that orders "should not contain any factual findings or decisional discussions", *New York Civil Practice Act*, §127; *New York Rules of Civil Practice,* 70-74. Similarly, there is decisional law to this effect, i. e., *White* v. *White,* 175 Misc. 66, 22 N. Y. S. 2d 776; and *Ayman* v. *Teachers Retirement Board,* 19 Misc. 2d 374, 193 N. Y. S. 2d 2, modified 9 N. Y. 2d 119, 172 N. E. 2d 571.

The Justice of the New York Supreme Court by signing the Appellee's counter-order did not make a substantive ruling as to the scope, extent and nature of the dispute submitted to the arbitrators and neither the District Court nor this Court are precluded from making such a substantive ruling on the summary judgment motions presented by the parties.

Based upon the language employed by the parties, particularly the Appellee in its demand for arbitration, and the form of the award made by the arbitrators, there is no doubt that the sole dispute that the parties submitted to arbitration was "the sum of $22,067.97 and each and every part thereof *to the extent that said claim exceeds the sum of $6,000.00.*" [Part II of the "Amended Demand for Arbitration against Albin Stevedore Company", TR p. 86.]

...l not determine sub-
... the order it signed,
...l the two causes of
...its moving affidavits
[TR pp. 115-118].
... New York County.
... the Appellee [TR
... the form of the
... improper in that
...al discussion. It
...should not contain
...ions", New York
... of Civil Practice,
... to this effect, i. e.,
... § 21.76; and Ayman
... 374, 193 N. Y. S.
... E. 2d 571.
... Court by signing
... make a substantive
... of the dispute
... the District Court
... such a substan-
... presented by
... the parties, par-
... arbitration, and
... trators, there is
... les submitted to
... each and every
... exceeds the sum
... Demand for
...", TR p. 86.]

II.

This Court and the District Court are required to presume that the arbitrators decided only the matters submitted to them and put before them.

The Presumption of Regularity of the Proceedings and the Award is so Great That no Parol Inquiry May be Made of the Arbitrators Either by the Court or the Parties.

The arbitrators' award in its clear and specific language stated:

> ". . . 1. Central Rigging & Contracting Corp. hereinafter referred to as Central, shall pay to Albin Stevedore Company, hereinafter referred to as Albin, the sum of NINE THOUSAND FIVE HUNDRED DOLLARS ($9,500.00) plus interest at the rate of six per cent (6%) per annum from September 18, 1959, to the date of this award *in full settlement of all claims submitted to this arbitration.*" [TR p. 95; emphasis supplied.]

The award relates solely to the claims ". . . submitted to this arbitration" and the sole matter submitted for the arbitration was the sum in excess of $6,000.00 (*supra,* p. 6; p. 4). Thus, it remained for the District Court to determine the rights of the parties as to the demand set forth in the first cause of action seeking damages in the sum of $6,000.00. That amount was admittedly due to the Appellant. The Appellant's motion for summary judgment should have been granted and the Appellee's cross motion for summary judgment should have been denied.

As previously stated in our first point, it must be presumed that the arbitrators decided only the matters submitted to them (*supra,* pp. 16-18).

It is a fundamental requisite of an award that it shall be coextensive with the submission. *Jones* v. *Welwood*

(1877), 71 N. Y. 208; 10 *Carmody on New York Pleading and Practice,* §1196-1198.

Except for certain statutory grounds, an arbitration award must stand. These grounds are set forth in Section 1462 of the Civil Practice Act of the State of New York.

Section 1462 of the Civil Practice Act of the State of New York sets forth the specific grounds authorizing the vacating of an award. These may be summarized as follows:

1. Where the award is procured by corruption, fraud or other undue means.

2. Where there was evident partiality or corruption in the arbitrators.

3. Where the arbitrators were guilty of misconduct in refusing to postpone a hearing upon sufficient cause; or in refusing to hear evidence pertinent and material to the controversy; or of any other misbehavior by which the rights of a party have been prejudiced.

4. Where the arbitrators exceeded their powers or so imperfectly executed them, that a mutual, final and definite award upon the subject matter submitted was not made.

5. Where there was no valid submission or contract and an objection had been raised under the conditions set forth in Section 1458.

The New York Courts have repeatedly held that they will not interfere with an award made by arbitrators who have acted impartially within the powers conferred upon them, in the absence of a showing that one of the grounds specified in Section 1462 of the New York Civil Practice Act exists. Illustrative of this view is *D. Goff & Sons* v. *Rheinauer,* 199 App. Div. 617, 192 N. Y. S. 82 (1s Dept. 1922) and *C. Stoh & Co.* v. *Bayer Oil Co.,* 198 App. Div. 881, 191 N.Y.S. 290 (1st Dept. 1921).

The New York Court of Appeals, a court of last resort, has similarly ruled in *Matter of Wilkins* (1902), 169 N. Y. 494 at page 496 (62 N. E. 575):

"When the merits of a controversy are referred to an arbitrator selected by the parties, his determination, either as to the law or the facts, is final and conclusive, and a court will not open an award unless perverse misconstruction or positive misconduct upon the part of the arbitrator is plainly established, or there is some provision in the agreement of submission authorizing it. The award of the arbitrator cannot be set aside for mere errors of judgment either as to the law or as to the facts. If he keeps *within his jurisdiction* and is not guilty of fraud, corruption or other misconduct affecting his award, it is unassailable, operates as a final and conclusive judgment, and however disappointing it may be the parties must abide by it. *Hoffman* v. *DeGraff,* 109 N. Y. 638; *Masury* v. *Whiton,* 111 N. Y. 679; *Sweet* v. *Morrison,* 116 N. Y. 19, 27; *Perkins* v. *Giles,* 50 N. Y. 228; *Fudicker* v. *Guardian Mut. Life Ins. Co.,* 62 N. Y. 393."

In 1956, the Appellate Division First Department, an intermediate appellate court, had under review a case where a party contended an arbitrator did not understand the full import of an award and had testimony taken to that effect. The Court in *Matter of Arbitration of Weiner (Freund),* 2 App. Div. 2d 341 said at pp. 342-3 [Later (1957) aff'd (no op.) 3 N. Y. 2d 806, 144 N. E. 2d 647].

"* * *

"In essence, the award gave respondent credit for unused materials returned and allowed the counterclaim in an amount in excess of the purchase price of the goods.

"Motions to vacate an award pursuant to section 1462 of the Civil Practice Act, or to modify or correct awards pursuant to section 1462-a of the Civil Practice Act, must be granted only for the specific reasons set forth in the enumerated sections (*Matter of Wilkins,* 169 N. Y. 494). The nub of this case is the claim that the impartial arbitrator did not intend the consequences of the award to which he agreed. The Civil Practice Act does not permit either vacating or correcting an award upon that ground.

"More than a century ago it was held that parol evidence, even of an arbitrator to contradict or impeach an award, was inadmissible. *Doke* v. *James,* 4 N. Y. 568, 575.

"An arbitrator should not be called upon to give a reason for his decision. Inquisition of an arbitrator for the purpose of determining the processes by which he arrives at an award finds no sanction in law. *Bernhardt* v. *Polygraphic,* 350 U. S. 198, 203; *Matter of Shirley Silk Co.* v. *American Silk Mills,* 257 App. Div. 375, 377.

"These parties by agreement selected arbitration as the method by which any dispute between them should be determined. The award in the forum of their choice is final and conclusive and a court should not disturb it except on the grounds of one of the statutory provisions. Absent such an exception, the award may not be disturbed for error either of fact or law not evident on the fact of the award. . . . (citing cases) . . . Judicial review of an award is more limited than judicial review of a trial. *Bernhardt* v. *Polygraphic, supra; Wilko* v. *Swan,* 346 U. S. 427, 435-438.

"If an arbitrator may not be questioned as to the reasons underlying an award in order to impeach it, then by the same token he cannot be heard to impeach it upon the ground it does not reflect his intention. . . .''

See also:

Shirley Silk Co. v. *American Silk Mills,* 257 App. Div. 375, 13 N. Y. S. 2d 309 (1st Dept. 1939).

"There is no authority which sanctions an inquisition of arbitrators for the purpose of determining the processes by which they arrived at an award. An arbitrator who is a quasi judicial officer should not be called upon to give reasons for his decision" (257 App. Div. at p. 377).

To the same effect

Lief v. *Brodsky,* 126 N. Y. Supp. 2d 657, 658 (Sup. Ct., Bronx Co.—1953);

N. Y. Omnibus, 189 Misc. 892, (Sup. Ct. N. Y. Co. —1947).

The irrefutable presumption is that the arbitrators decided only "all claims submitted to this arbitration" [TR p. 95]. The only dispute submitted to them was that which the Appellee set forth in its demand, "the sum of $22,067.97, and each and every part thereof, *to the extent that said claim exceeds the sum of $6,000 . . .*" [TR p. 86]. The arbitrators never had jurisdiction of that latter claim (the first cause of action); it remained always with the District Court.

Conclusion.

Appellee in its demand for arbitration did not place in dispute Appellant's claim to the $6,000.00 demanded in the first cause of action. The Appellee merely sought an arbitration of and disputed Appellant's claim for $22,067.97 solely to the extent that it exceeded $6,000.00. This submission and demand was not ambiguous. The Appellee has admitted that there is no dispute that the $6,000.00 was due the Appellant.

The Appellee's demand for arbitration and the Appellant's answering statement were "the source and definition of the authority exercised by the arbitrators" (*Matter of TWU, supra,* pp. 10-11). The parties submitted but one dispute, *i.e.,* the excess over $6,000.00, the claim set forth in the second cause of action. The arbitration award was solely "in full settlement of all claims submitted to this arbitration"; that submission did not include the first cause of action.

The District Court erred in granting Appellee's motion for summary judgment and dismissing the complaint. The District Court erred in refusing to grant Appellant's motion for summary judgment in the sum of $6,000.00 with interest, as demanded in the first cause of action. The District Court solely and not the arbitrators had jurisdiction over the claim set forth in the first cause of action.

Therefore, in the absence of any question of fact as to the amount due under the first cause of action and in light of the indisputable fact that the first cause of action was not before the arbitrators, this Court should reverse the District Court and enter an order granting Appellant's motion for summary judgment on the first cause of action and grant judgment in the sum of $6,000.00 with interest at 6 per cent from September 18, 1959, to date.

Respectfully submitted,

CLARKE, CLARKE, ALBERTSON & BOVINGDON,
Attorneys for Appellant, Albin Stevedore
Company.

GEORGE W. CLARKE,

JAMES B. DONOVAN,
THOMAS A. HARNETT,
(Both of the New York Bar),
Of Counsel.

question of fact a
of action and in li
first cause of action r
should reverse
granting Appellee
first cause of act
$5,000.00 with inter
, to date.
ed,
& BOVINGDON,
Albin Stevedo

No. 17609

United States Court of Appeals
For the Ninth Circuit

ALBIN STEVEDORE COMPANY, a Washington Corporation,
Appellant,

vs.

CENTRAL RIGGING & CONTRACTING CORPORATION,
Appellee.

ON APPEAL FROM THE UNITED STATES DISTRICT COURT
WESTERN DISTRICT OF WASHINGTON,
NORTHERN DIVISION

BRIEF OF APPELLEE

ROSLING, WILLIAMS, LANZA & KASTNER
JOSEPH J. LANZA
Attorneys for Appellee
1440 Washington Building
Seattle 1, Washington

KAISER & HOLZMAN
HENRY W. HOLZMAN
Of Counsel
21 East 40th Street
New York 16, New York

THE ARGUS PRESS, SEATTLE

United States Court of Appeals
For the Ninth Circuit

ALBIN STEVEDORE COMPANY, a Washington Corporation,
Appellant,

vs.

CENTRAL RIGGING & CONTRACTING CORPORATION,
Appellee.

ON APPEAL FROM THE UNITED STATES DISTRICT COURT
WESTERN DISTRICT OF WASHINGTON,

NORTHERN DIVISION

BRIEF OF APPELLEE

ROSLING, WILLIAMS, LANZA & KASTNER
JOSEPH J. LANZA
Attorneys for Appellee
1440 Washington Building
Seattle 1, Washington

KAISER & HOLZMAN
HENRY W. HOLZMAN
Of Counsel
21 East 40th Street
New York 16, New York

THE ARGUS PRESS, SEATTLE

INDEX

TABLE OF CASES

Page

TEXTBOOK

STATUTES

United States Court of Appeals
For the Ninth Circuit

ALBIN STEVEDORE COMPANY, a Washington
Corporation, *Appellant,*

vs.

CENTRAL RIGGING & CONTRACTING COR-
PORATION, *Appellee.*

No. 17609

ON APPEAL FROM THE UNITED STATES DISTRICT COURT
WESTERN DISTRICT OF WASHINGTON,
NORTHERN DIVISION

BRIEF OF APPELLEE

JURISDICTION

District Court.

This action was commenced by appellant in the Superior Court of the State of Washington for King
County to recover sums totaling $22,060.97 which it
claimed was due it from appellee for services performed in loading and stowing a cargo aboard the
"Despina C" at the Port of Seattle in August, 1959.
The complaint contained two causes of action: one for
$6,000, alleged to be the balance due under the written
contract; and the second cause of action for $16,060.97
for alleged extras pursuant to an alleged oral agreement therefor (Tr. 5-9).

Appellee promptly transferred the action to the
United States District Court for the Western District
of Washington, since the matter in controversy ex-

ceeded the sum of $10,000, and because of diversity of
citizenship (Tr. 1-3). The requisite bond for removal
was filed with the petition (Tr. 10). The District Court
had jurisdiction by virtue of 28 U.S.C.A., § 1332, and
§ 1441 (a).

Circuit Court.

Final judgment of the District Court herein granting appellee's cross-motion for summary judgment of
dismissal was entered August 24, 1961 (Tr. 134).
Notice of appeal therefrom was filed by appellant
September 21, 1961. This court has jurisdiction of this
appeal from said final decision of the District Court by
virtue of 28 U.S.C.A., §§ 1291 and 1294, and Federal
Rules of Civil Procedure, Title 28, Rule 73.

STATEMENT OF THE CASE

Appellant's Statement of the Case omits many facts
that are essential to the proper consideration of this
case. Appellee therefore feels compelled to make the
following counter-statement containing all of the essential facts.

A. The History of the Litigation.

On August 14, 1959, the parties entered into a written
contract whereby appellant undertook to perform certain stevedoring work in Seattle, Washington, for appellee. Portions of a certain written contract between
appellee and Howard International, Inc. dated April
28, 1959, were expressly incorporated by reference in
the written agreement between the parties (Tr. 48-67).

In substance the contract provided that appellant
was to load, stow and lash a particular cargo aboard the

"Despina C" at Ames Terminal, Port of Seattle, within ten days of August 17, 1959, and that appellee was to pay therefor as the agreed contract price the sum of $14,000 or a payment determined by an adjusted cost plus computation, whichever was lower.

Paragraph 10 of the agreement between the parties states:

"Upon completion of its work and within fifteen (15) days after receipt of the requisition from Albin, Central agrees to pay the balance due to Albin as agreed. As a further condition, Albin agrees to furnish to Central an affidavit by of (sic) Albin's principal officers certifying that full payment has been made and that there are no persons or firms who have or claim liens arising out of or with respect to the work and in addition Albin agrees to furnish Central with waivers of lien from all subcontractors and materialmen." (Tr. 50).

Paragraph 11 of the contract incorporated by reference Paragraph 22 of the underlying contract which with the required substitution of "Central" (appellee) for "Howard" reads as follows:

"Arbitration: Any controversy or claim arising out of or relating to this contract, or the breach thereof, shall be settled by arbitration, in accordance with the Rules of the American Arbitration Association, and judgment upon the award rendered may be entered in any court having jurisdiction thereof. The arbitration shall be held in New York City, New York, or in Seattle, Washington, at (Central's) option." (Tr. 51, 65-66).

Despite the foregoing arbitration clause, appellant saw fit to institute an action on or about January 4, 1960, to recover the sum of $22,060.97 which it claimed was due it from the appellee for the services it performed. The complaint contained two causes of action: one for $6,000, a balance due on the stipulated contract price of $14,000 (appellee having paid $8,000 on account) and the second cause of action for $16,060.97 for alleged extras (Tr. 5-9).

After completion of the work, appellant claimed that it was entitled to receive $16, 060.97 for alleged extras over and above the stipulated contract price, and prior to suit being commenced herein, appellee served and filed demand for arbitration with the American Arbitration Association seeking to arbitrate its differences with both Howard International, Inc. and appellant (Tr. 12, 34, 41, 43).

Subsequent to this demand for aribtration, appellant received from the American Arbitration Association a request for an answer, and appellant in the month of December 1959 notified the association that it objected to such arbitration upon the ground that the matters in dispute between the parties were not covered by arbitration, as well as upon other grounds (Tr. 42, 43). At or about the same time, appellant commenced the instant suit in the state court as heretofore mentioned. (The complaint was verified December 21, 1959 (Tr. 9) and served on appellee January 4, 1960 (Tr. 1).

Under date of January 7, 1960, the American Arbitration Association advised appellant that inasmuch as Howard International and appellant were not parties to the same contract with appellee and in the absence of an agreement by all three parties that the dispute be heard jointly, these matters would be heard separately unless stayed by order of court. Appellee was accordingly directed to file an answering statement by January 18, 1960 (Tr. 43-44).

After transferring the state court action to the District Court, appellee filed a motion for stay of the action until arbitration was had in accordance with the terms of the agreement between the parties on January 18, 1960 (Tr. 11). On January 19, 1960, appellant filed its motion to enjoin and restrain appellee from proceeding with the arbitration proceeding, and urging that the matters in dispute between the parties be determined in the present action before the District Court (Tr. 40-42).

Prior to the hearing date on said motions, appellee filed its answer on February 10, 1960, and with repect to the first cause of action, it denied that plantiff had fully performed its contract, and that a balance of $6,000 was owed thereon, or that defendant conceded said indebtedness, and in particular denied that plaintiff had conformed with the provisions of Paragraph 10 of the contract requiring it to furnish an affidavit of receipt of full payment as a condition for receiving any balance due thereunder. It likewise denied plaintiff's second cause of action, and alleged as an affirmative and complete defense to both causes of action the aforesaid arbitration agreement (Tr. 68).

Prior thereto, on January 21, 1960, it had filed an amended demand for arbitration against appellant only, which was substantially the same as that previously filed jointly against both Howard International and appellant, in accordance with the direction of the American Arbitration Association's letter of January 7, 1960 (Tr. 85-87).

The hearing on the repsective motions of the parteis was had before Judge Boldt on February 15, 1960, and he granted appellee's motion to stay the action pending arbitration, and denied appellant's counter-motion to restrain the arbitration proceedings (Tr. 72).

Thereafter appellant timely filed notice of appeal on March 14, 1960, from the order sustaining defendant's motion for stay and denying plaintiff's motion for restraner (Tr. 73). However, it voluntarily abandoned the appeal by filing its motion and affidavit for dismissal and for exoneration of the appeal bond (Tr. 74), and a formal order dismissing the appeal was entered by the court on February 7, 1961 (Tr. 76).

Thereafter no further steps in the litigation were taken until the arbitration proceeding was concluded by entry of judgment on the award by the Supreme Court of the State of New York on February 24, 1961 (Tr. 132). (The arbitration proceeding will be covered in subdivision B of this brief immediately following.)

On April 10, 1961, appellant filed a motion before the District Court to vacate the stay theretofore entered in the action, and to enter summary judgment in plaintiff's favor for the relief demanded in the first cause of action, i.e., for $6,000 (Tr. 77). This motion was predicated upon the conclusory statement contained in the moving affidavit of Thomas A. Harnett, Esq., sworn to on March 30, 1961, wherein he averred in paragraph 12 thereof that the three arbitrators were designated and

"a single controversy as framed by the 'amended demand for arbitration' and the 'answering statement,' to-wit, the sum, if any, in excess of $6,000 due and owing to Albin for work and services performed in the loading and lashing of the MV Despina C was submitted to arbitration by them.'' (Tr. 81).

Following this conclusory statement, Mr. Harnett asserted in paragraph 16 of the aforesaid affidavit that

"The sum demanded in plaintiff's first cause of action was conceded to be due and owing to the plaintiff in the defendant's 'amended demand for arbitration' *and hence was never submitted to arbitration,* and no jurisdiction thereof was conferred on the arbitrators and this would not and could not be included in the award made by the arbitrators on the controversy submitted to them.'' (Tr. 82) (emphasis ours).

In response to this motion, appellee filed a cross-motion for summary judgment of dismissal (Tr. 101) and supported same by the affidavit of M. Emanuel Kaiser, Esq., of counsel for appellee in which he set forth in detail the issues and proceedings before the arbitrators, including excerpts from the stenographic transcript of the proceedings, and of the post-award proceedings before the Supreme Court of the State of New York for confirmation of the award (Tr. 103-118).

Although served and filed on April 20, 1961, no reply affidavit was interposed by appellant or his counsel controverting any of the factual data asserted therein.

The repective motions for summary judgment were extensively argued before Judge Boldt on August 15, 1961 (this date is not shown by any documents in the transcript) and the matters were submitted to the court entirely on the pleadings, affidavits and exhibits that were filled in support of the respective motions.

Thereafter the court took the matter under advisement and on August 24, 1961 prepared and entered its own form of order granting appellee's motion for summary judgment (Tr. 134).

The court also concluded in said order that

"From a review of the entire record before the court, including the proceedings before the arbitrators, this court is satisfied that the arbitrators understood and intended that the agreed amounts owing plaintiff were included in the total award made to plaintiff."

The present appeal followed the entry of said order (Tr. 135).

B. Proceedings before the Arbitrators.

(1) Issues submitted.

In its amended demand for arbitration (Tr. 85-87) appellee set forth its disputes with appellant in the following language:

"CENTRAL RIGGING & CONTRACTING CORP. hereby disputes and contests the claim of Albin Stevedore Company for the sum of $22,067.97, and each and every part thereof, to the extent that said claim exceeds the sum of $6,000. Said claim has been made by Albin Stevedore Company against Central Rigging & Contracting Corp. for payment of the work performed which was required by the aforesaid contract. The said disputed claim of Albin Stevedore Company for sums in excess of $6,000 is based on the additional expense of Albin Stevedore Company in performing said contract caused by the alleged failure of Central Rigging & Contracting Corp. to furnish a ship with 45 ton boom and with other adequate loading equipment as allegedly required by the terms of the aforesaid contract.

Central Rigging & Contracting Corp. disputes and contests said claim on the grounds that the said contract provides for a maximum price of $14,000 of which $8,000 has heretofore been paid, and that there is no basis upon which Central Rigging & Contracting Corp. is liable for any sum in excess of $6,000; in addition, the amounts claimed by Albin Stevedore Company as such additional expenses are hereby disputed.''

In its answering statement (Tr. 89-92) appellant denied that the matter submitted was the subject of arbitration, but immediately added:

"Nevertheless, this answering statement is submitted in order that the issues may be framed and *that the merits of this controversy may be finally determined.*" (Tr. 89).

Appellant further stated therein:

"Albin Stevedore Company specifically denies that its claim under the written contract referred to in the demand for arbitration is for the sum of $22,067.97 because of certain facts which are not set forth in the demand for arbitration filed by Central Rigging & Contracting Corp. in its notice dated January 19, 1960, but avers that said amount of *$22,067.97 is due it pursuant to said written contract and a subsequent oral contract hereinafter referred to.* Moreover, Central Rigging & Contracting Corp. in its demand for arbitration admits that the sum of $6,000 is payable to Albin Stevedore Company for services rendered in loading and stowing of certain equipment on board the vessel 'Despina C'. *Accordingly, Albin Stevedore Company hereby demands that the said sum of $6,000 be paid to it forthwith.*" (Tr. 89-90) (our emphasis).

This answering statement concluded with the following prayer:

"Accordingly, Albin Stevedore Company requests:

"1. An award forthwith in its favor against Central Rigging & Contracting Corp. in the sum of $6,000, the undisputed amount due it pursuant to the terms of the written contract referred to in the arbitration agreement and in the demand for arbitration filed herein by Central Rigging & Contracting Corp., and further

"2. An award in the sum of $16,060.97 on the subsequent oral contract of August 21, 1959 together with interest on both awards at the rate of 6% per annum from September 3, 1959 until paid, together with the expenses incurred herein." (Tr. 91-92).

During the course of the hearing before the arbitrators, the following ensued with respect to paragraph 10 of the agreement pertaining to the certification required from Albin as a condition for receiving the balance due under the contract (the questions were put to Mr. Robert Albin, President of plaintiff corporation):

"Q. Under your written agreement with Central, were you to furnish to Central, before the balance of $6,000 was paid to you, an affidavit by Albin's officers certifying full payment and that there are no claims against or liens against the job? Were you supposed to file that with Central?

"A. There is a clause in the contract and I am prepared to do that. I was never asked to do the affidavit. I was unable to make contact with Central Rigging & Contracting Company.

"MR. THILLY (one of the arbitrators): You haven't done it, is that what you mean?

THE WITNESS: I haven't done so.

MR. THILLY: It provided for it, but you didn't do it so far?

WITNESS: Yes.

Q. You never provided wavers of lien before getting the $6,000?

A. No, sir." (Tr. 107).

Apropos to this item, Mr. Kaiser, who represented appellee at that hearing, made the following opening statement:

> "I don't want to burden the record with what we intend to prove. I do say that at the end of this proceeding it will become evident to this Board that there is a $6,000 balance due them. I don't want the Board to penalize us for not having paid the $6,000. We couldn't have paid the $6,000 because when we paid the $6,000 we were entitled to certain papers which they were unwilling to give us, certain releases, and an affidavit that there could be no claims against us for this work, so that we owe that $6,000." (Tr. 108).

(2) Excerpts of the stenographic transcript of the proceedings.

As stated in the affidavit of Mr. Kaiser which was filed in support of defendant's motion for summary judgment, it was agreed that a stenographic transcript of the proceedings before the arbitrators be recorded and the expenses thereof shared equally by the parties (Tr. 109). He then referred the court to the portions of the transcript pertinent to the instant motions.

In his opening statement before the arbitrators, he said at page 8 (Tr. 109):

"We say, gentlemen, you may assess the $6,000 which we owe on the contract, you may, further assess against us as damages up to an amount equal to $1500 on proof that the money was spent for overtime for that Saturday and Sunday; the dates, I think were August 22nd and 23rd of 1959.

"But over and above that, there is no claim that Albin can make against us."

Mr. Harnett, in his opening statement to the arbitrators, said at the bottom of page 18 and the top of page 19 (Tr. 109):

"We feel that we are entitled to an award for the aggregate amount of $22,060.97."

The court will note that this is the exact amount which the plaintiff sued for in its complaint in the District Court.

After this statement, Mr. Wallace Bock, the Tribunal Clerk of the American Arbitration Association, asked Mr. Harnett the following question at page 19 (Tr. 109-110)

"Does that amount include the $6,000?" (meaning does the $22,060.97 include the $6,000.00).

MR. HARNETT: Yes."

To substantiate its claim of $22,060.97 the following evidence was elicited by Mr. Harnett from Mr. Robert Albin, plaintiff's president, at pages 67 and 68 (Tr. 110):

"Q. Furthermore, the only sum that you have been paid against this contract is the $8,000 payroll advance that was made?

A. Yes, sir.

Q. The net due is $22,060.97?

A. Yes, sir.''

After both sides had rested in the arbitration proceeding, the following colloquy took place before the arbitrators, at page 336 (Tr. 110-111):

"MR. KAISER: Then, I think under the rules a decision may be made within thirty days.

MR. HARNETT: In view of the ten-day delay and the thirty-day delay, is it possible for an order of the Board that they pay the $6,000 of which there is no dispute, forthwith, without prejudice to their position in this litgation?

MR. KAISER: I am afraid that under the rules of Arbitration, if the Board were to order that, the subsequent decision of the Board would be void.

Am I correct that there can be only one award in an arbitration:

TRIBUNAL CLERK: Yes, that's right.

MR. KAISER: And they can not break it up into anything but one award?

MR. HARNETT: If the Tribunal Clerk so speaks, then I have no objection.

MR. KAISER: There can be only one award.''

Thus at the conclusion of the hearings before the arbitrators, Mr. Harnett renewed the demand he had made in the answering statement in the arbitration proceedings for two separate awards: one for $6,000 and the other for such damage as the board found. Since it was made clear that the arbitrators could make but one award for all clams made by the plaintiff, Mr. Harnett was satisfied that there could be but one award by the arbitrators under the Rules of the American Arbitration Association, and stated that he had no objection to one award which would include plaintiff's claim for $6,000.

In the pre-hearing memorandum submitted by Mr. Harnett to the arbitrators, he made the following statement:

> "This memorandum is submitted on behalf of Albin Stevedore Company in support of its claim in the aggregate sum of $22,060.97 for work, labor and materials." (Tr. 111).

Further, in said memorandum, Mr. Harnett made the following statement under the heading "CONTENTION":

> "Albin contends that pursuant to the agreements of the parties, the oral authorization of Central's president, the subsequent written approval by Central's pier representatives, and the performance of the work by Albin, that Albin is entitled to the sum of $30,060.97, less the $8,000 received, a net of $22,060.97 for its work, labor, materials and services." (Tr. 111).

At the conclusion of the hearings, Mr. Harnett asked leave to submit a memorandum setting forth the actual damages he claimed he had proved during the hearings. His request was granted and he submitted his computation of Albin's damages in writing as follows:

"1. Amount concededly due and not in
dispute ....$ 6,000.00

2. Amount of Albin's expenses in dispute $16,060.97

Claim Established

    (a) Total payroll costs including fringe benefits and other applicable costs (1)............$11,615.40

(b) Materials 20% of
$4,069.01 (2) 813.80

(c) Rent of Equipment 20%
of $543.22 (2) 108.64

$12,526.87   12,526.87

$18,526.87

Plus interest at 6% from September 3,
1959, to date of award........................ ...."

(Tr. 112)

An examinatoin of this computation indicates that instead of the gross amount of $22,060.97, Mr. Harnett maintained at the end of the arbitration proceedings that Albin had merely setablished damages of $18,-526.87, and he asked for an award in that amount plus six percent interest from September 3rd, 1959, to the date of the award, which line he left blank. Mr. Kaiser submitted a written reply to Mr. Harnett's computation of damage on behalf of Albin, and in said reply stated at the outset:

"Central Rigging & Contracting Corp. admits that it owes to Albin Stevedore Company the following sums:

$6,000.00 representing the balance due Albin Stevedore Company on the written contract of August 14th, 1959;

$1,291.05 representing payroll authorized by Harry Meyerson in a long distance telephone conversation on August 28th, 1959, for work, performed on Saturday, August 29th, 1959, the day the vessel sailed from Seattle." (Tr. 112-113).

Mr. Kaiser then analyzed and took exception to the

various claims which Mr. Harnett made in his computation of damage, and concluded his memorandum
with the following statement:

> "It is our positoin that the award to Albin
> should be for $6,000.00 plus $1291.05, or a total of
> $7291.05. No interest should be granted Albin be-
> cause it should not benefit by its presentation of an
> unjust and exaggerated claim for payment.

> "At best, if credence were to be given to Albin's
> claims for breach of the written contract, to-wit:
> damages sustained by reason of alleged defective
> vesel equipment, it would then become entitled to
> an additional sum of $243.14 for alleged lost time."
> (Tr. 113).

(3) The award.

The pertinent provison of the award of the arbitrators reads as follows:

> "1) CENTRAL RIGGING & CONTRACTING CORP.,
> hereinafter referred to as CENTRAL, shall pay to
> ALBIN STEVEDORE COMPANY, hereinafter referred
> to as ALBIN, the sum of NINE THOUSAND FIVE HUN-
> DRED DOLLARS ($9,500.00) plus interest at the rate
> of six per cent (6%) per annum from September
> 18, 1959 to the date of this award *in full settlement
> of all claims submitted to this arbitration.*" (our
> emphasis) (Tr. 113, 121).

It is fair to state at this point that neither side obtained the result it sought in the arbitration proceedings. Appellee wanted the arbitrators to limit their
award to the sum of $7,500. Appellant originally re-
quested the arbitrators to award it a total amount of
$22,060.97, and then by its post-hearing memorandum
limited its claim to $18,526.87. The arbitrators actually

awarded $9,500 "in full settlement of all clams submitted to this arbitration" together with interest, and saw fit to reject the determination sought by each of the parties.

(4) Post-award proceedings before the Supreme Court of the State of New York.

On or about December 30, 1960, Mr. Harnett, on behalf of appellant, made a motion in the Supreme Court of the State of New York, County of New York, wherein he prayed for the following relief:

> "WHEREFORE, deponent (Thomas A. Harnett) prays that an order be made herein confirming said award and directing that judgment be entered in the Supreme Court of the State of New York, County of New York and that Albin Stevedore Company be allowed the costs of this motion to confirm and that Albin Stevedore Company have such other and further relief as to this Court would seem proper." (Tr. 114).

On behalf of appellee, Mr. Kaiser submitted an affidavit to the Supreme Court of the State of New York, in which he consented to the confirmation of the award as rendered by the arbitrators, but opposed Mr. Harnett's request for costs on the ground that he had offered appellant the amount of the award, to-wit: $9,500 plus interest, in accordance with the award, of $672.90, or a total of $10,172.90, and that he had informed Mr. Harnett that the appellee had already deposited with his firm the aforesaid sum of $10,172.90 to satisfy the award of the arbitrators (Tr. 114-115).

The decision of the Supreme Court of the State of New York, confirmed the award without costs, and directed counsel to settle the order (Tr. 115).

Mr. Harnett then submitted an order for signature, the pertinent decretal portions of which read as follows:

"ORDERED that the award of Alvin A. Borgading, Frank D. Pillatt, Jr. and John E. Thilly, all of the arbitrators in the above entitled proceeding dated November 23, 1960, *whereby they determined a single dispute, to-wit, the sum, if any, in excess of $6,000 due and owing to Albin Stevedore Company* for work, labor, and services performed in the loading of the M. V. DESPINA C, and awarded that Central Rigging & Contracting Corp. pay to Albin Stevedore Company the sum of $9,500 plus interest at the rate of Six Per Cent (6%) per annum from September 18, 1959, to November 23, 1960, and that the administrative fees and expenses of the American Arbitration Association in the amount of $481.20 be borne equally by the parties, and it is further

"ORDERED that the said Albin Stevedore Company have judgment upon said award in the sum of $9,500 plus interest at the rate of Six Per Cent (6%) per annum from September 18, 1959, to November 23, 1960, and that said judgment be entered as a judgment in the Supreme Court of the State of New York, County of New York." (emphasis ours) (Tr. 115, 123-124).

Being of the opinion that this proposed order submitted by Mr. Harnett on behalf of the appellant did not conform to the arbitrators' award and the decision of the court, Mr. Kaiser submitted on behalf of appellee, a counter-order which he felt was in conformity with the court's decision, and each party submitted memoranda in support of their repective proposed orders. In his memorandum, Mr. Harnett advanced the same conclusory interpretation of the award that is now being advanced by appellant before this court, to-wit: that only "a single controversy to-wit, the sum, if any, in excess of $6,000, due and owing to Albin" was submitted for arbitration (Tr. 125-127 at p. 126).

In his memorandum to the court in opposition to Mr. Harnett's proposed order, and in support of appellee's proposed order, Mr. Kaiser set forth that the arbitrators "did not limit their award to a single issue as set forth in the proposed order" of Mr. Harnett. He further stated that the court, in its decision, did not determine that the arbitrators awarded Albin $9,500 on a single dispute. He further urged that "the aforesaid award was in conformity with the Amended Demand for Arbitration filed by Central, the Answering Statement thereto filed by Albin, and the issues presented to the arbitrators in the arbitration proceedings, as evidenced by the transcript of the proceedings before the arbitrators." (Tr. 128-129).

The court rejected Mr. Harnett's proposed order and entered the order requested by appellee (Tr. 130-131). The pertinent decretal portions of the order entered by the court read as follows:

"ORDERED that the motion of Albin Stevedore Company is granted to the extent that the award of Alvin A. Borgading, Frank D. Pillatt, Jr. and John E. Thilly, all of the arbitrators in the arbitration proceedings held before the American Arbitration Association, dated November 23rd, 1960, be and the same hereby is confirmed; and it is further

"ORDERED that the said Albin Stevedore Company have judgment upon said award against Central Rigging & Contracting Corp. in the sum of

$9,500.00 plus interest at the rate of six per cent
(6%) per annum from September 18th, 1959 to
November 23rd, 1960, without costs, and that said
judgment be entered by the Clerk of this Court."
(Tr. 131).

No appeal was taken by appellant from the aforesaid order dated February 1, 1961, and its time to do so
has long since expired.

On February 24, 1961, appellant caused the Clerk of
the Supreme Court of the State of New York, County
of New York, to enter a judgment on the order affirming the arbitration award, the pertinent decretal portion thereof reading as follows:

"Adjudged that the said Albin Stevedore Company to recover of the said Central Rigging & Contracting Corp., the sum of $9,500 with interest
thereon from September 18, 1959, to November 23,
1960, at the rate of six per cent (6%) per annum,
amounting in all to the sum of $10,172.90 and that
the said Albin Stevedore Company have execution
therefor." (Tr. 132-133).

On March 1, 1961, Mr. Kaiser's firm delivered its
check in the sum of $10,172,90 to appellant and received
in exchange therefor a satisfaction of the aforesaid
judgment, which was filed in the County Clerk's office
of the Supreme Court of the State of New York, County
of New York (Tr. 117).

SUMMARY OF THE ARGUMENT

1. The District Court's original order staying the action and refusing to enjoin the pending arbitration
proceedings, conclusively established that both causes
of action were covered by the arbitration clause. There-

fore, appellant was precluded from reasserting before the District Court that the first cause of action for $6,000 was never submitted to the arbitrators, but was the subject of further affirmative action thereon, following the award and payment thereof.

2. Appellant is estopped from challenging the jurisdiction of the arbitrators.

3. The issues and proceedings before the arbitrators clearly indicate that its award included appellant's claim for $6,000.

4. The confirmation of the award and the entry of judgment thereon is *res judicata* of appellant's claim for $6,000.

ARGUMENT

1. The District Court's original order staying the action and refusing to enjoin the pending arbitration proceedings, conclusively established that both causes of action were covered by the arbitration clause. Therefore, appellant was precluded from reasserting before the District Court that the first cause of action for $6,000 was never submitted to the arbitrators, but was the subjec of further affirmative action thereon, following the award and payment thereof.

Section 3 of the United States Arbitration Act (9 U.S.C. § 3) authorizes federal courts to stay proceedings involving an issue which is referable to arbitration under an agreement in writing for such arbitration.

In this case, appellee moved for a stay pursuant thereto (Tr. 11) and appellant moved to enjoin and restrain appellee from proceeding with the arbitration proceedings (Tr. 40). Said motions placed in issue the question whether each of appellant's causes of action was subject to arbitration under the written agreement.

Thus with respect to the first cause of action, appellant asserted in its motion to enjoin:

> "That under the original written agreement between the parties, dated August 14, 1959, there remains due, owing and unpaid to the plaintiff the sum of $6,000, which by the defendant's admission, in its demand for arbitration, remains unpaid and undisputed, and upon which there remains no ground for arbitration under said written agreement." (Tr. 42).

The District Court's order of February 18, 1960 (Tr. 72) resolved this issue in favor of appellee in sustaining its motion for stay, and denying appellant's motion to restrain appellee from proceeding with the arbitration proceedings.

Such order was appealable under Section 1292 (1) of the Federal Judicial Code (28 U.S.C. § 1292 (1)) which permits appeals from interlocutory orders "granting, continuing, modifying, refusing, or dissolving injunctions," etc.

> *Ross v. Twentieth Century-Fox Film Corp.* (C.A. 9th, 1956) 236 F.(2d) 632;

> *Shanferoke Co. & Supply Corp. v. Westchester Service Corp.*, 293 U.S. 449, 79 L.Ed. 583, 55 S.Ct. 313;

> *Baltimore Contractors, Inc. v. Bodinger* (1955) 348 U.S. 176, 75 S.Ct. 249, 99 L.Ed. 233.

In an annotation on "appealability of federal district court order granting or denying stay of action pending arbitration" in 99 L.Ed. 241, the author states at page 242:

"The decisions of the federal courts have established that Section 1292 (1) authorizes an appeal from a district court's grant or denial of a stay pending arbitration where (1) such grant or denial is ordered in the exercise of the district court's equitable powers, and (2) the effect of the order is to stay a common law action; under such circumstances, the grant or denial of the stay amounts to a grant or denial of an injunction."

In fact, appellant recognized the appealability of this order by filing notice of appeal therefrom (Tr. 73). Its subsequent abandonment of the appeal thereby conclusively established the correctness of the order, and was not only a tacit recognition on the part of appellant that *both* causes of action were to be arbitrated, but in law had the binding force of establishing that fact.

It is significant that on the day following the filing of notice of appeal, appellant filed its answering statement before the Arbitration Tribunal asserting therein that "this answering statement is submitted in order that the issues may framed and *that the merits of this controversy may be finally determined*" (Tr. 89). In accordance with this statement, it asked the Tribunal for an award "forthwith" in its favor in the sum of $6,000 pursuant to the terms of the written contract, and an award in the sum of $16,060.97 on the purported subsequent oral agreement (Tr. 91, 92).

It is also significant that while appellant's motion and affidavit for dismissal of the appeal was sworn to on August 30, 1960 (Tr. 75), it was not filed with the District Court until February 13, 1961 (Tr. 74), which was 13 days after the New York Supreme Court entered its order confirming the award of the arbitrators as per form submitted by appellee's counsel (Tr. 130-131).

The inference from this is irresistible that appellant believed that the present approach in moving for summary judgment on the first cause of action before the District Court would probably be more effective than the prosecution of its appeal. In the meantime it wanted to keep both avenues open, depending upon the amount that should be awarded to it by the arbitrators. Certainly, if it had been awarded the sum of $22,067.97 as originally prayed for, or for that matter the sum of $18,526.87 as computed in its memorandum at the conclusion of the hearings (Tr. 112), appellant would not have dared to seek an additional $6,000 from appellee, as was attempted in the later proceedings before the District Court.

In any event, appellant's present attempt, following arbitration and an award, to again asesrt that the first cause of action was never referred to the arbitrators, but remained always in the bosom of the District Court and subject to a summary judgment thereon, would nullify completely the binding effect of the District Court's original order.

It follows, therefore, that the granting of summary judgment of dismissal of plaintiff's action, following arbitration and the payment of the award thereon, was entirely proper and should be affirmed.

2. Appellant is estopped from challenging the jurisdiction of the arbitrators.

The record clearly establishes that appellant participated solely and on the merits in the arbitration proceedings that were conducted before the American Arbitration Association in the City of New York, the forum and place designated in the written agreement between the parties. Thus it not only asserted in its answering statement that it was being submitted in order "that the issues may be framed and that the *merits* of this controversy may be *finally* determined" (Tr. 89-92), but also prayed for an award in the total amount of $22,067.97 which it readily conceded included the sum of $6,000 (Tr. 109-110). After both sides had rested, appellant's counsel renewed the demand he had made in the answering statement for the immediate payment of the $6,000, and after being informed that there could be only one award stated:

"If the Tribunal Clerk so speaks, then I have no objection." (Tr. 110-111).

The cases are legion that hold that where a party participates in the arbitration proceedings on the merits, it waives any right to challenge the jurisdiction of the arbitrators and is estopped from so doing.

> *In re Iino Shipbuilding & Eng. Co. Ltd.,* 175 N.Y.S.(2d) 750;
>
> *Harris v. East India Trading Co.,* 144 N.Y.S. (2d) 894;
>
> *Smith v. Polar Cia De Navegacion, Ltda,* 181 N.Y.S.(2d) 368;
>
> *In re Simplex Machine Tool Corporation and Swind Machinery Company,* 144 N.Y.S. (2d) 595;

In re National Cash Register Company and Charles Wilson, 184 N.Y.S.(2d) 957.

Thus in the *Iino Shipbuilding* case, *supra,* the court said at page 753:

> "Indeed, participation in selection of the arbitrator is itself a waiver of objection to the items of dispute submitted."

Also:

> "The builder made clear its reservation about going into arbitration; but when it went in it must be deemed by the court to have yielded the reservation."

In *Harris v. East India Trading Co., supra,* at page 898, it was said:

> "There can be no doubt that under present law participation either in selection of the arbitrator or *in any of the arbitration proceedings* estops the raising of the jurisdictional issue as to the making of the contract providing for arbitration." (Emphasis ours)

3. The issues and proceedings before the arbitrators clearly indicate that its award included appellant's claim for $6,000.

Not wishing to reiterate what has already been stated in our statement of the case pertaining to the proceedings before the arbitrators, we believe that we can limit our argument on this point by making the following comments.

There can be no question but that the arbitrators understood that one of the issues presented to them for determination was the question of the payment of the sum of $6,000. This is clear from the questions asked by Mr. Thilly, one of the arbitrators:

"Q. Under your written agreement with Central, were you to furnish to Central, before the balance of $6,000 was paid to you, an affidavit by Albin's officers certifying full payment and that there are no claims against or liens again the job? Were you supposed to file that with Central?

A. There is a clause in the contract and I am prepared to do that. I was never asked to do the affidavit. I was unable to make contact with Central Rigging & Contracting Company.

MR. THILLY (one of the arbitrators) You haven't done it, is that what you mean?

THE WITNESS: I haven't done so.

MR. THILLY: It provided for it, but you didn't do it so far?

WITNESS: Yes.

Q. You never provided waivers of lien before getting that $6,000?

A. No, sir." (Tr. 107)

And by the question of Mr. Wallace Bock, Tribunal Clerk, to Mr. Harnett:

"Q. Does that amount include the $6,000?" (meaning does the $22,060.97 include the $6,000)

A. Yes." (Tr. 110)

It is also plain that from the outset all parties, including the arbitrators, clearly understood that the $6,000 was an item to be included in the ultimate award.

Thus, (a) appellant's original submission "that the merits of this controversy may be finally determined," (b) its repeated insistence upon an *aggregate award* of some $22,000 which included the $6,000 item, (c) its demand at the outset and at the end of the proceedings that the sum of $6,000 be paid "forthwith," (d) its acquiescence in the clerk's advise that this was not possible since there could be only one award, (e) its computation of the damages furnished the arbitrators at the conclusion of the hearings totaling $18,526.87, which included the $6,000 concededly due, — clearly belie appellant's contention that this item "was not submitted to the arbitrators for decision."

The fact that appellee conceded that $6,000, being the contract balance, could be assessed against it, does not mean that it was to be left out of the ultimate award. For that matter, appellee's counsel also conceded that the Board could assess damages against appellee in the sum of $1,500 (Tr. 109). To be consistent here, appellant should contend that that additional amount was likewise excluded from the ultimate award in view of appellee's concession.

The issue was fully and finally resolved in the making of the award wherein the arbitrators stated that it was "in full settlement of *all claims* submitted to this arbitration." The District Court's conclusion after reviewing the entire record, including the proceedings before the arbitrators, that it was "satisfied that the arbitrators understood and intended that the agreed amounts owing plaintiff were included in the total award," (Tr. 134) was therefore correct and should be affirmed.

4. The confirmation of the award and the entry of judgment thereon is *res judicata* of appellant's claim for $6,000.

Apparently, appellant was dissatisfied with the award, and by ignoring the pleadings in the arbitration, the proceedings therein, and the language of the award, sought to subvert the final determination of the controversy by subsequent proceedings in the Supreme Court of the State of New York. Thus, after its motion before that court to confirm the award was granted (except for costs), it sought to have the court make a determination that the award *did not embrace the claim of $6,000*. It not only filed a proposed order to that effect but likewise filed a memorandum in support thereof (Tr. 125-127). In effect, appellant sought the same relief in the New York Supreme Court as it is now seeking by its appeal from the order below which granted appellee's cross-motion for summary judgment dismissing the complaint. The Supreme Court of the State of New York rejected appellant's contention and confirmed the award which specifically stated that it was "in full settlement of *all claims* submitted to this arbitration." Thereupon, it duly entered a judgment against appellee on said award, which was promptly paid by appellee.

In all jurisdictions a party is foreclosed from litigating anew that which has already been determined by a court of competent jurisdiction. In Corpus Juris Secundum, Vol. 50, § 592, page 11, the rule is enunciated in the following language:

"Any right, fact, or matter in issue, and directly adjudicated on, or necessarily involved in, the determination of an action before a competent court

in which a judgment or decree is rendered on the
merits is conclusively settled by the judgment
therein and cannot again be litigated between the
parties and privies whether or not the claim or demand, purpose, or subject matter of the two suits
is the same. * * *

> "*Res judicata* is a rule of universal law pervad-
> ing every well regulated system of jurisprudence,
> and is put on two grounds, embodied in various
> maxims of the common law; the one, public policy
> and necessity, which makes it to the interest of the
> state that there should be an end to litigation—*in-
> terest republicae ut sit finis litium;* the other, the
> hardship on the individual that he should be vexed
> twice for the same cause—*nemo debet bis vexari
> pro aedem causa.* The doctrine applies and treats
> the final determination of the action as speaking
> the infallible truth as to the rights of the parties
> as to the entire subject of the controversy, and such
> controversy and every part of it must stand ir-
> revocably closed by such determination. The sum
> and substance of the whole doctrine is that a mat-
> ter once judicially decided is finally decided."

In fact, appellant very frankly concedes on page 17
of its brief that:

> "The moving papers submitted by the appellant
> at the time of the motion fully apprised the New
> York court of the position of the appellant, *which
> is the same here."* (Emphasis supplied)

Thus, it is clear that appellant has had its day in
court. It submitted this same issue to a court of competent jurisdiction. The ruling was adverse. No appeal
was taken therefrom. The ruling put an end to the controversy. It should therefore be *res judicata* of the
issue.

Discussion of Appellant's Authorities

The bulk of the decisions cited in appellant's brief deal with general principles applicable to arbitration proceedings and of the limitations placed upon arbitrators with respect to the issues submitted to them for determination. Appellant has no quarrel with these propositions. The question here is not whether the arbitrators exceeded their authority, but simply whether their lump award of $9,500 "in full settlement of all *claims* submitted to this arbitration" included the item of $6,000. The record is clear that this item was not only impliedly, but expressly submitted to them for their consideration. Therefore, discussion of appellant's citations becomes unnecessary. However, on page 11 of its brief, appellant refers to a collateral case in which appellee was involved in the New York Supreme Court and quotes from an opinion rendered on October 14, 1961. The fact of the matter is that the New York Court subsequently reversed itself on a motion to reargue and fully confirmed the award in that case. In view of the fact that appellant has seen fit to quote from the prior decision in MATTER OF CENTRAL RIGGING & CONTRACTING CORP. (HOWARD INTERNATIONAL, INC.), New York Law Journal, October 14, 1961, we feel it incumbent to quote the entire opinion of Mr. Justice Streit in the Supreme Court in that case, as published in the New York Law Journal on November 29, 1961, and append the same by way of an appendix to this brief.

The following quotation from one of appellant's citations at page 9 of its brief appears to answer appellant's contentions adequately:

> "The court will look at the language of the submission in its every part and from a consideration of the whole, will determine the matter of intent. If the reasonable construction appears to be that the parties intended to have everything decided, if anything should be, then a decision of all matters submitted will be imperatively required."—*Jones v. Welwood,* 71 N.Y. 208 (1877).

Appellee submits that looking at the language of the submission of appellant in its every part and from a consideration of the whole, including the proceedings before the arbitrators, appellant clearly indicated its intent to have everything decided and therefore the award rendered necessarily included the item in question.

CONCLUSION

Appellant's insistence that this claim was not submitted to the arbitrators, flies in the face of what actually transpired. It is aggrieved by the amount of the award and now would have this court ignore all of the facts and grant it a further sum of $6,000 although its claim for such sum has been fully litigated in the arbitration proceedings and was unquestionably included in the $9,500 awarded appellant on both of its claims.

This claim has now been fully and completely adjudicated on three occasions: (1) before the District Court on the original motion granting a stay and refusing to enjoin the arbitration, from which an appeal was taken and later dismissed by appellant; (2) before the arbitrators and included within its award; (3) before the New York Supreme Court, in its refusal to adopt the same contentions as are now being made before this court.

Litigation of the same issue must come to a halt, and appellant should not be permitted to flout the rule of *res judicata* by repeating the same arguments and raising the same issues again on this appeal.

The judgment of the District Court in granting summary judgment of dismissal should therefore be affirmed.

Respectfully submitted,

ROSLING, WILLIAMS, LANZA & KASTNER
JOSEPH J. LANZA
Attorneys for Appellee

KAISER & HOLZMAN
HENRY W. HOLZMAN
Of Counsel

APPENDIX

APPENDIX

Opinion of the Supreme Court of the State of New York, Strett, J., *Matter of Central Rigging & Contracting Corp. (Howard International, Inc.)* October 14, 1961, New York Law Journal, November 19, 1961:

"Matter of Central Rigging & Contracting Corp'n (Howard Internat., Inc.)—After careful study of the papers on this motion, and on the original motion, as well as the record before the arbitrators, the court is satisfied that the amendments allowed by the arbitrators, did not violate the rules of the American Arbitration Society and that the arbitrators were not guilty of an abuse of discretion in permitting the amendments. The amendments did not make 'any new or different claim,' within the meaning of section 8 of said rules, and respondent was afforded ample opportunity to attempt to meet them. It is accordingly unnecessary to determine whether, if the amendments had made 'new or different' claims, the arbitrators could reasonably construe the second sentence of section 8 (supra), as permitting them to consent to amendments at the hearing, without compliance with the requirements of the first sentence of the section.

"The contention that the award makes no disposition of the counterclaim is without merit, for the award states that it is 'in full settlement of all claims submitted to this arbitration *by either party against the other* (italics supplied).

"The contention that the award should be vacated, because it does not make a separate decision as to each claim asserted, is overruled. There is no legal requirement that an arbitrator make a separate determination of each separate claim, or even that a lump sum award state the manner in which the lump sum was arrived at.

"Respondent makes much of the contract provision limiting claims for extras to those evidenced by a prior written approval signed by respondent. *Even in a court of law,* such a provision does not prevent recovery for extras not so evidenced, on the theory of waiver (*La Rose v. Backer,* 11 App. Div.2d 314, 319-320; *Langley v. Rouss,* 185 N.Y. 201, 207-8; *Soloman v. Vallette,* 152 N.Y. 147, 151; *Arrow Plumbing Co. v. Dare Const. Corp'n,* 212 N.Y.S.2d 438, 441), or estoppel (*Imperator Realty Co. v. Tull,* 228 N.Y. 447, 453). A *fortiori,* arbitrators, who need not be lawyers and who are not bound to decide according to legal principles may permit a recovery for extras, notwithstanding the absence of written approval required by the contract, where the evidence permits them to find a waiver or an estoppel.

"The other points made by respondent, based on alleged misconduct of petitioner's counsel, alleged rewriting of the agreement by the arbitrators, the acceptance of affidavits as evidence, alleged partiality of the arbitrators, &c., do not require discussion. The court is satisfied that they do not warrant vacatur of the award.

"The motion for reargument is granted, and on such reargument, the motion to confirm the award, with the date of the contract, as stated in the preamble, corrected to April 28, 1959, is granted and the cross-motion to vacate award denied. Settle order."

United States Court of Appeals

For the Ninth Circuit.

Docket No. 17609

ALBIN STEVEDORE COMPANY,
a Washington Corp.,

Appellant,

v.

CENTRAL RIGGING & CONTRACTING CORPORATION,

Appellee.

On Appeal from the United States District Court
Western District of Washington : Northern Division

REPLY BRIEF FOR PLAINTIFF-APPELLANT.

CLARKE, CLARKE, ALBERTSON & BOVINGDON,
Attorneys for Plaintiff-Appellant,
1118 Alaska Building
Seattle 4, Washington

WATTERS & DONOVAN,
Of Counsel,
161 William Street
New York 38, New York

SUBJECT INDEX.

United States Court of Appeals

For the Ninth Circuit

Docket No. 17609.

Albin Stevedore Company, a Washington Corp.,
Appellant,

v.

Central Rigging & Contracting Corporation,
Appellee.

On Appeal from the United States District Court
Western District of Washington: Northern District

REPLY BRIEF FOR PLAINTIFF-APPELLANT.

Replying to Appellee's Arguments.

Except for the conclusory statement, of its position, Appellee's brief, in its entirety, neither disputes nor overcomes the basic point raised in and the authorities cited by the Appellant in its main brief, i.e., that the sole matter submitted to the arbitration was "the sum of $22,067.97 and each and every part thereof to the extent that said claim exceeds the sum of $6,000" [Tr. pp. 86, 87]. This is made manifest by the extensive argumentative approach employed by the Appellee throughout its brief.

The Appellee's brief concedes that its demand for arbitration, in fact its *amended* demand for arbitration, was solely with regard to the sum "in excess of $6,000". [Appellee's Brief, pp. 8, 9] Appellee's *amended* demand for arbitration, was that it:

"... disputes and contests the claim of Albin Stevedore Company for the sum of $22,067.97, and each
and every part thereof, to the extent that said claim
exceeds the sum of $6,000 ... and that there is no
basis upon which Central Rigging & Contracting
Corp. is liable for any sum in excess of $6,000; in
addition, the amounts claimed by Albin Stevedore
Company as such additional expenses are hereby disputed." [Tr. pp. 85-87, and set forth in Appellee's
brief, pp. 8-9.]

Thereafter, in its brief, the Appellee continues to crystallize
the Appellant's point when it quotes from Appellant's
answering statement in the arbitration proceeding and
italicizes the matter that the parties put into controversy
in the arbitration proceeding, i.e., "Nevertheless this
answering statement is submitted in order that the issues
may be framed and *that the merits of this controversy may
be finally determined.*" [Tr. p. 89 and Appellee's Brief,
p. 9—emphasis is theirs; however, we place further emphasis on the words "this controversy".] The answering statement in the arbitration proceeding related and referred to
"this controversy", i.e., the sum in excess of $6,000, as
chosen by the Appellee in its amended demand for arbitration. Appellee recognizes our point when it proceeds to
state that Appellant made a demand for payment forthwith
of the $6,000 concededly due it. [See Appellee's Brief,
p. 9; Tr. 89-90.]; there never was any dispute about it to
be arbitrated.

However, thereafter in its brief, the Appellee endeavors
to becloud the issues and skirt the question before this
Court, by showing that at the arbitration hearing, Appellant attempted to prove the entire claim of $22,067.97, not
merely the "extent said claim exceeds the sum of $6,000."
Appellant, of necessity, had to prove all of the $22,067.97
in order to determine what was "in excess of $6,000." This
is simple and basic arithmetic, i.e., the total must be proved
in order to establish the extent of the excess over the first
conceded item.

Moreover, the statement at page 13 of Appellee's brief that the arbitrators could make only "one award" is true and we concur in it. There could only be one award but that award, to be proper, may only be within the jurisdiction conferred upon the arbitrators in the controversy submitted to them by the Appellee's amended demand for arbitration, the Appellant's answering statement and nothing else. The award of the arbitrators, "in full settlement of all claims, submitted in *this arbitration*" [Tr. p. 113, emphasis supplied] shows the extent of the arbitration award and relates it to the dispute submitted by the parties.

The only controversy over which the arbitrators had jurisdiction was with regard to the sum "in excess of $6,000." The controversy was never changed by the parties; it was never increased by the parties.

With regard to the post-arbitration proceedings, the Appellee seeks comfort and repose in the form of the order signed by the Supreme Court, New York County [Tr. pp. 98, 99; and Tr. pp. 130, 131]. As we stated in our main brief, the only reason the Supreme Court signed the Appellee's order was that orders "should not contain any factual findings or decisional discussions." [See authorities at p. 18 of our main brief.] Nevertheless, now that the Appellee claims that the Appellant seeks to pervert the decision of the New York State Supreme Court, we answer it head-on. The Appellee's position and assertions in this regard are false. Since the Appellee has raised the question obtusely, let us look at the facts.

What did the Appellant submit to the Supreme Court, New York County on its motion to confirm? It used in addition to the notice of motion and certain exhibits the affidavit of one of its attorneys, Thomas A. Harnett [Tr. p. 114]. The affidavit reads in part as follows:

"7. Pursuant to the aforementioned written agreement dated August 14, 1959, and Central's "Amended Demand for Arbitration" dated January 19, 1960, a copy of which is annexed hereto, made a part hereof and marked Exhibit A [See in particular pages 2 and 3 thereof Re "II. DEMAND FOR ARBITRA-

TION."], and pursuant to Albin's "Answering Statement" in reply to the "Amended Demand for Arbitration," a copy of which is annexed hereto, made a
part hereof and marked Exhibit B, *a single controversy, to wit, the sum, if any, in excess of $6,000 due
and owing to Albin for work and services performed
in the loading of the Despina C, was submitted to
arbitration* by the Commercial Arbitration Tribunal,
administered by the American Arbitration Association, 477 Madison Avenue, Borough of Manhattan,
City and State of New York, under its rules and pursuant to the laws of the State of New York."
[Emphasis supplied: entire notice of motion and
affidavit attached and inserted in Appendix for clarity purposes only; cf. Tr. p. 126.]

The Appellee was apprised of the relief sought in the
Supreme Court, New York County, thirteen days before the
motion was returnable. The Appellee did not oppose the
motion, nor contest the factual statements in the affidavit
of Thomas A. Harnett, submitted in support of the motion
in New York County, Supreme Court. [See decision of
Supreme Court set forth in full in Appellant's affidavit in
the District Court, Tr. 115; reported N. Y. L. J. Jan. 24,
1962, p. 12, col. 7.]

The sole motion before the Supreme Court in the State
of New York was to confirm the award of a dispute relating
to "... a single controversy, to wit, the sum, if any, in excess
of $6,000 ... submitted to arbitration." [¶7 of Affidavit of
Thomas A. Harnett, *supra;* Tr. p. 126.]

We do not make any concession as Appellee states at
page 30 of its brief, but as at page 17 of our original brief
and referred to at page 30 of Appellee's brief, we reaffirm
that "the moving papers submitted by the Appellant at the
time of the motion fully apprised the New York Court of
the position of the Appellant, which is the same here." [In
its brief, Appellee put emphasis on the words "which is
the same here".] From the affidavit which is contained in
the Appendix of this brief, it is clear beyond peradventure
of doubt that the Supreme Court in New York was told that
there was a "single controversy". [¶7 of affidavit of

Thomas A. Harnett, *supra* and Appendix.] If the Appellee asserts the doctrine of *res judicata*, it binds appellee; it did not oppose the motion in the Supreme Court, New York County. The Appellee did not controvert the affidavit of Thomas A. Harnett there, nor did it oppose the relief the Appellant sought in its application for confirmation [Tr. 114, 115; N. Y. L. J., Jan. 24, 1962, p. 12, col. 7.]

Restatement of Appellant's Arguments.

The parties submitted but one dispute to the arbitrators, "The sum of $22,067.97 and each and every part thereof to the extent that said claim exceeds the sum of $6,000 . . . The said disputed claim of Albin Stevedore Company for sums in excess of $6,000 . . ." [Tr. pp. 86, 87].

Article 84 of the Civil Practice Act of the State of New York, and particularly Section 1462, limits the power of the arbitrators to those granted the arbitrators by the demand for arbitration. In the case at bar, neither the demand for arbitration [Tr. p. 38], the amended demand for arbitration [Tr. pp. 86-87], nor the answering statement [Tr. pp. 89-92] submitted any dispute other than the claim which "exceeds the sum of $6,000." We submit, these simple, precise facts sustain our conclusion.

For, under the principle of *contra proferentem*, the demand and amended demand for arbitration, both drawn by Appellee, must be strictly construed against it. *Taylor v. U. S. Casualty*, 269 N. Y. 360, 199 N. E. 620 (1936); *Marcus v. U. S. Casualty*, 249 N. Y. 21; 161 N. E. 571 (1928). If the Appellee desired to arbitrate the Appellant's entire claim, it could have used simple language to do so; it chose, however, simple language placing *only the excess of $6,000 in dispute*.

The plain meaning of the words "in excess of $6,000" does not include, by any stretch of the imagination, issues as to the sum of $6,000 which was concededly due the Appellant (there never was any dispute about it to be

6

arbitrated) nor did it permit the arbitrators thereunder to question the basic $6,000, i.e., the conceded amount due Appellant. The sole matter before the arbitrators was that "in excess of $6,000"; the arbitrators were powerless to include that $6,000 in their award. To do so would have been improper, and unfair to the Appellee. *William B. Logan & Associates* v. *Monogram Precision Industries*, 184 Cal. App. 2d 12; 7 Cal Rptr. (West's) 212 [set forth at pp. 13-15 of our main brief]; a situation that we would not countenance.

Apparently, it is the Appellee's contention, however, that the discussions relative to the sum of $6,000 concededly due Appellant at the arbitration hearing enlarged the jurisdiction of the arbitrators. This contention is without merit in fact or law and the cases referred to at page 25 of its brief do not sustain the conclusion appellee asserts.

Conclusion.

The demand for arbitration, i.e., "the sum of $22,067.97 and each and every part thereof to the extent that said claim exceeds the sum of $6,000" and "the said disputed claim of Albin Stevedore Company for sums in excess of $6,000" [Tr. pp. 86, 87] and the award of the arbitrators "in full settlement of all claims submitted to *this* arbitration [Tr. p. 95; emphasis supplied] fully sustains our position.

The Appellee's demand for arbitration and the Appellant's answering statement were the source and definition of the authority exercised by the arbitrators. *Matter of T. W. U.*, 187 Misc. 2d 247, 63 N. Y. S. 2d 17. The parties submitted but one dispute to the arbitrators, i.e., the excess over $6,000, the claim set forth in the second cause of action in the District Court suit. The arbitrators' award was solely "in full settlement of all claims submitted to *this arbitration*." [Tr. p. 95; emphasis supplied] The submission to the arbitrators did not encompass the first cause of action; the right to dispose of that action remained

exclusively in
and not the
forth in the

Therefore
the amount
light of the
was not be
the District
motion for
and grant j
6 per cent i

GEORGE W.

JAMES B. P
THOMAS A.

(Both o

exclusively in the District Court. The District Court solely, and not the arbitrators had jurisdiction over the claim set forth in the first cause of action.

Therefore, in the absence of any question of fact as to the amount due under the first cause of action and in the light of the indisputable fact that the first cause of action was not before the arbitrators, this Court should reverse the District Court and enter an order granting Appellant's motion for summary judgment on the first cause of action and grant judgment in the sum of $6,000 with interest at 6 per cent from September 18, 1959, to date.

Respectfully submitted,

CLARKE, CLARKE, ALBERTSON & BOVINGDON
Attorneys for Appellant,
Albin Stevedore Company

GEORGE W. CLARKE,

JAMES B. DONOVAN,
THOMAS A. HARNETT,

(Both of the New York Bar),
Of Counsel.

APPENDIX

Notice of Motion in Supreme Court, New York County,
and Supporting Affidavit of Thomas A. Harnett.

SUPREME COURT OF THE STATE OF NEW YORK,

COUNTY OF NEW YORK.

IN THE MATTER of the Application of ALBIN STEVEDORE COMPANY to confirm the award made in the arbitration proceeding between Albin Stevedore Company and Central Rigging & Contracting Corp. under the arbitration clause of a written agreement dated August 14, 1959.	Index No. 97/61

Sirs:

PLEASE TAKE NOTICE that upon the written award of all of the arbitrators in the above-entitled arbitration proceeding, dated and acknowledged the 23rd day of November, 1960, and delivered to and received by Watters & Donovan, the attorneys for Albin Stevedore Company at the office of said attorneys, 161 William Street, New York 38, New York, on the 28th day of November, 1960, and upon the annexed affidavit of Thomas A. Harnett, sworn to the 30th day of December, 1960, the Petitioner herein will move this Court at a Sepcial Term, Part I, thereof, to be held in and for the County of New York, at the County Courthouse, New York, New York, in the Borough of Manhattan, City of New York, on the 16th day of January, 1961, at 10 o'clock in the forenoon of that day or as soon thereafter as counsel can be heard, for an order:

1. Pursuant to Section 1461 of the Civil Practice Act confirming the award of the arbitrators made by a majority thereof; and

2. Pursuant to Section 1464 of the Civil Practice Act directing judgment to be entered in conformity therewith; and

3. Granting such other and further relief as to the Court may seem just, together with the costs and disbursements of this proceeding.

PLEASE TAKE FURTHER NOTICE that pursuant to Rule 64 of the Rules of Civil Practice, you are hereby required to serve upon the undersigned answering affidavits and other papers, if any, which you intend to submit in opposition to this motion not less than five days before the return day thereof.

Dated: New York, New York
      December 30, 1960.

Yours, etc.

WATTERS & DONOVAN
Attorneys for Petitioner,
Albin Stevedore Company
161 William Street
New York 38, New York

To:

KAISER & HOLZMAN, Esqs.
Attorneys for Central Rigging & Contracting Corp.
21 East 40th Street
New York 16, New York

SUPREME COURT OF THE STATE OF NEW YORK

County of New York

In the Matter

of the Application of

Albin Stevedore Company

to confirm the award made in the arbitration proceeding between Albin Stevedore Company and Central Rigging & Contracting Corp. under the arbitration clause of a written agreement dated August 14, 1959.

Thomas A. Harnett, being duly sworn, says:

1. I am an attorney and a member of the firm of Watters & Donovan, attorneys for Albin Stevedore Company, the Petitioner herein. I am familiar with all the proceedings herein.

2. Albin Stevedore Company, hereinafter called Albin, is a corporation duly organized and existing under and by virtue of the laws of the State of Washington.

3. Central Rigging & Contracting Corp., hereinafter called Central, is a corporation duly organized and existing under and by virtue of the laws of the State of New York.

4. On or about August 14, 1959, Albin and Central entered into a written agreement for the loading and lashing of a specified cargo on the *M. V. Despina C* at Ames Terminal, Seattle, Washington.

5. Paragraph 11 of the said written agreement contained the following provisions:

"The parties hereto hereby incorporate by reference as though fully set forth herein all of Paragraphs 14, 15, 17, 20 and 22 of the underlying contract between Howard International and Central dated April 28, 1959. Except that where the said contractor is referred to in said underlying contract there is hereby substituted the word 'Albin' and wherever the word Howard is referred to is substituted the word 'Central'.

6. Paragraph 22 of the aforementioned "underlying contract between Howard International and Central dated April 28, 1959," contained the following provisions:

Arbitration: Any controversy or claim arising out of or relating to this contract, or the breach thereof, shall be settled by arbitration, in accordance with the rules of the American Arbitration Association, and judgment upon the award rendered may be entered in any court for jurisdiction thereof. The arbitration shall be held in New York City, New York or in Seattle, Washington, at Howard's option."

7. Pursuant to the aforementioned written agreement dated August 14, 1959, and Central's "Amended Demand for Arbitration" dated January 19, 1960, a copy of which is annexed hereto, made a part hereof and marked Exhibit A [See in particular pages 2 and 3 thereof Re "II. Demand for Arbitration."], and pursuant to Albin's "Answering Statement" in reply to the "Amended Demand for Arbitration," a copy of which is annxed hereto, made a part hereof and marked Exhibit B, a single controversy, to wit, the sum, if any, in excess of $6,000 due and owing to Albin for work and services performed in the loading of the *Despina C*, was submitted to arbitration by the Commercial Arbitration Tribunal, administered by the American Arbitration Association, 477 Madison Avenue, Borough of Manhattan, City and State of New York, under its rules and pursuant to the laws of the State of New York.

Lightning Source UK Ltd.
Milton Keynes UK
UKHW020109051218
333419UK00006B/81/P

9 780260 625489